Building States to Build Peace

A project of the International Peace Institute

BUILDING STATES
TO BUILD PEACE

EDITED BY
Charles T. Call
WITH **Vanessa Wyeth**

LYNNE
RIENNER
PUBLISHERS

BOULDER
LONDON

Published in the United States of America in 2008 by
Lynne Rienner Publishers, Inc.
1800 30th Street, Boulder, Colorado 80301
www.rienner.com

and in the United Kingdom by
Lynne Rienner Publishers, Inc.
3 Henrietta Street, Covent Garden, London WC2E 8LU

Library of Congress Cataloging-in-Publication Data
Building states to build peace / edited by Charles T. Call with Vanessa
Wyeth.
    p. cm.
"A project of the International Peace Institute."
Includes bibliographical references and index.
ISBN 978-1-58826-456-5 (hardcover : alk. paper) — ISBN 978-1-58826-480-0
(pbk. : alk. paper)
  1. Nation-building. 2. Peace-building. 3. Nation-building—Case studies.
4. Peace-building—Case studies. I. Call, Charles. II. Wyeth, Vanessa.
III. International Peace Institute.
  JZ6300.B85 2008
  327.1—dc22
                                                2007049052

British Cataloguing in Publication Data
A Cataloguing in Publication record for this book
is available from the British Library.

Printed and bound in the United States of America

    The paper used in this publication meets the requirements
∞ of the American National Standard for Permanence of
    Paper for Printed Library Materials Z39.48-1992.

  5 4 3 2 1

Contents

Part 2 Cases

Part 3 Conclusion

Foreword

Terje Rød-Larsen,
President, International Peace Institute

The International Peace Institute is proud to present *Building States to Build Peace*, edited by Charles T. Call with Vanessa Wyeth. This timely volume makes an important contribution to the growing scholarship on post-conflict peacebuilding, with policy implications for the United Nations and other institutions.

Since the early 1990s, the UN has undertaken peacebuilding activities in more than two dozen peacekeeping operations and several peacebuilding-specific missions. Yet initial optimism about the UN's role in postconflict peacebuilding has been belied by a mixed record of success. In very few cases have the foundations for lasting and sustainable peace emerged. Efforts by other actors to consolidate peace in war-torn societies have fared no better, as headlines from Iraq and Afghanistan remind us on a daily basis. Clearly, there is a collective interest in improving this record.

In the face of these circumstances, policy analysts and scholars increasingly agree that there is no substitute for capable and legitimate states and that building or rebuilding state institutions is a sine qua non for peace to persist. Unfortunately, there are no blueprints for international actors seeking to assist postwar societies in developing states that can adequately protect and govern their populations. Building a legitimate and sustainable state is a complex, difficult, and lengthy task. Past experiences demonstrate that international assistance can have both positive and negative effects. External action alone is certainly not sufficient to rebuild the institutions of a war-torn state. Yet external statebuilders today find themselves, wittingly or unwittingly, the protagonists of efforts to build peace by building states.

Responding to some of these concerns, international actors in recent years have embarked on a wave of new postconflict programs and policies. These changes have been underpinned by the recognition that postconflict programming often lacks clear goals, effective coordination, and adequate

resources; tends to misjudge the necessary timelines; and can unintentionally produce negative effects. The creation of new US and UK coordinating
offices for postconflict reconstruction and stabilization and the creation of
a UN Peacebuilding Commission and a new Peacebuilding Support Office
in the UN Secretariat are emblematic of these reforms. This volume was
completed as these efforts were under way.

Divided into two main sections, the book investigates the principal challenges of institutionalizing states after conflict. The first section is theme-
driven, drawing on recent scholarship that addresses the most difficult demands of statebuilding. Beyond the practical aspects of institution building
in general, the challenges include not only building states in war-torn societies, but also constructing substate and suprastate authorities, in addition to
managing the important relationships among legitimacy, capacity, and security. Such challenges often require difficult choices by both national and international actors.

The second section consists of case studies, examining in-depth statebuilding in light of peacebuilding efforts in Afghanistan, Bosnia-Herzegovina,
East Timor, Liberia, Palestine, and Somalia. These six cases cover a range
of the most vexing and diverse challenges for international actors seeking
to foster sustainable peace. In all the cases, statebuilding played a particularly salient role in strategies to consolidate peace. In some cases, external
recognition was intertwined with questions of war and peace. In most cases,
internal state capacity and reach posed crucial obstacles to peacebuilders.
We hope that these chapters elucidate the issues, challenges, and successes
for international initiatives aimed at building states in the service of building peace.

This volume represents the culmination of several years of work on postconflict statebuilding and peacebuilding, drawing upon many scholars and
practitioners in the UN system and beyond. We at the International Peace Institute are deeply grateful to the many people who took part in the book's development, as well as to the authors and editors. The project was also undertaken as part of a broader program of work on statebuilding, including
dedicated support to the new peacebuilding architecture at the UN. The research and the publication of the book would not have been possible without
generous support from the Carnegie Corporation of New York, the John D.
and Catherine T. MacArthur Foundation, and the government of Canada. We
would particularly like to express our gratitude to Steve Del Rosso of the
Carnegie Corporation of New York and to IPI's core funders.

Acknowledgments

We are grateful to a number of people who were instrumental in the publication of this book and the project with which it was associated at the International Peace Institute (IPI, formerly the International Peace Academy). Our thanks go first and foremost to the contributors to the volume for their patience and dedication. We are extremely fortunate to have been able to draw on their expertise and collaboration.

Several people contributed to the initial impulse to organize an effort examining the need for a more state-centered understanding of postconflict peacebuilding, especially where the United Nations sought to improve its performance. We are grateful to the contributions of Simon Chesterman and Sebastian von Einsiedel in originating projects on transitional administrations and on statebuilding at IPI, and subsequently to the conceptual and organizational contributions of Kirsti Samuels, who carried the book project in its initial stages.

David Malone, Terje Rød-Larsen, Neclâ Tschirgi, and Ed Luck provided intellectual guidance and organizational support at various stages. We are indebted to Elizabeth Cousens, who was the project's champion during her tenure as IPI's vice president and a chief intellectual contributor before, during, and after her time at IPI.

Several individuals participated in early meetings to conceptualize the project, for which we are grateful: Michael Barnett, Shepard Forman, David Harland, Bruce Jones, Chetan Kumar, Thant Myint-U, Barney Rubin, and Teresa Whitfield.

An authors' meeting at Greentree, Long Island, helped clarify the concepts and contributions of the project. The meeting was enriched by the contributions of Salman Ahmed, Catherine Barnes, Michele Brandt, Bill Durch, David Haeri, Bob Maguire, Yezid Sayigh, and Laura Sitea, as well as those of the chapter authors. We are particularly grateful to colleagues at New York

University's Center on International Cooperation for their support in carrying out joint activities related to the project on statebuilding.

Many thanks are also due to colleagues at IPI and elsewhere who reviewed chapters, provided comments, and offered guidance as the book developed, including Abiodun Alao, Markus Bouillon, Kaysie Brown, Matt Bryden, James Cockayne, Rahul Chandran, Anthony Goldstone, Agnès Hurwitz, Gordon Peake, Jenna Slotin, Astri Suhrke, Susan Woodward, and two anonymous reviewers. Special thanks in particular to Amy Scott and Madalene O'Donnell for their frank and thoughtful feedback. The volume has benefited enormously from their involvement.

We are grateful to Clara Lee, Ellie Hearne, Alison Gurin, and Jeremy Dell for editorial assistance and to IPI editor Adam Lupel for his able handling of the entire publication process. Of course, we would also like to thank the staff at Lynne Rienner Publishers for their expert work, as well as Lynne Rienner herself for stalwart support.

Finally, our thanks to Tracy Fitzsimmons and John Wyeth, and Shayla, Jag, Dash, and Nate.

— Charles T. Call and
Vanessa Wyeth

1

Ending Wars, Building States

Charles T. Call

S cholars and practitioners have for centuries sought to improve our ability to end wars. For a number of reasons, however, this challenge has recently taken on new urgency. The classic peacekeeping model aimed at
consolidating a cease-fire between the armies of two warring countries
today seems a distant memory from simpler times. Civil wars—historically
more difficult to settle and to keep settled—now comprise 95 percent of the
world's armed conflicts. Even where countries go to war with one another
(witness recent wars in Afghanistan and Iraq), internal armed conflicts and
external war making become intermingled in messy ways.

Success also seems more elusive than in the past. Early successes in securing negotiated settlements after the Cold War—in El Salvador, Mozambique, Namibia, and South Africa—gave way to several cases in Africa and
the Middle East where apparent peace failed and war returned with a ven-
geance. Repairing the torn social fabric in such countries and preventing
numerous and often inchoate forces from reigniting war are difficult endeavors. The difficulty is compounded by people's rightful expectation that displaced persons will be able to return without fear, that human rights atrocities will be punished, and that infrastructure and economies will be rebuilt.
In addition, some postconflict countries experience high rates of criminal violence and host threats to transnational security.

The difficulty of ending wars today is matched by its urgency: the costs
of failing to secure peace are serious. Failed peacebuilding represents one of
the worst risk factors for new wars. Between one-quarter and one-third of
peace agreements ending civil wars collapse within five years.[1] In addition,
"backlash violence" after a failed peace agreement is often worse than before an accord was reached. If the implementation of only two peace agreements—the 1991 Bicesse Accords for Angola and the 1993 Arusha Accords
for Rwanda—had not failed, some 2 million people, roughly one-third of all

civil war victims during the 1990s, would not have died in subsequent internal violence.[2] War's disruption of people, economic production, and political certainty combine to produce what is known as "reverse development," or impoverishment that is difficult to staunch.[3]

Complicating the picture are war-torn countries where the institutions of authority have been destroyed or disrupted. In places as varied as Haiti in 1994, Kosovo and East Timor in 1999, Afghanistan in 2001, and Iraq in 2003, military interventions dismantled the state. These interventions left not only the usual human and material debris of warfare but also uncertainty about how and by whom millions of people would be governed. These international efforts, initially aimed at discrete objectives like ending ethnic cleansing or toppling a dictator, uniformly got more than they bargained for. Even in supposed peacekeeping success stories like Bosnia, East Timor, and Sierra Leone, external actors found themselves ill-equipped to foster a process that would result in a legitimate, sustainable authority.

Thus we come to a major concept and theme of this book: the state and its relationship to peace. US-led interventions in Kosovo, Afghanistan, Haiti, and Iraq suggested to those engaged in "postconflict" operations that rebuilding the state was the logical implication, perhaps even the moral obligation, of external interventions. Implementing peace agreements in places like Bosnia also underscored how important developing a viable state was for consolidating peace—and for enabling international troops to depart. Other factors—such as the specter of weak or "failed" states engaged in terrorism and the development community's emphasis on the institutional foundations for sustainable development—also brought the state and statebuilding to the fore of policy discussions. To quote the 2002 *National Security Strategy of the United States of America,* "America is now threatened less by conquering states than we are by failing ones."[4]

Afghanistan and Iraq illustrate the difficulties of building states after (and during) war, as well as its importance for international peace and security. The well-being of the peoples of these lands, of the regions where they are located, and indirectly of the rest of the world depends on whether effective and legitimate states emerge in these war-torn societies. Yet the peacekeeping successes listed above, as well as more problematic attempts to end wars as in Palestine, Somalia, and East Timor, point to problems in the process of building states in war-torn societies. Such experiences raise the question of how consolidating peace relates to recrafting the institutions of authority—or how building peace relates to building states.

The Main Questions and Contributions of This Book

Given these challenges, this book explores a number of questions. How does the process of building states relate to the process of building peace? Is statebuilding somehow essential to postwar peacebuilding? Are there functional priorities in fostering legitimate states in war-torn societies, and how should they be advanced? What are the tensions between peacebuilding and statebuilding? Where should policymakers look to identify and overcome the trade-offs and the not-so-apparent tensions that may arise between strengthening state institutions and seeking to address underlying causes of war?

The book seeks to address these questions. Academics and policy analysts have already written a good deal about both peacebuilding and statebuilding. Much of this literature consists of case studies, lessons learned, and advice for policymakers on building state institutions in postwar environments. Herein we initially sought to explore further how to build states more effectively in ways that sustain peace. Once completed, however, the chapters yielded different and more interesting results than anticipated. First, we do find guidance on what sorts of measures are likely to yield sustainable postconflict state institutions in different circumstances. The thematic chapters in Part 1 provide robust recommendations about which processes are most likely to foster legitimate and effective state institutions—and which processes are likely to be harmful.

Yet the most salient finding is that the relationship between peacebuilding and statebuilding is complicated, contingent, and context-dependent. That is not to say that the specifics of each case prevent generalizations from being drawn. However, peacebuilding cannot be boiled down to building state institutions. Enhancing state institutional capacity may potentially harm the chances for consolidating peace and vice versa. A number of tensions exist between the logic of building states and that of ensuring that war will not recur. The contributors here add conceptual depth and nuance to how we think about the relationship between strengthening states and consolidating peace and provide contingent guidance on handling the tensions and linkages between state consolidation and peace consolidation. The chapters in this book suggest that effective peacebuilding requires strategizing around several linkages (1) between negotiated deals and their consequences for a sustainable state; (2) between capacity and legitimacy; (3) between urgent short-term measures and long-term sustainability; (4) between international interests and recognition versus national interests and legitimacy; and (5) between the interests of elites, especially combatants, and of the population at large. This volume comes on the heels of important reforms in the international architecture for postconflict and statebuilding operations. In the early 2000s, a number of observers emphasized the serious limitations on external efforts to reweave social fabrics and to rebuild state structures after wars. Marina Ottaway, Roland Paris, and others criticized the overambitious "liberal democratic" prescriptions of international actors in postwar peacebuilding.[5] Successful peacekeeping (i.e., maintenance of cease-fires and the commencement of recovery) in places like Liberia (1997), Kosovo and East Timor

(1999), and Sierra Leone and Haiti (by 2000) had not readily led to peace-building successes whereby international troops could leave behind self-sustaining states. Frustrations with persistent gaps in international civilian capacities, the short attention span of donors once crises have fallen from the headlines, and problems of interagency coordination led bilateral donors and the UN system to restructure their organizations for such operations.[6] The United Kingdom, Germany, Canada, the European Union, and other donors are adopting "joined-up" approaches involving closer collaboration among their defense, foreign, and development ministries or offices.[7] The World Bank, which had created a Post-Conflict Unit in 1997,[8] opened a Fragile States Unit in 2002.[9] The debacle of postwar reconstruction in Iraq helped stimulate the United States to restructure its own institutions for weak states and postconflict reconstruction in 2004, creating an Office of the Coordinator for Reconstruction and Stabilization (S/CRS) in the State Department.[10] And with perhaps excessive fanfare, the UN created a new Peacebuilding Commission, a modest Peacebuilding Fund, and a Peacebuilding Support Office within the UN Secretariat aimed at strengthening strategies, resources, and diplomatic support for selected postconflict countries. All these changes reflected an international community struggling to find answers to the problem of creating sustainable states in the wake of war. We hope that this volume provides clarity and guidance on the relationship between enhancing state institutions and peacebuilding, including how not to do harm in trying to build states after war, that will aid in this process of international reflection.

Peacebuilding: What Is it?

One of the difficulties in analyzing peacebuilding is the reigning conceptual confusion about postconflict processes. A number of related terms, defined in the box on p. 5, differ slightly in their denotation and the values underlying them. The term *peacebuilding* entered public usage through the United Nations. Drawing on work by Johan Galtung and others, Secretary-General Boutros Boutros-Ghali's *Agenda for Peace* in 1992 defined "peacebuilding" largely in relation to a conflict continuum.[11] Passing from preconflict prevention to peacemaking and then peacekeeping, the *Agenda for Peace* associated peacebuilding with postconflict societies, defining it as "action to identify and support structures which will tend to strengthen and solidify peace in order to avoid a relapse into conflict" (para. 21).[12]

By the mid-1990s the concept of peacebuilding had entered academic and policy discourse and become more expansive, leading to confusion even within the United Nations. The "Supplement to an *Agenda for Peace*" (1995) emphasized that the term applies not solely to postconflict situations

Related Concepts and Terms

- *Peacebuilding:* actions undertaken by international or national actors to consolidate or institutionalize peace.
- *Peace implementation:* actions undertaken by international or national actors to implement specific peace agreements, usually in the short term. Where operable, it usually defines—and either enables or constrains—the framework for peacebuilding.
- *Statebuilding:* actions undertaken by international or national actors to establish, reform, or strengthen the institutions of the state and their relation to society (which may or may not contribute to peacebuilding).
- *Nation building:* actions undertaken, usually by national actors, to forge a sense of common nationhood (1) to overcome ethnic, sectarian, or communal differences; (2) to counter alternate sources of identity and loyalty; and (3) to mobilize a population behind a parallel statebuilding project. It may or may not contribute to peacebuilding. Confusingly, this term is often equated with either postconflict stabilization or statebuilding, especially in US policy and journalistic circles (as in President George W. Bush's injunction: "no nation building").
- *Stabilization:* actions undertaken by international actors to reach a termination of hostilities and consolidate peace, understood as the absence of armed conflict. A prevalent term in US policy usually associated with military instruments, generally reflecting a shorter time horizon than peacebuilding, and associated with a post-9/11 counterterrorism agenda.
- *Reconstruction:* actions undertaken by international or national actors to support the economic and, to some extent, social dimensions of postconflict recovery. It is also a familiar term in the World Bank (whose formal name includes the term) and US policy circles (e.g., US coordinator for reconstruction and stabilization) and reflects roots in the experience of postwar assistance in Europe after World War II.[13]
- *Peace operations:* operations undertaken by international actors in the midst of or after armed conflict, usually consisting of Security Council–mandated peacekeeping that usually encompasses a range of civilian and political tasks ("multidimensional peacekeeping" and peacebuilding).

Source: Adapted from Charles T. Call and Elizabeth M. Cousens, "Ending Wars and Building Peace." Coping with Crisis Working Paper Series. New York: International Peace Academy, March 2007, p. 4.

but to the conflict spectrum: preconflict prevention, actions during warfare, and postconflict measures. However, the Department of Political Affairs limited its analysis and work to "postconflict peacebuilding." Institutional turf battles also fueled the divergent understandings of peacebuilding within the UN system. For example, in 1997 the UN Economic and Social

Council (ECOSOC) stated that peacebuilding was "essentially a component of development activities," whereas the Department of Political Affairs defined it as "quintessentially a political task."[14]

In this volume *peacebuilding* refers to efforts at national, local, or international levels to consolidate peace in war-torn societies. Although peacebuilding often refers to efforts to create less conflictual relationships among different groups who have not taken up arms, we refer here to such efforts only in wartime or postwar societies.[15] As with other terms, such as *crisis management* (used by the EU) and *stabilization* (preferred by the United States), peacebuilding (used especially by the UN) is a value-laden term that privileges order over other values such as justice, social equity, and basic livelihood. In international operations, the degree and type of order considered sufficient for international resources and troops to be withdrawn is generally determined by the world's most powerful states, rather than by the local population. Therefore, even where undertaken by national actors, peacebuilding is not simply a neutral activity responding to the needs of the population at large. It privileges certain groups over others.[16]

Peacebuilding only ceases to be an ambiguous term when its standards of success are defined, and here even more confusion reigns. How do we know peacebuilding success when we see it? Virtually all concepts of the term go beyond what might be considered a traditional security studies approach, or a "negative peace" standard: once a cease-fire is reached and holds. A sustainable cease-fire may be an acceptable standard for *keeping* the peace (i.e., peacekeeping), but it is insufficient for having *consolidated* or *institutionalized* peace (i.e., peacebuilding).[17]

At the other end of the spectrum, some scholars and UN agencies advocate what we regard as a laundry list concept of peacebuilding. This approach, which also refers to universal "root causes" of war, includes numerous benchmarks such as the eradication of poverty and inequality, accountable governance, democracy, respect for human rights, and a culture of nonviolence.[18] These standards, associated with "positive peace," would be considered ambitious even for peaceful, industrialized societies.[19] Although this more ambitious concept admirably recognizes the complex, integrated nature of peacebuilding, it is too inclusive to be useful. It fails to distinguish between abject failures such as Rwanda and Liberia in the late 1990s and partial successes such as El Salvador and Mozambique, where peace is consolidated but root causes remain.

Instead, our standard of success strikes a middle ground that includes the lack of recurrence of warfare as well as some sustained, national mechanism for the resolution of conflict—signified by participatory politics. Participatory politics does not equate to liberal democracy, but refers to mechanisms for aggrieved social groups to feel that they have both a voice and a stake in the national political system. This standard is admittedly difficult to measure but excludes stable, authoritarian, and clearly illegitimate governments.

States: What Are They?

The editors of this volume draw on Max Weber to define the "state" as the collection of institutions that successfully claims the monopoly on legitimate authority and use of force over a given territory.[20] Truthfully, different contributors use the term "state" in different ways in the volume. Some emphasize the *legitimate authority,* as exercised and recognized over a territory either internally or externally. Others emphasize the *institutions* of government, the administrative capacity of governance. Still others emphasize the state as an entity that represents a territorial *political community* over and above the government.[21] This entity includes the institutions of government but goes beyond them, having its own character and (in some minimal way) speaking for the political community.

Our definition emphasizes the institutions of government, recognizing the links to international recognition and resources but stressing the relationship between the institutions of governance and the territory's citizens or population, also known as "empirical sovereignty."[22] This inward-looking exercise of authority is distinct from "juridical sovereignty," which refers to the external recognition accorded a state by other members of the international system and presently emblemized by membership in the UN General Assembly.[23] Juridical sovereignty plays an important role in the wars of several of the cases examined—Palestine, East Timor, Bosnia, and Somalia—and interacts with the degree to which states exercise authority internally. Nevertheless, the challenges of internal, or empirical, sovereignty seem to be especially important in peace processes and in the thematic chapters that follow.

Our emphasis on empirical sovereignty is consonant with a concept of the state as an exercise and embodiment of power, not a neutral, benign collection of executive agencies. Leon Trotsky once said, "Every state is founded on force."[24] Charles Tilly echoed this with his famous assertion: "War made the state and the state made war."[25] The state represents an order imposed on a territory by a particular class or group of elites, but one that usually involves some degree of consent—hence the importance of legitimacy both in the definition of a state and in the process of statebuilding. The accrual of legitimacy, through various means and both internationally and internally, is essential to contemporary state formation and a central theme of the contributions presented here. International actors, by recognizing certain actors diplomatically, by choosing to speak with or provide resources to certain groups, and by occasionally using force, are a salient interactive component of this process. Although some of the authors in this book at times adopt a neutral view of the state, which is common in the discourse of intergovernmental organizations, the cases presented and arguments made in thematic chapters belie these notions.

Statebuilding: State Capacity and State Design

Francis Fukuyama defines "statebuilding" simply as "the creation of new government institutions and the strengthening of existing ones."[26] Yet informed scholarship draws on different ideas about what the state is and what dynamics are most important. It is useful to distinguish between two different approaches to or aspects of the state. The chapters herein vary in the extent to which they implicitly assume, or draw upon, these two aspects.[27]

First, and most common, is a Weberian focus on *institutional capacity:* statebuilding as institutional capacity building.[28] That concept emphasizes formal state agencies. It subordinates informal or traditional institutions of authority as well as suprastate authorities that operate across murky or attenuated borders. In this view, "stateness" is visible predominantly in two state functions: (1) the institutions that can guarantee a monopoly on the coercive use of force (see the discussion of security in Chapter 2 by Barnett R. Rubin); and (2) those institutions that can collect revenues and govern expenditures, among other functions (see the discussion of public finance by Michael Carnahan and Clare Lockhart in Chapter 4).[29] But beyond the army, the police, and tax/customs collection agencies, the institutional understanding of the state extends to the capacity and reach of all state ministries and agencies, including those that formulate and administer policy in the areas of justice, finance, money, agriculture, trade, and so on.[30] Fukuyama delineates between two dimensions of statebuilding: state capacity across territory ("strength") and institutional capacity across functions ("scope").[31] Both fall into the concept of the state as institutional capacity.

One important element of state capacity is not simply service delivery but institutionalization of its various organizations. "Institutionalization" here means the process by which a cluster of activities acquires a persistent set of rules that constrain activity, shape expectations, and prescribe roles for actors.[32] Institutionalization means that sustainability does not depend on any single individual but on a shared commitment to the principles, procedures, and goals of the institution. The death or departure of an influential leader does not doom the institution, for generalized patterns relate to the expected roles played by all rather than roles assigned by one individual. Institutionalization presumes that roles and rules are taken for granted by those who execute them and are subject to them.[33] As discussed earlier, the predominant approaches to peacebuilding, humanitarian aid, and development have long neglected institutionalization of state agencies precisely because those agencies are deficient and thus obstacles to effective outcomes.

Instead, international actors often succumb to the temptation to shape strate- gies around an influential leader or Western-educated "reformer" as the shortest route toward capacity building. Unfortunately, although this ap- proach may work in the short term as an exit strategy for internationals, it is not a sustainable approach toward building the capacity of state institutions.

Second, apart from institutional capacity, the state can be understood in relation to particular *organizational arrangements*—what we refer to as "state design." Whereas capacity refers to the ability of the police or the govern- ment's tax collectors to discharge their responsibilities, state design refers to where and how these state powers are allocated or arranged.[34] States can ex- hibit decisionmaking authorities at different levels, granting national author- ities relatively reduced powers in a federal or confederal system, more pow- ers in a centralized system, or exceptions to their power through autonomous regions. Such arrangements shape popular expectations of the role of the state over time, as people come to expect the state to act, say, intrusively or minimally. State design may also distribute power across different branches of government (e.g., legislatures versus executives).

The design of states is generally so historically rooted that the state's organizational arrangement seems impervious to change. Indeed, changing the design of the state—from a federal to a centralized structure, from one with a strong executive to one rooted in parliamentary strength—is rare. However, the extraordinary circumstances of war and its termination both compel and provide windows of opportunity for national elites, or external powers where their troops are involved, to revisit the state's organization for better or worse.[35] The settlement of wars often requires that the state's insti- tutional structure be redesigned to grant regional autonomy (or indepen- dence, as in Bosnia) to the territory associated with a warring party.

In addition, state design issues are linked to questions of extrastate au- thority—both "below" the state with regard to local or tribal authorities and "above" the state in relation to regional or transnational arrangements that usurp some state functions (e.g., the EU and the World Trade Organization). In Chapter 7 William Reno confronts this challenge: How possible is it to build statelike structures below the national level? He shows that governance can be achieved without state institutions, something that discussions of state design should take into account.

It is virtually impossible for decisions about state structures not to favor certain social or political groups, as well as the process of selection of rulers, thus influencing regime type. Robust approaches to state design cannot side- step decisions and debate about regime type (e.g., democracy or authoritar- ian? What sort of democracy or authoritarian regime?). Whereas "regime" generally refers to how those who govern are selected and their power vis-à- vis other branches of government, the "state" refers to a broader set of insti- tutional rules and mechanisms, generally embodied in part in constitutions, that define the institutions and power of the entire governmental apparatus vis-à-vis society.[36] Statebuilding must minimally grapple with regime form and process, insofar as state structures and reforms provide the contour and foundation for the forms of democracy (e.g., parliamentary versus presidential, consociational approaches versus majoritarian, electoral systems, etc.). All the case studies in this volume implicitly illustrate the interface between design issues of states and the character of the political regime, as does Katia Papagianni's thematic treatment of legitimacy in Chapter 3.

The chapters in this volume each treat the interaction of state capacity with state design and legitimacy, some more explicitly than others. At certain moments in a society's history, the institutional arrangement of the state takes special precedence over capacity. These moments generally occur in the immediate aftermath of state or regime collapse (e.g., the great revolutions that prompted the rearrangement of states and regimes in France, China, Russia, and the United States, and in 1979 in Nicaragua and Iran, for instance). In recent decades, external actors often have played a crucial role in the overthrow of states and regimes, leading to constitutional conferences or other processes to redesign the state. We have seen such processes in a variety of postintervention territories: Haiti (1994, 2004), East Timor and Kosovo (1999), Afghanistan (2001), and Iraq (2003).[37]

Even though international actors exercise a role in state design in such cases, national actors still play a determinant role in decisions about state structures. During these formative moments, external ideas and interests conjoin with historical and regional trajectories to craft parliamentary systems, judicial systems, security systems, electoral systems, and the relationships among local and provincial powers. These issues of state design interact with state capacity. Elites may replace weak or undesirable repressive forces, as in Haiti. Or as in Afghanistan, the process of central state design and formation may reflect the weakness of all national institutions and the relative power of provincial actors. Yet once these constituting moments of state design pass, capacity once again becomes the fundamental characteristic of stateness and state power in the eyes of international organizations.

State design issues are profoundly political, not technical "constitutional design" questions that can be mapped in some scientific fashion. This book does not contain a separate chapter devoted to state design questions, since they are intertwined with capacity and legitimacy issues. Instead, the case studies treat these questions in their social context, and the thematic chapters address such design questions in conjunction with capacity. Chapter 3 explicitly addresses the challenges involved in institutional arrangements of the state at these crucial moments of design, as well as the broader issue of the cultural character of the state vis-à-vis social groups and actors.

Old ideas about reshaping society or citizens (i.e., "nation building") are no longer as compelling as they once were, for two reasons. First, citizen identification with the state is no longer the sine qua non for successful stateness. Modernization theory posited that successful states required a citizenry that identified itself with the state over other ethnic or religious allegiances; in other words, that statebuilding required nation building. Although social groups still aspire to nationhood and often independence, the power of external neighbors and the international system has made the idea of multinational states more common and accepted (and, of course, very few states come even close to being a single-nation state). Second, the idea that identity can be deliberately manipulated through external programs or intervention has lost the credibility it enjoyed in the 1960s. Large-scale programs to redefine a society's allegiances and identities seem silly or self-defeating in today's globalized world.

Nevertheless, the study of statebuilding is incomplete without examining society's evolving image of and expectations of the state. States are often analyzed in a vacuum, without reference to the social groups they purportedly represent and regulate. However, statebuilding involves the interface of state institutions with society. As Joel S. Migdal and his colleagues have pointed out, "States may help mold, but they are also continually molded by, the societies within which they are embedded."[38] State capacity necessarily involves the input and perceptions of citizens. The design of the state will in many ways shape and help define those interactions between state and society. The success of state designs ultimately depends on how well they mediate state-society negotiations.

Why Should Statebuilding Contribute to Peacebuilding?

In the wake of the international response to the attacks on September 11, 2001, questions about peacebuilding were conflated with, and largely eclipsed by, the problems of weak or "fragile" states. Despite early references to Somalia and Bosnia as "failed states" in the early 1990s, the term rose to prominence only in the twenty-first century after the weakness of the Afghan state under the Taliban was associated with the ability of Al-Qaida to operate freely.[39] Yet the state is important for reasons completely distinct from the potential threat posed by terrorism. Effective and popularly supported states are necessary for the provision of basic goods and services to the population of a given territory.

Most of today's political theories and policy frameworks, and even many peace agreements, assume the existence of a functioning state. The international human rights regime, for example, assumes that states not only exist but exercise full control over their agents and their territory.[40] In fields as disparate as development, humanitarian assistance, and conflict resolution, states are often assumed to be capable of developing policies and implementing them.

Nevertheless, states and state institutions have been neglected.[41] The very assumptions of statehood and states indicate that state institutions have been presumed to exist and function as designed on paper. The United Nations was created by and for states; there is no provision for "decertification" of states that fail to perform even minimal functions.[42]

States have not only been neglected; they have been actively undermined by international efforts at peace and development. Many humanitarians and development practitioners have tended to disdain the state as an impediment to their well-intentioned work. Humanitarian agencies, for instance, prize the delivery of aid to those most afflicted by natural or manmade disasters. They understandably prefer to deliver their aid directly to those most in need, rather than channel it through state agencies that may be corrupt, inefficient, or pursuing partisan or ethnic agendas. Consequently, the state is bypassed and atrophies as other entities assume its functions.[43] In Afghanistan during the 1990s, donors supplanted entire ministries throughout much of the country. Finally, neoliberal economic policies contributed to the weakening of the state during the 1980s and 1990s, when bilateral development agencies and international financial institutions (IFIs) pushed aggressively to limit the state in favor of the private sector.

Events in the late 1990s led peacebuilders to recognize that they had neglected the state to the detriment of postconflict societies. In places like Bosnia, Afghanistan, and Haiti, where wars seemed to end, self-sustaining peace proved elusive. External actors such as military peacekeepers, diplomats, and development experts turned increasingly to the state as a needed antidote to reversion to warfare. The weakness of state institutions proved elemental in poor outcomes of peace processes in Liberia, Sierra Leone, Haiti, and the Democratic Republic of Congo. Prevailing ideas about peacebuilding require more attention to strengthening legitimate and effective state institutions. Where peace processes involve security reforms or new human rights protections, it is necessary to create or strengthen the state institutions needed to sustain these important changes. Many poor countries emerging from warfare require greater human capacity and institutional capacity to function with minimal effectiveness. As Fukuyama stated in 2004, "State-building is one of the most important issues for the world community because weak or failed states are the source of many of the world's most serious problems."[44]

Theoretically, statebuilding should support the consolidation of peace in a number of ways.[45] First, it enhances sustainable mechanisms for security and conflict resolution at the national level that should carry legitimacy in the eyes of the populace and of the outside world. Such mechanisms—be they justice systems, policing systems, or service delivery agencies—provide a credible arena and framework (or at least a foundation for a framework) for social groups to express their preferences and resolve their conflicts nonviolently. If states function to provide these public goods, rather than contribute to private gain, they reduce the incentives to seek basic goods outside established channels or through violence. In postwar societies with an international presence, statebuilding should also accelerate the orderly withdrawal of international troops and civilians, ensuring stability and popular support for an emergent regime. From the perspective of sustainable economies, functioning and legitimate states also provide the infrastructure for sustainable development with a diminishing role for external actors. All of these factors point to a complementary relationship between peacebuilding and statebuilding, one that exists in many circumstances and should be nourished.

Yet the difference in values and emphasis between these two concepts should also be noted. Self-sustaining, legitimate, and effective states may be seen as an important, even necessary cornerstone of peacebuilding, but they are the end goal of statebuilding, whereas self-sustaining peace is the ultimate goal of peacebuilding. These overlapping concepts can diverge greatly when programs and aid policies are designed around their respective end goals, as we shall see.

What Are the Priorities in Statebuilding?
The Thematic Chapters

Are there certain priority state functions in the process of statebuilding in war-torn societies? Experience shows that current models of statebuilding are unlikely to fit local conditions. Many analysts suggest that the experience of the United Nations in setting up a transitional administration in Kosovo unduly influenced the UN strategy in East Timor, setting back the sustainability of that new state upon independence in 2002. Public pronouncements and policies of the United Nations and of major bilateral actors now embrace what scholars have insisted for years: there is no "one-size-fits-all" model of statebuilding. Experienced practitioners and UN member states repeated the call for attention to national and local context at the first informal gathering of the UN Peacebuilding Commission in May 2006.[46]

At the same time, experience has shown that certain state functions repeatedly prove to be essential to the viability of war-torn states. Unless a state can deploy these goods, its internal power in all areas is likely to be limited, even if it is propped up by external actors. In this volume, we draw upon and adapt the three types of resources that Charles Tilly identifies as crucial for statebuilders: coercion, capital, and charisma.[47] Statebuilders historically required some combination of these resources to consolidate state power. Our thematic chapters largely correspond to these core responsibilities of the state, including the provision of security and the accumulation and distribution of economic resources or capital. The third resource, charisma, is here interpreted as a resource for broader legitimacy, especially in the eyes of the internal population. Four thematic chapters address these three core issues. In addition we add a thematic chapter on the provision of justice as a core state function.[48] A word about each of these areas is in order.

Security

One of the most salient lessons of peace operations is "security first."[49] In Chapter 2, Barnett R. Rubin draws a distinction between the more conventional "national" or "state" security and "human security." Both are important, but especially the latter. Without security, other tasks of statebuilding and postconflict reconstruction are impossible. At the same time, the provision of other state goods like education, a regulatory environment for foreign investment, and the ability to extract resources and tax citizens all impinge on the state's ability to provide security. Each of these functions is interrelated. A conceptual focus on one without attention to their interaction with others can be disastrous. Similarly disastrous is the concentration of resources and attention solely on the provision of security, a mistake often made by those in the security business. Even where private actors are contracted to provide security, the regulation and oversight of these actors remains a core state function.

Legitimacy

Legitimacy is not so much a responsibility of the state as a necessary resource or characteristic. Because its presence is interlaced with every function of the state, legitimacy here is viewed as a resource that cuts across all state functions, rather than a role or sector of the state. The concept is difficult to analyze meaningfully. Legitimacy is often assumed or defined in a circular manner. By *legitimacy,* we here refer both to the normative acceptance and expectation by a political community that the cluster of rules and institutions that compose the state ought to be obeyed, as well as the degree to which the state is seen as the natural provider of core goods and services.

Emergent states will rarely enjoy a high degree of legitimacy, and new state institutions will thus need to acquire such legitimacy unless they have been established as a result of a successful insurrection that toppled a regime (in which case, the new regime may confer a problematic excess, rather than deficit, of legitimacy on the state). Where states have historically not been the natural providers of core goods and services (i.e., "weak" states), it is unrealistic to expect any newly recast state to acquire and effectively carry out such services in the space of a few years. Given the contemporary influence of external actors in legitimating transitional regimes, especially in armed conflicts, national actors require legitimation not only internally but also externally (the "dual legitimacy" problem referred to by Ghassan Salamé, or what Michael Barnett and Christoph Zuercher describe as the "peacebuilder's contract").[50] Katia Papagianni addresses the challenges inherent in establishing legitimacy and participation in Chapter 3.

Public Finance and Economic Policymaking

States require resources, and resources in turn make states. More specifically, the capacity to collect and distribute capital is one valid measure of "stateness." The more the state is the focal point for the collection and distribution of capital for public goods, the more the state carries weight vis-à-vis other quasi-public institutions (e.g., mosques, churches, tribal chiefdoms, neighborhood groups, etc.). International military and diplomatic actors tend to neglect the importance of state capacity for collecting, managing, and distributing taxes, customs, and the like, although international financial institutions have paid increasing attention to these state capacities.

In Chapter 4, Michael Carnahan and Clare Lockhart address the state's capacity to collect and expend revenues and the national budget process at the core of these decisions. As we will see, the case study on Liberia in Chapter 14 describes an innovative experiment in international intrusion into a core component of the state: the collection and distribution of customs duties. Distinct from the capacity for public finance, a country's economic policies—and its capacities for formulating such policies—affect the consolidation of peace. Paul Collier analyzes this issue in Chapter 5, adding a global level of analysis to the risk factors of particular economic policies in postconflict societies.

Justice and the Rule of Law

We have included a chapter on the rule of law in recognition of its importance as a state function in most contemporary postconflict societies. Historically, scholars have not viewed the capacity to administer justice and provide the rule of law as a core state function. Charles Tilly's core functions make no mention of justice. Yet global standards of justice and globalized communications have made state legitimacy more contingent on how well it delivers justice.

In Chapter 6, Erik G. Jensen cites the example of Cambodia, where everyday "micro"-injustices far outweighed Khmer Rouge atrocities in average people's complaints about the rule of law. Although he concludes that peace processes can survive a deficit in the rule of law, our case studies suggest that both legitimacy and security hinge somewhat on whether the populace is able to see everyday conflicts resolved peaceably, either in the state's courtrooms or through local mechanisms of justice. In cases where past atrocities occurred (as in Afghanistan, Liberia, Bosnia, and East Timor), important ethnic groups' views of state legitimacy often hinge on how past injustices are addressed. Widely established human rights norms, together with publicized trials of former heads of state, have created expectations for justice that did not prevail in earlier generations. Yet overzealous "victor's justice" may set back legitimacy among losing social groups. In either case, the state's capacity to mete out justice is today of fundamental importance.

Not every state requires these core functions in equal measure. Some state functions, such as meting out justice or providing health care, will assume greater importance in some societies under certain historical conditions. In some cases, external actors may opt to provide these resources. For example, the tacit commitment by the Organization of American States and the United States to provide for Costa Rica's security from invasion enabled that country to eliminate its armed forces in 1948. As a rule, however, these core resources and state functions are the starting point for analyzing the process of statebuilding, with appropriate attention to local and national context.

The intersection of peacebuilding and statebuilding poses special challenges. In most postwar societies, international actors deploy a high amount of resources for a concentrated time period, and then these resources will be diminished. The peculiar challenge of statebuilding in war-torn societies lies mainly in the generation of core and other state functions, with the expectation that external provision of those resources (be it in the form of "assistance" or occupation) will be withdrawn or dramatically reduced within a few years. As a result, international agencies develop a range of strategies that at times are self-defeating. In Chapter 8, Sarah Cliffe and Nick Manning address four common mistakes made in the institution-building process and offer clear, practical, and programmatic recommendations for avoiding these common errors. The chapter acts as both a summary of the prior thematic chapters and as a transition to the case studies.

A related challenge is the relationship between those external provisions of stateness and the emergent or extant providers of state goods and services, be they national, provincial, local, or supranational. Many wars take place in societies whose state functions have previously been carried out at the substate or suprastate levels. As mentioned earlier, to address this dimension of stateness and explore the concept of governance without state institutions, we have included Chapter 7 by William Reno, which explores both the advantages and challenges confronting substate authorities in terms of legitimacy and the provision of goods and services.

What Do the Case Studies Offer?

This volume contains not only the thematic chapters described above, but also case studies of statebuilding efforts in the context of peace processes or postwar societies. The case studies include rich and varied empirical material that sheds light on the relationship between statebuilding and peacebuilding in war-torn societies. Unlike those found in other edited volumes, the case studies here focus specifically on peace processes and their relationship with the trajectory of the state and its institutions. These exceptional studies raise new issues and point to interesting tensions in the relationship between statebuilding and peace consolidation. These findings are especially important in an international policy environment where statebuilding has become conflated with the promotion of peace.

The selection of the volume's cases—Somalia, Palestine, Bosnia, East Timor, Afghanistan, and Liberia—reflects a simple logic: they all involved internal (often internationalized) wars in which stateness—either juridical or empirical—and international actors (including the United Nations) played a crucial part in the war and the process of securing peace. Within this framework defined by three factors (civil war, salient questions of statehood, and prominent international roles), the cases exhibit important diversity along two dimensions.

First, they reflect a range of experiences with war and peace. International actors were prominent direct combatants in the conflicts in Afghanistan and East Timor. They acted as combatant third parties in Bosnia and Somalia and to a lesser extent Liberia, but they have played little military role in the Israeli-Palestinian conflict. Some wars ended in outright victory (East Timor and Afghanistan), whereas others produced peace agreements (the 1995 Dayton Accords for Bosnia, the 2003 Accra agreement for Liberia, and the 1993 Oslo Accords for Palestine). Some peace accords enjoyed success (Bosnia and Liberia to date), and others failed (the Oslo Accords). Somalia never experienced a formal peace, and East Timor and Afghanistan experienced postwar violence, albeit at very different levels.

Second, the cases represent diversity in the role of the state in war and peace. War centered on the creation of new juridical states in East Timor, Bosnia, and Palestine. How powerful and regional states treat populations in these territories depends greatly on whether they form part of another state or have achieved independence. The occurrence or recurrence of warfare was largely ascribed to weak empirical states in Afghanistan, Somalia, and Liberia (and, in 2006 after independence, East Timor). Indeed, the notion of "failed states" posing threats to international security received its greatest boost from the Al-Qaida presence in Afghanistan in 2001. In Afghanistan (as in Kosovo and Iraq), peacebuilding activities commenced not upon a cease-fire throughout the territory, but upon the withdrawal of one side from power and the collapse of state functions. In the case of Somalia, an armed conflict in the 1990s led to the collapse of the state itself, and the central political drama of the early twenty-first century centered on statebuilding rather than consolidating peace. The cases permit analysis not only of the relationship between peace processes and statebuilding but also of the relationship between renewed warfare (in the cases of Palestine, Somalia, East Timor, Afghanistan) and state formation.

Finally, powerful states and international organizations played an important role in all the cases; conversely, these countries also played a significant role in shaping the thinking and practice of international actors in postwar peacekeeping and peacebuilding. The United Nations was heavily involved in each case, either with a peacekeeping troop deployment or through a diplomatic presence (as in the Middle East and, after the withdrawal of its UN mission, Somalia). The cases present the chance to learn about the various roles played by the UN mission, UN agencies, regional organizations (specifically NATO in the context of Bosnia and Afghanistan), international financial institutions, donor countries, and nongovernmental and private actors in addressing the challenges of statebuilding in war-torn countries.

These case studies offer rich hypotheses about how processes of ending wars interact with questions of statehood and statebuilding. Because we exclude cases in which questions of juridical or empirical sovereignty were not salient (e.g., El Salvador) or in which international actors were not prominently involved (e.g., Peru, Burma, Costa Rica), the case studies yield neither structured comparisons nor confirmation or testing of hypotheses. The cases represent only a sample of the pool of cases in which issues of statehood and peace involved UN missions, and we found it unnecessary to include other recent cases that conformed to our criteria (e.g., Kosovo, Sudan, the Democratic Republic of Congo).

Four essential questions underlie our case study inquiries: Did statebuilding help build peace? Did peacebuilding help build states? If so, how? What can we conclude from these experiences? Each case study author was asked to address several other issues in an effort to answer the above interrogatories: If there was an agreement to reach and sustain peace, then what elements of statebuilding or state reform did it address? Which aspects or functions of statebuilding were included and omitted? What was the relationship of efforts to consolidate peace to efforts to design and consolidate state institutions? Were the same actors involved in each? How did these processes cohere, and how did they experience tensions or contradictions? If the state failed or persisted in weakness, how was the peace process affected? How did the success or failure of a peace process interact with efforts to strengthen the state and its institutions? How did efforts to build states or build peace involve and shape society and its salient groups?

The contributors bring diverse perspectives to bear on their analysis. All have field experience in war-torn societies and are relatively well-known in either policy or academic circles. Virtually all have provided expert advice on the issues or countries of their expertise or have acted directly as policymakers within international organizations such as the UN or the World Bank. Some chapters are written in the tradition of critical analysis that presents both insider and outsider perspectives, whereas others are written more from outside institutional perspectives. Some ground their analysis in the broad literature (mainly the thematic authors), whereas others concentrate on their findings from the field. Although we have sought common frameworks and questions, some contributions are more structured than others, longer than others, and more practice-oriented than others.

Processes of strengthening states and of consolidating peace may be nonlinear and fraught with contradictions. The book is intended to identify useful generalizations where possible and to highlight contradictions and conceptual problems where they are important for avoiding mistakes. It seeks to identify the tensions between ending wars and building states and to specify how policymakers can ease these tensions and deepen the mutually positive interactions between these processes. Consolidating peace is especially urgent in today's world. This book articulates how engaging in statebuilding can help, rather than harm, that endeavor.

Notes

1. Roy Licklider, "The Consequences of Negotiated Settlements in Civil Wars 1945–93," *American Political Science Review* 89, no. 3 (1995): 681–690; Paul Collier et al., *The Conflict Trap* (Washington, DC: World Bank and Oxford University Press, 2003), p. 7; Paul Collier, Anke Hoeffler, and Mans Soderbom, "Post-Conflict Risks," Working Paper 2006-12 (Oxford: Centre for the Study of African Economies, Oxford University, August 2006); Astri Suhrke and Ingrid Samset, "What's in a Figure: Estimating Recurrence of Civil War," *International Peacekeeping* 14, no. 2 (April 2007): 198.

2. Stephen John Stedman, "Introduction," in Stephen John Stedman, Donald Rothchild, and Elizabeth M. Cousens, *Ending Civil Wars* (Boulder, CO: Lynne Rienner, 2002), p. 1.

3. Collier et al., *The Conflict Trap,* p. 7.

4. The White House, *The National Security Strategy of the United States of America,* Washington, DC, September 2002, p. 1.

5. See, among others, Marina Ottaway, "Nation Building," *Foreign Policy* 132 (September–October 2002): 16–24; Roland Paris, *At War's End: Building Peace After Civil Conflict* (Cambridge: Cambridge University Press, 2004); Michael Barnett, "Building a Republican Peace: Stabilizing States After War," *International Security* 30, no. 4 (2006).

6. See, e.g., United Nations, *Report of the Panel on United Nations Peace Operations* (Brahimi Report), UN Doc. A/55/305-S/2000/809, August 21, 2000.

7. Stewart Patrick and Kaysie Brown, *Greater Than the Sum of Its Parts? Assessing "Whole of Government" Approaches to Fragile States* (New York: International Peace Academy, 2007).

8. It later became the Bank's Conflict Prevention and Reconstruction (CPR) Unit.

9. The office was originally dubbed the "Low-Income Countries Under Stress" (LICUS) initiative.

10. See Nora Bensahel, "Organising for Nation-Building," *Survival* (June 2007).

11. Johan Galtung, "Three Approaches to Peace: Peacekeeping, Peacemaking, and Peacebuilding," in his *Peace, War, and Defense—Essays in Peace Research,* Vol. 2 (Copenhagen: Christian Eljers, 1975), pp. 282–304.

12. The US government has eschewed the term in favor of others like *peace-keeping* and *reconstruction and stabilization,* although *nationbuilding* still prevails in popular discourse. See, e.g., James Dobbins et al., *America's Role in Nation-Building: From Germany to Iraq* (Santa Monica, CA: RAND, 2003).

13. See, e.g., Robert C. Orr, *Winning the Peace: An American Strategy for Post-Conflict Reconstruction* (Washington, DC: Center for Strategic and International Studies, 2004).

14. Quote from Margaret J. Antsee, "Strengthening the Role of the Department of Political Affairs as Focal Point for Post-Conflict Peacebuilding," report for the UN Department of Political Affairs, December 1998, para. 2. For a broader discussion of different UN concepts, see Charles T. Call, "Institutionalizing Peace: A Review of Post-Conflict Peacebuilding Concepts and Issues for DPA," review conducted for UN Department of Political Affairs, New York, January 2005. See also United Nations, "Supplement to *An Agenda for Peace,*" Position Paper of the Secretary-General on the Occasion of the Fiftieth Anniversary of the United Nations, UN. Doc. A/50/60, 1995.

15. See John Paul Lederach, *The Moral Imagination: The Art and Soul of Building Peace* (Oxford: Oxford University Press, 2005).

16. Elizabeth M. Cousens, Chetan Kumar, and Karin Wermester, eds., *Peacebuilding as Politics: Cultivating Peace in Fragile Societies* (Boulder, CO: Lynne Rienner, 2000).

17. See Michael W. Doyle and Nicholas Sambanis, "International Peacebuilding: A Theoretical and Quantitative Analysis," *American Political Science Review* 94, no. 4 (2000): 779–801.

18. "Statement by the President of the Security Council," February 20, 2001, UN Doc. S/PRST/2001/5.

19. The "Annotated Agenda" of the Fourth UN Regional Organizations High-Level Meeting, "Meeting the Challenge of Long-Term Peace-Building: Preventing the Outbreak and Recurrence of Violent Conflict," explicitly says, "The goal here is to promote a 'positive peace'" (para. 17), June 20, 2000. See also Roland Paris, *At War's End: Building Peace After Civil Conflict* (Cambridge: Cambridge University Press, 2004).

20. Max Weber, "Science as a Vocation," in H. H. Gerth and C. Wright Mills, *From Max Weber: Essays in Sociology* (New York: Oxford University Press, 1946), pp. 129–156. Originally a speech at Munich University, 1918.

21. Amy Scott, "The Image of the State and the Expansion of the International System," Ph.D. diss., New College, Oxford, 2006, Chapter 2.

22. Robert H. Jackson and Carl G. Rosberg, "Why Africa's Weak States Persist: The Empirical and the Juridical in Statehood," *World Politics* 35, no. 1 (October 1982): 1–24; Michael Barnett, "The New United Nations Politics of Peace: From Juridical Sovereignty to Empirical Sovereignty," *Global Governance* 1, no. 1 (Winter 1995): 79–97.

23. Jackson and Rosberg, "Why Africa's Weak States Persist"; Barnett, "The New United Nations Politics of Peace." Also see Jeffrey Herbst, *States and Power in Africa: Comparative Lessons in Authority and Control* (Princeton, NJ: Princeton University Press, 2000).

24. Max Weber, "Science as a Vocation."

25. Charles Tilly, "Reflections on the History of European State-Making," in Charles Tilly, ed., *The Formation of National States in Western Europe* (Princeton, NJ: Princeton University Press, 1975), p. 42.

26. Francis Fukuyama, *State-building: Governance and World Order in the 21st Century* (Ithaca, NY: Cornell University Press, 2004), p. ix.

27. These approaches or concepts overlap with the four concepts described by Katia Papagianni in Chapter 3. The "institutional capacity" and "organizational arrangement" approaches coincide largely with her concepts of states as bureaucracies and administrations, and as institutional arrangements reflecting power balances.

28. Implicit in this definition is a distinction between institutional capacity and the capacity of individuals within those institutions.

29. Tilly, "Reflections on the History of European State-Making," p. 42; Weber, "Science as a Vocation."

30. Ashraf Ghani, Clare Lockhart, and Michael Carnahan, "An Agenda for State-Building in the Twenty-first Century," *Fletcher Forum for World Affairs,* 30, no. 1 (Winter 2006): 101–123. See also Chapter 8 in this volume.

31. Ghani, Lockhart, and Carnahan, "An Agenda," pp. 11–14.

32. Here I have adapted Robert O. Keohane's definition of institutions, "International Institutions: Two Approaches," *International Studies Quarterly* 32, no. 4 (December 1988): 384. This definition encompasses informal rules as well as institutions that may not be specific organizations (e.g., the international human rights regime), though here formal rules will be most pertinent.

33. See John Rawls's discussion of the accretion of force of rules, "Two Concepts of Rules," *Philosophical Review* 64 (1955): 3–32, described in ibid., pp. 384–385.

34. For various perspectives on what is here called state design and its relation to war termination, see Daniel J. Elazar, *Federalism and the Way to Peace* (Kingston: Institute of Intergovernmental Relations, 1994); Michael Burton and John Higley, "Political Crises and Elite Settlements," in *Elites, Crises, and the Origins of Regimes,* edited by Mattei Dogan and John Higley (Lanham, MD: Rowman and Littlefield, 1998); Donald L. Horowitz, *Ethnic Groups in Conflict* (Berkeley: University of California Press, 1987); Nancy Bermeo, "What the Democratization Literature Says, and Doesn't Say, About Post-War Democratization," *Global Governance* 9, no. 2 (April–June 2003): 159–177.

35. See Charles T. Call, "War Transitions and the New Civilian Security in Latin America," *Comparative Politics* 35, no. 1 (October 2002). For an analogous view at the interstate systemic level, see John Ikenberry's *After Victory.*

36. Although states are defined as distinct from "regimes," it is difficult to disentangle the two in the area of state design. On the well-trodden distinction between states, regimes, and governments, see Stephanie Lawson, "Conceptual Issues in the Comparative Study of Regime Change and Democratization," *Comparative Politics* 25, no. 2 (January 1993): 183–206; Munroe Eagles, Christopher Holoman, and Larry Johnston, *Politics, Introduction to Democratic Government,* 2nd ed. (Peterborough, ONT: Broadview, 2004); Guillermo O'Donnell, Philippe C. Schmitter, and Laurence Whitehead, eds., *Transitions from Authoritarian Rule* (Baltimore, MD: Johns Hopkins University Press, 1986); Robert M. Fishman, "Rethinking State and Regime in Southern Europe," *World Politics* 42 (April 1990): 428.

37. Jamal Benomar, "Constitution-Making After Conflict: Lessons for Iraq," *Journal of Democracy* 15, no. 2 (April 2004): 81–95.

38. "Introduction," in Joel S. Migdal, Atul Kohli, and Vivienne Shue, eds., *State Power and Social Forces: Domination and Transformation in the Third World* (Cambridge: Cambridge University Press, 1994).

39. Gerald B. Helman and Steven R. Ratner, "Saving Failed States," *Foreign Policy* 89 (Winter 1993): 3–20.

40. The emerging norm of "responsibility to protect," however, reflects a growing awareness that not all states are capable of providing for their populations. See International Commission on Intervention and State Sovereignty, *The Responsibility to Protect* (Ottawa: International Development Research Centre, 2001).

41. Susan L. Woodward, "Fragile States," paper presented at the Peace and Social Justice meeting of the Ford Foundation, Rio de Janeiro, Brazil, November 29, 2004; and her "Peacebuilding and 'Failed States': Some Initial Considerations," paper presented at a conference in Coimbra, Portugal, March/April 2006.

42. Jeffrey Herbst proposes such decertification in *States and Power in Africa*.

43. Ashraf Ghani and others have written widely on the ways in which aid delivery undermines state effectiveness. See Ashraf Ghani, Clare Lockhart, and Michael Carnahan, "Closing the Sovereignty Gap: An Approach to State-Building," Working Paper no. 253 (London: Overseas Development Institute, September 2005); and Ghani, Lockhart, and Carnahan, "An Agenda for State-Building in the Twenty-first Century."

44. Fukuyama, *State-building,* p. 1.

45. See Woodward, "Peacebuilding and 'Failed States'"; and Simon Chesterman, Michael Ignatieff, and Ramesh Thakur, eds., *Making States Work: State Failure and the Crisis of Governance* (Tokyo: United Nations University Press, 2005).

46. International Peace Academy and Center on International Cooperation, "Next Steps for the Peacebuilding Commission: Seminar Report," June 2006.

47. Charles Tilly, *Coercion, Capital, and European States,* A.D. *990–1992* (Oxford: Blackwell Publishers, 1992). These three resources were emphasized by Barnett Rubin during a workshop attended by the editors and a number of scholars and practitioners who work on the state and statebuilding, including Tilly. The workshop was organized by the Center on International Cooperation and the International Peace Academy, December 16, 2004, New York. See Chapter 2 of this book for more by Rubin.

48. Others suggest more numerous state functions, such as Ghani et al., "Closing the Sovereignty Gap" and Chapter 8 herein.

49. Kofi Annan, "Learning the Lessons of Peacebuilding," speech at University of Ulster, Londonderry, October 18, 2004.

50. Ghassan Salamé, *Appels d'empire: Ingérences et résistances à l'âge de la mondialisation* (Paris: Fayard, 1996); Michael Barnett and Christoph Zuercher, "The Peacebuilder's Contract: How External State-building Reinforces Weak Statehood," discussion draft for Research Partnership on Postwar State-Building, www.statebuilding.org/resources/Barnett_Zeurcher_RPPS_October2006.pdf, 2006.

PART 1

Context

2

The Politics of Security in Postconflict Statebuilding

Barnett R. Rubin

The appropriate mandate for peacekeeping or security forces in postconflict or peacebuilding operations has been one of the most difficult and contentious issues since the end game of the Cold War led to the increasing involvement of the UN in multifunctional operations. The controversy over the enforcement of provisions on demobilization and human rights in Cambodia and, especially, the disasters that overtook UN forces in Rwanda and Bosnia-Herzegovina led to evaluations of what went wrong.[1] In one influential analysis, Steve Stedman argued against the assumption that international forces were always present to overcome security dilemmas and monitor compliance with an agreement; instead he argued there are often actors, labeled "spoilers," who use violence to prevent implementation and that mandates needed to change accordingly. The 2000 Brahimi report on UN peace operations adopted the category of "spoilers" and argued that troop deployments, mandates, and resources must correspond to a realistic threat assessment, rather than to existing doctrine or the degree of interest of the Security Council or troop contributors.[2]

The insurgencies and civil conflicts in Afghanistan and Iraq have similarly drawn attention to the primacy of security in statebuilding operations that take place without a comprehensive peace agreement (as in Afghanistan, where the Bonn Agreement did not include the apparently defeated Taliban) or with no agreement or international mandate whatsoever (as in Iraq). Many observers have argued that more security forces, better coordination, and other changes of strategy are needed for "success."[3] Yet even more troops in Iraq have been even less successful in providing security than in Afghanistan.

All such operations aim at political objectives, not just building "states," let alone "peace," and their success is crucially linked to the international and domestic legitimacy of those objectives and the ability of leaders to

mobilize people to defend them. The challenge of legitimacy is doubly difficult in such operations: statebuilding always requires a struggle for legitimation among citizens, but international operations must also meet a high standard of international legitimation, including appropriate authorization and
political support in each of the states that provide financial or military aid.
These various sources of legitimacy may contradict as well as complement
each other. Understanding the challenge of providing security in internationalized statebuilding or peacebuilding operations requires situating both the
operations and the accompanying efforts to provide security in their political
context.

In this chapter I examine first the concept of security in internationalized statebuilding operations and analyze its relation to other components
of the statebuilding process, legitimacy and finances. I then analyze how international actors can supply each of these components in different ways,
which may either complement their domestic supply (support national statebuilding) or substitute for domestic supply (undermine national statebuilding). Using this conceptual framework, I then explore several political issues
relating to security in such operations, including the legitimacy of the international security deployment among both the citizens of the affected state
and the international community; whether international deployments support
or displace the creation of national capacity; the relation of security sector reforms to both interim power-sharing arrangements and the transition to permanent institutions; priorities among different types of security and security
institutions; the need for legitimation among the general population but particularly within the security forces; and sustainable finance for the security
sector. Throughout these sections, I draw extensively on the case of Afghanistan, partly because I have followed the country for over two decades and
advised the United Nations during the transition period after the US-led coalition intervention in late 2001, but also because the case exemplifies many of
the key claims of this chapter. Finally, I draw on this analysis to discuss some
major questions over the sequencing and interrelationships of various components of peacebuilding and statebuilding operations, in particular the relationships among security, democratization, and reconstruction or development.
The interdependence of security, legitimacy, and economic development in the
statebuilding process provides a framework for a comprehensive analysis that
transcends the usual stove-piped discussions of peacekeeping, security sector
reform, reconstruction, and governance.

The Context: Internationalized Statebuilding Operations

As noted in Chapter 1 of this volume, operations known as "postconflict," "reconstruction," "peacebuilding," or "stabilization" do not form a homogeneous
group. Despite the recent emergence of some of these terms, such operations

have a long history. The use of international coercive forces as part of an operation aiming to build national capacity (rather than absorb a territory as an imperial or colonial possession) represents the latest historical iteration of interaction between powerful states' self-interest and the prevailing juridical forms of power, especially state sovereignty.[4] Internationalized statebuilding responds to the problem of maintaining security, however defined, in a global system juridically and politically organized around universal state sovereignty. With the construction of a more tightly linked system of mutually recognized and demarcated states in post-Westphalian Europe, the quest for security and profit on the periphery became an imperial—and ultimately global—extension of interstate competition among core states. The contemporary global framework for security developed with the foundation of the United Nations system after World War II. That system extended the international regime of national sovereignty enshrined in the Charter, both by legitimizing recognized states as actors on the international stage (the UN's "member states") and by delegitimizing colonialism and imperialism as legal doctrines.

During the Cold War, the struggle over building postcolonial states largely took the form of competing foreign aid projects by the alliance systems led by the United States and Soviet Union. The end of the Cold War freed the UN and some regional organizations to replace unilateral clientelism with multilateral statebuilding efforts, especially in countries emerging from internal wars. Agreement by the Security Council to entrust most such operations to the UN reflected both the end of zero-sum strategic competition and the lowering of stakes in who controlled these states.

The attacks of September 11, 2001, showed that the United States could now be attacked from even the weakest state and hence reignited the strategic interest of US nationalists in the periphery. Because the regime of universal sovereignty prevents such peripheral territories from being absorbed into more powerful units, however, international security after 9/11 requires the transformation or strengthening of existing national states. Consequently, current internationalized statebuilding operations, even those labeled "peacebuilding" or "stabilization," reflect the impulse of powerful Western states to exercise influence.[5] The terminology deployed, the very endeavor to "build" states, and the process by which international mandates are defined and undertaken all reflect an inherent political dimension, one that is not benign and selfless but self-interested and instrumental.

International Peacebuilding Resources: Complements or Substitutes for National Capacity?

International participants in peacebuilding or stabilization operations attempt to build states in accord with their interests in areas that pose a perceived threat to them. Such operations make use of the same types of resources as other processes of statebuilding: coercion, capital, and legitimacy. Building on the discussion in Chapter 1, in this section I describe the international tools used in statebuilding and the positive or negative effects of these resources (see Table 2.1). When the intervention occurs in a country where state power is weak or contested, preventing relapse to war requires the interveners to jumpstart the mutually reinforcing process of security provision, legitimation of power, and economic development by providing international resources or capacities to cover initial gaps in all three. *Coercion* includes transitional international security provision or intervention (peacekeeping, peace enforcement, security assistance, or occupation); the demobilization, disarmament, and reintegration (DDR) of at least some combatants; and the establishment of new security agencies or reform of existing ones (security sector reform, or SSR). *Capital* takes the form of both international financial assistance for recovery, reconstruction, and development and of efforts to invigorate the national economy and the fiscal capacity of the government. The *legitimacy* of the operations derives from both the legitimacy of the international operation or intervention and that of the system of rule that this operation tries to institutionalize. The outcome depends on initial conditions and the combination of national and international capacities in these areas.[6]

In the best case, such transitional assistance will help launch a new self-sustaining dynamic, but there is a danger, to borrow terms from public finance, of "crowding out" as well as "crowding in."[7] Crowding out occurs when international efforts or structures displace existing or potential new domestic-level state institutions that might carry out similar functions, thus hindering statebuilding. Crowding in occurs when international efforts or institutions provide the space for, the resources for, or the training and mentoring for domestic-level actors or institutions in ways that enhance their capacity and potential sustainability, thus promoting statebuilding. These possible interactions and their effects are illustrated in Table 2.1.

International security may provide a sheltered environment for building national security forces, or it may give contending factions the space to continue to feud without confronting the consequences. External financial aid may fund the creation of national capacities, institutions, and development or create parallel systems that suck capacity out of national institutions and create unsustainable white elephants: roads that cannot be maintained, overpasses to nowhere, schools with no teachers, or "security" forces with no salaries. International support may strengthen the legitimacy of interim or transitional arrangements through authorization by the Security Council and guarantees of respect for human rights and secure political participation for all, but it may also undermine legitimacy by weakening incentives for leaders to be accountable to citizens or exposing conflicts between local and international standards, as in the case of the apostate Abdul Rahman in

Table 2.1 Resources for Internationalized Statebuilding and Their Interactions

Resource	National	International	Promotes Statebuilding When:	Hinders Statebuilding When:
Coercion	Existing security forces; DDR; SSR.	Peacekeeping, security assistance, or occupation forces.	Supplying security and monitoring for DDR; training and equipping new forces (SSR); providing security for political process.	Security goals are contradictory; incentives to cooperate by externalizing costs of conflict are reduced; unsustainable security forces are established with foreign aid.
Capital	Domestic capital formation, resource mobilization, taxation.	International assistance for recovery, reconstruction, and development.	Building capacity, channeling resources through national budget, building sustainable physical and human capital.	Creating parallel systems that monopolize capacity; providing technical assistance without capacity development; supporting unsustainable projects that eat up funds for recurrent expenditures.
Legitimacy	Historically and socially embedded claims of nation, religion, ethnicity, values.	UN Security Council authorization of intervention; conformity of interveners to international law and norms; assistance with political transition and elections; legal and judicial reform; human rights standards and monitoring.	Enabling state to develop inclusive, fully representative, and capable government; protecting rights of broad participation; shielding vulnerable people from threats.	Coercive imposition of international norms conflicts with local values and culture; timetables for foreign political goals are rushed.

Afghanistan. To what extent states built in this manner exercise power as sovereigns, in the service of nationally determined goals, and to what extent they act as agents of externally defined interests constitutes the "dual legitimacy" problem of global state formation.[8]

In the 1990s, UN peacekeeping mandates underwent a shift that would prove crucial for understanding "security" in postconflict operations. In the early 1990s mandates presumed full agreement among warring parties and full legitimacy of the operation among all parties. This produced what some have called "warlord democratization," in which armed groups voluntarily demobilized in order to resolve a security dilemma, requiring confidence-building measures enforced by peacekeepers.[9] In such cases the main task was protecting the security of the former combatants. The disastrous UN operations in Rwanda and Bosnia led to more robust interventions.[10] Thereafter the UN expanded the scope of its missions, not only acting when it had consent, but also authorizing the use of force against "spoilers" seeking to block implementation of agreements or fight their way into a better deal.[11] But that change has required more than a revision of security mandates, which are always closely tied to legitimacy.

In 1985, UN special envoy Diego Cordovez told me that "the UN is not in the business of changing the governments of member states." Only two years later, in 1987, however, as the talks that led to the Geneva Accords on Afghanistan reached their end game, Cordovez himself became involved in just such an activity. Since then, internationalized "postconflict" operations have usually taken place after internal war, though some parties may continue fighting after the so-called postconflict operation starts. The stake is precisely the nature of the government and who controls it.

What Is Security?

The term *security,* like *peacebuilding,* contains an embedded political claim. Consistent with the use of technocratic language that obscures political issues, debates over security often neglect to define whose security is at stake and for what purpose. Conventional means of providing security through the use or threat of force rely on the paradox of security provision: making some people and institutions secure by making those who would threaten them insecure. In its conventional use to denote the goal of military and police operations, *security* means the use or threat of legitimate force to prevent illegitimate violence. The claim that any specific use of force creates "security" is a political claim that the force is legitimate and that those against whom it is directed are outlaws or spoilers. The transformation of coercion into security through the rule of law, like the transformation of predation into taxation through accountability and service provision, are essential to building legitimacy as part of the process of statebuilding.

The transformation from civil war to "peace," whether the latter is defined negatively as the absence of war or positively in terms of sustainable human security, requires transformation of the organization and control of the means of violence. In a state of civil war, at least some armed groups are outside state control. In the course of such wars, both states and non-state armed groups often create multiple, unaccountable, politicized armed forces. Other parts of the security sector, such as police, public prosecutors, and the judiciary, are likely to be weak, corrupt, or subordinate to the political demands of civil warfare. Armed groups rather than civilian political parties or institutions become the principal bodies for political contestation or gaining control of assets. The interrelated establishment and stabilization of control of the means of legitimate violence and authority, combined with the mobilization of resources to sustain these institutions, constitutes the process of statebuilding.

Parties to a civil conflict resolved by means other than partition have to be integrated into a common state. In the usual cliché, they must substitute "ballots for bullets," that is, settle differences through a civilian political system, in which violence is regulated by law for public purposes (security), not used as the premier tool of political competition. The process of building security institutions after a civil war is not only a technical task of building capacity, but is central to the distribution of political power that makes a settlement possible. It requires both political legitimacy and a fiscal basis that will sustain the institutions. Given the weakness of civilian institutions in states plagued by civil conflict, the very process of empowering them is political, independently of the explicit struggle over who controls those institutions. DDR and SSR are technical terms for historical processes essential for statebuilding, as they permit what Anthony Giddens describes as the "extrusion" of violence from politics and administration. This is the process through which military and police functions are distinguished, separating the inside of the state, regulated by rule of law, administration, and policing, from the external relations, regulated by diplomacy, international agreements, military violence, and balance of power.[12] This separation of a pacified internal regime from a more anarchic international regime in turn requires building states with sufficient legitimacy and capacity to allocate resources and resolve disputes without overt violence. In the rare event that international actors assist in establishing a new state (East Timor, potentially Kosovo), the previously subordinate territory needs support and aid to develop the capacity to exercise self-government.[13]

International Transitional Security Provision

The outcome of peacebuilding processes depends both on the degree of difficulty and the amount and effectiveness of international resources deployed.

Michael W. Doyle and Nicholas Sambanis analyze what they call the "Peace-building Triangle," which has three "sides" or dimensions: the severity of the conflict (measured by numbers of casualties and refugees, whether the conflict is ethnic, the degrees of ethnic and political fragmentation, and the outcome of the war before the operation), national capacities for peace (measured by levels and type of economic activity and human development), and international capacities (measured by type of mandate, and size of the international intervention).[14]

The first two dimensions define the initial conditions. One can characterize the initial security conditions as Charles Tilly characterizes challenges to statebuilding, namely the degree of accumulation and of concentration of violence. "Accumulation" refers to the amount of means of violence available, and "concentration" to how widely control over them is distributed. Afghanistan, for instance, had a high degree of accumulation and a low degree of concentration (many armed groups with a lot of weapons), whereas East Timor had a low degree of accumulation and a high degree of concentration (few armed groups with few weapons). These are roughly equivalent to Doyle and Sambanis's measures of conflict intensity and political fragmentation.

Since initial conditions (including severity of conflict and national capacities) as well as international capacities affect the outcome, there is a tradeoff between them, as Doyle and Sambanis argue exists among the three dimensions of peacebuilding: the greater the initial challenges (hostility and lack of national capacities), the more international resources will be required to attain an equivalent outcome. The tradeoff is not necessarily linear, however. The provision of international resources may affect the provision of national capacities, either positively or negatively. The most effective level and type of international force depends on the extent to which international security forces and their claims of legitimacy crowd in or crowd out—promote or hinder—national security capacity and legitimacy.

These resources include the nature of the mandate and the number of troops, but also the overall legitimacy of the effort and financial resources. In cases where the state has kept paramount control of the means of violence over most of the territory (Guatemala) or where a guerrilla movement captures the state (Uganda, Eritrea), international security provision is unlikely. Opposition or minority groups may want it, but the state can block it, and the state can protect international aid providers. In cases where the control of violence is more divided or fragmented, an international security mandate may be necessary. Low accumulation and high concentration of weapons combined with a high degree of legitimacy or consent constitutes the most favorable environment for peacekeeping. Higher accumulation, lower concentration, and less consent require more international forces with a more robust mandate. Factors such as the geographical distribution of hostile forces will also affect the size and nature of international security forces needed to achieve a given outcome with relative certainty.

The *supply* of international security provision, however, depends not only or even primarily on the need, but on the degree and nature of interest among those states with the capacity to supply it. Given the limited supply of deployable troops and the limited commitment to many operations, powerful states accept a higher risk of failure in cases of low strategic interest (often in Africa) by providing or paying for fewer troops than needed and insisting on weaker mandates in order to ensure availability of high-quality troops for cases they consider more important to their interests (the Balkans for Europe, Iraq for the United States).

Reluctant troop contributors may argue for lower levels of force on the grounds that international deployments crowd out local capacity. US secretary of defense Donald Rumsfeld originally argued against expansion of the deployment of the International Security Assistance Force (ISAF) in Afghanistan on the grounds that it might displace efforts to build the Afghan National Army.[15] Others argued that broader deployment of an international force with a mandate to demilitarize key political centers (the original mandate of ISAF in the Bonn Agreement) would have supported DDR and created a more favorable environment for creating professional security forces free of factional control. The latter argument eventually prevailed, with some limits, but it appears to be true that too large a deployment can be counterproductive. Special Representative of the Secretary-General (SRSG) Lakhdar Brahimi's argument for a "light footprint" in Afghanistan, although directed mainly toward civilian rather than military deployments, was based on opposition to crowding out. Too large a military deployment that appeared to be an invasion or occupation could provoke a backlash that would increase insecurity and undermine efforts to create national forces.

Whether international deployments provide security as a public good that strengthens national security capacity depends largely on the domestic legitimacy of the deployment. This legitimacy affects the likelihood that the political actors these forces protect will enjoy sufficient trust and access to build security institutions and the rule of law, if that is their goal. At one extreme, few contest the legitimacy of UN operations to assist in implementation of a peace agreement requested by parties to a conflict and approved by the Security Council. At the other extreme lies the war in Iraq, which launched rather than terminated a war and was conducted with neither the consent of the parties nor the approval of the Security Council. The international legitimacy of operations at the first extreme can crowd in domestic legitimacy. Involvement by the UN provides a more neutral and credible interlocutor for political groups than an occupying power, as the Bush administration found to its apparent surprise in Iraq. International approval also communicates to opponents of the operation that they are less likely to gain external support.

A process endorsed by the UN supposedly enjoys the support of humanity's global political body and hence should enjoy full legitimacy. Of course, no body or court has the power to overturn a decision of the UN Security

Council, but that body is nonetheless political, and its structure reflects the undemocratic reality of international power politics. The Bush administration is not alone in believing that its own definition of interest and legitimacy trumps decisions of the Security Council, though the United States is uniquely positioned to implement its defiant views. The United States was able to have the Security Council approve a UN "peacebuilding" operation in Iraq based on an invasion that most members considered illegal. Some cases of international intervention also involved armed actors who rejected the legitimacy of the intervention or the proposed (or imposed) political settlement, and others (notably Kosovo) also began with interventions not sanctioned by the Security Council. This point is more than a mere footnote: the effectiveness of all security operations and efforts to build security institutions depend on their local and international legitimacy as well as the volume of resources put at their disposal, as a comparison of the effectiveness of the operations in Iraq and Afghanistan illustrates. Because of conflicting goals and values, attempts to legitimate deployments with the national publics of troop-deploying states may conflict with attempts to legitimate those deployments where they take place. In Afghanistan the issue of narcotics exemplifies this problem: The British government has largely legitimated its deployment to southern Afghanistan by telling the British public that the troops are needed there to stamp out cultivation of the poppy that is the source for heroin sold in the UK, but the more these troops engage in direct counternarcotics action, especially crop eradication, the less Afghans will believe that the troops are present to provide for their welfare and security. The case of the Afghan who converted to Christianity posed an even more harsh conflict of basic values, as most Afghans appeared to insist that apostasy was a capital crime, whereas the countries supplying troops and assistance insisted on the basic human right to hold or change religious beliefs.

Security Sector Reform, Power Sharing, and Legitimacy

Almost by definition, international statebuilding operations begin under conditions in which states lack not only capacities to provide security and services but also legitimacy. Building national capacity for security and legitimate governance is key to sustaining peace.[16] The doctrines and organizational practices of these two tasks are usually stove-piped in different organizations, but in practice they are closely linked. Building legitimate institutions requires sufficient security for unarmed citizens and nonmilitary officials to participate. Building security institutions requires sufficient legitimacy to motivate participation, risk, and sacrifice. The interim power-sharing agreements that are often needed to start a transition process are just as likely, if not more likely, to involve participation in and control over the security forces as participation in and control over the ostensibly authoritative civilian positions.

The standard model for legitimizing international statebuilding operations is known as "democratic peacebuilding."[17] The predominant view of such operations links this political model to a legal model based on liberal human rights and an economic model based on the market. Therefore the entire package delivered to countries constitutes a "liberal" model of peacebuilding. Elections are the preferred path to establish such legitimacy, but elections can fulfill that function only when certain demanding conditions are met. They must be preceded by a constitutional process (whether or not the process eventuates in a formal constitution) to establish a broad consensus on the institutions of government and structure of the state to which officials will be elected, as well as on the electoral system and administration. Elections require security against both those who wish to disrupt and discredit them and those who wish to use violence and intimidation to win them; adequate administrative capacity (domestic or international) to ensure that the system is workable; and sufficient agreement on the rules and the mode of enforcement to ensure that losers accept the outcome and winners do not overstep their authority. It is no wonder that first postconflict elections therefore require international security forces and international civilian assistance, except where the incumbents' legitimacy is established through decisive military victory.

The liberal model, however, has no explicit linkage to the process of statebuilding needed to make the political, legal, and economic institutions meaningful. It also includes no basis of local or national legitimacy other than pure legal and electoral claims, which are generally insufficient to motivate people to sacrifice their lives. The success of SSR requires growing legitimacy of the state. The intense, quasi-religious esprit de corps of military organizations derives from the human need to believe intensely in something for which one risks one's life. Effective armies and police require formation of a national authority that can command such loyalty, not just technical training. The officer corps in particular finds its coherence and spirit in service to a mission. Hence, though effective security is necessary to carry out credible elections and other political processes, political processes that build credible, legitimate national leadership are essential to building effective security forces. Sacrifice usually requires strong religious, nationalist, or group loyalties, which may be more or less compatible with the liberal model but are not contained within or generated by it.[18] This model also separates the recognized political processes—elections, legislation—from the process of disarming militias and creating or reforming security institutions, as if the latter were an administrative or technical process. A fuller understanding of these operations, however, requires analyzing the politics of interim power sharing and restructuring the forces of violence, which often has greater political consequences than the ostensibly political institutions.

The first stage toward national legitimacy in an internationalized state-building operation is the establishment of an interim administration and agreement on a transition process. Besides a UN transitional administration or a foreign occupation regime, this may take the form of a coalition among national forces pursuant to an agreement or a monitored government consisting of previous incumbents. The main purpose of the transitional government is to preside over a process that establishes a legitimate legal framework for political contestation and rule (generally, a constitution) and to administer the first stages of the implementation of this framework. The transitional government normally must accommodate the claims for inclusion of a variety of parties to the conflict, though in some cases monitoring of the incumbents or the imposition of a UN transitional administration constitute alternatives. Though the UN, unlike some regional organizations, has no explicit standards for the type of government legitimate for its members, its operational doctrine requires that the transition lead to adoption of a constitution providing for at least an appearance of liberal democracy, with elections constituting the principal benchmark. The United States even more explicitly has made "democracy" (defined as a government elected by universal adult suffrage) as the goal of such operations.

Establishing a transitional government and implementing a political process often requires protection by international security providers, whether to ensure against defection, to defend the process from its enemies, or to provide the logistical support needed for the demanding task of holding national elections. Such a protected transitional government can then benefit from international assistance to build its legitimacy and capacity, including the legitimacy and capacity of the national security agencies. International security provision is particularly important in operations that provide for the dismantling or demobilization of some forces, as doing so is likely to generate a security vacuum and heighten tensions. Research indicates that the provision of international security assistance is most needed at the start of the process, while financial aid needs to expand for a considerable period afterward, as national capacity grows.[19]

Without the separation of politics from violence and the regulation of the latter by law, civilian politics and politicians are impotent and the usual power-sharing agreements of limited value. One of the most common complaints from citizens of postconflict societies against international actors is that despite the latter's rhetoric of peace and democracy, they speak mainly with warlords who are the enemies of both, instead of with "civil society." Depending on the weakness of civilian institutions, it may be more or less possible for international mediators or interveners to engage meaningfully with unarmed political forces. But as long as armed force constitutes the main currency of power, engagement with armed actors, backed up by sufficient international leverage, is the only means to transform their roles. Only the demilitarization of politics makes engagement with nonmilitarized political forces meaningful. The nature of the process for the demilitarization of politics (concentration of the means of violence in the state and the separation of unmediated violence from politics in favor of law enforcement) determines what forces can be engaged. An invasion force can choose its interlocutors until insurgents blast their way into the political arena. To the extent that DDR and SSR are negotiated with combatants, these combatants become the main interlocutors. The demilitarization of politics is at least as important to the political transition as the holding of elections; the latter are meaningless without the former.

Some states, such as Afghanistan or the Democratic Republic of Congo (DRC), have weak civilian institutions and strong armed groups that benefit from foreign aid or predation on global markets (narcotics, gold, diamonds, coltan) or both. In such cases, the security forces themselves, not the civilian institutions, constitute the chief arena of competition for power. On several occasions when the interim Afghan government wanted to neutralize the power of regional warlords without openly confronting them, President Hamid Karzai appointed them to senior government posts in the capital. By placing these individuals at the head of a largely powerless administration while separating them from their regionally based armed groups, the government had deprived them of power rather than sharing it with them. In doing so it gambled on legitimacy at the expense of capacity.

Building the capacity of security agencies can become technical only to the extent that the agencies are politically neutral and serve a legitimate state and its laws, not political leaders, factions, parties, or ethnic groups. Even in fully consolidated democracies, political struggles continue over the mission, role, financing, and recruitment of the security forces. In a country barely emerging from civil war, the transformation of the institutions of violence and coercion constitutes the main arena for power struggles. Actors devise and evaluate such proposals based not on their technical effectiveness—though they will use such arguments when they seem useful—but on the degree to which they maintain their power and their own security, not necessarily that of a politically neutral, inclusive—and elusive—"public."

Armed groups, which are the most powerful form of association in post–civil war situations, pursue political, military, and economic objectives simultaneously. By proposing the separation of these functions into different organizations, the liberal peacebuilding model threatens to undermine the society's most powerful individuals and threaten the welfare of their followers, unless local capacities for liberal development grow sufficiently to offer employment and new roles for exercising power and accumulating wealth to the elites that emerged during the war. Such elites may lose from open warfare, but they also stand to lose from consolidated peace, if it means undermining personal power. Hence they have a strong interest in resisting the full implementation of peace agreements, if not reversing them.

The negotiations over power sharing in the Bonn Agreement, DDR, and SSR in Afghanistan illustrate the centrality of the security sector to politics in postwar statebuilding. At the UN talks on Afghanistan in Bonn, international actors negotiated a government power-sharing deal with Shura-yi Nazar (the Supervisory Council of the North, the core of the Northern Alliance). The international actors accepted for the time being that faction's control of all "security" agencies (the Ministries of Defense and Interior and the intelligence agency), in return for its agreeing to measures of civilian power sharing. They included accepting a chair of the interim administration (Hamid Karzai) who was not from the Northern Alliance and was not a military commander; sharing civilian ministerial posts with other groups; promising to adhere to a process of gradual broadening of the base of the government, though without specific commitments to give up control of the security agencies; and accepting international monitoring of all these arrangements.

Afghanistan's experience after the Bonn Agreement illustrates several political features common to countries experiencing international efforts to build state security forces. Despite frequently agreeing to succumb to civilian political authorities, armed factions (including government armed forces) often fortify parallel or preexisting command or authority structures to weaken the actual power of nominal civilian control. The Northern Alliance, for instance, accepted civilian power sharing but resisted measures to dilute its control of the security organs or to disempower armed commanders.

Similarly, armed factions whose commanders are reluctant to relinquish control over their soldiers commonly employ tactics like formal delays, foot-dragging, efforts to interpret or rewrite agreed-upon depoliticization of security forces, and outright duplicity. Consider the negotiations over the composition and powers of the new Afghan National Army. These largely secret negotiations, which occurred in Kabul in 2002–2003, mainly involved the United Nations Assistance Mission in Afghanistan (UNAMA), the United States, a few members of the Afghan government, and the Shura-yi Nazar leadership of the Defense Ministry. The latter, led by Marshall Fahim, demanded full pay for the clearly exaggerated figure of 200,000 militia members. It also asked for a permanent army of the same size and insisted that the officer corps and rank and file of the new army come mainly from former members of mujahidin units. These demands would have ensured domination of the state by these armed groups, whatever civilian "power-sharing" measures were introduced. In the end, the Karzai administration and international allies were able to overcome most of these early efforts to undermine security sector reforms.[20] They did so not through simply formal or technocratic responses, but via the deployment of capital and limited coercion, as well as the legitimacy that internal and external recognition offered warlords.

Reform of the leadership of the main security institutions in Afghanistan illustrates how these politically sensitive appointments responded to the political context more than the technical demands of SSR and that such political criteria were not necessarily misplaced. Changing the Afghan ministers of defense and interior and the chief of intelligence, as well as key staff in each ministry, required difficult political decisions that threatened violent fallout in every case. These changes were closely associated with key political events: the minister of the interior was changed at the Emergency Loya Jirga; the chief of intelligence was changed after the Constitutional Loya Jirga; and the minister of defense was changed as a result of the presidential election.

The warlords accepted these appointments in Kabul in large part because of pressure from the US-led coalition, whose support they needed to protect them from the Taliban and other enemies. In this case the judicious application of internationally supplied coercive resources provided the government with the opportunity to build the state by ending the capture of the administration by informal power holders. The same changes had the potential to increase the legitimacy of the government, if it could deliver better than the warlords, and to increase the government's fiscal base, as it took direct control of major customs points. The removal of Fahim as minister of defense encouraged many commanders to demobilize and increased the supply of recruits to the Afghan National Army. These are examples of the political use of international forces in support of statebuilding.

Differing Security Priorities

Political interest affects the definition of security objectives and hence priorities among security tasks. International interests focus on challenges to international security, and international action therefore concentrates on military institutions, often equating building a large army with building "security." Often, interveners continue to treat the aftermath of a civil war as largely a military security problem, whereas the end of warfare often creates new security problems, such as crime and economic predation.[21]

In Afghanistan there was from the start a contradiction between the security objectives of the United States and the security imperatives of statebuilding and the political process. The United States and its coalition partners intervened in Afghanistan to protect their own security from Al-Qaida, not to protect Afghans from Al-Qaida, the Taliban, the Northern Alliance, militias, drought, poverty, and debt bondage to drug traffickers. The military strategy for accomplishing the former objective was to dislodge the

Taliban and Al-Qaida with air strikes while using the Central Intelligence Agency (CIA) and special forces to equip, fund, and deploy the Northern Alliance and other commanders to take and hold ground, including cities. Although the United States half-heartedly tried to prevent the Northern Alliance from seizing the capital, it inevitably did so, as the United States was not prepared to occupy Kabul itself anymore than it was later prepared to provide security in Baghdad.

The Bonn talks therefore had to prevent the victorious militias from looting, fighting with each other, and seizing power. Through an act of diplomatic ventriloquism by the UN team, the parties to the Bonn Agreement asked the Security Council to authorize deployment of a "United Nations mandated force to assist in the maintenance of security for Kabul and its surrounding areas." The agreement went on to note, "Such a force could, as appropriate, be progressively expanded to other urban centres and other areas." The participants in the talks also agreed "to withdraw all military units from Kabul and other urban centers or other areas in which the UN mandated force is deployed."[22] This UN-mandated force became known as the International Security Assistance Force. Since August 2003 it has been under the command of the North Atlantic Treaty Organization (NATO). Neither the withdrawal of militias from Kabul nor the expansion of ISAF to provinces began until then, largely because of opposition from the US Department of Defense, which wanted to ensure priority for its war-fighting goals over the internal security goals of ISAF.

The same hierarchy of priorities among security goals led to the establishment of the "lead donor" system for SSR, which delayed progress and blocked coordination. Because the United States initially wanted to devote resources solely to the counterterrorist operation, it took on responsibility for building the new Afghan National Army, while asking other Group of Eight (G-8) countries to take on DDR, police, justice, and counternarcotics. The Afghanistan Compact of January 2006 finally jettisoned this system after the United States and others realized, in the words of the compact, that "security cannot be provided by military means alone. It requires good governance, justice and the rule of law, reinforced by reconstruction and development."[23]

The specific circumstances of the intervention in Afghanistan, in particular the presence of a direct threat to the United States, intensified the contradiction between different security goals and means, but similar problems exist elsewhere. Nationals of the postconflict country often oppose the focus on armies and elections and ask for more efforts to be devoted to the rule of law, human rights, justice, the police, the development of political parties, and civil society.[24] These institutions would provide ordinary citizens with more security and genuine representation. They would make elections more meaningful in a way that building an army cannot. Charles Taylor was able to win a presidential election in Liberia in 1997 largely based on his control of extralegal "security" institutions that enabled him to intimidate the electorate. Former Liberian president Amos Sawyer has argued that the international community's focus on building an army for Liberia did little to improve the security of Liberians, who associate an army with insecurity rather than security. They were in much greater need of police and a justice system.[25]

Partly such decisions result from international actors doing what they know how to do rather than what needs to be done. Military institutions are easier to build with external aid than police, justice, and legal institutions, because military violence depends less on local knowledge and legal and social norms.[26] Previous analyses, however, have demonstrated the close interrelationship within the security sector of military and police reform, and the need for police reform to be coordinated with legal, judicial, and penal reform.[27]

Statebuilding and Security: Sequencing and Interdependence

If building security institutions, separating military from civilian roles, and strengthening civilian institutions and the rule of law are necessary conditions for electoral politics to meaningfully arbitrate among contenders for power, does statebuilding, or building basic local capacities for security or economic development, have to take primacy over holding elections or building other democratic institutions? Analyses of past operations suggest that holding elections before DDR, at least, can reignite conflict and be more likely to lead to destabilization, since the elections can be viewed as winner take all.[28]

Some have posed the question in terms of sequencing or priorities. International operations are too short and lack the long-term commitment (in time, mandate, or resources) needed to implement sustainable transformation of political structures and statebuilding. One study found that the single variable that best explained success in "nation-building" operations was the length of international engagement.[29] Providing security—including the demobilization of nonstate armed groups, the disempowerment of abusive groups that came to power through violence, the reform of official coercive capacities so that they enforce the rule of law rather than factional or personal interest or political agendas, and the establishment of new security agencies and administrative capacity—must precede elections and the broad political mobilization over conflictual issues that elections stimulate.

Marina Ottaway, challenging the viability of the democratic peacebuilding model in the DRC, Afghanistan, and other fragile states, has advocated an initial focus on core issues of security and state control, going so far as to oppose international pressure even to form a central state in Afghanistan, let alone a democratic one. A number of other analysts have argued that the emphasis on democracy is premature or misplaced. Jack Snyder and Edward Mansfield argue that elections often generate more conflict. Francis Fukuyama and Fareed Zakaria, in works on statebuilding and illiberal democracy, respectively, argue that the rule of law and basic institutions of governance must precede the development of institutions for contestation of power.[30]

Some practitioners echo these cautions. In a series of speeches, Lakhdar Brahimi has argued that UN operations are expected to accomplish a complete agenda of political, social, and economic transformation in some of the world's poorest and most violent countries on a tight schedule and with few resources.[31] Pressure for elections, transitional justice, accountability for human rights violations, and social reforms, notably with regard to women's status, builds early as a result of the commitments of donor governments and nongovernmental organizations (NGOs), as well as the high expectations of the beneficiary population. UN political officers often find that these pressures fail to take into account the time needed for basic social transformation, the difficulty (not to say impossibility) of social engineering according to a timetable, the unforeseeable consequences of or backlash from such engineering in divided societies, and the amount of resources needed to build the institutional capacity to implement such changes.

The burst of effort at the start of an operation and the mobilization of international actors with short-term time horizons fails to build local capacity or the basic institutions needed for sustainable peace, while focusing efforts on visible benchmarks like elections. Elections may accentuate differences and stimulate conflict before the society and state have the capacity to manage them. These capacities include both the institutional strength of rule of law institutions and the social capital of trust, built through postconflict reconciliation and cooperation in economic recovery.

Brahimi, in a "nonpaper" that he circulated to the diplomatic community before leaving Afghanistan at the beginning of 2004, noted that neither the provision of security, nor economic reconstruction, nor national reconciliation had kept pace with the political timetable. As the international community prepared to help Afghanistan hold elections, there was still no rule of law, the means of violence were still under the control of numerous armed groups, and there was still a gulf of mistrust among various groups. Nor had economic development and service delivery taken off enough to build the capacity of the state, bind people's loyalties to it, or provide alternative livelihoods to those involved in armed groups or the drug economy.

But although it is true that everything cannot be done at once with inadequate resources, sequencing alone is too simple a model to capture the relationship between security and political reform or democratization. There is often a mutually interdependent relationship between security and political legitimacy that makes it difficult to separate these functions in a temporal sequence. The international operation must be sufficiently legitimate that its protection helps to support rather than undermine the transitional administration. Such internationally provided transitional security is necessary for building the legitimacy of government institutions through participation and increasing the government's capacity to mobilize resources and deliver services through the state. Only governments enjoying a significant degree of legitimacy can build sustainable national capacity to deliver security.

Both commanders and ordinary combatants (including part-time combatants) also need an economy that can sustain them without recourse to armed predation. To build state capacity, to enable the state to create an environment conducive to economic growth, and to protect and support the initial processes of state fiscal reform require security and the establishment of the rule of law. The Ministry of Finance in Afghanistan was able to operate with some autonomy from the armed groups in the Ministry of Defense only because of the presence of ISAF and the coalition, which provided its personnel with a margin of security.[32] With their support, the Ministry of Finance could bargain from a position of confidence with the Ministry of Defense over the integrity of the payroll. These negotiations were key to DDR. The international protection extended to the central government by ISAF also made it possible to maintain the integrity of the Da Afghanistan Bank (the central bank) and enabled the Ministry of Finance to overcome strong resistance to centralizing revenue in a single treasury account. Without these measures, the Ministry of Defense and other factionally controlled armed forces could have intimidated, threatened, or even attacked the officials leading the reform, ensuring that systems that facilitated the capture of state revenues and payments by factions remained in place.

Once it had reformed its internal operations, the Ministry of Finance sought further assistance from the international security forces to help it gain control of customs points and provincial branches of state banks. Such control is essential if the national government put in place by the Bonn Agreement and now functioning under an elected president is to collect payments in the provinces and receive the revenues from import duties. The international forces, however, failed to see that as part of their mission, which left major obstacles to statebuilding in place. Control of state revenues and payment systems enables the state to establish and operate police, courts, and other institutions of the rule of law that can create the security of contract and operations that (according to the liberal model) will encourage investment, free markets, and economic development.

Elected governments presiding over a society that visibly supports them will be better able to mount campaigns for empowerment by international actors than interim governments of dubious legitimacy. Hence the first election of a legitimate government, although a key step in the statebuilding process, is far from its termination point and may mark its true beginning.

After his election, Afghan president Hamid Karzai openly opposed US plans for aerial eradication of opium poppy, showing greater independence than previously.

This analysis indicates that even though there is no simple formula for sequencing, there is a hierarchy of priorities. An international peacebuilding or stabilization operation must take as its first priority providing whatever transitional security assistance is needed to enable a transitional government to start the process of legitimizing state power. To do so, that operation must itself be legitimate. The negotiation of the security transition is as important, if not more important, to the success of the operation than the negotiation of what is usually called the "political" transition, which bears mainly on civilian authorities. The successful and mutually reinforcing action of international security provision and national legitimacy may then make it possible to build national capacity for domestic provision of security. Both international and domestic security provision can assist a legitimate government in building its capacity to provide other services needed for the welfare and security of the people and the growth of the economy.

Notes

1. United Nations, *Report of the Independent Inquiry into the Actions of the United Nations During the 1994 Genocide in Rwanda,* UN Doc. S/1999/1257, 1999; United Nations, *Statement by the Secretary-General on the Report of the Independent Inquiry into the Actions of the United Nations During the 1994 Genocide in Rwanda,* UN Doc. SG/SM/7263, 1999; United Nations, *Report of the Secretary-General Pursuant to General Assembly Resolution 53/35: The Fall of Srebrenica,* UN Doc. A/54/549, 1999.

2. Stephen John Stedman, "Spoiler Problems in Peace Processes," *International Security* 22, no. 2 (Autumn 1997): 5–53; United Nations, *Report of the Panel on United Nations Peace Operations* (Brahimi Report), UN Doc. A/55/305-S/2000/809, 2000.

3. On Afghanistan, see Michael Bhatia, Kevin Lanigan, and Philip Wilkinson, "Minimal Investments, Minimal Results: The Failure of Security Policy in Afghanistan," Briefing paper (Kabul: Afghanistan Research and Evaluation Unit, June 2004); James Dobbins et al., *America's Role in Nation-Building: From Germany to Iraq* (Santa Monica, CA: RAND, 2003); Seth G. Jones, "Averting Failure in Afghanistan," *Survival* 48, no. 1 (Spring 2006): 111–128.

4. Robert H. Jackson and Carl G. Rosberg, "Why Africa's Weak States Persist: The Empirical and the Juridical in Statehood," *World Politics* 35, no. 1 (October 1982): 1–24. See also Michael Barnett, "The New United Nations Politics of Peace: From Juridical Sovereignty to Empirical Sovereignty," *Global Governance* 1, no. 1 (Winter 1995): 79–97.

5. Classifying operations in one or another category can itself be a political claim. A term such as *peacebuilding* contains an implicit claim of legitimacy, since the goal is defined as "peace," a pure public good, rather than as reducing the level of violent contestation against a particular (and perhaps unjust) distribution of power and wealth. Different but related claims pertain to "postconflict" and "stabilization," for example.

6. Michael W. Doyle and Nicholas Sambanis analyze the success of UN peace operations (defined as the nonreversion to collective violence plus minimal democratization) using indicators of conflict intensity, national capacities, and international capacities. See Doyle and Sambanis, "International Peacebuilding: A Theoretical and Quantitative Analysis," *American Political Science Review* 94, no. 4 (2000): 779–801. This chapter suggests a theoretical basis for further conceptualizing and measuring those capacities, both national and international, and their interaction.

7. James Boyce, introduction to James K. Boyce and Madalene O'Donnell, eds., *Peace and the Public Purse: Economic Policies for Postwar State-building* (Boulder, CO: Lynne Rienner, 2007).

8. Ghassan Salamé, *Appels d'empire: Ingérences et résistances à l'âge de la mondialisation* (Paris: Fayard, 1996).

9. Barbara F. Walter and Jack Snyder, eds., *Civil Wars, Insecurity, and Intervention* (New York: Columbia University Press, 1999). See also Leonard Wantchekon, "The Paradox of 'Warlord' Democracy: A Theoretical Investigation," *American Political Science Review* 98, no. 1 (2004): 17–33.

10. United Nations, *Report of the Independent Inquiry into the Actions of the United Nations During the 1994 Genocide in Rwanda,* UN Doc. S/1999/1257, 1999; United Nations, *Statement by the Secretary-General on the Report of the Independent Inquiry into the Actions of the United Nations During the 1994 Genocide in Rwanda,* UN Doc. SG/SM/7263, 1999; United Nations, *Report of the Secretary-General Pursuant to General Assembly Resolution 53/35: The Fall of Srebrenica,* UN Doc. A/54/549, 1999.

11. See *Supplement to* An Agenda for Peace: *Position Paper of the Secretary-General on the Occasion of the Fiftieth Anniversary of the United Nations,* Report of the Secretary-General on the Work of the Organization, UN Doc. A/50/60-S/1995/1 1995, January 3, 1995; and United Nations, *Report of the Panel on United Nations Peace Operations* (Brahimi Report).

12. Anthony Giddens, *The Nation-State and Violence,* vol. 2, *A Contemporary Critique of Historical Materialism* (Berkeley: University of California Press, 1987).

13. Of course, these cases are most similar to decolonization, in which the UN played a major role, though not in exercising trusteeships or international transitional administrations. The challenge of transforming colonies into sovereign states has proved to be a difficult one.

14. Doyle and Sambanis, "International Peacebuilding," pp. 63–85.

15. In a press conference on February 20, 2002, Rumsfeld was quoted (http://transcripts.cnn.com/TRANSCRIPTS/0202/20/se.03.html): "The question is, do you want to put your time, and effort, and money into adding and increasing the International Security Assistance Force, go take it say from 5,000 to 20,000 people? That's—there's one school of thought that thinks that's the desirable thing to do. Another school of thought, which is where my brain is, is that, why put all the time and money and effort in that, why not put it into helping them develop a national army so that they can look out for themselves over time? Because otherwise, the International Security Assistance Force would be the thing providing peace and stability and security in the country, and at some point it would leave, or ought to leave, because it's an unnatural thing. You'd much prefer that countries look out for themselves and have their own force."

16. Doyle and Sambanis, "International Peacebuilding."

17. Marina Ottaway and Anatol Lieven, "Rebuilding Afghanistan: Fantasy Versus Reality," Policy Brief 12 (Washington, DC: Carnegie Endowment for International Peace, 2002), pp. 1–7; Marina Ottaway, "One Country, Two Plans," *Foreign Policy* 137 (2003): 55–59; Marina Ottaway, "Nation Building," *Foreign Policy* 132

(September–October 2002): 16–24; Roland Paris, *At War's End: Building Peace After Civil Conflict* (Cambridge: Cambridge University Press, 2004).

18. Benedict Anderson, *Imagined Communities: Reflections on the Origin and Spread of Nationalism* (London: Verso, 2006).

19. Paul Collier et al., *Breaking the Conflict Trap: Civil War and Development Policy* (Washington, DC: World Bank and Oxford University Press, 2003).

20. The total to be demobilized turned out to be closer to 60,000; the ultimate strength of the armed forces is now planned to be 80,000, which some think is still larger than the country needs or can afford; and fewer than 2 percent of the Afghan National Army's recruits are former mujahidin. The latter have been largely accommodated in the police, where their continuing group solidarity undermines attempts at reform. These data are from the authors' notes as a participant in these events.

21. Charles T. Call, "Conclusion," in *Constructing Justice and Security After War* (Washington, DC: US Institute of Peace Press, 2007), pp. 25–27.

22. "Agreement on Provisional Arrangements in Afghanistan Pending the Re-establishment of Permanent Government Institutions," Annex 1, "International Security Force," December 5, 2001; at www.un.org/News/dh/latest/afghan/afghan-agree.htm.

23. "The Afghanistan Compact," January 31, 2006; at http://www.ands.gov.af/ands/I-ANDS/afghanistan-compacts-p1.asp.

24. Amos Sawyer, comment during Center on International Cooperation and International Peace Academy [Institute] Conference on "Post-Conflict Transitions: National Experience and International Reform," New York, United States, March 28–29, 2005.

25. Ibid.

26. Francis Fukuyama, *State-building: Governance and World Order in the 21st Century* (Ithaca, NY: Cornell University Press, 2004). In his book, Fukuyama argues that some institutions are easier to transfer to new environments because the requirements for them to be successful are more general, since they function in more or less the same way everywhere. The central bank and the military are cited as examples, whereas other institutions, such as the judicial system, are more dependent on local norms and what the ancient Greeks called *metis,* the pragmatic wisdom of the practitioner (James C. Scott, *Seeing Like a State: How Certain Schemes to Improve the Human Condition Have Failed* (New Haven, CT: Yale University Press, 1998).

27. The Brahimi Report, for instance, suggested measures to ensure that UN transitional administrations are able to adopt an off-the-shelf legal system devised for such situations. See United Nations, *Report of the Panel on United Nations Peace Operations* (Brahimi Report).

28. Chester A. Crocker, "Peacemaking and Mediation: Dynamics of a Changing Field," Coping with Crisis Working Paper Series, International Peace Academy (March 2007); Simon Chesterman, Michael Ignatieff, and Ramesh Thakur, eds, *Making States Work: State Failure and the Crisis of Governance* (Tokyo: United Nations University Press, 2005); International Peace Academy and the Center on International Cooperation, "Post-Conflict Transitions: National Experience and International Reform," Meeting Summary, Century Association, New York, March 28–29, 2005.

29. Dobbins et al., *America's Role in Nation-Building.*

30. Fukuyama, *State-building;* Edward D. Mansfield and Jack Snyder, "Democratic Transitions and War: From Napoleon to the Millenium's End," in *Turbulent Peace: The Challenges of Managing International Conflict,* edited by Chester A. Crocker, Fen Osler Hampson, and Pamela R. Aall (Washington, DC: US Institute of

Peace Press, 2001), pp. 113–126; Fareed Zakaria, *The Future of Freedom: Illiberal Democracy at Home and Abroad* (New York: W. W. Norton, 2003).

31. See United Nations, *Report of the Panel on United Nations Peace Operations* (Brahimi Report).

32. Ashraf Ghani, Clare Lockhart, Nargis Nehan, and Baqer Massoud, "The Budget as the Linchpin of the State: Lessons from Afghanistan," in *Peace and the Public Purse: Economic Policies for Postwar State-building,* edited by James K. Boyce and Madalene O'Donnell (Boulder: Lynne Rienner, 2007), pp. 153–183.

3

Participation
and State Legitimation

Katia Papagianni

States emerging from long-term, destructive warfare face particularly significant challenges to their legitimacy. Political factions may contest the state's very existence and borders, while others may question the structure of its institutions and the rules governing the division of political power. The public, however, exhausted by the fighting and disillusioned with political leaders, often identifies the state with the crimes and mismanagement carried out by elites. Compounding these challenges is the fact that the state has a low capacity to perform the roles usually associated with it, such as providing public security and basic services, and therefore cannot easily bolster its legitimacy in the eyes of the public. Furthermore, contemporary state-building operates under tight time constraints, often imposed by the international community, which prevent lengthy negotiations aimed at achieving consensus among leaders about the role and structure of the state. As a result, new state institutions may lack the support of a segment of the political elites and suffer from serious legitimacy deficits.

In this chapter I first attempt to unpack the sources of state legitimacy by focusing on postconflict states and examining the challenges faced by postwar countries in gaining legitimacy in the eyes of political elites and the public. I then discuss the political processes taking place during the state-building period that contribute to the legitimacy of the state. I ask what type of processes are likely to lead to legitimate new constitutions and institutions and what role inclusion and public participation play in legitimating postwar states.

I define legitimacy as the normative belief of a political community that a rule or institution ought to be obeyed.[1] States are legitimate when key political elites and the public accept the rules regulating the exercise of power and the distribution of wealth as proper and binding. Legitimacy implies that the political community views the goals pursued by the state, the means selected to pursue them, and the decisionmaking process leading to both goals and means as proper.[2] Empirically, legitimacy is observed when rules and the decisions of rule-making and rule-applying institutions are observed. Furthermore, deference to the rules, even by violators, demonstrates the legitimacy of the rules.[3]

In attempting to understand how postwar states may come to be perceived as legitimate, I make four arguments. First, in order to gain legitimacy in the eyes of the public, a state needs to perform its key functions, such as delivering basic public services and maintaining public order. This is extremely difficult in the aftermath of conflict because infrastructure is often severely damaged and services have been disrupted for several years.

Second, for a state to be perceived as legitimate, it is crucial that a political process exists that creates space for debate and dialogue among powerful elites and includes all major political forces. Such a process has a chance of generating support among elites for the new rules and institutions and, thus, of contributing to their legitimacy.

Third, the participation of the public in the statebuilding process may also contribute to the legitimacy of the state but needs to be carried out with great care. Elites often pose obstacles to participation by controlling access, disregarding the outcomes of participatory processes, and manipulating the information available to the public. Disingenuous efforts to engage the public in the political process do not necessarily bolster the state's legitimacy.

Fourth, the domestic legitimacy of states and institutions is influenced but not determined by international standards and external actors. The legitimacy of institutions in the eyes of the local political community may differ from their legitimacy in the eyes of external actors. External legitimacy is crucial when it is accompanied by substantial international investment and intervention, as in Bosnia for example. However, in the cases in which the international community fails to invest the necessary resources in support of statebuilding, international norms such as sovereignty, respect for human rights, and democratic governance do not necessarily strengthen the domestic legitimacy of states.

My argument in this chapter, then, is that a statebuilding process is most likely to generate legitimacy for the state when it is inclusive of all major political forces and open to the participation of the public but also places a priority on maintaining public order and delivering services. This approach to the legitimacy of postconflict states relies on empirical observation of the willingness by domestic political elites and the public to support new state institutions and to pursue their interests through these institutions.

In this chapter I first discuss a number of internal and external sources of state legitimacy before addressing the concrete challenges to bolstering the legitimacy of postwar states. I then examine the opportunities and limitations of different efforts to give content to state institutions through inclusive elite-level dialogue and consultations and through public participation.

Internal and External Sources of State Legitimacy

States gain legitimacy in the eyes of their citizens from their ability to serve a number of purposes. States are complex entities performing many roles, which vary across time within the same state and across states. In this chapter I examine four of these roles, which I treat as complementary: states as bureaucracies and administrations, states as institutions embedded in legal orders, states as embodiments of normative orders, and states as institutional arrangements enshrining power balances.[4]

These four roles allow us to think of the state as a variable concept, as opposed to a fixed one.[5] They also remind us that statebuilding is the process of establishing or rebuilding an entity that combines these four roles and whose legitimacy is derived from performing all of them. These categories furthermore help us distinguish the state from other concepts such as nation, regime, institution, territory, or sovereignty. It is especially important to differentiate states from regimes and to recognize the wide array of functions that states perform in order to avoid reducing the long-term and complex process of statebuilding to a handful of elections or technical assistance programs.

The evaluation of a state's legitimacy is difficult in cases in which some state roles are performed well, but others are not. States perform their roles variably and in the context of variable expectations by the public, making the evaluation of state legitimacy and comparisons across cases difficult. Also, the underperformance of a particular state function does not necessarily imply complete absence of state legitimacy. Furthermore, especially in postconflict states, different social groups perceive the state's legitimacy differently, depending on the history of the conflict and the implications of the peace settlement for their group's interests. As a result, the state may be seen as legitimate by some groups but illegitimate by others. Finally, in some cases, external legitimacy contradicts internal legitimacy—mostly due to the fact that external sources of state legitimacy are often divorced from the state's capacity to perform its tasks, as will be discussed below. In other cases, different sources of external legitimacy offer variable verdicts regarding a state's legitimacy.

The State as Bureaucracy and Administration

The state as a bureaucracy responsible for administration, policy development, and implementation derives its legitimacy in the eyes of the public from its capacity to enforce laws, ensure public order throughout its territory, and promote economic development. The importance of the state's ability to maintain public order and security can be traced back to the Hobbesian idea that individuals accept the authority of the state, at least partly, in order to avoid the insecurity and violence to be found in the state of nature. It is also reflected in the most widely used definition of the state as phrased by Max Weber, according to which the state is the "human community that (successfully) claims the monopoly of the legitimate use of physical force within a given territory."[6]

States are also expected to create favorable conditions for economic development. A powerful example of the importance of economic well-being in state and regime legitimation is the Soviet system's loss of legitimacy following its failure to deliver economic welfare.[7] The demise of several African authoritarian regimes beginning in the late 1980s, including those in Benin, Zambia, and Niger, can also be traced to a large extent to their economic failures. The high degree of legitimacy of the largely undemocratic Singaporean regime, however, can at least partly be attributed to the success of its economic model. The evaluation by the public of state performance usually depends on comparisons with the past. For example, in Romania, the middle-ranking communists who replaced Nicolae Ceauşescu enjoyed legitimacy for several years thanks to their reliance on nationalist rhetoric, but also thanks to the improvement of living standards compared to the dismal conditions of the late 1980s. The systematic looting of the state by the post-Ceauşescu elite became evident to the voters only in the middle of the 1990s.[8]

External sources of legitimacy can cause problems when it comes to a state's performance of its administrative responsibilities. On the one hand, the state's ability to control its territory and maintain public order does not necessarily influence its chances of gaining international recognition. As discussed in Chapter 1, there is often a significant difference between juridical and empirical sovereignty. Thus, in the eyes of the domestic public, the state's legitimacy is closely linked with its ability to provide services, maintain public order, and promote economic prosperity. However, the international system contains contradictory norms, namely the norm of state sovereignty and of state responsibility for economic development, when it comes to the state's role as a bureaucracy and an administration.

The State as Legal Order and International State Legality

As a continuing tradition and heritage with roots in the country's history, the state's internal legal order serves as an important source of legitimacy. Provisional governments in postauthoritarian transitions often rely on the state's legality as a source of continuity until the representatives of the new regime are elected and installed in their positions. As Shain and Linz write, "legality may ensure the continuity of the state's normal administrative functions, if indeed the state itself remains intact."[9] The importance of legal legitimacy is exemplified by the example of the Baltic states in the late 1980s, which reverted to the legal orders of the interwar republics of the 1920s in search of legitimacy for their status as independent states and for their internal legal order before they adopted new constitutions. Similarly, Iraqi and Afghan leaders, in 2005 and 2003, respectively, consulted the constitutions of the early twentieth century in an effort to anchor their constitutional drafting in the legitimacy of a legal tradition. However, "when state institutions of repressive nature have lost any perceived legitimacy in the eyes of the opposition and the public at large, the chances of clinging to old-state legality are reduced dramatically."[10]

Externally, the international sovereignty regime has been "highly accommodating" in recognizing as sovereign those states emerging from decolonization. As a result, today states such as the Democratic Republic of Congo and Somalia are recognized as sovereign, despite their lack of key state characteristics, such as the ability to effectively control their territory. A state's international recognition as sovereign may bolster its internal legitimacy against certain actors, such as minority or secessionist groups, who contest its right to exist in its current borders. International recognition ensures the state's access to international resources, financial and otherwise, while denying recognition to the aims of its challengers. However, when states fail to perform their basic functions, international recognition needs to be accompanied with significant political and material investment in order to significantly bolster domestic legitimacy.

The lack of international recognition has had a variable impact on the ability of unrecognized entities to establish state functions. Kosovo's and the Palestinian Authority's lack of sovereign status explains some of the difficulties they have had in building institutions.[11] Taiwan overcame the same handicap, however, and succeeded in developing a functioning state, democratic system, and market economy. Also, substate entities, such as Iraqi Kurdistan and Somaliland, have to differing degrees achieved characteristics of stateness, including maintenance of public order and provision of public services, in the absence of international recognition. In the case of Somaliland, it has occurred with little, if any, external assistance, as discussed in Chapter 9 by Kenneth Menkhaus. However, Menkhaus also points out that the sustainability of such substate efforts is questionable without international and regional support and cooperation.

The State as Normative Order

The state's ability to symbolize and represent the existence and unity of the political community is one of its key sources of legitimacy. Historically as well as today, "political activity focused on the state sustain[ed] the ethical and moral needs of citizens, not just their material needs."[12] A number of sources of legitimacy, including ideology, ethnicity, and religion, offer the symbols and identities that define the legitimate modes of interaction among state institutions, citizens, and societal actors.[13]

During statebuilding especially, leaders rely on the common history, culture, and language of the nation or community to offer the public a sense of unity in the midst of intense disagreement on the state's future.[14] Shared ethnic and cultural identities offer a foundation upon which societies can begin to rebuild the weak institutions of the state.[15] Even ideologically based statebuilding projects such as the Soviet Union and communist China relied heavily on Russian and Han Chinese culture and identity to legitimize state rule. Ceauşescu's reign in Romania, also, relied on ethnic/cultural nationalism in addition to socialist ideology to gain domestic legitimacy.[16] However, in some countries, such as France and the United States, loyalty to the institutions of the state—as opposed to culture, ethnicity, or religion—forms the basis of what scholars call civic nationalism.[17] In these cases, the state still serves as the embodiment and guardian of society's shared principles and ideals, although these ideals are not based on shared ethnicity or religion, but on a shared understanding of and respect for the state's rules and institutions.

Externally, the normative basis of state legitimacy derives from the international normative order constructed partly under the auspices of UN human rights institutions. According to this normative framework, the exercise of state power is legitimate when it is based on consent and respects basic freedoms and human rights. Scholars have argued that this international normative framework influences state identity and behavior.[18] For example, the democratic formula for the legitimization of authority is often a source of internal legitimacy. It is telling that provisional governments or administrations attempt to gain legitimacy by promising free and competitive elections within a defined period of time.[19]

However, these standards and principles are applied inconsistently by the international community. In postconflict states, international actors have relied on less than demanding standards in order to bestow legitimacy on new states. Democracy is frequently measured in terms of holding elections, and respect for and protection of human rights are measured by the incorporation of international standards in laws and constitutions as opposed to the implementation of these standards. This formal application of international human rights and other standards does not contribute to domestic legitimacy in the absence of an inclusive and consultative political process and improvement in living standards.

The State as an Institutional Arrangement
Mirroring Power Balances

Historically, states emerged from long-term struggles among groups and elites.[20] Statebuilding is a competitive process that inevitably generates winners and losers (see Chapter 8 in this volume). The process results in a set of institutions that reflect the bargains struck between the various competitors and the power balances among them. The state's legitimacy in the eyes of political elites depends on the degree to which its institutions represent accurately the society's diversity and the power balance among the various political groups. When that is the case, groups opt to pursue politics within state institutions instead of using violence to revise or exit the state. Thus, institutions "cohere if they emerge out of existing social forces, if they represent real interests and real clashes of interest which then lead to the establishment of mechanisms and organizational rules and procedures which are capable of resolving those disagreements."[21]

Building or reforming state institutions requires agreement on multiple issues, including the centralization of coercive power, the division of power between center and periphery, and the administration of justice. In the particularly challenging circumstances of postwar states, parties to the conflict often favor institutions that share and divide power among them. The negotiations on how exactly to shape these institutions are torturous, lengthy, and marred by mutual suspicions. Antagonists hesitate to endorse institutional solutions because they know that, once in place, institutions tend to rigidify and reproduce themselves.[22] Even when agreements are reached, the new state institutions are fragile and need continued political engagement by the international community to ensure their survival. However, the international community frequently assumes that, after elections and brief constitutional negotiations, close engagement in postconflict states is no longer necessary. Later in this chapter, the implications of this assumption will be examined in more detail.

Challenges to State Legitimation

The previous section discussed the multiple sources of state legitimacy and some of the contradictions among them. These contradictions become more pronounced in the context of postconflict statebuilding as new institutions face great challenges in performing their roles.

Delivering Public Services and Maintaining Public Order

The postconflict state's ability to promote economic development and ensure public security contributes significantly to its legitimacy, whereas economic inequalities and the inability of states to offer tangible social and economic benefits challenge their legitimacy. This is the case even after elections have been held and the attributes of formal democracy are in place. The importance of the state's ability to deliver services is underscored by a number of contributors in this volume, including Chapters 9 and 14 on Somalia and Liberia, respectively.

Four main challenges to economic development, provision of social services, and wealth distribution are endemic to statebuilding. First, peace agreements often include provisions that protect the socioeconomic interests of privileged interest groups and render reforms and wealth distribution almost impossible. In El Salvador and South Africa, the peace agreements safeguarded the economic interests of the privileged economic classes. Thus, although such agreements enable the end of conflicts, they may prevent economic policies geared toward redistribution of economic benefits and thus endanger their own sustainability and the legitimacy of postconflict states.

Second, the policies pursued by the international community often challenge the capacity of nascent states to deliver services and promote growth. Postconflict states such as El Salvador have been called to implement stabilization and structural adjustment programs that limited their capacities to implement peace agreements, rebuild infrastructure, reintegrate combatants, and deliver services.[23] The willingness of international financial institutions to fund transitional states has increased following the lessons of the 1990s, although the impulse of stabilization programs persists. Moreover, as Chapter 4 of this volume illustrates, external aid often bypasses the public finance system, creating parallel or duplicate structures that can undermine efforts to build state capacity.

Third, predatory elites often remain in power and continue to mismanage their countries' natural resources and other sources of revenue for their private benefit. Some scholars have proposed "shared sovereignty" over specific state services and sources of state revenue between state institutions and the international community.[24] Chapter 14 of this volume discusses the Liberian Governance and Economic Management Assistance Program (GEMAP), which attempts to reduce the discretion of corrupt elites in managing the collection and management of state revenues. Interestingly, the Liberian example combines external intrusion in the form of GEMAP with a political process and an elected government.

The fourth challenge to delivering public services and ensuring public security in postconflict countries concerns states that fail to perform the functions usually associated with states but continue to receive international financial and other resources due to their status as sovereign states.[25] The dilemma for the international community is whether to assist substate entities in their role as service providers at the risk of forgoing the goal of strengthening the central state. Some scholars argue in favor of the former strategy.[26] Jeffrey Herbst, for example, argues that it was improvident for the World Bank and the International Monetary Fund (IMF) to offer no assistance to Somaliland following the collapse of the central government in Mogadishu. He argues that if new subnational entities are not assisted, they may turn into "institutionalized protection rackets [rather] than states that guard the rights of their citizens."[27]

It is often difficult to disentangle the contribution to legitimacy of a sound political process from the state's ability to ensure public security and deliver services. The provision of services and maintenance of public order, at a minimum, may allow the political process to stay on track. Also, service delivery and public order breed patience among the population, allowing people to develop long-term horizons and to consider investing in peaceful activities. In contrast, when public insecurity prevails, the political process is blamed for ineffectiveness, and public support declines.

The Iraqi example is instructive here. Following each significant landmark of the political transition, including the handover of sovereignty in June 2004 and the January 2005 elections, the Iraqi public was supportive of the political process but withdrew their initial support as the security and economic situations failed to improve. However, Iraq has not benefited from a political process that included all significant political actors and allowed for public participation. Thus, the country has suffered both from a less than perfect political process and from the deterioration of public services. The Bosnian model of statebuilding, in contrast, has also included minimal public participation outside of the multiple local and national elections held starting a year after the signing of the Dayton Accords. However, as Marcus Cox discusses in Chapter 11 of this volume, the enormous international military presence in the country succeeded in two years in disrupting the paramilitaries, preventing them from moving around the country, and eventually disbanding them, thus bolstering the legitimacy of the statebuilding effort. Arguably, however, the legitimacy of the Bosnian state was limited due to the continued domination of politics by nationalist elites.

Building a Legal Framework and Defining State Legality

Postconflict states often enjoy international legality but continue to face internal challenges to their existence and territorial integrity. In Iraq, international recognition of the state and its borders provided a formal source of stability and legitimacy, but the state's legality is challenged by the Kurdish question. In Bosnia, the existence of the illegal Bosnian-Croatian statelet, Herzeg-Bosna, openly defied the territorial integrity of the Bosnian state. Similarly, Bosnian Serb politicians envisioned a Republika Srpska independent of or incorporated into Yugoslavia. In other cases, legal questions have been postponed, for example in Kosovo and in southern Sudan, where the final status of various substate entities will be decided further along in the transition.

The question of recognizing breakaway areas in conditions of complete collapse of the central states has emerged since the 1990s. The traditional view in international politics favors territorial integrity and the strengthening of the precollapsed state over the recognition of substate entities.[28] Herbst, however, argues that substate entities should be recognized under certain conditions. Specifically, he argues that if the breakaway areas provide more order through functioning military, police, and judicial systems, over a significant period of time, than the central government, then they should be recognized.[29]

When states fail to perform their basic functions, international recognition may be translated into a meaningful internal order when substantial international political and material resources are invested. This occurred in Bosnia and, in a less invasive manner, in Macedonia. Both countries were challenged by internal spoilers as well as by their neighbors. Their international recognition as sovereign states as well as consistent international diplomatic and material support has helped them survive. However, in the many cases neglected by the international community or where inadequate resources are invested, international sovereignty at best remains an empty shell and at worst inhibits the development of alternative forms of internal order, as William Reno argues in Chapter 7 of this volume. Therefore, international actors need to be aware that the promotion of international norms, such as territorial integrity and state sovereignty, carries enormous responsibilities in terms of providing material and political resources.

Creating Institutions That Reflect Power Balances

Following civil conflicts, countries often reform their constitutions or restructure certain institutions, such as the judiciary and the police. Such constitutional overhauls and institutional reforms sometimes become part of peace agreements or are agreed upon by political leaders in subsequent transitional periods. These reforms aim to redistribute power among stakeholders in a new set of institutions and to strengthen their commitment to the agreement. Inevitably, institutional reform is an extremely contentious process as all actors try to secure as many privileges as possible in the new order.

The effort to create institutions that reflect power balances and enjoy legitimacy involves two key challenges. First, constitutional discussions and institutional reforms tend to take place in a hasty manner, which is often due to the deadlines imposed by the international community. External actors often view drafting constitutions and setting up new institutions as an exit strategy.[30] The hastiness is also due to the push for elections that comes from both national and international actors (see the next section of this chapter), despite the significant risks premature elections carry in the absence of strong institutions. The international community, although in principle appreciating the need for viable political coalitions to support institutional reforms, has not tended to devote the time needed for such coalitions to develop and be nurtured. Unlike postauthoritarian transitions in which political actors have time to debate in detail the timing of elections, electoral systems, and constitutional arrangements, in postconflict settings, decisions are rushed.[31]

The second, related challenge is that new constitutions and reformed institutions tend to result from limited discussions among political actors and minimal, if any, participation by the public. They often lack the support of those stakeholders excluded from the discussions, while limited public participation means that the public is unaware of the rationale behind institutional reforms and hesitates to support them. The importance of lengthy and inclusive domestic political processes for the construction of legitimate and effective institutions is usually underestimated. However, ample evidence and experience demonstrate the importance of not only the content of the constitutions but also the process that leads to their adoption.[32] In order for new institutions to be perceived as legitimate, they need to result from lengthy political processes inclusive of all major political actors.[33] In the next section I examine in greater detail the role of political processes in giving content to and bolstering the legitimacy of state institutions.

Building and Giving Content to State Institutions
Ideally, lasting and legitimate institutions result from political processes that create forums for negotiation and compromise, and allow for the participation of the public and civil society, in order to create common understandings of what the rules regulating political life should be. An inclusive and participatory political process can give content to state institutions so that actors will resort to these institutions to debate issues and resolve disputes. There are limitations to this strategy, however, which are discussed below.

The Timing and Significance of First Elections
In postwar countries, there is often a push for early elections. Following years of conflict and political disenfranchisement, the popular demand for political participation and representation is strong. The public wants to have a say in shaping the country's future and sees elections as an immediate and effective way of doing so. Also, political elites often push for early elections in order to capture perceived strategic advantages. This push for elections also suits the preference of the international community to produce democratically elected leaders with whom they can work and justify early international withdrawal. Dangerously, the international community often presents elections as important landmarks when they may signify little or no progress at all. Early elections very often lead to the election of wartime leaders (Bosnia) and to instability and renewed conflict (Angola, Liberia, Sierra Leone, and Rwanda).[34]

Although elections themselves may be problematic, the delay of elections can create legitimacy problems. In the absence of elections, transitional governments may be completely run by external actors, as in Kosovo and

East Timor under the UN and in Iraq under the US-run Coalition Provisional Authority. But national politics cannot simply be put on hold; political elites will begin to clamor for power.[35] Alternatively, transitional governments may be composed of national leaders appointed by external powers, such as the Iraqi Interim Government chosen by the United States and the UN in June 2004 or the Afghan Interim Administration put in place by the Bonn Agreement in 2001. The delay of elections offers ammunition for opponents of the peace process intent on damaging its legitimacy.

In order for electoral outcomes to be accepted by all, the costs of electoral loss must be made tolerable.[36] The techniques usually used to reduce the costs of electoral loss, some of which are exemplified in the Bosnian case, include power-sharing arrangements as well as the presence of third-party military actors who attempt to ameliorate the security dilemma. The importance of such guarantees was demonstrated in the Iraqi elections of January 2005, which were boycotted by the Arab Sunni community, whose leaders rejected the deal offered to them by the United States and its Iraqi allies.

Ideally, elections should not be held prematurely, and the period leading to elections should provide for inclusion and public participation in order to reduce the winner-take-all understanding of elections. For example, local elections were held in Kosovo and East Timor before national elections in an effort to bolster public participation and local institutions and to diffuse winner-take-all tendencies.[37] An appropriate compromise may be to delay elections according to a transparent, agreed-upon timetable that makes time for inclusive discussions among political elites and public forums. The Bonn process in Afghanistan, although not without its problems, was one such attempt to widen participation in the period before a representative government was elected (see Chapter 13 of this volume).

Regardless of the timing of elections, international actors must be clear about what elections can and cannot achieve in terms of legitimizing the political process. Elections may confirm the existing commitment of political actors to the political process and may confer legitimacy on this commitment by consulting the public. However, long-term legitimacy remains conditional on the continued participation of powerful elites in the political process. In Bosnia, as Marcus Cox discusses in Chapter 11 of this volume, the first elections of 1996 drew the political elites into the new constitutional order. By participating in the elections, hostile elites agreed to interact in the Dayton institutional framework. The election, then, enabled a political process to commence, although greater commitment to the Bosnian state by the leaders of all three communities only emerged several years later. However, in some cases, elections may have little or no impact on the legitimacy of the political process. The January 2005 Iraqi elections failed to bring the Arab Sunnis into the political process. Although the political process, including the drafting of the constitution, continued through 2005, Sunni participation was uneven. Ultimately, the constitution was adopted without their endorsement, and debate over its content continued. The Iraqi case demonstrates that if elections are simply one-time events that have not been preceded by political processes encompassing elites and publics, they can hardly legitimize state institutions.[38]

Consultative Mechanisms Among Political Elites

Given that in most postconflict countries the principal political actors do not agree on the shape or future of the state, it is crucial that transitional processes and institutions leading to elections and new institutions engage all political elites in discussions. Consultations and deliberations offer an opportunity to the signatories of agreements to settle outstanding issues and to bring nonsignatories into the process, thus expanding political participation beyond the narrow group of elites who sign peace agreements and to deepen the commitment of the nonsignatories to the agreement as well. Consultative mechanisms among elites serve as arenas where all sides assess whether the new order will protect their interests and whether agreements will be implemented.[39] Such mechanisms may be incorporated at several stages of transitional periods: the implementation of cease-fires and demobilization agreements, the appointment of transitional governments, the drafting of electoral laws, the establishment of electoral commissions, the administering of elections, the promotion of national dialogue, and the drafting of constitutions. Consultations and transitional institutions create intermediate steps in the process at which actors take binding decisions about the next stage of the process, guarantee the continued participation of opponents and their ability to influence decisions, and gradually develop agreements on constitutional questions.

Experience in a number of countries demonstrates that consultative and inclusive mechanisms which facilitate bargaining and negotiation among elites contribute to the acceptance of the transitional political process and its outcomes. There is also evidence that the absence of such mechanisms has harmed several transitional processes. For example, constitution-making processes that excluded major constituencies have usually led to contested constitutions that lack legitimacy and fail to resolve the major disputes in the country.[40]

The experiences of Iraq and East Timor demonstrate the consequences of noninclusive political processes for the legitimacy of new constitutions and state institutions. In Iraq, the policy of debaathification and the exclusion of former Baathists from the political process, as well as the absence of an inclusive political process until the 2005 elections, left the transitional period with a legitimacy deficit in the eyes of a substantial portion of the population. The adoption of an interim constitution, which was drafted by

the United States and its Iraqi allies, widened rather than bridged the legitimacy deficit due to the exclusion of anti-occupation constituencies from the
deliberations.[41] At each stage of the transitional process, the United States and
its Iraqi allies decided against wide inclusion in the political process, although
alternatives existed that would have created a political space for consultation
and dialogue.[42] Observers have noted, for example, that the constitutional discussions in the summer of 2005 were damaged by the time limitations imposed by the United States and by the insufficient inclusion of Sunni Arabs in
the deliberations.[43] Due to the absence of an inclusive political process, the
country was ill-prepared for the challenge of constitutional discussions. Ultimately, a majority of Sunni Arabs voted against the draft constitution at the
October 2005 constitutional referendum, which was adopted by 78.6 percent
of the total vote.[44]

In a different context, East Timor also demonstrates the detrimental impact of the minimal or complete lack of political consultations among national actors. As a result of multiple factors, the United Nations Transitional
Administration in East Timor (UNTAET) was slow in developing a strategy
for political transition and established a short transitional timetable, leaving
political parties little time to establish themselves. Importantly, the constitutional process was rushed, and the political institutions were relatively weak
at the time of independence. As a result, as Edith Bowles and Tanja Chopra
argue in Chapter 12 of this volume, UNTAET offered a limited contribution
to sustainable self-government and a democratic political environment.[45]

In contrast, the Bonn process in Afghanistan allowed for routine negotiations and consultations among Afghans during the transitional process. Before the adoption of the constitution in early 2004 and the presidential elections in October 2004, the transitional framework allowed for consultations
and negotiations among Afghans in the context of the Interim and Transitional Administrations, and in the Emergency Loya Jirga (ELJ) and later the
Constitutional Loya Jirga (CLJ). The Afghan transitional process did privilege the representatives of the Tajik-dominated Northern Alliance. However,
the Afghan transitional process provided forums within which political actors interacted and negotiated and drafted a constitution.[46]

In South Africa, a culture of bargaining and inclusion was instilled from
the early stages of the transition to democratic government. The 1993 interim
constitution was a political pact, a power-sharing agreement. Concessions
were made to potential spoilers of the pact to bring them into the power-
sharing agreement, the government of national unity. Importantly, the South
African power-sharing arrangement was designed to expire within five years,
and indeed it withered away and was replaced by a modified majority-rule
democracy. Nevertheless, the culture of intergroup bargaining persists and is
deeply embedded in many sectors of South African society, including its new
political institutions.

Of course, inclusion is not a foolproof strategy. Large coalitions tend to be diffuse and represent widely different interests, thus rendering decision-making difficult. In the Guatemalan constitution-making process, which started in 1997, the Partido de Avanzada Nacional (PAN) government opted for a "consensus strategy" with opposition parties, although it could form the necessary alliances to pass the reforms. Consensus was sought in order to give the reforms greater legitimacy and to avoid sabotage by other political parties after the referendum. However, the reforms quickly became hostage to, and were hijacked by, interparty disputes, disappeared from public view, and were lost in the Multiparty Platform. Following a rigorous antireform campaign, the public rejected the bloated constitutional reforms in the referendum, despite the support of civil society and indigenous people's organizations for the reforms.[47]

Taking the above risk into consideration, the goal of inclusion and elite bargaining in the transitional period is to secure the engagement of key political actors in the process and to channel differences among them through agreed-upon institutions and procedures. The long-term goal is that such interaction will lead to the acceptance of such institutions by political actors.

National Dialogue and Public Participation

Public participation may take place during several phases of the statebuilding process, including the appointment of interim governments, as in the example of the Afghan Emergency Loya Jirga and several West African national conferences; the drafting of constitutions, as in Eritrea, South Africa, Rwanda, and Afghanistan; or the implementation of peace agreements, as in Guatemala. Civil society may also participate in transitional governments as well as in discussions of electoral laws and on the reform of specific institutions, such as the police or the prison system. The goal of public participation is to create the space for civil society to gain strength and to develop skills in articulating positions and aggregating interests.[48] Public participation may also expand the issues negotiated during transitions among elites, as in the Afghan Constitutional Loya Jirga. Participation may also lead to the emergence of new national leaders from the ranks of civil society (as in Guatemala), create the political space for the entry of moderate actors in the political process, or expand the scope of contestation in the new regime. Furthermore, participation may develop the democratic characteristics of the individuals participating, namely their support for the democratic system and process, as well as their identification with the statebuilding process.[49]

The importance of process for the legitimacy of public participation efforts. In order to bolster state legitimacy, the process of public participation itself needs to be perceived by the public as legitimate. It is a challenging task: questions of who may participate and on what issues and who selects the participants are very sensitive. No straightforward answers exist on how to achieve a legitimate participatory process. The answers to the question are imperfect but point to the usefulness of multistep selection processes led by credible individuals and independent commissions and relying on publicly available selection criteria. Inevitably, however, inclusion "cannot be perfect or complete, since it will involve some group(s) choosing (and rejecting) others as partners when none of them has been tested electorally."[50] Other ingredients of a participatory process that enhances legitimacy include ample public information and education efforts that endow the process with openness and transparency.

The examples of several West African national conferences, which led the transition to democracy and appointed interim governments, are relevant here. These conferences were led by religious leaders or by commissions composed of all the major contending political forces.[51] In Benin, the incumbent president Mathieu Kérékou agreed under opposition pressure to call a national conference and appointed a diverse preparatory committee to decide the conference's agenda and composition. The committee identified the groups that would participate in the conference and specified how many representatives each would be allotted. The 500-member conference included both representatives of the government and the military as well as Kérékou's enemies in political exile.[52] It also included representatives of all trade unions, voluntary associations, and women's groups, as well as religious leaders, several former heads of state, and a variety of public figures.[53] The conference was followed by peaceful elections and a change in political leadership. In this case, the independence of the preparatory committee and its diverse membership lent legitimacy to the preparatory process and to the conference.

Similarly, the Constitutional Commission in Afghanistan achieved a reasonable degree of legitimacy and succeeded in establishing a representative Constitutional Loya Jirga, which was held in December 2003 and January 2004 and allowed the expression of diverse opinions.[54] The delegates deliberated on each of the 160 articles of the constitution and recommended revisions to a harmonization committee, in this manner contributing to changes in the draft constitution.[55] Also, the constitution-making process enjoyed a genuine public participation effort. The Constitutional Commission had the mandate to promote public information, to conduct public consultations, to prepare a report analyzing the views of Afghans gathered during the public consultations, and to educate the public on the draft constitution. The secretariat of the commission partnered with NGOs in order to disseminate information, distributed 450,000 questionnaires about key constitutional issues, and organized consultations between the commissioners and the public throughout the country. More than 15,000 citizens participated in these consultations.[56]

As discussed above, there are only imperfect answers to the questions of who should participate and through what selection process. The above examples demonstrate that selection processes that are independent of the major political factions, are transparent, and include genuine outreach efforts to the public are likely to be perceived as legitimate by the public and to bolster the legitimacy of the state.

The importance of outcomes for the legitimacy of public participation efforts. Examples abound of participatory and dialogue efforts that failed to achieve their goals and mandates. The Afghan Emergency Loya Jirga did not fulfill its mandate of appointing the Interim Afghan Administration, which was ultimately appointed outside the auspices of the ELJ. Much of the decisionmaking that fell under the ELJ's mandate took place "outside the tent." As a result, the vision of the Bonn Agreement of expanding the membership of the Transitional Administration following the ELJ was not fulfilled. Similarly, the Iraqi National Conference did not elect the Interim National Council, a body supervising the Interim Government, as mandated. The conference simply approved with a show of hands a closed list of candidates, which was also put together outside the tent, and formed the Interim National Council. Both of these processes failed to add legitimacy to the political process, generated bitterness and feelings of unfair treatment, and constituted missed opportunities.

Often, the decisions resulting from participatory processes are not implemented. For example, the Eritrean constitution was drafted through a model, multiyear participatory process but has not been implemented. Also, several West African national conferences (convened to facilitate a transition to democracy) were disbanded, often forcefully, by authoritarian leaders (as in Togo), despite being well-prepared in terms of representativeness and transparency.[57]

Other cases belong in a gray area in terms of their outcomes. Although the Afghan CLJ was fairly representative, it was "by no means fully democratic, in either its selection or its procedures."[58] The constitution's main parameters were in effect decided by the interim government and the international community and then submitted for ratification to the CLJ. In that sense, the constitution-making process was a top-down process and did not emanate from Afghan society.[59]

In Nicaragua, despite the overwhelming victory of the Frente Sandinista de Liberación Nacional (FSLN) in the 1984 elections and the continuation of armed conflict, public participation in the 1985–1987 constitution-making process was extensive. After the election of the National Constituent Assembly, a Constitutional Commission was appointed to prepare an initial draft constitution. The commission invited the input of civic groups before presenting a first draft to the assembly, which distributed 150,000 copies of the draft throughout the country. Subsequently, seventy-three town hall meetings were held around the country to solicit further public input on this first draft. Based on these public comments, a second draft was prepared and delivered to the assembly. The final draft was voted on by the assembly. Nevertheless, although the constitution-making process achieved significant levels of citizen involvement, it achieved only minimal elite consensus. The process of drafting the Nicaraguan constitution did not achieve a substantive agreement among key groups on the nature of the state and on key constitutional principles.

Obstacles to genuine participation due to self-interested political elites. The contribution of public participation to state legitimacy depends greatly on elite attitudes. Opening politics to the public in the aftermath of conflict creates opportunities for elite manipulation of a public that still lives in fear and forms opinions based on the information provided by ethnic or group elites.[60] Also, information regarding political developments tends to be either scarce or manipulated by elites.[61] Political leaders pose obstacles to participation by controlling access to participation and disregarding the outcomes of public participation efforts. Due to elite influence, public participation in the immediate postagreement period may not influence public attitudes toward the new political order, as the discussion of Uganda below demonstrates, or may create incentives for nationalist manipulation and extremist rhetoric.[62]

These issues are real and raise questions about how early in the postagreement period a political process should draw in civil society and the public. The somewhat unsatisfying answer to this question is that it depends on the context and mainly on the security situation in the country. In East Timor, for example, the UN could have initiated an expanded process in the first few months of the transitional administration, but in Bosnia a longer time-frame would have been needed following the 1995 Dayton agreement. The security situation in East Timor improved quite rapidly, and the divisions among the East Timorese were not yet destabilizing immediately after the referendum on independence. In Bosnia, however, it took years before public security was established, and the divisions among the three communities were too great for a genuinely inclusive political process to immediately commence. In this sense, the strategy of holding elections as a way of beginning to engage the leaders of all three groups in a joint process was sensible for the first post-Dayton years. However, by the end of the 1990s, a more locally driven political process was possible.

The Uganda constitutional process demonstrates the influence of elites over the public's perception of the transitional process and of its own participation. Following an eight-year constitution-making process with extensive public participation, the opinions of the Ugandan public on the legitimacy of the constitution (measured as whether it was good for the country or not) relied on the opinions of their community leaders. Devra Moehler argues that regional leaders influenced whether people came to view the constitution as legitimate. This was due to the scarcity of alternative sources of information, the difficulty individuals faced in interpreting information, and the leaders' deliberate efforts to influence public opinion. Also, the public was not informed about the impact of the participatory process on the content of the final document. Therefore, despite the opportunity to directly participate in the constitution, the public remained reliant on their leaders in forming their opinions.[63]

The Iraqi National Conference and the Afghan ELJ demonstrate how elites may prevent genuine participation by controlling who has the right to participate. The Iraqi National Conference of August 2004 was organized by a High Preparatory Commission (HPC), which was dominated by the political parties participating in the Interim Government. The HPC handled the preparation of the conference in secrecy and did not adequately inform the public about the process of selecting the participants.[64] Not surprisingly, the main political parties, which were well-organized and well-informed about the process, gained significant representation. As a result, civil society, independents, and small parties argued that the provincial process resulted in the underrepresentation of civil society and independents and the overrepresentation of the main political parties.[65]

The Afghan Emergency Loya Jirga, in June 2002, suffered from intimidation and other irregularities during its selection process. Furthermore, at the ELJ itself, the presence of provincial governors and warlords, the monitoring of voting and debating by security officers, and the use of Islamist rhetoric hampered the free expression of opinions and independent voting.[66] Observers of the ELJ agreed that it failed to embody democratic expression and to reduce the authority of the regional commanders and warlords.[67]

As the above examples demonstrate, self-interested elites may pose significant obstacles to public participation. Here the international community can play a role. It can contribute to efforts to educate the public about the political process, provide credible and reliable information, and create venues where the public may express its opinion.

Conclusion

In this chapter I have approached statebuilding as a process aiming to establish or rebuild the institutions of the state. I proposed that the state should be understood as a variable concept and that there is no one template of state or statebuilding. I also proposed four general categories of state functions with the goal of underlining the complexity of statebuilding, pointing out the centrality of the state's role as an administrative entity, and separating statebuilding from the different task of regime transition.

I argued that statebuilding, for the purpose of legitimating new state institutions, should be approached as a process as opposed to an event. It should also be seen as a process that meets the criteria of inclusion and participation. Although inclusive and participatory political processes are not foolproof strategies in terms of leading to legitimate outcomes, when managed well, they have a significant chance of bolstering the legitimacy of postwar states.

Notes

1. Ian Hurd, "Legitimacy and Authority in International Politics," *International Organization* 53, no. 2 (April 1999): 381.
2. Michael Barnett, "Bringing in the New World Order: Liberalism, Legitimacy, and the United Nations," *World Politics* 49, no. 4 (July 1997): 539.
3. Thomas M. Franck, "The Emerging Right to Democratic Governance," *American Journal of International Law* 86, no. 1 (January 1992): 51.
4. The choice of the four categories was greatly influenced by Stephen D. Krasner, "Approaches to the State: Alternative Conceptions and Historical Dynamics," *Comparative Politics* 16, no. 2 (January 1984): 223–246, reviewing Clifford Geertz's *Negara: The Theatre State in Nineteenth-Century Bali* (Princeton: Princeton University Press, 1981).
5. J. P. Nettl, "The State as a Conceptual Variable," *World Politics* 20, no. 4 (July 1968): 559–592.
6. Max Weber, "Science as a Vocation," in H. H. Gerth and C. Wright Mills, *From Max Weber: Essays in Sociology* (New York: Oxford University Press, 1946), pp. 129–156. Originally a speech at Munich University, 1918.
7. Anna Matveeva, "Democratization, Legitimacy and Political Change in Central Asia," *International Affairs* 75, no. 1 (January 1999): 37. See also Stephen White, "Economic Performance and Communist Legitimacy," *World Politics* 38, no. 3 (April 1986): 462–482.
8. Tom Gallagher, *Modern Romania: The End of Communism, the Failure of Democratic Reform, and the Theft of a Nation* (New York: New York University Press, 2005).
9. Yossi Shain and Juan J. Linz, *Between States: Interim Governments and Democratic Transitions* (New York: Cambridge University Press, 1995), p. 14.
10. Ibid., p. 15.
11. On Kosovo, see Alexandros Yannis, "The UN as Government in Kosovo," *Global Governance* 10, no. 1 (January–March 2004): 67–91; on Palestine, see Chapter 10 in this volume by Rex Brynen.
12. See Krasner, "Approaches to the State," p. 233.
13. Ibid., p. 228.
14. Rogers Brubaker, *Nationalism Reframed: Nationhood and the National Question in the New Europe* (Cambridge: Cambridge University Press, 1996), p. 63.
15. Ernest Gellner, *Nations and Nationalism* (Ithaca, NY: Cornell University Press, 1983); Mark Juergensmeyer, *The New Cold War? Religious Nationalism Confronts the Secular State* (Berkeley: University of California Press, 1993); Michael Hechter, *Containing Nationalism* (Oxford: Oxford University Press, 2000).
16. Katherine Verdery, *National Ideology Under Socialism: Identity and Cultural Politics in Ceausescu's Romania* (Berkeley: University of California Press, 1991).

17. Rogers Brubaker, *Citizenship and Nationhood in France and Germany* (Cambridge, MA: Harvard University Press, 1992).

18. Martha Finnemore, *National Interests in International Society* (Ithaca, NY: Cornell University Press, 1996); Martha Finnemore and Kathryn Sikkink, "International Norm Dynamics and Political Change," *International Organization* 52, no. 4 (Autumn 1998): 887–917; Alexander Wendt, *Social Theory of International Politics* (Cambridge: Cambridge University Press, 1999).

19. Franck, "The Emerging Right to Democratic Governance."

20. Krasner, "Approaches to the State," p. 225.

21. David Chandler, "Introduction: Peace Without Politics?" *International Peacekeeping* 12, no. 3 (Autumn 2005): 309.

22. Krasner, "Approaches to the State," p. 234.

23. Alvaro de Soto and Graciana del Castillo, "Obstacles to Peacebuilding," *Foreign Policy* 94 (Spring 1994): 69–83.

24. Stephen D. Krasner, "Sharing Sovereignty: New Institutions for Collapsed and Failing States," *International Security* 29, no. 2 (Fall 2004): 85–120.

25. Stephen D. Krasner, "Building Democracy After Conflict: The Case for Shared Sovereignty," *Journal of Democracy* 16, no. 1 (January 2005): 73.

26. Jeffrey Herbst, "Responding to State Failure in Africa," *International Security* 21, no. 3 (Winter 1996–1997): 131, 139. See also Richard Joseph and Jeffrey Herbst, "Correspondence: Responding to State Failure in Africa," *International Security* 22, no. 2 (Autumn 1997): 175–184.

27. Herbst, "Responding to State Failure in Africa," p. 139. Also, see William Reno, "Bottom-Up Statebuilding?" Chapter 7 in this volume.

28. William Zartman, "Putting Things Back Together," in *Collapsed States: The Disintegration and Restoration of Legitimate Authority,* edited by I. William Zartman, pp. 267–273 (Boulder, CO: Lynne Rienner, 1995).

29. Herbst, "Responding to State Failure in Africa," p. 136.

30. Marina Ottaway, "Rebuilding State Institutions in Collapsed States," *Development and Change* 33, no. 5 (November 2002): 1001–1023.

31. Charles T. Call and Susan E. Cook, "On Democratization and Peacebuilding," *Global Governance* 9, no. 2 (April–June 2003): 238.

32. Neil Kritz, "Constitution-Making Process: Lessons for Iraq." Testimony by Neil Kritz, director of the Rule of Law Program at the US Institute of Peace, before a joint hearing of the Senate Committee on the Judiciary, Subcommittee on the Constitution, Civil Rights, and Property Rights; and the Senate Committee on Foreign Relations, Subcommittee on Near Eastern and South Asian Affairs, June 25, 2003, 108th Congress, 1st session, http://www.usip.org/congress/testimony/2003/0625_kritz.html; Vivien Hart, "Constitution-Making and the Transformation of Conflict," *Peace and Change* 26 (2001); Jon Elster, "Constitution-Making in Eastern Europe: Rebuilding the Boat in the Open Sea," *Public Administration* 71, nos. 1–2 (1993); Michael Barnett, "Building a Republican Peace: Stabilizing States After War," *International Security* 30, no. 4 (2006): 16–17.

33. Marina Ottaway, "Rebuilding State Institutions in Collapsed States."

34. Edward D. Mansfield and Jack Snyder, "Democratization and the Danger of War," *International Security* 20, no. 1 (Summer 1995): 5–38.

35. Jack Snyder, "Empire: A Blunt Tool for Democratization," *Daedalus* 134, no. 2 (Spring 2005): 58–71.

36. Nancy Bermeo, "What the Democratization Literature Says—or Doesn't Say—About Postwar Democratization," *Global Governance* 9, no. 2 (April–June 2003): 165.

37. Call and Cook, "On Democratization and Peacebuilding," p. 37.

38. Marina Ottoway, "Iraq: Without Consensus, Democracy Is Not the Answer," Carnegie Endowment for International Peace Policy Brief no. 36, Washington, DC, March 2005.

39. Terrence Lyons, "Post-conflict Elections and the Process of Demilitarizing Politics: The Role of Electoral Administration," *Democratization* 11, no. 3 (June 2004): 36–62.

40. Neil Kritz, "Constitution-Making Process: Lessons for Iraq."

41. Andrew Arato, "Interim Imposition," *Ethics and International Affairs* 18, no. 3 (Winter 2004–2005): 25–50. For an overview of the Iraqi process, see Larry Diamond, "Building Democracy After Conflict: Lessons from Iraq," *Journal of Democracy* 16, no. 1 (January 2005): 9–23.

42. Katia Papagianni, "State-Building and Transitional Politics in Iraq: The Perils of a Top-Down Transition," *International Studies Perspectives* 8 (August 2007): 253–271.

43. Jonathan Morrow, "Iraq's Constitutional Process II: An Opportunity Lost," Special Report 155 (Washington, DC: United States Institute of Peace, November 2005).

44. Ottoway, "Iraq."

45. See Ian Martin and Alexander Mayer-Rieckh, "The United Nations and East Timor: From Self-Determination to State-Building," *International Peacekeeping* 12, no. 1 (Spring 2005): 136.

46. On the Afghan transitional process, see Chapter 13. See also Barnett R. Rubin, Chapter 2 in this volume; Rubin, "Crafting a Constitution for Afghanistan," *Journal of Democracy* 15, no. 3 (July 2004): 5–19; Larry Goodson, "Building Democracy After Conflict: Bullets, Ballots, and Poppies in Afghanistan," *Journal of Democracy* 16, no. 1 (January 2005): 24–38; International Crisis Group, "The Afghan Transitional Administration: Prospects and Perils," Asia Briefing no. 19, Kabul and Brussels, July 30, 2002.

47. Roddy Brett and Antonio Delgado, "Guatemala's Constitution-Building Processes," paper submitted to International IDEA's Democracy-Building and Conflict Management program, 2005, p. 22, http://www.idea.int/conflict/cbp/upload/CBP-Guatemala.pdf (accessed July 28, 2007).

48. For the role of civil society in postconflict countries, see Daniel N. Posner, "Civil Society and the Reconstruction of Failed States," in *When States Fail: Causes and Consequences,* edited by Robert I. Rotberg, pp. 237–255 (Princeton, NJ: Princeton University Press, 2004). See also Zartman, "Putting Things Back Together," p. 269.

49. Jarat Chopra and Tanja Hohe, "Participatory Intervention," *Global Governance* 10, no. 3 (July–September 2004): 292.

50. Arato, "Interim Imposition," p. 29.

51. Michael Lund and Carlos Santiso, "National Conferences," in *Democracy and Deep-Rooted Conflict: Options for Negotiators,* edited by Peter Harris and Ben Reilly, pp. 252–262 (section 4.8), Handbook Series 3 (Stockholm: International IDEA, 1998); Jacques Mariel Nzouankeu, "The Role of the National Conference in the Transition to Democracy in Africa: The Cases of Benin and Mali," *Issue: A Journal of Opinion* 21, nos. 1–2 (1993): 44–50.

52. John R. Heilbrunn, "Social Origins of National Conferences in Benin and Togo," *Journal of Modern African Studies* 31, no. 2 (June 1993): 277–299, 286; Samuel Decalo, "Benin: First of the New Democracies," in John F. Clark and David E. Gardinier, eds., *Political Reform in Francophone Africa* (Boulder, CO: Westview Press, 1997), pp. 43–61, 54.

53. Kathryn Nwajiaku, "The National Conferences in Benin and Togo Revisited," *Journal of Modern African Studies* 32, no. 3 (September 1994): 429.

54. For a detailed discussion of the CLJ, see International Crisis Group, "Afghanistan: The Constitutional Loya Jirga," Asia Briefing no. 29, December 12, 2003.

55. Michele Brandt, "Constitution-Making in Cambodia, East Timor and Afghanistan," UNDP/BCPR, May 2005, p. 16 (unpublished report on file with the author).

56. For a criticism of the constitution-making process, including of the public information and participation effort, see International Crisis Group, "Afghanistan's Flawed Constitutional Process," Asia Report no. 56, June 12, 2003.

57. John R. Heilbrunn, "Togo: The National Conference and Stalled Reform," in *Political Reform in Francophone Africa,* edited by John Clark and David E. Gardinier, pp. 225–245 (Boulder, CO: Westview Press, 1997).

58. Anatol Lieven, "Afghan Democracy Must Be More Than Skin Deep," *Financial Times,* January 6, 2004, p. 13, Comment.

59. Ibid.

60. James D. Fearon and David D. Laitin, "Violence and the Social Construction of Ethnic Identity," *International Organization* 54, no. 4 (Autumn 2000): 845–877.

61. Jack Snyder and Karen Ballentine, "Nationalism and the Marketplace of Ideas," *International Security* 21, no. 2 (Autumn 1996): 5–40.

62. Devra C. Moehler, "Public Participation and Support for the Constitution in Uganda," manuscript.

63. Ibid.

64. The HPC made decisions on the composition, agenda, and rules of procedure of the conference without adequately consulting with political and social groups. See Katia Papagianni, "National Conferences in Transitional Periods: The Case of Iraq," *International Peacekeeping* 13, no. 3 (September 2006): 316–333.

65. "Last Chance for Inclusion in Iraq," *New York Times,* August 2, 2004.

66. Furthermore, there were procedural obstacles to meaningful dialogue and participation. The rules of procedure according to which individuals would be nominated and selected for the various positions in the Transitional Administration were made public only the day before the ELJ began and were not widely known.

67. International Crisis Group, "The Loya Jirga: One Small Step Forward?" Asia Briefing no. 17, May 16, 2002.

4

Peacebuilding and Public Finance

Michael Carnahan and Clare Lockhart

A sustainable system of public finance is foundational to the building and ongoing operation of a stable state. The state's capacity to collect and expend revenues underpins its ability to deliver basic services to its citizens, including security, social services, and infrastructure. The ability of the state to collect revenues depends on whether its citizens perceive it to be legitimate; the state will be increasingly seen as legitimate if it can allocate resources and manage expenditures effectively and equitably. Rebuilding the public finance system can, therefore, both underpin and reinforce a virtuous cycle as part of broader efforts to build a legitimate and effective state. However, external aid that bypasses the public finance system can undermine efforts to build state capacity, turning a potentially virtuous cycle into a vicious one.[1]

In this chapter we examine the centrality of public finance to building a functioning state. The first section outlines why an effective public finance system is integral to statebuilding, and the second section analyzes what a functioning system of public finance entails. Those sections provide the context for a two-part discussion of how interventions led by the international community undermine statebuilding efforts by channeling funds outside the government and relying on parallel mechanisms of their own creation. The final section proposes some ways forward that offer an alternative approach that places the public finance system at the center of international statebuilding interventions.

Why Focus on Public Finance?

A functioning public finance system is the backbone of an effective and legitimate state. A public finance system is integral to statebuilding because it underpins the ability of the state to perform its core functions, which necessarily supports efforts to build state capacity across other domains.[2] By building up the public finance system in a postconflict country, the capability for strategic planning can be developed through the budget process, which should be the locus for formulating, coordinating, and monitoring policy. A holistic approach to developing the public finance system, with a particular focus on balance between revenue and expenditure, is essential to ensuring the public finance system can meet its potential as the foundation for an effective state.

The key to success in restoring state functions is well-sequenced and coherent progress across economic, political, security, and administrative domains. Progress—or failure—across these domains tends to be mutually reinforcing. Improvements in the security situation are reinforced by a functioning, representative, and inclusive political system. Economic growth will only occur if security is improving and the political situation becomes more stable, but increased economic growth is itself the foundation upon which a sustainable politics and security can be built over the longer term. Forward movement on all these fronts generates a mutually reinforcing process that can contribute to the creation of a stable and prosperous society.[3]

Building a sustainable public finance system is a fundamental part of this mutually reinforcing process. Domestic revenue must be collected and spent in priority areas, including the investments in human, physical, and institutional capital that lay the foundations for economic growth. When the government is seen to be delivering services and reporting transparently on revenue and expenditure, its legitimacy is further enhanced. In a postconflict situation, where trust between groups is low, a mechanism that ensures the transparent and even-handed allocation of resources can be especially important. When the government allocates resources in a transparent and accountable way, the influence of spoilers and competing actors can be undermined.

In the absence of a strong public finance system, a vicious cycle can fast be reinforced. Revenues will be inadequate to meet expenditure needs, and the revenues that are collected are likely to be misallocated or stolen and may be used to fund illicit activities that generate instability. Unlike domestic revenue collection, which often spurs calls for accountability in government expenditure, citizens have little stake in the efficacy of foreign aid expenditure, reinforcing a culture of lack of accountability. Alternative sites of authority emerge and are reinforced, and the authority of the state is weakened.

Developed countries have traditionally engaged with fragile, failing, or failed states by compartmentalizing issues into clearly defined silos. The United Nations typically takes the lead in political reform, including designing and implementing peace processes. This political process is supported by security arrangements, usually provided by combinations of forces sponsored by varying groups, including the North Atlantic Treaty Organization (NATO) and the Organization for Security and Cooperation in Europe

(OSCE). Responsibility for ongoing law and order has had a range of champions. Economic reform has been the responsibility of the International Monetary Fund (IMF), the World Bank, and regional development banks. UN agencies and nongovernmental organization (NGOs) have tended to focus on the delivery of social services.[4]

Interventions are further complicated because multilateral actors are joined in any exercise by a number of bilateral partners. In most cases each individual donor country is represented by a different agency within its government: the political domain may be covered by a foreign ministry, the security domain by a defense ministry, the economic domain by a finance ministry, and the social domain by a development ministry, with no guarantee that representatives from each ministry will agree on the way forward.

There have been calls for both domestic and international actors to employ a more strategic approach to planning, underpinned by core statebuilding imperatives, in a postconflict period.[5] The budget is the instrument most likely to ensure that any such strategy gets traction in practice. The budget is the mechanism binding the state to transparency and accountability in the use of finances: through the transparent preparation of a budget and tracking of its implementation, actors can most effectively be held accountable for playing by new rules of the game.

In Afghanistan, extensive studies undertaken by NATO strategic planners during 2004 demonstrated that the creation of a public finance system and credible institutions were fundamental to the creation of a secure environment over the medium to long term. Supported by a team of strategic planners and international experts, the government of Afghanistan led the preparation of a twelve-year statebuilding plan and programs to which resources would be pledged.[6] The budget underpinned this plan, which itself focused on reinforcing the ability of the state to collect revenues and plan effective expenditures.

In political or security discussions ambiguity can often be a useful way to garner an initial consensus, enabling incremental progress over time.[7] In contrast, questions of public finance, such as the rate of customs duty to be levied on goods or the amount of money that would be spent in a given year on the defense force, require early precision. Early in the life of a new government, budgets are prepared, revenues collected, and expenditures made. The allocation of scarce resources is among the first concrete decisions that a new administration must take. The exercise of preparing and agreeing on a budget can be an important tool in consensus building and capacity building for cabinet governance. In this way, the public finance system generally, and the budget more specifically, provide a tangible discourse that drives change in the sphere of political decisionmaking. The budget process should accordingly become the locus for the formulation, coordination, and monitoring of policy, and a critical tool of strategic planning in any statebuilding effort.[8]

Within the public finance sphere, balanced progress must occur across different domains. A strong budget that precisely allocates spending to high-priority areas is worthless if there are no staff in ministries who can effectively run these programs. Indeed, without the capacity to spend effectively, domestic revenue collection may undermine the statebuilding agenda as patronage and corruption become institutionalized. Balanced support is required between the revenue and expenditure sides of the public finance system. For example, Kosovo faces particular challenges because the revenue system was built up rapidly and effectively, but the expenditure side received less attention. Consequently, Kosovo collected revenues of around 30 percent of gross domestic product (GDP); a figure of around 15 percent is considered by the international financial institutions (IFIs) to represent a strong revenue effort in a postconflict context. Considerable public sector hiring took place, and several programs commenced without careful planning. Now, Kosovo faces difficult decisions on what areas to cut back as revenues are not growing fast enough to match the growth in expenditures.

In concluding this section, it might be helpful to consider two different views of statebuilding. One view posits that political legitimacy can be created and shored up through the use of patronage to support specific groups. In a postconflict situation, there is a risk that this approach leads to the consolidation of a criminal-mafia regime, because the groups that most need to be appeased are often those that thrived during war and became connected to international money laundering, weapons supply, and other illegitimate global interests. Another view posits that unless a rules-based system is instituted as soon as possible, based on the realization of citizens' rights and duties through transparent, accountable rules and systems, these criminal networks and their interests will capture the state. A functioning public finance system is the key catalyst to the latter process.[9]

What Constitutes a Functioning and Sustainable System of Public Finance?

Public finance involves estimating available resources, allocating resources to priority needs through a budget, collecting revenue, expending resources against the budget, and monitoring and reporting on these collections and expenditures.[10] The key to building a sustainable public finance system is to design a system that is clearly rules-based, with very little room for individual discretion. The system should provide predictable and transparent management, requirements for regular reporting to the public and the legislature, and limits on opacity. These features must be developed across the entire public finance system, including the domains of revenue, expenditure, and public debt. This section offers a brief overview of each of these domains.

Revenue

The government must have the capacity to estimate the amount of revenue that will be collected under existing legislation, enact legislative changes if revenue needs to be increased or decreased, and then administer the system to ensure that the revenue is collected. Estimating the available revenue involves analyzing data from previous years, estimating the changes in major macroeconomic parameters (such as GDP and inflation), and then estimating the impact of these changes on likely revenue collections.

The two key aspects of revenue administration are tax and customs. There are four key elements in taxation administration: registering and accounting for payments from taxpayers; assessing and reconciling the amounts paid by taxpayers with overall obligations each year; educating taxpayers; and enforcing the tax laws, which generally involves a focus on large taxpayers, an active program of audits, and court-based prosecutions. Customs administration involves the collection of all relevant duties and levies, including customs and excise duties. This work includes valuation of goods, determination of eligibility for exemption, export/import procedures, controls of import quotas, and physical examination of goods.

A cursory consideration of these aspects of revenue administration shows the intimate link between public finance and the other domains of statebuilding. Without a functioning security sector, the enforcement and compliance needed to operate a revenue system will be inadequate. In the absence of broad political support for the administration and an acceptance of its legitimacy, there will be such a high volume of willful noncompliance that only an extremely draconian enforcement effort will yield any revenue (and will itself further undermine the government's legitimacy).

There are two major challenges to building a sustainable revenue system. First, there must be adequate economic activity from which revenue can be extracted. In the absence of productive activity, there is nothing to tax, and there will be no revenue. Therefore, economic growth and sound macroeconomic and microeconomic policies are critical. Second, the tax and customs administrations require a strong cadre of public officials who are well trained, adequately remunerated, and committed to building a strong revenue service.

In postconflict economies there is often no shortage of international assistance to develop physical and technological infrastructure.[11] However, there is usually a shortage of experienced and well-trained revenue officials. This constraint dictates the way in which the revenue collection capacity in postconflict countries is likely to develop.

Most postconflict countries have tended to follow a four-stage sequence, driven by the initial shortage of trained revenue officials. There is usually an initial focus on customs collection, particularly where there are a limited number of border points that can be policed with a relatively small staff. The next development is usually the introduction of a services tax, generally on services consumed by the expatriate community, such as hotels, restaurants, and telecoms. The third development is the creation of a large taxpayer unit, focusing generally on the 100 to 500 largest taxpayers, as they provide the bulk of the corporate income tax revenue. The fourth development is personal income taxation, often with pressure to introduce a comprehensive personal taxation system in advance of the first major civil service pay raise under the new administration. Subsequent developments will depend on the individual country's circumstances and can include resource taxation or more comprehensive indirect taxation.

Expenditure

A functioning public finance system uses the available revenue to provide services to individuals and communities, including social services, safety and security of person and property (including police and a justice system), and access to essential physical infrastructure services. There are three distinct phases in an expenditure system: budget preparation, budget execution, and monitoring and auditing expenditure. The first component in public expenditure management is the preparation of the expenditure plan. Preparing a budget involves bringing together all spending proposals, evaluating them for their cost-effectiveness, and presenting them in a complete and coherent form so that decisions on priorities can be taken by the relevant political decisionmaking body—usually a cabinet or a group of senior ministers working with the president or prime minister. This is generally coordinated by a ministry of finance, in close consultation with other ministries. Then, depending on the structure of the legislature and the relationship between the legislature and the executive branches of government, there may be additional modification of the spending plan.

The international development community lacks a well-developed understanding of the need for a unified expenditure plan in the form of a budget. Rather, the majority of international actors often seem to resent a budgeting process that limits their freedom to do what they want with their aid money. Each international partner allocates expenditure in its own interest, or in its perception of the national interest of the recipient country, inevitably leading to a whole that is less than the sum of its parts. A comprehensive and coherent budgeting process is vital to ensuring that overall expenditure meets the national interests, rather than a collection of sectional interests.

Governments use budgets to prepare expenditure not because some things are unimportant, but because everything is important. Budgets allow prioritization among competing goods: they allow questions to be asked and choices to be made about what is more important and what is most important. The relevant question is not whether reducing maternal mortality or improving farm access to markets is important. Rather, in a world where resources are limited, the question is what level of resources should be allocated to each activity. Preparing expenditures in a piecemeal fashion, in which each organization has its plan, does not allow for this overall perspective and prioritization, nor does it allow for easy coordination. Planning expenditure through a budget process ensures that trade-offs can be made and balance maintained across dimensions. Balance must be maintained between sectors, between capital and operational expenditures, between staffing and operational costs, and across geographically and ethnically diverse communities. The budget, in sum, is the site where trade-offs between multiple and competing aims can be analyzed and managed.

Once the budget has been legislated, the next step is to carry out the spending program in accordance with the legally approved budget, which is generally the responsibility of the treasury within the ministry of finance. It involves preparing monthly or quarterly allotments for different budgetary units of the government and processing their expense reports. When expenditures are legitimate, payments are issued to the claimants. The treasury must also manage cash flow on an ongoing basis to ensure that government finances do not go into deficit, unless there is legislated approval to borrow. Management of cash flows is complicated when there are multiple sources of funds, such as special accounts or dedicated multilateral trust funds.

Creating a single treasury account, into which all resources of the state flow and from which all payments are made, will facilitate cash-flow management. A particular challenge in many countries, including Afghanistan, has been the presence of multiple accounts, with many ministries having their own accounts. This makes it very difficult to assess the country's overall fiscal position and trade-offs between different spending priorities. Moreover, given the limited auditing and accounting capacity in Afghanistan, the presence of multiple accounts makes effective oversight and monitoring very difficult.

The final task is monitoring and reporting on expenditure, which includes the preparation of monthly, quarterly, and annual expenditure statements that report on expenditure by each ministry against its budget allocation. Trained staff can use these expenditure reports as the basis for assessing the effectiveness of expenditure. The expenditure report indicates how much money was spent on a particular project, but additional analysis is needed to determine whether the expenditure actually delivered the benefits or provided the services that it was designed to. Additionally, targeted auditing programs are needed to ensure that public funds are spent in accordance with the budget and the law.

Regular reporting on revenue and expenditure to the organs of government and to the public fosters transparency and accountability in governance. Regular and timely reports on primary expenditures must be institutionalized.

In Afghanistan, monthly reports are submitted to the cabinet on revenues and expenditure, and regular reports from international auditors are submitted to cabinet-rank ministries on the proportion of their expenditure that was ineligible according to the laws of the country. The degree to which ineligible expenditures occurred and the extent to which abuses were addressed led to reductions in future funding allocations to that organ of government. Pending the creation of parliamentary oversight mechanisms, regular reports were made to the nation through press conferences and at the *loya jirgas* to summarize the same issues.

Public Debt

The goals of debt management policy include managing the net debt portfolio of the country at the lowest cost over the medium term and supporting market efficiency through borrowing operations in the financial markets. The government needs the capacity to issue a range of debt instruments of varying maturities to ensure that it can access sufficient funds to continue operations.

Countries that have experienced regime change often face the issue of liabilities incurred by previous regimes. There may be questions about whether the previous regime was legitimate, or cases in which borrowed resources were squandered. If a previous regime received military hardware and training on credit that were later used to oppress the population, should that population have to pay for the bullets that killed their families after the regime is ousted?[12] The prevailing position has been that the new regime inherits the liabilities of the old regime. This approach protects the fiscal rights of citizens in lending countries at the expense of citizens in borrowing countries.

The period after regime change or conflict poses a range of challenges to the indebted country. A new beginning provides an opportunity for major debt write-offs and the possibility of obtaining donor support to fund any arrears in repayments—a prerequisite for obtaining new multilateral funding. Although there may be external pressure for the new government to enter into a Paris Club process to have the debts consolidated and repaid at a highly concessional rate, this decision should be made with care. To enter into such an arrangement requires the new country to acknowledge that the debts are legitimate, when they may not be.

Other Economic and Financial Functions of the State

The focus of this chapter is the relationship between building the institutions of public finance and statebuilding. There are also a range of economic and financial state functions outside the domain of public finance per se that should be considered in any discussion of statebuilding. When carried out effectively, these functions support a growing and dynamic economy. Several of these functions are briefly summarized below, although to fully capture each of these issues is beyond the scope of this chapter.

Monetary affairs. The institutional arrangements around the monetary authority need to be well designed, including its degree of independence from the rest of the government and its associated reporting responsibility and accountabilities. There will be other challenges in a postconflict environment: ensuring that the financial architecture is operating, setting the overall goals of monetary policy, and making the instruments available to the monetary authority to conduct that policy and potentially the choice of currency.

Management of state assets. The management of the tangible and intangible assets of the state is a second key area requiring attention in the immediate aftermath of war. It is ironic that, as donors pledge billions of dollars to postconflict countries, billions of dollars in state assets can be transferred into private hands, entrenching and empowering a criminalized elite. Tangible assets can be transferred through the granting of rights over assets, including rights over forests, oil, gas and minerals, antiquities and cultural heritage, land, and fishing. Public assets can also be transferred into private hands through the granting of monopoly rights over key sectors. Sadly, monopolies of this kind can destroy value by entrenching inefficient and costly market structures. Poor management of state assets in this way entrenches a winner-take-all mentality, with public assets treated as spoils to be divided. Such an approach is opposed to a more cooperative growth-based model for development and is likely to undermine stability and contribute to ongoing conflict.[13]

Transforming the illegal economy. In developed countries, the market and economic institutions can be assumed to exist. Often the task becomes one of ensuring the right balance between free market activity and government direction or regulation. In developing countries, and, more specifically, in postconflict countries, the market and economy do not exist as functioning institutions. During the conflict, networks of criminality are likely to have flourished and thus, the networks of an *illegal* economy have become entrenched and institutionalized. The creation of a legitimate economy as an institution is an essential task for economic policymakers in a postconflict situation. It is clear that the international community has not yet identified the mechanisms to do this. The current mechanisms—including drafting legislation and establishing anticorruption units—may be insufficient. If the challenge is to create a legitimate capitalist class who will be both willing and able to pay taxes—and will demand a functioning state— other mechanisms need to be identified.[14]

The Impact of Development Resources on State Capacity

To understand how the international assistance community can support or undermine the creation of a sustainable public finance system, it is important to understand how funds flow and how decisions are made in the current system. Funding for development assistance starts as domestic revenue collected by donor countries and is designed to provide assistance, either directly or indirectly, to developing countries. The channels through which the funds flow, and the modalities through which they are spent, will determine how much money trickles down to the beneficiaries and how much is diverted to meet other objectives. These decisions will also determine whether the international development industry supports or undermines the building of state capacity. Fieldwork across six countries, reviewed by leaders of postconflict transitions at a conference at Greentree Estates in September 2005, found that the majority of current international practice undermines the statebuilding agenda.[15]

How Resources Can Flow: The Architecture

The prevailing understanding of the flow of funds in the international development system is illustrated in Figure 4.1 below. It delineates five elements in the process: the original funding sources, the conduits through which the funds pass, the decisionmakers, the implementers, and the beneficiaries.

The main *sources* of development funding are the private citizens and companies in donor countries. Some funds are collected in the recipient country through taxation of domestic economic activity, license fees, or the sale of state assets. However, the bulk of public spending in postconflict countries comes from revenue collected in donor countries and then allocated by the donor government to the recipient country. In some cases, international

Figure 4.1 The Flow of Resources in Developing Countries

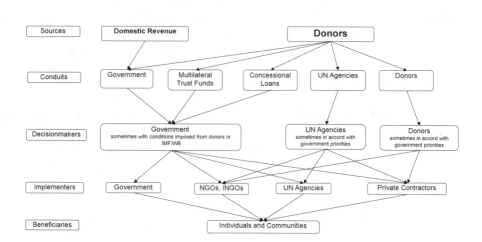

nongovernmental organizations (INGOs) collect funds directly via donations, but the majority of their funds come from donor governments.

Funding conduits are the channels through which funds flow on the way to their final destination. Domestic revenue is channeled directly to the government. Donor funds can pass through several possible channels. Some funds are provided directly to the host government from the donor in the form of tied or untied budget support. In the case of untied budget support, the donor simply deposits the money in the government account, and for all intents and purposes it can be treated like domestic revenue. Otherwise, the donor may direct funds toward a specific portion of the budget (e.g., earmarking it to pay teachers' salaries). In some cases, donors may wish to provide direct support to the operations of the government but may use a multilateral channel. Multilateral trust funds have been established for many countries to provide budgetary support, often with conditions attached (e.g., funds could not be used to purchase lethal weapons).

Some donor funds are used to support the operations of development banks and other international financial institutions, including concessional lending operations. Donors also provide funds to development banks, either directly or by funding endowments that the development banks then provide as grants. In some cases, donor governments provide money directly to United Nations agencies or NGOs. That is, a donor government will agree to fund a project that has been designed by a United Nations agency. Finally, the development agency or other agencies from the donor government may choose to retain and program the money itself.

Decisionmakers determine how and where the money will actually be spent. There are at least three possible decisionmaking loci. The first decisionmaker is the recipient government itself. Theoretically, the government has full control over how it spends its domestic revenue. In the case of budget support, the government presents a proposed expenditure plan, and if donor governments support it, they may provide resources for the plan.

A second possible decisionmaker is intergovernmental organizations, including IFIs and UN agencies. When the government borrows or receives grants from IFIs, the government is the notional decisionmaker, although the preferences of IFIs, especially where conditionality is exercised, often shape government's expenditure patterns.[16] For UN agencies, funding is often provided from donor governments against very general project proposals, with great pressure on donors to disburse. Under such a general remit, a UN agency can often determine unilaterally where it works, what type of services or benefits it provides, and who the beneficiaries of the services will be.[17]

A third possible decisionmaker is a donor government's development agency, which can allocate funds as it wishes. In some cases, donor funds are earmarked to particular sectors, but even within those sectors the development agency can decide on issues such as the location and precise nature of the projects.

Implementers are the organizations that actually produce things: delivering services, building infrastructure such as roads or schools, or digging wells. Generally, implementation is carried out by one of four groups: the government, a small number of UN agencies, NGOs, or private contractors. There are several important points to bear in mind regarding implementation. First, development agencies and UN agencies almost never actually implement programs directly; they contract other organizations (usually NGOs or private contractors) to do so. Second, the distinction between NGOs and private contractors is often blurred. Many private contractors will register as NGOs in order to receive preferential tax treatment. Third, regardless of which conduits the money goes through, donor agencies, UN agencies, and the government all end up using the same implementers. Where implementation capacity is limited, these actors compete with each other to ensure *their* projects are implemented.

The *beneficiaries* are the individuals or communities who receive the services that are delivered. That is, the beneficiaries are people who are treated at the clinics, who can travel on the improved road network, or who have better access to potable water.

How Resources Flow in Practice

In postconflict countries the vast majority of resources flow outside government channels. Some resources flow to the government in the form of budget support or development bank credits and grants, but these funds are often eclipsed by the money that flows outside the government. In the case of Afghanistan, for instance, over 80 percent of funds bypassed the government system during the first three years. Even in the case of East Timor, where the international community initially served as the government, over 55 percent of resources were channeled outside the government, with a further 35 percent being provided through a multilateral trust fund. Figure 4.2 represents this dynamic.

In this situation, the only source of funds available to the national government is domestic revenue, apart from any funds received in the form of direct budget support or through trust funds. In a fragile state, and particularly in a postconflict situation with weak economic activity, domestic revenue is often quite low. For political and practical reasons, the highest priority for domestic revenue is generally the payment of civil service salaries. So in the absence of other resources, domestic revenue can simply become entrenched as a source of patronage with no concept of service delivery.

Typically, donor governments provide the money directly to UN agencies or program it themselves by contracting NGOs or private companies. This approach undermines the building of a sustainable state by reinforcing parallel mechanisms rather than state institutions, by spending inefficiently

Figure 4.2 Flow of Funds in Practice

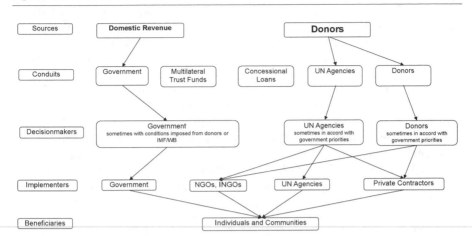

due to a lack of coordination among donors, by exacerbating intergroup tensions through an inequitable distribution of assistance, and by creating expectations that cannot be sustained. Moreover, in response to the argument that operating outside the government is faster, it is not clear that bypassing the government actually allows international organizations to deliver services more quickly or more cheaply. The same contractors on the ground are used as implementers regardless of the channels through which the funds pass.

Parallel mechanisms undermine state structures and government authority. By establishing parallel decisionmaking structures, the international community undermines the creation of these structures within the state apparatus. This is particularly pertinent in the case of the cabinet or senior political decisionmaking body. A functioning cabinet is a critical ingredient for a stable state. When given the opportunity to make real decisions, over real resources, institutional capacity can be dramatically strengthened. Too often, major decisions are made without recourse to this body. Even more problematic is when donor countries take advantage of nascent decisionmaking capacity by seeking bilateral deals with elements within the government in order to claim "government" support for their priorities.

Parallel mechanisms also prevent bonds of citizenship from forming between the government and its citizens. These bonds are developed and strengthened through consultation on the use of state resources and through the ability of citizens to hold the government to account for its decisionmaking on public expenditure. If the government does not manage the funds, it cannot be held accountable.

The public expenditure system in a postconflict or fragile state often resembles a set of old pipes. There are a series of leaks in the system, but until water is flowing in the system it is not possible to identify the leaks and patch them so the funds flow effectively. By keeping funds out, the opportunity to strengthen the financial management system—including budget execution, auditing, and accounting—is lost. Critics may argue that funds will be wasted in this process, but unless the system is repaired and functioning, the state will never be able to function independently.

Parallel mechanisms undermine capacity building. Not only do parallel mechanisms undermine the exercise of government authority, but they also draw human resources out of the government and undermine attempts to build the capacity of public officials. When donors contract UN agencies or NGOs to manage projects, each of these actors must hire financial managers, accountants, administrative staff, and project managers.

Unfortunately, postconflict and fragile states often have a very limited supply of skilled labor to fill these positions. When donors or agencies offer salaries well above what the government can pay, they undermine the ability of the government to recruit skilled staff and develop the capacity to operate the public finance system. In situations in which each donor and each UN agency is operating a series of projects, these scarce human resources are dispersed across a number of small projects, rather than being in a position to manage the overall spending portfolio. Even more ironic is when international organizations fund large and expensive technical assistance projects to build government capacity. The highly paid international consultants that are flown in to manage such projects often recruit the most talented civil servants to work as their assistants, while the less talented staff remain in the government to attend the trainings. This impact is particularly pronounced when there is a large UN mission present, for example in Cambodia, Kosovo, or East Timor.[18] Although studies have not been undertaken on the effects of a large *non-UN* international presence, the results can be extrapolated from studies of UN missions because bilateral donors regularly pay even higher wages than multilateral organizations.

Uncoordinated expenditure planning leads to ineffective expenditure. Generally, the host government prepares a budget based on an estimate of the resources that donors may provide. These resources are then disbursed to the government during the course of the year, but often in an uncoordinated and unpredictable manner. There are two strongly negative consequences of this approach. First, after preparing a budget and ensuring its passage through the legislature, the Finance Ministry then must spend much of the year chasing donors for funds to ensure that the pledges of budget support are actually delivered. Second, the nebulous offer of support that many donors make is often interpreted by less experienced ministers as meaning budget support. What this has meant in practice is that when the finance minister presents the draft budget, with difficult trade-offs, to the cabinet, other ministers suggest that, rather than prioritize within a spending envelope, the government should seek additional funds from the international community. In this way the presence of unpredictable budget support from donors undermines the development of good public finance decision-making. Similarly, there is little support for politically unpopular revenue measures when ministers see the donors as an easier source of revenue.

When expenditure takes place in this uncoordinated fashion, the benefits of budgeting will be lost. In particular, the balance between spending in different sectors; between investment, operations, and maintenance expenditure; and between popular and essential expenditure will no longer be maintained.

This approach undermines the building of a sustainable state in at least two distinct ways. First, effective public spending is a critical component of creating an environment for strong economic and employment growth. It can play a key role in creating a virtuous cycle where stronger economic activity and employment growth helps create stakeholders in a stable society, drawing people from illicit or destabilizing activities into productive employment. Stronger economic performance also supports the collection of the domestic revenue needed to fund an adequately remunerated security force.

Second, despite the fact that the funds are not channeled through the government, the citizens in the recipient country are aware of the pledges of assistance from the international community. They may then apportion some blame to their government for the way in which these funds are spent. When the funds are spent in a haphazard manner and services are not delivered effectively, the legitimacy of the government and the trust that the people place in it will be harmed.

Geographic and ethnic inequity in spending compromises political and security developments. Lack of coordination leads to spending and service delivery that takes places in a geographically and ethnically unbalanced manner. International organizations prefer to deliver their programs in areas of the country that are close to major population centers in order to reduce costs and speed up the delivery. They also want to work in the safest areas of the country. In the absence of coordinated nationwide programs, the benefits of the influx of foreign funds will only be felt in selected areas. This disparity is likely to fuel existing political and security tensions and inhibit progress in bridging these critical divides and is particularly problematic where there are ethnic and geographic disparities in access to the benefits of foreign funds. These situations are likely to engender a vicious cycle in which the initial disparity of resources fuels additional political and security tensions, further reducing the likelihood that donor programs will operate in these areas.

Short-term delivery of services by external actors may create expectations that cannot be sustained. Delivery of expensive services may create expectations that cannot be sustained. For example, the creation of externally funded new armed forces may not be fiscally sustainable. In addition to creating unrealistic expectations, services may erode traditional coping mechanisms, leaving communities in a worse position than before. For example, the United States Agency for International Development (USAID) undertook a major health program in Afghanistan, funding clinics to deliver basic health services. These clinics operated at a significantly higher cost than other clinics: the unit cost was estimated to be more than double the cost for service provision under a World Bank grant to the government. Unless donors fund these clinics in perpetuity, the service level will be reduced when operation of these clinics reverts to the government.

Does this approach deliver better results? International actors generally choose to use channels outside the government because they are trying to avoid corruption or to allow more rapid implementation. In rare cases, channels outside the government are needed because the government actually opposes the program (e.g., girls' education and some women's health services under the Taliban) or because the project is designed to support civil society or the media to increase government accountability.

One particular irony in the development industry is that, regardless of the way the funds flow, it is the same group of implementers (either NGOs or private contractors) that do the work. The difference is whether they are contracted by the government, by a UN agency, or directly by the donor. It is not as if donors or UN agencies have access to a range of contractors that the government cannot access. The same people end up doing the work; the only question is who is paying them.

Thus the major difference between donors who channel the money through the government or those who go around it is how long it takes to contract the implementing partner and how much money is lost due to corruption or leakage. Assessments of risks and the challenges of channeling money through the government suffer from the use of a flawed counterfactual: a perfect system is assumed. But the outside channel is also flawed.

It would be a useful exercise to assess the time it takes different actors to move from the stage when funds become available to the stage when contracts have been signed. It is not at all clear that donors or UN agencies move more quickly than the government. Certainly in the case of Afghanistan, the government's two major programs—the National Emergency Employment Program and the National Solidarity Program—were implemented more rapidly than any other major program, except for emergency food distribution and refugee repatriation programs.

A second useful exercise would be to compare the amount of money that reaches the beneficiaries when funds are channeled in different ways. Those who favor bypassing the government often cite corruption in their defense. These claims need to be accurately assessed and compared against the significant costs of going outside the government, including the cost structure of individual UN agencies and international NGOs. When a share of the funds is sliced off the top in a nontransparent fashion by a host government, it is referred to as corruption. When a UN agency or an international NGO takes 10, 15, or 20 percent as "overhead," no questions are asked by donors. This effect is compounded when funds cascade through several intermediaries, each charging their own overhead costs. When international technical assistance companies bill an overhead of 100 percent in addition to the amount paid to their contractors, it is often accepted as "industry standard." Private contractors can charge similarly high rates.

Donors may prefer to work outside the government in order to use their aid budget to pursue their foreign policy objectives or because of domestic political considerations—for example, in response to lobbying by their domestic aid stakeholders or to protect the interests of domestic companies who win contracts to provide goods and services to developing countries. They are certainly entitled to do so, but the consequences of these decisions, in terms of the negative impact on peacebuilding, should be understood, and the accuracy of the justifications for their policies should be examined. Channeling funding through the national government does not necessarily mean that fiduciary standards will be compromised or that planning will be less effective; various mechanisms can be put in place to ensure checks and balances in the system. These will be examined later in the chapter.

How Development Partners' Policies Undermine the Domestic Revenue System

The sustainability of the public finance system is undermined not only by the way development funds are allocated and spent. The policies that international organizations advocate, and the way they do business, can also undermine the creation of a sustainable revenue base.

The fundamental problem is the prevailing attitude of the majority of international actors: that revenue comes from donors, and taxes are to be avoided at both a personal and an institutional level. There is little expertise among international development agencies on revenue policy or revenue collection issues, let alone an understanding of the centrality of domestic revenue collection to sustainable development.[19] Donors generally insist that donor-funded activities be exempt from all taxes.[20] That is, donors, international organizations, and NGOs argue that, at a minimum, their international and local staff should be exempt from income tax; any materials they bring into the country should be exempt from customs or excise duties; and they should be exempt from any other government charges or fees (e.g., license or registration fees, inspection fees, etc.). In many cases, bilateral donors will further insist that these concessions be provided to any organization that they contract to perform a service. As a result, the single largest source of economic activity, and generally the largest employer of labor and other resources—the reconstruction effort—provides no revenue. Consequently, the rest of the economy, which is generally in a far more fragile state than the reconstruction and development sector, is burdened with the entire taxation effort.

This blanket demand for exemptions has several indirect impacts that substantially undermine the creation of a sustainable revenue system. First, in an environment of already weak administrative capacity, granting exemptions for certain groups adds an additional layer of complexity to the system, making it harder to administer. It also opens a new area for corruption by giving officials discretion to apply these exemptions more broadly than they were originally intended. These two impacts reduce the capacity of the system to operate effectively.

Second, other impacts reduce the amount of revenue collected. There is considerable anecdotal evidence of goods being brought into postconflict countries by exempt groups and then being sold in the market for use in other activities.[21] After all, the same lumber can be used to build emergency shelters or sold to build luxury homes. Moreover, granting exemptions to NGOs from either income or customs taxation gives these organizations a competitive advantage when bidding for contracts, thus inhibiting the development of the private sector, which cannot easily compete with the tax-exempt NGO.

Third, the domestic revenue system is undermined by donors that promote poor economic policies that do not foster long-term, sustainable economic growth. In many cases, the commercial arms of bilateral partners seek tax concessions for particular investors from their country.[22] In other cases they push for sweetheart deals, such as monopoly rights, for investors from their home countries. Although they meet the goals of the bilateral donor, such approaches do not serve the long-term needs of the country.

Fourth, this no-tax attitude is so pervasive that it manifests itself in demands for concessions or refusals to cooperate with the revenue system that go well beyond legally established conventions. In the case of the United Nations, the Convention on Privileges and Immunities relates to taxation; it does not apply to the payment of user fees for services provided. Yet in East Timor, UN staff regularly extended this blanket exemption to user fees and charges. On several occasions in Afghanistan, large and politically influential

NGOs had their cargoes held at customs points because they did not have the legally required documentation. Yet these cargoes were often cleared following the subtle application of diplomatic influence at varying pressure points. The prevailing attitude is that raising revenue is someone else's problem.

Opportunities to Move Forward

Tools for the International Community
If the international community wants to channel its resources through the government to leverage institution-building benefits, it has a number of options to ensure that the resources continue to be used appropriately. These interventions range from explicit red lines that, if crossed, will see support withdrawn through explicit and implicit conditionalities, to a partnership approach.

At one end of the spectrum, donors, collectively or individually, can impose a series of specific political conditions on the recipient country. They may include requirements that certain people be excluded from positions of authority (e.g., those who have committed human rights violations or who have criminal connections) or that the government not undertake certain activities (e.g., use of force) or employ discriminatory policies (e.g., access to public services determined by ethnicity or gender). Red lines are a negative sanction: the donor indicates that if the lines are crossed, it will disengage.

The next level of intervention is conditionalities. In contrast to red lines, they are generally positive. Donors indicate that if certain actions are taken or certain results obtained, then the recipient government will be rewarded. A common form of explicit conditionalities revolve around credits or grants from multilateral institutions, including the development banks and the IMF. When the recipient government meets certain conditions, funds are released. The conditionalities may be more implicit. For example, a donor may indicate that if the recipient government passes a particular budget, then funds will be released to support its implementation. As will be discussed below, there is scope to use explicit conditionalities to ensure that a transparent and accountable public finance system is built when funds are channeled through the government.

At the other end of the spectrum are partnerships that apply a consensus-based approach to the planning and implementation of expenditure. This could include some sort of expanded consultative group process in which donor representatives and their government counterparts sit along with representatives from relevant multilateral organizations on sector-based groups to plan the programs in each sector. After the sector programs are combined, the donor representatives and senior ministers meet to agree on the overall spending and implementation program. The sector-based consultative groups then assume a monitoring and reporting role, again based on a joint donor-government approach.

An Alternative Approach

As an alternative to the financing modalities outlined earlier, the international community could use its assistance not only to deliver services to citizens, but to do so in a way that supports the development of sustainable state structures. Doing so requires a fundamental reorientation of the development community away from substituting for functions toward building the capacity of that state. Such a change will occur only if the current silo mentality is broken down and replaced by an approach that treats the country as a whole, providing assistance across domains, through government systems, with the flow of funds as the organizing principle. In order to do so, the international community will have to place a greater focus on helping the government to fulfill its key roles, rather than substituting for the government. The objective would be to support and build up the government through this process.

As outlined in Figure 4.3, this process would involve channeling international funds through a multilateral trust fund or directly to the government. Allocation decisions would be made through a unified process whereby donors would support the various government departments as they undertake expenditure planning. This process would conclude with a single budget for all expenditure, approved by both domestic political decisionmakers and representatives of the international community.[23]

This approach resembles the concept of shared sovereignty outlined by Stephen D. Krasner.[24] Although it may appear that requiring the agreement of the international community impinges on the sovereignty of the host government, in fact it serves to increase its sovereignty. The genuine counterfactual in most countries is that the host government has little real control. However, in contrast to Krasner's position, this approach would see the government increase its "share" of sovereignty over time, rather than having sovereignty over some domains shared indefinitely. As capacity increases, the overall goal would be full sovereignty.

Once the budget has been decided, the government would use a transparent process to contract program fulfillment to all implementing partners, including international NGOs, local NGOs, private companies, and UN agencies. This competition ensures that the government (and therefore the donors who are providing the funds) receives the best value for its money. One option is to require that for all expenditure resourced from a trust fund or provided through budget support there exists international management or oversight of internal procurement, financial management, and auditing

Figure 4.3 Government-Preferred Model

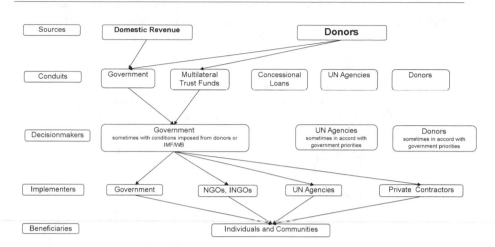

processes, enabling the government to operate as quickly and to equally highstandards as an international agency. Such an approach must be coupled with a strong skill transfer program to ensure that the process is sustainable in the long term.

This approach has been applied with some success in Afghanistan. The United Nations Office for Project Services (UNOPS) and Care International were contracted by the Afghan government to deliver aspects of the National Emergency Employment Program. In the case of the National Solidarity Program, more than twenty local and international NGOs were contracted to deliver services, and other organizations (first a UN agency and then a consortium of two private development agencies) were contracted to provide oversight of the twenty NGOs, while block grants were delivered directly to the villages.[25]

The benefits of this approach, in terms of delivering services, supporting the public finance system, and supporting statebuilding, are considerable. Rather than using resources to establish parallel systems of financial management, the international community could use these resources to support the development of this capacity within government, leveraging its financial contributions by making transparent financial management and reporting the conditions of receiving support. In this way, good practices can be entrenched while the volume of assistance is high, giving donors maximum leverage; as international aid declines and domestic revenues fund an increasing share of overall expenditure, the practices can continue. The same is

true with regard to entrenching open and transparent procurement and ten-
dering practices; donors can use their financial leverage to ensure that the
government tenders out contracts to the most cost-efficient implementer.

By channeling resources in this way, government decisionmaking practices are strengthened, and concerns about ineffective expenditure are addressed by balancing needs across sectors, between groups, and between investment and operational expenditure. The legitimacy of the state grows as
the government is seen to be providing services, which in turn will support
the peace and security processes. Most importantly, the government and its
institutions will have their capacity enhanced through a "learning by doing"
approach—a far more effective teaching tool than abstract capacity-building
methods with no real resources attached.

Service Delivery with Weak or Corrupt Governments

In certain instances channeling all resources through the government may
not be possible or desirable, including cases in which a government is committing human rights violations, is incapable of administration, or is otherwise unwilling to engage constructively in policy formulation. Indeed, where
services are severely limited or nonexistent and the needs are pressing, the
benefits of delivering goods and services directly to people in need may out-
weigh the costs of bypassing state institutions. In these cases, there are alternatives to unconditional support for state institutions.

First, international actors enjoy a range of foreign policy tools, including
sanctions and, in extremis, military intervention. Second, under the responsibility to protect doctrine, the international community has the option to provide humanitarian services directly. Such services are traditionally delivered
independently of the government, through mechanisms such as refugee assistance and food delivery. Although such assistance may be necessary and helpful to avert imminent suffering and provide emergency assistance in the short
term, there is a clear need to examine the medium- and longer-term impact of
the ways in which such assistance is provided. Those providing goods must be
aware of the impact on the domestic market for goods such as food and the
impact on local coping mechanisms that may not reestablish themselves when
the aid dwindles. A culture of dependency, or indeed lack of transparency in
resource delivery, may become entrenched. As discussed above, the establishment of a large infrastructure of organizations and staff for delivery of such
assistance may reduce the efficacy of state institutions. Thus, although such
assistance may be necessary and unavoidable, mechanisms need to be identified to limit the adverse impacts of such assistance in the long term. It is worth
noting that central to the responsibility to protect doctrine is the notion that the
state is the primary duty-bearer of citizens' rights, and the international community should only step in to provide services with that in mind.

Where external actors have determined that humanitarian needs are substantial and pressing and that national service-delivery capacity is too weak

or corrupted, it may be useful to include a clear cost-benefit analysis of the institutional impact of providing such assistance. Determining the cost of service provision, as well as agreement on the scope of, equity of, and exit strategy for such assistance would be essential. Mechanisms might include policy frameworks such as the Strategic Partnership mechanism used in Afghanistan under the Taliban or the social funds widely used by donors to aggregate financing, policy preparation, and contracting modalities.

A useful tool might be to prepare a "substitution matrix" that would specify, for each function of the state, which actor has responsibility for its provision, for what period of time, to which citizens, at what level of service, and for what costs. At the same time, credible mechanisms for building state capacity to provide these functions could be identified. The period when political conditions do not permit direct engagement should be used for contingency planning and training for state capacity to be generated in the interim. For example, in a case in which the government in question is providing no health services, an agency may take over policy and implementation responsibility for that function for a specified period of time or until certain criteria are met. At the same time, credible capacity-building mechanisms could be developed, including preparation of policy frameworks and options and training for health workers and managers. If necessary, some of these measures could be undertaken outside the country. In cases in which the government is unable to keep the peace, security forces or peacekeepers might be deployed, but at the same time, pathways to create the capacity for policing and maintaining a national army should be identified.

The international community may also require that the government contract out some key services, using either domestic or internationally provided funds to finance such contracts. For example, management of revenue collection, security, or key national programs could be contracted to international firms or agencies. This approach might work in a case in which the government was relatively weak and the administration eroded and corrupt. In these cases, responsibility for financial management would be out of the state's hands, but the government could still participate in policy formulation.[26]

As discussed in the previous section, there is scope to develop creative strategies for routing resources through the government without giving up control and oversight. The approach described above proposes a system of dual controls whereby international assistance channeled through a multilateral trust fund or to the government is subject to verification by an external agent to ensure that proper accounting standards have been met prior to the release of funds. Similarly, procurement and auditing processes can be subjected to external verification. The government's internal budgeting process would, however, remain the locus for prioritization and planning for both domestic and international actors. This type of approach maintains oversight while building capacity for an effective, accountable, and transparent public expenditure system.

Some Specific Ways Forward

In addition to the alternative approach described earlier, several concrete changes could be considered in the area of public finance and the management of resources to advance the statebuilding agenda. Some of these options have been tried; others have not. Questions are often raised as to the applicability of these recommendations across different contexts. It is not the case that the prescriptions require strong and charismatic leadership from an individual, as they are designed to provide institutional mechanisms even where enlightened leadership is absent. Where governments are particularly corrupt, abusive, or predatory, the international community may need to build in additional safeguards, as described above. However, if the fact of a corrupt regime at one point in time is taken as a reason to perpetuate the elements of a vicious cycle, the conditions to alter the trajectory will never be created.

Making the budget the central instrument of strategy and policy formulation. As argued above, the budget is the framework through which essential policy trade-offs are made and strategies of the government articulated and thus the framework through which the government can coordinate decisionmaking. However, when the international community bypasses government institutions, making its aid allocation decisions unilaterally, the capability of the government to guide policymaking is undermined. Thus, the budget must be the central instrument of policy and strategy formulation for both internal and external actors. Although the annual rhythms of a budget may be insufficiently long-term for an institution-building agenda, a medium-term expenditure framework or a long-term statebuilding strategy may be an ideal framework through which to coordinate international strategy and policy in which the budget can be rooted.[27]

The international policy community is currently searching for mechanisms to ensure coherence in strategic planning across the domains of security, political, and development interventions. Although strategic planning exercises may be very useful and the participation of all key stakeholders in such processes essential, they must be linked to and underpinned by budgets in order to have traction. The budget and its associated processes and instruments provide the critical linkage between vision and strategy on the one hand and implementation on the other.

Making budget support more effective. In most postconflict countries, bilateral donors provide cash support to finance the budget of the host government. In the early years this can represent well over half of the resources for the ordinary or operating budget.[28] However, the uncoordinated and unpredictable way that assistance is provided often undermines efforts to build public finance capacity.

Rather than offering budget support that could reduce the imperative to collect domestic revenue, donors could offer collectively to tie their budget contribution to the level of domestic revenue that is collected. For example, donors could agree that in the first three years of a new government they will match the domestic revenue collected, up to a certain level.[29]

By doing this, donors achieve several things. First, they provide enough certainty to the host government to allow effective budget planning. Second, they require the government to face the genuine trade-offs between spending programs. Third, they encourage the introduction of politically difficult revenue measures, because revenue collection now has the added benefit that each additional dollar of domestic revenue makes two additional dollars available for expenditure.

Such an approach also addresses many of the IMF-style conditionalities—measures such as establishing a large taxpayer unit or reforming the customs rates—that are designed to encourage the government to build a robust revenue system. However, a direct approach, in which the government is rewarded for actually collecting more revenue rather than for interim steps, would be more effective. Such an approach ensures that reforms to the revenue system are demand-driven and domestically owned rather than externally imposed, significantly enhancing their chances of success.

Adopting a comprehensive capacity-building approach that enhances leadership and management skills. Capacity building is an essential component of any statebuilding effort. However, the deployment of technical assistance through expensive companies in the name of capacity building, whose incentive is to perpetuate their own existence, does not tend to lead to the creation of capacity. A different approach is needed. Alternative mechanisms include a focus on enhancing leadership and management skills, a focus on rules for recruitment of capable leaders and managers, and twinning arrangements with officials from other countries who face similar challenges and experiences.

Both international and domestic actors must focus on building the core functions of a public finance system. Doing so will include a focus on the organization and institutions of the ministry of finance, but it is also linked to financial management systems and personnel across many functions and levels of government, including other line ministries, local administrations, and municipalities. As experience shows, institution building requires a focus on functions, systems, and rules as expressed in laws and manuals, as well as recruitment, training, and resourcing. Interventions must treat capacity building in a holistic manner, rather than relying on the provision of technical assistance alone.

A postconflict state is rarely a tabula rasa. Accordingly, approaches must be designed to suit the context and to build on existing institutions and capacities. Afghanistan, for example, had a system of public administration staffed with approximately 200,000 civil servants at the time the Bonn Agreement was concluded, making it essential to map and build on existing systems. In southern Sudan, the Comprehensive Peace Agreement of 2004 required the establishment of new public finance institutions drawn ostensibly from scratch; however, even in such a case, historical practices and institutional memories can be drawn upon in establishing new institutions.

The need to build on existing systems, some of which may be out of date or have been corrupted during the war years, must be balanced with introducing new technologies and practices aligned with international systems. Experience has shown that importing proprietary software packages immediately after conflict may be counterproductive; rather, the use of simple solutions on commonly used software platforms such as Microsoft Excel may be more appropriate.

Reducing coordination problems by managing donor participation. A particular problem in a fragile state is that every donor wants to operate in every sector. Regardless of the overall size of their financial contribution, each donor wants to spread that contribution over many different sectors in the developing country. Often they do so in response to NGOs and other lobbies in their home countries who are publicly critical of the donor government for failing to work in a particular sector. Not only does this dispersal of resources and effort across numerous sectors via minor projects lead to ineffective spending, it also produces a coordination nightmare that often falls on the government. In response to this, the government of Afghanistan came up with a system of coordination that included clear government-led rules for terms of donor engagement and systems and processes for simplifying, channeling, and monitoring donor activity that has been widely copied across other countries.

Contracting out for service provision. A key criticism of channeling funds through the government is that the government will use the funds to finance a bloated and inefficient bureaucracy. To counter this criticism and to ensure good value for the money, it is critical that the government build up a solid record of contracting out for service delivery at an early stage. It may be easier to do that in a postconflict or failed state environment, when the government's actual capacity to in-source activities is limited. As discussed above, this was the approach inherent in the National Emergency Employment Program and the National Solidarity Program taken by the Ministry of Rural Development and the Ministry of Public Works in Afghanistan. This approach also enhanced the extent to which the productive capacity, both in the NGO and private sector, was being used to deliver on the government's agenda rather than on the ad hoc ideas of bilateral donors.

Imposing taxes on international agencies. A final approach to building a sustainable public finance capacity is to remove tax and customs exemptions enjoyed by international agencies and their affiliates and reduce the amount of budget support provided to offset this revenue. Such an intervention would not change the overall level of support provided to the country: the increased amounts needed by the international agency to cover the tax and customs obligations would be offset by the lower requirements for budget support. This approach would enhance the capacity of the domestic revenue system, as it would decrease administration costs and reduce the scope for corruption and abuse of the system.

There are some practical challenges in changing the machinery of government to move forward in this way. These challenges would be minor compared to the challenge of changing the prevailing attitude of the international community regarding the centrality of revenue collection and sustainable public finances to effective and lasting poverty reduction.

Conclusion

The focus of this chapter has been on conditions in postconflict and conflict-affected countries, but many of its lessons may be applicable to weak states that face many of the same constraints. There are significant differences between postconflict situations and weak states, of course, and accordingly, as with any institutional reform program, approaches must be designed to fit the context. However, a better understanding of approaches to building effective public finance institutions in any state, on the part of both domestic and international actors, could have immense payoffs. Many of the same issues addressed above occur with equal visibility in discussions on donor harmonization, policy coherence, and fragile states. In all these contexts, the use of public finance as the central lifeblood of an administrative and political system has equal potential and relevance.

Notes

1. Ashraf Ghani, Clare Lockhart, and Michael Carnahan, "An Agenda for Statebuilding in the 21st Century," *Fletcher Forum of World Affairs* 30, no. 1 (Winter 2006): 101–123. See also the "Conclusion" by James Boyce and Madalene O'Donnell, in their *Peace and the Public Purse: Economic Policies for Postwar Statebuilding* (Boulder, CO: Lynne Rienner, 2007), pp. 271–296.

2. See Ghani, Lockhart, and Carnahan, "An Agenda," which draws on work with the Bonn Agreement and Afghanistan's National Development Framework, and proposes ten core functions that the state must perform in the contemporary world. Of these, the public finance function is one of the three foundational state functions.

3. See also Joel S. Hellman, Geraint Jones, and Daniel Kaufmann, *Seize the State, Seize the Day: State Capture, Corruption, and Influence in Transition,* Policy Research Working Paper no. 2444 (Washington, DC: World Bank, 2000).

4. For a more detailed description of this in practice, see the discussion of the mission planning and implementation arrangements for Kosovo, East Timor, and

Afghanistan in Conflict, Security and Development Group, *A Review of Peace Operations: A Case for Change* (London: Kings College, 2003).

5. See Ashraf Ghani, Clare Lockhart, and Michael Carnahan, "Closing the Sovereignty Gap: An Approach to State-Building," Working Paper no. 253 (London: Overseas Development Institute, 2005).

6. See the National Development Framework (2002) and Securing Afghanistan's Future (2005), which elaborate a framework, financing plan, and budget for a long-term statebuilding plan.

7. For example, in Afghanistan the size of the defense force was particularly contentious. Suggestions ranged from 20,000 to 700,000. The issue was not decided for several months, at which point a long-term vision for a force of 70,000 was accepted. Its composition remained ambiguous, which allowed the parties to move forward without getting bogged down in controversial details.

8. For a further discussion on the centrality of budgets to broader decision-making, see János Kornai, "The Soft Budget Constraint," *Kyklos* 39, no. 1 (1986): 3–30.

9. Indeed, it was interesting that the promise to reform customs drew considerable cheers from the delegates to the Constitutional Loya Jirga held in December 2003 in Afghanistan; their response demonstrated that the issue of public finance reform is related in the minds of the population to rules-based, transparent, and effective governance.

10. A more detailed discussion of this topic can be found in many places. Two examples are Ehtisham Ahmad, Piyush Desai, Thierry Kalfon, and Eivind Tandberg, "Priorities for Reform in Post-Conflict Finance Ministries," in *Reforming Fiscal and Economic Management in Afghanistan,* edited by Michael Carnahan, Nick Manning, Richard Bontjer, and Stephane Guimbert (Washington, DC: World Bank, 2004); and International Monetary Fund, *Rebuilding Fiscal Institutions in Post-Conflict Countries,* prepared by the Fiscal Affairs Department, approved by Teresa Ter-Minassian (Washington, DC, 2004).

11. In fact, comparing the amount of money spent on providing technical and physical assistance for revenue collection as a share of revenue collected does not provide flattering benefit-cost ratios. This figure is somewhat misleading, however, if the technical assistance is providing training—hence it will deliver an ongoing benefit. But technical assistance that does not deliver an ongoing increased capacity needs to be very carefully considered.

12. There does not even need to be a direct link for this issue to be problematic, given the fungibility of aid: loans need not have been specifically for the purchase of military hardware, but loans could have paid for teachers' salaries, allowing revenue that would have been spent on salaries to be spent on weapons.

13. There is a growing strand of literature that examines the extent to which "greed or grievances" leads to conflict. Although grievances (e.g., high inequality, chronic unemployment, ethnic and religious clashes) have traditionally been perceived as the primary factors, this literature argues that greed (access to finance, the capacity to gain from extractive industries, access to diaspora funding) could have greater explanatory power. See, for example, Gilles Carbonnier and Sarah Fleming, eds., *War, Money, and Survival* (Geneva: International Committee of the Red Cross, 2000); Paul Collier and Anke Hoeffler, "Greed and Grievance in Civil War," *Oxford Economic Papers* 56, no. 4 (2004): 563–595.

14. The challenges posed by high unemployment in the immediate period post-conflict require the consideration of different and innovative policy responses that have not traditionally found favor with economists. It is critical that the fundamental

policy settings for economic growth are put in place, including a reliable property rights regime, stable and predictable monetary and fiscal policy, and sound regulatory policies. While these policies support and enable growth, they may not encourage rapid enough growth in inclusive employment-generating industries to stop the country from slipping back into conflict.

15. See conference proceeding in Ghani, Lockhart, and Carnahan, "An Agenda for State-building in the 21st Century."

16. Although IFIs do exert pressure on all governments to adopt specific economic policies, they generally play a positive role in building the public finance architecture. Because of their charter, they are required to enter into agreements with the national government, and grants and credits in most cases must flow through government systems and thus help build national institutions of public finance. Thus, the IFIs are not able to circumvent the government architecture in the same way that bilateral donors and other international development agencies do.

17. Project proposals often specify general areas, such as provision of potable water or emergency shelter, but give little more detail.

18. In the case of Cambodia, see "The Short Term Impact of UNTAC on Cambodia," unpublished report prepared by the Economic Adviser's Office, UNTAC, 1992; and for East Timor, see Michael Carnahan, William Durch, and Scott Gilmore, *The Economic Impact of Peacekeeping: Final Report,* prepared as part of the Economic Impact of Peacekeeping Project commissioned by PBPS/DPKO, published in partnership with Peace Dividend Trust, March 2006.

19. This comment does not apply to the Fiscal Affairs Division of the IMF, which has a strong understanding of these issues, or to some parts of the World Bank or the Asian Development Bank.

20. The way in which different donors request different exemptions also highlights their lack of understanding of revenue systems. First, while they demand exemptions for their staff from income taxation, they do not, in general, demand exemptions for their staff from indirect taxation (e.g., services tax). Similarly, while they insist on exemptions for their own staff and for their contractors, they vary in how far down the subcontracting chain they require exemptions. Yet if their primary argument that aid dollars should not be used for paying domestic taxes was to be applied, then these exemptions would need to be traced through the entire economy.

21. In East Timor the reselling of tax-exempt alcohol led to the introduction of a tax stamp system so that tax inspectors in the marketplace could quickly identify alcohol on which tax had not been paid. In Sierra Leone entire markets have appeared selling tax-exempt items obtained from UN peacekeepers.

22. Tax concessions undermine a sustainable revenue system, since granting a concession to one industry effectively imposes a penalty on all other industries. Conceptually, the best system for both economic development and revenue generation involves the lowest possible rate structure and the broadest possible tax base, both consistent with the revenue needs of the state.

23. Often there is a distinction between what is referred to as the operating or recurrent budget and the development or investment budget. This distinction is not consistent with best practice in budgeting. It is often used simply because the donors will not allow the government much say in the development expenditure. So the development budget simply represents a catalog of what donors are going to do anyway, rather than a process and document that reflects government decisions on spending priorities.

24. Stephen D. Krasner, "Sharing Sovereignty: New Institutions for Collapsed and Failing States," *International Security* 29, no. 2 (Fall 2004): 85–120.

25. A particular challenge in this regard is the attitude of many international organizations, which see themselves as part of a vertically integrated industry—they identify a need, design a project, advocate for the funding of that project, obtain the funding through their own organization, and then contract for the project's implementation. Building a sustainable state actually requires that this vertical integration be removed, with competition introduced at each level of the process, from competition over priorities to competition over the implementer. There is no natural reason why a group that is good at designing projects will also be good at implementing them.

26. See Michael McGovern's discussion of the Governance and Economic Management Assistance Program in "Liberia: The Risks of Rebuilding a Shadow State," Chapter 14 in this volume, for an example of one such approach.

27. Ashraf Ghani, Clare Lockhart, and Michael Carnahan, *Closing the Sovereignty Gap: An Approach to State-Building,* Working Paper no. 253 (London: Overseas Development Institute, September 2005).

28. The operating budget pays civil and military salaries and funds the ongoing operational costs of the government. In the case of East Timor, budget support represented around half of the resources needed to fund the government in the first three years. In Afghanistan, budget support funded around 75 percent of the operating budget in 2002, just under two-thirds in 2003, and around 50 percent in 2004.

29. For a more detailed discussion on this issue see, for example, Michael Carnahan, "Options for Revenue Generation in Post-Conflict Environments," *Public Finance in Post-Conflict Environments: A Policy Paper Series,* Center on International Cooperation, New York, and the Political Economy Research Institute, Amherst, MA, 2007.

5

Postconflict Economic Policy

Paul Collier

Civil wars occur disproportionately in low-income countries with stag-
nant or declining economies. Superficially, the postconflict situation in
such countries looks very similar to the general problem of statebuilding in
low-income environments with poor policies, weak institutions, and limited
local capacity. Indeed, until recently, the organizations dedicated to economic development did not systematically distinguish postconflict settings
as requiring a distinctive approach. Yet policy in the postconflict phase
needs to be distinctive, both that of the government and that of the donor
agencies. It should not be simply development as usual. Of course, policy
always needs to be tailored to circumstances, and circumstances differ mas-
sively between postconflict countries. The purpose of this chapter is not to
lay out postconflict policies for economic recovery as a set of iron principles, but rather to show some features that generally do need to differ systematically from those appropriate for equally poor countries that are not
postconflict.

The suggestions in this chapter are not a substitute for thorough knowledge of a particular situation and may well be seriously inappropriate in
particular instances. They are based on statistical analysis of what is currently an inevitably limited number of postconflict observations. Nevertheless, they may be a useful supplement to practitioner expertise, which is itself necessarily limited: service in the reconstruction of East Timor may
have only limited applicability to the reconstruction of Afghanistan. The
new UN Peacebuilding Commission provides the opportunity to introduce
a greater degree of standardization into postconflict interventions while dif-
ferentiating them from other situations in which the state is in some sense
"failing." Indeed, that will presumably be one of its tasks.

A key reason why policy should be distinctive in postconflict settings is
that the legacy of civil war implies that objectives should be distinctive. One

legacy is that there is a high risk of further violent conflict. Typically, there is a 23 percent risk that peace will collapse within the first four years and a 40 percent risk that it will collapse over the first decade.[1] These risks are much higher than for the typical low-income country with a history of peace—the five-year risk for such a country is "only" around 14 percent. These high risks of conflict relapse occur partly because the countries that have had a conflict have underlying and persistent characteristics such as low income, "ethnic dominance," and natural resource dependence that make them prone to conflict.[2] Additionally, something happens during conflict that increases the risks. Thus the high level of risk is equally due to these two factors—preconflict characteristics and the legacy of the conflict.

It is imperative to bring down this initially high risk of further conflict, both as an objective in itself and because perceptions of high risk will be deeply damaging to economic recovery. Hence, all policies have to be assessed in terms of whether they will reduce or worsen this risk.

A second legacy of civil war is that the economy is severely damaged. The typical conflict reduces gross domestic product (GDP) by around 15 percent by the end of the conflict. The adverse economic legacy of civil war is sometimes obvious: capital—physical, human, and social—gets destroyed. Typically, skills were already in short supply prior to conflict, but, as I will argue, in postconflict conditions a major temporary collapse in the supply of skills confronts a major temporary increase in their demand. Some effects are more subtle and so more likely to be missed in prioritizing policy. Government expenditure gets diverted away from economic services into the military. Private economic actors shift their capital abroad. The government resorts to debt accumulation in order to finance the need for military spending and more generally sacrifices future gains from good economic policies to snatch short-term gains from policy deterioration. Because of increased uncertainty, time horizons shorten, reducing the value of reputation. This, combined with the decline in policing, encourages opportunism and predation. In response to all these developments, people shift their economic activities into subsistence, which is less reliant upon other parts of the economy.

In this chapter I focus on what economic actions the postconflict government and international actors—donors and security providers—can undertake to address these distinctive problems. What policies are likely to be appropriate to reduce the risk of repeat conflict and to speed the economic recovery?

Priorities for the Postconflict Government

Reducing the Risk of Conflict

During the conflict, skills, organizations, and investments build up that are only of use through violence. Peace is costly for these interests, and so they will look for opportunities to revert to conflict. In practical terms, these interests have to be opposed by military force. Typically, postconflict governments do exactly this by maintaining very high levels of military spending. Indeed, spending on the military during the postconflict decade is almost as high as during the conflict, and nearly double its normal peacetime level.

Postconflict governments cannot be blamed for prioritizing their spending in this way, nor donors for financing it. The typical justification is the sensible one that risks are indeed high: governments are well aware that they face spoilers, both within the society and harbored by neighbors. The question is not an ethical one but rather a brutally practical one: is such high military spending effective in deterring further rebellion?

Together with Anke Hoeffler, I have tried to answer this question statistically.[3] The task is difficult because military spending in postconflict settings tends to be highest where the risks are highest. Hence, an incompetent researcher can blunder into the mistake of confusing the direction of causality: in fact, high risk causes high spending, but without proper precautions it will be misinterpreted as high spending causing high risk. The proper precautions are to consider only those components of military spending completely unrelated to the risk of civil war.[4] We find that high military spending by the government in postconflict societies is counterproductive—it significantly and substantially *increases* the risk of further conflict. This adverse effect is distinctive to military spending in postconflict situations. Why might military spending in postconflict situations have this distinctive effect?

We get some insight from the literature on the problems of achieving and sustaining a peace settlement.[5] It stresses what economists term the "time consistency" problem. As the peace is prolonged, rebel forces inevitably decline, whereas the government can keep its own forces together. After all, the normal state for a government army is to be at peace, but there is no example in history of a rebel army staying intact as a fighting force over a prolonged period of peace. Thus, as the peace continues, the government faces a growing temptation to renege on the explicit or implicit terms of any settlement. Indeed, the government is unlikely to have been united in its enthusiasm for a settlement: there will be voices urging that now is the time to abandon aspects of the settlement that it regarded as unreasonable. Conversely, since the rebels will be well aware how the balance of power is changing, there will be those on the rebel side who were never peace enthusiasts who will be urging a preemptive return to war. Even those rebels who have supported the peace will be worried. They will be watching government behavior closely for signs of its intentions. Of course, the government can, and should, make reassuring statements, but the problem with words is that they are relatively easy to reverse. The key aspect of government behavior is those actions that cannot be easily reversed and are therefore good leading indicators of government intentions. Military spending is the central such action. A government that intends to renege upon a settlement does not drastically cut its military spending: on the contrary, aware that reneging will increase the risk of rebellion, it needs to maintain its military capability at a high level. A deep cut in military spending is therefore an excellent signal that a government does not intend to renege. It can be read as such by rebels and used by those rebels who supported the peace to win the argument against those rebels that did not. Conversely, the maintenance of high military spending is inadvertently a signal that the government means to rely upon repression.

The most common policy error of postconflict governments is to maintain military spending at about conflict levels. Whether due to the explanation given above or for some other reason, a deep cut in military spending radically reduces the risk of further conflict. Hoeffler and I simulate the effect of different postconflict spending strategies upon risk. We find that a policy of deep cuts would reduce the risk of conflict recurring from around 39 percent to around 24 percent. Nor is it hypothetical: it was precisely the strategy of the postconflict government of Mozambique. Not only has Mozambique remained at peace, but it has had very fast growth, in part because the cut in military spending has released resources for economic priorities.

If large military forces under the control of the postconflict government actually increase the risk of conflict, what should be done? The government and its supporters can hardly be defenseless, given that spoilers are to be expected. I think, however, that defending the peace from spoilers is the proper role for international actors, and I return to it below.

Although a radical downsizing of the army therefore makes a lot of sense, it may not need to be as expensive a process as is commonly the case with programs of demobilization, disarmament, and reintegration (DDR). Two very different statistical studies of demobilized soldiers both tend to the conclusion that complex and protracted reintegration projects are either unnecessary or ineffective. A study of demobilized soldiers in Uganda, where demobilization provisions were rudimentary, found that contrary to popular concerns there was generally no tendency for demobilization to increase crime.[6] An increase in crime was discernable only in the one district in which soldiers had stated prior to demobilization that they had no access to land. A second and more recent statistical study focused on the reintegration of the beneficiaries of DDR programs in Sierra Leone, where such programs had become substantial. It found that the programs had had no discernable effects on the ability to reintegrate.[7] To my knowledge, these are currently the only statistical studies of DDR programs. Since the late 1990s, DDR programs have become an industry with the consequent vested interests in their further expansion. Although the statistical evidence is currently far too thin to conclude that they are excessive, it does suggest that a serious quantitative evaluation using modern techniques of random sampling is overdue.

Managing Expectations

Peace commonly occurs in the context of hype. All the normal woes of poverty will have been attributed to the overarching problem of war. Additionally, donors and peace negotiators will—quite sensibly—have tended to exaggerate the immediate benefits of peace in order to get the conflicting sides to agree to peace. Unfortunately, all this tends to produce exaggerated short-term expectations of what peace can bring in terms of economic benefits. The bitter reality is that whereas bad politics can destroy an economy with great speed, even the best politics can only facilitate a gradual recovery. That hard truth can rapidly lead to a sense of disillusion and skepticism on the part of the population. People are also habituated, during conflict, to a short-term perspective: this is a consequence of high uncertainty. The best the government can do, perhaps, is to articulate a credible medium-term growth strategy: what the economy could look like after one or perhaps two decades. Such a credible medium-term vision was implicit in Eastern and Southeastern Europe through the prospect of accession to the European Union. It has clearly proved valuable, both as a stabilizer and as an incentive for reform. Few postconflict societies have such a high-credibility ready-made vision, but that only increases the importance of government efforts to create one.

Other than reducing military spending, the most effective thing a post-conflict government can do to reduce conflict risk is to accelerate economic recovery. If the growth rate can be raised, it is even more effective in reducing risks than it is in conflict prevention.[8] Growth directly reduces conflict risk and also cumulatively raises income and diversifies the economy, both of which also reduce risk. The instruments that the government has to raise growth are a range of economic policies. These policies appear to have no direct systematic effect on the risk of conflict but indirectly lower risks by raising growth. How should they be deployed?

Raising the Growth Rate Through Policy Reform

The inheritance from conflict is that overall economic policy and institutions are typically very poor. Commonly, overregulation of formal economic activity coexists with a large illegal economy; there are high trade barriers, widely evaded by criminals; the budget is badly structured and poorly executed; commercial law is unreliable; and property rights are confused. Such a legacy poses a large agenda for reform and institution building. Further, growth during the postconflict decade is much more sensitive to such policy reforms than in other circumstances, which can be seen from the very wide range of postconflict growth outcomes—some countries recover rapidly, but others continue to decline. So, economic policy is much more important in postconflict settings than in other settings. Further, in one important sense—political constraints—reform is relatively easy. Together with Lisa Chauvet,

I have analyzed statistically the likelihood of successful "statebuilding": a substantial and sustained improvement in policies and institutions starting from a situation in which they are very weak.[9] In our studies we relied upon World Bank ratings. With respect to policies, these ratings cover macroeconomic management, such as inflation; structural policies, such as trade restrictions and the regulation and scope of private activity; and social inclusion, such as broad-based education and health care. With respect to institutions they assess the standard of honesty and efficiency in governance. A "substantial" improvement would be the sort of transformation that Uganda went through during the 1990s, with the country starting from a position of unambiguous weaknesses and attaining a standard that, although it might not be good, is not manifestly a severe handicap to development. We have included all low-income countries with such policies and institutions, whether they are postconflict or not, covering the period from 1975 to 2003. We find that other than in postconflict conditions, the chances of such a turnaround are very low: conditions may be bad, but they are stable. By contrast, during the postconflict decade the chances of a quantum improvement are much higher. Postconflict conditions provide the political opportunity for radical improvement in policies and institutions. A likely reason is that the political equilibrium that usually blocks the reform of dysfunctional policies and institutions has been broken. Vested interests may be weakened by conflict, and in the aftermath of peace people expect change. Starting from its medium-term vision, the government should therefore chart out step-by-step reforms that get there. Even when the political conditions for radical reform are propitious, the technical capacity for change may be radically limited. Having acknowledged that, for the moment I defer the discussion of how to resolve it.

Which policies are priorities? Some actions are obvious, for example, the reconstruction of damaged infrastructure. Other priorities are less obvious: the retreat into subsistence needs to be reversed and this reintegration of the rural economy into the market may require both reform of the market and repair of rural roads. The rise of opportunistic behavior will need to be countered by rebuilding institutions in both the private and the public sectors.

In the private sector, at a minimum, opportunism should be countered by a swift resolution of property rights, supported by the establishment of a functioning system of commercial law to enforce contracts. The resolution of property rights may help to reverse capital flight. Typically, capital flight continues during the postconflict decade, but in some cases governments have managed to attract substantial repatriation during the decade.

In the public sector the effective check on opportunism is not the legal system but a set of procedures that contribute to accountability. Accountability is a public good and like all public goods is radically undersupplied because nobody has an incentive to provide it. The decline in the ability to cooperate typical of conflict further undermines the capacity to deliver public goods. Accountability faces an even more severe problem than other public goods in that its supply faces not just a free-rider problem: those with power have an interest in actively opposing accountability because of the restraints that it would impose upon their conduct. Generating accountability in post-conflict conditions is therefore difficult.

There are three processes for building accountability: top-down, bottom-up, and sideways. All three are needed. Top-down involves bureaucratic systems of authorization and audit. During conflict these are usually opportunistically undermined, and restoring them requires getting into the bowels of civil service procedures: Who authorizes whom to do what, based on what information, and supported by what paper trail? Reform of these practices has to maintain a delicate balance: recreating responsibility without paralyzing civil servants into defensive inactivity. Bottom-up involves giving citizens power over service providers, such as having representation on school boards and electricity-generating companies. The empowerment of citizens requires information, which is aided by a free and competent press, something that is surely absent in postconflict conditions. Citizen power generally collapses during civil war if, indeed, it ever existed in the first place. Sideways accountability involves generating some peer pressure. For that to work there must be peers: the decisionmaking system must be sufficiently decentralized that different parts of government can reasonably be compared against each other. Peer pressure works if the peer group shares information on relative performance: nobody wants to be worst. The government's instinct after civil war is often to concentrate power so that there are insufficient peers, and even where there are decentralized entities they may not see themselves as a peer group but be fragmented by wartime divisions.

Effective accountability is the best defense the society has that its politics will not degenerate into patronage. If political parties cannot embezzle public funds, they simply cannot finance a patronage system and so are more likely to be driven to compete for votes by effective provision of public goods. In the absence of accountability, given the conditions of low income, valuable natural resource rents, and ethnic voting allegiances that are common in postconflict settings, the politics of patronage is likely to triumph over the politics of ideals. The postconflict period is the best time to get accountability established. People expect change, and so change is easier. Once patronage politics has taken hold, it will be defended by the vested interests it creates.

Among the broad categories of macro, structural, and social policies, there is some evidence as to which should be priorities.[10] Inclusive social expenditures such as the expansion of primary health care and education are atypically important for growth in postconflict settings, whereas macro policy is atypically less important. I do not mean that macroeconomic policy is in some absolute sense less important than social inclusion. The point is simply that comparing a postconflict society with an otherwise similar but peaceful failing state, there should be relatively greater emphasis upon social inclusion and relatively less on macroeconomic management. The legacy of collapsed public health systems and the high levels of illness consequent upon the mass movement of populations typical of conflict conditions provides one explanation for the high priority that should be attached to expenditures on public health. A further reason for the prioritization of social expenditures relates to the signaling problem discussed above. High expenditures on social inclusion signal that the government does not intend to run a patronage system for its core support base and so reinforce the signal given by a sharp reduction in military spending.

Priorities for International Actors

International actors face the same two areas for intervention—military provision and raising the growth rate. However, their instruments (external military force and aid) differ from those of the government.

Reducing Risk with an External Military Force

Given that some military force is needed in postconflict situations, but that force provided by the postconflict government is counterproductive, there is an inescapable need for external military force. However, UN forces operating under Chapter VI rules have not proved very successful. Countries are willing to supply forces under these terms, but they are often not willing to see their troops exposed to significant levels of risk, and Chapter VI does not permit an adequate level of force to be deployed to discourage rebel groups.

A spectacular demonstration of this problem was the capture by the Revolutionary United Front (RUF) of 500 UN troops in Sierra Leone. The more recent deployment of British troops under Chapter VII rules has, by contrast, been remarkably successful. Over a four-year period, the operation has cost only around $180 million, and the payoff has already been four years of secure peace in what was surely a high-risk situation. If the costs of the typical civil war are taken to be on the order of $50 billion, the payoff to this respite from risk, even if only temporary, is enormously greater than its costs.[11] The Sierra Leone model is therefore worth taking seriously. Its basic elements are the participation of a power with sufficient interest in the situation to risk taking casualties, an invitation from the government, and authorization under the UN to use sufficient force to secure the peace (Chapter VII), not merely for the immediate self-defense of troops (Chapter VI).

In contrast to the British intervention in Sierra Leone, the French intervention in Côte d'Ivoire has to date been radically less successful. Arguably, this intervention came too late: the proper moment was probably immediately following the military coup d'état against President Henri Konan Bédié on December 24, 1999. The French authorities had the military capability to reverse this coup but decided not to do so, partly because of hesitations over neocolonialism, partly because the incoming military leader, General Robert Guéï, had strong links with the French military, and partly because he promised to hold elections within six months. Surprisingly, the French government failed to recognize the "time consistency" problem inherent in this promise. Once the French had missed their window of legitimate opportunity to put down the coup, General Guéï was able to make a "modest amendment" to the terms of the forthcoming election: he himself would be a candidate, and all other candidates of any importance would be debarred. From that point on there was no legitimate government to restore and so no overarching objective for external military intervention.

Implementing Change Through
Technical Assistance and Capacity Building

The reform of economic policies and institutions cannot happen simply by decree. Even in the most hopeful postconflict circumstances, in which one or two ministers may appreciate the need for economic reform, there will be a severe shortage of the people qualified to implement reforms. Typically, even prior to conflict, such countries were acutely short of these people, and during conflict the more qualified citizens are those most likely to leave. Further, those few in the country are unlikely to be attracted to the public sector: they are more likely to be recruited by international NGOs and donor agencies. Yet the reform of economic policies and the building of economic institutions requires skilled people. This combination of an acute lack of supply with an explosion of demand has the potential for chaotic change that is at best ineffective and may even become difficult to undo.

The most realistic solution is a massive influx of technical assistance. In our study of turnarounds, Chauvet and I indeed find that large-scale technical assistance very early in an incipient reform process is highly cost-effective in improving the chances of achieving and sustaining a substantial improvement. It seems reasonable to suppose that gradually over the decade the provision of technical assistance should be replaced by a corresponding capacity-building effort. However, capacity building is not the appropriate response to an initial skill shortage of crisis proportions. First, some of the surge in demand for skills is temporary. Reform of policies and the building of institutions are both highly intensive in skills that are scarce even internationally, and largely unnecessary once conditions have been restored to normal. A normal society simply does not need the skill set appropriate for rapid change. Second, capacity building is too slow a process to meet the acute needs for skills that arise in the early years of the postconflict period. For both reasons the skill crisis is best resolved by temporarily importing foreign technical assistance. The exception to this is capacity building *outside* the civil service. Recall that a crucial component of accountability is bottom-up scrutiny by civil society. This function cannot be replaced, even temporarily, by foreign technical assistance. It is therefore, paradoxically, more urgent to build capacities outside the civil service than within it.

Capacity building within the public sector is, of course, necessary. However, it should probably attempt neither to recreate the civil service as it was nor even to create a conventional structure of ministries. In some postconflict situations, such as Liberia and the Democratic Republic of Congo, the attempt to build genuinely functioning ministries for service delivery is likely to be forlorn. A better approach may be to use a leapfrog technology, analogous to the way in which mobile phones have obviated the need to establish land-line systems. Even societies in the Organization for Economic Cooperation and Development (OECD) have begun to establish quasi-independent public agencies that contract out for services. Such agencies, or independent service authorities (ISAs), can be held to account by government, donors, and civil society, but they are not within the civil service, which frees them to hire afresh under far superior incentive systems. ISAs do not themselves deliver services. Rather, their role would be to contract with multiple, distinct types of service providers—private groups, NGOs, and local governments. An ISA's core functions are competitive allocation of contracts and rapid and continuous evaluation of performance. Thus, the key capacities to be built include contracting and evaluation, skills that are quite different from those of a traditional civil service.

Accelerating Growth Through Aid

Historically for the postconflict decade as a whole, aid has not been significantly higher than if there had been no conflict, although it is significantly higher in the first two or three years. Recent analysis of the effect of aid on growth in postconflict situations finds that aid is superb at raising growth in those situations.[12] However, this finding only applies during the middle of the decade. Hence, from the perspective of growth, aid should taper in during the first few years postconflict, whereas actually it tapers out. During its present peak in the early postconflict years, it is not particularly effective. Probably that is because although needs are great, the postconflict government lacks the capacity to spend aid effectively. Hence, bigger aid budgets overall that were better timed (in the middle of the decade) would have a more positive effect. Since politically the moment for committing to postconflict aid is clearly around the time of the peace settlement, the right approach is probably to allow much greater flexibility in the timing of aid disbursements. Long lags between commitment and disbursement should become normal in postconflict situations.

Unfortunately, the enhanced growth effect of aid depends upon the quality of policy, governance, and institutions. That is, aid effectiveness is much more sensitive to these characteristics in postconflict situations. Normally, effectiveness increases quite rapidly during the decade, which reinforces the idea that aid should taper in rather than taper out. It also provides a rationale for focusing international attention heavily upon improving these characteristics. Typically, considerable attention has been paid to political design in postconflict situations, especially in encouraging elections. Although that may be desirable in itself, the evidence is that elections per se do not reduce risks in postconflict situations. Indeed, changes in political arrangements appear to increase the risk of renewed conflict. I do not mean to imply, of course, that we should forget about promoting democracy, but rather that we should see it as broader than mere electoral competition. Accountability and checks and balances are the hidden part of mature democracy. Competitive elections can be put into place very rapidly, as in Afghanistan and Iraq. Accountability cannot be put in place so rapidly, and it lacks the glamorous urgency of an election. Yet without it, as I have argued, electoral competition will deliver the divisive and growth-inhibiting politics of patronage.

Encouraging Reform Through
International Models of Economic Governance

The enormous importance of good economic policies and the restoration of accountability in postconflict settings, and their previous neglect, suggest that the international community may want to establish models of reasonable practice. The models might cover key areas such as transparent management of the budget and accountability to the domestic population for public expenditure. Although donors are now rightly reluctant to insist upon ad hoc policy reforms, the existence of such internationally accepted models would enable donors to coordinate around them and would also assist governments in knowing what they should be aiming for.

In many postconflict settings, the governance of resource rents particularly matters, because they are one of the risk factors in initiating conflict. Further, the postconflict situation, with its resolution of property rights and restoration of peace, is likely to induce companies to prospect for new deposits and to work previously known but untapped deposits. For example, East Timor will receive large new revenues from offshore gas; the postconflict government of southern Sudan receives around $1 billion per year in new oil revenues; and oil prospecting is underway off the coasts of Liberia, Côte d'Ivoire, and Sierra Leone. Managing such revenues is difficult, and the low-income democracies typically do it even worse than other types of government.[13] An international model of good economic governance is urgently needed specifically for these situations. What should it contain?

Reasonable harnessing of resource rents requires four steps. The first is the process by which contracts are awarded to companies in the extractive industries. The record here is dreadful. A recent study of international diamond companies in Angola investigated the effect of peace upon their stock prices.[14] Specifically, taking all the diamond companies quoted on the New York market that had interests in Angola, the study estimated the impact of news of the death of Jonas Savimbi, and of the subsequent peace, on the price of their stocks. It found that peace significantly *lowered* stock prices: these companies were indeed "doing well out of war." More generally, contracts should be awarded in a transparent and competitive context, as is standard practice in developed societies: an international template of standard practice should stipulate the parameters of what is acceptable.

Once international actors have policed how contracts are awarded, their second concern for a model of good practice should be what the contracts say. Here, the key issue is distribution of price risk. Commodity prices are volatile, and if the postconflict government bears the risk, it will be faced with revenue volatility that is likely to be destabilizing. At present, ridiculously massive international companies are passing on the price risk to incompetent, impoverished, and fragile governments. A model should require a more reasonable distribution of this risk. If companies do not want to bear it, they can use their sophisticated market knowledge to enter derivatives contracts that pass the risk on to others. No postconflict government has the competence to engage in such derivatives contracts.

Having policed what contracts say, the international community must ensure that payments and the expenditures they support should be transparent. The "Publish What You Pay" campaign has focused on the former, resulting in the Extractive Industries Transparency Initiative. However, transparency in revenues is only an input into the scrutiny of expenditures. Thus, a model of good economic governance needs to spell out the parameters of budgetary transparency.

The final component of a model involves managing revenue volatility. At present, price crashes lead to growth collapses that substantially heighten the risk of conflict. Better design of contracts, as in the second step, would reduce revenue volatility, but it is unlikely to eliminate the problem. At present, each government makes up its own ad hoc scheme for smoothing expenditures. East Timor and Chad even use elements of Norway's approach to oil revenue—accumulating financial assets for future generations. Such a feature is surely ill-advised for low-income postconflict countries, which will need to finance major public capital formation if they are to transform their economies. Long-term financial assets are only appropriate for a capital-abundant economy such as Norway or Kuwait. What is needed in terms of *financial* asset accumulation is a reasonably simple rule for medium-term expenditure smoothing so that governments faced with either a boom or a bust would not have to invent a policy rule from scratch. Many resource discoveries last for finite periods of two or three decades. Partly, such short time horizons result from the economics of resource discoveries: it is simply not efficient for an oil company to "prove" reserves beyond a horizon of around thirty years. However, even if there is good reason to think that resources will only last for a relatively short period, that is not a reason to accumulate *financial* assets. If resources will expire, it is indeed imperative for the society to *save* them, but the right choice of asset in low-income societies is overwhelmingly likely to be domestic capital formation. Low-income societies simply face a different decision than does Norway, which already has plenty of domestic capital.

Why might such an international model of good economic governance be effective? From the perspective of the international companies, the biggest risk in postconflict settings is not political or commercial: it is the potential for loss of reputation. An international model or standard creates strong pressures for companies to abide by it. By following the standard they protect themselves even if things go wrong: they have a solid alibi. Those not adhering to the standard heighten their risk of loss of reputation: when things go wrong, their position is indefensible. From the perspective of donors, a standard provides a similar defense of reputation and also a clear criterion for aid allocation: the standard becomes a condition for big aid. Such conditioning upon the processes of governance has a legitimacy that the intrusive conditioning upon economic policies lacked. Policy conditionality transferred to donors the power that should have belonged to governments. In the process it muddied the attribution of accountability: Who should citizens blame if things go wrong, their government or their donors? By contrast, governance conditionality seeks to make governments more accountable to their own citizens. From the perspective of postconflict governments, a model of economic governance would guide reformers and reduce the scope for unproductive argument. Economic reform is complex, and there are always multiple opinions. In the typical postconflict conditions of an acute shortage of resident citizens with skills, and high levels of suspicion, self-guided reform is likely to be fraught with disputes even among people who should be on the same side. In addition to reducing frictions among those who want reform, an international standard is likely to raise the bargaining power of reformers as a group against both international companies and domestic vested interests. The utility of standards to reformers would be analogous to role of the *Aquis Communautaires* for reformers in the potential accession countries of the European Union. Who, however, would play the role of the European Union—that is, who would promulgate the standards? The obvious answer is that the new UN Peacebuilding Commission should play such a role.

Conclusion

Postconflict situations have historically been times of high risk: indeed, half of all civil wars result from postconflict situations gone wrong. Postconflict situations have also featured major policy errors, both by postconflict governments and the international community. Fortunately, by avoiding the mistakes of the past, it should be possible to do much better and so bring these risks down.

Economic factors are at the heart of conflict risk. With better policies, better priorities for reform, and bigger and better-timed aid, it should be possible to restore the economies of postconflict countries considerably more rapidly. Yet even with the best choices, economic recovery takes time. The risks of the postconflict decade cannot be solved by economic choices. What good economic choices can do is ensure that those risks do not persist beyond that decade. Hence, economic strategy can only complement other strategies for keeping the postconflict peace. I suspect that there has been an overemphasis upon political design, perhaps because that is the skill base of most of those who write about the topic. I favor a dual strategy in which external military forces are used to maintain a credible peace during the postconflict decade, while others take the opportunity to pursue the economic recovery strategy with vigor. In turn, this strategy gradually brings risks down to acceptable levels by the close of the decade.

Notes

1. Paul Collier, Anke Hoeffler, and Mans Soderbom, "Post-Conflict Risks," *Journal of Peace Research,* forthcoming.

2. "Ethnic dominance" can occur where ethnicity is central to social identity. Statistically, it is defined as the largest ethnic group being between 45 percent and 90 percent of the society. See Paul Collier and Anke Hoeffler, "Greed and Grievance in Civil War," *Oxford Economic Papers* 56, no. 4 (October 2004): 563–595. In effect, the largest group has the potential to dominate minorities, and the minorities are sufficiently large to be worth exploiting. Where religion is central to social identity, it can function in the same way as ethnicity.

3. Paul Collier and Anke Hoeffler, "Military Expenditure in Post-Conflict Societies," *Economics of Governance* 7, no. 1 (January 2006): 89–107.

4. Unfortunately, this technique cannot be given a full description accessible to a noneconomist that is sufficiently brief for a footnote. However, in summary, the researcher estimates an "instrumentation regression" that predicts military spending, including some factors unrelated to the risk of civil war, and then uses this prediction in the regression of the risk of conflict.

5. Barbara F. Walter, *Committing to Peace: The Successful Settlement of Civil Wars* (Princeton, NJ: Princeton University Press, 2002).

6. Paul Collier, "Demobilization and Insecurity: A Study in the Economics of the Transition from War to Peace," *Journal of International Development* 6, no. 3 (May–June 1994): 343–351.

7. Jeremy Weinstein and Macartan Humphreys, "Disentangling the Successful Determinants of Demobilization and Reintegration," Working Paper no. 69 (Washington, DC: Center for Global Development, 2005).

8. Betty Bigombe, Paul Collier, and Nicholas Sambanis, "Policies for Building Post-Conflict Peace," *Journal of African Economies* 9, no. 3 (October 2000): 323–348.

9. Lisa Chauvet and Paul Collier, "What Are the Preconditions for Turnarounds in Failing States?" Forthcoming, *Journal of Peace and Conflict Management.*

10. Collier and Hoeffler, "Greed and Grievance in Civil War."

11. Costs are all in US dollars. Paul Collier and Anke Hoeffler, "Aid, Policy, and Growth in Post-Conflict Societies," *European Economic Review* 48, no. 5 (October 2004): 1125–1145.

12. Collier and Hoeffler, "Greed and Grievance in Civil War."

13. Paul Collier and Anke Hoeffler, "Democracy and Natural Resources" (Oxford: Center for the Study of African Economies, Department of Economics, Oxford University, 2005).

14. Massimo Guidolin and Eliana La Ferrara, *Diamonds Are Forever, Wars Are Not: Is Conflict Bad for Private Firms?* Discussion Paper no. 4668 (London: Center for Economic Policy Research, 2004).

6

Justice and the Rule of Law

Erik G. Jensen

The love of rationalistic simplification . . . leads people to think that in the mere technicalities of law they possess the means and the power to effect unlimited changes. . . . [Such an illusion is] cherished by lawyers who imagine that, by drafting new constitutions and laws they can begin the work of history all over again, and know nothing of the force of traditions, habits, associations and institutions.[1]
                                                    —Guido de Ruggiero, 1927

Development policy is a matter of both contestable political choices and sharp economic analysis—for neither of which is "law" a substitute.[2]
                                                    —David Kennedy, 2003

I have three motivations in writing this chapter. First, undoubtedly shared with all of the contributors to this volume, I have an interest in improving the practice of statebuilding. Second, I'm struck by ghettoization in the development industry whereby "statebuilding" has become a nested specialty insufficiently connected to the general development literature and experience.[3] Third, the development industry's thirst for reinvention often takes us far from the historical context of local institutions, which should be central to the development of strategies to strengthen the rule of law, not incidental to it.

Since the 1990s, the concept of "rule of law" has been enthusiastically embraced by international development actors and touted as the key to consolidating peace in postconflict societies. Rhetorical overuse of the term has been matched by a proliferation of rule of law programs purporting to do everything from legislative, judicial, and police reforms to land and property administrations and market reforms. These programs, with their outsized ambitions, rely on a contested definition of what constitutes rule of law and what can be accomplished through international assistance. So-called comprehensive rule of law programs are routinely favored over limited and more strategic interventions with a manageable set of dependent variables.[4] And funding tends to get stove-piped in institutions like judiciaries

119

whether they are, can, or should be the causal agents to achieve the outcomes identified.[5]

Expectations and assumptions about the rule of law have led to a patchy record of performance in rule of law projects. The development industry expects too much from technical assistance projects that install formal laws and legal institutions. These expectations are driven by a set of assumptions about the *number* of outcomes that can be achieved through rule of law assistance and *when* they can be achieved. The number is unrealistically high and the timing unrealistically short. We expect too much, too soon, with too little money, too much emphasis on technical precision, and too little on the embedded political, economic, and cultural dynamics that surround institutional change. In the worst cases, we support the wrong institutions to achieve the articulated goals and objectives. When this happens, institutional support to strengthen the rule of law mimics the drunk looking under the lamppost for his keys, not because he lost his keys there, but because that is where the light is. In the wake of unrealistic expectations emerges a record of performance that led the World Bank to conclude that "less overall progress has been made in judicial reform and strengthening than in almost any other area of policy or institutional reform."[6] If goals and objectives were more modest and built soundly on the historical evolution of existing institutions, perhaps funding would be more proportionate and our record of performance better.

I have divided this chapter into two sections. The first section is organized around four key analytical questions associated with building the rule of law and the strategic implications that flow from the answers to those questions. Building on those answers, the second section discusses the political economy of institutional change and the challenges that rule of law shares with other public institutional reform efforts. It also suggests practical interventions and approaches that can surmount those common challenges in rule of law programs.[7]

Key Analytical Questions

In this section, I ask and answer four basic questions: (1) What orders behavior? (2) What is the "rule of law"? (3) What is a "legal system"? and (4) What are the goals of strengthening rule of law? Understanding the answers to these questions directly shapes the design of rule of law programs—the goals, strategic objectives, and project activities that advance those objectives and goals.

On one level, the answers seem rudimentary. But on another level, the answers to these questions are messy and complex. Gerhard Casper once wrote that "the messy phenomena of life" cannot "be made to fit [a legal]

Code."[8] My answers to the four questions posed are messy. But from this messiness emerges straightforward advice to

- understand and appreciate the complexity and messiness inherent in strengthening the rule of law;
- clearly define and sequence a *limited* set of strategic dependent variables (outcomes); and
- then support and build a mix of institutions and regulations that are critical causal agents for progress on the dependent variables.

Let me be very clear. I am not "pro" informal institutions (e.g., community-based mediation) or "anti" formal institutions (e.g., judiciaries). I am pragmatic. Formal institutions are expensive to build. Enforcement through formal institutions is complex. It requires the coordination of multiple agencies (e.g., judiciary, police, and prosecutor). Formal enforcement is also expensive. These realities, among others analyzed in this chapter, lead to a very practical approach. Figure out what informal institutions are doing; which types of disputes are handled reasonably well by informal institutions and which are not; and tailor formal institution building to handle matters that are not being handled well by informal institutions yet are crucial to the strategic dependent variables or outcomes identified. This advice may strike some as rudimentary, yet it is too frequently ignored.

What Orders Behavior?

A key question that should be answered before defining the rule of law is, What orders behavior? It's a prior (and messy) question because it turns out that law (or rules) is just one potential mechanism by which behavior is ordered, and often not the most robust mechanism, especially in postconflict situations.

Custom and convention play predominant roles in ordering behavior, even in rule-based societies, and an overwhelming role in statebuilding contexts where formal institutions are often weak.[9] Custom relates to habit, behavior that is taken for granted in a given cultural context.[10] Convention is shaped by groups seeking approval or fearing disapproval. Norms "specify how things should be done; they define the legitimate means to pursue valued ends."[11] Norms incorporate custom and convention and also may be incorporated and codified in rules.[12]

The roles of self-enforcement and coercive enforcement in ordering behavior. Custom, convention, and norms enjoy a high level of self-enforcement. That is, state institutions do not need to coercively enforce them. Self-enforcement is motivated by, among other things, a fear of *ostracism* if one fails to comply with custom, convention, norms (and perhaps rules); concern about *reputation* in conducting relations; appreciation for the value of a good reputation and the negative consequences of a bad reputation; and *kinship* ties or close personal relations in a group.

Coercive enforcement is at the other end of the spectrum from self-enforcement. In the context of rule of law, it is called *legal coercion:* coercive action of the state based on law. However, as Max Weber understood so well a century ago, the state always has limited capacity for legal coercion:

> Legal coercion, where it transforms a custom into a legal obligation . . . often adds practically nothing to its effectiveness, and, where it opposes custom, frequently fails in the attempt to influence actual conduct. (320) The chance of legal coercion which, . . . motivates even "legal" conduct only to a slight extent, is also objectively an ultimate guaranty for no more than a fraction of the actual course of consensually related conduct. (324–325) . . . Only a limited measure of success can be attained through the threat of coercion supporting the legal order. (334)[13]

One practical implication of Weber's insight on legal coercion is the following: rules that run contrary to custom, convention, and norms must be very strategically *targeted* if there is to be a realistic expectation of enforcement.[14] If new rules and institutions are developed, they should be tied to—or have the potential of being tied to—behavior over time in the context of prevailing informal constraints. Some argue that ambitious law making and law reform "does no harm." But too many rules in low-capacity regimes can undermine public support and state legitimacy. Public cynicism will grow if rules are introduced without attention to pace, sequence, local context, and, of course, implementation. Where rules are not self-enforcing in a statebuilding context, selective enforcement or no enforcement should be expected outcomes. This is so because *legal coercion is a scarce commodity.*[15] Or, stated another way, *credible enforcement by public actors is expensive.*

Axiomatically, since legal coercion is a scarce commodity and credible enforcement is expensive, another practical implication for the rule of law practitioner in statebuilding contexts is that one needs to understand what is being handled well through informal mechanisms based on custom and convention and what strategic issues are not being handled well through those mechanisms or not being handled at all.

What Is the "Rule of Law"?

According to a *Jakarta Post* account in January 1998, Larry Summers, then secretary of the treasury, "blew into Jakarta for a few hours," after which he climbed the stairs to his plane, looked out over the unwashed, and said, "Indonesia needs the rule of law." What did Larry Summers mean? "Rule of law" is bandied about by politicians and development professionals alike as if we have a common conception of the term. We don't. It is hotly contested. At a minimum, just being aware of the basic elements of the rich definitional debate about the rule of law should improve the practice of strengthening it.

A detailed discussion of rule of law is well beyond the parameters of this chapter.[16] But it is important to be aware that there is a definitional spectrum associated with the rule of law. Some of us describe this spectrum as a range from the *thinnest* definition of the rule of law to the *thickest*.[17] Broadly, theories either focus on *form* or on *substance*.

Form. From thinnest to thickest, the three levels of formal rule of law include rule by law, formal legality, and democratic rule of law.[18] The thinnest form may be characterized as "whatever the sovereign utters is law" or "all government action must be authorized by law." It may also be called rule *by* law because it does not set any limitations on government action. A second form, which many adopt, is "formal legality"; it requires laws to be general in their scope, prospective in their application, clear in their formulation, and certain in their application. The most important outcome of formal legality is predictability: people can plan their activities with advance knowledge of potential legal implications. Formal legality is neutral about substance. Some argue that formal legality has a moral component because it prohibits governments from acting in an entirely arbitrary fashion. Others argue that formal legality does not include a moral dimension: "Like a knife, which is neither good nor bad in itself, but can be used to kill a man or to slice vegetables, the morality of law is a function of the uses to which it is put."[19] Therefore, many would argue that legal formality would be satisfied in circumstances where you have the clear and consistent application of a law, even an immoral one like slavery. Democratic rule of law is the thickest of the formal types; it focuses on the *consent* of the governed to the laws. Unanimous consent to laws is impractical, if not impossible. The goal in democratic legal formality is to maximize to the extent possible the consent of persons affected by the law enacted.[20]

Substance. Substance overlaps with form. Substantive rule of law includes the formal attributes discussed above: general, prospective, clear, and consistent. In addition, even thin substantive rule of law has content requirements, such as some specification of individual rights. Thin views on content stress limitations on government action. A thicker social welfare version of substantive rule of law includes the affirmative duty of the government to make the lives of citizens better, distribute resources justly, and recognize the right to dignity. There are at least two interrelated problems with the thickest conception of rule of law: one is conceptual; the other is purely pragmatic. Conceptually, if all that is good is bundled into "rule of law," then rule of law simply becomes a "proxy battleground," as Brian Taman-aha calls it, for disputes about broader social, political, and economic is-sues. Pragmatically, some of us have argued that a thick social welfare ver-sion of the rule of law is impractical in developing countries, in any event, because enforcement capacity, certainly in the courts, is weak and must be targeted *and* because the resource distribution issues behind social welfare are more effectively handled by other branches of government.

What Is a "Legal System"?

Defining what constitutes a legal system turns out to be a messier exercise than most imagine. Contrary to popular development discourse, justice is not a sector, it is an institutional phenomenon. "Justice" is not neatly bounded either in content or institutional framework. Both the substantive content and the institutional patterns that may perform functions that implement jus-tice are diverse and dynamic.[21] There is no bright demarcation between the functions that a formal legal system should perform and those that semifor-mal or informal institutional arrangements should carry out.

Let us put aside for the moment semiformal institutions (e.g., state-sponsored mediation) and informal institutions (e.g., community-based tradi-tional mediation) and just focus on the complexity of functions of formal institutions. Francis Fukuyama's analysis of public administration in a state-building setting makes the important point that there is "no optimal specifica-tion of formal institutions and thus no optimal form of organization, particu-larly for public sector agencies."[22] Challenges to specifying the organization of formal institutions include the following: (1) goals in public institutions emerge from complicated interactions between organizational players; (2) for-mal systems of monitoring and accountability entail high transaction costs; (3) the appropriate level of delegated discretion within and across public institu-tions is dynamic and variable; and (4) domestic constituencies for institutional reform are weak.

These general challenges are magnified in the reform and building of rule of law institutions in at least four respects. First, in institutions associ-ated with the rule of law, these interactions are much more complicated than other functions often associated with public service delivery because the functions have *low specificity* compared, for instance, to an institution charged with building roads or providing health services. Essential system components—judicial integrity, for example—are more elusive and harder to measure than the tensile strength of a metal beam or trends in infant mor-tality. Second, rule of law functions require high levels of *interagency co-ordination* to achieve credible enforcement (e.g., the courts, police, prose-cutors, public defenders, and other civilian agencies). Third, rule of law functions often include actors that by definition function with *low levels of transparency* (e.g., courts, investigative police). Consequently, the technical components of reforming a construction ministry or public health system are less complex than those involved in reforming a judiciary. And they are more readily subject to monitoring, oversight, and demands for transparency. Finally, political *constituencies* for the reform of legal systems tend to be even lower than for the reform of other public agencies.

Again, limiting ourselves to the sphere of formal public institutions, the scope of "judicialized" functions and bureaucratic functions varies. This is true even in developed countries. For example, several years ago, the Netherlands externalized no-fault divorce from the judicial system; such divorces were diverted to the bureaucracy, where the parties simply filed their divorce papers.[23] Thus, the bureaucracy can and often does carry out effectively functions that judiciaries might otherwise perform. Yet, too often, law projects simply assume the virtue of the large-scale migration of power from the bureaucracy to the judiciary. This is important to understand in a statebuilding context, where a scarcity of formal legal actors is common. Some law projects recognize this danger and try to avoid unnecessarily burdening the judiciary with functions that can be handled by the bureaucracy. For example, nascent commune councils in Cambodia, a local-level bureaucratic institution, are handling a growing portfolio of conflict resolution functions that might otherwise be considered judicial.

For rule of law reformers, the implications of this discussion on what defines a legal system should be clear. Too often, logical frameworks assume that formal legal institutions perform a broad set of similar functions across countries. The functions that are judicialized, however, should be carefully targeted for at least three reasons. First, judicialized functions are more expensive than bureaucratic functions. Second, the general challenges of institution building are even greater in rule of law institutions. Third, legal coercion, apart from being an expensive and scarce resource, is often ineffective if it runs counter to custom and convention. Programs aimed at strengthening the rule of law should therefore be carefully designed to focus on what institutions actually do and might realistically do, rather than on what they say they do, what their organization chart says they do, or what we may imagine they should do.

What Are the Goals of Strengthening Rule of Law?

The goods or outcomes that one expects from stronger rule of law should directly affect the prioritization of objectives and activities. Five of the most commonly articulated goals in donor-assisted rule of law programs are citizen security and stability, protection of human rights, dispute resolution, economic growth and development, and protection from bureaucratic caprice and corruption. The breadth of outcomes reflects, in part, the fact that rule of law has become a proxy for political, economic, and social choices. In postconflict countries the prominent debate about competing priorities is between those who emphasize stability, order, and regularized administration (security) and those who emphasize rights and redress for past abuse (justice).[24] Stability and justice are not mutually exclusive goals; pervasive and violent injustice may spark instability. Nevertheless, a sense of prioritization among these five "goods" is necessary to pace and sequence the building of rule of law.

Ensuring security and stability. Statebuilding requires a state. Basic order—a Weberian state that has the ability to monopolize violence—is the first priority. Iraq and Afghanistan have poignantly demonstrated the importance of establishing security and stability before taking on more ambitious statebuilding goals. Based on his experience in Iraq, Larry Diamond recognizes as a sine qua non "the fundamental importance of a coherent, capable state."[25] Based on my experience, the chances of succeeding at institution building are greatest for functions on which the common understanding is strongest and the need most observable. A common understanding of "security" is always stronger than a common understanding of "justice"—what is just and what is unjust.

Of course, if institutions are to strengthen security credibly, they must act with some restraint. As Larry Diamond asks, "What if the safety and rights of Iraqi citizens are threatened by the very security forces we have helped to stand up?"[26] Comprehensive treatment of the dilemmas Diamond frames is beyond the scope of this chapter, but for a discussion of some of these dilemmas, see Barnett R. Rubin, "The Politics of Security in Postconflict Statebuilding," Chapter 2 in this volume. A growing body of literature analyzes the challenges and policy options in restoring a restrained security apparatus in an environment where both military (in response to violence directed against the state) and police skills (in response to crimes affecting the general population) are required.[27] As David Bayley, among others, has argued, violence against the state will take priority over crime against the general population. At least at this broader level, the ordering of security priorities is obvious.

Especially at the early statebuilding phase, one of the most consequential tasks is distinguishing between good and bad actors within security forces. The task is, or should be, highly nuanced. We know that blunt purging efforts such as debaathification in Iraq yield counterproductive results. They create virtually insurmountable shortfalls in trained staff through the medium term. More importantly, wholesale purging swells the ranks of trained, disaffected, mobilized, and often armed constituencies of resistance. Interventions short of full-scale purging carry their own risks, however. If the screening of good and bad actors is inadequate, the compact reached between the state and the security forces (including factions within) may be marked by insufficient commitment. Moreover, if institutional incentives to encourage good behavior are not implemented, the result will be varying degrees of poor or inimical performance.

Competing and complex security demands call for targeted solutions. Despite an abundant critique of the performance of the Serious Crimes Unit in East Timor, the effort to significantly limit the jurisdiction of that tribunal and, at the same time, strengthen traditional dispute resolution mechanisms for lesser crimes was, in principle, a good idea under the circumstances.[28] That institutional design tacitly recognized the limits of legal coercion and eventually took advantage of the strengths of traditional institutions.

Protecting human rights. In the practice of development (and the literature on transitional justice), the desirability of representative government and enhancement of rights and participation are assumed.[29] Surprisingly, in the transitional justice literature one finds no empirical proof of the effectiveness of trials in deterring human rights violations or truth commissions and amnesties in contributing to reconciliation. Rather, as Leila Sadat observes, "What appears to be at issue is a competition over the values underlying the normative claims."[30]

All the challenges that attend formal legal institution building discussed in this chapter suggest that a generalized rights-based approach is ill-advised. (By "rights-based approach" I mean the assumption that by creating a right, demand will follow, institutions will respond favorably to the demand, and then social, economic, or political change will happen.)[31] A more nuanced approach with a higher likelihood of success would ask and answer three questions: Which human rights/crimes are the highest priority and which violations most serious? Are there ways to modify the functions of preexisting institutions to address the rights violation/crime? If not, can formal institutions effectively target the rights violations identified? To illustrate the sequence, take domestic violence, which is committed at alarming rates in East Timor. In a study conducted in 2003 under the auspices of the International Rescue Committee, "24.8 percent of women had experienced violence from an intimate partner in the past year," and "51 percent of women consulted stated that in the last 12 months they felt unsafe in their relationship with their husband."[32] The violation is widespread and serious. Can preexisting institutions (usually informal) address the problem? As robust as traditional justice is in East Timor, most would agree that it does an inadequate job of addressing the problem, and it is unlikely that traditional justice institutions can significantly improve their performance in addressing the problem. The next question is, Can formal institutions address the problem?

Settling common disputes. Beyond the security-on-the-one-hand-justice-on-the-other debate is a wide and largely ignored swath of disputes that citizens may care the most about after basic security: that is, small debt, small property, small inheritance, and family matters.[33] Interestingly, in a recent survey conducted by the Asia Foundation in Cambodia, when respondents were asked to cite examples of justice and injustice both inside and outside the courts, the cases cited were consistently "micro"-level cases, involving issues of justice that directly affect people's daily lives, rather than examples of "justice" as the protector of abstract values. Land disputes that ultimately result in murder or other serious crimes were the most common types of cases cited.[34] One might have expected some reference to the Khmer Rouge Tribunal (KRT), the prospect of which has been a major media attraction. Although the data do not support the broad conclusion that the KRT is unimportant to Cambodians, it is absolutely striking that the Khmer Rouge atrocities were *not* cited as an example of injustice by respondents.[35]

Apart from assessing which functions matter most and which configuration *across* institutions might deliver those functions, a realistic assessment of change potential *within* institutions is necessary. Which changes can be made relatively easily, and which will face more resistance? Which changes are most essential to build the legitimacy of the state? And will the benefits of progress on the dependent variable justify the costs?

Promoting economic growth and development. A convincing argument could be made that, after citizen security and stability, the most important rule of law priority should be the facilitation of economic growth and development. Many of us have been influenced by the positive effects of a new "Asian drama" over the past twenty-five years in the most rapidly developing region of the world.[36] We find salience in what I call a "Lipsetean" progression in economic and political development. Back in 1960, Seymour Lipset argued that political development tends to follow economic development, the consequent expansion of the middle classes, and their rising political demands.[37] In other words, get economic growth going, rapid economic growth if you can; the middle classes will then expand and demand a reduction in the scope of the patrimonial state, among other positive political benefits. Many of us who focus on Asia have seen Lipset's hypothesis successfully tested time and time again.

Some argue that statebuilding donors and the international bureaucrats that staff their agencies fail to learn from the Asian development experience and do not emphasize enough the importance of unleashing private sector initiatives. As a result of this oversight, statebuilding efforts often have the inadvertent results of creating institutional barriers to private sector development. John MacMillan called it the "blind spot" in the foreign advisers' view of nationbuilding as he analyzed the lack of private sector development in East Timor.[38] East Timor is ranked as the 174th worst country out of 175 countries surveyed for ease of doing business, nudging out last-place Democratic Republic of Congo.[39] The rules on business, originally written by the United Nations Transitional Administration in East Timor (UNTAET), specify a $100 annual business registration fee with a $500 fine and closure for failing to register, in addition to a $200 health ministry approval and a $300 business license. According to the study, "The applicant [for business registration] must visit six different government agencies, deposit in a bank a sum of nine times per-capita income, and pay fees that add up to 125 percent of per-capita income."[40]

In the face of this impediment to economic growth, MacMillan criticizes the bureaucratized and top-down approach to private sector development taken by donor agencies in East Timor and zeroes in on the World Bank's 2005 East Timor country assistance program. The linchpin in the strategy is a public works program to create jobs in the short term. The blind spot involves not appreciating the private sector's *immediate* value. Although MacMillan acknowledges the need for public works to create jobs and supply infrastructure, he argues that the most effective way to create jobs would be to rewrite the rules that stand in the way of business. MacMillan may be overstating the impact that a change in the rules would have on the economy. Still, such a rule change is a cost-benefit no-brainer; it would do no harm, cost little, and may do some or a substantial amount of good.

Combating corruption. Many rule of law projects assume that institutional support for formal rule of law institutions will translate into less corruption. A closely associated assumption is that an independent judiciary must fulfill the functional need for credible third-party enforcement. But the empirical evidence for both assumptions is weak. Indeed, the evidence shows that reliance on legal institutions such as judges and police to enforce and strengthen accountability in the public sector is misplaced.[41] And, in general, countercorruption commissions have failed to fill the function of credible third-party monitoring.[42]

Private enforcement, contracting out enforcement, and citizen enforcement are alternatives to public enforcement. Citizen enforcement based on easy access to information on public programs can serve to create demand for transparency, monitor service quality, and challenge abuse by public officials. A significant example of such access is what is contemplated in East Timor's oil-revenue management. According to the Extractive Industries Transparency Initiative assessment, East Timor is off to an excellent start:

> From the outset the Government of Timor Leste has pursued a rigorous approach to transparency. Revenues and contracts are in the public domain. The Government has conducted thorough public consultations on several initiatives on transparency and management of oil and gas revenues. . . . In February 2005, the Government launched public consultations on a Law

to create a fully transparent and audited Petroleum Fund, which the Government plans to bring into full operation for the next fiscal year. All petroleum revenues will flow through the Fund.[43]

Certainly one of the most important ways to reduce corruption and improve economic growth is the credible and transparent management of a country's natural resources—a form of economic justice. If East Timor manages its oil and gas reserves responsibly, it will have a greater positive effect on strengthening the rule of law in the country than any other single issue, enhancing citizen security and stability as well as economic growth and development. And, importantly, it will demonstrate effective and legitimate government by protecting against bureaucratic caprice and corruption. So far, East Timor seems to be dodging the "resource curse" and setting an international example in its transparent management of oil and gas reserves among "statebuilding states."

Surmounting Institution-Building Challenges

Although rule of law institutions have distinct challenges, as outlined above, they also share common challenges to institution building that Sarah Cliffe and Nick Manning identify in Chapter 8: failure to take account of what institutions already exist, lack of prioritization of institution-building efforts, nontransferability of international models of capacity, and unintentional collateral damage caused to domestic institutions through the international presence.[44] This section of my chapter reflects on institutional change and interventions that can surmount those common challenges in rule of law programs, drawing extensively on experiences in Cambodia and East Timor. More specifically, this section:

- suggests empirical baselines needed for problem diagnosis and the design of successful interventions;
- discusses the barriers to obtaining this information through traditional staffing of rule of law assessment teams;
- pinpoints problems in capacity building;
- raises elements of the political dynamics of institutional change beyond capacity building; and
- summarizes the problem of transplantation of laws and legal institutions.

Institution Mapping and Dispute Mapping

I have argued elsewhere that "the most urgent need is for more thick descriptions of local context regarding the role, functions and substance of formal and informal legal institutions."[45] Both institution mapping and dispute mapping—identifying which institutions exist and which types of disputes are most common—are essential first steps. Central to the challenge of identifying which institution-building efforts to prioritize are concerns about public demand and need on the one hand, and legitimacy of institutions on the other. Mapping exercises can help to answer these questions and form the basis for an informed set of priorities. Such a mapping exercise needs to include both bureaucratic and judicial institutions as well as informal institutions, and disputes that cut across all (e.g., high and low courts, bureaucracy and judiciary, urban and rural judiciary, judiciary and various local tribunals).

Institution mapping should capture preexisting practices (such as the use of hand-written administrative notes at a rural subdistrict level in East Timor, as discussed by Edith Bowles and Tanja Chopra in Chapter 12), and avoid, to the extent possible, the introduction of inappropriate technology and forms that do not connect to prior local practice. Such mapping would also capture practices such as the custom of registering citizens by the local police in "family books" in Cambodia. During the Khmer Rouge period, family books were used to track and control populations. After 1979, family books became important evidence of citizenship and legal identity.[46]

Likewise, institution mapping can begin to capture who the actors are within institutions and provide an explanation for the performance and legitimacy of those institutions. For example, according to Kim Ninh and Roger Henke's report on the commune councils in Cambodia, "most of the former commune chiefs have made the switch to the new system" and "half of these former commune chiefs have returned as chair of commune councils."[47] This finding, together with the high percentages of council members who have held prior positions as civil servants or as local officers, may suggest that the Cambodia commune council project relies on national staff that understand prior institutions.

Opinion surveys of the public, disputants, and "would-be" disputants (i.e., those who are systematically avoiding a dispute resolution forum because of perceived bias) can also be useful tools in establishing baselines. Opinion surveys can be a useful technique in mapping disputes, twinned with an analysis of other data points, such as relevant records kept by state, religious, or community organizations. In order to assess community norms and ascertain self-enforcing behavior, as opposed to behavior that requires a degree of coercive power, ethnographic data on local justice and injustice can be invaluable. Objectives of this research include, among others:

- assessing the frequency, nature, and severity of civil disputes and crimes;
- identifying actions taken in response to such disputes (violence, other types of retaliation, etc.);
- determining motivations for taking or refraining from action in various dispute forums;
- assessing demand for various types of dispute resolution mechanisms so that the institution-building agenda dovetails with demand; and

- assessing citizens' confidence in, and satisfaction with, various dispute resolution mechanisms.

Much has been written about the failure of the UNTAET mission to take account of what institutions already existed at the time of transition in East Timor. I will not reconstruct this critique, but it strongly supports my argument for the mapping and analysis of informal institutions. Edith Bowles and Tanja Chopra's critique in Chapter 12 in this volume highlights the *terra nullius* fallacy. UNTAET was slow to realize the role and value of traditional justice, perhaps because some presumed that the traditional system of justice lacks mechanisms to meet international standards of human rights, especially gender equality. A more pragmatic way forward would be to take advantage of existing informal institutions to the extent possible and to seek other institutional arrangements on targeted issues where the traditional system seemed problematic.[48]

A survey commissioned by the Asia Foundation in East Timor illustrates the care that must be used in analyzing survey data that assesses satisfaction with preexisting institutions as well as demand for institutions old and new. When asked to agree or disagree with the statement, "I prefer to settle disputes by going to the formal system," 62 percent of respondents agreed. The finding, taken in isolation, seemed to favor formal over informal legal institutions. But this finding contradicts other findings within the survey that enjoy a much higher level of plausibility, given East Timor's history. The survey was much stronger on revealing the demand for and legitimacy of traditional justice mechanisms and processes. Of those who actually had taken disputes to the traditional *adat* process, 83 percent expressed satisfaction. Overall, 94 percent expressed confidence or were "somewhat confident" in the traditional justice system.[49] The point is that developing baseline assessments of preexisting institutions and public demand for institutions, both old and new, requires a nuanced understanding of the strengths and limitations of the empirical instruments employed.

Whatever research technique is used, the danger of bias needs to be controlled for. Certain donors and consultants have a strong bias for formal, centralized institutions irrespective of the dependent variables that are sought. Likewise, others may have a bias for preexisting informal, decentralized institutions.

Staffing Rule of Law Assessment Teams

Another related practical problem is achieving the right mix of skills in baseline assessment teams that identify and analyze institutions that already exist, examining formal and informal legal systems in a local context. Generally, the international development industry takes far too narrow an approach to what constitutes a "legal expert" and places disproportionate emphasis on expert legal advice. Lawyers and judges are necessary but insufficient. They tend to have very strong skills in what Max Weber called "legal dogmatics"[50]—that is, they examine legal propositions and try to determine whether each is logically correct and, taking multiple legal propositions together, whether they are logically coherent. They also have a good working knowledge of procedural law and how it works. Court administrators, often trained as lawyers, are accustomed to analyzing in great detail the technical requirements of courts. These skill sets, as important as they are respectively to the evolution of law and the technocratic administration of courts, are not well suited for many of the functions outlined above that require the empirical skills of social scientists.[51]

Of course, staffing rule of law assessments with local social scientists and legal experts may be a challenge: local expertise may be scarce or nonexistent at the onset of statebuilding activities. Local expertise is preferred, but international expertise with appropriate skill sets may be necessary. Political scientists, economists, anthropologists, and historians are not as common on assessment teams as they ought to be. For example, economists and political scientists can be incredibly competent in designing survey instruments, tabulating results, and analyzing disputants' incentives. Anthropologists can greatly enhance survey insights with microanalysis of case studies. As obvious as it seems, an essential "X factor" in the success of multidisciplinary assessment teams is the ability of team members to communicate effectively across disciplines.

Capacity Building

By way of background, Timorese court actors were all appointed by the UN before independence in 2002. Most agreed that permanent appointment should be contingent upon a successful evaluation. The membership of the Council of Coordination—the minister of justice, prosecutor general, and president of the Court of Appeal—endorsed the evaluation process.

Some judicial training projects carried out in East Timor soon after independence failed to take even modest account of local circumstances and failed to build capacity. Donor accountability for such failures was low. In these courses, prosecutors and trial judges were not given special training in the kinds of crimes they might confront. An evaluation was conducted and determined that no one was adequately qualified. Some think that poorly tailored training programs directly caused probationary judges to fail their exams. The East Timorese government disqualified *all* Timorese judges, prosecutors, and public defenders in 2005.

Some have alleged that the process was nontransparent and biased against Indonesian-trained lawyers and judges. Others argue reasonably that even if the evaluation process is not biased, at a minimum, one needs to look at various training programs to assess more thoroughly why, after three-plus years, not one local judge or lawyer was able to pass the evaluation. With that kind of result, training programs should invite as much scrutiny as the trainees.

This is a generic story of ineffective judicial training. My point is not the details of the story in East Timor, because it is a story retold across most developing countries. Rather, my point is that, as a general matter, donors do not critically evaluate capacity-building efforts. Training programs are popular in the development industry because they can absorb significant resources, the accountability for such programs is relatively low, evaluative mechanisms are weak, and the likelihood of collateral damage is thought to be remote.

The Political Dynamics of Institutional Change

Development strategies tend to start with a construction of perceived political will for change. Too often, the discussion of political will ranges from naive to disingenuous. Planning documents, government edicts, the passing of laws, or representations made by a key political, legal, or economic actor over a meal are often taken at their face value as demonstrating elite commitment.[52] Ironically, sometimes the representations themselves are drafted by donor-supported consultants and then cited as evidence by the same donor community of the political will of local political elites.[53]

Four key indexes of change potential in institution building, including rule of law institutions, are the following: leadership, elite commitment (or at least lack of strong resistance), incentives of users and internal actors (including enforceable performance standards), and institutional competence. Development too often focuses on the last item. Yet the "capacity gap" by itself turns out to be a weak justification for setting priorities. Capacity building needs to be closely tied to leadership dynamics, elite commitment, meaningful constituency mobilization, and compatible incentive structures. For purposes of assessing change potential within institutions, leadership and elite commitment with meaningful constituency mobilization are key. Of course, opportunities are sought when leadership is present.[54] But it is important to also ask, Is there elite commitment, and can constituencies be built?

Elite commitment. Charles Tilly has usefully observed that three variable elements of what he calls a regime's social environment strongly affect its organization: coercion, capital, and commitment.[55] Strengthening the balanced accumulation of all three elements is essential to statebuilding. This chapter has analyzed the practical ramifications of *coercion* in the context of Weber's notion of "legal coercion." It has also discussed the primal importance of *capital* in the context of promoting economic growth and development. Threaded throughout the chapter are references to the political economy of development that require *commitment.* Commitment includes "those webs of connection on which people rely when engaging in long-term, high-risk, socially contingent activities."[56]

A set of elites—neither international nor purely domestic—featured prominently in East Timor's statebuilding process; they were returning exiles from Mozambique, Portugal, and Australia. Most in this group, now prominently represented among the governing elite of the country, had lived in exile for decades. The contributions of this group to East Timor's postindependence phase are unquestionable. However, coming from a lusophone exile background, this group seemed eager to establish formal justice structures, giving much less attention to traditional justice mechanisms.[57] Moreover, this group is largely responsible for installing Portuguese as the mandated language in courts and legislation, despite the fact that only 5 percent of the population speak it. Language is a common and contentious issue in the history of colonial courts.[58] Some would argue that few measures can alienate people from their public institutions more effectively than to create language barriers to access. And scarce human resources must learn not only the basic skills of the job but a new language as well.

On the positive side, this group of returning exile elites played a crucial role in ensuring the inclusion of Section 2(4) of the constitution, acknowledging the role and value of customary law not contrary to the constitution. Section 2(4) provides formal cover for the use of customary law and could provide for legal pluralism in essential and pragmatic ways. In practice, however, some argue that informal systems enjoy insufficient elite commitment and are systematically undermined.

A less qualified success could be in the making: if the returning exiles set a transparent and credible course of conduct in managing the country's oil and gas reserves, their contribution to rule of law will have been enormous. Juxtaposing the Portuguese-only policy in courts with the provision for customary law in the constitution and the credible management of oil and gas reserves, the lesson is that elite commitment is not monolithic; it can simultaneously impede certain reform efforts while facilitating others.

Mobilization of constituencies. Can more generalized public participation mobilize constituencies? The answer is yes, but only in targeted ways.[59] Generally, domestic demand for public institutions and institutional reform is diffuse or weak because of classic collective action problems. On the one hand, citizens incur high transaction costs to organize collectively; on the other hand, their gains are modest and speculative.[60] In diffuse institutional reform programs with few short-term gains, collective action problems abound.

One key way to mobilize constituencies is to couple rule of law activities with provision of essential services, which is what seems to be happening in the evolution of commune councils in Cambodia. Some data suggest that the commune council project is doing a relatively good job of providing essential services while generating a high trust rating, which may indicate that they are also addressing the legitimacy issue. Cambodians polled showed a high awareness of the provision of services, especially the building of roads and schools by the commune councils.[61] The councils are unexpectedly providing conflict mediation services at the village and the communal level, and citizens find their provision of this service "easier, cheaper, and more effective than at higher levels."[62] A somewhat similar phenomenon took place in the 1990s in an initiative in Bangladesh funded by the US Agency for International Development, in which legal awareness programs were attached to the provision of reproductive health services through a network of reproductive health NGOs.[63]

Transitional justice mechanisms, such as the Serious Crimes Unit in East Timor and the Khmer Rouge Tribunal in Cambodia, should at least include as a factor in their establishment an empirical assessment of the strength of domestic constituencies. The data regarding local demand for a KRT, for example, are unclear. If Cambodians are asked whether they would like to see the rascals tried, of course, they will respond affirmatively. However, if they were asked whether $56 million should be spent to try this group of seven to eight defendants, their answer might well be different.

Transplantation of Laws and Legal Institutions

The long-term global historical experience with the transfusion of laws and evolution of legal systems is subtle and complicated. Since at least the times of the Romans, laws have been transplanted across borders. Transplantation of legal institutions often occurs at watershed moments of political change: installation or defeat/withdrawal of colonial powers, economic crisis, importation by elite reformers who wish to modernize their country, or upon the demand or suggestion of international institutions.

The transplantation of laws and legal institutions is not always wrong, but formalistic transplantation should come with a caveat emptor. Anthropologists have long understood the problems of transferability.[64] Extensive regressions have been run to determine the conditions on which successful legal transplantation depends. The two key findings in these regressions are (1) if law and legal institutions are adapted to local needs, they will be used and resources will be allocated to enforcing and developing them; and (2) intermediary authorities can be more effective if they work with a law that is broadly compatible with the preexisting legal order.[65] These data show the strong logical coherence among local context, prioritization of institutions, and transferability and adaptability of international models.

In order for transplantation to be effective, it must meet a basic test articulated earlier: if new rules are developed, they must be tied to—or have the potential of being tied to—behavior over time in the context of prevailing informal constraints. And the new institutional arrangements must make those rules effective and self-enforcing.

Conclusion

In this chapter I identified key analytical challenges in strengthening the rule of law in a statebuilding context and then examined practical implications that flowed from the challenges. Discourse on statebuilding and the rule of law tends to be schizophrenic. One moment, conversation is probing the customs and conventions of society, followed in the same breath by confidently suggesting technocratic and formalistic interventions to modify customs and conventions. If nothing else, I hope that this chapter has exposed some of the details of that schizophrenia and possible ways to bridge theory and practice. The bridges that I've suggested might seem rudimentary, yet the implementation of advice along these lines has proven surprisingly elusive. Between the politics of donor assistance and the complex politics of domestic internal institution building and change—both of which discourage critical learning and response—we waste scarce international assistance resources. More importantly, purported beneficiaries of rule of law projects lose security, opportunities, and hope. In an effort to overcome these pathologies, I call for setting standards for minimum levels of due diligence and probity in the design of rule of law programs in statebuilding contexts.

Notes

1. Guido de Ruggiero, *The History of European Liberalism,* trans. R. G. Collingwood (London: Oxford University Press, 1927), pp. 25–26.

2. David Kennedy, "Laws and Developments," in John Hatchard and Amanda Perry-Kessaris, eds., *Law and Development: Facing Complexity in the 21st Century* (London: Cavendish Publishing, 2003), pp. 17–26.

3. Clearly, however, there are special issues and matters of degree in the statebuilding process where basic order is not achieved because the Weberian test of a state—the ability to monopolize violence—is not met.

4. A large body of literature parrots the virtues of "comprehensive" legal and judicial reform. See, e.g., "Comprehensive Legal and Judicial Development: Towards an Agenda for a Just and Equitable Society in the 21st Century," World Bank Conference, June 5–7, 2000.

5. At the risk of tautology, the single greatest challenge to comparative law is *comparability.* See the discussion answering the question "What is a legal system?" later in this chapter.

6. James H. Anderson, David S. Bernstein, and Cheryl W. Gray, *Judicial Systems in Transition Economies: Assessing the Past, Looking to the Future* (Washington, DC: World Bank, 2005).

7. The second section considers common challenges to institution building that Sarah Cliffe and Nick Manning identify in Chapter 8 in this book and the implications

of those challenges for rule of law institutions: failure to take account of what institutions already exist, lack of prioritization of institution-building efforts, nontransferability of international models of capacity, and unintentional collateral damage caused to domestic institutions through the international presence.

8. Gerhard Casper, "The United States at the End of the 'American Century': The Rule of Law or Enlightened Absolutism?" *Washington University Journal of Law and Policy* 4 (2000): 153.

9. See, for example, Robert C. Ellickson, *Order Without Law: How Neighbors Settle Disputes* (Cambridge, MA: Harvard University Press, 1991).

10. W. Richard Scott, *Institutions and Organizations* (Thousand Oaks, CA: Sage Publications, 2001). See also John L. Campbell, *Institutional Change and Globalization* (Princeton, NJ: Princeton University Press, 2004).

11. Scott, *Institutions and Organizations,* p. 55.

12. Of course, norms are not bound by state borders. Norms may diffuse, through the "neighborhood effect," into and out of postconflict states. See, e.g., Kristian Skrede Gleditsch's *All Politics Is Local: The Diffusion of Conflict, Integration, and Democratization* (Ann Arbor: University of Michigan Press, 2002). Apart from scholarship on EU enlargement and some of the literature on human rights norms, the rule of law industry has paid insufficient attention to the neighborhood effect. For the neighborhood effect on economic growth, see note 38.

13. Max Weber, "The Economy and Social Norms" and "Summary of the Most General Relations Between Law and Economy," in his *Economy and Society: An Outline of Interpretive Sociology,* edited by Guenther Roth and Claus Wittich, 2 vols. (Berkeley: University of California Press, 1978).

14. Some developmentalists imagine rather elaborate public institutional arrangements in the statebuilding project. Others argue that one of the most obvious imperatives today in developing countries, based on post–World War II development experience, is to reduce the scope of government.

15. In statebuilding contexts, that capacity for credible legal coercion may be an even scarcer commodity due to the scarcity of formal legal actors. At the end of the Khmer Rouge era in Cambodia, for example, there were seven lawyers in the country; upon independence in East Timor, there were forty lawyers.

16. For those who are interested in the great historical debates about the definition of rule of law, see A. V. Dicey, *Introduction to the Study of the Law of the Constitution,* 10th ed. (London: Palgrave MacMillan, 1985); Lon Fuller, *The Morality of Law,* 2nd ed. (New Haven, CT: Yale University Press, 1969); a number of publications by Fredrik Hayek, including *Law, Legislation, and Liberty,* 3 vols. (Chicago: Chicago University Press, 1973–1979); Joseph Raz, "The Rule of Law and Its Virtue," in *The Authority of Law: Essays on Law and Morality* (Oxford: Clarendon Press, 1979), pp. 210–229; and a good synthesis of the history of rule of law scholarship in Brian Z. Tamanaha, *On the Rule of Law: History, Politics, Theory* (Cambridge: Cambridge University Press, 2004).

17. Erik G. Jensen, "The Rule of Law and Judicial Reform: The Political Economy of Diverse Institutional Patterns and Reformers' Responses," in *Beyond Common Knowledge: Empirical Approaches to the Rule of Law,* edited by Erik G. Jensen and Thomas C. Heller (Stanford, CA: Stanford University Press, 2003), pp. 336–381.

18. There are many different stratifications of rule of law, but the three identified here provide a good illustration of the spectrum.

19. Brian Z. Tamanaha, *On the Rule of Law,* p. 95.

20. See generally, Larry D. Kramer, *The People Themselves: Popular Constitutionalism and Judicial Review* (Oxford: Oxford University Press, 2004).

21. That is why economic historian Avner Greif, in his groundbreaking work on the evolution of institutions, focuses on functions and motivations rather than structures: for example, "coercion constraining institutions" and "contract enforcing institutions." Avner Greif, *Institutions and the Path to the Modern Economy: Lessons from Medieval Trade* (Cambridge: Cambridge University Press, 2006).

22. Francis Fukuyama, *State-building: Governance and World Order in the 21st Century* (Ithaca, NY: Cornell University Press, 2004).

23. Erhard Blankenburg, "Judicial Systems in Western Europe: Comparative Indicators of Legal Professionals, Courts, Litigation, and Budgets in the 1990s," in *Beyond Common Knowledge: Empirical Approaches to the Rule of Law,* edited by Erik G. Jensen and Thomas C. Heller (Stanford: Stanford University Press, 2003), p. 75.

24. See Charles T. Call, "Ending Wars, Building States," Chapter 1 in this volume.

25. Larry Diamond, "Promoting Democracy in Post-Conflict and Failed States: Lessons and Challenges," paper prepared for the National Policy Forum on Terrorism, Security and America's Purpose, Washington, DC, September 6–7, 2005, p. 2.

26. Larry Diamond, *Squandered Victory: The American Occupation and Bungled Effort to Bring Democracy to Iraq* (New York: Henry Holt, 2006).

27. See, for example, Charles T. Call, "Democratisation, War, and State-Building: Constructing the Rule of Law in El Salvador," *Journal of Latin American Studies* 35, no. 4 (November 2003): 827–862; David H. Bayley, *Changing the Guard: Developing Democratic Police Abroad* (Oxford: Oxford University Press, 2006); Robert M. Perito, *Where Is the Lone Ranger When We Need Him? America's Search for a Postconflict Stability Force* (Washington, DC: US Institute of Peace Press, 2004).

28. See, for example, David Cohen, *Indifference and Accountability: The United Nations and the Politics of International Justice in East Timor,* East-West Center Special Reports no. 9 (Honolulu, HI: East-West Center, 2006).

29. But see Jennifer Widner's critical look at the Commonwealth "best practices" for constitution-making and its usual admonitions about the crucial need to have broad participation in constitution-making. In particular, Widner looked at the relationship of participation in the constitution-making process (independent variable) on lower levels of violence (dependent variable) in postconflict states. She found that in some cases participation mattered empirically, in many other cases it did not, and in other cases it negatively affected progress toward the desired dependent variable. See Jennifer Widner, "Constitution Writing and Conflict Resolution," UNU-WIDER Research Paper no. 2005/51 (Helsinki: UNU-WIDER, 2005). See also Devra Coren Moehler, *Distrusting Democrats: Outcomes of Participatory Constitution Making* (Ann Arbor: University of Michigan Press: forthcoming 2008).

30. Leila Nadya Sadat, "Universal Jurisdiction, National Amnesties, and Truth Commissions: Reconciling the Irreconcilable," in *Universal Jurisdiction: National Courts and the Prosecution of Serious Crimes Under International Law,* edited by Stephen Macedo (Philadelphia: University of Pennsylvania Press, 2004), p. 206. My thanks to Allen Weiner for a useful discussion about this topic.

31. See, for example, Raymond C. Offenheiser and Susan Holcombe, "Challenges and Opportunities in Implementing a Rights-Based Approach to Development: An Oxfam America Perspective," *Nonprofit and Voluntary Sector Quarterly* 32 (2003): 268–306.

32. Aisling Swaine, "Traditional Justice and Gender-Based Violence," International Rescue Committee Research Report, August 2003, p. 13.

33. See, for example, Patricia Ewick and Susan S. Silbey, *The Common Place of Law: Stories from Everyday Life* (Chicago: University of Chicago Press, 1998);

Hazel Genn, *Paths to Justice: What People Do and Think About Going to Law* (Oxford: Hart Publishing, 1999); and Richard Roberts, *Litigants and Households: African Disputes and Colonial Courts in the French Soudan, 1895–1912* (Portsmouth, NH: Heinemann, 2005), see esp. the introduction, "'Disputes Without Significance': African Social History and Colonial Courts at a Time of Social Transformation."

34. Roger Henke, Erik G. Jensen, and Debra Ladner, *Public Perceptions of Justice in Cambodia,* Asia Foundation for the Asian Development Bank, 2004, p. 5 (on file with the author).

35. Ibid.

36. Gunnar Myrdal, *Asian Drama: An Inquiry into the Poverty of Nations* (New York: Pantheon Books, 1968).

37. Seymour Martin Lipset, *Political Man: The Social Bases of Politics* (New York: Doubleday, 1960).

38. John MacMillan, "How Not to Rebuild an Economy: The Lesson from East Timor," Graduate School of Business, Stanford University, June 20, 2006. A related blind spot among donors is inadequate optimization of the regulatory environment to capitalize on the "neighborhood effects" of regional growth. That is, countries close to fast-growing economies experience faster growth in aggregate demand for their exports, stimulating faster domestic growth. See, Josep M. Vilarrubia, "Neighborhood Effects in Economic Growth," Working Paper no. 627 (Madrid: Banco de Espana, 2006). If that is true, it bodes well for the long-term prospects for Cambodia, less strong prospects for East Timor based on this criterion, and rather weak prospects for Afghanistan.

39. World Bank Group, *Doing Business: Economy Rankings,* 2007, http://www.doingbusiness.org/EconomyRankings/.

40. See MacMillan, "How Not to Rebuild an Economy," p. 3.

41. Jakob Svensson, "Eight Questions About Corruption," *Journal of Economic Perspectives* 19, no. 3 (Fall 2005): 19–42.

42. Martin Tisné and Daniel Smilov, *From the Ground Up: Assessing the Record of Anticorruption Assistance in Southeastern Europe,* CPS Policy Studies Series (Budapest: Center for Policy Studies, Central European University, 2004).

43. Extractive Industries Transparency Initiative, "Timor Leste," May 30, 2007, www.eitransparency.org/section/countries/_timorleste (accessed June 12, 2007).

44. Interestingly, Cliffe and Manning's chapter on institution building uses a framework that differs from my previous work on rule of law and institutions in terminology only. It does not differ in conceptualization, or in the experience that has caused the convergence. See Jensen and Heller, eds., *Beyond Common Knowledge.*

45. Jensen and Heller, eds., *Beyond Common Knowledge,* p. 340.

46. Debra Ladner, Erik Jensen, Caroline Vandenabeele, and Christine V. Lao, "Legal Identity for Inclusive Development" (Manila: Asian Development Bank, 2007).

47. Kim Ninh and Roger Henke, "Commune Councils in Cambodia: A National Survey on Their Functions and Performance, with a Special Focus on Conflict Resolution," Asia Foundation, 2005, p. 59, available at: http://www.asiafoundation.org/pdf/CB-CCSurvey.pdf.

48. The Commission for Reception, Truth, and Reconciliation in Timor-Leste (CAVR), a UN-supported initiative, took a more differentiated approach to disputes, drawing on the strengths of the traditional justice system in certain kinds of disputes, rather than trying to supplant it. By all accounts, CAVR has been one of the most successful internationally supported justice efforts in East Timor. It evidenced

significant learning by the UN, distinguished from the UN's more *terra nullius* modus operandi in the country immediately after independence. See Spencer Zifcak, *Restorative Justice in East Timor: An Evaluation of the Community Reconciliation Process of the CAVR,* Asia Foundation, 2004.

49. For an excellent description and analysis of traditional justice in East Timor, see Dionísio Babo-Soares, "*Nahe Biti:* Grassroots Reconciliation in East Timor," in *Roads to Reconciliation,* edited by Elin Skaar, Siri Gloppen, and Astri Suhrke (Lanham, MD: Lexington Books, 2005), pp. 225–246.

50. Max Weber, *Economy and Society: An Outline of Interpretive Sociology,* edited by Guenther Roth and Claus Wittich, 2 vols. (Berkeley: University of California Press, 1978), p. 311.

51. The history of competition between legal experts and social scientists is extensive and well beyond the scope of this chapter. Although many law schools in the US have for some time demonstrated their commitment to interdisciplinary legal studies by hiring political scientists and economists as faculty, the rule of law industry is dominated extensively by legal experts.

52. Economic actors, as Weber recognized, influence the creation of law and legal institutions. See Weber, *Economy and Society,* p. 334. A stylized example of "empirical" research that evidences the interests of economic actors in rule of law would be a survey of a very small group of business leaders that asks a series of questions along the following lines: Does the judiciary work? If not, would you like it to work? To what extent does the judiciary's failure to work affect your bottom line—10 percent, 20 percent, 50 percent? Again, empirical work along these superficial lines really doesn't help in prioritizing institution-building efforts.

53. This chapter self-consciously avoids use of the term *political will.* As implied here, the term is typically defined very loosely with reference to characteristics thought to be inherent in individual leaders. In the aggregate this is notoriously unhelpful shorthand for an exercise that requires a disaggregated analysis of the political pressures that arise from various interest groups and how these pressures are managed by those in authority to secure and advance their interests. Political will is deterministic rather than dynamic: either you have it or you don't. And it is tautological because, at the end of the day, political will broadly writ, or the lack thereof, is a core feature of virtually every development problem.

54. For an extensive account of the importance of the leadership of the chief justice of Tanzania to building the rule of law, see Jennifer Widner's *Building the Rule of Law: Francis Nyalai and the Road to Judicial Independence in Africa* (New York: W. W. Norton, 2001).

55. Charles Tilly, *Contention and Democracy in Europe, 1650–2000* (Cambridge: Cambridge University Press, 2004).

56. Ibid., p. 47.

57. The Asia Foundation sponsored a workshop on traditional justice in East Timor in July 2002 at which participants stressed the lack of legal acknowledgment of the traditional justice system. See Judicial System Monitoring Programme, *Findings and Recommendations: Workshop on Formal and Local Justice Systems in East Timor* (Dili: JSMP, 2002). Although USAID did not initially invest in the development of traditional justice mechanisms, the organization has been a leader, through the Asia Foundation, in investing in research on this subject.

58. See, for example, Roberts, *Litigants and Households.*

59. Public participation in development processes is often poorly conceived and ineffective. See Erik G. Jensen, "Meaningful Participation or Deliberative Deception:

Realities and Dilemmas in Legitimating Legal and Judicial Reform Projects Through Consultative Processes," paper presented at World Bank Lawyers' Forum, November 4–5, 1999, Washington, DC.

60. See Santos Pastor, *Ah de la justicia: Politica judicial y economia* (Madrid: Civitas and Ministerio de Justicia, 1993).

61. Data in Ninh and Henke, "Commune Councils in Cambodia," p. 22.

62. Ibid, p. 61.

63. Karen L. Casper and Sutana Kamal, *Evaluation Report: Community Legal Services Conducted by Family Planning NGOs* (Dhaka: Asia Foundation, 1995).

64. James C. Scott, *Seeing Like a State: How Certain Schemes to Improve the Human Condition Have Failed* (New Haven, CT: Yale University Press, 1998), p. 311.

65. Daniel Berkowitz, Katharina Pistor, and Jean-Francois Richard, "Economic Development, Legality, and the Transplant Effect," *European Economic Review* 47, no. 1 (February 2003): 174–181.

7

Bottom-Up Statebuilding?

William Reno

Collapsed and fragile states are primary targets for international intervention. Just since the turn of the century, interventions under the guidance
of the UN and the North Atlantic Treaty Organization (NATO) in Afghanistan, Bosnia, the Democratic Republic of Congo (DRC), East Timor, Haiti,
Kosovo, Liberia, and Sierra Leone have taken on a wide range of functions
conventionally thought of as core state tasks. They include law enforcement, defense, delivery of services, coordination of foreign aid, and management of relations with international agencies and foreign governments,
often under the direct command of foreign experts. Bilateral interventions,
such as Australia's in the Solomon Islands and Papua New Guinea, extend
the list of these interventions.

Most interventions occur where state institutions fail to provide for basic
human security. For example, UN officials reported in 2004 with regard to
Somalia that "crime in Mogadishu has continued unabated. This is in addition
to inter- and intra-clan fighting that continues to claim lives."[1] But intervention does not occur in a vacuum. Where state institutions fail to provide security, basic public security is often provided by other actors—private networks,
local militias, guerrilla armies, or customary authorities. These nonstate actors often generate their own insecurities. Nevertheless, partly due to their
success in providing security, these substate groups often become the most legitimate political authority in areas that they control.[2]

In northern parts of Somalia, for example, officials of the Republic of Somaliland advertise their "government of law and order" that regulates and
taxes trade, holds regular elections, issues a currency, and provides citizens
with basic personal security.[3] This authority is not a state in an international
legal sense, as no other government recognized it as of mid-2007. But it is a
state in the sense of maintaining local order to a degree that local people support its authority and contribute to its maintenance. Other substate groups
maintain order in otherwise conflict-ridden areas. Local militias in Sierra Leone

defended communities against attacks of the Revolutionary United Front (RUF) during their 1991–2002 war. The Oodua People's Congress and other Nigerian groups that call themselves vigilantes fight crime, adjudicate disputes, provide other services, and collect taxes in cities where state agencies exercise a weak hold. Youth militias protect communities in Côte d'Ivoire and in the DRC. Prior to the 1999 NATO intervention in Kosovo, a shadow government run by the Democratic League of Kosovo (LDK) maintained its own police force, schools, and clinics and ran its own elections.

The legitimacy that these groups enjoy often carries a price. Militia leaders, for instance, often mobilize networks of ethnic solidarities to fight enemies during war. In warfare, these ties that were so integral to maintaining local order often translate into exclusionary ethnic definitions of community. Armed substate groups may bear responsibility for serious violations of international humanitarian law during warfare, such as collective punishment of civilians and the use of child soldiers. This is especially true in conflicts in which combatants lacked large-scale hierarchically organized armies and relied instead upon small units under the immediate command of charismatic leaders with little or no formal training. Substate leaders often propagate illiberal political programs that violate interveners' concerns about equal access on the basis of gender, for example.

These realities pose serious dilemmas, with practical import for intervention programs. Though wholesale acceptance of the interests of these substate groups on the part of interveners in some instances would contradict core principles of interventions designed to halt conflict, these groups remain important actors in local politics. To the extent that outsiders try to rebuild state institutions, pressures to incorporate these groups into their statebuilding strategies grow. Leaving them out of such plans, along with the effect of massive shifts of resources on local balances of political power, entangles outsiders in the intricacies of conflicts between local factions. Interveners face choices between expediently completing scaled-down statebuilding missions at an acceptable cost, versus taking on substate groups in political and military terms as new enemies.

As I argue below, most intervention administrations try to build parallel state institutions to provide security, deliver services, and mobilize citizens' organizations. These actions can duplicate or even circumvent the efforts of locally popular substate groups in some instances. To the extent that substate groups are shut out of formal programs to rebuild state institutions, some local people may interpret that as the political marginalization of their communities.

The solution is not just a matter of identifying and incorporating indigenous substate structures of governance. Some cannot be ignored, as the decision of diplomats to deal directly with the Sudan People's Liberation Army (SPLA) in the negotiations that led to the 2005 peace agreement showed.

That process conferred diplomatic legitimacy on SPLA structures on the ground in southern Sudan that are integral to any international postconflict intervention there. But the majority of substate groups, especially if armed, do not receive such support from international actors.

All substate entities are not equal, and the approach taken in Sudan may not be valid in some circumstances. But international actors must develop the tools to deal with the political consequences of ignoring or undermining political entities that, for better or worse, enjoy a certain amount of legitimacy among the populations they purport to serve. It is to these dilemmas that I turn, first in terms of the role of substate groups in the politics of conflicts surrounding state collapse, and then in terms of their situation in the context of large-scale international intervention.

Local Political Economies at the Substate Level

The availability of military hardware and easily exploitable natural resources play major roles in the breakdown of civil order and the rise of armed groups where central government authority collapses. But this collapse does not always result in complete disorder. There are often significant local variations even within the context of the same central state's collapse. As the Somalia case study in this volume demonstrates, shared clan politics, language, prewar experiences of dictatorship, and similar resource endowments still produced widely differing outcomes in different parts of the territory (see Chapter 9). Likewise, clandestine diamond mining in Sierra Leone's Kenema district helped to sustain Civil Defense Force (CDF) home guard units that protected some communities from predation, while sixty miles to the north, diamonds spurred the predations of RUF fighters. Both armed groups mobilized young men of similar social backgrounds in the context of a shared experience of a corrupt and violent national government. But one became a substate authority, while the other became an easy target for interveners because it lacked a durable base of public support. The RUF candidate in the 2002 presidential election, for example, received only 33,000 votes, a figure indicating that even many of its own former fighters failed to vote for the organization's standard-bearer.[4] In contrast, several years after the war, CDF leaders still were able to mobilize thousands of supporters for protests and other political action. Similarly, in Bosnia, the militias of some local commanders disintegrated in the mid-1990s as opportunities for looting decreased. But leaders of other ethnic militias still enjoy enough local support, more than a decade after fighting has ended, that they are able to evade international efforts to apprehend them.

These differing outcomes draw attention to the importance of local social structures for shaping how resources like guns and the proceeds of clandestine trades are integrated into different political economies, which in turn sheds light on the nature of existing substate political authorities once interveners arrive. Indeed, more capable groups among these substate actors may simply represent the continuation of a historic process of autonomous statebuilding. Left to themselves, collapsed states may "fix themselves," but with outcomes that supersede old frontiers and that are based upon the formation of new political communities. But contemporary diplomatic norms that privilege existing states and reject changes in international borders are barriers to this process.[5] The unsettling implication is that in the eyes of some local people, especially those who lead substate groups, intervention poses an obstacle to achievement of their political destinies. Some condemn intervention as a deeply reactionary force that imposes particular values and institutions and even contemporary international frontiers, sometimes linked in local minds to episodes of colonial rule.

Moreover, some substate networks and practices that contemporary interveners regard as obstacles to postconflict order historically have had positive effects for future state strength when they have been incorporated into state rulers' political strategies. Charles Tilly has demonstrated how coercion and violence have long been important tools in the repertoire of statebuilders.[6] David Kang concludes that corruption among state officials has not necessarily been injurious to economic growth, especially if corruption takes place within a small clique and the beneficiaries trust their associates enough that they are willing to invest ill-gotten gains in their home economies.[7] Informal institutional structures often draw upon ethnic and cross-border bases, a fact that clashes with interveners' ideas about ethnic exclusion and concerns about clandestine international trade, both of which are blamed as catalysts of conflict. That is not to say that corrupt political cliques with roots in clandestine economies always provide order and build strong states. But sometimes they do.

Closer examination of local variation, including analysis of Somalia and Sierra Leone in the next section, produces some generalizations that can be applied to instances in which substate groups use access to arms and clandestine economies to promote local order for at least some communities amid general state collapse. First, substate groups that share their control of clandestine commercial networks with longstanding indigenous "customary" authorities are more likely than others to develop as alternative legitimate political authorities during conflicts and after. They share structures and practices based on ethnic solidarities and historical cross-border commerce, which can provide new ways to maintain order and mobilize local identities. Second, the more marginal these local authorities were to prewar capital-based political networks, the more likely they will resist the interventions of predatory entrepreneurs (including from their own communities) and reduce the local risks of armed conflict. But this means that these people are most likely to lack the ties to global languages and culture that facilitate links to interveners and international diplomats.

Differences in popular legitimacy stem partly from the fact that regime-backed predators appear to benefit from the willingness of distant political patrons to manipulate the enforcement of laws, deploy the police, and distribute state assets for the benefit of loyal followers. Local armed groups associated with these patrons may not need the cooperation of other local notables such as clan or religious leaders, since their access to resources is based upon the favor of the president. Once the power of their central patrons declines, some of those regime strongmen simply take over segments of these networks. Thus many "warlords" in places like Liberia, Democratic Republic of Congo, and Somalia held key positions in prewar governments that enabled them to develop clandestine commercial connections and to build private armies. Since their political positions and access to resources did not hinge upon any particular relationship with local authority figures, or popular legitimacy, they do not suffer decisive material or social sanction for violent predatory behavior, even if directed against their own communities.

Local strongmen who might be equally inclined to be greedy and violent, but who spent prewar years desperately trying to shelter their activities from interference from the president and his favored associates, are in very different positions once central government control begins to collapse. They are forced to make deals with local authority figures to shelter their illicit transactions from the gaze of officials in the capital. In the absence of an ability to manipulate the application of laws or call police or paramilitaries to their aid, they need local help to guarantee their contracts with other operators and fend off "official" predators. Often these mediators take advantage of their roles as protectors of this kind of local political economy to articulate local grievances. Once conflict becomes more widespread, these strongmen may find that local mediators are in positions to deny them the resources needed to fight, unless they also heed the interests of these communities and observe terms that local authorities set.

This dichotomy recalls historical patterns of statebuilding. For example, Mancur Olson observed that "roving bandits" simply looted areas through which they passed; they did not need a long-term relationship with local people to get the resources they needed to fight rivals. Contemporary strongmen who use distant connections to operate businesses and exploit local resources occupy much the same situation as the roving bandit. The "stationary bandit," however, had few options but to consider the future ability of his victims to continue getting resources.[8] Like the contemporary marginalized strongmen, they had to negotiate with local mediators to get repeated access to resources, even through overseas commerce. This stands in contrast to those whom they might have considered their luckier counterparts, who could survive on far-flung commercial connections, regardless of the interests of local people. Local mediators have their own stakes in the exploitation of resources, including illicit activities like smuggling or contacts with international criminal networks. It is not the source of wealth that matters as much as the legitimacy of the social relations that force different actors to engage in relations of reciprocity. Thus it is possible to maintain order and build a locally legitimate administration on proceeds from illicit trades such as drug trafficking.

This production of locally legitimate order does not follow a virtuous design. Some strongmen who provide local communities with these public goods leave a trail of prewar appeals and promises designed to gain the favor of capital-based rulers.[9] Often they or their fathers supported a political party in the decades before the war that either lost power or that a ruler found threatening. Many protested their loyalty. But field investigations and archives uncover pasts in which these strongmen had to contend with more than the average interference from the capital, were more insecure in their positions of power, and faced disproportionate punishment and falls from grace. Once conflict started, however, such "burdens" translated into mechanisms for organizing resources and armed young men in ways that maintained a semblance of order and security in local people's everyday lives. The cases of Somalia and Sierra Leone, discussed in detail below, highlight the extent to which this informal sector of local governance is intertwined with clandestine economies and past human rights violations as it contends with interveners' statebuilding plans.

Somalia and Sierra Leone:
Local Variations in Order and Violence

Conflict in Somalia provides a good example of the relationship between substate social control and the nature of violence. Long before widespread fighting started in the late 1980s, President Siad Barre (1969–1991) found a way to match an ambitious modernization of the country's agricultural sector with his concern to build a loyal political powerbase among the Mogadishu elite and in the military that had helped him to seize power. These plans centered on agricultural areas in the south of the country that already had attracted the attention of colonial-era officials. First, a 1975 land tenure reform measure placed all land at the disposal of the state and legalized individual lease-hold ownership. In practical terms it meant that the president could distribute valuable land to people on the basis of his political calculations of their support. Even though the most valuable farmland was situated in southern river valleys, the main beneficiaries of this reform were notables in cities and from the president's distant home area. These people had the easiest time getting officials to recognize their efforts to register their claims for titles of ownership.[10]

This commercialization of agriculture quickened in the late 1970s, when Somalia shifted its strategic alliance from the Soviet Union to the United States. Suddenly World Bank and bilateral loans to finance large-scale commercial farming appeared. The Shabelle and Juba Valleys in the south became prime targets of these projects. Projects in the latter region, for example, involved 42,000 acres in which land use rights shifted from local pastoralists and small farmers to capital-based entrepreneurs who had the president's confidence. These entrepreneurs organized their own militias to evict local communities.[11] Since many of these people were from the president's home area in the northeast of the country, they were free to import ethnic kinsmen to fight on their behalf. The appearance of unemployed young men in the capital also provided these strongmen with access to outsiders to recruit to these militias in return for political support for the president.[12] Prewar economic initiatives further strengthened the position of this politically favored group. For example, foreign currency and import regulations appeared in the mid-1980s, giving the president the capacity to manipulate new laws, enforcing them selectively to harm the commercial prospects of suspect or disloyal groups while granting exemptions to his political supporters. It opened up new rackets and gave tacit presidential sanction to otherwise clandestine commercial operations.[13]

This type of patronage victimized local communities. Local strongmen's commercial success depended upon the political favor of their patron in the capital, not the consent or even the productive energies of local people. The fact that outsiders recruited other outsiders to become members of militias meant that both could use violence in the pursuit of their business and political goals with little fear of local consequences. Customary institutions such as elders' councils, local forms of negotiation, and local land use practices all could be swept away in the process of building new estates. Once widespread fighting began, those who already controlled local resources were in an advantageous position to fight and could act even more coercively toward local communities, since their access to resources—including weapons—did not depend upon support from those communities. They could continue their activities even after their president fled in 1991, since their positions in the old patronage network had given them access to local assets and to commercial networks that they could convert to their exclusive use as fighting erupted. These people found that war and predation were the easiest ways to maximize their material assets and personal security. By extension, the imported militias associated with these strongmen failed to protect local community interests and preyed upon them instead.

The consequences of this settler elite's freedom from local social control emerged more recently in negotiations since 2002 to create a national government for Somalia. The unwillingness of these groups to countenance the return of property, including land, has become a major obstacle to the conclusion of negotiations and the return of a transitional government from Kenya. The main port city in the south saw battles in 1999, 2001, and 2004, long after other parts of the country had become relatively calm. Some of the strongmen were accused of hijacking several cargo ships, even after they were incorporated into the interim government.[14] These strongmen can count upon armed followers and call upon kinship connections for aid. But it is easy for outsiders to convincingly characterize them to other Somalis as human rights abusers and obstacles to peace to the extent that they lack widespread local legitimacy as providers of security or other services.

At first glance, northern Somalia also seemed to follow this path of predatory violence in the early 1990s. Fighters loyal to Abdirahmaan Ali Tuur, Somaliland's first leader, for example, looted markets and ports in their hometowns in 1992. Further violence of this sort occurred in 1994 and 1995. But then it stopped. Local notables succeeded in asserting control over the ports. Why did local notables have this capacity to force armed groups to change their behavior? The answer lay in the marginality of the local political elite, at least compared to their southern counterparts. The primary "mistake" of this community was to have been a base of support for the old Somali Youth League during the 1960s. After taking power in a coup in 1969, Barre feared that northern Somalia might support a challenger and that therefore it posed a threat to his hold on power.

Under the Barre regime this marginality was a serious liability, since it meant that elites in the north received few resources from the state. For example, about 40 percent of state investment, largely funded through foreign aid programs, was slated to be spent in Mogadishu. Of the remaining 60 percent, four-fifths went to politically favored regions in the south and northeast, such as to the commercial farming operations discussed above.[15] Even more important, the political untrustworthiness of the northern elite meant that the president gave few of them large-scale access to the rackets that enriched the bank accounts of more favored politicians and state officials. Since projects were not directed toward the north, local strongmen also did not benefit from the manipulation of land tenure laws to the degree that their southern counterparts did.

This marginal position meant that if local northern elites participated in the same rackets that their more favored counterparts enjoyed, they would have to find local protection that could shield them from the predations of those who received direct regime support. They sought protection from local brokers, many of whom also held customary positions of authority in local communities. In the view of prewar northerners, it may have seemed like an inefficient way of doing business. For example, the predations of the president's political network forced some local businessmen to seek partners in neighboring Djibouti and among ethnic kinsmen abroad to shield clandestine transactions from rival operators who enjoyed presidential favor. Since they were more often the targets rather than beneficiaries of manipulations of official laws, they needed these local intermediaries to guarantee their transactions with partners inside and outside Somalia. In turn, these intermediaries ultimately controlled this elite's access to resources, acquiring the capacity to undermine these transactions among local strongmen if they misbehaved. Thus strongmen in that region had to negotiate with community notables in exchange for their support, a very different relationship from that found to the south.

From a perspective that considers only the results rather than the organization of violence, the north was a very poor candidate for stability as Somalia disintegrated. By 1990, the army had killed about 50,000 people in the north. But once the central government had collapsed and army officers sought their fortunes in their home bases, many of the remaining fighters hailed from the region. Since local notables already played a key role in controlling access to resources, local strongmen could not sustain those fighters if they preyed on their own communities. That gave community authorities the means to impose control over their use of violence. Some misbehaved, but a visitor noted "the difficulty of shooting young apprentice shiftas because their clan and family backgrounds had to be taken into account and the same holds for any person who might kill."[16] The outcome was armed young men who could be integrated into community defense forces and not into predatory gangs.

Sierra Leone exhibited a similar dynamic during its 1991–2002 war. The political economy of preconflict government patronage, especially where it was rooted in illicit commercial networks, shaped the wartime substate order (or its absence). Presidential patronage involved partnerships between state officials and foreign firms. This business joined the interests of politically reliable chiefs in diamond-mining areas, the main source of wealth and revenues in the country, to capital-based politicians. These partnerships were most extensive in the Kono District mining areas. Not only was it a key diamond mining area, but also it was home to many local chiefs who had been eager to support the ruling party that won an election in 1967 and then returned to power in 1968 after a countercoup had reversed the army's attempt to reverse the election results.

Local chiefs initially supported what became a single-party regime that ruled until 1992 because they feared the power of a populist party that arose in the 1950s. That party questioned government regulation of small-scale alluvial mining operations that local people considered their right and the government labeled as illegal. These popular politicians also challenged the prerogatives that chiefs enjoyed under Sierra Leone's political system. Chiefs in Kono were especially vulnerable to these criticisms, as they had used their official positions to sell protection to illicit miners whom they could shield from government prosecution. Therefore, the prospect of presidential patronage after 1968 to engage in larger-scale official mining was welcome among many of these chiefs. Now that they had support from the capital, they had no need to negotiate with local mining gangs. They could simply call upon police and the military to chase them off. This new relationship with political power in the capital also released them from customary obligations as "landlords" to protect and provide for outsiders—including illicit diamond miners— who worked in their territory.[17]

This situation contrasted with earlier practice. People who mined diamonds in the 1950s and 1960s had their complaints: "Stories are frequently repeated of large sums paid to Chiefs for a permit" that supposedly was free.[18] But so long as the colonial government intended to enforce the letter of the law, these chiefs had to deal with local mining gangs if they wanted to have a stake in the illicit mining economy, such that officials in the capital reported that "Chiefs and their courts are not cooperating in control of either strangers or illicit mining."[19] Ultimately this situation made the introduction of large-scale industrial mining a seemingly sensible policy for controlling illicit mining. Moreover, the postcolonial government's political strategy of including local chiefs in these deals looked like a good way to cultivate political loyalties of chiefs while giving them incentives to suppress local people's illicit mining. Once chiefs stopped backing illicit miners against capital-based politicians, these new partners supported periodic military efforts to expel strangers who had previously looked to chiefs to protect them.

This arrangement did not end small-scale illicit mining. Instead, it meant that those miners had to find their places in clandestine channels that central government officials, including the president, controlled. By the 1970s, this required supporting the single-party regime. Patronage occurred in a much more hierarchical fashion in this context, compared to areas where local elites remained in opposition to the government. It marginalized autonomous local intermediaries and put the control of resources in the hands of officials in the distant capital. From a prewar perspective, it might have seemed like a good way of extending political control over the countryside, and especially over the main source of wealth in the country. But it also meant that when central control began to collapse in the late 1980s, local mining gangs did not depend upon chiefs for protection as they became more autonomous of their political bosses in the capital. Since some were given weapons to intimidate government opponents and freelance miners, these gangs could easily convert these weapons to personal use to defend and extend their own mining operations.

The practical consequence for the Revolutionary United Front rebels in the early 1990s was that once their agents arrived in the area, they found ready recruits among youth who mined diamonds amid the collapsing capital-based patronage network. In addition, the RUF enjoyed the support of Charles Taylor, head of Liberia's National Patriotic Front (NPFL), and after 1997, Liberia's president. Thus it was not surprising that local fighters regarded customary authorities such as chiefs, long allied with corrupt national politicians, as easily removed impediments to their control of local diamonds. RUF recruiters recognized this antagonistic relationship and reportedly exploited it when recruiting local supporters. Prior to RUF attacks, operatives infiltrated communities to determine who harbored personal grievances against local authorities.

In contrast, communities near Kenema, a community about 60 miles away where gangs of youth also mined alluvial diamonds, RUF recruitment was less effective. This area also was a heartland of support for a political party that lost its hold on power in 1967. Prior to that critical election, chiefs in this region were poised to join in the benefits of diamond mining, both formal and illicit, as it was managed from the capital. But once the old party was swept out of power, a local historian noted that the new administration systematically interfered in chiefdom politics to advance the new president's favored candidates. The president's allies sponsored armed youth gangs to contest local chief decisions and to interfere in legislative elections. Nonetheless, some local chiefs could resist these provocations with their own youth gangs.[20] But since these chiefs did not enjoy presidential sanction to mobilize youth on their own or particularly favored or secure positions in the president's patronage network, they were forced to turn to local youth initiation societies to discipline these recruits. These local religious authorities in turn required that chiefs uphold customary expectations that they would provide for their welfare and protect these youth as a consequence of their landlord obligations. Combined with landlord traditions, this initiation custom enabled the integration of outsiders into local communities. It also meant that this web of locally legitimate obligations to defend and protect depended upon recruiting and arming youth—child soldiers in contemporary global parlance.

The implication of this relationship became clearer during the 1986 *ndogboyosi* uprising during the country's single-party elections, when local youth were armed to protect local favorites.[21] By the early 1990s, when the RUF had begun to appear in downriver communities, the local historian helped mobilize these youth that he had studied as *kamajoisi,* or "traditional hunters" associated with the initiation society and in collaboration with Chief Sam Hinga Norman and several head initiators. Though their intellectual backer was killed in early 1994—his grave maintained as a venerated shrine in the main square in Kenema—the armed group joined with similar groups elsewhere in the country to form the Civil Defense Forces.

CDF fighters, many of them under eighteen years old, played a key role in defending a civilian government after the UN-endorsed peace agreement resulted in elections in 1996. Soon after, army units and the RUF mined diamonds, occasionally in collaboration. They continued to loot local communities and went to war with the new government. After an RUF-dominated coalition launched an invasion of the capital in May 1997, only CDF-controlled areas remained outside RUF control. CDF fighters continued to play an important role in defending the government when a foreign intervention force returned it to power in early 1998, up to the end of widespread fighting in 2001 and again in 2002, when it appeared that core RUF forces would infiltrate from Liberia. CDF fighters were responsible for considerable human rights violations. But this did not obviate the fact that they administered areas under their control and that many people in those places considered them to be legitimate and trusted, or at least expected them to exercise violence on their behalf.

The Dilemma of International Norms and Local Self-Determination

These examples show that a local group that takes on tasks of governance—a provider of public goods—can do so even if its members do not look like government officials. Postage stamps, letterheads, and even ministries and orders of rank are artifacts of custom and practice. History shows governments that take other forms that reflect the diversity of human cultures can find local legitimacy. Moreover, those whom local people regard as legitimate rulers may engage in behavior that others consider odious. For example, the Taliban rulers of Afghanistan gained considerable local support for their capacity to control local violence. To its followers, the Taliban also promoted virtue and fought to banish sin from Afghan society, which according to their perspective were public goods. In this lies a major challenge for substates and other indigenous efforts to create public order, especially in conflict zones where they must fight enemies and make decisions about who belongs in their definition of community while confronting the rest of the world's ideas about what makes an armed group recognizable as a government.

Some scholars propose that diplomats simply acknowledge the legitimacy of local self-determination movements and allow them to construct more viable states on the ruins of old ones. They recognize that the struggle to establish new political communities and new international borders would lead to violence in the short run but would have the long-term benefit of creating legitimate governments able to mobilize citizens to solve many of the problems that have beset contemporary weak states.[22] But this is an extreme alternative to conventional interventions that seek to restore failing states and build administrations that will conform to global standards of governance. Nearly all diplomats and incumbent political leaders of these countries recognize that such struggles would recreate conditions such as those that accompanied the collapse of Yugoslavia. Many citizens are aware of these dangers, even in societies where local self-determination movements and wartime militias receive considerable popular support.

Yet the standard approach of international actors—one focused on restoring state institutions and instilling respect for global standards of administration—encounters significant problems in recognizing and integrating existing legitimate groups and structures. Indeed, to the extent that their behavior clashes with norms of human rights and governance, political engagement with these groups is even more unlikely. This becomes even more apparent as the implementation of norms has become more uniform in the course of interventions.

Returning to the Sierra Leone example, during wartime the country's elected civilian president remained in office only through significant support that he received from the CDF. In fact, this militia played a key role in restoring him to office in 1998, nine months after the RUF and renegade elements of the army launched a coup against him. The international community had a stake in the president's return, too: no country extended diplomatic recognition to the rebel junta, and the UN Security Council imposed sanctions against it. The president himself expressed his gratitude to the CDF upon his return to power: "As you have seen, it is because of the high professionalism of these magnificent men and the gallant efforts of our Civil Defense Forces that we are here today."[23] In 2001 he again offered his thanks "to all those throughout the country—civilians, soldiers, members of the CDF, the Police, as well as our ECOMOG and UNAMSIL" for defending his government against rebel attacks in 2000.[24]

Yet less than two years later, a hybrid international-national court issued indictments against CDF leaders charging them with serious violations of international and Sierra Leonean law. The court described a criminal conspiracy that involved rape, torture, and the use of child soldiers: "The plan, purpose or design of Samuel Hinga Norman et al. and subordinate members of the CDF was to use any means necessary to defeat the RUF/AFRC and to gain and exercise control over the territory of Sierra Leone."[25] Substate groups are likely to be subject to stringent international demands that they comply with global norms of warfare and governance or risk prosecution. Despite the fact that the CDF had joined with UN peacekeepers for a common purpose, noted above in the president's words of praise, they are more easily singled out for their misdeeds.

Substate groups are treated differently for structural reasons. Since the CDF, like many vigilantes and home guard militias, was built upon initiation institutions that armed and mobilized youths, their community norms and operations clashed with global norms prohibiting the recruitment of child soldiers. Substate groups also lack sovereign status. The Special Court ignored the fact that loyal elements of Sierra Leone's army and officials supported this substate group during the war, for the simple reason that the international court, the UN, and foreign governments require an interlocutor with whom they can coordinate the postwar intervention and statebuilding exercise. Likewise, officials in Somaliland suspect that the absence of global recognition of their authority leaves them exposed to more intense criticism of their conduct during their battle for self-determination in the early 1990s than otherwise would be the case. Moreover, if interveners seek to prosecute sitting state officials, it destabilizes their primary interlocutors in the country and risks creating severe political turmoil. Conflict management and state-building under those conditions require that international interveners occupy countries directly and administer people without the aid of an indigenous government. Doing so would be extremely expensive and would require considerable local knowledge in order to carry out—the kind of help that sub-state groups can provide.

The Sierra Leone court's officials do not acknowledge this inconsistency, but it is apparent to most citizens, who distinguish between the intensities and uses of violence, regardless of whether child soldiers were involved. A countrywide survey, for example, attributed 6 percent of all reported incidents of human rights violations to the CDF, compared to 60.5 percent to RUF fighters.[26] Even leaving aside the issue of intensities of violence, many people remain willing to distinguish between violence exercised on behalf of what they regard as a public good and violence perpetrated against communities simply to advance the interests of fighters.

It would be extremely difficult for interveners to incorporate these indigenous political perspectives into their local strategies. They strive to remain above local political divisions while still providing a framework to strengthen the local rule of law. Yet not taking sides is perceived locally as favoring one side or another. Local people's willingness to evaluate different substate groups (and also their own government) on the basis of legitimacy and their uses of violence complicates interveners' tasks. International actors may protest otherwise, but it remains true in all cases of state collapse where substate groups assume responsibilities for community protection and basic services.

Solutions to the Dilemma?
Substate groups will remain as obstacles to the creation of postconflict orders—at least in the view of most international actors. They imagine a secure state that possesses capable military and police who do not violate the rights of citizens, a state able to provide social services to communities, and leaders who support the rule of law. But as the continuing political dominance of substate groups like the remnants of the Kosovo Liberation Army (KLA) show, even the most intensive international interventions—with one soldier for every fifty people in the province—cannot remove the influence of substate groups that claim the support of local populations. Complaints from interveners in places like Liberia and Sierra Leone that local state officials lack the skills or

political will to implement serious reform also masks the extent to which substate groups either challenge what they consider infringements on their prerogatives or even claim the allegiance of significant numbers of state employees, including in the security services.

These dilemmas point to two solutions. The first involves boosting the state to replace substate groups in the provision of services and in the affections of local people, which is the preference of most international interveners. The second involves simply recognizing the authority of these groups and incorporating them into international actors' political strategies.

The first solution entails building up state security forces to the point that they can provide protection to local people without abusing their rights and requires strengthening the capabilities of judicial systems to prosecute misdeeds among state agents. In turn, police, soldiers, and judges have to be paid and provided with enough resources to perform their duties, such that they will have political autonomy from other groups in society that would challenge their performance of their duties. Moreover, it requires that local people support this project and the regime that carries it out. Challenging substate groups then involves gaining the allegiance of citizens, and boosting the capacity of states to provide social services becomes an integral element of this strategy. Taken together, these tasks constitute a comprehensive statebuilding project, requiring lengthy outside commitments, a lot of money, and the political will to use force in the event that some local substate groups defy these plans.

The most pragmatic way to accomplish these tasks is to pursue tight coordination between different elements of outside intervention forces. Since the tasks of statebuilding are so huge, the scope of intervention has to be broad and include not only conventional peacekeepers and development agencies but also specialized military trainers from the armies of powerful countries. They ensure the security of state officials and foreign experts who help to build stronger states. The US government recognizes this form of intervention as an integral component of conflict prevention that boosts the capacities of states to provide security while preventing the rise of challengers. It is broadly applied, with forty-four out of forty-seven sub-Saharan African states currently participants in US military training programs, police and border patrol capacity building exercises, or the transfer of weapons.[27]

Moreover, outside interveners in these security sectors are increasingly likely to team up with development agencies, including international organizations, to coordinate efforts. In Sierra Leone, for example, the Department for International Development (DfID) helps to coordinate an extensive British military training program that guarantees the security of the government and UN development agencies. More broadly, the Millennium Challenge Account (MCA), a US effort, coordinates directly with security programs, though it more often promotes US interests than postconflict statebuilding interests. As

Paul Applegarth, chief executive officer of the Millennium Challenge Corporation (MCC) and MCA's director, said: "MCC and development assistance more generally are a key component of US national security strategy. As the 9/11 Commission Report itself says, 'A comprehensive US strategy to counter terrorism should include economic policies that encourage development, more open societies and opportunities for people to improve the lives of their families.'"[28]

Members of NGOs and international agencies complain that this association with military aid compromises their neutrality. But as I pointed out above, intervention, especially amid existing substate groups, is generally not regarded as neutral in local eyes. Furthermore, these associations are likely to be the most effective way for these international actors to achieve their ambitious goals of building the kind of local governance that meets their standards and to maintain a critical level of popular support for this project. Either this strategy will produce early success and members of substate groups will desert their old organizations for the promise that the new regime offers, or international actors will have to take a more coercive approach to protect their local allies from continued challenge as their statebuilding effort encroaches on substate turf.

Intervention of this sort, especially in the midst of conflict, is expensive. The United Nations peacekeeping force in Sierra Leone, for example, cost about $2.8 billion for six years (up to its withdrawal at the end of 2005) and deployed 17,500 soldiers at its peak.[29] Even then, the success of that intervention depended upon the intervention of British troops in 2000 and the continued presence of British military trainers. The UN intervention in Liberia cost $864 million for half of 2005. Deployment of 10,000 UN peacekeepers in Congo cost $709 million for the same period.[30] The US operation in Kosovo cost $8.1 billion from 1999 to mid-2003.[31] In each instance, peacekeeping forces on the ground still made pragmatic choices to cooperate with "good" substate groups that were compatible with the overall mission of bringing a minimum of order and stability to these places. To confront these groups simply was beyond the military and fiscal capabilities of interveners, even given the fairly high levels of political commitment in the case of Kosovo.

Moreover, these interventions occurred in very small states (or territories, as in Kosovo). Although most attention to intervention focuses on very weak states in sub-Saharan Africa, the reality since 1987 shows that fairly large middle-income states are at risk too. Yugoslavia collapsed, while Zimbabwe, Venezuela, Bolivia, and some of the states of Central Asia are considered by certain scholars as candidates for state collapse.

The alternative strategy puts more focus on integrating substate groups into externally led statebuilding plans, which would be compatible with scholars' recognition that creating democracy and the rule of law have been generational projects in other states. Where outside interveners succeeded in imposing it by force, as in Germany and Japan after the end of World War II, closer examination turns up numerous examples of compromises and incorporation of substate groups, including illiberal ones, that possessed legitimacy and reciprocity in their internal relations that external actors desired to transplant to new regimes. These compromises imparted distinctive features particular to the political cultures of those societies that aided the legitimacy of the new democratic order.

Integrating ethnic vigilantes and exclusionary substate groups into post-conflict orders in contemporary weak states poses considerable problems. Outside interveners will have to decide which groups are incompatible with overall goals and which are likely to adapt. These choices also involve taking a flexible approach to the question of prosecution for past wrongs. If groups prove to be useful allies in a statebuilding process that provides multiple long-term benefits for the entire population, should their leaders be prosecuted for past human rights abuses? These decisions also will confront differences between how local communities define appropriate state tasks and how state rulers and foreign interveners define them. For instance, the leaders of the Sudan People's Liberation Army have a very different idea about the distribution of authority and tasks than the government of Sudan in Khartoum. But international agencies that intervene in that conflict already have confronted these issues, culminating in an internationally brokered peace agreement between the SPLA and the Sudanese government in Kenya in January 2005.

It also may be preferable to accept that some states should not be rebuilt. Put differently, some substate groups and the territories they control should be recognized as states. In fact, it is already happening. On February 17, 2008, Kosovo declared independence, ending months of uncertainty after negotiations over the province's final status ended in deadlock. A month later, twenty-eight states had recognized independent Kosovo, including sixteen of the twenty-seven EU member states and six of the UN Security Council's fifteen members. The willingness of diplomats to engage the SPLA in negotiations, which led to a peace treaty for Sudan that includes the option of a referendum on independence in 2011, is further evidence of this trend. Furthermore, UN aid agencies deal with Somaliland authorities, and US officials support them because of their arrests of alleged Al-Qaida members. In each instance, engagement has involved selective acceptance of these groups on the basis of current local support and performance, even though most are responsible for significant human rights abuses in the past.

This recognition poses risks to existing international borders. But as these precedents show, it need not challenge borders between the collapsing state and its neighbors. The dissolution of Yugoslavia, for example, did not necessarily infringe on the territories of states outside Yugoslavia. This process would be more strenuously resisted among the rulers of Africa's weaker states, lest the precedent extended to their realms could also increase incentives for substate groups to press demands for secession. At the same time, interveners are unlikely to be willing to bear the costs of the forcible reassembling of old states. In these instances, recognizing and negotiating with at least some substate groups is the lesser evil.

Notes

1. United Nations, *Report of the Secretary-General on the Situation in Somalia,* UN Doc. S/2004/469, June 9, 2004, para. 34.

2. This, of course, approximates Max Weber's classic definition of a state, in *Economy and Society: An Outline of Interpretive Sociology,* edited by Guenther Roth and Claus Wittich (Berkeley: University of California, 1978), vol. 1, pp. 904–908.

3. Republic of Somaliland, *Submission on Statehood and Recognition of the Republic of Somaliland* (Hargeisa: Ministry of External Affairs, 1996), p. 16; and statements at www.somalilandgov.com/.

4. Vote tally reported by IFES (formerly the International Foundation for Election Systems) on http://www.electionguide.org/results.php?ID=434. The UN provides a figure of 57,000 ex-combatants registering for its programs, with about 40,000 from the RUF. United Nations, *Fourteenth Report of the Secretary-General on the United Nations Mission in Sierra Leone,* UN Doc. S/2002/679, June 19, 2002, p. 4.

5. Classic statements are found in Robert H. Jackson, *Quasi-states: Sovereignty, International Relations, and the Third World* (Cambridge: Cambridge University Press, 1990); Christopher Clapham, *Africa and the International System: The Politics of State Survival* (Cambridge: Cambridge University Press, 1996); Jeffrey Herbst, *States and Power in Africa* (Princeton, NJ: Princeton University Press, 2000).

6. See Charles Tilly, "War Making and State Making as Organized Crime," in *Bringing the State Back In,* edited by Peter B. Evans, Dietrich Rueschemeyer, and Theda Skocpol (Cambridge: Cambridge University Press, 1985).

7. David Kang, *Crony Capitalism: Corruption and Development in South Korea and the Philippines* (Cambridge: Cambridge University Press, 2002).

8. Mancur Olson, "Dictatorship, Democracy, and Development," *American Political Science Review* 87, no. 3 (September 1993): 567–576. Similarly, Tilly likens statebuilding to protection rackets in his "War Making and State Making as Organized Crime," pp. 169–191.

9. The author has found many such petitions and apologies in government files in Sierra Leone and Liberia, for example.

10. African Rights, *Land Tenure, the Creation of Famine, and the Prospects for Peace in Somalia* (New York, 1993).

11. Kenneth Menkhaus, "From Feast to Famine: Land and the State in Somalia's Lower Juba Valley," in *The Struggle for Land in Southern Somalia: The War Behind the War,* edited by Catherine Besteman and Lee V. Cassanelli (Boulder, CO: Westview, 1996), pp. 133–153.

12. Roland Marchal, "Forms of Violence and Ways to Control It: The Mooryaan of Mogadishu," in *Mending Rips in the Sky: Options for Somali Communities in the 21st Century,* edited by Hussein M. Adam and Richard Ford (Lawrenceville, NJ: Red Sea Press, 1997), pp. 193–208.

13. For a detailed description of this "official" clandestine economy, see Norman Miller, "The Other Somalia," *Horn of Africa* 5, no. 3 (1982): 3–19.

14. "Kenya Probes Somalia Ship Hijack," *BBC News,* October 12, 2005, http://news.bbc.co.uk/2/hi/africa/4334220.stm.

15. Michael Roth and Jon Unruh, *Land Title, Tenure Security, Credit and Investment in the Lower Shabelle Region, Somalia* (Madison, WI: Land Tenure Center working paper, 1990), p. 12.

16. Gerard Prunier, "A Candid View of the Somali National Movement," *Horn of Africa* 13, nos. 3–4 (1991): 108.

17. On landlord customs, see Vernon R. Dorjahn and Christopher Fyfe, "Landlord and Stranger: Change in Tenancy Relations in Sierra Leone," *Journal of African History* 3, no. 3 (1962): 391–397.

18. "Secret Telegram from Sir Dorman to Sec. State for Colonies," December 31, 1958, in CO 554/1508, "Disturbances in the Sierra Leone Selection Trust Concession in the Kono Area," London, Public Records Office.

19. Telegram No. 57, Governor to Colonial Office, August 22, 1959, in CO 554/1506, "Alluvial Diamond Mining Sierra Leone," London, Public Records Office.

20. Alpha Lavalie, "SLPP: A Study of the Political History of the Sierra Leone People's Party with Particular Reference to the Period, 1968–1978," MA Thesis, University of Sierra Leone, 1983.

21. Marianne Ferme, "Studying *Politisi*: The Dialogue of Publicity and Secrecy in Sierra Leone," in *Civil Society and Political Imagination in Africa: Critical Perspectives,* edited by John L. Comaroff and Jean Comaroff (Chicago: University of Chicago Press, 1999), pp. 160–191.

22. Jeffrey Herbst, "Let Them Fail: State Failure in Theory and Practice: Implications for Policy," in *When States Fail: Causes and Consequences,* edited by Robert Rotberg (Princeton, NJ: Princeton University Press, 2004), pp. 302–318.

23. Sierra Leone Press Release, "Address to the Nation by His Excellency the President of Sierra Leone, Alhaji Dr. Ahmed Tejan Kabbah," March 10, 1998.

24. President Alhaji Dr. Ahmed Tejan Kabbah, "Address to the Nation on the First Anniversary of the May 8, 2000, Incident in Freetown," May 8, 2001.

25. Special Court for Sierra Leone, "The Prosecutor Against Samuel Hinga Norman, et al., Indictment," Freetown, SCSL-03-14-I, February 5, 2004, p. 5.

26. Sierra Leone Truth Commission, *Witness to Truth: Report of the Sierra Leone Truth and Reconciliation Commission, Statistical Appendix 1* (Accra: GPL Press, 2004), pp. 27–28. The report can also be found at http://www.trcsierraleone.org/pdf/APPENDICES/Appendix%201%20-%20Statistical%20Report.pdf.

27. US Department of State, *Foreign Military Training and Department of Defense Engagement Activities of Interest* (Washington, DC: Bureau of Political-Military Affairs, May 2005).

28. Paul Applegarth, CEO, Millennium Challenge Corporation, testimony before the House Appropriations Subcommittee on Foreign Operations, Export Financing, and Related Programs, Hearing on FY2006 Appropriations, 109th Congress, 1st Session, April 13, 2005, http://www.interaction.org/files.cgi/4234_CONGRESSIONAL_TRANSCRIPTS_4_14_05.doc.

29. United Nations, "Sierra Leone—UNAMSIL—Facts and Figures," http://www.un.org/Depts/dpko/missions/unamsil/facts.html.

30. United Nations, *Fourth Progress Report of the Secretary-General on the United Nations Mission in Liberia,* UN Doc. S/2004/725, September 10, 2004, para. 55; United Nations, *Third Special Report of the Secretary-General on the United Nations Organisation Mission in the Democratic Republic of Congo,* UN Doc. S/2004/650, August 16, 2004, para. 105.

31. Nina Serafino, "Peacekeeping: Issues of US Military Involvement," CRS Issue Brief IB94040 (Washington, DC: Congressional Research Service, August 6, 2003), p. 16.

8

Practical Approaches to Building State Institutions

Sarah Cliffe and Nick Manning

In this chapter we describe some of the problems encountered in previous postconflict institution-building efforts and attempt to lay out elements of a different approach. We write from the perspective of practitioners involved in postconflict reconstruction for the World Bank. In the first section we introduce the centrality of state institutions to sustained postconflict recovery. Next we lay out four particular problems encountered in previous reconstruction and recovery efforts. In the third section we propose remedies for these problems. We conclude by laying out practical steps to strengthen the focus on institution building in postconflict recovery.

The Centrality of Institutions

Although much of the current international aid architecture was created to deal with reconstruction needs in the aftermath of World War II, conflict and postconflict reconstruction were largely peripheral issues to development discourse from the 1950s to the 1980s. The 1990s saw a number of high-profile postconflict reconstruction cases—including the West Bank and Gaza, Bosnia and Herzegovina, Haiti, Kosovo, Sierra Leone, and East Timor—where political imperatives led to a renewed high level of international support for postconflict reconstruction. The early thinking among development policymakers when faced with this demand for reconstruction assistance tended to focus on initiatives to consolidate peace and achieve physical reconstruction—just as the Marshall Plan in postwar Europe had done.

Yet war not only demolishes schools and bridges: it destroys institutions of all kinds. It can fatally weaken central government institutions through insecurity, which keeps public services from operating, and through economic pressures that distort or stop payment of civil servants or the supply of basic goods. It can destroy social capital and local institutions through displacing populations, widening ethnic divides, or heightening communal conflicts. It can create a culture of impunity and breakdown in the rule of law. And it may spur large-scale migration of skilled personnel abroad, which is difficult to reverse when peace is finally won.

Furthermore, in the conflicts of the 1980s and 1990s, this damage occurred to institutions that were relatively weak or new, in marked contrast to World War II Europe and Japan, where a long tradition of public administration existed. In the examples given above, either peak-level institutions common to states had never existed, or they had been distorted and weakened by decades of conflict and poor governance. Early reconstruction initiatives paid relatively little attention to this institutional vulnerability.

Recent research has demonstrated that many postconflict recovery efforts are not sustained—there is a 23 percent risk that peace will collapse within the first four years after a peace agreement and a 40 percent risk that it will collapse over the first decade.[1] This discovery has led to renewed attention to the role of institution building in preventing the renewal of conflict, reflecting the broader shift in the development community toward viewing governance and institutions as central to change in all developing societies.[2] Effective institutions are now widely viewed as critical to address both the "capacity deficit" and "legitimacy deficit" faced by fragile states—since only strong national institutions can ensure that the state is associated with provision of positive services to the population and can be held to account by its citizens.

Recognition of the problem, however, has not led to proven solutions. Institution building in postconflict societies has had at best a mixed record. A recent study of four internationally supported postconflict operations highlighted the persistence of key weaknesses in managing postconflict statebuilding, in particular a lack of comprehensive planning of public administration initiatives, weak sequencing of institution building, failure to make rhetoric on capacity building a reality on the ground, and continued failure to plan and deliver effective rule of law.[3] Within the World Bank's Country Policy and Institutional Assessment (CPIA) rating system, of the nine countries with CPIA scores that were classified as postconflict since 2000, eight have not yet attained a "satisfactory" rating.[4]

Four Particular Problems

Some overarching difficulties stand out in postconflict reconstruction experiences. First, many reconstruction efforts have been insufficiently informed by what institutions already exist and so have tended to reinvent the wheel (or worse, invent an extra wheel) based on the assumption of *terra nullius,* rather than build on the preexisting institutional architecture. Second, efforts to support institution building have typically been quite diffuse, spread across all sectors and all areas of the state. Third, there has been little attention paid to the relation between transitional oversight and delivery mechanisms and long-term national institutions. Last, donors' own good intentions to support rapid recovery after a conflict have all too often unintentionally undermined long-term institution building by sapping the skills base available to national institutions and bypassing national decisionmaking structures. These four recurrent problems are elaborated below.

The Fallacy of Terra Nullius

Newspaper reports on reconstruction operations often include comments from international representatives—and sometimes national leadership—to the effect that "we were left with nothing" or "we had to start from zero." Although it is certainly true that conflicts such as in Rwanda, Afghanistan, or East Timor produced near-total state collapse and immense physical and human destruction, these countries were not an institutional blank slate. Community and traditional structures are often resilient to conflict, and some institutions—such as resistance structures—may actually be brought into being and strengthened by conflict. Basic administrative practices continue in the minds of current or ex-civil servants, even where structures have ceased to function and paper records have been lost.

Why has it often proven so difficult to identify and make use of this existing institutional capacity? Part of the problem may be the change of political and decisionmaking actors. The end of a conflict often brings to power a new political leadership who may be unaware of prior practice and the capacities of existing systems and personnel—in addition to viewing all previous institutions as tainted by the previous regime. Diplomatic and donor representation also frequently changes at the beginning of a postconflict operation: too few international staff and policy makers have knowledge of the strengths and weaknesses of the institutions that existed prior to their arrival. Hence the temptation to treat postconflict countries as a *terra nullius* where no positive institutional practices existed before the onset of peace.

Prior practices may indeed be imperfect: corruption and bias in the public administration or abuse by political and security sector institutions may have been a cause of the original conflict. Yet many existing practices are likely to be sound and can be quickly restored to working order because they are familiar to national staff: it is much more difficult to introduce entirely new models. Existing practices are also likely to be well adapted to constraints in communications, logistics, and staff skills. Even where prior institutional practice is deeply flawed, new institutional initiatives will need to take account of it because it can act as an implicit barrier to reform: reform efforts need to understand previous models to identify which changes can be made relatively easily and which will face more resistance.

Lack of Prioritization

Even before institution building came to the fore in discussions of postconflict recovery, there was little agreement as to what sequence should be followed in addressing the range of urgent needs in postconflict situations. Add the relatively new concern for statebuilding or institution building, and the set of priorities that donors and fledgling governments need to act upon in fragile postconflict settings becomes more complex and more contested. The sphere of institution building brings its own set of choices and trade-offs: Which institutions matter most for stability and recovery? Where do we start when resources are scarce, but we need everything at once? Should we build a reformed security architecture to prevent recurrent instability? Effective rule of law to arrest and punish criminal offenders? Anticorruption initiatives to restore credibility in the eyes of the population and secure new investor confidence? Functional public services to deliver education, health, and infrastructure? Decentralized systems, when a history of centralized government has been at the root of conflict?

This lack of consensus over priorities has led to highly fragmented institution-building programs. A scattergun approach may not achieve the critical mass necessary: when faced with institution-building challenges as difficult as security sector reform in Democratic Republic of Congo or restoration of accountable public financial management in Afghanistan, focusing policy dialogue and financial resources on a narrower set of priorities may be necessary to achieve a lasting impact. A fragmented approach may also have the unintended consequence of weakening government capacity by requiring a small pool of skilled government workers to devote a large amount of their time to the implementation and reporting of many small institution-building efforts.

Confused and Ineffective Use
of "Transitional Institutions"

Nascent national institutions in the aftermath of a conflict often lack the capacity to deliver results and ensure good governance in critical functions of the state such as the justice and security sectors, basic services, or the management of public finances and natural resource revenues. Because of this institutional deficit, one of the most important characteristics of postconflict institutional arrangements is that they tend to be transitional in nature: for a variety of reasons, state institutions are not ready to take on the full range of functions and outputs that they will fulfill in the longer term, or a specific transitional institutional configuration is necessary to address the political legacy of conflict. Two types of transitional institutional arrangements are generally present in postconflict situations:

• De jure/Formal. The postconflict settlement itself may specify certain institutional arrangements to address the legacy of conflict, such as the formation of a transitional government prior to the conduct of elections; of special agencies to address finite tasks such as demobilization or truth and reconciliation; or of externally provided peacekeeping missions to monitor or enforce a cease-fire or to prepare initial elections (or, in extreme cases such as Kosovo or East Timor, to take on a transitional administrative role).

• De facto/Informal. Humanitarian needs and lack of capacity in state institutions may have already led to a situation in which basic services (security, social protection, water, education, health) are being provided by international agencies, religious and nonreligious nongovernmental organizations (NGOs), and various types of quasi-formal substate authorities, such as tribal elders and community councils.[5] The state may not have the capacity to take on all of these functions immediately after the signing of a peace accord.

Transitional institutional arrangements can draw on both national and international capacity and can substitute for some of the *core executive and delivery functions* of the state, or focus only on the *oversight* of existing state systems. Some transitional arrangements directly affect the configuration of a core government or state institution (for example, the establishment of a transitional government), while others supplement state functions with nonstate capacity for a transitional period (for example, large-scale NGO service provision). Table 8.1 provides some examples of transitional institutional arrangements that have been used in the past in postconflict countries.

Postconflict situations often require transitional institutional arrangements—either to create rapid improvements in the perceived political neutrality and governance of the state, or because humanitarian and reconstruction needs are broad and immediate and existing capacity within government structures is insufficient to take on all the core functions of government at once. Transitional institutions and capacity, however, have often arisen in an ad hoc manner and proven difficult to translate into longer-term national institution building.

Overall, the incentives and political dynamics surrounding transitional governments have at times militated against their ability to lead a strong institution-building agenda. At a sectoral level, difficulties have emerged in transferring responsibilities to national actors: NGOs run the bulk of postconflict health and education services, for example, but national accountability is lacking and services collapse when international funding is withdrawn. Or international advisers generate all the documentation, which is issued by their national "bosses," but fail to put in place a long-term system managed with confidence by their national counterparts.

Such results have generally been perceived as a failure of "skills transfer," and the incentives for skills transfer certainly play a part. They may also represent an inappropriate choice of where international models can be imported. Francis Fukuyama, building on an earlier paper by Michael Woolcock and Lant Pritchett, argues:

Table 8.1 Examples of Transitional Institutions

	Regular Country Systems	Transitional Institutional Arrangements Using National Capacity	Transitional Institutional Arrangements Using International Capacity
Delivery	• Elected executive • Core government fiduciary systems • Public health and educational systems • Local government provision of local services and infrastructure	• National transitional government • Special agencies for transitional tasks such as truth and reconciliation or demobilization • Autonomous agencies or project implementation units employing national staff outside regular salary scales and treasury systems • NGO or faith-based provision of education or health services • Community-driven provision of local services or infrastructure prior to the establishment of local government structures	• International transitional administration • International agency or NGO provision of health or education services • International procurement or financial management agencies • International peacekeeping or police forces • International staff in line management or advisory roles • Project implementation units using international capacity • International management contracts for utilities or facilities management
Oversight	• Parliamentary oversight • Auditor-general, audit office, or ombudsman	• Civil society oversight or verification committees	• Mixed international-national oversight committees • International audit • Full (Kosovo, East Timor) or partial (Bosnia) oversight of executive decisions

There are some high-specificity activities with low transaction volumes like central banking that do not permit a high degree of variance in institutional structure or approach. These are the areas of public administration most susceptible to technocratic reform, where . . . "ten bright technocrats" can be air-dropped into a developing country and bring about massive changes for the better in public policy. . . . By contrast, the hardest areas to reform are the low specificity activities with high transaction volumes like education or law. There is no legal system in the world that can be "fixed" by ten technocrats, however bright. These are also the areas of public administration that are likely to be the most idiosyncratic and subject to variance according to local conditions.[6]

International agencies and staff tend to bring with them institutional models from other countries. Although in some areas of public sector activity these models may be relatively easy to transfer to a new setting, in others local social and cultural dynamics can create barriers to their effective implementation. We would therefore add to the Woolcock and Pritchett/Fukuyama model a factor related to "international professionalization." It captures the reality that for some sectors, although the activities and outcomes are intrinsically hard to specify and tend to lead to high transaction volumes, they are organized according to principles that are underpinned by a strong international professional consensus. Doctors and hospital managers, for example, although dealing with fairly high transaction volumes in their work, have professional bonds and a shared international community of practice that tend to cross borders. That is not generally true for teachers. Equally, there is a body of relatively common defense doctrine and a shared sense of professional skills among senior military officers, which is much less the case for police forces and police personnel.

Reflecting these aspects, the experience of postconflict reconstruction across countries shows that some sectors are more responsive than others to the transfer of international models, which tends to come with large numbers of international personnel. Table 8.2 shows specificity, transaction volumes, and international professionalization in different sectors. Sectors with high specificity, low transaction volumes, and a significant degree of accepted international professionalization—such as central banking and defense—are in principle likely to be more receptive to rapid and intensive international support. This presentation is of course highly stylized, in that there is also significant variance between subsectors on the factors shown here, but it does give a sense of the structural reasons that prevent a one-size-fits-all approach.

Collateral Damage

Donor efforts to help postconflict countries meet basic needs may in some cases have actively undermined longer-term national institution-building goals.[7] Massive amounts of donor aid largely provided off-budget, which

Table 8.2 State Sectors: How Readily Can External Capacities and Models Be Applied?

Sector	Indicator	Barriers to Applying External Models/Capacity		
		High	Moderate	Low
Central banking	Specificity			X
	Transaction volumes			X
	International professionalization			X
Public finance	Specificity			X
	Transaction volumes	X		
	International professionalization		X	
Defense	Specificity			X
	Transaction volumes			X
	International professionalization			X
Police	Specificity	X		
	Transaction volumes	X		
	International professionalization	X		
Judiciary	Specificity	X		
	Transaction volumes	X		
	International professionalization			X
Education	Specificity	X		
	Transaction volumes	X		
	International professionalization	X		
Health	Specificity			X
	Transaction volumes	X		
	International professionalization			X
Infrastructure	Specificity			X
	Transaction volumes		X	
	International professionalization		X	

dwarf government budgetary resources, and the associated existence of a large and well-paid "second civil service" consisting of consultants, advisers, and employees of international agencies and NGOs, can constitute a major hindrance to national institution building. High salaries paid by international agencies make it difficult to retain skilled individuals in the civil service: every time some success in establishing a new function or implementing institutional reform is achieved, it is put at risk when national managers succumb to the temptation of inflated salaries in donor agencies.

Services provided entirely outside government institutions, unless very carefully managed, may actually decrease the credibility of the state in the eyes of the population: unpopular functions such as taxation are recognizably attributed to the state, whereas popular functions are perceived to stem solely from donors or NGOs. Even where institutions are in principle "transferable," transfer will not happen unless the incentives of national and international staff are aligned with this outcome. The role, influence, and funding flows of international agencies and NGOs in a postconflict society—as well as of individual consultants—may depend on lack of national capacity, which justifies the continued substitution of their services. These agencies may at best have conflicting objectives: the genuine desire to see increased national empowerment clashes with the need to protect their organizational role and turf.

Huge waves of international staff and consultants, many of them unaware of local political dynamics and social and administrative practices, may result in reform proposals that are unworkable and, in the worst case, damaging to the underlying institutional capital that the country has retained.

Elements of a Different Approach

In this section we examine ways to mitigate the four problems discussed in the previous section: building on the institutions that already exist; focusing on functions critical to the survival of the state; using transitional institutional arrangements judiciously; and avoiding collateral damage by using international capacity to support rather than undermine longer-term local institution building.

Build on What Exists

It is important to ensure that institutional models take account of the local hardwiring that comes from prior practices, sociocultural norms, physical conditions, and existing local skills and capacities. As noted above, there are few states, however weak, that become an institutional blank slate after conflict. The coherence of fiscal and administrative systems, the common understanding of how they are intended to work, and any remaining entrenched discipline of staff are valuable resources. The overarching principle that must underpin statebuilding is to work with these strengths, nurturing the discipline that has remained despite years of conflict in many settings. Reform proposals that modify existing, well-entrenched, and well-understood procedures present serious risks of confusion and parallel structures. In a setting in which the overwhelming majority of administrative and fiscal procedures are not written but are well known to most serving officials, the introduction of new arrangements must pay very careful attention to how they will overlay existing practices.

Incorporating awareness of existing institutional strengths and weaknesses begins with the selection of personnel involved in discussions on the institutional elements of peace agreements and early reconstruction planning. Notwithstanding the political difficulties of managing divisions between people who served the previous regime and those who were in opposition to it, national leadership would be well advised to involve in their early planning

exercises a number of technical staff who are familiar with the legal framework, organizational structures, and administrative practices of the previous
regime. This can avoid unintentionally "throwing the baby out with the
bathwater," ensuring that sound existing practices are not discarded solely
because of their association with previously existing oppressive or dysfunctional institutions.

On the side of donors, more effort should be made to field personnel
who have a strong knowledge of the country context and institutional evolution over time. Donors can also help identify existing institutional practices by ensuring that postconflict needs assessments carried out at the beginning of reconstruction programs include an analysis of prior or existing
institutions such as laws, organizational structures, systems and processes, and
capacities and skills. Postconflict needs assessments are typically good at
documenting the number of physical facilities that still exist but are less
successful at doing the same analysis for institutions. More emphasis on documenting existing institutions right at the beginning of a transitional process
may help avoid the temptation to reinvent the wheel that has been so characteristic of many postconflict endeavors. A more systematic effort to provide
orientation to new international staff would also assist in building awareness of existing institutional strengths and weaknesses.

Prioritize Functions Critical to the Survival of the State

National leadership and donors face a difficult challenge in states that have
suffered partial or total collapse: of the multitude of institutions that will be
needed for development in the longer-term, where should they focus efforts
in the early period? In attempting to sequence or prioritize the broad array of
institution-building needs in a postconflict environment, it may be helpful to
think in terms of the key functions and outcomes that are necessary for the
survival of the state and sufficient to restore credibility to the state. Thus institutions that support political statebuilding objectives (in particular, to avert
the risk of renewed conflict) should have priority in the early postconflict
period, although political statebuilding objectives are served by security, economic, and social functions, so priorities still fall across all four areas.

Which functions are really critical from the perspective of ensuring
survival and restoring the credibility of the state? As the chapter topics of
the thematic portion of this volume reflect, the four areas below emerge as
key in postconflict contexts.

Basic political functions. Political leadership and a functioning process to
mediate between interests and peacefully resolve disputes is critical to stabilization after a conflict. If key actors do not participate in the political
process and do not take responsibility for leading the recovery, then postconflict stability is unlikely to survive. We suggest three priority functions

---

Ten Critical Functions of the State

Political functions

- a representative process that delivers credible leadership at the national and local level
- the ability to take and implement collective decisions in the executive
- the ability to hold the state to account for decisions made and actions taken

Security and rule of law functions

- provision of safety and security to citizens in an impartial manner
- ability to arrest, prosecute, and punish wrongdoers in a way perceived to be fair by the population

Public finance functions

- ability to manage natural resource revenues and taxation
- ability to manage expenditures
- ability to employ and pay staff

Service delivery and economic recovery functions

- ability to restart services in place before the conflict and to provide limited new services in areas previously outside the reach of the state
- economic management to stabilize consumer and producer prices and to enable domestic entrepreneurs to take advantage of economic recovery

---

and results in this area, no matter what particular form of political institutions is adopted: (1) a functioning representative process that delivers credible transitional leadership at the national and local levels; (2) the ability to take and implement collective decisions in the executive; and (3) the ability to hold the state to account for decisions made and actions taken. Institution building in these core political functions involves technical systems (for example, establishing cabinet processes), but more importantly requires support for leadership inside and outside government to transform the mindset of opposition, resistance, or armed struggle into a framework of consensual decisionmaking and the peaceful mediation of competing political interests.

Basic security and rule of law functions. Success in statebuilding will be measured by the degree to which the government can regain control over national policies and implementation across the country. Often, this process is made more difficult by the financial and military strength of regional warlords and local commanders, widespread criminal activities, or the existence of a large and underpaid national army that may be viewed by the population as more of a predator than a beloved national institution. The restoration and reform of core rule of law functions are a crucial prerequisite for state-building. We suggest two core functions/results in this area: the provision of safety and security to citizens in an impartial manner and the capacity to arrest, prosecute, and punish wrongdoers in a way perceived to be fair by the population. "Arrest-prosecute-punish" is described as one function here because many postconflict programs have suffered from poor sequencing in balancing institutional development of the police, justice, and corrections systems—resulting in one part of the criminal justice system causing a bottleneck in the functioning of the system as a whole.

Basic public finance functions. The ability to tax, spend, and employ staff is a central function of the state—not only because it makes possible the other functions, but also because an effective monopoly over taxation and core public services is critical to prevent the financing of parallel state structures or private armies by political competitors. Failure to pay salaries to civil servants may also be a key factor in causing social unrest or facilitating renewed conflict. In the early postconflict period, much of the state's revenues may come from aid; guarding against corruption in the taxation/expenditure function is also important to ensure continued aid flows and maintain a level of credibility in the eyes of the population. Budget, customs and taxation, treasury, recruitment, and payroll are the core functions in this area.

Basic service delivery and economic recovery functions. The three areas above could be described as the defining functions of a state: the areas in which there is little argument over the limits of state versus private or community action. On their own, however, they are insufficient to restore the credibility of a postconflict state: the state must also be perceived to be delivering more positive "peace dividend" benefits to the population in order to consolidate peace and avert social tensions. Spoilers to a peace agreement will take advantage of any failure to quickly restart services. In most postconflict environments, it is important to rapidly restart state service delivery in two areas: (1) services in place before the conflict,[8] and; (2) limited new services in areas previously outside the reach of the state.[9] It is important to keep in mind that the priority is for the state to be associated with the delivery of these key services—not that the state necessarily must deliver them itself. In the economic area, policy measures to stabilize consumer and producer prices and to enable domestic entrepreneurs to take advantage of economic recovery help to restore a sense of confidence in the state's economic management.

Focus on functions and outcomes rather than form or inputs. Within each of these priority areas, a focus on functions and outcomes (rather than the form of laws and organizational structures in place) forces further prioritization and helps avoid the pitfall of supporting "paper" institutions that fail to deliver any tangible benefits of peace on the ground. This represents a change in approach: not "We need institution building of the Department of Budget," but rather "We need to build a functioning budget process that is transparent and enables government to avoid unexplained over- or underexpenditure"; equivalently, not "We need to build the capacity of the Ministry of Justice and the courts," but "We need to build a functioning impartial criminal justice system capable of following standard basic investigative and arrest procedures, processing the resulting caseload in the courts within a reasonable timeframe, and housing prisoners in appropriate conditions." Ambitions in the early postconflict period should be realistic given baseline capacity: in the example above on the public finance system, for instance, a second-generation objective might be "a functioning budget process based on identified poverty reduction priorities and performance," but this outcome may be attainable only at a later level of institutional strength.

A focus on functions and outcomes also helps to make effective use of technical assistance, which is most likely to benefit the country when international consultants have incentives to deliver a fully functioning system in the area of government in which they work, managed and operated by national personnel. Technical assistance focused solely on "paper" outputs—drafting a law or set of procedures—will often not be carried through into implementation.

Managing the trade-off between capacity and legitimacy objectives.
In addition to prioritizing sectors and functions, there is an inevitable trade-off between institution-building initiatives that directly address the "legitimacy deficit" and initiatives that address the "capacity deficit." An institution that has high capacity but low legitimacy may undermine other governmental objectives, including peace and stability; an institution that has high legitimacy but does not deliver results may not survive long enough to demonstrate the benefit of the institutional framework that has been put in place. Is it, for example, more critical to eliminate corruption in procurement practices, thus demonstrating that the state can be held to account, or is it more critical to ensure that government can spend its budget rapidly, thus associating the state with the delivery of important services? Is it more important to ensure that education policy is strategic, coherent, based on local needs, and supportive of national unity, or is it more important to rapidly rebuild schools and train teachers?

In reality, of course, in most cases both alternatives are crucial, but they are not always mutually supportive: introducing a new procurement system and training staff may delay the delivery of goods and services to the population; policy workshops and the drafting of legislation takes time from government officials who are then unavailable to meet urgent needs. Perhaps the most important principle here is to ensure that legitimacy and capacity move in tandem. There is little point in rapidly establishing a function perceived to be illegitimate by the population because of corruption or bias. At the same time, it is unproductive to devote intense efforts to establishing institutional systems, procedures, and controls when national institutions are unable to spend any money or deliver any services.

Use Transitional Institutions and Capacity More Effectively

Identify the right transitional institutional arrangements. Identifying a set of state functions and results as critical does not mean that all will be delivered by the state institutions that play this role in the longer term. As discussed earlier, postconflict countries may also use capacity from outside government on a temporary basis to fill an institutional gap while public sector systems are developed and staff trained.

Incorporating an institutional assessment and specific transition plans for institution building in early postconflict planning processes can help establish a shared understanding between government, the population, and the country's international partners on what it is realistic to expect government to provide in the short and medium term—and can focus the efforts of all partners on creating long-term capacity and accountability in the state. The following questions are generally important in determining whether—and for which functions—the use of transitional institutional arrangements makes sense in a particular local context:

• How did existing or recent institutional arrangements work? How did senior public servants and others understand the machinery of government? It is important to understand which arrangements can be built on, particularly bearing in mind that the possibility of retraining large numbers of staff in new or complex systems is likely to be limited.

• Is there a need for rapid service delivery or improvements in perceived neutrality and governance that can only be achieved through the use of transitional institutional arrangements? If the core executive, legislative, and judicial structures can deliver the desired results (or can rapidly develop capacity) in any of the ten critical functions of the state listed earlier, it will make more sense to strengthen that capacity than to create new transitional arrangements. Where there is a need for rapid delivery of results or improvements in governance that cannot be provided through regular government institutions, it will generally be necessary to put in place transitional institutional arrangements.

• Are existing capacity and accountability problems so deep-rooted that exceptional transitional *management and delivery* measures are needed, or could transitional *oversight* mechanisms for core government systems provide sufficient reassurance to key domestic constituencies, the wider population, and donors? Where government services have entirely collapsed and skilled personnel are no longer available, a relatively longer period of delivering services through transitional arrangements may be needed while public sector institutions are established and staffed. Equally, where a national institution is viewed by the population as deeply corrupt or biased, more active transitional management may be needed in order to effect a large-scale reform of the institution. In many postconflict situations, however, a reasonable level of existing capacity and reform orientation may exist within several core state functions, alongside weaknesses of capacity, corruption, or bias. Where that is the case, a better solution may be to augment core government systems with transitional oversight structures to provide an additional level of external verification and technical assistance to supplement capacity gaps.

Use international capacity wisely in transitional institutional arrangements. A strong statebuilding focus in postconflict reconstruction would imply keeping transitional institutional arrangements as light as possible and as reliant as possible on national capacity. Where core executive, legislative, and judicial institutions are capable of carrying out core functions with additional technical assistance or special transitional oversight mechanisms, they should be left to do so. Where national capacity is available to provide transitional oversight or technical assistance, it should be tapped before international assistance is requested.

Although too heavy a reliance on international capacity should always be avoided, there are some situations in which the use of international capacity for transitional delivery or oversight can be key to the success of a long-term statebuilding strategy.[10] Three rationales for the use of temporary international management or oversight capacity are presented in the box on p. 178.

The experience of international transitional administrations has made many decisionmakers doubt the capacity of international institutions to take on wide-ranging administrative functions. Even in very small territories such as Kosovo or East Timor, the UN and its international partners faced major challenges in deploying sufficient numbers of experienced staff to provide credible and efficient management services in every area from policing, justice, and public finances, to agricultural extension and vehicle registration. This caused tensions with local leadership and technical counterparts, who in many cases felt that they were able to perform functions more efficiently than the highly paid international personnel sent to their ministries.

Conversely, postconflict operations that lacked the ability to provide any international management or oversight in key state functions (for example, public finances in Liberia, police in Haiti, the security sector in post-independence East Timor) have highlighted the substantial challenge of letting institutions with a track record of corruption and illegitimacy in the eyes of the

**Using International Executive or
Oversight Capacity for a Transitional Period**

Reform rationale: Internal resistance to reform may be so strong that post-conflict leadership will have difficulty in delivering the desired results without international executive or oversight assistance. The two areas in which this is most likely to be the case are public finance reform (in particular reforms that touch upon vested interests and individuals or groups who are profiting from large-scale corruption in the state) and security sector reform (both with regard to the disarmament of nongovernment militia and reform of the state security sector). International executive or oversight involvement in reform is more likely to be successful in processes that are low in transaction intensity and therefore do not overstretch the capacity of international institutions—monitoring large-scale public finance contracts and concessions, for example, rather than aiming to eliminate petty corruption in the civil service.

Capacity rationale: Using international institutions or personnel may enable delivery at greater speed or quality levels than relying on national capacity. This is not a given: international agencies also suffer constraints in capacity and quality of personnel and may be little better equipped to deliver rapid results than national institutions. Where there is a generalized skills deficit (both inside and outside the state) in certain technical areas, such as health systems or utilities management, importing capacity from abroad on a transitional basis may produce real benefits. The capacity rationale works only for functions that have relatively low local variance: for example, functions such as education are deeply rooted in the local context and generally not susceptible to effective international management. On the negative side, international agencies, companies, and personnel can cause substantial tensions with national stakeholders, in particular if the former are perceived to be biased, overpaid, or otherwise inefficient. It is important to make a realistic assessment of capacity in international agencies prior to committing to a transitional solution of this type.

Neutrality rationale: International institutions may reassure the population or parties to a conflict on the neutrality of interventions. For this reason, many postconflict political settlements have provided for partial international executive or oversight capacity within three of the ten critical functions described earlier: (1) provision of safety and security (through the deployment of a peacekeeping operation); (2) the initial postconflict representational process (conducted with international management or monitoring of elections); (3) and international tribunals to prosecute war crimes. In principle, partial international oversight could also be applied to other key functions in public finance, rule of law, or service delivery, provided that constraints in international capacity and political tensions caused by reliance on international agencies or firms are taken into account.

population reform themselves. The experience of weaknesses on both sides of the spectrum has led to a recent increase of interest in "partial" executive or oversight interventions on the part of the international community. The "shared sovereignty" model of the Office of the High Representative in Bosnia is one example. To a lesser extent, the use of international agencies for procurement and financial management in countries such as Afghanistan, or the deployment of international line managers in regional stabilization operations such as the Solomon Islands, or mixed national and international oversight committees such as the Cash Management Committee in Guinea-Bissau also follow the same logic. The specific use of international capacity to bolster transitional institutions will always vary by country, but it is worth ensuring that national leadership and their international interlocutors are aware of the options early in the process.

The choice of transitional arrangements should also take into account the lessons learned on international transferability of institutional approaches, summarized in Table 8.2. It indicates that sectors with high specificity, relatively low transaction volumes, and strong shared professional practice across countries (such as central banking, some areas of defense and health, some public finance or revenue collection functions) may be more susceptible to rapid and intense international institution building than sectors where the opposite conditions prevail (education, police). In the latter sectors, a slower and more deliberate process, which allows national stakeholders to produce their own ideas on institutional design to fit their underlying societal conditions and preferences, is likely to be more successful than the import of ready-made international models.

Insist on an exit strategy. Lack of clarity on the use of transitional institutional arrangements and their relation to longer-term state institution building has often led to

- an absence of understanding among government, the population, and international donors on the role of transitional institutional arrangements and when and how the shift will be made to longer-term delivery through core government systems; and
- an inability to translate capacity and results generated through transitional arrangements into long-term institutional strength and development outcomes.

Clearer transition plans for national institution building may assist in producing more effective outcomes. Explicit transition plans can also diminish suspicion that international actors intend to stay on beyond their initial welcome, dominating important areas of the economy, service provision, or administrative decisionmaking.

A transition plan for institution building (as part of an overall reconstruction plan) may include the definition of clear state institution-building targets and timelines; identification of transitional institutional arrangements where necessary; a list of supporting actions (by national authorities and donors); and funding requirements. It will also be important that this type of transition planning establish incentives for national and international institutions and individuals—for example, making funding flows to international entities dependent on their meeting institution-building and capacity-building targets. Insisting on this type of transition planning at the beginning of an institution-building exercise implicitly forces donors to hold their interventions to the test of whether there is an exit strategy from dependence on international capacity (or nongovernmental capacity subsidized by international funding flows).

Clear transitional planning is more likely to take place where there is a clear international counterpart structure for sectoral institution building. We do not mean that each sector must have only one donor partner but that the development of a transition plan for national institution building will be facilitated where donors coordinate their support to service delivery or technical assistance in each sector.

Avoid Collateral Damage

In addition to taking positive action to foster long-term institution building, donors need to anticipate and avoid the unintended negative consequences of aid projects on national institutions. Respect for emerging national institutions, collective decisionmaking, and the mediation of competing interests—such as cabinet and budget processes—are particularly important after a conflict. International organizations and staff should work within these nascent domestic decisionmaking institutions, not around them. To do so, they must ensure that major aid-financed projects are discussed at the policy level in the cabinet (or other collective governmental decisionmaking body) and incorporated into the budget.

Maintaining sensible limits on the number of local staff employed by international agencies and their salaries is also important. Large numbers of local staff in service delivery or project functions (except where it has been agreed on as a short-term transitional strategy under overall government management) can constitute a parallel civil service that undermines the credibility of the government. Where they are working in recurrent service delivery or development functions, they also pose a contingent liability for the government, which will be under pressure to underwrite these services when international funding is withdrawn. Setting the salaries of local staff of international agencies substantially higher than the salaries of civil servants may also undermine the civil service, by creating a brain drain of senior managers and technical personnel into the international sector. Lower salaries, of course, affect the efficiency of international organizations: but the efficacy of a strategy that produces capable international agencies at the expense of the national institutions whose strengthening they intend to support must be questioned (see Chapter 4 in this volume). Of course, the question of salaries creates a dilemma for international organizations that are, on the

---

**Transitional Institution-Building Strategy
for the Health Sector in East Timor**

The transition strategy in the health sector in postconflict East Timor can be divided into four phases, through which the health authorities gradually moved toward an integrated public health management system.

Phase I: During the initial emergency phase, NGOs reestablished essential services, saving lives and alleviating the suffering of a population traumatized by the recent violence. An Interim Health Authority (IHA) was established in February 2000, comprising sixteen senior East Timorese health professionals in Dili and one in each district, along with a small number of international experts. IHA staff made assessment visits to all districts in preparation for a first sectoral planning exercise.

Phase II: The health authority (now called the Department of Health Services, or DHS) started work on the establishment of a policy framework, medium-term planning for the sector, and national preventive programs, including immunization campaigns. During the second half of 2000, DHS signed memoranda of understanding with NGOs for each district, formalized district health plans' service standards, and initiated a basic system for distribution of essential pharmaceuticals.

Phase III: In April 2001, the Ministry of Health took over the financing of a majority of the NGOs in the districts. By the third quarter of 2001, the first round of recruitment of health staff had been completed. Most of these staff had previously worked with NGOs or on government stipends prior to finalization of the recruitment process. Several senior staff members in the department were also sent for public health management training.

Phase IV: At the request of the government, NGOs gradually withdrew from the districts between September and December 2001, and the management of all health facilities was placed under the control of the Ministry of Health. International doctors were hired to replace departing NGO practitioners while Timorese doctors were being trained overseas, and public health specialists were deployed to serve as liaisons between the ministry and district health centers. A few NGOs remained to provide specialized services on a countrywide basis.

---

one hand, under pressure to recruit proven experts, and on the other are also required to ensure more parity between international and local staff and to draw on local staff wherever possible (as was Special Representative of the Secretary-General Lakhdar Brahimi's approach in Afghanistan).

Rethinking the provision of technical assistance is also long overdue. The donor habit of providing a large number of short-term technical advisers in many small, uncoordinated projects can actively undermine national institution building because national reformers are forced to dedicate substantial time and effort to managing this unruly priesthood. Technical assistance projects are also frequently designed to be measured by the production of inputs (for example, the drafting of recommendations, laws, and procedures) rather than concrete results in improved counterpart performance. Better matching of technical assistance with statebuilding priorities, design of programs to focus on outputs in improved performance by national institutions, and stronger coordination—ideally through the pooling of donor funds for technical assistance—is needed.

Conclusion

The previous sections have reviewed some common problems in postconflict institution building and the elements of a different approach. A more central focus on institution building in postconflict countries would argue for the inclusion of a clear statebuilding strategy in the early stages of postconflict reconstruction. A step-by-step approach to this could include the following recommendations:

1. Involve personnel (national and international) with knowledge of existing state institutions to provide input in peace talks and to participate in postconflict needs assessments and recovery planning. Conducting a basic institutional assessment early in a peace process will help ensure that new agreements and plans build on strengths and take account of institutional constraints.

2. Consider the implications of political agreements for the functioning of state institutions and of institution-building efforts for peace and stability. Peace agreements often contain provisions for the creation or composition of key transitional institutions, at times without sufficient consideration of later difficulties (both technical and political) that these commitments may cause. Early identification of the likely trade-offs between political agreements and institutional strengths and weaknesses may assist in making the right decisions between short-term political stabilization and the longer-term institutional strength, which is critical to avoid a renewal of conflict.

3. Identify priority institutional functions and results to be achieved. The list of ten functions outlined in this chapter will not necessarily match the priorities in each and every country: early dialogue between national leadership and international actors (either at peace talks or in parallel and subsequent postconflict needs assessments) will help establish clear priorities tailored to the country context. Early discussions should cover

- priority areas where rapid improvements in perceived neutrality, good governance, or delivery of services will be critical in the immediate postconflict period;

- a realistic assessment of the timing necessary for the state to take on these functions, in full, at an acceptable level of performance; and
- an initial sense of acceptable transitional arrangements, including transitional oversight versus transitional management or delivery, and the role and capacity of national and international actors.

4. As part of the postconflict recovery planning process, develop specific transition plans for sectors with major institutional shortcomings. Likely to be done during an initial postconflict needs assessment, transition plans may include the definition of clear state institution-building targets and timelines, identification of transitional institutional arrangements where necessary, supporting actions (by national authorities and donors), and funding requirements. The development of transitional plans should include a realistic assessment of the capacity of international actors and consideration of whether the institutional models they bring with them will be easily transferable to the specific country context.

5. Aim for early agreement between national authorities and donors on key donor policy issues that affect national institution building, such as approval processes for aid projects, technical assistance coordination, and local staff salary scales.

6. Include provisions to measure institution- and capacity-building outcomes within agreements and contracts made for temporary service provision and technical assistance with international agencies and companies.

7. Institution building in a postconflict context is likely to be a long, uphill struggle. In addition to the collapse of systems, loss of staff, and destruction of physical facilities, many postconflict countries face a legacy of distrust of the state and institutional malpractice. Such conditions are difficult to transform within a short time. Greater emphasis on institution building within peace agreements and early recovery planning processes will not be a magic bullet, but it offers significant potential to address one of the central constraints on successful peacebuilding.

Notes

1. See Paul Collier, Anke Hoeffler, and Mans Soderbom, "Post-Conflict Risks," *Journal of Peace Research,* forthcoming.

2. Daniel Kaufmann, "Governance, Security and Development: An Initial Exploration," Paper presented at joint Rand Corporation/World Bank seminar on security and development (Santa Monica, CA: Rand Corporation, 2004).

3. Conflict, Security, and Development Group, *A Review of Peace Operations: A Case for Change* (London: Kings College, 2003).

4. Up until 2004, a CPIA rating of three was defined as "moderately unsatisfactory" and a rating of four as "moderately satisfactory."

5. See Paul Kingston and Ian S. Spears, eds., *States Within States: Incipient Political Entities in the Post–Cold War Era* (New York: Palgrave Macmillan, 2004).

6. Francis Fukuyama, *State-Building: Governance and World Order in the 21st Century* (Ithaca, NY: Cornell University Press, 2004), p. 84. See also Michael Woolcock and Lant Pritchett, "Solutions When the Solution Is the Problem: Arraying the Disarray in Development," Paper 10 (Washington, DC: Center for Global Development, 2002). By "specificity" Fukuyama means the ability to monitor a specific output; "transaction volume" refers simply to the number of decisions that need to be made by an organization (p. 56). Central banking, certain health and public finance functions, the administration of justice and prisons, the construction and maintenance of large-scale infrastructure, and the management of utilities tend to have relatively low local variance; political systems, policing, legal reform, education, and social protection services tend to have high local variance.

7. See, for example, Organization for Economic Cooperation and Development, Development Assistance Committee, *Fragile States: Policy Commitment and Principles for Good International Engagement in Fragile States and Situations* (Paris, 2007).

8. Services provided before the conflict may not have been provided equitably: restitution of services such as electricity and water to large urban settlements may therefore not be the most poverty-reducing intervention. However, the benefits, in political stabilization terms, of rapidly restoring a minimum level of service provision in urban areas may be long term, if they serve to reduce poverty and prevent the conditions that facilitate a reversion to conflict and instability.

9. This may include areas previously under active conflict and/or isolated rural areas.

10. International management or oversight is unlikely to be successful in eliminating petty corruption in the civil service. Even if one assumes that a large group of international administrators who are themselves clean and efficient could be recruited (which is questionable), the numbers of staff required to monitor this level of small transaction would likely exceed the benefits in terms of protection of public finances. Effective international oversight aimed at preventing "grand corruption" is more feasible (although still difficult)—since it involves in general a limited number of concessions, monopoly agreements, or the award of major contracts.

PART 2
Cases

9

Somalia:
Governance vs. Statebuilding

Kenneth Menkhaus

Since January 1991, Somalia has been without a functional central government, making it the longest-running instance of complete state collapse in postcolonial history. Over a dozen national peace conferences to revive the Somali state have been launched, including several sponsored by the massive UN Operation in Somalia (UNOSOM) in 1993–1995. None has succeeded. This track record has earned Somalia the dubious distinction of being the world's foremost graveyard of externally sponsored statebuilding initiatives. One peace conference, held in August 2000 in Arta, Djibouti, resulted in a Transitional National Government (TNG), but the TNG faced strong opposition and never became operational. The most recent effort to broker a new central government in Somalia, the Kenya peace accords, produced an agreement on a Transitional *Federal* Government (TFG) in October 2004, the culmination of two years of negotiations and considerable external pressure. But three years after its establishment, the TFG's future does not look promising. The TFG was a stillborn government for its first two years of existence and only succeeded in establishing itself in the capital Mogadishu in January 2007 on the coattails of its external patron, Ethiopia, which militarily defeated the Council of Islamic Courts (CIC), the TFG's main armed rejectionist group. Since assuming power in Mogadishu, the TFG has faced a "complex insurgency" of clan and Islamist militias that, along with a harsh Ethiopian and TFG counterinsurgency campaign, has plunged the capital into the worst armed violence and displacement it has seen in over a decade. The TFG has been unable to establish even a rudimentary administration, remains dependent on Ethiopian troops for its protection, and is viewed as an illegitimate puppet of Ethiopia by most Somalis. Few observers are optimistic that the TFG will succeed in its final two years as a transitional government, a scenario that is likely to produce still more years of de facto state collapse in Somalia.

Somalia is not, however, merely a repository of lessons learned on how not to pursue statebuilding. In some respects, Somalia is at the forefront of an important but poorly understood trend—the rise of informal systems of adaptation and governance in response to the prolonged absence of a central government, driven by the evolving role of coalitions of business groups, traditional authorities, and civic groups in promoting more "organic" forms of public order and rule of law. Recent research findings on systems of localized, ad hoc governance in other zones of protracted state collapse suggest that the Somali experience is not unique.[1] Whether the informal mosaic of local authorities and coping mechanisms that have emerged in Somalia constitutes nascent statebuilding is debatable. But the repeated failure of top-down efforts to revive central government in Somalia must not obscure the fact that significant "governance-building" efforts have made progress within local Somali communities.

In this assessment of the challenges of state revival in Somalia, I review the roots of state collapse in Somalia; attempt to explain the repeated failure of statebuilding projects; track trends in contemporary governance in Somalia and Somaliland; and consider prospects for integrating local, "organic" sources of governance with top-down, "inorganic" statebuilding processes. I make the following arguments. First, I observe that the prolonged and complete collapse of central government in Somalia has produced a uniquely difficult context for state revival. The Somalia case suggests that for a variety of reasons statebuilding is exponentially more difficult where the state has collapsed for an extended period of time. This finding points to the need for more context-specific statebuilding strategies in zones of protracted state collapse. It also serves as a cautionary note that delayed external action to revive and support failing states only compounds the difficulty of statebuilding down the road.

Second, I conclude that although Somalia remains a collapsed state, important changes have occurred since the early 1990s in the nature of armed conflict, governance, and lawlessness, rendering the country less anarchic than before. Contemporary Somalia is, in other words, without government but not without governance. The rise of informal systems of governance and rule of law is driven by evolving interests and adaptations on the part of a range of Somali actors. More Somali constituencies today have economic and political interests in a certain level of predictability and security, and a greater capacity to advance these interests, than in the days when Somalia was dominated by a war economy and warlordism. All that may be producing a political climate more conducive to state revival than was the case in the past, as was in evidence with the broad popular support extended to the Council of Islamic Courts (CIC) when it controlled most of south-central Somalia for six months in 2006 and briefly provided an impressive level of rule of law and public order in the capital. But the downfall of the CIC and the subsequent failure of the TFG to extend its authority could reinforce the public's lack of patience with efforts to revive a central government and increase its reliance on informal means of securing basic security and services. The very success of local adaptation to state collapse could actually impede statebuilding by reducing local incentives to support a revived state.

Repeated failures to revive a central state have been due in part to the enduring "veto power" of spoilers and to risk aversion on the part of political and economic elites who have made their fortunes in a context of state collapse and for whom the reintroduction of a central state poses risks they have, to date, been unwilling to assume. Analysis that pays special attention to the role of shifting interests and strategies of risk management in Somalia are likely to produce better explanations of both changes and continuities in the political landscape.

Third, statebuilding has been and will continue to be a conflict-producing exercise, due to the zero-sum view most Somali political actors have of control of the state. Statebuilding and peacebuilding can and do work against one another in the short term. Statebuilding in Somalia has consistently been pursued via power-sharing accords without serious attempts at reconciliation of conflicts such as land occupation and conquest in southern Somalia, which may partially account for the high failure rate of these accords.

Likewise, the broad distribution of power and the notoriously fissurable, centrifugal nature of Somali lineage politics make it very unlikely for statebuilding in Somalia to come about as the result of a victor's peace and imposition of rule by one coalition over others. "Picking a winner" and backing it as a means of reviving the Somali state is thus not an especially promising strategy, though it sometimes appeals to external actors informed by self-declared "realist" thinking. At least during the transitional period of state revival, a government of national unity is the only option for rebuilding trust and co-opting potential spoilers in Somalia. Unfortunately, Somali political elites—including both the CIC and TFG leadership—have consistently sought to impose a victor's peace rather than accept power-sharing formulas.

Paradoxically, in the short to medium term the process of reviving a central government in Somalia may work against, not toward, objectives in counterterrorism, by creating a "weak state" environment within which terrorists can more easily operate. External sponsors of statebuilding in Somalia whose interests are animated by security concerns must consider ways to manage the long transitional period Somalia will require before it possesses a capable internal security capacity.

External actors—specifically, the United States and Ethiopia—have come to play an important but ambiguous role in statebuilding in Somalia. Both are publicly committed to building the capacity and legitimacy of the

TFG, yet both pursue counterinsurgency and counterterrorism policies that have had the effect of undermining the fledgling government by working through and empowering unaccountable and predatory local security forces. Somalia is not the only instance in which the United States pursues statebuilding with one hand and undermines it with parallel security partnerships with paramilitaries with the other—Afghanistan is a better known case—but it too serves as a vivid example of the need for the United States to address the contradictions between its statebuilding and counterterrorism strategies.

Apart from these broad structural obstacles to state revival in Somalia, practical impediments also seem daunting. One such impediment is budgetary. Statebuilding in Somalia is constrained by the extremely modest revenues a government can secure from taxes. Most efforts at state revival have relied on external sources of funding, which have been unpredictable and unsustainable. Externally funded statebuilding has also created a disincentive to govern, has reduced government accountability to the Somali people, and has tended to promote unrealistically expansive, patronage-based visions of the state that are entirely out of line with Somalia's very weak tax base. Barring a major discovery of energy reserves or other windfall profit to the state, in the near-term a successful state structure in Somalia will have to be minimalist in size and mandate and will hence not be an especially useful tool of political patronage. Real consensus building, rather than mere purchasing of political allegiance and co-opting of rivals, will be required to hold the state together. That makes the task for Somali political leaders even harder.

Given that existing informal and local systems of governance have enjoyed real success and that a central government will necessarily have to be minimalist in nature in the near term, the most promising formula for success in statebuilding in Somalia is likely to be some form of a "mediated state" in which the government relies on partnership (or at least coexistence) with a diverse range of local intermediaries and rival sources of authority to provide core functions of public security, justice, and conflict management in much of the country. Whether this mediated state formula becomes an enduring part of the Somali political landscape or is merely a necessary transitional phase toward consolidation of formal state authority would remain to be seen.

The Barre Regime and the Civil War of 1988–1992

Somalia's descent into civil war and state collapse can be traced to a number of underlying factors that were at work in the 1980s but which only culminated in political catastrophe in 1991. The harsh repression and police state tactics of the government of Siad Barre fueled sharp resentment toward and fear of the state itself in the Somali public. Divide-and-rule tactics used by the Barre regime stoked deep interclan animosities and distrust, and are partially responsible for the failure of clans to unite in a post-Barre government.[2] The high levels of Cold War–generated foreign aid that Somalia earned funded an expansive but unsustainable patronage system and civil service. The subsequent freezing of that aid by Western donors in 1988–1989 led to the rapid withering of a central government left virtually devoid of resources. Funded almost entirely from external sources (100 percent of the development budget and 50 percent of the recurrent budget was covered by foreign aid), the Somali state was a castle built on sand.[3] While complete state collapse in Somalia was not inevitable in the post–Cold War period, a general condition of state failure was.[4]

Indeed, ample evidence exists that by the mid-1980s, Somalia was already a failed state. Most of the institutions of the Somali government not related to the security sector began to atrophy in the years following the disastrous Ogaden War with Ethiopia in 1977–1978. Fierce government repression, heightened clan cleavages and animosities, gross levels of corruption, and low salaries all combined to accelerate state decline. The public school system, a source of pride and progress in the 1960s and 1970s, crumbled. Production on state-run farms and factories plummeted. Government ministries were almost entirely dysfunctional despite a bloated civil service, due in part to chronic absenteeism and cronyism; effective and committed civil servants were seen as a threat and removed.[5] Externally, the Somali state became "a ward of the international aid community."[6] Internally, it devolved into an instrument of repression and expropriation, a tool to dominate political opponents and rival clans, expropriate resources, and above all serve as a catchment point for foreign aid that was then diverted into the pockets of those civil servants clever, powerful, or well-connected enough to place themselves at strategic spigots in the foreign aid pipeline.

After the fall of the government in January 1991, factional warfare devastated southern Somalia. There, an economy of plunder developed, featuring violent banditry by armed gunmen and warfare waged principally over opportunities to loot. An estimated 250,000 Somalis died in famine and warfare, and over 1 million fled as refugees.[7] In the northwest, a unilateral declaration of secession established the state of Somaliland in May 1991.[8]

The legacy of the 1988–1992 period of civil war is profound and disastrous. It includes unaddressed war crimes and deep interclan grievances over atrocities committed; massive levels of stolen property, unresolved property disputes, and occupied territory; the rise of warlords and others with vested interests in continued lawlessness and impunity; near-universal spread of armaments; destruction of much of Mogadishu; the looting of nearly all public goods and state properties; the flight of up to 1 million Somalis abroad; massive internal displacement; and an unresolved secession in the north. This level of destruction, displacement, and division is an enormous challenge to statebuilding in Somalia. Revival of the Somali state must proceed from rubble.[9]

International Intervention, 1993–1995

In November 1992, the United States announced it would lead a multinational peace enforcement operation in Somalia aimed at protecting humanitarian aid. The more challenging tasks of brokering national reconciliation, demobilizing and disarming militia, and reviving local and national government were left for the UN Operation in Somalia, which took over in May 1993. UNOSOM was intended to serve as a precedent for a more "muscular" post–Cold War peace enforcement and nation building. Instead, it was quickly plunged into a crisis—armed conflict with the strongest warlord in the country, General Mohamed Farah Aideed—from which it never recovered. UNOSOM withdrew in early 1995, leaving Somalia still in a state of war and state collapse.

The lessons of UNOSOM's failed attempts at statebuilding and national reconciliation in Somalia are well known and need not be repeated here.[10] The failure in Somalia led to strong international (and especially US) reluctance to engage in "nation building" elsewhere; the entire enterprise of reviving failed states was widely viewed as a fool's errand thanks to the costly misstep in Somalia. But in the haste to write UNOSOM's eulogy, observers overlooked a legacy of the intervention that came to have a positive impact on governance and statebuilding in later years. The large UN operation poured an enormous amount of money, employment, and contract opportunities into the country and inadvertently helped to stimulate and strengthen legitimate business, shifting business activities away from a war economy toward construction, telecommunications, trade, and services. In the process, it helped to reshape local interests in security and rule of law, and eventually local power relations as well.

State Collapse and Governance in Contemporary Somalia

Somalia has since UNOSOM's departure remained a collapsed state—notwithstanding current efforts to animate the Transitional Federal Government.[11] But subtle, important changes have marked many aspects of contemporary economic and political life in Somalia since the early 1990s. Most of these trends are driven by gradual shifts in the interests of key local actors and in the manner in which they seek to protect and advance those interests. The general trend is toward greater interest in improved security, rule of law, and predictability, an agenda increasingly embraced by businesspeople, neighborhood groups, professionals, and even some militiamen, who over time prefer the stability of a paid job in a private security force to the dangers of banditry. The catastrophic levels of armed violence and displacement in Mogadishu since 2006 are all the more tragic in light of the palpable hunger of the population for basic peace and security.

In many instances, these changes constitute potential opportunities for reconciliation and statebuilding. Equally as important, they reflect what could be described as an "organic," local revival of governance. Collectively, this mosaic of overlapping informal and formal systems does not add up to anything approaching a central state—thus it is not necessarily accurate to depict it as a natural process of "statebuilding"—but it does provide Somalis with a modicum of rule of law and predictability in a dangerous environment. However vulnerable these local systems of governance are, they have the added advantage of enjoying a high degree of legitimacy and local ownership, something that cannot always be said of the inorganic, top-down statebuilding projects associated with national reconciliation conferences, which have not only failed but which often undermine local polities in the process, leaving the country worse off than before.

Subnational Governance

The most visible manifestations of subnational governance in Somalia are the formal, self-declared administrations. A quick inventory reveals four levels of such polities—transregional, regional, district, and municipal.

A number of regional and transregional authorities have come into existence since the 1990s, following the termination of the UNOSOM operation. Somaliland (a separatist state in the northwest, discussed below) and Puntland (a nonsecessionist, autonomous state in the arid northeastern corner of the country), are the only two such entities that have achieved much functional capacity over an extended period of time, but a number of others—the Rahanweyn Resistance Army's (RRA) administration of Bay and Bakool regions from 1998 to 2002, the Benadir Regional Authority in 1996—showed some initial promise. By far the most interesting and robust such subnational polity was the CIC's administration of most of south-central Somalia from June to December 2006, an experiment in Islamist rule that was abruptly terminated when CIC forces were defeated by neighboring Ethiopia.

Strictly speaking, most of these regional and transregional polities are or were essentially clan homelands, reflecting an inclination among the Somali political elite to pursue a "Balkan solution"—or, more appropriate to the Somali context, "clanustans." Puntland's borders, for instance, are explicitly drawn along clan lines, encompassing the territory of the Harti clans in the northeast and contested sections of Somaliland. Even authorities that appear to be based on a prewar regional unit are often thinly disguised clan polities. The CIC's brief tenure over south-central Somalia in the latter half of 2006 was a partial exception to the rule, in that the Islamists drew on support across clan lines and espoused an Islamist/nationalist ideology rejecting clannishness. But a close look at the CIC power base and range of territorial control clearly shows that even the CIC was to an important degree a movement controlled by, and advancing the interests of, one lineage—in this case, the Hawiye clan.[12] In addition, though the CIC never expanded its control beyond south-central Somalia, it had explicit national ambitions to govern all of Somalia and in that sense was more an aspiring national government than a regional polity.

Transregional states in Somalia were at their high point in 1999, when both Somaliland and Puntland were operational and a nascent Rahanweyn administration in Bay and Bakool regions looked promising. The "building-block" approach to Somali statebuilding, a policy favored by external donors at the time, actively promoted these incipient states.[13] The declaration of the TFG as a federal government in 2004 again energized regionalized state-building in Somalia.

Nonetheless, Somalis remain deeply divided between centralist and federalist camps, a split not easily papered over in the declaration of a Transitional Federal Government. Those advocating some form of decentralized, federal, or even confederal system claim that only that approach can guarantee to local communities (read "clans") protection from a central state dominated by another lineage. Unitarians, including the Islamists, fear that decentralization will balkanize Somalia, destroying any hope of reviving Somali nationalism and providing neighboring states with ample opportunity to play divide and rule.[14] Among Somalis, preference for either the decentralized or unitarian vision of a future Somali state tends to be closely linked to the perceived advantages the options afford one's lineage. Clans such as the Rahanweyn, which are relatively weak politically but claim as their home territory some of the most valuable riverine and agricultural land in the country, are strong proponents of a federal solution. They view "self-rule" as their only form of protection against the land hunger of more powerful clans. Conversely, the Hawiye clan-family is now the dominant lineage in the capital city of Mogadishu and has come to occupy some of the most valuable riverine land in Somalia; many of its members view federalism as a thinly veiled attempt to rob them of the fruits of victory.

The fact that some variation of a federal system is increasingly viewed as inevitable will set in motion renewed efforts to form or consolidate regional states in coming years. Puntland is the most legitimate functional regional polity in Somalia, but a number of other regional authorities—in Middle Shabelle, Lower Shabelle, Hiran ("Midland state"), the Kismayo/Lower Jubba area, and Benadir (encompassing the greater Mogadishu area)—have been declared and exercise at least token authority over the main town in their region. If these regional states are formed as "clanustans," however, they will trigger conflict and, at worst, ethnic cleansing. In southern Somalia—where, thanks to decades of migration and settlement, much of the ethnic topography resembles the patchwork quilt of a Bosnia-Herzegovina rather than the ethnostate of Puntland—the building-block approach is viable only if regional polities are ethnically heterogeneous experiments in coexistence and power sharing rather than tools of ethnic hegemony.

Unfortunately, the period since the late 1990s has produced worrisome evidence throughout Somalia that localized politics are not necessarily more benign to minorities.[15] Instead, regional and local administrations have tended to be tools of domination used by the larger or more powerful clan against weaker groups, especially in southern Somalia, where a good deal of the self-declared authorities have installed themselves as an occupation force. In Gedo region, for instance, the Marehan clan monopolizes political and economic life at the expense of Rahanweyn and other clans there. The Rahanweyn return the favor by declaring non-Rahanweyn clan members to be "outsiders" in Bay region, even though a sizable population of non-Rahanweyn Somalis lived and worked in Bay region prior to the war. The important port city of Kismayo was for years militarily occupied by a loose alliance of outside clans, the Marehan and Haber Gedir/Ayr, under the banner of the Jubba Valley Alliance, in order to profiteer from monopoly control of import-export activities at the port. The recently deposed governor of Lower Shabelle region, Shaikh Indha'adde, presided over a regional administration entirely dominated by the Haber Gedir/Ayr clan, which controlled the region mainly by military occupation. These anecdotes suggest that at present the trend toward political decentralization has the potential to degenerate into armed conflict and even ethnic cleansing if not executed with considerable sensitivity to local realities.

The political administrative unit that has received the least amount of external support but has produced the most actual day-to-day governance in Somalia is at the municipal and (in Mogadishu) neighborhood level. In the immediate post-UNOSOM period, this "radical localization" of politics tended to manifest itself mainly in informal, overlapping polities loosely held together by clan elders and others.[16] During the second half of the 1990s, these local polities often became more structured and institutionalized. Different types of local polities have emerged in Somalia, but the most common manifestation has been a coalition of clan elders, intellectuals, businesspeople, and Muslim clergy to oversee, finance, and administer a sharia court. These coalitions are themselves shaky, laced with tensions over power and resources. But when conditions are right, these groups can cobble together a modest judicial and law enforcement structure.

Several features of these sharia courts stand out. First, they have been widely embraced and supported by local communities as a means of restoring rule of law. Second, until recently they remained under the control of traditional, moderate elements—the clan elders, businesspeople, and sheikhs making up this system are usually staunchly opposed to radical Islamists. In 2004 a growing network of sharia courts in Mogadishu and the countryside fell under the control of hard-liner Islamists, led by Hassan Dahir Aweys, eventually forming part of the CIC authority. Third, these sharia court systems remained eminently local in nature, rarely able to project their authority beyond a town or district level or to exercise jurisdiction over clans that are not parties to the court administration. They thus offer rule of law within, but not between, clans, though they often facilitate interclan relations. In 2006, the CIC leadership sought to transform the clannish nature of the individual courts by recasting them as neighborhood rather than lineage-based, a risky experiment that was interrupted by the Ethiopian offensive against the CIC. Fourth, the sharia courts have proven to be fragile and very susceptible to spoilers. Where they have succeeded in curbing lawlessness, it has never been via a tactic of direct confrontation with a powerful warlord. Instead, it has tended to occur in areas where the powers of local warlords and militia have already been on the wane for other reasons. Finally, the sharia courts appear to come and go in cycles—following a decline in the 1999–2001 period, the courts were in a period of expansion and ascendance in 2004–2006, but with the Ethiopian victory over the CIC, no local sharia courts were permitted to operate in southern Somalia in 2007.[17] Their reemergence in parts of southern Somalia in 2004–2006 was linked in part to the failure of the Transitional National Government in 2001 and the related rise of insecurity, and in part as a tactic by hardliner Islamists to build an integrated public security and judicial system and an alternative power base to challenge the TFG.

In some locations—most notably, the towns of Borama, Hargeisa, Luuq, Jowhar, Beled Weyn, and Merka, to name a few—the local polities that have emerged constitute incipient municipalities that do more than simply keep the peace via a sharia court. They also have at times managed to provide some basic services, operate piped water systems, regulate marketplaces, and collect modest levels of taxes and user fees to cover salaries. Typically, these successful municipalities have been led by dedicated, professional mayors working closely with local nongovernmental organizations (NGOs), clan elders, and businesspeople. In addition, these success stories usually involve partnership with an enlightened set of UN agencies and international NGOs that are committed to local capacity building and provide much of the funding for municipal projects. In some cases, innovative partnerships have resulted—the management of several municipal piped water systems supported by the United Nations Children's Fund has been outsourced to a multiclan consortium of businesspeople, who have run the water system effectively and transparently as a money-making venture. As with the sharia courts, effective municipalities have enjoyed enormous popularity in the local community but have also proven to be vulnerable to the machinations of warlords and jealous politicians and to the vagaries of clan tensions. Most of the municipalities mentioned above have risen and fallen (and sometimes risen again) since the mid-1990s.

What has emerged in Somalia by way of "governance" since the late 1990s has not so much resembled the "jagged-glass pattern of city-states, shanty-states, nebulous and anarchic regionalisms" depicted in Robert Kaplan's famous 1994 portrait of failed states, but rather a loose constellation of commercial city-states and villages separated by long stretches of pastoral statelessness.[18] In the towns, the sharia courts and municipal authorities do what they can to impose basic rule of law. Across the towns, business partnerships weave extensive commercial ties that transcend clan and conflict across the countryside. This imbues Somali society with a dense network of communication and cooperative relations that are often critical in managing conflict and taking the edge off what appears to be anarchy. The pastoral zones have never come under the effective control of a state, so the collapse of the state has not been as traumatic for nomadic populations as outsiders often presume. There, protection and access to resources in a political world that loosely approximates the "anarchy" of the international system have long been secured through a combination of blood payment groups (*diya*), customary law (*xeer*), negotiation (*shir*), and the threat of force—mirroring in intriguing ways the practices of collective security, international "regimes," diplomacy, and recourse to war, the principal tools of statecraft that modern states use to manage their own anarchic environment. Since the 1990s, clan elders in pastoral areas have at least partially restored their authority and devote most of their energies to managing relations with neighboring clans. Where clan territory abuts an international border, the clan elders have also assumed the role of diplomatic envoy to neighboring state authorities in Ethiopia or Kenya, working out cooperative relations on policing banditry, smuggling, and spillover from local disputes.

These extensive and intensive mechanisms for managing conflict and providing a very modest level of security in a context of state collapse are virtually invisible to external observers, whose sole preoccupation is often with the one structure that actually provides the least amount of rule of law to Somalis—the central state. There is perhaps no other issue on which the worldviews of external actors and Somalis are more divergent than their radically different understanding of the state. For external actors, the conventional wisdom is that a responsive and effective state is an essential prerequisite for development, a proposition enshrined in virtually every World Bank and UN strategy on development. For many Somalis, the state is an instrument of accumulation and domination, enriching and empowering those who control it and exploiting and harassing the rest of the population. These different perceptions of the state often result in external and national actors talking past one another rather than with one another in discussions about the rebuilding of the central government.

Armed Conflict

Evolution in local and regional governance has been accompanied by other important changes in the Somali political landscape, including the nature of warfare. Armed conflict continues to plague much of Somalia, but since 1995 the nature, duration, and intensity of warfare has changed significantly. Until the dramatic explosion of armed conflict in 2006–2007 in Mogadishu, armed conflicts were devolving into more local disputes, pitting subclans against one another in an increasingly fragmented political environment. This devolution of clan warfare meant that armed clashes tended to be much shorter and less lethal, in part because of limited support from lineage members for such internal squabbles and in part because clan elders were in a better position to intervene. Atrocities against civilians were much less common than in the past. Armed clashes in Somalia were increasingly difficult to distinguish from armed criminality and blood feuds. The heavy and indiscriminate fighting between the insurgents and the TFG and then Ethiopian forces since 2006 in Mogadishu shattered this trend and reintroduced a much bloodier and more indiscriminate form of armed conflict into Somalia.

One important reason for the reduction in duration and scope of armed conflict from 1995 to 2006 was the erosion of the power of warlords. Since the late 1990s, the fortunes of most militia leaders have fallen, in part because their own clans are reluctant to provide them with financial support. But an even bigger reason has been the "coup" that leading businesspeople mounted against Mogadishu-based warlords in 1999. In the latter half of the 1990s, commercial opportunities surged in Somalia, vastly increasing the movement of goods across the countryside and placing a premium on security along main transportation corridors and in ports and urban markets. Frustrated with having to pay tribute to militias that provided no security in return (and were usually the source of insecurity and banditry), leading businesspeople in Mogadishu refused to pay taxes to the warlords associated with their clans. Instead, they bought out the militiamen from beneath the warlords and assigned the gunmen to the command of local sharia courts. The sharia militias promptly became an impressive source of law and order, at the expense of the much-weakened warlords. The establishment of the TNG in 2000 led to the temporary decline of the sharia militias, as the businesspeople shifted their support to the TNG. Since the failure of the TNG, the businesspeople have built large private security forces, which they directly control, to protect their assets; these private security forces now constitute the most powerful militias in Mogadishu. For their part, militia leaders who possess independent sources of revenue such as airstrips and seaports (i.e., those who double as businesspeople), or who head up regional administrations where they can collect taxes (i.e., those who double as governors and presidents), have maintained a greater level of influence than those dependent on their clans and external patrons for resources. But none could match the military capacity of their main rivals—the large private security forces of business-people, the CIC militia, and now the TFG security forces.

Criminality

Lawlessness remains a serious problem in Somalia, but the egregious levels of violent crimes and level of impunity associated with the early 1990s are generally a thing of the past for several reasons: the reassertion of gover-nance systems noted above, which punish and deter crime; the rise of private business militias, which protect most of the valuable assets in the country; and the procurement of arms by previously weak social groups (such as the agricultural communities of southern Somalia). Many former gunmen who earned a living from banditry have since demobilized, often shifting into jobs as security guards. The most dangerous street crime is now kidnapping for ransom, which is endemic in Mogadishu. Less visible but more destructive is the "white-collar crime" committed by some of the top political and busi-ness figures. It includes the damaging export of charcoal, the introduction of counterfeit currency, land grabs, complicity in dumping of toxic waste in So-mali territory, drug running, gun smuggling, embezzlement of foreign aid funds, and incitement of communal violence for political purposes. Since 2004, the most dangerous source of criminal violence has been a small cell of Somali jihadists in Mogadishu responsible for dozens or more assassina-tions of prominent Somali figures and several foreign aid workers and jour-nalists.[19] Ironically, in 2006 the CIC drew on some of these hard-line Islamist fighters, known as the *shabaab,* as part of their highly successful campaign to clean up crime and improve public order in the capital. With the collapse of the CIC, lawlessness and armed criminality are again the norm in Mogadishu. In some instances, the chief source of public insecurity and crime are the TFG's undisciplined security forces.

Economy

Statebuilding—whether organic or inorganic—is constrained by the eco-nomic base of the country. Somalia's economy remains one of the poorest in the world. Its productivity is based mainly on pastoral nomadism and in some regions agriculture; both sectors are mainly subsistence-oriented and profoundly impoverished. Somalia's human development indicators are among the lowest as well. The country is heavily and increasingly dependent on remittances, which total somewhere between $500 million and $1 billion annually. Remittances have been the key to impressive growth in money transfer and telecommunication companies, commercial imports of con-sumer goods, the transportation sector, real estate investment and housing construction, and a range of service industries. Nearly all this economic growth and entrepreneurism occurs in the largest cities, worsening the urban-rural wealth gap in the country. The prolonged absence of a central government has meant the private sector (and in some services, the non-profit sector) is generally the only provider of what services are available in sectors like health care and education. The private sector has stepped into many of the functions normally associated with the state, operating sea-ports, airports, and local electric and piped water grids. Sectors in which businesses either see no profit or are discouraged by problems of collective goods (road maintenance and public sanitation are two notable examples) are immediately visible "market failures" that only a revived state authority can address. This "privatization of everything" in Somalia has also created a largely unregulated economy in which criminal economic activity (such as smuggling and drug production) flourishes. The absence of customs taxes and poor border patrols in the region has transformed Somalia into a major entrepôt economy for commercial goods flowing into East Africa.[20] The dynamism and cross-clan collaboration of the private sector stands in stark contrast to Somalia's long-running impasse in formal statebuilding. This dynamism is threatened, unfortunately, by TFG officials demanding extortionate up-front taxes from Somali businesspeople at the main seaports.

Governance in Somaliland

Somaliland provides an intriguing contrast to the prolonged collapse of the state in south-central Somalia. After weathering a turbulent period of political crisis and armed conflicts from 1991 to 1996, the unrecognized secessionist/separatist state of Somaliland has enjoyed impressive successes. It maintains a high level of public security—most of Somaliland is as safe as anywhere in the Horn of Africa. Economic recovery in Somaliland has been equally impressive, with millions of dollars of investments by the Somali diaspora in service sector businesses and real estate; Somaliland has attracted thousands of migrant laborers and hundreds of business investors from both southern Somalia and Ethiopia as well. Somaliland has also built up a modest but functional state structure, with ministries, municipalities, police, and a legislature all performing at variable but not inconsequential levels. The national budget is very modest, typically between $20 and $30 million per year, much of which is derived from customs revenues collected at the seaport at Berbera, taxes on importation of the mild narcotic stimulant *qaat* from Ethiopia, and landing fees. Much of that budget (currently around 50 percent) has been devoted to the military, in the form of salaries to demobilized militiamen. A case can be made, in fact, that the Somaliland government's principal role has been as a large demobilization project.[21] Still, the government has also been able to build functional ministries, a public school system, a respected police force, and municipal governments that in a few instances have been among the most responsive and effective formal administrative units in all of Somaliland and Somalia.

In the period since 2000, Somaliland consolidated its statebuilding accomplishments in a very impressive manner, attracting the attention of even hardened skeptics. It made an imperfect but successful transition from clan-based representation to multiparty democracy, holding local, presidential, and legislative elections; it resolved a disputed, extremely close presidential election without violence; and it executed a peaceful, constitutional transfer of power upon the death of President Mohamed Egal in 2002.[22] In October 2005, the two opposition parties forged a coalition to gain a majority in the parliament, making Somaliland one of the only governments in Africa with "cohabitation" between rival parties in the executive and legislative branches—yet another example of democratic consolidation there. These accomplishments, juxtaposed with the ongoing armed conflicts and diplomatic impasse in southern Somalia, have led a growing number of observers to call for exploration of some sort of recognition for Somaliland.[23] It is, according to this view, increasingly absurd for the international community to refuse to grant juridical sovereignty to a state that has clearly established empirical sovereignty on the ground, while granting recognition to a transitional government in Mogadishu (the TFG) that is unable to exercise authority over more than a few neighborhoods in the capital. Opponents of Somaliland secession hotly dispute the extent of the political accomplishments made by Somaliland, claim that only a national referendum would give Somaliland the legal right to secede, and argue that external recognition of secession there would have far-reaching and negative consequences across much of Africa.

For all its successes, Somaliland has also had its share of setbacks since 2003. Domestically, Somaliland faces worrisome challenges. Internal political divisions between the government and opposition remain acute, resulting in sporadic efforts by the government to repress the media and jail critics. In addition, a military standoff with Puntland over control of parts of Sool region remains unresolved, and many to most of the population of Sool and Sanaag regions express support for a united Somalia rather than Somaliland. Poor performance by the government, including corruption in the judiciary, has reduced public confidence in the state. Finally, five foreign aid workers were assassinated by Islamic radicals (mainly from southern Somalia) in a four-month span in late 2003 and early 2004, temporarily damaging Somaliland's reputation for security, and a rising jihadist threat from Mogadishu seeks to destabilize Somaliland. The Somaliland government is poorly equipped to cope with this latter threat due to lack of resources, corruption, and strong pressures from clans to protect their lineage members from state arrest and prosecution.

Regardless of Somaliland's ultimate political dispensation, however, its accomplishments in statebuilding and reconciliation since 1991 serve as potentially valuable lessons for Somalia as a whole. Analysts are not in full agreement about the Somaliland statebuilding experiment. Some emphasize the critical role played by clan elders as peacebuilders, in demobilization, and in legitimizing the government. Others point to the leadership and experience of President Mohamed Egal as essential in consolidating Somaliland governance. Still others emphasize the role of the leading Isaaq businessmen in financing the Egal administration. Nearly all concur that the level of economic recovery, peace, and public security in Somaliland cannot be directly attributed to the existence of a formal state structure there. In some respects, these accomplishments have occurred despite, not because of, the Somaliland administration. What sets Somaliland apart from south-central Somalia is a very strong commitment by civil society to peace and the rule of law, which serves as a strong deterrent to would-be criminals, warlords, and politicians tempted to exploit clan tensions. Somalilanders often lament the fact that they are "prisoners of peace," willing to tolerate corruption and other political vices by their leaders for the sake of maintaining the state of peace in Somaliland.

There is additional irony in the fact that Somaliland has achieved so much by way of statebuilding with no external recognition and with only modest, perhaps even incidental levels of external assistance. Somaliland serves as a reminder that external assistance may not be as central to the success or failure of statebuilding as international organizations often presume. Some pro-Somaliland advocates actually fear the negative impact that too much external assistance may have on Somaliland. That will be an especially relevant concern in the event that Somaliland does receive some form of external recognition in the future, a possibility that now appears increasingly likely.

General Challenges of Statebuilding in Somalia

It is a truism that state failure is ultimately at the root of many of the security threats and crises of underdevelopment, both in south-central Somalia and in other zones of state collapse. To the extent Somalia is exploited by local and international terrorists, the lack of an effective government provides terrorists with a safe haven beyond the reach of law enforcement. To the extent that economic development requires an effective government to provide a dependable legal and security environment for the private sector, obtain international development loans, provide essential public goods, and catalyze economic growth, the absence of a responsible Somali government directly contributes to the country's enduring underdevelopment, which in turn produces social environments conducive to crime, violence, and radicalism. This analysis has stressed the impressive successes of local communities and businesses in forging informal systems of rule of law, but that assessment cannot be taken to imply that a central government is somehow unnecessary for Somalia.

It follows, then, that any long-term strategy intended to address security and development concerns in Somalia must focus first and foremost on statebuilding and governance. Yet in the short to medium term the process of reviving a central government in Somalia may paradoxically work against objectives in both counterterrorism and reconciliation. In other words, the period of transition between failed state and fully functional state—a category now being referred to in the development community as "fragile states"— poses special challenges and requires a specific set of policies designed to cope with the problems of transition from complete state collapse to consolidated government.

Another general challenge of reviving a functional state in Somalia is that statebuilding has been and remains a conflict-producing exercise because the stakes are so high for Somali actors. The state in Somalia has historically been the primary source not only of power but of wealth—as the catchment point for foreign aid, the point of control of government contracts and parastatals, and the coercive instrument with which empowered clans and coalitions have expropriated the assets of rivals. The repressive and predatory character of the Somali state under Siad Barre left a legacy of deep distrust among Somalis toward the state as an institution. For that reason, though almost all Somalis understand clearly the benefits a revived central government brings, they are reluctant to see control of the state fall into the hands of rival clans or factions. As a result, efforts to revive a central government since 1991 have been viewed as a zero-sum game by Somali actors and have provoked rather than mitigated conflict. This dynamic was evident as early as 1993, when the formation of local (district) administrations by UNOSOM produced sometimes deadly conflicts among communities that had coexisted in the absence of a formal government.

This zero-sum mentality toward the state has contributed to the virtual absence of "loyal opposition" groups in regional and transitional governments. Instead, those who find themselves out of the circle of power tend to become armed rejectionists, spoilers who opt to bring down an entire government rather than risk seeing it used against them. External actors, then, must proceed very carefully with statebuilding initiatives so as not to produce armed conflict; alternatively, they must accept the fact their interventions may produce casualties and in so doing violate the "do no harm" principle that has become such a popular but in some ways problematic nostrum among foreign aid donors. It also means that in the short term, external support for statebuilding will almost never be a neutral exercise but will instead entail taking sides in internal Somali disputes, since virtually all administrations face rejectionist groups.

Statebuilding in Somalia also faces the fundamental challenge of financial viability and the related question of the scope of the state itself. Unless the transitional government secures a windfall of foreign assistance at high and sustained levels—a scenario currently considered unlikely—it will have to operate mainly on tax revenues. The combination of modest levels of foreign aid, a very poor economy, the ease of evading tax collection, and possible resistance by private or regional authorities to handing over control of valuable seaports and airstrips where customs could be collected all point to the fact that the transitional federal government will be forced to work with an extremely modest annual budget. Statebuilding will thus necessarily be minimalist in scope—perhaps even radically minimalist—not by preference but by force of circumstances. The leadership will be forced to focus only on the most essential functions of government that cannot be left to (or subcontracted out to) the private and nonprofit sectors. The small budget will also severely hamper the capacity of the government to use state revenues for political patronage purposes, an important tool in maintaining a government of national unity. A minimalist state structure and a non-patronage-based state flies in the face of the existing political culture among Somali elites and civil servants, whose past experience of the state was as a bloated patronage machine fed by Cold War foreign aid. The fact that the TFG cabinet in 2006 consisted of about eighty ministers and deputy ministers—including, of all things, a minister of tourism—is one indication that the Somali political elite remains wedded to an old, maximalist view of the state utterly out of sync with Somali fiscal realities. Given this sobering financial picture, the natural temptation for the TFG leadership will be to devote its energies toward prospecting for external assistance rather than engaging in the arduous task of statebuilding and revenue collection.

The question of how much external assistance ought to be provided to a newly declared government in Somalia has been the subject of considerable debate, both during the establishment of the TFG and in the early phases of previous attempts to set up a central government in Somalia. One school of thought has argued that without essential foreign aid to "prime the pump" and give the new government the resources to begin operating, efforts to establish a central government will be doomed to failure. A second school of thought has urged that before it pours foreign aid into statebuilding, the international community insist first that a newly established government demonstrate a serious effort to actually govern, pointing to Somaliland as a case of locally supported statebuilding. Both positions have some merit. In practice, what consistently occurs is that a portion of the international community takes a "wait and see" approach, while others jump in and provide aid that is generally not carefully monitored and ends up in the pockets of political leaders. In the case of the TFG, some international groups fear that foreign aid given to the Yusuf administration, without insistence that the TFG reconcile with its most important political rivals and form a more inclusive government, will be wasted on a stillborn government.

Spoilers and "veto coalitions" are another enduring challenge of state-building in Somalia. Statebuilding repeatedly encounters resistance from groups and individuals who perceive that their economic and political interests are threatened by revival of a functional state. One category of spoilers includes clans, factions, or leaders who feel they have not been adequately represented or rewarded in the government and who withdraw from the TFG in anger or disappointment at not getting a "fair share of the cake." This category of spoiler can be managed with astute diplomacy, political bargaining, and external pressure. More problematic is a second category of spoilers who reject the statebuilding project because it poses a fundamental threat to their political or economic interests: so-called warlords who might be marginalized or even arrested for war crimes upon the return of the rule of law, businesspeople engaged in illicit activities, and whole clans who have benefited from armed occupation of valuable real estate during the war.

Statebuilding in Somalia does not enjoy the luxury of poor performance. The new government will lack the military capacity to use coercion to impose its rule; it will lack the financial resources to maintain itself in power through extensive political patronage. It will thus have to earn its legitimacy with the Somali people through performance—consensus building, provision of key services, and accountability. A government that is tempted to transform the state into an instrument of clan hegemony, is indifferent to provision of public security and other key state services, or engages in widespread corruption or predatory behavior will sow the seeds of its own demise by provoking rapid and widespread withdrawal by most of the population. Under current circumstances, Somalis are easily able to resort to an "exit" option if dissatisfied with a transitional government. In this respect, the popular wisdom in some diplomatic circles that "a bad government is better than no government at all" is quite misleading. Somalis make a very clear distinction between "weak" government, which they expect in the short term and will tolerate, and "bad" government, which they will swiftly reject. In this sense, good governance is not so much an ideal goal as it is a precondition for state survival.

A final general challenge is the level of commitment of the TFG political and economic leaders to the goal of reviving the state. Evidence from the failed TNG experiment in statebuilding in 2000–2003 suggests that many political and business leaders supported the *declaration* of a transitional government, but not the actual *establishment* of a functional state.[24] Instead, they approached the TNG as an opportunity to create a "paper state"—one that would attract foreign aid, which they could then divert, but not one powerful enough to enforce laws and regulations that might threaten their economic and political interests. It is worth recalling that the entire business class in Somalia has made its fortune in a context of state collapse; for some, the transition to an environment of state governance proved too risky to accept. State collapse may be unpalatable, inconvenient, and undesirable on any number of counts, but for some political and economic actors who have survived and thrived in a stateless setting, embracing a statebuilding agenda appears to constitute a leap of faith they were unwilling to take with the TNG in 2000. Most appeared even less interested in taking that risk with the TFG in 2005.

Specific Challenges of Statebuilding

In addition to the broad dynamics outlined above, Somalia faces a number of specific statebuilding challenges, some of which will require difficult decisions and have the potential to trigger serious armed conflict.

Federalism and Decentralization

The charter drafted at the Kenya peace talks in 2004 enshrines the principle of decentralization in the very title of the new government, the Transitional *Federal* Government. But little, if any, consensus exists inside Somalia about the merits and meaning of federalism, and none of the key details of federalism has been resolved. Almost all these unresolved issues of federalisms have the potential to trigger armed conflict. The delineation of boundaries of regional states is one example. Will the TFG fall back on the eighteen prewar regions as the basis of federalism or draw up new regions to better reflect current political realities? Many of the prewar regions are poor, remote, and not viable; some are also riven by clan conflicts. But any attempt to draw up new regions (or recognize existing ones such as Puntland) runs the risk of triggering disputes over valuable real estate such as port towns or even causing ethnic cleansing. What is intended as an exercise in political devolution could quickly degenerate into a violent struggle to carve out separate "clanustans." Another challenge is the scope of actual devolution of power to federal states. Some Somali clans—such as the Digil-Mirifle—are forceful advocates of regional autonomy, fueled by resentment of political domination and land expropriation by stronger clans. Others, such as the Haber Gedir/Ayr clan, hail from the very arid and remote central regions of Somalia but now control much of Mogadishu and are understandably fierce advocates of a more unified system of government. The controversy over residency and political rights in Somalia is also linked to federalism. Who may claim residency, property ownership, and full legal rights in regional states? Inside Somalia, a lively debate exists over residency and rights, a debate premised on the notion that clans have "home areas" where "guests" do not enjoy the same rights to representation, power, and protection.

Ownership of National/Regional Assets

Much is at stake in the question of control over tax and customs revenues. Some regions of Somalia enjoy income-generating seaports; others do not. Regions or militias controlling income-generating seaports and airports may be unwilling to see those revenues redistributed to other regions or even to cede control over port revenues to a national government, and may fight to maintain control over what they perceived to be "their" asset. Whether controlled locally or nationally, tax or customs revenue collection capacity and accountability will need strengthening.

Outstanding Reconciliation Issues

The TFG is the result of statebuilding without reconciliation; delegates at the Kenya peace talks found conflict issues too sensitive and divisive to manage and opted to postpone addressing them in favor of moving directly to power-sharing talks. As a result, extremely sensitive issues such as the return of stolen or occupied real estate, political control over towns and regions by military force, the right of all clans to return to live safely in Mogadishu, and the handling of charges of war crimes must now be dealt with by the transitional government. Failure to address these issues will almost certainly derail statebuilding—the creation of legitimate regional administrations in Lower Shabelle or Kismayo, for instance, cannot proceed until the conflicts over land and militia occupation in those areas are resolved, and a government of national unity will be virtually impossible to maintain if long-standing conflicts divide members of the cabinet.

The Role of the Legal Opposition

The TFG is currently configured as a government of national unity, though in reality it is a narrow clan coalition that marginalizes important constituencies. The benefits of unity governments in postconflict settings are obvious, but one of the costs is that such arrangements tend to conflate the government in power with the government as a whole. That does not provide space for a loyal opposition that might oppose the government in power but not the very idea of the TFG. Inasmuch as the TFG claims to be a unity government when in fact it is not, the need for legitimate and protected political space for a loyal opposition is even more urgent. To reduce the rise of spoilers and to deepen the democratic culture and practices of the parliament, legitimate space for opposition groups must be carved out.

Democratization and the Rule of Law

One of the TFG's principal statebuilding tasks during its five-year mandate (2004–2009) is to craft and agree upon a constitution. The fact that the TFG has made no progress on key transitional tasks after three years in power is one of many reasons observers worry about its likelihood of success. The constitution is critically important to Somalia's future, providing the framework for a return to the rule of law, the protection of civil liberties, and democratic governance in Somalia. For example, the constitution must address the structure and principles of democratic representation in Somalia. The current, temporary practice is "consociational"—that is, political representation based on fixed clan and subclan proportional representation. Somalis may opt to adapt the consociational model to democratic practices by holding elections within lineage groups (as occurs in Lebanon). Alternatively, they may opt for the more common practice of district or regional representation. The latter will raise important questions about district residency, district borders, voting rights, and voter registration, all of which can produce conflict and all of which will require a trusted and effective national electoral commission. Presuming regional administrations are democratically elected, these issues will be revisited at the regional level as well.

The Security Sector and the Judiciary
The Somali public consistently cites personal security as its most pressing need and expects improved public security from a central government. Creating an effective and accountable police force and judiciary is a critical statebuilding task, one that will catalyze positive developments in the economy and earn the state legitimacy in the eyes of the public. The challenges to the revival of an effective security sector are considerable. The expense of standing up even a modest police force nationally is straining the TFG's budget. Setting aside the robust insurgency forces in Mogadishu, private and clan militias will in all likelihood continue to exist in coming years and will possess firepower superior to that of the police. To effectively advance public security, the formal police and judiciary will need to establish innovative partnerships with local security and justice practices, including neighborhood watch forces, private business security forces, practices of customary law, and sharia courts.

Though severe financial constraints make the very existence of a standing national army a costly and controversial proposition, it is very likely that a revived Somali state will have as one of its central features a relatively large standing army. If the Somaliland experience is any guide, the army will be used mainly as a means of controlling, paying for, and de facto demobilizing clan militias that might otherwise become a force for destabilization or crime.

The Capacity of the Civil Service
Most members of the trained professional class of civil servants from the 1980s now live in the diaspora, and even though a number have been willing to return to assist in statebuilding efforts, Somalia suffers from very low

numbers of qualified professionals. Especially if the Somali state is to feature a lean, minimalist civil service, the skill level and dedication of those hired into the government will need to be quite high.

The Disposition of Somaliland

In the short run, Somaliland will almost certainly remain outside the statebuilding project of the TFG. In the longer run, however, the status of Somaliland's secessionist claim looms large and at some point risks provoking conflict. If Somaliland succeeds in winning external recognition, it will require creative rethinking about the notion of citizenship in Somalia and Somaliland, possibly including some innovative ideas on the status of the disputed areas of Sool and Sanaag.

The Radical Islamist Challenge

The repeated failures of conventional statebuilding projects in Somalia raise the prospect of a radical Islamist challenge to the secular state. Though the CIC was defeated in December 2006 and its leadership went into exile, ample evidence indicated that Islamists were a major part of the armed insurgency in Mogadishu and retained at least some level of political organization. If, as many expect, the TFG gradually fails, the Islamists are very likely to make a renewed bid for political power. Whereas in 2006 the CIC was a broad umbrella group of moderate, progressive, conservative, and radical Islamists, a post-TFG scenario would likely see the dominance of hardline Islamists tapping into a much more radicalized population. Somalia's hard-line Islamists openly reject any state that does not enshrine sharia and are dismissive of notions of popular democracy and political devolution as Western impositions on Somalia. If the TFG fails, the next major initiative to build a national government in Somalia will likely take on a much more explicitly Islamist tone.

The Prospects for a "Mediated State"

Two political trends have clearly emerged in Somalia since the collapse of the state in 1991. The first is the abject failure of repeated external efforts to revive a conventional central government in the country via a top-down process of power sharing among Somalia's quarreling political elites. Though this track record of failed statebuilding can partially be attributed to myopic Somali leadership and uninspired external diplomacy, it is also apparent that efforts to revive a central government in Somalia face important structural obstacles as well. One of the main obstacles is the extremely weak resource base a Somali state can draw on, a constraint that makes the revival of a large, conventional state claiming "omnicompetence" across a wide range of policy areas a pipe dream. Though insistence on such a state structure is understandable from the perspective of Somali leaders desperate to revive an expansive patronage system and build a capacity for repression—the only means of securing political control they have ever known—it is simply untenable for the near future.

The second trend is the rise of local, informal polities that have, in fits and starts, increasingly provided many Somali communities with variable levels of governance, public security, and even social services. The problem with this mosaic of informal polities is that it does not add up to anything resembling a conventional state and at this point in time does not appear capable of serving as the building blocks for an organically developed state. Local polities in Somalia have remained eminently local. And even the most impressive, functional examples of subnational or informal governance in Somalia cannot perform some badly needed functions of an internationally recognized sovereign state, from the issuing of passports to the securing of loans from international financial institutions.

Until now, Somalia's informal systems of governance have generally been accorded little to no role in external efforts to revive a conventional state.[25] International aid projects have channeled some funds to regional and municipal authorities as part of governance capacity-building programs; some aid agencies have been successful in building up the capacities of civic and professional associations; and a few groups, such as Interpeace (formerly the War-Torn Societies Project), have promoted much greater involvement of nonstate and substate authorities in shaping local policies and reconstruction preferences. But the UN in particular has been quick to abandon subnational polities the minute a national government is declared. The accepted, unspoken wisdom has been that local, informal systems of governance are of little significance, mere variations on a broader theme of anarchy. They are viewed as short-term coping mechanisms to be replaced by formal state authority once the elusive statebuilding project succeeds.

An alternative approach to statebuilding is possible, however, one that combines what is already working locally with what is essential nationally. In fact, this approach may be not so much a policy option as the only viable route to statebuilding in Somalia under the present circumstances. Specifically, Somalia's best hope for state revival may lie in the explicit pursuit of a "mediated state"—that is, a state in which a central government with very limited power relies on a diverse range of local authorities to execute core functions of government and "mediate" relations between local communities and the state. In this approach, the top-down project of building a central government and the organic emergence of informal polities are not viewed as antithetical (though they are invariably political rivals, coexisting in uneasy partnership), but are instead harmonized or nested together in a negotiated division of labor. The nascent central state limits itself to a few essential competencies not already provided by local, private sector, or voluntary sector actors. Central state authorities resist the temptation to insist on sovereign control over social and political realms and entire communities they cannot realistically exercise. For their part, local mediators gain recognition from the state through what today we call "good governance"—effectively providing core functions of public security or other services demanded by local communities and earning legitimacy as a result. Somali citizens retain the services already provided by local authorities while gaining the advantages afforded by a functional central government. A "thin" central government has the added advantage of reducing the threat it poses to opponents of the government in power, thereby reducing the likelihood of spoilers. Over time, of course, if the central government grows in capacity and resources, its reliance on local intermediaries to govern can be renegotiated. The mediated state need not be a long-term solution to the crisis of governance in Somalia, but rather a lengthy transitional strategy.

The notion of the mediated state is rooted in the study of premodern and early modern state formation in Europe, where ambitious monarchs with limited power were forced to manipulate, maneuver, and make deals with local rivals to their authority. Those rivals, notes Swen Voekel, "often mediated state authority, and did so both as over-powerful purveyors of royal prerogatives, as 'private' citizens exercising 'public' jurisdiction, or as members of extra-national bodies like the Catholic Church."[26] This produced situations in early modern Europe that sound oddly familiar in contemporary Somalia—France, for instance, is described as "a nation characterized by parcellized and overlapping jurisdictions, multiple legal codes, and a plethora of internal tariffs and taxes."[27] As such, the mediated state is considered by historians as a major obstacle to statebuilding, a syndrome to be overcome, usually by superior force of arms. Charles Tilly observes that European state formation "consisted of the states' abridging, destroying, or absorbing rights previously lodged in other units."[28]

By contrast, in Somalia—and perhaps in other cases of state collapse—a mediated state would not be so much an obstacle to statebuilding as a promising variation on the theme, or at least the last, best hope for something remotely approaching effective governance in communities desperate for a more predictable and secure environment and the core functions of a central state. In fact, something akin to a mediated state appears to be emerging in a number of failed or weak states in the Third World.[29] Many of the functions normally associated with a central state are now "subcontracted" out to a wide range of substate or nonstate actors. In neighboring Kenya, for instance, years of communal armed violence in lawless border areas with Uganda, Sudan, and Ethiopia have produced casualty levels akin to civil war. The Kenyan government, unable to exercise meaningful control over these badlands, left them to their own fate for a number of years in the 1990s. Recently, however, the government has actively partnered with coalitions of local nongovernmental organizations, traditional leaders, and other civic groups to manage and prevent armed conflict. In some locations, these "peace and development committees" (PDCs) have made dramatic improvements in public security and rule of law, allowing a government that is willing but not able to extend its authority into its frontier zones the capacity to do so.[30]

The notion of a mediated state should not be confused with the neoliberal trend toward subcontracting out state functions to the private sector, though the two practices overlap in some ways. When states opt to contract out functions (such as operating seaports) to private companies, usually they do so as a matter of public policy choice, ostensibly with the objective of providing the service more efficiently. That is the choice of a state authority that "has acquired the competence to decide the limits of its own competence."[31] By contrast, a mediated state strategy is the recourse of a state authority that lacks options. It has no choice but to work through local intermediaries if it is to have even token jurisdiction in an area within its borders. In the case of Kenya, the decision to work with PDCs to help govern and manage the country's lawless border areas was not a choice between direct state intervention or the PDCs; it was a choice between the PDCs or complete anarchy.

Precisely how a formal, top-down state structure can and should coexist with existing practices and structures of informal governance would be a matter for Somali authorities to work out, town by town, district by district. The result would be quite complex and, from a statebuilding perspective, invariably "messy," with a wide range of parallel, overlapping, and, in some cases, contested political authorities. External actors tasked with supporting statebuilding in Somalia would simply not be able to import fixed statebuilding project templates, could not insist on standardized judicial and other systems, and would have to learn to work with local polities in Somalia on their own terms, rather than attempt to transform them into images in their own likeness. That level of programmatic flexibility and local knowledge has not been a strong suit of international aid agencies in the past. This is especially true of statebuilding programs, which are among the most formulaic, unimaginative, workshop-infested enterprises in the entire foreign aid portfolio.

In sum, the problem in Somalia is not that statebuilding itself is doomed to fail; it is rather that the *type* of state that both external and local actors have sought to construct is unattainable and has as a consequence set up Somali political leaders and their external mediators for failure time and again. Statebuilding that focuses as a medium-term strategy on a minimalist state and harmonizing state authority with local systems, rather than displacing them, is much more realistic and likely to enjoy success in Somalia's current context of constrained authority and sharply limited resources. As Letitia Lawson and Donald Rothchild recently observed, Africans "have begun moving away from colonially designed juridical statehood to fashion empirical formulas that respond to the messiness of their current realities. Only time will reveal whether these new, flexible structures prove an effective response to . . . state weakness."[32] In this sense, Somalia could be at the forefront of a seismic shift in the recrafting and reconceptualization of the nature and scope of the sovereign state in Africa.

Notes

1. Koen Vlassenroot and Tim Raeymaekers, "The Politics of Rebellion and Intervention in Ituri: The Emergence of a New Political Complex?" *African Affairs* 103, no. 412 (July 2004): 385–412.

2. Among the many excellent studies of this period, see Ahmed Samatar, *Socialist Somalia: Rhetoric and Reality* (London: Zed Books, 1988); and Terrence Lyons and Ahmed Samatar, *Somalia: State Collapse, Multilateral Intervention, and Strategies of Political Reconstruction* (Washington, DC: Brookings Institution, 1995).

3. David Rawson, *The Somali State and Foreign Aid* (Washington, DC: Foreign Service Institute, US Department of State, 1993).

4. By "state failure" I mean a situation in which a quasi-state continues to enjoy juridical sovereignty but is not able to perform most basic functions associated with a state. Most of the literature on "collapsed states" actually describes variations on the theme of partial state failure.

5. Somalia's state failure in the 1980s closely mirrored the analysis of purposive state failure later described by William Reno in *Warlord Politics and African States* (Boulder, CO: Lynne Rienner, 1998).

6. David Laitin, "Somalia: America's Newest Ally" (unpublished paper, 1979), p. 8.

7. The most careful empirical study of the total casualty figures in Somalia's 1991–1992 famine and civil war is Refugee Policy Group, "Hope Restored? Humanitarian Aid in Somalia, 1991–1994" (Washington, DC, 1994).

8. Somalilanders argue that their May 1991 declaration was a not a secession but a dissolution of union. Their claim is technically correct. British Somaliland was a separate colony from Italian Somalia and earned its independence four days earlier than the Italian colony before joining it as a single state.

9. Most general observers are unaware of the extent to which public goods have been looted. Gravel under the runway at Mogadishu's international airport has been removed in places by contractors for building projects elsewhere; the old Parliament building has been entirely dismantled, its valuable red bricks now serving a new purpose in hundreds of ovens in the city; the largest industry in Somalia, the $250 million Jubba Sugar Project factory, was dismantled and sold for scrap metal in Kenya for $1 million.

10. See, for example, Walter Clarke and Jeffrey Herbst, eds., *Learning from Somalia: The Lessons of Armed Humanitarian Intervention* (Boulder, CO: Westview, 1997).

11. Portions of this section are adapted from Kenneth Menkhaus, "Somalia: State Collapse and the Threat of Terrorism," Adelphi Paper no. 364 (Oxford: Oxford University Press, 2004), chap. 1.

12. For a closer assessment of the CIC and the role of clans in it, see Kenneth Menkhaus, "The Crisis in Somalia: Tragedy in Five Acts," *African Affairs* 106, no. 424 (July 2007): 357–390.

13. Matt Bryden, "New Hope for Somalia: The Building Block Approach?" *Review of African Political Economy* 26, no. 79 (March 1999): 134–140.

14. International Crisis Group, "Negotiating a Blueprint for Peace in Somalia," Africa Report no. 59, March 6, 2003, p. 8.

15. The term *minority* is politically loaded in the Somali context. In its more general usage, it refers to members of "low-caste" lineages, including and perhaps especially "hard-hairs" (*jereer*), who are physically distinct from ethnic Somalis; some of them are descendents of Bantu-speaking slaves from East Africa. In this paragraph, I use the term minority in the strictly numerical sense—a clan that is only 20 percent of the population in one district is a minority there, although it may be the majority lineage in the adjacent district.

16. Kenneth Menkhaus and John Prendergast, "Governance and Economic Survival in Post-Intervention Somalia," CSIS Africa Notes no. 172 (Washington, DC: Center for Strategic and International Studies, 1995).

17. International Crisis Group, "Somalia: Countering Terrorism in a Failed State," Africa Report no. 45, May 23, 2002.

18. Robert Kaplan, "The Coming Anarchy," *Atlantic Monthly* 273, no. 2 (February 1994): 44–76.

19. International Crisis Group, "Counter-Terrorism in Somalia: Losing Hearts and Minds?" Africa Report no. 95, July 11, 2005.

20. Detailed analysis of these economic trends can be found in United Nations Development Programme, *Somalia Human Development Report 2001* (Nairobi, 2001).

21. Kenneth Menkhaus, "Vicious Circles and the Security-Development Nexus in Somalia," *Conflict, Security, and Development* 4, no. 2 (August 2004): 149–165.

22. Mark Bradbury, Adan Yusuf Abokor, and Haroon Ahmed Yusuf, "Somaliland: Choosing Politics over Violence," *Review of African Political Economy* 97 (2003): 455–478.

23. David Shinn, "Somaliland: The Little Country That Could," CSIS Africa Notes no. 9 (Washington, DC: Center for Strategic and International Studies, 2002); International Crisis Group, "Somaliland: Democratisation and Its Discontents," Africa Report no. 66, July 28, 2003.

24. Andre Le Sage, "Somalia: Sovereign Disguise for a Mogadishu Mafia," *Review of African Political Economy* 29, no. 91 (March 2002): 132.

25. A few analysts and organizations have recently produced excellent reports calling for "harmonization" of traditional/informal and formal governance in the Somali judicial sector; this is an especially important topic in any discussion of a mediated state because almost all justice in Somalia is meted out via informal mechanisms (customary law and blood payments, or sharia courts). See Andre Le Sage, "Stateless Justice in Somalia: Formal and Informal Rule of Law Initiatives" (Geneva: Centre for Humanitarian Dialogue, January 2005); and Puntland Development Research Centre, "Pastoral Justice: A Participatory Action Research Project on Harmonization of Somali Legal Traditions: Customary Law, Sharia, and Secular Law" (Garowe, Somalia: PDRC, 2002).

26. Swen Voekel, "Upon the Suddaine View: State, Civil Society, and Surveillance in Early Modern England," *Early Modern Literary Studies* 4, no. 2 (September 1999): 1–27, available at http://purl.oclu.org/emls/04-2/voekupon.htm.

27. Ibid.

28. Charles Tilly, "Reflection on the History of State Making" in Charles Tilly, ed., *The Formation of National States in Western Europe* (Princeton, NJ: Princeton University Press, 1975), p. 35. Importantly, the use of coercion by emerging states in Europe had the essential secondary effect of consolidating actual administration

(as opposed to mere warlordism) over the citizenry, in order better to tax it to finance the war efforts. That salutary political effect of war waging is absent in cases like Somalia, where armed conflict is financed largely by a combination of international funding and pillaging.

29. I am indebted to Professor Michael Barnett for identifying the mediated state concept as a tool for understanding problems of contemporary statebuilding. For a recent work which helps advance this concept, see David Waldner, *State-Building and Late Development* (Ithaca, NY: Cornell University Press, 1999).

30. Details of this experiment with a mediated state in Kenya's border areas are the subject of a forthcoming report by the author, sponsored by Development Alternatives. This behavior by the Kenyan government, due in part to the costs imposed by violent and lawless border areas (decline in tourism, rise in terrorist activities in those zones), is distinct from the more common state response to ungoverned border zones of low economic value, which is to ignore them. Jeffrey Herbst makes a persuasive argument that this form of state negligence is due to the fact that modern states enjoy juridical sovereignty over territories within their border whether they govern them or not, in contrast to earlier periods, when states that failed to control border areas risked losing them to rival neighboring states and empires. See Jeffrey Herbst, *States and Power in Africa* (Princeton, NJ: Princeton University Press, 2000).

31. Wolfgang Reinhold, introduction to *Power Elites and State Building,* edited by Wolfgang Reinhold (Oxford: Oxford University Press, 1999), p. 1.

32. Letitia Lawson and Donald Rothchild, "Sovereignty Reconsidered," *Current History* 104, no. 682 (May 2005): 228–235, 228.

10

Palestine:
Building Neither Peace Nor State

Rex Brynen

A s the World Bank has noted, the Palestinian territories have received "the highest sustained rate of per capita disbursements to an aid recipient in the world since the Second World War."[1] This, coupled with small size (comparable to that of the US state of Delaware), a small and relatively educated population (3.5 million), the absence of internal ethnic cleavages, a popular and well-developed nationalist movement, only a limited prior history of internecine violence, and relatively high levels of development (gross national income per capita of $1,850 in 1999, and a life expectancy of over seventy-two years), might seem to make the West Bank and Gaza (WBG) an "easier" case of statebuilding compared to some others examined in this volume. Yet, no Palestinian state has been established.

In this chapter I argue that major weaknesses have afflicted statebuilding in Palestine. Many relate to the impact and legacies of neopatrimonial politics under Yasser Arafat, who promoted patronage and cronyism at the cost of effective democracy, political institutionalization, and the rule of law. Others relate to the effects of Israel's military occupation, an occupation that did not end with the establishment of the Palestinian Authority (PA). The limited territorial and sectoral authority enjoyed by the PA under the various interim agreements meant that it could only be considered a proto-state at best, lacking in both juridical and empirical sovereignty.[2] Donors made mistakes too. On the one hand, aid was too politicized: political stabilization and conflict management were the clear priorities, and for several years weaknesses in Palestinian institution building were overlooked in the hopes of rapid progress toward peace. In this sense, the apparent demands of peacebuilding and statebuilding pulled in opposite directions.

Conversely, aid was also too depoliticized (or at least, politicized in different ways): rather than confront some of the difficult and highly sensitive issues at stake in the conflict, the international community often preferred to

focus its attentions on the less controversial process of providing development assistance. Yet, as the Palestinian case makes clear, statebuilding is
not simply a technocratic exercise in capacity building, but rather one that
is profoundly embedded in difficult, controversial politics.

The result was a deeply flawed architecture of Palestinian statebuilding. With the eruption of a new Palestinian intifada (uprising) in September
2000, and the failure of permanent status negotiations in 2000–2001, such
weaknesses in PA institutions were sometimes pointed to as the reason for
the collapse of the peace process.

Such a view is overstated, however. The peace process collapsed for political reasons: because of the failure of political negotiations and an escalating spiral of violence. Indeed, it is important to emphasize that *the PA was
not a failed state in the making:* had negotiations succeeded, the structures
of Palestinian governance would have been more than adequate to sustain
independence. Although the resulting state would have been less democratic, less efficient, and much less transparent and accountable than most
Palestinians hoped, it still would have been no worse (and probably better)
than many other functioning third world states and regimes. Indeed, prior to
the intifada, many Palestinians reported substantial improvements in public
services as a consequence of donor aid and PA rule.[3]

Where the weaknesses of Palestinian institutions did make themselves
especially felt was in the extent to which political patronage infiltrated
many aspects of governance, and the corresponding rapidity in which many
institutions unraveled amid the intifada and Israel's reoccupation of Palestinian areas. Moreover, those legacies remain even after Arafat's death in
November 2004, undermining the efforts of a new Palestinian leadership to
move toward statehood and self-determination. Instead, Palestinian politics
found itself overwhelmed by growing political tensions and internecine
conflict that threatened to tear the PA apart.

In exploring these issues, I first provide an overview of the Palestinian-
Israeli peace process, and its implications for Palestinian statebuilding in
the Oslo and post-Oslo eras.[4] Thereafter, the chapter will examine four key
dimensions of Palestinian statebuilding: public finance; the security sector,
justice, and the rule of law; development, development assistance, and economic policymaking; and questions of governance, legitimacy, and public
accountability. It will conclude by suggesting the ways in which the institutional aspects of Palestinian reform and statebuilding may be both inti-
mately tied, and substantially disconnected, from the prospects for Palestinian statehood.

Situating the Palestinian Case

Unlike Cambodia, Somalia, Haiti, Afghanistan, or most other cases of peacebuilding, the West Bank and Gaza have never enjoyed recognized statehood.

Nowhere in the 1993 Palestinian-Israeli Declaration of Principles is the establishment of a Palestinian state even explicitly mentioned—at the time, the idea was thought to be too sensitive within Israel to accept directly or immediately.[5] Instead, the agreement called for an interim period of Palestinian self-government, with a newly established Palestinian Authority to enjoy partial powers over some (but not all) of the WBG. That period would be followed by eventual permanent status negotiations. Statehood was always the presumed outcome, although the geographic extent of that state and potential constraints on its sovereignty were always in question.

In this respect, the Palestinian territories have more in common with East Timor (which underwent a transition from Indonesian occupation to independence under international auspices) or Kosovo (whose current juridical status and political future remains unclear, even if eventual independence now seems most likely). However there are stark differences here in the extent of local administrative power. The PA was first established in Gaza and the West Bank city of Jericho in May 1994, and over the next few years several interim agreements established and extended its power and its territorial authority.[6] By March 2000, the Palestinian Authority exercised civil and security control over 17 percent of the West Bank (Area A) and about three-quarters of the Gaza Strip, exercised civil control over 24 percent of the West Bank (Area B), and had no authority over the remaining areas or any of its international borders. This patchwork quilt of limited powers and territorial control—all in the shadow of Israeli military occupation—has no parallel in any other attempted war-to-peace transition.

Another stark difference relates to the role of the international community. In East Timor and Kosovo the international community assumed a leading role, deploying peacekeepers and assuming transitional administrative responsibility under the authority of the United Nations Security Council. In the WBG, Israel has, with US support, strongly resisted any such international role. The international community disbursed massive levels of development assistance, but it did not assume responsibility for the transitional delivery of public goods of any type (political, social, economic, or security) and consequently was never confronted with the question of how to devolve such responsibility to local actors and agencies. This was true despite the West Bank and Gaza being host to perhaps the largest per capita UN civilian presence anywhere, in the form of the United Nations Relief and Works Agency (UNRWA). Its routine delivery of education, health, and other social services to Palestinian refugees predated the peace process by more than four decades, however, and its future could not really be addressed until a future permanent status agreement resolved the long-standing Palestinian refugee issue.[7] The UN also took a back seat politically. Israeli objections to the appointment of a traditional Special Representative of the Secretary-General led to the establishment instead of the Office of the UN Special Coordinator for the Middle East Peace Process (UNSCO), with a nominal coordination function.[8]

Despite the absence of any prior state structures, the PA did inherit many of the bureaucratic structures of the former Israeli administration in the Occupied Territories, a rich and vibrant civil society, and the existing structures of the Palestine Liberation Organization (PLO) in exile. They were more than sufficient for self-government. Consequently, at no time were international officials embedded in Palestinian institutions, other than as short-term consultants lacking any sort of decisionmaking authority.

Thus, the PA was formed in 1994 by absorbing and expanding the existing Palestinian civil service (some 23,000 persons), which had been run under the Israeli Civil Administration (a branch of the Israeli Military Government in the WBG), with its existing rules, regulations, and procedures. The PLO brought in its own administrative personnel, especially experienced political managers (who filled many of the senior civil service posts in the new government), and the core of the newly formed Palestinian security forces (comprising some 7,000 former PLO guerrillas and administrative personnel). The PA quickly recruited thousands more civil servants and police/security personnel, as well as co-opting significant numbers of the local intelligentsia and professional sectors into senior government positions, thus consolidating its political legitimacy and social control. The PA did not attempt to displace UNRWA's delivery of health and education services, but it extended its political reach in the camps through large-scale recruitment into the security services and civil service and through the sponsorship of nongovernmental organizations (NGOs). With most camps located in or adjacent to urban areas, camp populations themselves increasingly accessed PA services.

Overseeing all the institutions of the Palestinian proto-state was a democratic political structure of sorts. In 1996, elections were held for both the PA presidency and the Palestinian Legislative Council. These were overwhelmingly won by Arafat and his Fateh party in voting that the international community duly certified as free and fair. However, even though he was democratically elected, Arafat was no democratic ruler. Instead he shrugged off legal constraints and centralized power in his hands, exercising influence through patronage (and occasional bouts of intimidation) while acting carefully to avoid the rise of alternative power centers.

Negotiating for Statehood?

The Oslo process envisaged an extended period of interim (and circumscribed) Palestinian self-government prior to the eventual negotiation and conclusion of a permanent status agreement. This extended period was intended to serve as a confidence-building mechanism, allowing the Palestinians to reassure Israel that its security could be protected, allowing Israelis to come to grips with the idea of a Palestinian state in the WBG, and fostering an interaction between the two entities based less on occupation and resistance and more on cooperation and compromise. Most fundamentally, the extended transitional period reflected the reality that, in 1993, the parties were still far too far apart on critical issues (territory, Jerusalem, refugees) to have been capable of reaching a permanent peace settlement at that time.

In practice, however, the extended nature of the intended transition was as much confidence-corroding as confidence-building. The rapid and illegal[9] growth of Jewish settlements on occupied Palestinian territory was seen by the latter as evidence of continued Israeli hunger for Palestinian land.[10] The continued existence of the militant Islamist group Hamas (and other armed rejectionist groups), coupled with periodic acts of violence and terrorism, were seen by Israelis as evidence of a dubious Palestinian commitment to peace.[11] Delay in the onset of meaningful permanent status negotiations further exacerbated such doubts.

Both domestic politics and negotiation dynamics provided little incentive for either side to offer compromises or signal eventual moderation. The Labor Party was assailed by Likud and the Israeli right for weakness, and on the Palestinian side, Fateh found itself in constant competition with the Islamist opposition. Rather than articulating a common vision that might appeal to both societies, political leaders believed it better to maintain a tight hold over bargaining "cards" (such as the fate of settlements or refugees' right of return) that would not be negotiated until the closing stages of the final deal.

Permanent status negotiations began in the spring of 2000, with cautious back-channel contacts between the two sides. Then followed the Camp David summit negotiations between Israeli prime minister Ehud Barak, Palestinian leader Yasser Arafat, and US president Bill Clinton in July 2000. Camp David failed to achieve a breakthrough, however, and instead ended with mutual recriminations. Extensive secret Palestinian-Israeli meetings followed in the subsequent months in Jerusalem and elsewhere. However, they were soon overtaken by the eruption of the intifada in late September, a rapidly escalating spiral of violence, and the political implosion of Barak's own government. In December 2000, outgoing US president Bill Clinton laid out his own views of the center ground between the parties and the so-called Clinton parameters provided much of the basis for a final round of intensive negotiations in Taba in January 2001. They were also unsuccessful, and the following month Barak lost office to a new right-wing Israeli government under prime minister Ariel Sharon.

With this, the Oslo era of the peace process essentially ended. The intifada continued, the death toll mounted on both sides, and most of the West Bank was reoccupied by Israeli forces from April 2002 until the present. During the first four years of the uprising, some 3,000 or more Palestinians and around 1,000 Israelis were killed, thousands of Palestinians were detained, and tens of thousands were injured.[12] Despite the combined pressures of partial reoccupation, widespread mobility restrictions, and severe economic and fiscal retrenchment, some components of the Palestinian proto-state (education, health care) showed remarkable resilience. Many others, however, all but collapsed. That was particularly true of the security sector, as well as the increasingly ineffectual institutions of democratic governance. Israel's frequent destruction of Palestinian security installations, jails, and government offices as punitive or retaliatory targets was seen by many Palestinians (and external aid officials) as a deliberate effort to hasten this political collapse and create a more compliant Palestinian entity.[13]

It was in this context—a context also reshaped by the terrorist attacks of September 11, 2001, intervention in Iraq, and renewed US attention to the Middle East peace process—that several new sets of political initiatives emerged. On March 13, 2002, the UN Security Council adopted Resolution 1397, formally (and for the first time) affirming "a vision of a region where two States, Israel and Palestine, live side-by-side within secure and recognized borders." Subsequently, President George W. Bush explicitly endorsed Palestinian statehood, but made Palestinian reform—and Palestinian leadership change—the sine qua non for US support. In his Rose Garden speech on June 24, 2002, the president called upon Palestinians "to elect new leaders, leaders not compromised by terror . . . to build a practicing democracy, based on tolerance and liberty." He also promised, "If they energetically take the path of reform, the rewards can come quickly. If Palestinians embrace democracy, confront corruption and firmly reject terror, they can count on American support for the creation of a provisional state of Palestine."[14]

Anticipating US pressure and with strong internal support for reform building, the PA released its own "100 Days Reform Plan." Donors soon followed by establishing their own senior-level Task Force of Palestinian Reform, as well as a series of local reform support groups intended to push forward the reform process on a sectoral basis (market reform, financial accountability, ministerial and civil service reform, judicial reform, elections, local government, and civil society). Some conditionality was also applied, especially by the EU and by the World Bank's Public Financial Management Reform Trust Fund, both of which linked emergency budget support for the PA to the implementation of reform measures.

Shortly thereafter, a new, post-intifada vision of transition to Palestinian statehood was unveiled by the diplomatic "quartet" (US, EU, UN, and Russia) in April 2003. Their Performance-Based Road Map to a Permanent Two-State Solution to the Israeli-Palestinian Conflict envisaged three phases: first, the termination of violence, a return to more normal conditions, and reform of the institutions of Palestinian governance; second, transition (originally scheduled for June through December 2003) to "an independent Palestinian state with provisional borders and attributes of sovereignty, based on

the new constitution, as a way station to a permanent status settlement."
Third, all that would be followed by negotiations leading to full Palestinian
statehood.[15]

Despite constant rhetorical reference to it by all of the parties thereafter,
the road map made little progress. The Palestinian leadership was unable
and/or unwilling to address many of the security and reform issues that were
required in the first stage of the plan, and Israel had little enthusiasm for either freezing settlement activity or encouraging any rapid advance to Palestinian statehood. For its part, the international community failed to exert the
pressure required to move the process forward—even assuming that international pressure could overcome the reluctance or incapacities of the local
parties. In particular, US policy soon veered away from the road map, especially in Washington's explicit acceptance of permanent Israeli control of
some areas of the Occupied Territories and its implicit acceptance of some
forms of continued settlement activity.[16]

Washington, as well as other capitals, also lent support to Israeli prime
minister Sharon's plan to unilaterally disengage from Gaza by withdrawing
Israeli forces and Jewish settlements.[17] Despite the absence of any linkage
between this plan and the road map, the international community hoped that
the momentum of territorial withdrawal in Gaza could carry through to larger
future withdrawals in the West Bank. Conversely, most Palestinians feared
that Sharon's withdrawal from Gaza, coupled with continued Israeli settlement activity and the construction of the separation wall in the occupied
Palestinian territories, was intended to help consolidate long-term Israeli
control over much of the West Bank.

Arafat's death in November 2004, and the subsequent election of Mah-
mud Abbas (Abu Mazen) to the PA presidency in January 2005, marked another important development in Palestinian statebuilding efforts. Abbas had
long been a critic of the armed intifada, as well as a proponent of reform
(including during his brief stint as PA prime minister in 2003, when his reformist agenda soon clashed with Arafat's efforts to preserve the political
status quo). His accession to the presidency was widely seen as a boost to
both reform efforts and the peace process. As a first step, he secured the agreement of Hamas to a year-long "period of calm" (*manakh al-tahdi'a*), linked to
Hamas entering the formal political process as well as to similar restraint on
the Israeli side.

Still, the challenges facing Abbas were immense. On the one hand, the
Sharon government sought to delay permanent status negotiations as long
as possible and in any case appeared to hold a vision of Palestinian statehood that likely would be unacceptable to the Palestinians. On the other
hand, political reform and proto-statebuilding continued to be complicated
by both realities on the ground and the legacies of the Arafat era. Widespread Palestinian public dismay at corruption, institutional inefficiency,

and severe economic conditions served to erode Fateh and bolster popular support for Hamas, only further increasing the political pressures on the new president.

It was in this context that, in January 2006, Hamas won 44 percent of the vote and 74 of 132 seats in elections to the Palestinian Legislative Council. Competing as the "List of Change and Reform," the Hamas campaign appealed to a Palestinian public dissatisfied with Fateh by stressing issues of good governance rather than those of the peace process.

Israel, under the leadership of Prime Minister Ehud Olmert after Sharon suffered a serious illness in early 2006, responded to the subsequent formation of a Hamas-led cabinet by halting the transfer of Palestinian customs taxes that it collected. International donors also suspended budget assistance to the PA, as well as bilateral cooperation. Instead, some aid (as well as security assistance) was provided to President Abbas and institutions that he still controlled.

In early 2007, against a backdrop of skirmishes between Hamas and Fateh militants in Gaza, Saudi Arabia brokered an agreement to form a Hamas-Fateh national unity government. It failed, however, to win cooperation from the quartet, Israel, or even local hardliners. Hamas—angered that it had been denied the fruits of democratic victory and fearing a US-Israeli plot to unseat it—decided to strike. In June, its forces launched a rapid and intense assault against the Fateh-controlled security forces, routing them and seizing control over the Gaza Strip. In response to what he termed a "bloody coup," Abbas then announced the formation of a new emergency government.[18] His decision confirmed the emergence of a bifurcated PA, with Hamas and Fateh controlling Gaza and the West Bank, respectively. Israel and international donors responded by pledging to resume tax transfers and aid to the new emergency government, hoping that the contrast between a well-financed Fateh and a poor, isolated, Hamas-controlled Gaza would blunt the appeal of the Islamists.

Dimensions of Palestinian Statebuilding

Public Finance

Palestinian public finance has undergone several periods of evolution. In the initial years following the establishment of the PA in 1994, revenue generation was clearly inadequate to meet the start-up costs and recurrent expenditure needs of the new Palestinian administration. Consequently, substantial budget support was required from donors. Between 1994 and 1997, some $212 million was therefore channeled to the PA through the World Bank's Holst Trust Fund.[19]

By 1998–1999, the PA had managed to balance its recurrent budget. Revenue collection totaled $942 million in 1999, representing an impressive 20.8 percent of gross national product—a level of resource mobilization much superior to that of most war-torn countries. Of this, approximately $360 million were collected by the PA from domestic taxes (value-added, petroleum, income), license fees, and other sources. Israel collected $580 million in customs and excise fees on goods imported into the Israeli-Palestinian customs union and then remitted them to the PA.[20] Although this Israeli collection of customs revenues was a major reason for the overall high collection rate, it was also associated with substantial tax leakages as well as political vulnerabilities.[21]

Despite the balanced PA budget, however, there were problems. For a start, almost all capital investments were financed by donors, and a significant portion of health and education costs were covered by UNRWA services to refugees. In this sense, the budget was rather less balanced than it looked.

More important, the emerging public finance system was heavily distorted by the politics of neopatrimonialism. Arafat relied heavily on political patronage to maintain political control and influence events. Public sector hiring grew rapidly, with the PA employing some 98,500 persons (54,100 civil employees and 44,400 security personnel) by 1999. At 15.2 percent of gross domestic product (GDP) and 49.3 percent of government expenditure, it represented perhaps the highest relative wage bill in the region.[22] Substantial budgetary funds (about 8 percent of the total) were allocated to the office of the president, where they were largely used for patronage purposes. Moreover, many funds never even reached the Ministry of Finance but instead were diverted into accounts under Arafat's direct or indirect control. According to International Monetary Fund (IMF) estimates, approximately $709.6 million were diverted this way between 1995 and April 2000.[23] Many of the security forces also ran their own "taxation" schemes, monopolies, and extortion rackets, both for private gain and because Arafat encouraged a degree of self-financing.

Since the earliest days of the PA, donors and Palestinian reformers alike have made repeated efforts to promote greater accountability and transparency. The first of these took the form of the Tripartite Action Plan on Revenues, Expenditures, and Donor Funding (TAP), signed by the PA, Israel, and donors in April 1995. The TAP committed each of the parties to specific actions. In the case of the PA, these included such measures as bringing all fiscal accounts under Ministry of Finance control and providing more information on the PA's shadowy private sector investments. The agreement was revised and updated several times from 1995 to 1999 and was formally monitored through a series of periodic reports by the IMF. Although the TAP proved useful in repeatedly focusing attention on the most important shortcomings in PA fiscal management, it achieved only limited success in ending some of the most objectionable practices.

A major reason for this failure was Arafat's determination to maintain his neopatrimonial political habits. However, both Israel and the United States also tended to overlook such activities in the interests of political stability. As former US ambassador to Israel Martin Indyk has noted, "The Israelis came to us and said, basically, 'Arafat's job is to clean up Gaza. It's going to be a difficult job. He needs walking-around money,' because the assumption was he would use it to get control of all of these terrorists who'd been operating in these areas for decades."[24] Indeed, Israel directly financed such activities through the diversion of the PA petroleum excise revenues that it collected to a private bank account in Tel Aviv controlled by Arafat and his financial henchmen.[25]

For Arafat, this subversion of public finance was largely motivated by political considerations, not personal greed. Some diverted funds (about $119 million) were reallocated back to PA ministries on an ad hoc basis, thereby bolstering the president's discretionary power. Others were used for dubious but nonetheless public purposes, such as offshore investments and patronage employment.[26] Even as Palestinian anger at corruption grew throughout the 1990s, incidents of bribe paying and similar corruption in Palestinian daily life seem to have been less frequent than in most developing countries, and certainly well below the averages for most neighboring countries.[27] At the same time, many did enrich themselves at public expense.

Over time, pressures for reform mounted. Further impetus was provided by an independent task force report by the Council on Foreign Relations,[28] as well as critical reports by the World Bank and other donors.[29] By early 2000, significant progress had been made on some fiscal management issues.

With the eruption of the second intifada in September 2000, the fiscal position of the PA changed dramatically. Due to conflict and Israeli restrictions on mobility, the WBG economy entered into a severe recession, with per capita GDP dropping from $1,493 in 1999 to $879 by 2002. During the same period, unemployment grew from 12 percent to 31 percent, and the (under $2/day) poverty rate from 20 percent to 51 percent.[30] Not surprisingly, Palestinian domestic revenue collection plummeted, even as the PA budget grew rapidly as it sought to address mounting humanitarian needs. Compounding this, Israel started to withhold tax transfers. The result was a massive PA budget deficit that could only be sustained by massive transfers of international budget support, coupled with local borrowing by the PA and growing arrears to suppliers.

Such fiscal compression had profound political effects as Arafat found himself increasingly unable to fund the pyramids of patronage that he had created. His influence over Fateh subgroups and other erstwhile clients weakened substantially. This fragmentation of political power was aggravated still further by reoccupation, closure, the near destruction of the Palestinian security forces in the West Bank, and Arafat's personal confinement in Ramallah—all of which made it difficult to assert command and control in the periphery. Much of the political machinery of Fateh collapsed into semi-anarchy and a profusion of armed gangs, some of whom threatened or impeded the already weakened or dysfunctional institutions of the PA and local municipalities. In short, the very patronage machinery that had been key to consolidation of Arafat's power in 1994–2000 proved to be a fundamental weakness when conflict erupted.

Israel gradually resumed some tax transfers in 2002, and in 2003–2004 the WBG economy stabilized but made only a limited recovery. June 2002 also saw the appointment of Salam Fayyad, a former IMF official, as PA minister of finance.[31] Fayyad undertook wide-ranging reforms of Palestinian public finance, centralizing revenue collection in the Ministry of Finance, reorganizing PA investments into a transparent and accountable Palestinian Investment Fund, and replacing cash payments to government workers with direct deposit through local banks, thus severely limiting payroll fraud. Substantial improvement was also achieved in the efficiency of the ministry itself, as well as its collection of domestic taxes.[32]

Arafat continued to resist other reforms, however, and PA employment continued to grow even through this period. By the first half of 2003, public employment reached 130,610. In a context of massive recession and high unemployment, public sector employment became a key mechanism for keeping the Palestinian economy afloat—indirectly financed, in part, through (predominately Arab and European) donor budget support.

By June 2004, reforms in Palestinian public finances were sufficiently successful that the World Bank was able to evaluate the risk level in the PA public financial management system as merely "significant"—that is, the same or better than twenty-two of twenty-six developing countries evaluated in the previous year. If reforms continued, moreover, the Bank projected that the risk level would fall to "moderate."[33]

Despite this, the fiscal position inherited by the President Abbas remained precarious. A structural shortfall in the budget (depressed revenues, high recurrent payroll costs) was complicated through 2005 by the electoral success of Hamas in local government elections and fear of its possible success in Palestinian Legislative Council elections. This intensified political pressures on the PA to win popularity through public finance, whether by acceding to public sector pay demands or by spending funds on new social safety nets (intended to offset the effects of Islamist social service provision). Pressures to absorb intifada activists through security sector employment and to hasten security sector reform by retiring old guard officers with generous pension schemes only further exacerbated the fiscal picture. The 2005 PA budget anticipated revenues of $1.058 billion (of which $662 million would be from Israeli tax clearances), and expenditures of $1.962 billion (of which $938 million would be wages and $625 million retirement costs), plus up to $240 million for the proposed social safety net. This left a funding gap of between $904 million and $1.144 billion, or about two to three times the level of external budget support that might reasonably be expected.[34]

This structural budget gap would prove even more catastrophic with the suspension of Israeli tax transfers and international aid that followed Hamas's 2006 electoral victory. For much of the next year and a half, most Palestinian public sector employees would go unpaid most of the time. Palestinian public institutions, already eroded by years of conflict and fiscal compression, would be further eroded by the budget crisis. Donors, having once stressed transparency, accountability, and the rule of law in Palestinian financial affairs, now reversed course. In an attempt to weaken Hamas and strengthen Abbas, they shunned the Hamas-controlled ministries and instead sought to direct funds to Abbas through the president's office, the Palestine Liberation Organization, and other channels. Only with the formation of an emergency government (ironically, led by newly appointed Prime Minister Salam Fayyad) did they once more return to dealing with the Ministry of Finance.

Security, Justice, and the Rule of Law

The Oslo process constructed a paradoxical relationship between security and stability, one that would bedevil the peace process throughout. On the one hand, Palestinian protection of Israeli security interests was a sine qua non for Israeli acceptance of eventual Palestinian statehood. On the other hand, the domestic stability of the transitional proto-state PA required that the authority not be seen as the subcontracted gendarme of the Israeli occupation. Indeed, this perception of Fateh and its policies contributed to the debilitating violence of 2007 that ended a long-standing pluralist norm in Palestinian society against internecine violence.

Complicating matters still further, the negotiating dynamics of the Oslo period meant that Arafat found it useful to maintain some reserve capability to inflict violence against Israel (whether through Fateh or through the continued existence of rejectionist groups) as a source of threat and potential pressure, while Israel found it useful to retain the parallel—and, indeed, much more powerful—threat of occupation, reoccupation, and the structural violence inherent in the appropriation of Palestinian lands through Jewish settlement activities.

The original Oslo Accords authorized the deployment of some 9,000 lightly armed Palestinian police, a number that was later increased to 30,000 under the 1995 Interim Agreement. In practice, police numbers far surpassed this, reaching 44,000 by 1999 and approximately 58,000 by early 2005 (representing around one-third of the budget, almost 10 percent of GDP, and one police officer for every sixteen persons). The vast majority of these are locally recruited, although many commanders are Fateh veterans who returned to Palestine from exile after the establishment of the PA.

Part of the reason for this growth in security force personnel was strategic: Arafat certainly saw more armed personnel as a potential bargaining chip,

as well as a way of deterring Israeli reoccupation. Patronage and employment generation were an even greater motivating factor, however, with the
security services being used as a way to absorb both the 7,000 or so PLO
military personnel returned from exile and a generation of street activists
who had sustained the first Palestinian uprising (1987–1991). The security
force payroll also provided financing to Fateh party cadres and a mechanism
to co-opt former supporters of other groups.[35] Although the security services
sometimes went after Hamas and other rejectionists in the Oslo period, or
even (but more rarely) outspoken critics of Arafat, their primary role was
one of co-option and political consolidation. In order to prevent the emergence of possible political challenges from within their ranks, Arafat was
also careful to create up to a dozen rival security organs under him. This further spurred police recruitment while at the same time severely weakening
the command, control, and coherence of the security sector.

Security concerns and the challenges posed by rejectionists have led to
violations of the law and of human rights by the security services, including
occasional physical abuse and detentions without trial. The PA also established special security courts that swiftly meted out sentences with scant regard for due process. (When politically convenient, Arafat also released
prisoners just as quickly.)

Prior to the intifada, there had been some progress in improving the standard of civil policing in PA areas. In general, however, the security forces
were poorly trained, disciplined, and led. Many were involved in corruption,
extortion, or the enforcement of economic monopolies/protection rackets.

When confrontation erupted with the intifada, some security force personnel were active, as individuals, in attacks against Israeli targets. At the same
time, the security forces failed to halt Israeli reoccupation of PA areas. Security force buildings, equipment, and personnel were among the first to be targeted by Israel in retaliation for violence. Many personnel were disarmed, and
outside Gaza, few could appear in uniform or deploy without risking Israeli
attack. Meanwhile, control of the Palestinian street in many areas of the West
Bank soon passed to local armed gangs, many linked to Fateh (through the al-
Aqsa Martyrs Brigade) but often refusing to obey unpopular instructions from
the central leadership. The rule of law deteriorated sharply.

Although donors pressed for security sector reform, Arafat was unwilling to undertake such measures. Under Abbas, however, the security forces
were reorganized in March 2005 into three entities (police forces, under the
Interior Ministry; the paramilitary National Security Forces; and a general
intelligence agency). A number of senior officers were also retired. With Israeli approval, armed and uniformed police officers began to reappear in the
streets of some West Bank cities.

The process of security sector reform faced serious challenges, however. For a start, despite the formal consolidation of services on paper, real

consolidation was slow to take place. Many services remained loyal to current or former commanders, and substantial divisions between the West Bank and Gaza existed with the command structure. The quality of discipline and training remained poor in most cases, with weak central command and control and lingering loyalties to individual commanders' security chieftains. In the West Bank, Israeli mobility restrictions prevent PA security forces from deploying outside a few small urban areas. Finally, although the thrust of reform was to develop a smaller, more professional, more coherent, and more fiscally sustainable security apparatus, the demands of politics and the demobilization of combatants pushed in other directions. Abbas could ill afford to alienate the rank and file of the services by firing too many personnel.[36] On the contrary, the PA sought to gain control over ex-intifada activists by integrating them into the security forces, a process that further inflated personnel numbers. Similarly, generous pension arrangements for retirees (100 percent of salary) were hardly affordable but were seen as necessary to help thin out older former PLO officers.

The establishment of a Hamas-led cabinet in 2006–2007 further complicated things. When the Fateh-dominated security forces refused to obey the new cabinet, Hamas established its own semi-official paramilitary unit, the so-called Executive Force.

Although security sector deficiencies inhibited (and even undermined) the development of the rule of law in the WBG, they have not been the only source of weakness in this area.[37] The PA inherited a complex and confusing legal environment, with laws variously deriving from outdated Ottoman, British, Jordanian (in the West Bank), and Egyptian (in Gaza) sources, as well as Israeli military regulations. They did provide a functional foundation for both criminal and commercial law, but they were far from ideal. Efforts were therefore made to unify and modernize Palestinian legal codes in all areas. Legislative action was often slow, however, either for political reasons or because of the enormity of the task and the finite availability of technical resources. Limitations on the territorial extent and authority of the PA further complicated matters.

Judicial institutions have been relatively weak, both in quality and physical infrastructure. Judges have also been subject to political challenges to their independence, and there have also been charges of bribery and influence-peddling. In some cases, the executive—and especially the security services—have simply ignored court orders. One World Bank survey of the Palestinian private sector found the judicial sector to be the most poorly rated of all public institutions, with over half of all businesspersons rating it "bad" or worse.[38]

Arafat's tendency to use patronage and cronyism to establish extralegal networks of power and influence, to ignore the Palestinian Legislative Council, and to make his own law through presidential decrees all sent signals that were highly corrosive of legal institution building. This was evident in the long struggle to establish a constitutional Basic Law for the PA. For years after its preparation by the Palestinian Legislative Council, Arafat refused to sign it. When he finally did so in 2002—under much international pressure—he seems to have unilaterally modified a few clauses. Ironically, Abbas—the reformer—would also use unconstitutional measures, when in the aftermath of the Hamas "coup" he appointed his own emergency government in clear violation of the Basic Law he had helped to craft.

Finally, in many rural and even urban areas, formal legal institutions also competed with informal family- and clan-based systems of adjudication and dispute resolution. Indeed, these informal family-based networks often overlapped with formal institutions, such that families could call upon members in the security services or the armed factions to bolster their influence.

The large numbers of active NGOs helped to highlight human rights abuses or weaknesses in the rule of law. However, Arafat in particular tended to see the NGO community as political opponents, and the PA showed occasional interest—although never much success—in bringing them to heel.

External donors sought to address these weaknesses through a myriad of programs during the Oslo era, including support for the Palestinian Legislative Council, technical assistance for legal modernization, human rights training and capacity building for police, physical and technical support to the judiciary, and support for human rights NGOs.[39] Progress was slow, however. Moreover, key donors (more specifically, the United States) seemed willing to overlook abuses if carried out in the name of security. It was by no means a universal attitude among donors, or even on the part of US officials. Nevertheless, there was a sense throughout much of the Oslo era that the peace process trumped all and that the imperatives of peacebuilding were more pressing than those of building the future institutions of the new Palestinian state.

When the intifada began, civil policing collapsed in most of the West Bank and deteriorated in Gaza. Corruption and intimidation became more widespread, and judicial institutions became increasingly marginal. When the police or courts were unable to act, many (re)turned instead to informal mechanisms. As the international community started to place more emphasis on reform, judicial reform and promotion of the rule of law became a key area of donor assistance. Unlike Arafat, Abbas supported and encouraged such efforts.

In February 2005 the United States appointed Lieutenant General William Ward as security envoy, with a mandate to assist the PA in improving security, reining in (or suppressing) militants, and undertaking security sector reform. This mission was later taken up by his successor, Major-General Keith Dayton, in November 2005. However, it proved difficult to undo the legacies of the Arafat era, especially given Abbas's own political weaknesses as well as the broader political uncertainty surrounding the peace process. The failures of both security sector reform and of the security forces in general were amply evident in the fighting in Gaza in June 2007. A much smaller number of (better motivated and disciplined) Hamas fighters quickly routed the larger Fateh-controlled security forces in only a few short days. With that, hopes of immediate security sector reform faded. Hamas moved to consolidate its own position, and some Fateh militants in the West Bank went on a rampage against Hamas-aligned institutions.

Development, Development Assistance, and Economic Policymaking

From the outset, both the PA and donors alike recognized that a robust Palestinian economy would be a critical element of the transition to Palestinian statehood, both by legitimizing the transitional process (and the PA itself) and by providing a base for long-term sustainable development of the new state. Their efforts were shaped, however, by several important sets of constraints.

Constraints on economic policymaking.   First, the PA itself has never exercised real economic sovereignty. Rather, it has enjoyed only circumscribed economic powers, which were gradually expanded during the Oslo era through the various interim agreements. In particular, the 1994 Paris protocol prevented the PA from issuing its own currency (thus tying the WBG economy to Israeli price structures) and locked it into customs union with Israel (making it dependent on Israeli revenue collection and starkly limiting its control over trade and tariff policy). There were, admittedly, solid economic arguments that could be made for both of these provisions.[40] However, as with most elements of Palestinian-Israeli economic relations, political calculations triumphed: Israel was unwilling to allow the interim PA the statelike symbolism of its own currency, and the absence of agreed Palestinian-Israeli borders made it difficult to envisage any trade regime other than a customs union.[41]

Second, there were no institutions of Palestinian economic policymaking prior to the establishment of the PA. The functions of many new PA ministries and institutions were poorly demarcated (for example, between the Palestinian Economic Council for Development and Reconstruction, the Ministry of Economy, and the Ministry of Planning). Turf fights and inefficiencies were common, especially in the early years. Weaker sectoral ministries (such as agriculture or housing) tended to have little impact on the formulation of Palestinian development plans. Stronger ministries (such as education and health) tended to go their own way. Although the PA produced a series of development plans, many looked more like shopping lists than statements of a prioritized and integrated development strategy. Moreover, it was difficult to engage in any long-term planning when the PA could predict neither the immediate effects and fluctuations of Israeli closure policy nor the ultimate territorial extent of a future Palestinian state.

Third, and most important of all, were the economic legacies of occupation. Israel had done little to create a coherent development vision for the WBG after its occupation of the area in 1967. Moreover, the Palestinian economy was (and continues to be) highly dependent on Israel. Prior to the Oslo agreement, over 85 percent of the WBG's exports went to Israel, and 89 percent of its imports came from there. More than 100,000 Palestinians also worked in Israel daily, representing about one-quarter of the employed labor force in 1991.[42]

This dependence would have devastating economic consequences in the context of Israeli security measures. Increasingly through the Oslo years, Israel responded to acts of rejectionist violence by limiting the mobility of goods and persons between and within the West Bank and Gaza ("closure") and by curtailing the number of Palestinian workers within Israel. This depressed economic growth through much the 1990s, especially during periods of intense closure in 1996.[43] The economy began recovering toward the late 1990s, but only returned to pre-Oslo levels by 1999. With the eruption of the intifada, these measures were intensified: labor flows to Israel dropped to a trickle, scores of checkpoints and roadblocks slowed or prevented internal movement in the West Bank, West Bank/Gaza linkages grew ever more difficult, and Palestinian exports were further constrained by delays and security inspections. As noted earlier, this led to a sharp drop in per capita income and dramatic increases in unemployment and poverty, in what the World Bank characterized as "one of the deepest recessions in modern history."[44] Although education and health services were more or less maintained despite extraordinarily difficult conditions, other PA institutions all but collapsed under the strain.

This, in turn, had political consequences. Palestinian public resentment grew, directed at both the PA for its policy failures and at much of the "old guard" elite for their perceived corruption and inefficiency. As a result, support for militant opposition groups (most notably Hamas) grew not only in reaction to Israeli occupation but also in response to the perceived failures of Fateh and the Palestinian Authority.

The role of the international community. From the outset of the peace process, donors "agreed that to help transform the Declaration of Principles into an enduring agreement, the Palestinians needed to see the tangible benefits of peace."[45] General improvement in the standard of living, it was hoped, would reduce the risk of dissident violence, stabilize the interim period, and promote a positive environment for permanent status negotiations. The usual developmental priorities of aid agencies—poverty alleviation, child welfare, capacity building, environmental concerns, gender equity, or economic policy reform—shaped many aid interventions. So too did more explicitly political objectives, such as fostering potential areas of shared Israeli-Palestinian common interest (e.g., water management) or building the institutional foundations for eventual statehood. The language of statebuilding was almost completely absent from donor discourse, however, since the issue had yet to be formally resolved through Israeli-Palestinian negotiation. A major assessment of donor efforts written by the World Bank on behalf of the entire aid community in June 2000, for example, does not mention statebuilding at all, but rather makes vague and euphemistic references to "the development of Palestinian institutions of self-governance."[46]

Nevertheless, the sheer volume of assistance to the West Bank and Gaza has been almost unparalleled in international peacebuilding and statebuilding, totaling around $8 billion (for up to 3.8 million Palestinians in the WBG) between 1994 and 2004, or over $2,000 per capita during this period. Over time, however, the volume and composition of aid has changed substantially (Figure 10.1). Annual assistance was a little over $500 million per year during the Oslo era but later rose to over twice that amount since the eruption of the intifada in late September 2000. In 1994–1995, a significant proportion of aid went to support the institutional start-up costs of the PA, as well as transitional budget needs. That proportion began to decline, although the intensification of Israeli closure policy in 1996–1997 cut PA revenues and required some additional emergency budget aid (including some emergency job creation funds). With the start of the second intifada, the PA once more required budgetary life support. It also required, for the first time, a substantial influx of humanitarian assistance as malnutrition rates began to climb.

It is difficult to disaggregate how much aid went to Palestinian statebuilding (that is, support for building governmental capacity) versus other development needs (such as NGOs, economic infrastructure, or other sectors). According to the PA, approximately 22 percent of all donor investment during the Oslo period was directed toward institution building, which was considerably more than the 8–10 percent typically called for in various Palestinian development plans.[47] Institutional and statebuilding issues were given a boost in June 2002, when US president Bush called for Palestinian reform and leadership change, and the PA unveiled its own reform program. It is unclear, however, what level of assistance these reform efforts have received and whether it differs markedly from the pre-intifada levels. In any case, interest in statebuilding effectively stopped in January 2006, when the focus of US policy shifted to undermining the democratically elected Hamas government.

Well over forty bilateral donors have been involved in supporting statebuilding and development in the WBG, together with international financial

Figure 10.1 Donor Assistance to the WBG, 1994–2002

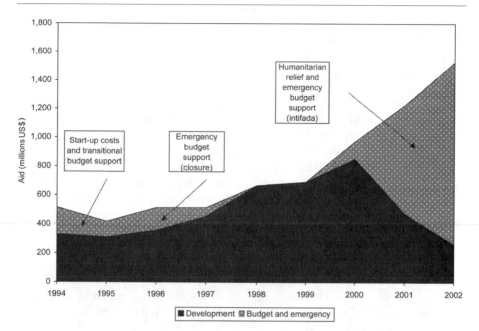

Sources: World Bank, *Aid Effectiveness in the West Bank and Gaza* (Washington, DC, June 2000); World Bank, *Twenty-Seven Months—Intifada, Closures, and Palestinian Economic Crisis: An Assessment* (Washington, DC, May 2003); Stephen Lister and Ann Le More, *Aid Management and Coordination During the Intifada* (Oxford: Mokoro, 2003).

institutions, dozens of UN agencies, and many scores of NGOs. The EU and United States accounted for by far the largest share, together with the post-intifada budget support from the Arab League.

The coordination mechanisms that have emerged to support donor engagement have been complex but relatively efficient by global standards. They comprised a complex series of interlinked coordination groups with varying membership, operating at both the headquarters and field levels.[48] Later, this original structure was overwritten by the establishment of emergency coordination structures (developed to deal with the immediate needs of intifada-related relief efforts), as well as a short-lived Task Force on Palestinian Reform and a number of reform support groups (to support reform efforts). Pooled funds flowing through multilateral channels represented another, implicit form of donor coordination. In practice, only 10–20 percent of donor aid to the WBG probably flowed through the World Bank, UN agencies, or other multilaterals during the Oslo era.[49]

Two problematic aspects of donor assistance in the WBG have been the degree of host ownership of the development process and the extent to which donor assistance distorted local institutional development. Donors often seemed to play the leading role in setting aid priorities, doing so either unconsciously or citing Palestinian inefficiencies as a reason for weak PA input. At times, the complexity and multiplicity of coordination mechanisms, coupled with the large number of bilateral and multilateral donors active in the WBG, could overwhelm weak Palestinian institutions, further limiting their role in effectively shaping Palestinian development priorities.

Donors also tended to flock to the robust, well-run ministries (such as health and education) and municipalities (Gaza, Ramallah, Nablus) rather than more problematic or lower-capacity partners (such as the Ministry of Agriculture or smaller towns and village councils). This created a statebuilding catch-22 whereby weak ministries received the least help. Donor support could also distort bureaucratic growth, with the development of bureaucratic units and technical capacities often being driven by the supply of donor aid for salaries or the provision of externally financed consultants in a given area, rather than by Palestinian assessment of need. Publicly, Palestinian officials praised technical assistance from donors, hoping that such positive words would bring more aid; privately, many were very critical of the quality and relevance of the help that they were given.[50] They also often lamented what they saw as an excessive volume of technical assistance (over a quarter of all donor assistance in the pre-intifada period), compared to the provision of infrastructure investments.[51]

It is important to recognize that such problems are not unique to the WBG, however. On the contrary, most are common to official development assistance, especially in conflict areas. In general, donor assistance to Palestine was of high quality, and overall the aid process probably ran more smoothly than in almost any other comparable case.[52] To the extent that donors erred in supporting Palestinian statebuilding during the Oslo era, it was not in the way that technical assistance and support for capacity building were provided, even if substantial room for improvement existed. Rather, donors failed in their frequent unwillingness to confront the parties on key issues such as problems of Palestinian patronage and governance or continued Israeli settlement construction. The difficult challenges of statebuilding—and with it, ending Israeli occupation of the Palestinian territories—cannot be addressed with technocratic aid efforts. Political engagement is key.

Gaza Disengagement: Past as Prelude

After 2004, the dynamics of Palestinian development and economic policymaking were altered by Israel's decision to withdraw from the Gaza Strip and parts of the northern West Bank. Gaza disengagement also underscored the importance of correctly understanding past mistakes of the Oslo era.

Proponents of disengagement hailed it as an opportunity for the Palestinians to prove that they were able to run a statelike administration, as well as a possible prelude to further Israeli territorial withdrawals. Although welcoming the withdrawal of approximately 7,000 Israeli settlers, however, the PA was deeply suspicious of the move. First, the plan called for Israel to retain direct or indirect control of Gaza's airspace, seas, and borders for an indefinite period—essentially maintaining many aspects of the occupation. Second, the PA was understandably concerned that there would be no corresponding withdrawals in the West Bank and that Sharon hoped to leave the Palestinians with little more than a Bantustan-like quasi-state in Gaza and isolated West Bank cantons (excluding Jerusalem).

In support of disengagement, the World Bank undertook a series of analytical studies in 2004, which stressed that the sustainability of Gaza would depend on an improved security situation, continued Palestinian reform, but most importantly on improved access to the West Bank and the rest of the world.[53] Although Israeli disengagement from Gaza did present new opportunities, they were ultimately squandered. Israeli mobility restrictions continued to smother prospects for sustainable economic growth, and at the same time Israel continued to consolidate its territorial control in the West Bank. The PA failed to press forward political and institutional reform. Radicals continued to engage in periodic violence. The quartet, and especially the United States, failed to advance any sort of credible diplomatic plan for addressing the core political issues in the conflict. The ultimate result was the growth of radical Islamist influence, internecine conflict between Hamas and Fateh, and the eventual emergence of rival "Hamastan" (Hamas-controlled Gaza) and "Fatehland" (in the West Bank) amid the near collapse of the PA altogether.

Legitimacy, Governance, and Public Accountability

Questions of legitimacy and Palestinian statebuilding can be seen from two perspectives: the legitimacy of the negotiation process with Israel that was to give birth to a Palestinian state and the legitimacy of the institutions of governance established in the interim period. *Moreover, the two are also dialectically interlinked, affecting each other.*

The Oslo peace process was largely negotiated and conducted behind closed doors. Indeed, the rationale for (and success of) the original Oslo backchannel lay precisely in the difficulty of reaching agreement in the much more public Palestinian-Israeli negotiations held in Washington in 1992–1994 under the official auspices of the Madrid peace process.[54] Even after the Declaration of Principles, negotiations on the various interim agreements remained the purview of Palestinian officials and usually occurred without public notice of their likely contents or any systematic input from either the Fateh rank and file, civil society, or (after its establishment in 1996) the Palestinian Legislative Council.

Did the lack of inclusion delegitimize the process? It may have, and civil society and opposition groups criticized the Palestinian leadership for exactly that. Some constituencies—notably Palestinian refugees—grew increasingly suspicious as to what the negotiators, and negotiations, might have in store for them. Palestinian public support for a negotiated two-state solution to the conflict remained high, however, even after the eruption of the intifada and collapse of the peace process. Indeed, polls repeatedly suggested that Palestinian public support for the peace process was just as strong as (and sometimes stronger than) Israeli public support, despite the arguably more open political process in the latter.[55]

Leaving aside the issues of legitimacy, inclusion, and the peace process, what about the broader question of constructing participatory institutions in the WBG that could act as the foundations for a future democratic Palestinian state? The WBG enjoyed the preexisting strengths of a relatively diverse and vibrant civil society, multiple political parties, high levels of education, and years of exposure to the tumult of Israeli democratic politics. Popular support for democratic values and practices was high.[56]

Democratic elections for the presidency and Palestinian Legislative Council were called for in the interim agreements and were held in 1996 under rules that magnified Fateh's preexisting strength but nonetheless made for a reasonably accurate reflection of public opinion. Some non-Fateh groups and many independents participated, but the main secular/left party (Popular Front for the Liberation of Palestine) and the Islamist opposition (Hamas) boycotted the polls, both out of opposition to the Oslo process and out of a more cynical calculation that they would fare badly at the ballot box in any case. Up to the 2006 elections won by Hamas, donors generously supported the development of the council and continued to provide substantial levels of support to Palestinian civil society groups.

The results were mixed, however. Much of the mid- and upper-level Palestinian leadership was suspicious of genuine grassroots participation, seeing it either as a constraint on their political freedom of action or as a threat to their power. Arafat himself circumvented the authority of the Palestinian Legislative Council whenever it suited him, variously refusing to sign duly passed legislation or issuing executive decrees or informal orders that essentially circumvented the quasi-constitutional order. None of that enhanced the reputation of the council, which (like other Palestinian official institutions) suffered further in public opinion as it proved unable to deal with the challenges of the intifada, reoccupation, the breakdown of security and many public services, economic collapse, and the fading prospect of peace negotiations.

Structures of administration suffered as much as did structures of democracy. *Wasta*—the politics of patronage and political/personal connections—undermined appointments and promotions based on qualifications and merit, rather than political allegiance or kinship, and burdened the PA with a massive public sector payroll. It exacerbated a marked reluctance to develop organizational plans, recruitment criteria and targets, and job descriptions for PA ministries and agencies. Underlying and overshadowing everything was

Arafat's personal style of neopatrimonial management, which combined concentration of bureaucratic and financial powers in his hands with excessive micromanagement. This undermined institution building and the development of administrative routine and procedure in all branches of government. The PA was therefore less a *system* of government, a set of functionally differentiated but coordinated agencies, than a collection of multiple, nominal structures formally designated as "ministries" and inflated with bloated payrolls but rarely, if ever, held to account for actual performance. Arafat's success in marginalizing the Palestinian Legislative Council and circumventing the justice system removed any countervailing force within government, both perpetuating and deepening the problem. Similarly, oversight institutions, both official (such as the PA's supposed financial oversight body, the General Control Institute) and civic (such as the local press) generally did a poor job of providing independent information and analysis of either public accounts or administrative performance.

Eventually, it all proved highly delegitimizing for the entire PA, with the credibility of the Palestinian administration dropping in tandem with growing public concern at the lack of public accountability and transparency (see Figure 10.2). By September 2004, polls showed that no public institution enjoyed a positive appraisal of its performance by the public: not the Palestinian Legislative Council (30 percent), the PA cabinet (33 percent), security services (35 percent), judiciary (39 percent), nor the presidency (42 percent). Fully 88 percent of Palestinians believed that corruption existed within the PA, only 29 percent offered a positive evaluation of Palestinian democracy, and 93 percent supported calls for political reform.[57]

Issues of legitimacy would loom large in the mounting political chaos that slowly overwhelmed the PA in 2006–2007. However objectionable its political views and support for violence, Hamas had clearly won the 2006 legislative elections. Yet, despite that victory, Fateh, Israel, and the international community alike seemed determined to isolate and undermine the Islamists with the aim of driving them from power. For many Palestinians, it was the height of hypocrisy. It certainly did little to boost Fateh's credibility while further radicalizing many Hamas supporters.

Conclusion

It is possible to engage in an almost endless series of "what ifs" about the Palestinian-Israeli negotiating process, most of which lie outside the scope of this chapter. What if the election of Israeli prime minister Benjamin Netanyahu in 1996, and Ehud Barak's later pursuit of the Syrian track in 1999–2000, hadn't delayed serious Palestinian-Israeli permanent status negotiations? What if publics on both sides had been better prepared for the compromises that they would have to make to secure peace? What if there had been better preparation and initial negotiations for the July 2000 Camp

Figure 10.2 Trends in Public Assessments of Accountability, Transparency, and PA Approval

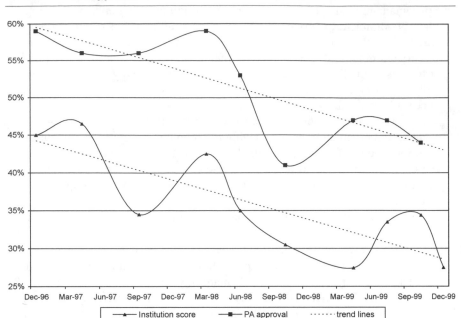

Source: World Bank, *Aid Effectiveness in the West Bank and Gaza* (Washington, DC, June 2000), Figure 3.25.

Note: The "institution score" represents an amalgam measure of accountability (democracy and respect for human rights) and transparency (perceptions of PA corruption). PA approval reflects the approval rating of the PA cabinet.

David summit? What if Arafat had responded more creatively to US and Israeli positions at Camp David? What if Israeli settlement activity had not continued, or Ariel Sharon hadn't made his provocative visit to Haram al-Sharif/the Temple Mount in September 2000? What if Arafat had actively discouraged intifada violence instead of passively encouraging it? What if Barak had a stronger coalition base, or a new US administration had maintained American commitment to the so-called Clinton parameters? A review of missteps by the United States, Israel, and the Palestinians alike makes it hard to escape the conclusion that, with different decisions, peace and statehood were within reach in 1999–2001.[58]

In any case, and as noted at the outset, the PA was hardly a failed state (in the making) in the period between its inauguration in July 1994 and the start of the al-Aqsa intifada in September 2000. The statebuilding process was marred by a number of internal flaws, but they were for the most part avoidable. Rather, the critical context for the weaknesses of Palestinian (proto-)statebuilding was the unresolved political and territorial dispute with Israel and the manner in which it was handled by the PA, Israel, the United States, and other members of the international community.

The PA indisputably bore direct and primary responsibility for the inherent weaknesses of its system of government. Among the most serious problems was uncontrolled and haphazard hiring in the public sector, driven in large part by Arafat's desire to exercise widespread political patronage and in part by cronyism in his close circle and tolerated more widely within the PA and society as a means of addressing unemployment.

However, Israeli policy also played a direct part in weakening Palestinian statebuilding during the Oslo era of 1994–2000 and subsequently became a primary factor in fostering a near collapse of the PA through its withholding of tax transfers and its targeting of Palestinian infrastructure during the intifada. Israeli actions (notably settlement construction) also delegitimized the broader peace process, helping (along with Arafat's own strategy and tactics) to set the stage for the collapse of negotiations and the onset of the intifada.

It is within this framework that the role of the international community should be assessed. The international community, finally, had limited impact on Palestinian statebuilding in the Oslo era, in part, ironically, because of the high premium it placed on the peace process. That is, its interest in seeing the peace process take root and progress was such that it was willing to tolerate tacitly the more retrograde practices and trends of the PA and its head and also to focus on compensating the Palestinians, especially financially, for the negative effects of Israeli policies and measures rather than confront Israel frankly over its actions. Support for statebuilding was therefore reduced to mainly technical assistance and capacity building. To the extent that peacebuilding and statebuilding were necessarily linked—and indeed often portrayed as such by the international community to justify focusing political efforts and financial investments on one or the other—the link was in practice ignored. When the demands of peacebuilding and statebuilding seemed in contradiction, external actors often seemed to tilt to the former—and in doing so, paid little attention to the trade-offs involved. The problem, therefore, was neither the insufficiency of international technical or financial assistance nor the inadequacy of policy advice in regard to legislation, the economy, or social policy, but rather the failure to tackle the core political faults of both PA and Israeli policies. Assistance to the PA failed to buy the international community critical leverage with respect to domestic governance or negotiations with Israel, any more than it was able to influence Israel by avoiding a head-on confrontation over settlements and collective punishments.

Today, the process of Palestinian statebuilding seems more difficult and distant than ever. The Palestinian Authority has been torn asunder by the conflict between a discredited Fateh and a rising Hamas. In this context, the best that can be done for a while may be to work to preserve the institutions of potential statehood from further harm and reform some of the most egregious weaknesses in the fractured PA, while turning priority attention to the key *political* issues that stand in the way of reestablishing a meaningful peace process. Since the Islamist challenge will not simply evaporate, working to moderate Hamas and to find a new modus vivendi between Fateh and Hamas is one such task. Regional actors need to articulate a clear and appealing vision of a two-state solution, possibly building on the Arab League's "Beirut Declaration" of March 2002.[59] The international community, and especially the United States, need to spell out the broad parameters of an acceptable negotiated outcome, possibly based on the December 2000 Clinton parameters. Israel needs to stop actions, such as illegal settlement activity and excessive mobility restrictions and security measures, that lessen the prospects for peace. The danger is that, as in the past, the "easy road" of aid and technical assistance will be pursued, rather than (and almost as a substitute for) the more challenging path of pushing the parties toward a political solution.[60]

Paradoxically (given the focus of this book) for now, the imperatives of diplomacy trump processes of statebuilding. The latter can even serve as something of a distraction from the former. Yet this in no way means that statebuilding will not eventually be an essential element of peacebuilding in Palestine. Indeed, without a Palestinian state and without addressing the political and national aspirations of an occupied and dispersed Palestinian people, it is hard to imagine how peace can ever be achieved.

Notes

1. World Bank, *Four Years—Intifada, Closures, and Palestinian Economic Crisis: An Assessment* (Washington, DC, 2004), p. 64.
2. See Chapter 1 in this volume on the distinction between juridical sovereignty and empirical sovereignty. Although the literature has paid considerable attention to entities that possess the former and lack the latter ("quasi-states"), Palestine is unusual in having a political administration that lacks both but is intended—somehow, sometime—to achieve them.
3. A 1999 public opinion survey conducted for the World Bank found Palestinians reporting significant improvements in education, roads, solid waste disposal, and health care. Conversely, the evaluation of PA institutions was mixed, and that of the rule of law was negative. World Bank, *Aid Effectiveness in the West Bank and Gaza* (Washington, DC, 2000), p. 66.
4. The Palestinian Authority has been afflicted by considerable political instability and uncertainty since the 2006 Palestinian Legislative Council elections. Consequently, it is harder to draw conclusions about developments in 2006–2007, and less attention will be devoted to this period.
5. Indeed, in comments to the Knesset (Israeli parliament) on October 5, 1995, then prime minister Yitzhak Rabin suggested: "We view the permanent solution in the framework of the State of Israel which will include most of the area of the Land of

Israel as it was under the rule of the British Mandate, and alongside it a Palestinian entity which will be a home to most of the Palestinian residents living in the Gaza Strip and the West Bank. *We would like this to be an entity which is less than a state,* and which will independently run the lives of the Palestinians under its authority" (emphasis added).

6. They were the April 1994 (Paris) Protocol on Economic Relations, which established a customs union and detailed the PA's interim economic relationship with Israel; the May 1994 Agreement on the Gaza Strip and Jericho Area, which outlined Israel's withdrawal from these two areas; the August 1994 Agreement on the Preparatory Transfer of Powers and Responsibilities, and the August 1995 Protocol on Further Transfer of Powers and Responsibilities, both of which transferred additional civil administrative functions to the PA; the September 1995 Palestinian-Israeli Interim Agreement, which extended the scope of Israeli withdrawals and PA geographic authority in the West Bank; the January 1997 Protocol Concerning Redeployment in Hebron; and the October 1998 Wye River Memorandum, which called for additional Israeli redeployments (which were only partially implemented). The text of the various agreements can be found on the Israeli Ministry of Foreign Affairs website, http://www .israel-mfa.gov.il/mfa/peace percent20process/reference percent20documents/.

7. As of June 2004, UNRWA counted some 12,501 local staff (most of them teachers) and 73 internationals in the West Bank and Gaza, out of a total staff of 25,307 in all its areas of operation. See "UNRWA in Figures: Figures as of June 30, 2004," Gaza, UNRWA Headquarters Public Information Office, August 2004, www .un.org/unrwa/publications/pdf/uif-june04.pdf. UNRWA expenditures in the WBG exceed 3 percent of total Palestinian gross domestic product. When and if a Palestinian state is established, UNRWA services in the WBG would be incorporated into the new Palestinian government. Up to the present, however, UNRWA has played no role in Palestinian statebuilding, nor has the PA shown any desire to have it play such a role for fear that it would facilitate a premature wind-down of the agency prior to a full resolution of the refugee issue. In the aftermath of Israel's August 2005 disengagement, some donors did quietly moot the possibility of a gradual transfer of UNRWA services to the PA as a form of Palestinian institution building, but business has generally continued as usual. For further analysis on UNRWA's possible role in a final status agreement, see Palestinian Refugee ResearchNet, "Workshop on the Future of UNRWA: Minister Lovell (UK), 19–20 February 2000," March 25, 2000, http://www.arts.mcgill.ca/MEPP/PRRN/prunrwa3.html.

8. In practice, UNSCO (especially under the tireless Terje Røsd-Larsen) largely played a very useful role as energizer and political fixer during the Oslo era, but was less effective as a coordinator of UN actors. Later, the formal role of the UN would increase with its inclusion within the diplomatic quartet, but UNSCO's impact on the ground would diminish. In his May 2007 "end of mission" report, the then outgoing UN Special Coordinator was highly critical of Israel, the Palestinians, and the Quartet alike. "Secret UN Report Condemns US for Middle East Failures," *Guardian,* June 13, 2007, http://www.guardian.co.uk/israel/Story/0,,2101677,00.html.

9. None of the Israeli-Palestinian agreements explicitly mentioned settlement activity (at Israeli insistence), although they did commit the parties not to undertake unilateral measures that would prejudice permanent status negotiations. However, according to Article 49 of the Fourth Geneva Convention (1949), "The Occupying Power shall not deport or transfer parts of its own civilian population into the territory it occupies." The Rome Statute of the International Criminal Court (1998) reiterates this prohibition, classifying such action as a war crime (Article 8.2.b.viii). The illegality of settlement activity was confirmed by the International Court of Justice in

244   *Cases*

its July 2004 advisory ruling on Israel's separation barrier, which noted that "the Israeli settlements in the Occupied Palestinian Territory (including East Jerusalem) have been established in breach of international law" (para. 120).

10. During the period of the Oslo peace process (1993–2001), the number of Israeli settlers in the West Bank and Gaza almost doubled, from approximately 120,000 to 208,000 in 139 settlements. These figures exclude occupied East Jerusalem and areas of the West Bank illegally annexed to Israel after 1967, where approximately 170,000 Israeli Jews resided by 2001. See Foundation for Middle East Peace, http://www.fmep.org/settlement_info/stats_data/settlements_and_land/settlement _localities_2001.html, citing Israeli Central Bureau of Statistics.

11. According to Israel, between 1993 and 1998 some "279 men, women and children [were] killed in 92 lethal attacks carried out against Israelis by Palestinian terrorists. This is 50 percent more than the number of Israelis killed in the six years of the [first] intifada (1987–93), and surpasses the number of those killed in the entire 15 years preceding the signing of the agreements." See Israeli Ministry of Foreign Affairs, "Terrorism and the Peace Process: Background Paper," September 14, 1998, www.mfa.gov.il/mfa/peace%20process/guide%20to%20the%20peace%20 process/terrorism%20and%20the%20peace%20process.

12. For a comparison of different data sources on casualties, see "Losses on the Four-Year Anniversary of the al-Aqsa Intifada: A Comparative Statistical Table," pp. 98–99, in Michele K. Esposito, "The Al-Aqsa Intifada: Military Operations, Suicide Attacks, Assassinations, and Losses in the First Four Years," *Journal of Palestine Studies* 34, no. 2 (Winter 2005): 85–122.

13. On this see Palestine Emergency Committee, "Destruction of Palestinian Public Institutions: First Preliminary Report," April 13, 2002, http://www.jmcc.org/ new/02/apr/destruction.htm.

14. "President Bush Calls for New Palestinian Leadership," June 24, 2002, www.whitehouse.gov/news/releases/2002/06/20020624-3.html.

15. US Department of State, "A Performance-Based Roadmap to a Permanent Two-State Solution to the Israeli-Palestinian Conflict," Office of the Spokesman Press Statement, April 30, 2003, available at www.state.gov/r/pa/prs/ps/2003/20062 .htm.

16. "In light of new realities on the ground, including already existing major Israeli population centers, it is unrealistic to expect that the outcome of final status negotiations will be a full and complete return to the armistice lines of 1949." See "Letter from President Bush to Prime Minister Sharon," April 14, 2004, www.whitehouse .gov/news/releases/2004/04/20040414-3.html.

17. Israel Ministry of Foreign Affairs, "The Cabinet Resolution Regarding the Disengagement Plan," June 6, 2004, as published by the Prime Minister's Office, www .mfa.gov.il/MFA/Peace+Process/Reference+Documents/Revised+Disengagement+ Plan+6-June-2004.htm.

18. "Palestinian President Rips Hamas' 'Bloody Coup,'" CNN, June 22, 2007, http:// edition.cnn.com/2007/WORLD/meast/06/20/gaza/index.html?eref=rss_topstories.

19. Rex Brynen, *A Very Political Economy: Peacebuilding and Foreign Aid in the West Bank and Gaza* (Washington, DC: US Institute of Peace Press, 2000), see esp. Table 6.4, p. 180. The Holst Fund was simply a spend-and-replenish account, whereby the PA budget would be reimbursed against proof of allowable expenditures. Later post-intifada budget support mechanisms typically involved greater conditionality.

20. International Monetary Fund, *West Bank and Gaza: Economic Performance and Reform Under Conflict Conditions* (Washington, DC, 2003), p. 68.

21. Israel collects taxes on goods imported through Israel directly for the WBG. However, in many cases Palestinians import through Israeli middlemen. In such cases, customs and excise taxes accrue to Israel, not the PA.

22. IMF, *West Bank and Gaza,* p. 92.

23. Ibid, p. 91.

24. Quoted in "Arafat's Billions: One Man's Quest to Track Down Unaccounted-For Public Funds," *CBS News Sixty Minutes,* November 9, 2003, www.cbsnews.com/stories/2003/11/07/60minutes/main582487.shtml.

25. Some $486 million was diverted to Arafat by Israel in this way in 1995–2000. See IMF, *West Bank and Gaza,* p. 91.

26. In particular, Muhammad Rashid (Khalid Salam), Arafat's moneyman, ran a shadowy network of publicly owned private investments, thus maintaining an off-the-books war chest and political insurance/rainy day fund of sorts for Arafat and Fateh. These funds made an estimated $307 million in profit in 1995–2000, most of which was sunk back into investments. IMF, *West Bank and Gaza,* p. 91.

27. The World Bank's 2000 World Business Environment Survey of local businesses found much less evidence of commercial bribe paying in the WBG than in most other places. On a 6-point scale (where 1 = never pay bribes, and 6 = always pay bribes), the WBG produced a rating of 1.7, compared to an average of 2.7 in Latin America, 3.7 in India, 4.3 in transitional Europe, and 4.8 in Egypt. See "Figure 5: Frequency of Informal Payments, WBG and Elsewhere," in David Sewell, "Governance and the Business Environment in the West Bank/Gaza," Working Paper Series no. 23 (Washington, DC, 2001), p. 8.

28. Yezid Sayigh and Khalil Shikaki (principal authors), *Strengthening Palestinian Public Institutions,* Independent Task Force Report (New York: Council on Foreign Relations, 1999).

29. World Bank, *West Bank and Gaza: Strengthening Public Sector Management* (Washington, DC, 1999).

30. World Bank, *Stagnation or Revival? Israeli Disengagement and Palestinian Economic Prospects—Overview* (Washington, DC, 2004), p. 32, http://siteresources.worldbank.org/INTWESTBANKGAZA/Resources/WBG-Overview-e.pdf.

31. For a profile, see James Bennet, "The Radical Bean Counter," *New York Times,* May 25, 2003, p. 36.

32. The success of reform under Fayyad owes much to Fayyad's initiative and leadership in this area, coupled with effective coalition building with other Palestinian reformers (and supportive nonreformers), a substantial degree of public support, and mounting external pressure from international donors. Although there are impressive Palestinian human and technical resources available locally, well-targeted, demand-driven external technical assistance from the IMF, World Bank, and bilateral donors has also been useful.

33. World Bank, *West Bank and Gaza: Country Financial Accountability Assessment,* Report No. 28990-GZ (Washington, DC, 2004), p. 6.

34. PA Ministry of Finance, Press Release, March 16, 2005; interviews with donor officials, WBG, May 2005. Figures in US dollars.

35. According to former US security envoy General William Ward, only some 22,000 or so of the 58,000 persons on the PA security force payroll actually show up for work. See Mary Curtius, "US Envoy Says Palestinian Forces Unprepared for Pullout," *Los Angeles Times,* July 1, 2005, p. 3-A.

36. Several events illustrate how complex and sensitive this process was. In July 2004, while Arafat was still alive, a wave of pro-reform demonstrations swept Gaza.

Although reform sentiments were widespread, many of the demonstrators were actually former security service employees who had been terminated as a result of Salam Fayyad's payroll reform measures. The demonstrations were also encouraged by Muhammad Dahlan, the ambitious former commander of the Gaza Preventive Security Force (PSF). Clashes also occurred between PSF and military intelligence personnel, the latter under Arafat loyalist Musa Arafat. Musa Arafat was later retired by Abbas in April 2005, whereas Dahlan became minister of civil affairs. In June 2005, several hundred military intelligence personnel demonstrated against personnel cutbacks by briefly seizing the Palestinian Legislative Council, possibly with the encouragement of their former commander. That same month, armed Fateh gunmen in Nablus stormed government buildings to demand that they be offered positions in the PA security forces in exchange for supporting a cease-fire with Israel.

37. For an excellent examination of the situation and development of the legal framework within the WBG, see the Office of the United Nations Special Coordinator in the Occupied Territories (UNSCO), *Rule of Law Development in the West Bank and Gaza Strip: Survey and State of the Development Effort* (Jerusalem: UNSCO Gaza, May 1999), www.arts.mcgill.ca/programs/polisci/faculty/rexb/unsco-ruleoflaw; and Nathan J. Brown, *Palestinian Politics After the Oslo Accords: Resuming Arab Palestine* (Berkeley: University of California Press, 2003).

38. Sewell, "Governance and the Business Environment in the West Bank/Gaza," p. 16.

39. UNSCO estimated that donors had committed some $100 million to this area by May 1999. For a more detailed breakdown, see UNSCO, *Rule of Law Development in the West Bank and Gaza Strip.*

40. Replacing the Israeli (and Jordanian) currency in use in the WBG with Palestinian currency might have been fraught with risk, and a customs union was an efficient way for a weak PA to manage both revenue collection and trade.

41. The PA was allowed to issue its own passport-like travel documents, as well as postage stamps. Israel attempted to block Palestinian efforts to obtain its own internet suffix (.ps) and insisted that Gaza airport use an Israeli call sign. After much delay, the PA won both arguments.

42. Brynen, *A Very Political Economy,* Table 2.3, p. 40.

43. Up until 2000, all available data on the Palestinian economy suggested a sharp decline in per capita GDP throughout the Oslo years. In 2001, however, the Palestinian Central Bureau of Statistics released corrected and updated figures that indicated a modest increase during this period. The willingness and ability of the PCBS to correct its figures (even when it was not politically convenient to do so) points to the maturity and sophistication of some PA institutions.

44. World Bank, *Disengagement, the Palestinian Economy, and the Settlements* (Washington, DC, 2004), pp. 1, 30.

45. Speech by (then US Secretary of State) Warren Christopher, "Widening the Circle of Middle East Peace," October 15, 1993, available at http://www.washington institute.org/templateC07.php?CID=62]. Indicative of how widespread this discourse was, the linked terms Palestinians/peace/tangible benefits appear on Google some 7,910 times (searched May 2005).

46. World Bank, *Aid Effectiveness in the West Bank and Gaza,* p. 52.

47. Brynen, *A Very Political Economy,* p. 167.

48. For a more detailed discussion, see Brynen, *A Very Political Economy,* pp. 87–111.

49. Author's estimate: Although the Ministry of Planning and International Cooperation maintained semiregular aid matrixes prior to the intifada, they do not lend themselves to easily estimating the aid flow via multilateral agencies.

50. Andrew Bird and Stephen Lister, *Planning and Aid Management for Palestine* (Oxford: Mokoro, 1997); Brynen, *A Very Political Economy,* pp. 185–187.

51. World Bank, *Aid Effectiveness in the West Bank and Gaza,* pp. 107–109.

52. For a systematic evaluation of the pre-intifada aid process, see World Bank, *Aid Effectiveness in the West Bank and Gaza,* as well as Brynen, *A Very Political Economy.*

53. See World Bank, *Stagnation or Revival?,* which consists of an overview paper and four technical papers on borders and trade logistics, industrial estates, export possibilities under a reformed trade regime, and settlements.

54. Mahmoud Abbas (Abu Mazen), *Through Secret Channels* (Reading: Garnet Publishing, 1995), p. 94. Abu Mazen, one of the main figures in the Oslo negotiations, also stresses the greater flexibility and informality of back-channel talks.

55. See, for example, the joint polls of the Palestinian Center for Policy and Survey Research (PSR) in Ramallah and the Harry S. Truman Research Institute for the Advancement of Peace at Hebrew University, http://www.pcpsr.org/survey/.

56. Surveys showed that Palestinians overwhelmingly favored periodic elections (95 percent), presidential term limits (82 percent), freedom to form political parties (76 percent), no state censorship (74 percent), an independent judiciary (78 percent), and an overall democratic political system (89 percent). See Palestinian Center for Policy and Survey Research, "Survey Research Unit: Results of Poll no. 6," November 14–22, 2002, www.pcpsr.org/survey/polls/2002/p6a.html.

57. Palestinian Center for Policy and Survey Research, "Survey Research Unit: Results of Poll no. 13," September 23–26, 2004, www.pcpsr.org/survey/polls/2004/p13a.html.

58. On the failures of the negotiation process, see Hussein Agha and Robert Malley, "Camp David: The Tragedy of Errors," *New York Review of Books,* August 9, 2001, together with Benny Morris, "Camp David and After: An Exchange (1. An Interview with Ehud Barak)," and Hussein Agha and Robert Malley, "Camp David and After: An Exchange (2. A Reply to Ehud Barak)," *New York Review of Books,* June 13, 2002; Charles Enderlin, *Shattered Dreams: The Failure of the Peace Process in the Middle East, 1995–2002,* translated by Susan Fairfield (New York: Other Press, 2003); Jeremy Pressman, "Visions in Collision: What Really Happened at Camp David and Taba?" *International Security* 28, no. 2 (Fall 2003): 5–43; Dennis Ross, *The Missing Peace: The Inside Story of the Fight for Middle East Peace* (New York: Farrar, Straus, and Giroux, 2004); and Clayton E. Swisher, *The Truth About Camp David: The Untold Story About the Collapse of the Middle East Peace Process* (New York: Nation Books, 2004).

59. Beirut Declaration, March 28, 2002, http://www.fmep.org/resources/official_documents/the_beirut_declaration.html.

60. New Palestinian-Israeli permanent status negotiations were launched on November 27, 2007, with a US-hosted peace meeting in Annapolis. Talks between the parties then continued in the Middle East into 2008. Washington, however, took a relatively hands-off approach, largely contenting itself with the fact that talks were occurring at all.

11

Bosnia and Herzegovina: The Limits of Liberal Imperialism

Marcus Cox

In the thirteen years since November 1995, when the General Framework for Peace in Bosnia and Herzegovina ("the Dayton Agreement") was concluded, Bosnia and Herzegovina has changed beyond recognition. The paramilitaries have been disbanded, the opposing armies reduced in size and influence and gradually integrated, and the threat of violence has disappeared from political life. The effects of ethnic cleansing have been eroded through restitution of property and the return of minorities, slowly erasing the military frontlines that divided the country into ethnic enclaves. All the major ethnic groups and political parties participate in the electoral process and the state institutions. When Bosnia and Herzegovina concludes a Stabilization and Association Agreement with the European Union—the first milestone on the path toward promised membership—sometime in the next year, it will be anchored into a European structure that will make a return to conflict almost unthinkable.

During this postwar decade, the international presence in Bosnia has had nothing if not a "heavy footprint." The international mission arrived with 60,000 troops equipped robustly in both weaponry and rules of engagement—a force so overwhelming in the Bosnian context that it never needed to be used in combat. An array of special institutions (notably the Office of the High Representative, or OHR) and multilateral agencies—including the Organization for Security and Cooperation in Europe (OSCE), the United Nations, the European Commission, the World Bank—participated in a complex mission structure, together with hundreds of nongovernmental organizations (NGOs) engaged in humanitarian and reconstruction work. During the first five years, the international community mobilized more than $5 billion in reconstruction aid, making Bosnia for a period of time the highest per capita recipient of international assistance in the world. The mission was not a transitional administration of the type seen in Kosovo or East Timor and initially had no executive authority within the domestic constitutional sphere. Over time, however, the position of the leading civilian official, the High Representative, was strengthened with the power to overrule domestic authorities, impose laws, and ban individuals (even elected representatives) from public office. Bosnia and Herzegovina thereby became a protectorate of the international community, with formally sovereign institutions subject to external supervision and control.

The scale of the international presence and the benign security environment has enabled a grand experiment in *liberal imperialism*—the use of international authority to dictate the process of statebuilding according to a democratic blueprint. If liberal imperialism can work anywhere, it is surely here, in this small country in the midst of the European Union. The legitimacy of the international presence is uncontested, being part of the peace agreement itself, and the protectorate operates with the consent (or at least acquiescence) of Bosnia's leaders, who may from time to time object to particular international actions but have tolerated and often welcomed the existence of the protectorate itself.

Yet there is no consensus as to whether statebuilding in Bosnia has been a success and, if so, which aspects of the complex international peace operation should take the credit. The central institutions of the Bosnian state remain weak and artificial, lacking both legitimacy and real governance capacity, and the political discourse is fractious and insubstantial. The High Representative has dominated the political landscape, convinced that the new state needs to be defended with a firm hand against elements of its own elected leadership. Yet there are also clear signs that the protectorate is fostering dependency by distorting the fragile democratic process and suppressing the emergence of effective institutions. To many observers, the international protectorate continued well beyond its useful life and became a constraint on the statebuilding process. However, fears of regional instability following Kosovo's unilateral declaration of independence in February 2008 have led the international community to extend its authority over Bosnia indefinitely.

In this author's view, the question of whether statebuilding in Bosnia has been successful requires a rather nuanced answer. In the first few years of the peace process, the strong international mission was remarkably successful at a number of core peacebuilding tasks—demilitarization, exclusion of war criminals from power, restoration of freedom of movement, and return of property. These were achievements with real strategic significance, helping to clear some of the most dangerous obstacles to the peace process. The international mission has also helped to put in place a basic set of institutions for the new state. The strategy implicit in the Dayton Agreement was to allow the ethnically defined, wartime regimes to consolidate their separate spheres of influence within a highly decentralized federal structure while creating an institutional framework at the central level in which they would gradually begin to interact. Statebuilding via this route is a slow process, with the central institutions necessarily beginning as weak and artificial constructs. However, incentives have been created for the progressive transfer of power and resources to the center, in a process that will be strengthened as Bosnia progresses through the European integration process.

However, the contradictions of liberal imperialism have also become very apparent. Democratization by decree involves an evident clash of ends and means. The use of undemocratic and unaccountable power—sometimes in defiance of the human rights standards the international mission was sent to uphold—has undermined the goal of establishing the rule of law. In fact, the concept of the rule of law, which is so fundamental to the statebuilding process, has at times been reduced in Bosnia to a crude rhetoric of law and order. The departing High Representative, Paddy Ashdown, former leader of the British Liberal Democrats, offers this as the first lesson of Bosnia: "You must establish the rule of law and do it fast. Be tough at the start in order to relax later on. We got that wrong here. We toughened up towards the end, but we should have been tough from day one."[1]

Heavy-handed interventions from the international mission across a very broad range of subjects have blurred the lines of accountability and created disincentives for compromise among the ethnic blocs. *External statebuilding*—a process done to Bosnians, rather than by them—has come to interfere with the organic development of a new politics of compromise and accommodation within legitimate structures, which is essential to making the new state succeed.

An Ambiguous Solution to a Bitter Conflict

According to an old definition, an international treaty is a disagreement reduced to writing. This is an apt description of the peace treaty concluded in an air force base in Dayton, Ohio, in November 1995. The document contained numerous possible futures for the people of Bosnia and allowed all the warring parties to claim a degree of victory, however contradictory their objectives.

The collapse of the Socialist Federal Republic of Yugoslavia after its first free elections in 1990 followed a decade of drastic economic decline, when the system of socialist self-management that had been widely admired around the world began to implode. As living standards fell precipitously, the unity and authority of the League of Communists shattered, leaving the decentralized federation without its primary mechanism for resolving conflicts.[2] Taboos on the politicization of ethnic differences were swept away by a new generation of leaders whose power came from ethnic constituencies in individual republics. As the end of the decade approached, Slovenia and

Croatia moved toward secession, objecting to the heavy-handed attempts of Serbia's Slobodan Milosevic to control the federal institutions. When it became clear that Yugoslavia was unraveling, Milosevic shifted strategy and tried to carve a Greater Serbia from the areas where Serbs were concentrated, tipping Croatia into war in 1991.

The collapse of the Yugoslav federation left Bosnia and Herzegovina in an untenable position. Its government was divided among three ethnically defined parties, with the Serbs insisting that Bosnia remain within Yugoslavia and the Croats demanding secession. As the government fractured, armed enclaves began to form. Conflict was stoked by Bosnia's more powerful neighbors, Serbia and Croatia, who conspired to partition Bosnia's territory between them.[3] A clumsy recognition policy on the part of the international community pushed the remains of the Bosnian government toward a declaration of independence in an apparent attempt to win international protection of Bosnia's territorial integrity. At the insistence of the European Community, a referendum was held on February 29–March 1, 1992, to "establish the will of the peoples" of Bosnia and Herzegovina, which in the face of a Serb boycott achieved a 63 percent majority in favor of independence.[4] International recognition followed on April 6, coinciding to the day with Bosnia's descent into armed conflict.

Over the next four years of bitter conflict, some 100,000 people lost their lives and 2.3 million—more than half of the population—were displaced from their homes.[5] Ethnic cleansing was not a side effect of war but an explicit aim of the Bosnian Serb and Croat armies, designed to shatter Bosnia's complex ethnic mosaic and establish claims to territory. From the shelling of civilian populations in Sarajevo and other besieged cities to the use of rape and torture in concentration camps to destroy communities and their ties to their homes, the brutality of the conflict surpassed anything seen in Europe for a half century. The international response was palliative and largely ineffective. A lightly armed UN force (United Nations Protection Force, or UNPROFOR) dispatched to protect humanitarian aid convoys found itself playing witness to continuing atrocities, while the declaration of "safe havens" in eastern Bosnia, combined with the failure to demilitarize or protect them, contributed to the massacre at Srebrenica. In an official report, the Secretary-General has acknowledged a degree of culpability on the part of the UN:

> The United Nations experience in Bosnia was one of the most difficult and painful in our history. . . . Through error, misjudgment and an inability to recognize the scope of the evil confronting us, we failed to do our part to help save the people of Srebrenica from the Serb campaign of mass murder. . . . When the international community makes a solemn promise to safeguard and protect innocent civilians from massacre, then it must be willing to back its promise with the necessary means. Otherwise, it is surely better

not to raise hopes and expectations in the first place, and not to impede whatever capability they may be able to muster in their own defence.[6]

Having agreed to recognize the new Bosnian state at its moment of disintegration in 1992, the one principle to which the international community held firm was its refusal to permit changes to the external boundaries. On all matters of internal organization, however, the approach was purely pragmatic. Successive peace initiatives took the form of horse trading over territory, creating perverse incentives for the parties to keep on fighting in order to improve their position at the negotiating table. As one Bosnian observer put it: "The maps of a divided Bosnia-Herzegovina passed around at international conferences have become more of a continuing *cause* for the tragedy that has befallen us than a *solution*."[7] By 1995, air strikes by the North Atlantic Treaty Organization (NATO) and US military assistance to Croatia and the loose Bosnian Muslim (Bosniac)–Bosnian Croat alliance had tipped the military balance against the Bosnian Serbs, creating an opening for an internationally brokered (or coerced) peace agreement. For the Bosnian Serbs and Croats, the peace agreement was an opportunity to consolidate and legitimate territorial gains, and may have been seen more as a tactical maneuver than a final settlement. For many Bosniacs, by contrast, accepting the existence of Republika Srpska, widely seen as a genocidal creation, was a bitter pill to swallow, and many continued to believe that the international community should forcibly restore a unitary state.

At Dayton, the parties signed a complex document with numerous annexes, including a constitution for the new state. The documents were drafted in English by State Department lawyers, and no one wanted to take the risk of submitting them to any democratic process within Bosnia.[8] The most important features of the agreement are as follows.[9]

1. It retained the existing military frontlines, adjusting them only where necessary to make up the agreed formula of 51 percent of territory to the Bosniac-Croat Federation and 49 percent to the Bosnian Serbs.[10] It thereby left intact the ethnic enclaves created through conflict, leading to widespread criticism that it rewarded ethnic cleansing.[11]

2. It left in place the three armies (with the Bosniac and Croat armies nominally merged into a single federation army), separated by a demilitarized zone of separation, with an agreement on maximum force levels between them. Integral to the settlement, although not mentioned in the agreement, was the US-led train and equip program, which built up the Bosniac forces to create a rough balance. To many observers, this security structure seemed more suited to keeping the peace between separate states than to supporting a common statebuilding project.

3. It created an extremely loose federal structure with a minimum of authority at the central level. The constitution incorporates a range of consociational devices, including ethnic representation, special majorities, and vital interest vetoes. The structure of representation at state level assumes continuing geographic separation of the ethnic groups; for example, the constitution specifies that there must be five *Serb* representatives from Republika Srpska in the upper house of parliament, and five *Bosniac* and *Croat* representatives from the federation.

4. It provided for elections at the earliest possible date. The OSCE was given the rather contradictory mandate of certifying that the conditions existed for free and fair elections, but nonetheless conducting them within nine months.[12]

5. It contained extensive provisions on individual human rights, incorporating the European Convention on Human Rights with priority over all other law and establishing a number of internationally controlled adjudication and monitoring mechanisms. Some observers noted the tension between the protection of individual rights and the constitutional entrenchment of territorially based group rights.[13]

6. It gave all refugees and displaced persons the right to return to their homes or to receive just compensation in lieu of return. It seems unlikely that many people expected that a highly autonomous Republika Srpska would accept the return of more than 600,000 Bosniacs and Croats to its territory. Burg and Shoup note that the reference to compensation was "diplomatic code for acknowledgement that many refugees or displaced persons were not likely to return."[14]

The Dayton Agreement was thus an ambiguous, even contradictory, document. This is not necessarily a criticism of its framers: the lead negotiator, US ambassador Richard Holbrooke, may have made Dayton, but it was hardly in circumstances of his own choosing. Perhaps ambiguity was the best strategy available. However, it is fair to say that Bosnia under Dayton could have developed in various directions: toward permanent partition, with the lines of division hardening as they have in Cyprus or Kashmir, the state remaining purely a nominal structure and dispossession of property causing tensions for generations to come; or toward the gradual erosion of boundaries and the creation of a common political space. The move toward gradual integration is a result of statebuilding strategies pursued in the post-Dayton period.

Peace Implementation

The most striking successes of international intervention in Bosnia and Herzegovina were in core peace implementation tasks: demilitarization, restitution of property and return of refugees, and political transition.

Demilitarization

Of these three areas, only in the security sector was there a clear strategy from the outset, backed by a strong mandate and plentiful resources. In Bosnia and Herzegovina in 1996, the three military blocs were potentially highly disruptive forces, linked to smuggling of weapons, fuel, and food-stuffs. Armed paramilitary groups were active across much of the territory, intimidating civilians and opposition politicians and severely restricting freedom of movement. These forces were well placed to hold the peace process hostage.

Within approximately six months, the multinational Implementation Force (IFOR), later renamed the Stabilization Force (SFOR), had confined the three armies to their barracks and begun their demobilization to peace-time levels. Heavy weapons were placed in cantonments and subject to regular inspection, with the destruction of weaponry used as a sanction to enforce compliance with IFOR instructions. By 1998, SFOR had asserted a right of veto over the appointment of senior officers and established an inspectorate general to discipline any officer who engaged in "anti-Dayton activities." The paramilitaries were disrupted, prevented from moving around the country, and eventually disbanded. Many of the demobilized soldiers were absorbed into the police forces, which became overmanned and acted as a constraint on ethnic reintegration. A United Nations International Police Task Force (IPTF) monitored the police (unlike the UN Civilian Police [CIVPOL] in Kosovo, it had no executive policing mandate) and undertook a long process of vetting police personnel, gradually cross-checking names against witness statements made before the International Criminal Tribunal for the Former Yugoslavia (ICTY) and decertifying those implicated in war crimes and other criminal activity. In January 2003, an EU Police Mission (EUPM) took over from IPTF the role of police training and reform.

The overwhelming force available to the military mission ensured that it never needed to be used, and the stabilization of Bosnia was achieved without a single casualty among international troops or any significant flare-up between the former warring parties. Nonetheless, the price of this security strategy was that the international military presence, heaviest along the Inter-Entity Boundary Line, tended to reinforce the division of the country. In the first few years of the peace process, the international military was not usually supportive of efforts to restore freedom of movement and reintegrate the population for fear that it would lead to violence against civilians—an eventuality for which the peacekeepers were ill-prepared. Only later, when there was a clear international commitment to ethnic reintegration, did the military mission become willing to support civilian objectives.[15] Over the longer term, changes in the regional environment cemented progress in stabilization. Regime change first in Croatia, with the electoral defeat of the wartime government in January 2000, and then in Serbia, with the overthrow of Milosevic in October 2000, meant that Bosnia's two powerful neighbors were no longer working against the integration of the country. In December 2004, the EU took over the military mission with a force of 7,000 soldiers.

Even given the size of international military force, it is remarkable how quickly the armies ceased to play a role in political life. Severe budgetary constraints forced successive rounds of demobilization, and military spending became dominated by social benefits for soldiers. Although the Dayton constitution had not provided for any military capacity at the state level, international pressure led first to the creation of a common Ministry of Defense in 2003, placing the separate armies under a common civilian command, and then gradually to the integration of the military forces themselves. Financial pressures were the major driver of change, with Republika Srpska becoming increasingly unable to support the cost of its own standing army. Creating linkages between the Bosnian armies and the outside world also helped to create incentives for military integration. For a new generation of professional soldiers, participation in NATO's Partnership for Peace program and international peacekeeping missions around the world now offers the best chance for military experience and career advancement.

Restitution and Reintegration

Perhaps the most visible success of peace implementation in Bosnia has been the gradual reversal of ethnic cleansing through the restitution of property and the return of refugees and displaced persons. In 1996, the displacement of more than half the population appeared to pose an insurmountable obstacle to the peace process. Each of the parties had adopted laws reallocating abandoned housing to displaced persons of their own ethnic group, ostensibly for humanitarian purposes, creating an impossible tangle of property rights.[16] The destruction of more than a third of the housing stocks magnified the problem. For some years after Dayton, Bosnian Serb and Croat authorities engaged in aggressive campaigns to consolidate Serbs and Croats into areas under their own control, using a combination of fear tactics and inducements such as free land and building materials. The large numbers of displaced persons living in property that did not belong to them were easily mobilized to protect the status quo, and for several years murder, arson attacks, and riots against minorities who attempted to return were daily events.

Even though the Dayton Agreement was explicit on the right to return, for the first two years the international mission itself was ambivalent about ethnic reintegration, which many observers thought would be infeasible, destabilizing, or too risky for the individuals concerned. Bosnian refugees compelled to return following the termination of temporary asylum in Western Europe tended to relocate to majority areas, rather than return to their original homes. In 1998, however, the international mission made a clear decision to mobilize efforts behind return and repossession of property. The problem was recast not in terms of ethnic reintegration (an essentially political objective), but as a question of individual property rights and the rule of law. The High Representative used his authority to overturn wartime legislation and create an administrative claims process for repossession of property. The basic principle (*svako na svome,* which means "each to his own") was easy to communicate to the public and accorded with a bedrock respect for property rights in Bosnian society. In what became the mission's most intensive field operation, the implementation of the property laws was supported by close monitoring, constant political pressure, and targeted reconstruction assistance. To keep up the momentum, a list of property implementation statistics was published on a monthly basis, putting pressure on each of the 142 municipalities to keep up with the average in order to avoid being labeled as obstructive. Once the system had been institutionalized into a clear set of procedures and legal entitlements, the displaced persons themselves became a strong lobby in their own interest, and the machinery ground on to a successful conclusion.

By March 2004, of 217,000 claims for return of property, more than 200,000 had been successful, and the claims process was brought to a conclusion.[17] Not everybody chose to go back. Many local factors influenced return patterns, especially economic conditions. Faced with the poverty of decaying industrial centers and underdeveloped rural areas, often it was the elderly or those with no alternative who chose to return. By the end of 2005, according to UNHCR, 454,220 people had chosen to return and live in areas where they now represent an ethnic minority—enough to transform the postwar demographics of Central Bosnia, Herzegovina, and the western half of Republika Srpska.[18] No other factor has done more to change the political environment. A town like Modrica in Republika Srpska, the scene of wartime atrocities, retained a reputation as a "black hole" of violence and extremism for several years after Dayton. By 2002, around half of the prewar Bosniac community had returned. The two communities now mingle in the streets and attend the same primary schools. Opening up daily contacts among former neighbors quickly erodes ethnic hostility. Talking to people in Modrica now, they describe the horrors of the war as a kind of hysteria that, thankfully, has passed.

Political Transition

One of the most criticized aspects of the Dayton Agreement was its insistence on early elections. The first election in 1996, at a time when freedom of movement was limited and the media environment hostile to reintegration, returned wartime leaders to power across the country. It is often said that early elections in Bosnia were a mistake that retarded the pace of political transition. However, that conclusion deserves careful scrutiny.

If the expectation was that Bosnians would "vote for peace" by throwing their wartime leadership out of office, clearly that did not happen. However,

that was never a realistic prospect; a decade on, credible political alternatives to the wartime nationalist parties are still slow to emerge. In retrospect, the real function of the election was to draw the existing political
elites into the new constitutional order. Common institutions at the state
level could not be convened until there were elected representatives to fill
them. The nationalist leaders who took up these posts obtained the legitimacy of an electoral mandate in exchange for acknowledging the legitimacy
of the new institutions. Though this struck many observers as a devil's bargain, it created the political space in which hostile elites could begin to interact, with careful international mediation.

The Dayton Agreement did not exclude any political force from participating in the postwar government—even those that had violently opposed
the Bosnian state. It did, however, prevent individuals indicted by the ICTY
from holding public office. The tribunal offered a slow but methodical
process, backed by a strong international mandate, for removing from public life those most closely associated with wartime atrocities. Excluding indictees helped to initiate an evolution of the nationalist regimes by marginalizing some of their most extreme elements. It forced Radovan Karadzic
from the presidency of Republika Srpska, triggering a factional split in his
party, the Serb Democratic Party (SDS), and the emergence of a more moderate Bosnian Serb leadership willing to participate in the peace process.
Across the country, as indictees were arrested or driven into hiding, it cleared
the way for political change at the local level and the beginnings of ethnic
reintegration. Though there was intense frustration at the slow pace of arrests,
the process gradually acquired legitimacy as it went, and around 200 individuals have now been transferred to The Hague in connection with the Bosnian
conflict.

In retrospect, the strategy of focusing on individual rather than collective responsibility has proved highly effective. Attempting to exclude any of
the main nationalist parties from power at the outset would have provoked
major confrontation. It would have left the most powerful political actors
clinging to power outside the constitutional structure, undermining the statebuilding process. Instead, the Dayton Agreement drew the wartime regimes
into the new constitutional order, beginning a process of political evolution
that is still unfolding.

The Dynamics of Statebuilding

Much of the literature on postconflict statebuilding displays an exaggerated
faith in the power of constitutional design, as though the right configuration
of electoral systems and representative structures can determine the behavior of political elites, almost against their own better judgment. It suggests a
rather mechanical view of the statebuilding process, based on prefabricated
constitutional models.

In practice, when a new constitution is thrust onto a severely divided society through a peace settlement, the first question is whether it will take root. Institutions built up during the conflict (and, of course, those predating the war) do not disappear overnight. The political elites do not at the outset depend on the new political institutions for their authority, and whether they choose to pursue their interests within, or in opposition to, the new constitutional order depends upon their political incentives. If the incentives favor participation, the new institutions will gradually take on a life of their own, adapting through compromise and accommodation to the needs of the postwar society. An international mission—even one with strong executive powers—cannot compel participation. It can, however, influence the incentives in important ways.

The Dayton constitutional design accommodated the demands of the warring parties for regional autonomy by establishing a highly decentralized federal structure with a minimum of responsibilities and resources at the center.[19] The wartime entity of Republika Srpska became a federal unit, with its own constitution, parliament, judiciary, and executive government—an arrangement seen by many Bosnian Serbs as independence in all but name. The Bosniac-Croat Federation had originally been intended as a federal structure for the state as a whole but ended up as the second federal unit in the Dayton constitution—a federation within a federation. Neither its "federal" institutions nor its ten cantons existed at the time of Dayton, and in practice were soon divided into separate Bosniac and Croat spheres of influence. The central institutions at state level depended on financial transfers from the two entities and were constrained by rules requiring interethnic consensus for most decisions. That gave the separate ethnic political structures an effective right of veto over the development of the state. In this way, the Dayton design enabled the wartime regimes to occupy the new constitutional structure at the level of government (entity or canton) where they exercised a majority, while preserving substantially separate institutional identities.

Most of the new constitutional order was a novelty. Only the municipalities predated the war; other levels of government had to be either built from scratch or assembled from fragments of prewar and wartime institutions. The new central institutions, convened at the insistence of the international community, initially had few resources and could be ignored with impunity. In the first few years after the Dayton Agreement, they served mainly as venues for political gamesmanship: boycotts and symbolic disputes to impress hard-line constituencies, followed by concessions to preserve relations with the international community, neither of which had much effect on how Bosnia was actually governed. It was a frustrating period for the international mission, which found itself babysitting new institutions that seemed to be achieving little. Creating new institutions from scratch—finding personnel and premises, developing work programs and procedures, securing budgetary resources, defining working relationships with stakeholders and political masters—takes years to accomplish even in the best of circumstances. The international mission was able to use its influence to prevent the new structure from collapsing, by mediating disputes and threatening any party that withdrew from the constitutional process with the suspension of assistance. However, it did not seem to be able to make the new institutions into effective governance structures.

Consequently, the Dayton design has been widely criticized for several reasons: (1) preserving territorial divisions and institutional structures based on ethnic cleansing, (2) allowing wartime leaders to remain in power, (3) indulging in complexity and institutional duplication, and (4) creating central institutions too weak to hold the new state together. There have been persistent calls, both from within Bosnia and internationally, for revision of the Dayton Agreement (if necessary, by international imposition) and a more robust constitutional model.

However, taking a longer view of the process, allowing the wartime regimes to establish their separate institutional spheres within the new federal structure set the stage for their political evolution over a period of several years. It was most visible in the case of Republika Srpska, which at the time of Dayton had a minimum of civilian structures and no formal revenues. It sustained itself mainly through smuggling and other criminal activity. In 1997, a split in the SDS led to a change in leadership, the shift of the capital to Banja Luka, and an end to Republika Srpska's international isolation, allowing reconstruction assistance to flow. By 2002, Republika Srpska had created its own public administration, with over 60,000 public servants and an annual budget of around $550 million.[20] Through a process which might be called "bureaucratization," Republika Srpska became a different political animal. The ability to offer public employment became a key source of legitimacy, and preserving its bureaucratic structures became a political imperative. This ushered in a new era of more pragmatic politics, driven by economic interests more open to negotiation and compromise. With a very weak economy of its own, the political establishment of Republika Srpska came to accept participation in the Bosnian state as an acceptable means of sustaining its institutions. By 2004, it had agreed to shift responsibility for collecting indirect taxes (customs, excise, and value-added taxes are Bosnia's most important revenues) to the center. This was a key concession that increased the financial viability of Republika Srpska over the longer term but also tied it more firmly to the Bosnian state.

In the case of Herzeg-Bosna, the wartime Bosnian Croat republic that had fought to join Croatia, political changes in Croatia compelled a gradual reconciliation with the Bosnian state. Herzeg-Bosna had been closely linked to the Croatian military establishment and had used funds from the Croatian defense budget to operate its institutions, provide benefits to its military personnel, and create inducements for Bosnian Croats to relocate to Croat-controlled areas of Herzegovina.[21] After 2000, a newly elected Croatian government began to eliminate these subsidies. Once it ceased to be a conduit for external funds, Herzeg-Bosna began to lose its political coherence. Though the Bosnian Croat nationalist party (the Croatian Democratic Union, or HDZ) remained the dominant political force among Bosnian Croats, its ability to sustain an isolationist posture rapidly declined. A last-ditch attempt by hardliners in 2001 to withdraw from the constitutional order and declare Croat "self-rule" ended in failure when the HDZ was no longer able to pay its military personnel. The powerful Bosnian Croat business lobby, which controls much of Bosnia's import trade, together with the leadership of some of the Bosnian Croat–majority cantons, refused to support the initiative. As a result, though the HDZ has remained in power, it has been forced by the changing strategic environment to pursue its agenda within the Bosnian constitutional system.

These incentives structures have played a critical part in overcoming resistance to the Bosnian state. They point to a key source of influence at the disposal of the international community: conditioning access to international assistance and other benefits on progress in statebuilding. It took some time for the international mission to identify and exploit these levers. For example, reconstruction funds were originally disbursed at local or entity level, bypassing state institutions. The World Bank initially provided reconstruction assistance to the three, ethnically divided electricity utility companies because it was seen as the most pragmatic way to get the electricity system functioning. It was only from 2001 onward that the mission came to understand that the way international assistance was channeled could influence the statebuilding process in a positive way.[22]

The more that Bosnia becomes integrated, politically and economically, with the outside world, the greater the opportunities for conditioning access to the international community and its benefits on the existence of a coherent state. Bosnians readily agreed to create national sports federations (an important symbolic area), in order that Bosnian teams would be allowed to compete internationally. After strong resistance, they agreed on a common, ethnically neutral vehicle licensing system (a key step to restoring freedom of movement) after the international community decided that no other license plates would be permitted to cross international borders. They agreed to place the three armies under the control of a single, state-level ministry of defense as a condition for participating in NATO's Partnership for Peace program.[23] These developments point to a promising strategy for external support for the statebuilding process. By conditioning access to those benefits on compliance with constitutional structures, the international community can create strong incentives for the political elites to pursue their interests within the new constitutional order.

Ultimately, it is the powerful incentives associated with the European integration process that will ensure the long-term viability of the Bosnian state. The European Union demands not a centralized state (most of the EU's body of law is implemented by subnational governments), but an efficient and rational state, capable of meeting the complex regulatory demands of the single market. In the coming years, the Bosnian state will need to acquire a whole array of new functions, from labor market policies through environmental standards to food-labeling regulations. What is distinctive about the EU's process of "member state building" is that it leaves the Bosnian political elites to devise their own working arrangements across a wide range of functional areas, rather than dictating particular institutional forms.[24] It concentrates on *function,* rather than *structure,* leaving Bosnians to work out the necessary compromises.

Statebuilding by Decree

During much of the peace process, however, the international mission followed a very different strategy of using its executive powers to dictate specific institutional outcomes. Bosnia became a complex laboratory experiment in the use of international authority within the domestic constitutional sphere. It often appeared that statebuilding under the international protectorate was something done *to* Bosnians, rather than *by* them.

The international mission in Bosnia obtained its protectorate powers only gradually. Originally, the mission had no formal authority over domestic institutions, and the mandate of the High Representative was limited to mediation among the Dayton signatories.[25] From 1997 onward, in frustration with the weak performance of the central institutions, the multinational Peace Implementation Council that oversees the Bosnian peace process gave its approval for the High Representative to make decisions on behalf of Bosnian institutions and to take action against elected politicians or public officials who were in violation of their obligations under the Dayton Agreement.[26] This authority was never clearly defined, and its legal basis remains obscure.[27] In practice, it was interpreted as power to dismiss public officials summarily and to impose legislation at any level of government—even constitutional amendments at the entity and cantonal levels.

The powers were initially used to push through peace implementation measures to which the parties were already committed under the Dayton Agreement—particularly concerning refugee return, where the powers were used to establish a legal framework for repossession of property. Over time, however, their scope was expanded to include economic reforms (e.g., privatization, banking, foreign investment, labor laws) and the shape and composition of domestic institutions, from the number of ministries at state level to the representation of ethnic minorities in government. By the end of 2005, the High Representative had issued 770 binding decisions, including 400 laws and 187 dismissals[28] of public officials.[29] These powers enabled the international mission to become the dominant political actor in postwar Bosnia, dictating the agenda of Bosnia's governments and parliaments.

International powers of this kind are a controversial tool. Some observers saw them as necessary to overcome deadlocks and remove obstructions to the peace process. In the view of this author, they had unintended and often negative consequences for the statebuilding process. At the most basic level, they undermined the principles of democratic accountability and the rule of law that the mission was supposed to uphold. The dismissal powers were exercised without any form of legal process. The individuals were informed of the accusations against them only in the most general of terms, after the dismissal decision had already been taken. They had no right of response, let alone appeal. The High Representative always insisted that the dismissals were a "political matter," rather than a judicial one, and did not require due process. However, the punishment was draconian—those dismissed were not only banned from any further participation in political life but also from public employment.[30]

In June 2004, the Parliamentary Assembly of the Council of Europe, Europe's oldest club of democracies, concluded:

> The scope of the OHR is such that, to all intents and purposes, it constitutes the supreme institution vested with power in Bosnia and Herzegovina. In this connection, the Assembly considers it irreconcilable with democratic principles that the OHR should be able to take enforceable decisions without being accountable for them or obliged to justify their validity and without there being a legal remedy.[31]

Several days later, the High Representative embarked on the most sweeping use of his powers ever, dismissing fifty-nine SDS politicians, including most of its senior leadership. The stated reason was the continuing role played by the party in hiding its wartime leader, the indicted war criminal Radovan Karadzic. Robust measures against war criminals play well in the press, making the international mission sound moral and resolute despite its own continuing failure to arrest Karadzic. However, according to the OHR's press releases, most of those dismissed were not alleged to have been individually involved in protecting Karadzic, but simply members or appointees of a political party whose financial affairs, according to an investigation commissioned by the High Representative, were "a catalogue of abuse, corruption and tax evasion." OHR concluded that, because of an absence of proper financial controls, "we cannot be confident that the party is no longer providing financial assistance to its indicted founder, Radovan Karadzic."[32] The punishment was therefore collective rather than individual.

As the High Representative at the time, Paddy Ashdown, put it: "The RS [Republika Srpska] has been in the grip of a small band of corrupt politicians and criminals for too long. We have to get rid of the cancer of obstructionism and corruption in the RS structures and nothing less than major surgery will do."[33] This is a debasement of the idea of the rule of law as it is understood in Western democracies—that political power should be subject to constitutional principles and legal processes. The rule of law cannot be imposed through the use of unaccountable power without conveying precisely the wrong lesson.

The use of international powers also caused visible distortions to the emerging democratic process. Domestic politicians often preferred to allow the High Representative to make difficult choices, rather than take responsibility before their own constituencies. That was apparent not just in contentious interethnic matters, but also on general questions of governance. A telling example occurred in 2000, when reform of the Bosnian pension funds was set as a condition for a World Bank loan. Unwilling to undertake an unpopular reform in an election year, the Bosnian parliaments refused to adopt the necessary legislation. The High Representative then stepped in and did so on their behalf, in order to prevent a suspension of the World Bank's lending program and a consequent budgetary crisis. As a result, the OHR office in Sarajevo was besieged by angry pensioners. What had been intended as a measure to encourage the Bosnian authorities to adopt fiscally responsible policies in fact taught precisely the opposite lesson—that difficult decisions could be avoided without consequence. Tellingly, the World Bank was among those pushing the High Representative to intervene, in order to prevent its lending program from going off track. The High Representative found himself under constant pressure, both from international agencies and from allies within Bosnian society, to use his powers to advance particular reform goals. Without any rules or principles to determine when he should intervene, these pressures were very difficult to resist.

Interventions such as these had the effect of blurring the lines of accountability between the Bosnian authorities and their electorates. Civil society came to see lobbying the international mission as the most effective strategy for advancing its interests and turned away from the Bosnian political process. Bosnian citizens become increasingly disaffected with national politics, expecting little from their politicians. As one Bosnian put it,

> international bodies and organisations should increase their efforts to make sure that, to the degree possible, decisions for which state authorities are responsible are made in the responsible organs. . . . Should this not happen, government bodies will increasingly find themselves in an inferior, second-rank position and will lose even basic authority in the eyes of the people of BiH, a very undesirable scenario for any state.[34]

The protectorate contributed to what the European Stability Initiative describes as "the passive state."[35] Bosnia is in a deep social and economic crisis, whose roots stretch back well before the conflict. It has suffered a devastating collapse of its industrial base, leading to unemployment rates of over 40 percent and depriving whole communities of their livelihoods. Today, Bosnia's economic landscape is dominated by decaying industrial towns and underdeveloped rural areas, where much of the population has been forced back into subsistence agriculture. Bosnia's postwar governments at all levels have singularly failed to face up to this social and economic crisis. In the most critical development areas—industrial policy, agriculture, natural resources, social welfare—there is almost a complete vacuum of credible government policy.

The passivity of Bosnia's institutions in these key governance areas is a result partly of the institutional legacy of Yugoslav socialism and partly of the novelty of Bosnia's postwar institutions. Yet it is also apparent that the protectorate has exacerbated the problem. The international mission has pursued its own policy agenda so aggressively that it has displaced the domestic political process. Yet the mission has by and large not focused on building the institutional capacity that Bosnia will need if it is to address its severe social and economic crisis. Had it focused on building *governance capacity,* rather than reshaping *government structures,* the mission would have had to engage in the statebuilding process in a very different way.

For example, in 2005, High Representative Ashdown lobbied hard for the transfer of policing powers from the entities to the state—a highly contentious reform that was a substantial departure from the Dayton Agreement and earlier international strategy. Though the High Representative did not impose the reform, he insisted on it becoming a precondition for a Stabilization and Association Agreement with the EU (the first step towards EU accession). He presented the reform to the Republika Srpska parliament in the following stark terms.

> BIH and the RS are at a historic crossroads. The decisions you take in the next few days and weeks, will open up BiH's future; or close it down. It's as simple—and as brutal—as that. There are two options. A bright future and a dark one. . . . [If you choose the latter] then BiH and the RS will be the only country left behind as all the rest of the Balkans moves down the path to Europe. And let me tell you what that means—BiH being left out and left behind. No new jobs. No foreign investment. No foreign travel. No end to the haemorrhage of your youngest and your brightest and your best—who see no future here. No change to the heavyweight foreign presence here, whose job will be, not to help you move forward, but to prevent you moving backwards and creating instability in a region moving away from the path to Europe. And if that's the choice you make—here in the RS National Assembly—then you will, no doubt, be able to meet here as frequently as you like to celebrate the fact that you have perfectly resisted change and perfectly preserved the past—in a darkened cellar.[36]

That speech is characteristic of what could be called "the rhetoric of the permanent emergency." The international priority of the moment was always presented as a make-or-break issue on which there could be no legitimate disagreement. In this way, the mission alienated those who held different views and left little space for Bosnia's governments to work out their own compromise solutions. Passivity and stubborn intransigence were the inevitable result. In the end, the EU decided to drop the condition and proceed with the Stabilization and Association Agreement.

The field of constitutional reform has often exemplified this dynamic. Most observers agree that the fairly rudimentary federal structure agreed to at Dayton needs to develop further if Bosnia is to become an effective state. One would hope to see a process of constitutional evolution, as the former warring parties hammer out the modalities of government in many practical areas. However, there are many in the Bosniac political establishment who believe that the Dayton Agreement yielded far too much to the wartime aggressors and would like to see the High Representative use his authority to abolish the entities and recreate a unitary state. They believe they have more to gain from international imposition than from negotiation with the Serbs, and they welcome each new constitutional crisis for its potential to force another intervention by the High Representative. As a result, even among those who are strongly supportive of a multiethnic Bosnian state, there has been little, if any, attempt to reach out across ethnic divides and seek compromise on constitutional issues. In this way, the existence of the protectorate works against an organic statebuilding process.

During 2005, the unlimited powers of the international mission began to seem increasingly anomalous. In April 2005, the International Commission on the Balkans, a group of elder statesmen led by former Italian prime minister Giuliano Amato, concluded:

> the powers and activities of the High Representative continue to dominate Bosnian politics. This has blocked the development of self-government which is a precondition to becoming an EU candidate state. As long as the Bonn powers of the High Representative exist, they form the core of postwar Bosnia's unwritten constitution, and all political calculations are shaped by them. The talks in Bosnia convinced us that the OHR has outlived its usefulness.[37]

In January 2006, Christian Schwarz-Schilling, a former German government minister and international mediator for Bosnia and Herzegovina, was appointed High Representative. He immediately announced a dramatic change in policy on the use of the international powers, and his goal of bringing the OHR as an institution to a successful closure.

> If the BiH institutions do not work in a proper way there are [two] instances where I'd use these powers to the full extent. First, if someone threatens

peace in the state, and secondly, if the BiH institutions do not co-operate with The Hague tribunal. Most probably I will not use them when it comes to legislation, administration and tasks in the fight against corruption and the bureaucracy. I will surely not issue decrees to make the State function better while local politicians sit idle.[38]

Two years later, however, following tensions associated with Kosovo's unilateral declaration of independence, the Peace Implementation Council decided to prolong the protectorate indefinitely, making the closure of OHR conditional on a number of open-ended conditions, including the fiscal sustainability of the state, entrenchment of the rule of law, and its own "positive assessment" of the situation in Bosnia.[39] It appears that, once the international community has taken up the protectorate role, there are strong disincentives to setting it down again.

With several other comprehensive statebuilding missions now under its belt, it seems unlikely that the international community will venture another experiment in liberal imperialism along the lines of the Bosnian model. The protectorate helped to put in place the basic institutional structures of the new Bosnian state, but in displacing the domestic political process, it proved quite unhelpful in promoting effective government and a healthy democratic process. Yet within the Bosnian experience, there are valuable lessons to be drawn—in particular, the various ways in which access to the international community and its benefits can be used as a lever to promote the creation of a unified state. Although the former warring parties have not disappeared, a set of incentives has been created for them to pursue their interests inside the new constitutional order. This has made a return to open conflict now a very distant prospect.

Notes

1. Lord Ashdown, on BBC Radio 4's "The World at One," April 7, 2004.

2. Among the extensive literature on socialist Yugoslavia's declining years, see Susan Woodward, *Balkan Tragedy: Chaos and Dissolution After the Cold War* (Washington, DC: Brookings Institution, 1995); Harold Lydall, *Yugoslavia in Crisis* (Oxford: Clarendon, 1989).

3. Laura Silber and Alan Little, *The Death of Yugoslavia,* 2nd ed. (London: Penguin, 1996), p. 144.

4. Arbitration Commission of the Peace Conference on Yugoslavia (Badinter Commission), "Opinion No. 4," *International Legal Materials* (Paris) 31 (January 11, 1992).

5. The death toll for many years has been reported in the media as around 200,000, but more recent research puts the figure at closer to 100,000. See Ewa Tabeau and Jakub Bijak, "War-Related Deaths in the 1992–1995 Armed Conflicts in Bosnia and Herzegovina: A Critique of Previous Estimates and Recent Results," *European Journal of Population* 21, nos. 2–3 (June 2005): 187–215.

6. United Nations, *Report of the Secretary-General Pursuant to General Assembly Resolution 53/35: The Fall of Srebrenica,* A/54/549, November 15, 1999, paras. 503–504.

7. Kemal Kurspahic, "Is There a Future?" In *Why Bosnia? Writings on the Balkan War,* edited by Rabia Ali and Lawrence Lifschultz (Stony Creek, CT: Pamphleteer's Press, 1993), p. 16.

8. Carl Bildt, *Peace Journey: The Struggle for Peace in Bosnia* (London: Weidenfeld and Nicholson, 1998), p. 139.

9. For a detailed description of the agreement, see Marcus Cox, "Building Democracy from the Outside: The Dayton Agreement in Bosnia and Herzegovina," in *Can Democracy Be Designed? The Politics of Institutional Choice in Conflict-Torn Societies,* edited by Sunil Bastian and Robin Luckham (London: Zed Books, 2003).

10. The federation was created by the Washington Agreement of March 1, 1994, principally as a military alliance. Steven L. Burg and Paul S. Shoup note that the Croats agreed to the alliance with the Bosniacs only following promises of US support for Croatia's territorial integrity, an international loan for reconstruction, membership in the NATO Partnership for Peace program, and accession to the Council of Europe. An agreement to integrate the Bosniac and Croat armies was concluded on March 12, and a federation constitution was negotiated in the US Embassy in Vienna and concluded in Washington on March 18, 1994. See Burg and Shoup, *The War in Bosnia-Herzegovina: Ethnic Conflict and International Intervention* (New York: Sharpe, 1999), pp. 292–298. The federation has ten cantons.

11. Earlier peace settlements had failed in part because of US objections to recognizing territory acquired by force. In 1995, it was US acquiescence on this point that made the Dayton Agreement possible. Burg and Shoup note: "The NATO air campaign protected US policymakers from the charge of having given in to the Serbs, at least in the short run. But the US policymakers paid a price for achieving an end to the fighting—the tacit recognition and partial institutionalization of partition and of ethnic cleansing." Ibid., p. 413.

12. The timetable was linked to a promise by the Clinton administration that US troops would remain in Bosnia for no more than a year.

13. Fionnuala Ní Aoláin, "The Fractured Soul of the Dayton Peace Agreement: A Legal Analysis," *Michigan Journal of International Law* 19, no. 4 (Summer 1998): 957; Zoran Pajić, "A Critical Appraisal of the Human Rights Provisions of the Dayton Constitution of Bosnia and Herzegovina," in *Human Rights in Bosnia and Herzegovina after Dayton: From Theory to Practice,* edited by Wolfgang Benedek (Kluwer: London, 1998).

14. Burg and Shoup, *The War in Bosnia-Herzegovina,* p. 358.

15. For example, in October 1997, in response to inflammatory broadcasts against the peace process, SFOR seized control of Bosnian Serb radio-television towers and held them until the Office of the High Representative had forced the resignation of the board of directors of the public broadcasting agency.

16. See Marcus Cox and Madeline Garlick, "Musical Chairs: Property Repossession and Return Strategies in Bosnia and Herzegovina," in *Returning Home: Housing and Property Restitution Rights of Refugees and Displaced Persons,* edited by Scott Leckie (Ardsley, NY: Transnational, 2003).

17. UN High Commissioner for Refugees, Office of the High Representative, and the Organization for Security and Cooperation in Europe, "Statistics: Implementation of the Property Law in Bosnia and Herzegovina," June 30, 2004, http://www.ohr.int/plip/pdf/PLIP_06_2004.pdf.

18. For return statistics, see http://www.unhcr.ba/return/index.htm.

19. The Bosnian state has authority for foreign affairs and trade policy, customs and monetary policy, immigration, air traffic control, inter-entity communications and transportation, and crime. Originally, it had no revenue-raising powers of its own and was dependent on transfers from the entity budgets. However, the constitution allows the entities to agree to transfer additional authority and resources to the state.

20. Including soldiers, police officers, teachers, health workers, and administrators. World Bank, "Bosnia and Herzegovina: From Aid Dependency to Fiscal Self-Reliance," Report no. 24297-BIH, Washington, DC, 2002, www.worldbank.ba.

21. For further discussion, see European Stability Initiative, *Reshaping International Priorities in Bosnia and Herzegovina, Part 1: Bosnian Power Structures,* Berlin, 1999, www.esiweb.org.

22. Declaration of the Peace Implementation Council, Brussels, May 23–24, 2000, www.ohr.int.

23. Despite the creation of a common ministry of defense, Bosnia's entry into the Partnership for Peace was turned down in 2004 due to the failure of Republika Srpska authorities to arrest Radovan Karadzic.

24. Gerald Knaus and Marcus Cox, "Building Democracy After Conflict: The 'Helsinki Moment' in South Eastern Europe," *Journal of Democracy* 16, no. 1 (January 2005): 39–53.

25. The High Representative is mandated to "coordinate the activities of civilian organizations and agencies in Bosnia and Herzegovina" but is admonished to "respect their autonomy within their spheres of operation." With respect to the military, he is instructed in strict terms not to "interfere in the conduct of military operations or the IFOR chain of command." Dayton Agreement, Annex 10, Art. II, para. 9.

26. Peace Implementation Conference, "Bosnia and Herzegovina 1998: Self-Sustaining Structures," Bonn, December 9–10, 1997, Article XI, para. 2, www.ohr.int.

27. The Dayton Agreement makes the High Representative the final authority in interpreting his or her own mandate. The Peace Implementation Council was careful to avoid stating that it was changing the mandate. Rather, it "welcomed" the High Representative's aggressive reinterpretation of the mandate—an endorsement later repeated by the UN Security Council.

28. In December 2005 and January 2006, the High Representative issued decisions lifting the ban on holding public office from thirty-seven dismissed individuals, on the basis that the threat to the peace process that justified their dismissal had passed.

29. For the list of decisions, see http://www.ohr.int/decisions/archive.asp.

30. On November 28, 2005, the High Representative issued a decision allowing dismissed officials to be employed in the public administration, although not in the security sector or in senior management positions.

31. Parliamentary Assembly of the Council of Europe, "Strengthening of Democratic Institutions in Bosnia and Herzegovina," Resolution 1384, June 26, 2004.

32. OHR Press Release, "Financial Review Reveals Abuse, Corruption, Tax Evasion in SDS," July 1, 2004, www.ohr.int.

33. OHR Press Release, "High Representative Announces Measures Against ICTY Obstructionists," June 30, 2004, www.ohr.int.

34. Nedo Milicevic, quoted in United Nations Development Programme, *Early Warning System,* July–September 2000.

35. European Stability Initiative, "Governance and Democracy in Bosnia and Herzegovina: Post-Industrial Society and the Authoritarian Temptation," Berlin, 2004, www.esiweb.org.

36. Speech by the High Representative to the RS National Assembly, Banja Luka, April 21, 2005, http://www.ohr.int/ohr-dept/presso/presssp/default.asp?content_id=34540.

37. International Commission on the Balkans, "The Balkans in Europe's Future," Sofia: Centre for Liberal Strategies, April 2005, http://www.balkan-commission.org.

38. Interview in *Vecernje Novosti,* February 21, 2006.

39. Press Conference by High Representative Miroslav Lajcak following the Peace Implementation Council Steering Board session in Brussels, February 26–27, 2008. Transcript available at: http://www.ohr.int/ohr-dept/presso/pressb/default.asp?content_id=41353.

12

East Timor: Statebuilding Revisited

Edith Bowles and Tanja Chopra

In May 2006, East Timor called on Australia, Malaysia, New Zealand, and Portugal to send troops to restore order following clashes between the new nation's police force and army. The call came just a year after the last of the UN peacekeepers had left, in June 2005, and seven years after Australia had led the original intervention force to stem the violent response by Indonesian-backed militias to East Timor's vote for independence in 1999. Largely confined to the capital, Dili, the renewed violence of 2006 constituted a multifaceted political, social, and security crisis, leading eventually to the fall of the first prime minister, Mari Alkatiri, and his replacement with Foreign Minister and Nobel Laureate José Ramos Horta. Some state agencies continued to function during the crisis, but East Timor came dangerously close to state failure. Central to the crisis were the weakness of the security institutions, the waning legitimacy of the first government, and socioeconomic factors such as unemployment and poverty. The crisis persisted into 2007, with daily community violence in Dili, ongoing displacement, and impaired functioning of already weak state institutions.

The international community had often presented East Timor as a success story.[1] Several factors seemed to make East Timor a promising example of statebuilding success: unity in overcoming occupation against enormous odds, a charismatic first president, a technocratically skilled first prime minister, a government committed to prudent use of oil revenues, generous international support, and reasonable levels of success in some areas of service delivery. The existence of a unifying common identity, based on a relatively unified struggle for independence, appeared to be a foregone conclusion. East Timor achieved obvious benchmarks—especially those set by the international community—such as the drafting of a constitution, elections, demobilization of former guerrillas, and formal creation of institutions. In particular, the creation of very sound petroleum revenue management arrangements inspired confidence in the international community.

However, these early successes masked weaknesses in the statebuilding process. An independent East Timor did not emerge out of a collective vision of the state or a coherent national identity. In order to build a state in a few short years, vast international resources in the form of funds, peacekeepers, administrators, and advisers—as well as leadership gathered home from the diaspora—were poured into East Timor. The first, diaspora-led government of Prime Minister Mari Alkatiri led an ambitious statebuilding process, but one poorly linked to and communicated with Timorese society. Reliance on external assistance was intended to quickly deliver state institutions, ready-made. However, it has resulted in a Timorese state that is not rooted in an organic relationship with Timorese society. Efforts to build a collective understanding of the state have been limited, as have attempts to create popular support for a development agenda.

The attenuated time frame and heavy reliance on external assistance were arguably necessary to quickly launch the statebuilding process. However, within this framework, choices could have been made to better link the statebuilding process to Timorese reality. Neither the UN nor the first government drew on or brought existing social structures, including kinship networks and the resistance structures, into the nation-building process. In setting up the administration, they similarly failed to build on the effective and familiar elements of the Indonesian administration. Although politically understandable, failure to build on what existed in such a low-capacity post-conflict setting further complicated the already difficult process of building an administration.

Achievements in consolidating peace were similarly weaker than they appeared. International attention tended to focus on potential conflict with Indonesia and its proxies, without recognizing the very significant fault lines within Timorese society. The international community and Timorese elites did go through the motions of creating participatory political processes that might have addressed these fault lines, but in reality, political space was limited by the actions of the Alkatiri government, which failed to communicate with the full range of stakeholders, sidelined the opposition, and marginalized some groups, including the powerful Catholic Church. Critical examination of elements of success and failure in East Timor is required to encourage both international actors and national leaders to develop more skilled and innovative approaches to statebuilding challenges while also recognizing their limitations.

Following a short historical discussion of the role of the United Nations Transitional Administration in East Timor (UNTAET), we explore several thematic aspects of statebuilding efforts in East Timor in this chapter. Although we examine decisions made during the transition era and their impact on the later fragmentation and politicization of the state, the majority of our analysis will focus on statebuilding efforts after independence.

Historical Background

Prior to 2002, East Timorese had never experienced an effective, broadly legitimate state. Occupying a mountainous half-island, East Timor was traditionally divided into a series of small polities, each ruled by a hierarchy of clans who based their legitimacy on primacy of claim to a local area and proximity to founding ancestors.[2] East Timor was nominally colonized by Portugal for 400 years, although it was really only in the early twentieth century that the territory was "pacified" and colonial rule established over all areas. Portugal did little to develop the territory. In the mid-1960s, paved roads and electricity did not extend beyond Dili, and the vast majority of the population was illiterate. Portuguese rule was followed by the brutal occupation by Indonesia from 1975 to 1999. Throughout the foreign occupations, lineages and networks of blood and marriage affiliations, organized socially and spiritually around a hierarchy of clan "houses," have remained the basis of the sociopolitical fabric.[3] Proving remarkably resilient, traditional notions of what constitutes a legitimate local ruler have persisted and adapted readily and still largely determine local leadership.

Following the fall of the dictatorship in Portugal in 1974, political parties formed in East Timor. The most popular party, Fretilin, called for independence from Portugal and emerged victorious from a brief but bloody civil war with the rival Timorese Democratic Union (UDT) in mid-1975.[4] Following the civil war and the departure of the Portuguese colonial administrators, Fretilin assumed control. Correctly anticipating an Indonesian invasion, the party unilaterally declared East Timor's independence and swore in a government on November 28, 1975. Four members of the first government survive—Mari Alkatiri, José Ramos Horta, Rogerio Lobato, and Francisco Xavier do Amaral. Indonesia invaded in December 1975, with tacit support from the United States and Australia. The invasion led to a twenty-four-year brutal occupation, costing between 108,000 and 180,000 Timorese lives.[5]

After the invasion, East Timor's anticolonial nationalists transformed themselves into a successful resistance to the Indonesian occupation, characterized by strong coordination between the armed wing, Falintil, civilian activists, and overseas representatives.[6] After the decimation of resistance base areas in 1978 and 1979, the resistance changed to a small guerrilla force with a large network of civilian supporters, under the leadership of José Alexandre "Xanana" Gusmão. In 1987, the different resistance groups were unified under the umbrella of the Conselho Nacional de Resistência Maubere (CNRM), which was changed to the Conselho Nacional de Resistência Timorense (CNRT) in 1998. Originally the armed wing of Fretilin, Falintil became the armed wing of the entire resistance in 1987.

The CNRM/CNRT provided a structure to the resistance, from the grassroots to the Falintil high command. At the same time, the CNRT also functioned as a shadow administration during the Indonesian occupation. In many cases, the same *chefe do suco* could be appointed by the Indonesian authorities but also clandestinely serve the CNRT representative.[7] At the highest level, Xanana Gusmão was president of CNRT as well as supreme commander of Falintil, while East Timor's long-time representative to the UN, José Ramos Horta, was vice president. CNRT also included a resistance organization of Timorese students studying in Indonesia, which produced much of the younger generation of political and civil society leaders.

Following the resignation of long-time Indonesian dictator Suharto in 1998, Indonesia agreed to give East Timor a choice between greater autonomy within the Indonesian state or independence. A referendum was administered by the United Nations Mission to East Timor (UNAMET). Despite intimidation by the Indonesian military and their Timorese militia proxies, the vast majority of Timorese took part in the referendum, recognizing that it might be East Timor's only chance to become an independent nation. In the August 30, 1999, ballot, 78 percent voted for independence. The vote was followed by an orchestrated campaign of destruction, which was stopped only by the arrival of the Australian-led International Force for East Timor (INTERFET) in September 1999. On October 19, 1999, the Indonesian parliament, the Peoples' Consultative Assembly, renounced Indonesia's territorial claim to East Timor, and the last of Indonesia's troops departed later that month.

It had been anticipated that a vote for independence would lead to the UN overseeing an orderly transfer of government functions from the Indonesians to a Timorese administration. Instead, post-referendum violence left hundreds dead, almost the entire population displaced, and 70 percent of buildings in ruins. Infrastructure built by the Indonesian administration was systematically destroyed. Office buildings were burned, water pipes torn up, television transmitters sabotaged, and public telephones ripped out. The institutions of governance ceased to function, and the economy collapsed.

There was also a dramatic loss of experienced professionals. Under the Indonesian administration, most mid- and high-level positions in the civil service were occupied by Indonesians. The departure of the Indonesian administration left the country with very few engineers, accountants, administrators, lawyers, doctors, and other professionals. In 1999, East Timor had approximately forty lawyers, twenty doctors, and one surgeon, among approximately 800,000 citizens. Although East Timor's physical infrastructure could be gradually restored, building human capacity posed a fundamental challenge.

Statebuilding Under International Administration

East Timor was the quintessential experiment in international statebuilding, with UNTAET assuming authority over the territory from October 1999 to

May 2002. This enormous intervention by external actors may arguably have been necessary to solidify peace and ensure Indonesian withdrawal from East Timor. However, despite the massive amount of international resources committed to East Timor since 1999, the attempt to build state institutions and functions has been fraught with difficulties ranging from the uncertain legitimacy of the state to the execution of the basic functions of administration.

UNTAET marked the first time the United Nations assumed full executive, judicial, and legislative powers and sovereign authority over a territory.[8] In addition to peacekeeping, UNTAET was mandated to administer the country while simultaneously working to establish a government and public administration that would eventually be handed over to the Timorese. Its mandate further included development of the civil service, coordination of aid, capacity building for self-government, and the establishment of conditions for sustainable development.[9] UNTAET encompassed a peacekeeping force with an authorized troop level of 9,150 soldiers and a police component of 1,640, as well as 700 civilian staff, at a cost of approximately $44 million per month, about 60 percent of which was spent on peacekeeping.[10] Following two and a half years of UN administration, East Timor became independent on May 20, 2002.

UNTAET was succeeded by the United Nations Mission of Support in East Timor (UNMISET, 2002–2005), the United Nations Office in Timor-Leste (UNOTIL, 2005–2006), and the United Nations Integrated Mission in Timor-Leste (UNMIT, 2006–2007). These missions continued the statebuilding work of UNTAET, albeit with varying mandates. UNMISET retained executive policing authority until 2004 and fielded large numbers of advisers to government and a small peacekeeping force. UNOTIL's one-year mandate included not security responsibilities but rather training for the police and key advisory or line positions in the judiciary, parliament, and ministry of finance. In response to the crisis of 2006, UNMIT was established with a far broader mandate, including elections support, good offices, the strengthening of democratic institutions, humanitarian assistance, and a renewed executive policing mandate, with 2,500 personnel, including 1,600 UN police officers. Over 1,000 Australian and New Zealand troops provide additional security under a trilateral arrangement between the Timorese government, the UN, and the international forces.

The large international presence, particularly under UNTAET and UNMISET, provided an essential stabilizing force through the peacekeeping component. In 1999 and 2000, peacekeepers were enthusiastically received by the population, who saw them as the guarantors against militia aggression, if not possible civil war. The conflict was essentially resolved with the withdrawal of Indonesian troops, the renunciation of Indonesia's claim to East Timor, and the neutralization of pro-Indonesian militias. However, Timorese anxiety about security and stability remained very high. After independence, the UN-authorized troop strength was gradually reduced to a few hundred, the last of whom departed in April 2005 at the transition from UNMISET to UNOTIL. However, as late as 2005, the Timorese government and most of the population did not want the peacekeepers to depart, feeling that even a small troop presence provided a stabilizing influence.

Despite the UN's success in keeping the peace, the notion of an international administration capable of establishing and running a state was arguably overly idealistic. In such a mission, staffing challenges alone are potentially enormous, ideally requiring the mobilization of internationals with a thorough understanding of the history and culture of the country in question, language skills, and relevant technical expertise. Most UN missions face other constraints, including short mandates, short mission-planning time frames, and limitations on the use of mission budgets.

In addition to the logistical constraints, UNTAET, as a foreign administration, faced obvious limitations in its ability to command legitimacy among Timorese. An international administration inherently lacks an organic relationship with the people of a country and risks being rejected as an imposition. Moreover, reliance on just a few leaders for legitimacy can prejudice space for exchange with these leaders, as international administrators become beholden to them. UNTAET could have met this challenge by seeking out as many local and national leaders as possible, especially in the early period of the mission, in order to legitimate itself through association. Unfortunately, the mission failed to build a robust working relationship with Timorese institutions or broad segments of society.

At the national level, the Timorese leadership sought a partnership with the UN. However, UNTAET leaders did not establish a systematic working relationship with members of the CNRT headquarters located nearby. UNTAET relied on a small group of leaders, primarily Gusmão, Horta, and later Alkatiri, for consultation. Although on an individual basis, some UNTAET staff would consult with other CNRT members, the mission made no attempt to do so on a systematic basis.

UNTAET brought in a large international administration at the district level. Some enterprising UNTAET district staff built strong relationships with Timorese at the local level. However, an official, systemic collaboration between UNTAET and Timorese at the community level was never established. Instead of forming an official partnership with CNRT or other existing local authorities, UNTAET leadership in the early days failed to properly address the issue, and UN staff at the district level was explicitly ordered not to engage with the CNRT. The decision to keep CNRT at arm's length was informed by the belief that CNRT essentially constituted a party to the conflict, rather than a view of CNRT as an umbrella organization of a successful nationalist struggle.

At both the national and local levels, Timorese leaders could have been part of the administration from the outset. It is true that the CNRT did not constitute a state, but it did provide a basic local-level administration. CNRT was significantly weakened by the departure of Fretilin in mid-2000, to start acting as an independent party again. If the CNRT had been given a more formal role in the formal administration, it is possible that Fretilin would have waited until closer to the elections to make its break. Instead, Timorese formally assumed positions of power only after the creation of the East Timor Transitional Administration, the establishment of the first transitional cabinet in mid-2000, and the appointment of Timorese as district administrators in 2001.

A genuine partnership that placed Timorese in governing positions early on would have at the very least provided Timorese with an extra two years of experience in the mechanics of administration and decisionmaking. Many Timorese wanted the international administration to remain longer, fearing unrest, but elements of the leadership, particularly Fretilin, wanted to quickly assume power. This tension could have been reduced by putting Timorese in leadership positions, supported by international advisers. To do so, UNTAET could have appointed a transitional government or held "quick and dirty" bottom-up elections in the first months of 2000 to produce a two-year interim government.[11]

Both the UN administration and the diaspora-led first Timorese government notably failed to build on existing institutions, customs, and capacities, including kinship networks and the resistance structures that existed throughout the country. In building an administration, they did not use familiar procedures and systems from the Indonesian administration but instead sought to create all state institutions from scratch. Although Timorese were impatient for the benefits of a modern state, such as services, employment in the formal sector, and guaranteed rights, many had little understanding of the mechanisms for achieving them. East Timor's statebuilders ignored the lessons learned from the most successful developing nations, which have pragmatically adapted international models to their own societies. Instead, models were imported wholesale, particularly in the form of laws cut and pasted from other countries. The few projects grounded in local context have led to much better outcomes. For example, a well-researched land law project funded by the US Agency for International Development (USAID) led to an appropriate body of legislation that will help address the country's complex land tenure challenges.

The UN, bilateral programs, and the Timorese government could also have made greater efforts to find staff and advisers with more relevant international experience. As former prime minister Alkatiri has pointed out: "We also inherited an administration created with the assistance of people hailing from different backgrounds, origins and institutional cultures . . . the overwhelming majority had never faced a similar challenge, the challenge of setting up the administrative bases for an independent and democratic State." Greater attempts at strategic knowledge sharing and joint policymaking might have helped Timorese leaders and administrators tackle some of the practical and conceptual challenges of statebuilding while being supported by those with similar experience.

UN officials made correspondingly little attempt to foster a basic understanding within the Timorese public of a state and its functions. International administrators and bilateral program staff came mostly from countries and socioeconomic backgrounds that never gave them occasion to ask, "What is a state?"—much less explain such a concept to others.[12] It was an oversight in an environment where most Timorese had only ever experienced the state as an oppressor rather than a guarantor of basic rights and services. As a small society in the midst of social change, East Timor faced critical challenges in building modern institutions. For most Timorese, access to employment in the formal sector and interaction with state institutions was extremely limited in the Portuguese era, and expanded only marginally under the Indonesian administration. Local norms, customary sociopolitical structures, and belief systems remain very strong. The UN made few attempts to bridge gaps between local norms and modern institutions. In particular, and relevant to the youth violence of 2006, little attention was given to the fact that the large number of youth migrating to Dili existed in a world where neither traditional authorities nor the formal sector nor state institutions provided social control or access to opportunities.

Political Development

The transition from a relatively unified resistance army to political parties competing in a democracy proved difficult for Timorese leaders. Their lack of familiarity with the mechanics of parliaments, independent branches of government, and elections was unsurprising, and multiparty competition was highly contradictory to the local concepts of political authority. However, this transition was made more difficult in East Timor by elite political tensions and increased fragmentation, particularly in the wake of the violence in 2006.

The parties that emerged from the resistance struggle were underdeveloped, as party politics were subsumed under the larger goal of independence.[13] By 1999–2000, as Timorese began to contemplate their political future after the Indonesian occupation, individual political parties had to be created or rebuilt. Fretilin had been the first advocate of independence from Portugal and, following the civil war, initially led the resistance. Gusmão and Ramos Horta, the most prominent national leaders, had both left Fretilin in 1987. Compared to other political parties, however, Fretilin enjoyed far superior name recognition and organization in 2001, based on its historical role during the resistance, as well as plans, platforms, and policies—including a draft constitution—developed by those in exile.

During UNTAET's initial two and a half years of administration, before independence, the Timorese leadership gained little practical experience in governing. UNTAET established a succession of two quasi-parliamentary political bodies. First came the fifteen-person National Consultative Council, created in December 1999. It was superseded by the National Council (NC), a thirty-three-person body, in 2000. Both functioned only in an advisory capacity and had no formal veto powers. They neither gave real power to the Timorese membership nor provided substantial training in the assessment of legislation and parliamentary process. Those appointed by the UN did not necessarily enjoy popular legitimacy, as was later demonstrated by the failure of several members of the NC to win seats in the later Constituent Assembly.

After recognizing that there would be no genuine power sharing with the UNTAET administration, Timorese political leaders pushed for an accelerated timetable for elections and transfer of sovereignty. Their efforts coincided with UN member state pressure to wrap up the costly mission and UNTAET's own desire for a transfer of power. The CNRT put forward an ambitious electoral timetable, endorsed by the NC, which UNTAET used in 2001 as the basis for an election law, which would set up a Constituent Assembly to draft a constitution. The essential process of drafting the law was sound, incorporating input from a wide range of political parties, which were just beginning to organize, and civil society groups, including the church. In order to address popular fears of political party rivalry, a Pact of National Unity was signed shortly before the elections.

With the logic that it was necessary to promote the development of individual political parties and multiparty democracy, UNTAET backed the dissolution of CNRT. CNRT was dissolved in June 2001, just six weeks prior to the elections, leaving little time for new parties to establish themselves. Fretilin had already left the CNRT earlier, in 2000. The opposition party, Partido Democratico (PD), was formed immediately afterward, drawing in many leading CNRT members and seeking to capitalize on their networks. Importantly, Gusmão did not join or publicly throw his weight behind any party, in keeping with his established stance as a national unifier, but was widely seen as sympathizing with PD. The decision to dissolve CNRT and Gusmão's decision not to join a party removed any serious competitor for Fretilin for 2001.

All these factors contributed to an easy victory for Fretilin in the 2001 elections. During the campaign, Fretilin presented itself as the main resistance organization that had fought successfully against the Indonesian occupation. Its campaign was largely based on traditional and historical symbols, and it called upon people to pay tribute to the resistance fighters by voting for Fretilin. As the main figurehead of the party, the internal resistance leader Lu Olo appeared on the slate, although many of the figures topping the party list were drawn from the diaspora, such as Mari Alkatiri. In their eagerness to promote multiparty elections, internationals failed to grasp that the elections did not fit the local paradigm of selecting political leaders. The Timorese voted for Fretilin in tribute to the main resistance party, rather than for the candidates specified on the party lists, and were later surprised to find relatively unknown diaspora figures leading the country.[14] Fretilin won 57 percent of the vote, which translated into fifty-five seats in the constituent assembly, giving it a commanding majority after the remaining vote was fragmented among the twelve remaining opposition parties.

The constitution-drafting process commenced in 2001 and was completed in March 2002. There were two clear flaws in the process. First, the law that created the Constituent Assembly allowed for that body to transform itself into the National Parliament, which it did. It was officially sworn in at independence in May 2002. Thus those who were writing the constitution anticipated themselves holding power, which removed an important element of independence.[15] Fretilin used its own draft constitution as a basis for the process. The representatives did not have the time or the skills to bring serious debate or caucus for changes.[16] Even though UNTAET and some international nongovernmental organizations (NGOs) marshaled an impressive amount of expertise, it proved difficult to inject advice into an inexperienced body dominated by one party.

Second, there was insufficient consultation surrounding the constitution. Although a National Constitutional Commission was created (over the objections of Fretilin), and constitutional hearings were held in every district, local understanding of what a constitution is was limited. Furthermore, the commission results were not used in the actual constitution-drafting process. Instead, a week-long consultation was carried out following the completion of the draft constitution. Although this process involved wide distribution of the constitution and members of the Constituent Assembly traveled all over the country to conduct public hearings, the time was insufficient and the forums were too crowded for real debate. As a result, many Timorese did not understand, for example, that the constitution would create a semi-presidential system with a largely ceremonial presidency, but that the prime minister would be chief executive.

Following the election of the Constituent Assembly in August 2001, the second transitional government was formed, with Timorese in all cabinet positions and internationals in advisory roles. UNTAET, Gusmão, and many opposition members had pushed for a government of national unity, formally including other parties. Fretilin rejected that idea, although some opposition members were given posts in the new government. Although the Special Representative of the Secretary-General (SRSG) still technically held supreme executive authority, SRSG Sérgio Vieira de Mello now deferred to Alkatiri on major policy matters, based on the misperception that Alkatiri enjoyed widespread popular legitimacy. There was no further promotion of the opposition parties in their role as the opposition. The signing of the constitution in March 2002 was quickly followed by the first presidential elections, won by Gusmão, and independence on May 20, 2002.

By 2006, some of the flaws in the constitution-drafting process and the constitution itself came home to roost. The opposition and much of the public were less than totally committed to the constitution. During the 2006 crisis, the opposition called on the president to dissolve parliament and government, which legally he could not do, and assume extraordinary powers. Many Timorese now question the semipresidential system, expressing preference for a presidential system as a clearer and simpler configuration of executive power more appropriate to a small country without a well-developed political culture. Just as important, the constitution is vague or silent on some critical points. When Alkatiri's government fell in 2006, it was not clear from the constitution how a new government was to be formed. In 2007, constitutional ambiguity led to a political impasse because it was not clear whether the right to form a government as a result of a plurality of votes referred to the single party (in this case, Fretilin) or to the coalition of parties with the most votes.

By 2007, Fretilin's historical advantage had dissipated. Many voters were dissatisfied after five years of poor development and service delivery, very poor communications between government and public, and perceived arrogance on the part of the Fretilin leadership. Additionally, the Alkatiri government had failed to transform its parliamentary majority into the broad legitimacy required to shore up public faith in the institutions of the new state. In 2007, 70 percent of voters voted for change, with an 80 percent turnout.

The results of the 2007 elections were moderately encouraging. The fact that no party won a majority or even a commanding plurality may indicate that people did not simply choose according to historical loyalties and, critically, that political leaders could not take the people for granted. Fretilin suffered a large reversal, going from winning 57 percent of the vote in 2001 to 29 percent in 2007. At the same time, younger candidates and their parties did well, particularly in the presidential election. The political landscape of 2007 was rendered more complex by Gusmão's decision to form a new political party, using the old CNRT acronym but signifying the National Congress for Timorese Reconstruction. Gusmão's party came in second to Fretilin with 23 percent of the vote. Following a protracted political impasse due to ambiguity in the constitution, a coalition of four parties led by Xanana Gusmão formed a government with Gusmão as prime minister.

Critical to East Timor's future will be the separation of political parties from the violence of the past. East Timor's civil war in 1975 left a profound fear of partisan politics among the population, and since 1975, political party development has added an overlay to preexisting conflicts and power relationships. It is encouraging that the elections of 2007 were largely free of violence, although the presence of the large UN mission and other international observer organizations undoubtedly helped.

As a body, the National Parliament remains weak. Members lack the time, skills, and staff for real legislative drafting, and most laws have been drafted by government. Although receiving far less international support than the executive or judiciary, the legislature nonetheless remains dependent on foreign advisers for drafting laws and writing committee reports. Its ability to put forward solutions to national problems is very limited, and as a result, the public makes few demands on parliament. Many parties now agree that strengthening the role of parliament and, in particular, formalizing the role of the opposition are critical if Timorese politics are to mature.

Building an Administration

East Timor's public administration experienced its most important development after independence, albeit with bilateral, multilateral, and UN mission support. At the outset UNTAET lacked a coherent strategy for enhancing public administration and achieving other reconstruction goals, despite the fact that the Joint Assessment Mission in October–November 1999—encompassing the World Bank, the Asian Development Bank, donors, and Timorese specialists—had produced a strategy for reconstruction and the restoration of essential government services. Although UNTAET did not have a competing strategy, it sought to improvise rather than embrace the results of the Joint Assessment Mission.[17] Critically, UNTAET failed to develop a strategy that included institution building as the core element of statebuilding. This strategic failure undermined UN and Timorese efforts to develop a working public administration.

Although certain of East Timor's ministries function much better than others, many public institutions function at a low level. At the time of their appointment, many civil servants had a limited understanding of the role of their institutions. With systems, procedures, and institutional visions underdeveloped, low-level officials have tended to identify more with individual ministers or other senior officials rather than the institution itself. At the leadership level, this has led to a view of institutions as an extension of personal power.[18]

UNTAET was hampered by its own administrative and financial management systems, which were not easily adapted to the needs of an executive body supporting the development of nascent government institutions. For example, due to rules imposed by UN member states on the peacekeeping budget, UNTAET could not use its own administrative, procurement, and engineering services to establish the country's administration. At a practical level this led, for instance, to Timorese district administrators taking over from UNTAET staff, only to find that all furniture, computers, and phones had been removed.

In many areas, UNTAET did not seek to work closely with Timorese to design appropriate institutions, preferring instead to set up institutions run by UNTAET staff, which would purportedly be handed over to Timorese administrators through a process of "Timorization." Implicit in the notion of "hand-over" were expectations of skills and ideas about the function of a given institution that were often out of step with Timorese reality. For example, instead of recreating the previous system of written notes, international administrators introduced electronic filing into rural subdistricts. Upon UNTAET's withdrawal, Timorese district administrators were left with computers that they may or may not have been trained to operate, in locations without access to reliable electricity. All too often, Timorese appointees were handed the keys to an office, a pile of documents in English, and no training. This invariably left them dependent on the next international adviser, which did little to build capacity or confidence.

Despite this general trend, certain areas were much more successful than others in becoming operational and laying the groundwork for future capacity building. Where an institution-building approach was adopted at the outset, then job descriptions, systems and procedures, and skills-training development took place within the framework of what the institution itself was ultimately supposed to look like. The customs regime and service, established by UNTAET in 1999 and early 2000, is one example. In other areas, UNTAET entered into effective partnerships with bilateral and multilateral agencies. In the area of financial administration, UNTAET quickly drafted a series of laws while providing its own advisers to fulfill line functions, supplemented by secondments from Australia.

East Timor's Ministry of Health has consistently outperformed other ministries in terms of service delivery and policy development. Among the elements for success was the fact that the ministry enjoyed strong Timorese leadership, high-quality international advisers, and strong support from donors. Importantly, the ministry also built on existing capacity. Timorese health professionals, which included members of the Joint Assessment Mission, formed a working group soon after Indonesian withdrawal and started developing a strategy for the development of the country's future health care system.

At the local level, early attempts to build a public administration were less fruitful. With the CNRT sidelined, UNTAET created district administrations with large complements of international staff. During the first phases, Timorese were only employed as translators and drivers. Later, district- and subdistrict staff were selected based on merit, contradicting local conceptions of political authority, which were based on an elaborate system of kin relations.[19] The credibility of these authorities was also undermined by the fact that they could not draw on their peacekeeping-funded budgets for service delivery functions, such as buying school or medical supplies or rehabilitating destroyed buildings. Rather, expenditures for what were intended to be government functions were supposed to come from development assistance, state revenues, or trust funds, all of which took time to arrive. In many cases, proactive UN staff could only hope to facilitate the delivery of humanitarian relief and to seek donor funds for community projects. Given the existence of credible local authorities and uneven skill levels among UNTAET staff, it would have been preferable to rely on official cooperation with the CNRT.

Supplementing the UN's democratization and institution-building effort, the World Bank launched a program in early 2000 to support local governance and participatory decisionmaking processes. Through the Bank's Community Empowerment and Local Governance Project (CEP), the villages of East Timor elected councils that were supposed to serve as local-level institutions that could later be formalized and integrated into the local governance structure. The actual agreement on the creation of the councils only happened after great delay, after UNTAET twice rejected the project in negotiations and only signed up to it after intervention from the UN and World Bank leadership. UNTAET was not in favor of decentralizing its power.[20] These difficulties resulted in a lack of cooperation between the CEP structure and the official administration from which the program never truly recovered. In addition, local power structures resisted the short-term attempt to create a new institution.[21] The CEP was a lost opportunity to overcome the challenge of local participation and representation of local actors.

Human resource development represented one of the biggest challenges to statebuilding in East Timor. Due to inadequate education and inexperience, Timorese at all levels of the civil service lacked appropriate skills, with particular impact at the middle and upper levels. This is unsurprising, given that few Timorese gained high-level administrative experience during the Indonesian administration. Deficits ran from basic skills, such as use of computers, scheduling, and filing, to more sophisticated skills, such as policy development, analysis of data, and planning. Poor capacity affects service delivery.

In the years since independence, capacity building has had mixed results despite large amounts of international support. The primary approach to capacity building by subsequent UN missions has been the provision of adviser posts from the assessed budget. Between 2002 and 2004, UNMISET provided 100 "stability" posts considered critical to the functioning of the state, while the United Nations Development Programme (UNDP) managed 200 "development" posts. In some cases these were line functions, but in most cases, internationals were intended to serve as advisers to Timorese counterparts. In 2004–2005, these numbers were reduced to 58 and 118, respectively. A total of $7.9 million of UNMISET's budget was devoted to the 58 advisers, at an average cost of $126,000 apiece. In total, donors had provided a total of $13 million for UNDP-managed advisers by the end of 2004.[22] Additional advisers have been provided directly by bilateral and multilateral donors.

Many of these posts were never filled or filled only after long delays, and in some cases advisers had their contracts extended from mission to mission without apparent review. Some advisers have proved very capable and effective, but the overall approach has had several flaws. Rather than mentoring staff, advisers have often directly performed tasks at the request of overworked and inexperienced ministers. Lack of language skills, short contract times, insufficient coordination, and lack of training experience among advisers have all compromised effectiveness. The recent *Report of the Secretary-General* also noted challenges in finding the required skill sets and pointed out that adviser positions were identified and their performance evaluated by specific ministers, which affected the independence of advice.[23]

Like UNTAET, the postindependence government could have done more to tap local capacity. Despite their technocratic skills, many of the younger Timorese educated under the Indonesian occupation were not engaged due to lack of Portuguese language skills and prejudice against the Indonesian education system. East Timor's significant organizational capacity at the community level—as witnessed in the implementation of the CEP program and many other church- or NGO-run activities—was likewise not tapped.

The hasty implementation of Portuguese—in which only 12 percent of the population is literate—as an official language has created additional challenges in numerous areas.[24] It has meant that inexperienced civil servants need to carry out new jobs while simultaneously learning a new language, effectively narrowing an already thin human resource base. According to the constitution, Portuguese and Tetum are the official languages, whereas English and Bahasa Indonesia may be "working languages," to be used in government offices but not on official, public documents. In practice, only Portuguese has been used for almost all official documents, although officially entry into the civil service does not require Portuguese. Tetum, which 42 percent of the population can speak, read, and write, is very underdeveloped, limiting its utility as a legal and administrative language.

In parliament, almost all the debate takes place in Tetum, but laws are produced only in Portuguese, with the result that few parliamentarians can actually read and absorb the draft laws they are passing. The exclusive use of Portuguese for documents effectively shuts out many skilled staff and narrows the range of consultations. Portuguese is the language of education for most classes in school, despite the fact that many teachers speak it very poorly. More pragmatic use of Bahasa Indonesia, in which 38 percent of the population is literate, as a working language of the administration might make for improved communication and effectiveness, within and between state institutions.

The development of effective public administration has been further constrained by a high degree of centralization in both operations and decisionmaking, which was a tendency of the Alkatiri administration but also reflects the example set by UNTAET. UNTAET's structure was highly centralized, with decisions taken top-down by the SRSG. In spirit, this style of decisionmaking contradicted the position of transitional administrator as head of state, theoretically subject to a separation of powers. Overcentralization has fed the natural reticence of inexperienced staff to question superiors or be proactive. It also resonated very poorly with the strong Timorese preference for face-to-face interaction and dialogue with leaders, politically damaging the Alkatiri administration. Poor sharing of information or integration of views beyond a small group of decisionmakers contributed significantly to the Alkatiri administration's inability to rally public support for government policy.

Despite all these challenges, capacity has improved significantly in many areas. In addition to the UN adviser program, there have been bilateral and multilateral capacity-building programs funded in different sectors. The government has also conducted its own training for civil servants on skills ranging from language and computers to planning. Naturally, many civil servants have learned on the job. Program officers who four years ago were hesitant to take charge of scheduling meetings now regularly chair meetings and produce planning documents. Many office directors can now prepare and monitor essential programmatic and financial plans.

Relying on international advisers as a route to capacity building produces a set of dilemmas. The expertise of international advisers is often necessary to produce planning, policy, and legal documents, but too much reliance on internationals can lead to a lack of ownership. For many reasons, local counterparts may not feel part of the process, or ministers may reject policy advice, even when sound. Recognizing this, some programs have sought to create formal agreements on outputs and achievements. More subtly, the large number of advisers carrying out policy and planning tasks has meant that the highest levels of the administration are not forced to consult with subordinates or with other stakeholders or rely on national capacity. In future statebuilding endeavors, it will be important for the UN and other international agencies to develop a broader range of tools to support institution building. If UN peacekeeping operations, due to the nature of their budgeting, are best placed only to provide short-term personnel, then creative strategic partnerships with other donors may produce the more comprehensive kind of assistance needed for institution building.

Establishing Justice

The justice system remains the weakest of East Timor's state structures. Already a technically very difficult area, the justice sector has suffered from a lack of coherent planning and drastic changes in policy from the UNTAET to the Timorese administrations. Further, neither UNTAET nor the Timorese government promoted the pragmatic use of existing customary justice mechanisms in combination with efforts to build the formal system. UNTAET had hardly any knowledge of the existence of customary law, and members of the first government, many of whom came from the diaspora and were unfamiliar with local systems, prioritized the creation of the formal justice system. UNTAET thus lost an opportunity to adapt judicial sector reforms to local realities.

UNTAET's first regulation created a basic legal framework by declaring that Indonesian law obtained, except insofar as it contradicted international human rights law, and that new regulations passed by UNTAET and a future Timorese government would supersede the Indonesian law. (In 2003, the president of the Court of Appeals issued an opinion attempting to overturn this regulation and to rule that Portuguese law obtained. Recognizing that implementation of this opinion would have led to legal chaos in East Timor, the parliament issued a regulation reaffirming UNTAET regulation 1999/1.)

Although UNTAET appointed internationals to almost all high-level positions, in early 2000 the transitional administration chose to install Timorese judges, prosecutors, and public defenders. East Timor had sixty individuals with law degrees in 1999, but very few had substantial work experience, and none had ever served as a judge. UNTAET provided a very short initial training, and Timorese judges assumed their posts in early 2000.[25] In most other sectors, early appointments of Timorese allowed them to learn on the job. However, given the highly specialized nature of the justice sector, it would have been more effective to appoint internationals to these positions for a two- to three-year period, acknowledging that the fast and "fair" provision of justice was an urgent priority.

Appointing internationals would have gotten the system up and running more quickly, while providing time for the inexperienced but enthusiastic Timorese legal professionals to be trained. Even though law is specific to each country, many developing countries have successfully relied on international judges. Instead, inexperienced legal professionals struggled to make the system operate while also attending training courses run by UNDP and NGOs. By 2002, the justice system had developed a formidable backlog, two of the four district courts had never started, and judicial decisions were of mixed quality.

The functioning of the legal system was complicated by the imposition of Portuguese as the court language. In early 2004, the Court of Appeals issued an administrative order stipulating that all court documents must be in Tetum or Portuguese. However, Tetum is not sufficiently developed to serve as a legal language in all instances, nor is it spoken by international legal professionals, which means that in effect, all documents must be written in Portuguese. This adds an extra step to each transaction for the Indonesian-educated Timorese legal professionals, who write most fluently in Tetum or Bahasa Indonesia but must then render documents and comprehend legal texts in Portuguese.

In 2004 and 2005, the government administered an evaluation process that resulted in the disqualification of all of the Timorese legal practitioners appointed by UNTAET. They all then attended full-time training funded by UNDP until mid-2006, when they were reappointed. A standard complaint about the training is that it focused too heavily on Portuguese legal language skills, without paying sufficient attention to legal concepts and operations. Approximately twenty Portuguese-speaking international judges, prosecutors, defenders, and court clerks were introduced in 2004–2005. The addition of the international personnel has led to some improvements in the functioning of the system, but it still remains very slow, with large backlogs in both courts and prosecution, particularly for civil cases. The country is likely to rely upon international staff until at least 2009 and possibly as long as 2012.

Another crucial oversight has been the failure of both UNTAET and the first, diaspora-led Timorese government to build upon East Timor's customary conflict resolution mechanisms, which are an integral part of Timorese society.[26] Justice in Timorese communities is traditionally dealt with through nonstate systems aligned with local social structures and worldviews. Nearly every conflict beyond the family is brought to specialized elders, who can evoke ancestral linkages in negotiating a resolution to the case. Definitions of crime and appropriate punishment differ significantly from formal systems, leading in some cases to individuals being detained under the formal sector for deeds that they themselves did not perceive as wrongdoing. Customary punishments generally involve the provision of goods or labor or both by the guilty party, whereas jail sentences often do not "satisfy" victims. Additionally, formal justice systems simply cannot address certain kinds of issues, such as disputes over bride price, which underlie some local conflicts.

There is great demand both for a formal justice system and for customary systems to be recognized, particularly as the formal justice system remains inaccessible even for the middle class in Dili. Customary law remains both highly legitimate and the only system to which most Timorese have access, particularly in rural areas.[27] This issue demonstrates the fault line between institutions of the state and local practices, and the failure of the state to penetrate society or to respond to society's needs by providing pragmatic, accessible institutional arrangements that also relate to societal paradigms.

No adequate approach to the customary system has taken place under the Timorese administration, although there has been a significant amount of analytical work on the subject.[28] Based on this work, jurisdiction of customary justice practices could be defined to cover certain categories of crimes, such as petty theft, petty vandalism, and other common but minor infractions, as well as disputes revolving around customary practice such as bride price. For example, customary figures—*chefe do sucos,* groups of elders, or traditional rulers—could be legally empowered to render binding decisions in these cases, with the provision that either party would still have recourse to the formal system if not satisfied.[29] Such a system would be highly pragmatic, giving the desired legal legitimacy to local systems while keeping minor cases out of the formal courts. In designing such a system, East Timor could have drawn on expertise from other countries that have sought to recognize their customary systems in the interest of furthering access to justice.

In addition to the challenges of establishing a functional justice system, many Timorese and international actors sought redress for atrocities before Indonesia's withdrawal. In the absence of an international tribunal, UNTAET regulation 2000/15 created a special unit of international and Timorese judges, called the Serious Crimes Unit (SCU), to pursue crimes against humanity and cases of murder and serious sex offenses committed between January and October 1999. Following an initial period of poor management, the SCU ultimately issued 392 indictments against 440 defendants and won 84 convictions.[30] Unfortunately, the defendants in all the high-level indictments were in Indonesia, where many were tried in an inadequate process that yielded only two convictions, one of which was overturned.[31] The SCU ended in 2005 with the departure of UNMISET. Finally, a United Nations Independent Special Commission of Inquiry recommended approximately seventy cases for prosecution and dozens more for further investigation in connection with the 2006 violence. Very little progress has been made to date on these cases.

Managing Public Finance

East Timor's central economic challenge is to transform its significant oil revenues into economic growth. The macroeconomic situation has changed dramatically since 2002. For the first three years of independence, the country was dependent on international assistance to fund 40 percent of its modest annual budget. In addition to the resources devoted to UNTAET and subsequent UN missions, the United Nations, the World Bank, the International Monetary Fund, bilateral donors, and NGOs poured approximately $500 million in financial assistance into East Timor between 2000 and 2004.[32] UNTAET also managed an initial trust fund covering the recurrent and capital expenditures for nascent governmental structures, and the World Bank and the Asian Development Bank managed the Trust Fund for East Timor (TFET), which covered the costs of reconstruction and development in health, education, agriculture, infrastructure, microfinance, and community development.[33]

As of 2007, however, East Timor had in two years acquired $1.2 billion in savings from petroleum revenues, far more quickly than had been anticipated at independence, due in good part to the high global price of oil. Although per capita gross national income is rising rapidly due to petroleum revenues, going from $352 in 2002 to an estimated $847 in 2006, non-oil per capita gross domestic product is stagnant, going from $343 to $356 during the same period.[34] According to a poverty assessment carried out in 2001, 20 percent of Timorese live on less than $1 a day.[35] According to the 2004 census, unemployment rose from 6.2 percent in 2001 to 8.5 percent nationwide but is far higher in the urban areas of Dili and Baucau, at 23 percent in 2004.

After an economic recovery during the transition era, fueled in large part by internationally funded reconstruction projects and the large international presence, economic growth has been very slow, and it suffered a further setback with the 2006 crisis. A 2003 Demographic and Health Survey and census revealed that not only was the population, at 925,000, larger than expected, but East Timor also has one of the highest fertility rates in the world, at 7.8 children per woman.[36] At this rate, the population will double in just seventeen years, with approximately 10,000 new entrants into the labor market every year—making it challenging for the state to maintain the delivery of basic services.

The people of East Timor paid a huge economic price for independence in the destruction of 1999 and in the loss of the state subsidies and services of the Indonesian administration. Indonesia maintained a civil service of approximately 27,000 in East Timor. The state guaranteed the purchase of agricultural goods at subsidized prices. By contrast, East Timor in 2006 had a far smaller public service of only 17,000 public servants, including army and police. Programs such as USAID's Temporary Employment Program, which paid workers for small public works projects, and the World Bank's Community Empowerment Program, helped infuse some cash into the rural economy immediately after the 1999 crisis, but the rural population has had to adjust to a reduced state.

Given a lack of private investment, state spending will be the most important source of job creation and growth in the short term. The government has made moves in this direction, increasing the state budget from approximately $75 million in fiscal year 2005 to approximately $330 million in fiscal year 2007. Given poor budget execution, however, only a fraction of this sum was spent.

The public finance system was initially created by a joint effort involving UNTAET, the World Bank, the International Monetary Fund, Portugal, and Australia. Of the thirty-four regulations passed by UNTAET in 2000, twenty related to the state's finances, paving the way for the establishment of the treasury and central bank and for collection of tax and customs revenues. Although the combination of UNTAET and bilateral assistance produced a functional system, it remains dependent on internationals—a pragmatic option for the medium term but unsustainable in the long run. In the postindependence era, the strong, comparatively well-coordinated projects of bilaterals, international financial institutions, and UN missions have continued to support capacity building. In mid-2006, the World Bank and other donors launched a five-year, $40 million, financial management capacity–building program.

To date, East Timor has shown far greater capacity to collect than to spend revenues. Capacity constraints throughout the civil service, combined with a highly centralized system, have led to very poor budget execution—a situation that is frequently and erroneously mistaken for excessive rigidity in the petroleum savings arrangements. The government's inability to execute the budget has strangled many areas of service delivery and contributed to a sense of increasing dilapidation. Salaries are paid, but roads are not repaired. Schoolbooks remain undelivered, and broken photocopiers sit unrepaired. The problem is not failure to appropriate funds, but challenges in effective spending.

Financial management is highly centralized in the Ministry of Planning and Finance. The ministry was organized that way based on the view that the combination of low capacity and underdeveloped systems creates the potential for mismanagement. All procurement is carried out by a central procurement office, and each commitment voucher—even for five dollars—is signed by the minister. Petty cash allocations are low and can take weeks to be replenished. This effectively leaves civil servants without the basic goods and services necessary to do their jobs, much less undertake major capital development.

By contrast, the creation of a management regime for the country's oil revenues was the most significant statebuilding achievement of the Alkatiri government, which was determined to avoid the corruption, poverty, and conflict that have affected so many resource-rich countries. As Alkatiri noted in a speech at the Extractive Industries Transparency Initiative in 2004: "In this whole process we have been patently aware that our major challenge is to draw on the experience from other petroleum producing countries. Their experience today gives reason for serious concerns."[37]

With an agreement concluded between Australia and East Timor over maritime boundaries, East Timor stands to earn an estimated $12 to $15 billion in petroleum revenues from 2008 through 2028. In mid-2005, East Timor's parliament unanimously passed the Petroleum Fund Act, creating a Petroleum Fund into which all petroleum revenues will be deposited. The petroleum reserves are only projected to last for twenty-seven years, but the fund's assets will be invested offshore in order to provide an annual income of $200–300 million in perpetuity. All oil revenues must flow into the fund, which can only be used to support the national budget.

East Timor has also adopted measures to ensure transparency in line with the Extractive Industries Transparency Initiative, including publication of quarterly reports and annual financial statements of oil revenues, external audits, publication of company payments, and the creation of an independent Consultative Council to advise parliament on issues related to the Petroleum Fund. Signature bonuses are illegal. Expenditures and transfers from the fund can only be made as part of the routine budget process, not to exceed a ceiling set by parliament.

The relatively poor development performance of the first government and the rapid acquisition of substantial savings has led to political pressure for relaxation of revenue management arrangements, as witnessed by statements made by political figures during the 2007 elections. Because the country has no other significant source of revenue or investment, sustained state revenues and budgeting require continuing the petroleum savings and management arrangements.

Ensuring Security

Although UNTAET did well overall in providing the security and stability that allowed statebuilding to proceed—which, in East Timor, was less challenging than in other peacekeeping operations—the UN and other international actors have been less successful in building security institutions. Following independence, there was a steady decrease in the attention of international agencies to the security forces. A limited number of donors assisted the security forces, but security problems remained low-level concerns, and the security forces were not typically part of the discussion at formal and informal donor meetings. In addition, although some international organizations and diplomats did express concerns about developments within both the police and army prior to the 2006 crisis, the international community proved unwilling or unable to make the government pay attention to the matter.

A survey carried out in 2001 on perceptions of change since 1999 found that 85 percent of East Timorese perceived progress in safety and physical security.[38] The crisis of 2006 and continuing community violence in 2007 shattered this improved sense of security for those in Dili. East Timor's security institutions were at the core of the renewed conflict in 2006. The conflict started within the army, included prolonged and violent clashes between the police and army, and led to the collapse of the police force in Dili. Although the proximate causes of the violent clashes were miscommunication and poor decisions, the crisis also reflected deeper weaknesses in both institutions.

The Army

Unlike most other successful liberation forces of the postcolonial era, the East Timor resistance force, Falintil, did not automatically become the national army. From 1999 to 2001, Falintil remained in the cantonments where

Xanana Gusmão had ordered them to stay during the referendum, recognizing that Falintil engagement with the militias would prompt Indonesia to present the 1999 violence as a Timorese civil war.[39] Falintil posed a challenge for UNTAET, as its mandate included no reference to Falintil or security sector development other than police.[40] Additionally, elements of the UNTAET leadership failed to grasp that the conflict in East Timor was not a civil war but a successful nationalist struggle. The UN did not stand between two antagonistic armed groups—that is, Falintil and the militias—but rather had to find a way to deal respectfully with those whom the community regarded as the heroes of the resistance. UNTAET also faced an institutional challenge in the uncertainty surrounding the role of the UN in the development of defense forces. The problem was eventually dealt with by the creation of the Office of Defense Force Development, which was eventually folded into the Ministry of Defense (MOD).

There had initially been some debate as to whether East Timor would have a national army at all. But as a result of the 1999 violence, the Timorese leadership demanded that a national army be established and would only agree to demobilize Falintil in conjunction with the formation of a new force, which occurred on February 1, 2001. The force was initially named simply Forças de Defesa de Timor Leste (FDTL) but "Falintil" was added to the name in the constitution (Falintil–Forças de Defesa de Timor Leste, or F-FDTL).[41] Of the approximately 1,900 members of Falintil, 650 were selected to join the new army and the remainder were demobilized.

Early missteps by the international community in dealing with Falintil limited the space for frank dialogue on whether East Timor actually needed a defense force and on the establishment of F-FDTL itself. Additionally, neither UNTAET nor the Timorese leadership carried out public education campaigns to explain why Falintil needed to be demobilized and a new force created, nor were there public consultations on the need for or shape of a national defense force.

The selection process for F-FDTL produced an officer corps largely from the east of the country, which proved to be a factor in the 2006 crisis. Decisions on who would join the defense force and who would be demobilized were made by the Falintil high command, without reference to clear, publicized criteria. The preponderance of easterners in the officer corps reflected the historical fact that the armed resistance had survived most strongly in the east due to its greater distance from the Indonesian border and more favorable terrain. By 1999, the longest-serving officers were overwhelmingly from the east, although some central-western districts contributed large numbers of soldiers. The army subsequently corrected the overall balance through new recruits, with F-FDTL reaching its planned strength of 1,500 in 2004. However, the top officer corps remained largely eastern, opening officers to charges of regional favoritism in personnel decisions.

Despite international assistance to the defense force, including help with drafting laws and regulations, the Timorese government neglected to develop an institutional framework for the F-FDTL. Five years after its creation, F-FDTL still had no disciplinary law. The country had no threat assessment or defense policy. The army was effectively without a mandate. The F-FDTL force development plan, drafted in 2001, was only updated in 2006. There was no law or regulation on military service, which would have, for example, provided a framework for addressing the real or perceived grievances of soldiers from the west with respect to promotion and leave policy. Following the 2006 crisis, a number of laws that had been drafted earlier were hastily passed by the Horta government.

Even less institution building occurred within the Ministry of Defense. Four years after independence, the MOD had hired only four staff out of over thirty budgeted positions. Both F-FDTL and the MOD depend on international technical assistance, with up to twenty international advisers at any given time. F-FDTL officers widely perceived the government as devoting more attention and resources to the police force, fueling animosity between the two forces. On numerous occasions, officers, international advisers, and independent observers warned of these serious institutional problems. For example, an investigation into a clash between army and police in Los Palos in 2004 found that the army suffered from poor morale and discipline because of issues ranging from the lack of a mandate to the fact that the army used three different kinds of uniforms donated by three different countries.

Following independence, one of the government's most significant achievements was its rapid move to recognize and assist former combatants from the struggle against the Indonesian occupation. The months surrounding independence in 2002 saw agitation for assistance and recognition by groups purporting to represent veterans. Recognizing the issue as potentially destabilizing, President Gusmão established a series of commissions to register veterans and formulate policy recommendations. Included in the registration were veterans of the unarmed clandestine resistance, a group typically neglected in postconflict settings. The parliament passed a veterans' law in March 2006; award ceremonies for veterans commenced in late 2006. The law also contained provisions for payment of pensions, scheduled to start in 2007. The fact that veterans' grievances did not feature prominently in the political discourse surrounding the instability in 2006 and 2007 is a testament to the progress that had already been made in this area.

The Police

UNTAET moved quickly to establish a Timorese police force in 2000. Under UNTAET, the roles of operational policing and the training of the Policia Nacional de Timor-Leste (PNTL) were combined under the approximately 1,300 international UN Civilian Police.[42] However, UNTAET prioritized rapid deployment over institution building. For example, only after the first PNTL officers had been deployed in 2000 did UNTAET realize the police had no equipment to work with and had to request an emergency allocation from the Consolidated Fund for East Timor.[43] As of 2004, the PNTL had reached its planned strength of 3,000 officers. Thanks to UNTAET recruitment policy and gender equality efforts, 18–20 percent of PNTL officers are women, which is high by international standards.

The government of East Timor assumed full operational responsibility for internal and external security functions exactly two years after independence. The dual operational and training role of UN Police had a number of weaknesses as a model for creating a police force.[44] Most conspicuously, it impeded the development of a coherent policing model and esprit de corps. Generally lacking specialized training skills or a common language with the Timorese, the UN Police encompassed officers from forty different countries who lacked a common model of policing or sufficient knowledge of applicable law in East Timor. As a result, PNTL operated with and according to systems that often differed from district to district, rather than developing its own institutional systems and procedures. The UN Police approach never fostered the development of an institutional identity within the PNTL. This lack of institutional identity arguably contributed to the splintering and collapse of the police force in Dili during the 2006 crisis.

On the whole, the UN Police did not prioritize helping Timorese counterparts to build PNTL into an institution appropriate to Timorese social and fiscal realities. Instead, UN Police carried out their duties as the territory's police force and then "handed over" districts to PNTL. The notion of handing over disregarded the enormous differences in policing skills, management capacity, funding, and equipment resources between the PNTL and UN Police. Under subsequent UN missions, rapid turnover in advisers has meant constant changes in advice, training, and the development of institutional systems.

The UN approach to police development left the PNTL with weak administrative systems and management and an unformed legal and policy framework.[45] Some progress has been made in these areas since 2002: the organic laws for the PNTL and for the Ministry of the Interior, as well as the Police Disciplinary Regulation, were passed in July 2004, supplanting previous UNTAET laws. However, operational policies have not been developed. Australia and the UK have provided AUS$33 million for a four-year program (July 2004 to December 2008), and Japan, Malaysia, the United States, China, and Indonesia are all providing assistance, as have Canada, Portugal, and Brazil in the past.

The UN missions and other international agencies in East Timor have succeeded in instilling awareness of human rights in Timorese communities, through the presence of human rights officers in the districts, community workshops, cooperation with Timorese human rights NGOs, and targeted training for the police and other professional groups. Nevertheless, in April 2006, Human Rights Watch published a critical report, *Tortured Beginnings: Police Violence and the Beginnings of Impunity in East Timor,* detailing increases in police abuses. With respect to the PNTL, aspirations regarding adherence to human rights norms have not been met, indicating that far greater attention must be given to building the systems and incentives necessary to prevent abuse as well as creating normative demand for good police behavior.

The functioning of the police varies from district to district. In many stations, delegation and implementation of basic tasks are patchy. However, there have been improvements in some areas. For example, the notion of a limited pretrial detention period is now better understood and adhered to by the police, although this gain has unfortunately been offset by weaknesses in the prosecution and court systems. In some areas, police have shown an increased ability and willingness to work with community leaders and customary authorities. In the 2006 crisis, the police collapsed in Dili but continued to function in the districts.

Arguably the most serious problem facing PNTL in the years immediately following independence was the civilian administration. The PNTL falls under the Ministry of the Interior, and under former minister Rogerio Lobato, the distinction between civilian oversight and executive policing was regularly blurred, compromising the independence of the PNTL.[46] Lobato contributed to the fragmentation of the PNTL, as well as tensions between east and west, by promoting police officers from the west and fostering client-patron relations with circles of officers personally loyal to him. Further, there was little development of the Ministry of the Interior as an institution and neglect of ministry responsibilities other than the police, such as civil security and disaster relief.

In addition to the challenges faced by the army and police as institutions, their poorly articulated mandates, particularly of the army, have led to confusion and perceived overlap in the respective roles of police and army. In 2003, with the sanction of UNMISET, which retained overall authority over the police, the government created the Police Reserves, a paramilitary unit stationed outside Dili. This unit and the Rapid Intervention Unit were armed with automatic rifles. The move infuriated the army, contributed to tensions between the forces, and raised concerns within the public about clashes between army and police.

The 2006 Crisis
In January 2006, 400 soldiers went on strike, alleging discrimination against soldiers from the west by commanders from the east, ill treatment, and poor conditions. The striking soldiers, their ranks having swelled to 591, were

dismissed in early March 2006. The split cut the army by over one-third, leaving only 850 soldiers. It was followed by the desertion of Major Alfredo Reinado, head of the army's military police, a westerner, with a significant number of weapons and men.

At the end of April 2006, a demonstration by the "petitioners," as they came to be called, turned violent. After the failure of the police to maintain order, the army was called in. Following a few weeks of relative calm, violence erupted at the end of May with a series of violent clashes between army and police. Despite the arrival of international troops, the clashes were followed by days of serious communal violence, which broadly pitted easterners against westerners. The entire crisis led to scores of dead, the destruction of approximately 2,000 homes, and, at its height, the displacement of the majority of Dili's population. Although some order was restored by early June, violence continued at the community level into 2007, with long periods of daily clashes between gangs taking advantage of the breakdown of law and order, which the UN Police and international military forces were hard put to restore.

The crisis left both the police and army of East Timor operationally and institutionally damaged. During the rioting and arson, the police force in Dili collapsed, although the force continued to function in the districts. The standing of the army as a national institution and symbol was badly compromised. The crisis highlighted the institutional weaknesses and lack of overall policy and oversight frameworks for both forces, as well as the politicization and cronyism that had evolved within the police force.[47]

Conclusion

The challenge for the people of East Timor has been to create a functioning state amid the economic and physical destruction of 1999 and a legacy of colonial occupation. The international community has provided indispensable financial and technical assistance to this effort, as well as security in the form of peacekeepers. However, state institutions built by both the original UN administration and the Timorese government have not been able to prevent the most recent outbreak of violence. Even though the situation of East Timor is in many respects unique, some lessons emerge about statebuilding for international actors.

The example of East Timor shows that the involvement of the population and the reflection of its ideas and values in the governance system is essential to the creation of a successful state. Unfortunately, UNTAET started with the misperception that there was a political vacuum in the country. The mission decided at a crucial early stage not to create systemic mechanisms for sharing power with Timorese, relying instead on consultations with a relatively small number of people. A more formalized partnership between UNTAET and the CNRT could have helped the Timorese leadership gain experience in governing at all levels. If the situation permits—and in East Timor it did—local leadership needs to be given the lead in the statebuilding exercise. Statebuilding has a better chance of succeeding when there is legitimate local leadership and broad popular support.

Establishing security and constraining violence through rule of law is one of the primary functions of the state. There will always be conflict, but what is important is that society develops the tools to handle conflict and provides room for nonviolent opposition. Constructing these tools is at the very heart of building state institutions. However, the act of establishing democratic institutions does not mean that democracy instantly replaces other political paradigms.

Two crucial issues arise: how to create fast and efficient local representation, and how to ensure that one has the "right" local leadership? To ensure that statebuilding incorporates local visions requires the creation of mechanisms that can rapidly involve local actors. The challenge for statebuilders is to devise systems that are first based on an understanding of the political environment, thus ensuring that local interlocutors are legitimate leaders in the eyes of the population, and, second, can guarantee some form of representation. In some cases, this might entail quickly arranging elections from the bottom up. In other cases, elections might not be seen as a fair means of selecting leaders, requiring other appropriate mechanisms.

Any international effort to support statebuilding must be grounded in an understanding of local forces, norms, and values: ignorance of them will render such efforts irrelevant. And the international community must be realistic about challenges, responsibilities, and expectations. It is very difficult to build institutions or initiate reforms that are not based on local realities. As Francis Fukuyama points out, "The majority of cases of successful statebuilding and institutional reform have occurred when a society has generated strong domestic demand for institutions and then created them out of whole cloth, imported them from the outside, or adapted foreign models to local conditions."[48] The East Timorese experience demonstrates that ideas and models imported from the international community are most influential when there is national demand, in which case timely and competent international assistance can lead to speedy results. The creation of East Timor's Petroleum Fund Act and other measures for managing its oil revenue are good examples.

The international community must also recognize the limitations of its influence in a sovereign state. Greater innovation on the part of the statebuilders in drawing on local models and injecting more voices from countries that have experienced similar conflicts, transitions, and institution-building challenges could expand the repertoire of tactics and strategies used in creating institutions appropriate to local realities. Ideally, international advisers should play a facilitative role, helping local counterparts to explore international models while building on their own experiences and norms.

Fragile postconflict countries might require a sensitive third party to maneuver in a delicate political environment. In these cases, it is of utmost importance to cooperate with the local population and to design systems that reflect local views. The case of East Timor demonstrates that the legitimacy of an international transitional administration rapidly erodes if it is not based on local ownership. Foreigners can temporarily fulfill many state functions, lend critical financial and technical support, and contribute to security, but they lack local legitimacy and local knowledge and cannot substitute for local leadership very long.

Notes

Edith Bowles worked from 2000 to 2002 for USAID's Office of Transition Initiatives and from 2003 to 2007 for the World Bank in East Timor. Tanja Chopra was a political affairs officer with UNTAET. The authors are grateful to Elisabeth Huybens, Jim Della-Giacoma, Jarat Chopra, and Joaquim Fonseca for their insights and discussions in the writing of this chapter.

The views expressed in this chapter are solely those of the authors.

1. See, for example, "East Timor Independence: Annan's Speech," *BBC News,* May 20, 2002, http://news.bbc.co.uk/2/hi/not_in_website/syndication/monitoring/media_reports/1997322.stm.

2. See, for example, David Hicks, *Tetum Ghosts and Kin: Fieldwork in an Indonesian Community* (Palo Alto, CA: Mayfield, 1976); Brigitte Renard-Clamagirand, *Marobo: Une Société Ema de Timor* (Paris: SELAF, 1982); Elisabeth G. Traube, *Cosmology and Social Life: Ritual Exchange Among the Mambai of East Timor* (Chicago: University of Chicago Press, 1986).

3. Andrew McWilliam, "Houses of Resistance in East Timor: Structuring Sociality in the New Nation," *Anthropological Forum* 15, no. 1 (March 2005): 27–44.

4. Fretilin comes from Frente Revolucionária do Timor-Leste Independente (Revolutionary Front for an Independent East Timor); UDT's full name in Portuguese is União Democrática Timorense. For a history of these parties, see Jill Jolliffe, *East Timor: Nationalism and Colonialism* (St. Lucia: University of Queensland Press, 1978).

5. The Commission for Reception, Truth, and Reconciliation Timor-Leste, better known by its Portuguese acronym CAVR, released its final report in January 2006. See *Chega! The Report of the Commission on Reception, Truth, and Reconciliation Timor-Leste* (Dili: CAVR, 2006).

6. Forças Armadas de Liberatação National de Timor-Leste (Armed Forces of National Liberation of East Timor).

7. Head of the *suco,* lowest level of public administration in East Timor. Additionally, *chefe do suco* often come from traditional ruling families.

8. There is an extensive literature on UNTAET, its mandate for intervention, and its successes and failures. See Astri Suhrke, "Peacekeepers as Nation-Builders: Dilemmas of the UN in East Timor," *International Peacekeeping* 8, no. 4 (Winter 2001): 1–20; Simon Chesterman, *East Timor in Transition: From Conflict Prevention to State-Building* (New York: International Peace Academy, 2001); Paulo Gorjão, "The Legacy and Lessons of the United Nations Transitional Administration in East

Timor," *Contemporary Southeast Asia* 24, no. 2 (August 2002): 313–336; Anthony Goldstone, "UNTAET with Hindsight: The Peculiarities of Politics in an Incomplete State," *Global Governance* 10, no. 1 (2004): 83–98; and Conflict, Security and Development Group, *A Review of Peace Operations: A Case for a Change* (London: King's College, 2003).

9. See UN Security Council Resolution 1272 (1999), UN Doc. S/RES/1272.

10. "United Nations Transitional Administration in East Timor," http://www.un.org/peace/etimor/etimor.htm (accessed August 29, 2005).

11. This was suggested by some observers. See Jim Della-Giacoma, "The Next Step: East Timor Deserves Democracy," *Asian Wall Street Journal*, June 22, 2000, p. 7.

12. The authors are indebted to Joaquim Fonseca for some of these insights.

13. This also reflected the general atmosphere of political repression in Suharto-era Indonesia.

14. Tanja Hohe, "Totem Polls: Indigenous Concepts and 'Free and Fair' Elections in East Timor," *International Peacekeeping* 9, no. 4 (Winter 2002): 69–88.

15. Most obviously, Fretilin has been accused of deliberately creating a weak presidency, having correctly anticipated that Xanana Gusmão, rather than a Fretilin member, would win the presidential election. Overall the constitution draws heavily from the Portuguese and other lusophone constitutions.

16. The drafting process was originally supposed to take only three months.

17. Conflict, Security, and Development Group, *A Review of Peace Operations: A Case for Change* (London: Kings College, 2003), p. 251.

18. See also United Nations, *Report of the Secretary-General on Timor-Leste Pursuant to Security Council Resolution 1690*, UN Doc. S/2006/628, August 8, 2006.

19. Tanja Hohe, "The Clash of Paradigms: International Administration and Local Political Legitimacy in East Timor," *Contemporary Southeast Asia* 24, no. 3 (December 2002): 569–589.

20. Jarat Chopra, "Building State Failure in East Timor," *Development and Change* 33, no. 5 (November 2002): 992–994; La'o Hamutuk, "The World Bank in East Timor," *La'o Hamutuk Bulletin* 1, no. 4 (December 2000), www.etan.org/lh/bulletin04.html; and Joel C. Beauvais, "Benevolent Despotism: A Critique of U.N. State-Building in East Timor," *New York University Journal of International Law and Politics* 33, no. 4 (Summer 2001): 1126.

21. Tanja Hohe, "Local Governance After Conflict: Community Development in East Timor," *Journal of Peacebuilding and Development* 1, no. 3 (2004): 45–56.

22. *La'o Hamutuk Bulletin* 6, no. 3 (August 2005).

23. Secretary-General, *Report of the Secretary-General on Timor-Leste pursuant to Security Council Resolution 1690*, para. 94.

24. National Directorate of Statistics, *Timor-Leste: Census of Population and Housing 2004* (Dili, 2006). Figures refer to percentage of population over six years of age who report being able to speak, read, and write.

25. Suzannah Linton, "Rising from the Ashes: The Creation of a Viable Criminal System in East Timor," *Melbourne University Law Review* 25, no. 1 (2001): 6.

26. The first analytical work on the issue in the UNTAET period was conducted by David Mearns in 2001. See Mearns, "Variations on a Theme: Coalitions of Authority in East Timor: A Report on the Local and National Justice Systems as a Basis for Dispute Resolution," prepared for Australian Legal Resources International, December 2001.

27. See also Tanja Hohe, "Justice Without Judiciary in East Timor," *Conflict, Security and Development* 3, no. 3 (December 2003): 335–357.

28. See, for example, Timor-Leste Land Law Program, *Report on Research Findings and Policy Recommendations for a Legal Framework for Land Dispute Mediation,* prepared with funding provided by USAID, February 2004; Aisling Swaine, *Traditional Justice and Gender-Based Violence* (New York: International Rescue Committee Research Report, August 2003); Judicial System Monitoring Programme, "Findings and Recommendations: Workshop on Formal and Local Justice Systems in East Timor" (Dili, 2002); Spencer Zifcak, *Restorative Justice in East Timor: An Evaluation of the Community Reconciliation Process of the CAVR* (Dili, Timor-Leste Asia Foundation, 2004).

29. The USAID-funded land law project proposed a very well-designed system for the mediation of land disputes involving three levels, starting with local/customary practices and ending with courts if disputes could not be settled at a lower level.

30. This resulted in an investigation of the SCU leadership, which ultimately did not find wrongdoing, but the effectiveness of the unit was seriously affected for its first eighteen months of operation.

31. The other, Eurico Guterres, seems unlikely to serve his sentence.

32. World Bank, *Country Assistance Strategy for the Democratic Republic of Timor-Leste, for the Period FY06–FY08* (Washington, DC, 2005). UN contributions to these figures encompass advisers to government. This figure does not include the approximately $1.85 billion spent on successive UN missions. Approximate total costs by mission: UNTAET, $1.2 billion; UNMISET, $565 million; UNOTIL, $22 million. See Center on International Cooperation, *Annual Review of Global Peace Operations 2006* (Boulder, CO: Lynne Rienner, 2006), p. 170.

33. Since its establishment in 2000, eleven donors have contributed to TFET, and the fund had committed over $177.85 million as of February 2006. See Trust Fund for East Timor, *Report of the Trustee: Executive Summary,* March 31, 2006, http://siteresources.worldbank.org/INTTIMORLESTE/Resources/TFET_Work_Program_April2006-March2007_cleared_final.pdf (accessed June 14, 2007).

34. International Monetary Fund, Public Information Notice, No. 07/24, http://www.imf.org/external/np/sec/pn/2007/pn0724.htm (accessed July 30, 2007).

35. The Poverty Assessment Project drew on three different sources of data, including the Suco Survey, the Participatory Potential Assessment, and the Household Survey, an analysis of which was published in *Poverty in a New Nation: Analysis for Action* (2003).

36. Timor-Leste Demographic and Health Survey.

37. Former Prime Minister Mari Alkatiri, *Remarks Made to EITI Conference,* London, March 17, 2004.

38. See United Nations Development Programme, *Timor-Leste Human Development Report 2006: The Path Out of Poverty—Integrated Rural Development* (Dili, 2006), p. 7.

39. Initially in 1999, Falintil set up camp in several cantonments; after the entry of the international forces, Falintil gathered in the Aileu cantonment south of Dili.

40. Conflict, Security, and Development Group, *A Review of Peace Operations: A Case for Change* (London: Kings College, 2003), p. 47.

41. Symbolically, the name will make it harder to reform or dismantle the force, as some have called for in the wake of the 2006 crisis. If the force had remained "FDTL," disbanding it as an experiment of the transitional era that was no longer needed might have been possible. The hyphenated name links the force to the historical legacy of the resistance, making it harder to entertain a full range of options for the future of the force.

42. After UNTAET ended, the UN Civilian Police were renamed the UN Police (UNPOL), in keeping with a new UN practice.

43. Conflict, Security, and Development Group, *A Review of Peace Operations: A Case for Change* (London: Kings College, 2003), section 2.G.

44. The general operation challenges associated with UN policing operations, such as the wide range of policing models and poor coordination, have been well-documented, including in the Brahimi report. See United Nations, *Report of the Panel on United Nations Peace Operations* (Brahimi Report), UN Doc. A/55/305-S/2000/809, August 21, 2000. For a discussion of the strengths and shortcomings of the UNPOL policing operations in East Timor, see Conflict, Security, and Development Group, *A Review of Peace Operations: A Case for Change* (London: Kings College, 2003); and Ronald A. West, "East Timor," in Charles T. Call, ed., *Constructing Justice and Security After War* (Washington, DC: US Institute of Peace Press, 2007).

45. Timor-Leste Police Service, *Joint Assessment Mission Final Report, 2002.*

46. From the central-western district of Liquica, Lobato is the younger brother of Nicolau Lobato, the first president of Fretilin and commander of Falintil, who was killed by Indonesian forces in late 1978. He is currently serving a seven-and-a-half-year sentence in prison for his role in the 2006 crisis.

47. See United Nations, *Report of the United Nations Independent Special Commission of Inquiry for Timor-Leste,* Geneva, October 2, 2006.

48. Francis Fukuyama, *State-building: Governance and World Order in the 21st Century* (Ithaca, NY: Cornell University Press, 2004), p. 35.

13

Afghanistan: Nationally Led Statebuilding

Jake Sherman

Throughout the 1990s, international involvement in weak or fragile states was viewed as a humanitarian or moral imperative rather than a strategic interest. Military intervention, championed on a case-by-case basis, was reserved for the most egregious cases of human suffering, if used at all. Complex statebuilding exercises were viewed with skepticism by nations wary of committing forces to risky, open-ended missions without clear strategic or domestic political interests at stake. The attacks of September 11, 2001, altered this calculus. Absent serious international engagement to end the civil war and redress state failure after the end of the Cold War, Afghanistan had become a base for international terrorists capable of striking across the world. To Western policymakers, the attacks demonstrated the importance of investing in statebuilding operations lest fragile or "failed" states provide fertile ground for terrorism and other threats to international security.

The complexity of statebuilding in Afghanistan brought about innovations, including the concepts underlying how UN peace operations relate to host states and the interface of international civilian missions and military operations. Moreover, as the first statebuilding mission since the beginning of the "war on terror" and the UN's first peace operation after the 2000 Brahimi Report on peace operations, Afghanistan offers important lessons for both current and future peacebuilding and statebuilding exercises.[1]

Primary among these lessons is the challenge of executing a peace operation in parallel with ongoing warfare. Under US command, the Coalition Forces continue to fight Taliban and other antigovernment insurgents in Afghanistan. This agenda at times has been at odds with the peacebuilding and statebuilding objectives pursued by the UN and wider assistance community. Tensions exist between the international community's twin goals of establishing a strong state capable of maintaining order and resisting terrorism, on the one hand, and its ideals of democracy and respect for human rights

303

on the other hand. The decision to continue to rely upon Afghan militias after the removal of the Taliban, a key example, strengthened warlords opposed to the emergence of a strong central state and ostracized a majority of the population.

Afghanistan demonstrates that in a highly unstable security environment, peacekeeping forces, whether provided by the UN, a regional organization, or an ad hoc grouping of states, must provide an immediate, nationwide security umbrella for civilian reconstruction and political activities. Security is the sine qua non for delivery of services; both are essential to building and maintaining state legitimacy. Without such a force, the vacuum was filled by armed factions and insurgents. The latter have directly targeted nascent government institutions, reconstruction projects, major political events, and national and international staff responsible for their implementation. Insecurity has severely restricted access by UN and nongovernmental organization (NGO) staff to large areas of the country, limiting the peace dividend enjoyed by local communities and, in places, undermining confidence in the new government.

Inadequate security forces also have required compromises in the political arena that, although necessary in the short term, have had negative consequences for long-term stability. The decision to allow political participation by factional leaders prevented spoilers from emerging, but it has marginalized moderates and impeded extension of the national government. Unable to stand up to factional leaders on its own, the government, too, has been forced to make deals damaging to its own interests. This, in turn, affects other critical issues, from ethnic and political reconciliation, emergence of rule of law, and checking the growing drug trade, to maintaining public confidence in government and collecting the revenue needed to attain fiscal sustainability.

The UN's "light footprint approach" has been a central feature of statebuilding in Afghanistan. Unlike the UN transitional administrations in Kosovo and East Timor, power was transferred to an Afghan-led Interim Administration after the departure of the prior regime. Under the circumstances, the light footprint may have been the only option for the UN, given that its engagement was limited by the scale of the country and the war-fighting priorities of the United States and its military partners in the "war on terror." By defining the space and role for other international actors' involvement in Afghanistan, the coalition hindered deployment of a larger-scale UN mission and, at least initially, an international security force beyond Kabul.

Nationally led statebuilding has played a critical legitimizing role for the Afghan government. The UN has assisted the consolidation of state authority by working through—and simultaneously building up—state institutions. This in turn has increased government legitimacy and accountability. At the same time, the emphasis on a lead role for the government has created unreasonable expectations among Afghans about what it is able to deliver, as its capacity is not yet equal to their needs. The cautious optimism that was built during the Bonn process has subsequently eroded, as Afghans increasingly question the ability of the central government to exert control in the provinces and resent missteps by international troops.

Measuring the UN's accomplishments against its mandate—admittedly, a narrow test—the light footprint has proven the right approach in Afghanistan. The political objectives of the 2001 Bonn Agreement largely have been realized. Afghanistan has a new constitution, an elected president, and a parliament. Key Bonn-mandated commissions, such as the Afghan Independent Human Rights Commission (AIHRC), are functioning. But the real measure of successful statebuilding in Afghanistan, of course, is not completion of Bonn, nor is it the UN mission's record. Rather, it is whether the state can provide for the safety and well-being of its people and whether it is perceived as legitimate by its citizens. The elusiveness of security in Afghanistan is emblematic of shortcomings in the wider statebuilding approach of the international community. Likewise, maintaining a light footprint required compromises—for example, scaling down certain UN responsibilities, divesting some to other international actors—that diminished the effectiveness of the mission. These warrant consideration before such smaller, integrated missions become the new paradigm for UN statebuilding. Ultimately Afghanistan underscores the importance of security, both as an enabling environment and an end in itself.

Historical Background

During more than two decades of armed conflict, the Afghan state and its institutions exhibited great weakness. Rapid modernization policies and political repression instituted by the communist government that seized power in 1978 sparked Islamist-oriented rebellions in the countryside. As the rebellions spread and the Afghan army disintegrated, the Soviet Union invaded in December 1979, seeking to stabilize the country. Yet, from the early 1980s, increasing swaths of the countryside fell under the control of the externally supported mujahidin guerrillas, eventually forcing the withdrawal of Soviet Union in 1989 and, in 1992, the collapse of the Afghan communist government. Under the mujahidin government, the political and economic situation worsened as rival factions turned on one another. The anarchy and lawlessness of their rule created the conditions that swept the Taliban to power during the 1990s.

The Taliban instilled strict Islamic order over Afghans' daily lives but demonstrated little interest in administering the state. By the late 1990s, evidence that the Taliban were harboring international terrorists, as well as the regime's repressive treatment of women, earned it increasing isolation in international circles, leading to UN sanctions in 2000.[2] Afghans had to rely on the UN and NGOs to provide basic services. This assistance, channeled through local communities and military commanders, further weakened the state. Although there were attempts by the UN to secure peace talks between the Taliban and the opposition United Front, without international commitment, these efforts met no success.[3] Indeed, since the collapse of the Soviet Union, Afghanistan had languished as a forgotten victim of the Cold War with little help in sight.

International apathy toward state failure and humanitarian disaster in Afghanistan ended after the September 11, 2001, attacks on the United States. Afghanistan's pariah status had provided a safe haven for the radical, anti-Western Islamic terrorists who planned the attack. The Taliban had welcomed their foreign guests to use the country for this end. When they refused to expel the leadership of Al-Qaida, a US-led international coalition undertook UN Security Council–approved military action to remove the Taliban from power and eliminate Al-Qaida. That enabled the transfer of UN recognition from the de jure government of President Burhanuddin Rabbani to an interim administration.

On December 5, 2001, representatives of the United Front and other Afghan constituencies meeting in Bonn, Germany, on the future of Afghanistan signed an agreement on the composition of the Interim Administration, to be led by Hamid Karzai; a legal framework based on the 1964 constitution; and a three-year timetable for a transition to a freely and fairly elected democratic government.[4] The Bonn Agreement mandated several specialized commissions to facilitate this process and called on the UN to provide assistance. Critical issues, including reconciliation with the previous regime, the timetable for disarmament, and transitional justice, were excluded from Bonn and, consequently, would have to be redressed later on.

UN Statebuilding "Lite"

Following the Security Council authorization of the use of force against the Taliban, there was overwhelming agreement that the UN would play a key role in the political transition and economic reconstruction of Afghanistan. The question was what *kind* of role. The model of recent missions in Kosovo and East Timor, where the Special Representative of the Secretary-General (SRSG) was vested with executive authority in UN-run transitional administrations, might not be a good fit for Afghanistan for several reasons. They included a large country with rudimentary transportation and communication networks, complex domestic politics, a hostile security environment in which international military forces not only operated outside UN command but also defined the political space within which it would operate, and the existence of a recognized Afghan government.

The outcome was shaped by the selection of Lakhdar Brahimi, a former UN Special Representative in Afghanistan and chairman of the Panel on UN Peace Operations, as SRSG.[5] The UN Assistance Mission in Afghanistan (UNAMA), established in March 2002, was given a three-part mandate. First, it had a major role in assisting the government in meeting the benchmarks laid out in the Bonn Agreement.[6] Second, it was to promote national reconciliation through the good offices of the SRSG. Third, UNAMA was to lead the UN country team and coordinate the work of the UN agencies assisting relevant government ministries with relief, recovery, and reconstruction in accordance with the government's own priorities.[7]

In theory, the Bonn Agreement endowed the Afghan government with overall responsibility for statebuilding. The "light footprint" meant that the primary strategy of the UN would be to work through the Afghan government, relying on as few international—and as many Afghan—staff as possible. The approach explicitly recognized that a transitional government run by Afghans would have far greater credibility than a UN administration. In practice, however, the Afghan government had to relearn how to govern while simultaneously administering the state. Certain institutions have proved more adept at this than others. Under the initial leadership of Ashraf Ghani, the Ministry of Finance emerged as a strong advocate of government-led policy formation. Elsewhere, a weak civil service and limited authority outside Kabul restricted what the government was able to provide.

In effect, the government's international partners retained responsibility for delivering results, even if the government would be held accountable by the Afghan people. The dearth of qualified Afghan civil servants and civil society required the UN and the World Bank to place international technical advisers within the Bonn commissions and the Afghan ministries. At the provincial and district levels, even fewer qualified civil servants severely limited the capacity of the central government to deliver essential services on its own. The reality of the light footprint was further complicated by the fact that, although UNAMA had few staff on the ground, the myriad UN agencies and programs had a relatively heavy footprint, creating parallel service delivery mechanisms. Other international partners were needed to take on areas beyond the remit of the UN, including security sector reform. Having so many different actors has required better coordination mechanisms, although they have not always produced coherent results.

Large, internationally staffed and administered transitional administrations may be better able to implement services and consolidate security, but they do so without necessarily preparing inexperienced national institutions for actually governing and without giving the nascent government the opportunity to build legitimacy. Karzai and the reformists have gained the support of an overwhelming portion of the population who see them as an alternative to the "warlords." The trade-off is that they are now in danger of losing popular support the longer delivery of essential services—especially security—is delayed.

The Bonn Agreement: A Road Map for Peace?

If Brahimi influenced the UN's strategy for statebuilding in Afghanistan, the Bonn process provided its road map. The Bonn Agreement was not a peace agreement, nor did it provide a basis for national reconciliation. Instead, it was an agreement among victors. When the Taliban regime collapsed, the overwhelming majority of its foot soldiers simply returned to their villages. The exclusion of Taliban representatives ensured that a significant portion of the predominantly Pashtun population supportive of the old regime were unrepresented. The entrenchment of ethnic Tajiks in state security institutions exacerbated the sense of exclusion from the new government among Pashtuns, who had traditionally governed in Afghanistan, and other ethnic groups. At the same time, the United States and other international actors have worked behind the scenes to engineer their preferred outcomes. To the international community, the political process was a means of steadily conferring legitimacy on the new government. In contrast, the various groupings represented in Bonn—Islamists, modernizers, monarchists, and republicans—envisioned the political process as a means of advancing their own visions of the future of the state vis-à-vis one another. Encouraging would-be spoilers to remain in the political process while simultaneously eroding their authority and balancing public demands for holding them accountable has been the fundamental political challenge facing President Karzai.

The political transition outlined in Bonn contained now-standard instruments of statebuilding—choosing a transitional government, drafting a new constitution, holding national elections—but tailored to the traditional representative decisionmaking role of the *loya jirga,* or grand council, in Afghanistan. Convened in June 2002 to make decisions about a Transitional Administration, an Emergency Loya Jirga (ELJ) provided a political forum for discussions on the future of the country among a wider constituency than the Bonn talks.[8] During the run-up to the ELJ, consultations and public delegate elections were held throughout the country in an effort to make the process as inclusive as possible. By the time it gathered, though, intimidation, vote buying, and political appointments had ensured domination by the country's factional leadership over the proceedings, angering Afghans who hoped that the new political process would mark a break from the past.

The primary responsibility of ELJ delegates was to choose a transitional government. By subjecting the selection to a wider, more public body than that which appointed the Interim Administration in Bonn, the ELJ aimed to choose a president broadly representative of national aspirations, thereby generating more legitimacy for the transitional government. The stakes were high. The ELJ offered factional leaders, particularly Islamists regarded as antidemocratic, and other political blocs the opportunity to gain power. Openly and behind the scenes, the United States worked to influence the proceedings. US envoy Zalmay Khalilzad, later appointed as ambassador in Kabul, persuaded former king Mohammad Zahir Shah to stand down as a candidate for head of state and back Karzai. With their preferred candidate overwhelmingly reconfirmed as head of state, the United States and UNAMA were able to ensure that military commanders would be appointed to key positions in the cabinet, giving them a stake in the peace process and encouraging them to resolve differences with the government peacefully rather than by force.[9] However, the only modest changes from the Interim Administration's cabinet underscored to Afghans that representative democracy, let alone defactionalization of the government, was not on the agenda.

The next step under the Bonn Agreement was to draft and ratify a new constitution. With tacit approval from the United States and UN, the initial draft delivered by the constitutional commission was altered by the small, predominantly Pashtun reformist bloc within the cabinet, led by Karzai and including several Western-educated returnee ministers. A system of checks and balances on the power of the presidency and Supreme Court was removed from the final version in favor of a strong, centralized presidential state.[10] The reformists, the United States, and the UN believed that a single head of state, directly elected by the people, would be vested with the authority to stand up to the warlords and would not be subject to fractious challenges from within the government that might render it ineffective. In rejecting checks on the power of the executive, the draft also ignored concerns, largely from ethnic minorities in a still divided society, that a president representing only part of the nation—especially if that part were Pashtun—would wield too much authority over its whole.[11]

The alteration delayed publication of the draft, limiting public consultation ahead of the Constitutional Loya Jirga (CLJ). Fewer consultations meant fewer opportunities for the public to review, critique, and demand changes to the draft. Stricter criteria were placed on candidates for the CLJ in an attempt to lessen the presence of warlords and to increase that of individuals with the knowledge to engage in legal debates. Special elections were also held for women, nomads, refugees, and certain other constituencies to ensure that they were given a voice in deciding the nation's new fundamental law. The additional measures resulted in greater transparency, though many factional leaders were still elected or appointed.

The CLJ was convened on December 14, 2003, amid concerns that it would be the target of terrorist attacks. Highly contentious debates inside the tent, including over the role of Islam, a unitary versus devolved state, and presidential versus parliamentary government, nearly brought the assembly to deadlock. The final document, adopted with near unanimity, contained several concessions to factional powers. Importantly, it increased the power of parliament but retained a strong presidency and a unitary state. Given the crippling influence of a divided cabinet during the Interim and Transitional Administrations, as well as the likelihood—later borne out—that factional leaders would do well in the parliamentary elections, consolidating power in the presidency appeared a sensible choice.

Yet, debate over the constitution also made manifest divisive issues within Afghan society. The nontransparent manner in which reformists in the cabinet and international community sought to determine the outcome is likely to have a lasting imprint on national politics. Pashtuns reemerged as a political force during the CLJ, but to a sizable group of other ethnic minorities, the process demonstrated that the advocates of democracy were willing to subvert its ideals to ensure their own agenda. Power sharing and checks and balances that might have advanced the cause of reconciliation but risked state capture by factional leaders were forgone in place of a winner-take-all arrangement under a strong president. The constitution committed the central government to pulling back together a country fragmented by war by taking on powerful regional warlords. The process by which it was agreed ensured that disillusioned ethnic minorities, stirred by ambitious factional leaders, would continue to exploit national government weaknesses.

The constitution defined the parameters for national elections, the final stage of Bonn. It called for presidential and parliamentary elections to be held simultaneously, but with large areas of the country inaccessible to the UN due to insecurity, there were serious questions as to whether the conditions necessary for free and fair elections existed. Given legal, technical, and security deficiencies, parliamentary and local council elections were postponed. Presidential elections were held on October 9, 2004, four months later than the Bonn deadline. Different quarters argued that the Bonn timetable was unrealistic and that the quality of even a technically successful election—and its impact on the political transition—would have been greater if the elections were further delayed, as it would have enabled more time for disarmament and strengthening of political organizations.[12] However, the alternatives—such as allowing the CLJ to extend Karzai's mandate, or assembling a new *loya jirga* to extend Karzai's term or function as an interim parliament—were complicated by political realities and pressure for a nationally sanctioned government.

On the technical side, the light footprint meant that the Joint Electoral Management Body (JEMB) was staffed by relatively limited numbers of international UN electoral professionals, with Afghan "counterparts" at every level. Security and financial concerns prompted the further "Afghanization" of many field electoral staff, necessitating the hiring of large numbers of personnel in a short time frame, as well as the outsourcing of operations and logistics to the UN Office for Project Services and a private security firm called Global Risks.

Given these constraints, the elections were an impressive achievement. Over 8 million Afghan men and women—nearly 70 percent of registered voters—turned out to the polls and were largely able to freely cast their ballots for a diverse field of candidates. The feared violence by Taliban against polling sites on election day itself did not materialize, although there were indications of attempted fraud (e.g., multiple voter registration cards, ballot boxes that had been tampered with) and, in the days leading up to the election, vote buying and intimidation. Though candidates had to foreswear connections to military factions, past violations of human rights were not considered, enabling factional leaders to enter the political fray and pick up large numbers of votes from co-ethnics. President Karzai won an outright majority with more than 55 percent of the vote. His victory underscored that, whatever his failings to bring warlords to heel or security and services to the countryside, Karzai retained the promise of change. Winning granted him a mandate to continue his agenda, including further defactionalization of the government. Progress in defactionalizing the state had strengthened it relative to the ELJ two years prior. The leading runners-up in the election, finding themselves shut out of government but having attracted sizable constituencies, instead would seek a role through the parliamentary elections.

Parliamentary and provincial council elections were held on September 18, 2005. Incidents of intimidation were reported, but polling day passed without serious violence or technical problems, despite the far greater complexity of the elections. Nearly three months to the day later, the first Afghan parliament in forty years was inaugurated. Former commanders linked to armed groups or human rights violations comprised up to 60 percent of parliamentarians.[13] Presidential runner-up Yunnis Qanooni was elected leader of the lower house. Although Qanooni's election had the markings of a political showdown with Karzai, Qanooni resigned as leader of the opposition National United Front soon after his election and pledged to work with the government on behalf of the people. Overall, Karzai garnered sufficient support among the loose blocs in parliament to avoid major problems.

With the parliamentary and provincial council elections, the process laid out in Bonn ended. Bonn's aim of fostering the emergence of a government broadly representative of all Afghan people had been gradually, if imperfectly, realized. The national elections have heightened expectations from Afghans about the pace of service delivery and the exclusion of warlords from the cabinet, ministries, and provincial administration. There is, however, a long way to go before the underlying objective of the Bonn Agreement—to "promote national reconciliation, lasting peace, stability, and respect for human rights in the country"—is achieved.[14]

Center-Periphery Relations
and the Expansion of State Authority

A critical challenge of the present statebuilding effort in Afghanistan is extending the writ of the central government into the provinces. In much of Afghanistan, there is little, if any, state presence, whether for delivery of security, justice, or other services. Nonetheless, state administrative bureaucracies survived the decades of conflict more intact than expected.[15] These institutions, however, are often atrophied or controlled by factional networks, ranging from ministers down to loyal district-level cadres, who subvert the state to their own interests. The establishment of legitimate state political authority will mean monopolizing force, delivering fair, appropriate, and dependable basic services, and convincing citizens that it is in their interest to support rather than challenge state institutions.[16] This process has been hindered by the absence, and later weakness, of national security institutions with which to challenge the de facto control on the ground by factional militias, the Taliban, and other insurgents.

The central government in Afghanistan historically maintained only a tenuous hold over the provinces. A study on governance in Afghanistan points out that "the interplay—and at times conflict—between the two has been one of the recurrent themes of Afghan history."[17] The decades of conflict reversed the gains made by prewar regimes, resulting in a highly fragmented state in which different regions—even down to the subdistrict level—were controlled by factional commanders, who exercised near total control over the political, economic, and military realms. It was these commanders, with support from the Coalition Forces, who filled the power vacuum created by the ouster of the Taliban. The decision by the Coalition Forces to support factional militias proved to be a questionable strategic partnership when carried forward beyond the removal of the Taliban, since the emergence of a strong central state was inimical to the interests of many of these commanders. This decision had a lasting impact on the political environment inherited by the Afghan government, prompting the derisive commentary that, though the president, Karzai functioned more like the mayor of Kabul.

Within the Interim Administration, Shura-i-Nazar controlled the Ministries of Defense, Foreign Affairs, and Interior, and the National Security Directorate (NSD).[18] This in effect split the institutions of state between a pro-jihadi camp, interested in maintaining the status quo, and a pro-reform camp, led by Karzai, that wanted to marginalize the commanders and reorient the country toward democracy. The former's control of the state security apparatus created an environment of mistrust in which most Afghans believed that the government would pursue a factional rather than a national agenda—one in which Pashtuns would be marginalized for their common kindred with or past allegiance to the Taliban.

Parallel to reclaiming authority over state institutions, the central government had to challenge the control of warlords in the provinces. In May

2003, the National Security Council issued a directive aimed at reining in twelve of the most powerful regional commanders, including Governor Ismail Khan of Herat.[19] The decree mandated an end to the recruitment of unofficial militias and a cessation of their military action. It reaffirmed that government officials could not hold both civilian and military posts. The government, however, simply did not have the teeth to back up its demands, nor was the international community ready to provide any.

Ismail Khan is illustrative of the difficulty the pro-Karzai reformists have had in weaning power away from the mujahidin commanders and the opportunistic strategy they have taken to do so. Khan, a religiously conservative, fiercely autonomous commander, tightly governed the country's western province as a personal fiefdom. He regularly disregarded central edicts and withheld lucrative customs revenue from the national treasury, but provided services—from pay phones to police cars—unrivaled even in Kabul. In defiance of the central government, throughout most of his tenure he held not only the post of governor, but also formal military command of the western army corps and control of a loyal jihadi brigade. Both enabled him to exert considerable influence on political developments in surrounding provinces and resist pressure from the center. In March 2004, serious fighting erupted between forces loyal to Ismail Khan and a rival in the capital of Herat province. The government, with assistance from the US ambassador and UNAMA, was able to secure an agreement between the two sides but failed in its efforts to replace provincial officials implicated in the violence. The fighting enabled Ismail Khan to eliminate his rivals in Herat and temporarily consolidate his authority.[20] This provoked a combined attack from Khan's opponents in August 2004, which left the governor severely weakened and prompted a massive intervention by Kabul with the support of the United States. On September 12, 2004, President Karzai ordered the replacement of Ismail Khan as governor. Khan complied with the request and was later appointed a minister in the post–presidential election cabinet, the only major factional commander to be awarded such a post, though a position that finally brought him out from Herat to Kabul.

Factional violence like that in Herat, or in Mazar-i-Sharif in October 2003, has provided openings for the central government to deploy the Afghan National Army (ANA) and Afghan National Police (ANP) and to replace provincial and district officials. Changes have frequently required a combination of deal making, weakened militias, and international military support. As centrally loyal security forces develop—and as international military forces become more attuned to the threat of factionalism—the state has made advances against the militias. The reformists have gradually marginalized or co-opted factional figures through a combination of incentives and coercion, including the constitutional and electoral processes, the use of government positions as carrots and sticks, defactionalization of the Ministry of Defense (MOD), disarmament of militias, and the establishment of the ANA. The electoral process provided further impetus, as some factional leaders hoping to register their political parties opted to comply with demobilization, disarmament, and reintegration (DDR) and heavy weapons cantonment. In fact, many factional figures, including former president Rabbani, aligned themselves with Karzai in order to back the probable winner. Kabul's ability to appoint its choice of officials, collect revenues, and enforce national law is still hindered by the warlords and local militia leaders, but further marginalization or co-option of high-level factional leaders should facilitate state expansion by weakening the political protection afforded to these lesser commanders.

Security and the Rule of Law

Security Challenges

Six years into the statebuilding process, establishing public security remains the greatest challenge facing Afghanistan. Insecurity hinders efforts by the government to promote its authority beyond provincial capitals, to initiate reconstruction, and to guarantee the safety and well-being of its citizens. Insecurity also provides an enabling environment for narcotics production and other criminal activities that finance insurgency. Ultimately, if the state cannot establish order, then more and more Afghans will again abandon it in favor of those who can, as they did in response to the lawlessness of the pre-Taliban era.

The principal causes of insecurity are threefold: terrorist activities and armed attacks by Taliban and other antigovernment forces; factional clashes, the intensity and incidence of which have waned as DDR and heavy weapons cantonment proceeded; and drug-related violence, which appears to be on the rise. (The threat posed by the illegal drug economy is addressed in a separate section below.)

All these threats connect to wider regional dynamics.[21] Historically, Afghanistan was the crossroads of Asia. It remains so today. Porous borders make it susceptible to movement of drugs, weapons, and fighters. Neighboring countries pursue strategic interests via networks of support and control across the border. There are regular reports of Pakistani military and intelligence support for insurgents. The Durand Line—the border agreed upon between Afghanistan and British India, but one still not recognized by many Pashtun nationalists on either side—remains an obstacle to improving Pakistan-Afghan relations. Iran and Russia support other factions within the country. Growing licit regional trade should have a positive effect on regional relations, but for now, its impact is still overwhelmed by that of wartime economic activity.

Taliban, Hizb-i-Islami, and Al-Qaida. Taliban, insurgents loyal to Gulbuddin Hekmatyar's Hizb-i-Islami militia, and foreign fighters are able to operate deep into the Pashtun belt, to freely cross the Afghanistan-Pakistan border, and, increasingly, to strike within Kabul itself. From early 2002 through early 2007, insecurity in the south of the country worsened with attacks by Taliban and other antigovernment forces on government institutions, international military targets, and the civilian assistance community. In response to military action by the coalition and ANA, insurgents have switched tactics from open confrontation to smaller, more mobile methods—drive-by assassinations, suicide bombings, ambushes, improvised explosive devices, and the distribution of "night letters" threatening retribution against those who cooperate with the central government, international military, or aid communities. Their reach has spread, launching attacks against provincial reconstruction teams (PRTs) in the northeast. The threat forced the UN and NGOs to severely restrict travel by international and national staff alike, denying them access to communities for political and reconstruction purposes. Cumulatively, these activities maintain a perception of threat great enough to discourage the return of aid workers and sow fear in local populations. Coalition commanders have repeatedly asserted the diminishing ability of antigovernment elements to launch "military" operations. Some government and international military officials see positive signs in changes in insurgent tactics and the failure of a threatened offensive to materialize. Growing international casualties have called such optimism into question.[22]

As long as the Taliban are excluded from the state, they will have no reason to support it. Recognizing this, President Karzai has sought a dialogue with moderate members of the movement. In 2004, he offered amnesty for all but some 150 militant leaders and invited them to reenter the political fold. An Independent National Commission for Peace in Afghanistan was created to facilitate the process of reconciliation with former Taliban. Efforts are also underway to demobilize former Taliban fighters. Although initial negotiations with the Taliban were met with hostility, particularly among non-Pashtuns, the effort has shown results; two former Taliban officials were elected to parliament in September 2005.[23] These initiatives marked the first real steps toward national reconciliation between the previous and current regimes and their respective supporters, though it remains to be seen whether welcoming former Taliban and their supporters into the new Afghanistan will translate into diminished attacks.

Factionalism and armed groups. Political rivalries over territory and influence between armed factions have often erupted into deadly violence. Most prevalent in the north and west, the incidence and intensity of factional fighting have waned with the conclusion of DDR and, more importantly, heavy weapons cantonment. Political and ethnic tensions, stirred up by the CLJ and electoral outcomes, do still occasionally flare into violence—for example, pitting ethnic Uzbek supporters of General Abdul Rashid Dostum against the perceived Pashtun-dominated government. Factional conflagrations no longer end with tanks in the streets, because government forces backed by the International Stabilization Assistance Force (ISAF) now deploy to contain, if not quell, the violence. But they do demonstrate the ability of factional leaders to summon supporters to their political causes and their resistance to consolidation of central government authority.

Yet military commanders and their militias pose a more daily threat to countless communities. They are still able to act with impunity and exercise arbitrary rule in most areas of the countryside. Responsible for human rights violations, from illegal taxation to rape and murder, they cause greater harm to Afghans than terrorism by antigovernment forces. They are often integrated into the structure of the state, serving as provincial and district governors, chiefs of police, line department heads, and, until DDR, official military commanders. Many are well armed despite the DDR process, maintaining militias outside the formal MOD military structure. They interfere in the selection and decisionmaking of district and provincial administration, and they support and protect the drug trade and other illicit economic activities. State and private assets, including land, natural resources, and factories, have been appropriated. Illicit revenues are used to further invest in new business ventures, winning commanders an increasing slice of spoils.[24] This has deeply undermined public trust in state institutions, government officials, and, to a certain extent, the international community.[25]

International Security Actors

The Afghan government depends upon international forces to protect state institutions, to provide public security, to backstop and train nascent institutions like the ANA, and to fight insurgents. Until late 2005, the US-led Coalition Forces focused on defeating Taliban and Al-Qaida insurgents, only rarely using force to bring factional clashes under control. By early 2007, the structure of the international military forces in Afghanistan looked markedly different from that following the fall of the Taliban. Stretched thin in Iraq, US forces transferred greater control to the NATO-led International Stabilization Assistance Force. Once the North Atlantic Treaty Organization (NATO) began expanding its area of operation in 2003, it gradually assumed command of the Coalition Forces and the provincial reconstruction teams. In September 2006, some 12,600 US troops were brought under ISAF. It is now the primary international military presence in Afghanistan, though the coalition continues to maintain some forces outside ISAF command.

At the request of the Bonn signatories, the Security Council authorized ISAF, a non-UN-led international security force, to provide security for the political process until Afghan security institutions could be developed. Its presence stabilized the capital, reducing the risk of factional violence and crime as well as the threat of terrorism. This security, unfortunately, was not shared by the rest of the country. From the outset, there were calls by all sectors of Afghan society and the international community for the expansion of ISAF to the provinces to deter factional violence and provide political space for the expansion of central authority. Although an ISAF presence in the provinces outside of Kabul was envisioned by Bonn, calls for a greater ISAF role went unheeded until August 2003, when NATO assumed control of ISAF in its first out-of-area operation.[26] ISAF troop-contributing countries were wary of sending troops into potentially insecure areas, but sizable deployments from the UK, Canada, Germany, and others have since enlarged the force from 5,000 troops in 2002 to 32,600 by October 2006.[27] The force absorbed the coalition-led civil-military PRTs and has set up new ones as its area of responsibility has grown.

PRTs were a civil-military innovation conceived by the Coalition Forces in late 2002 as a relatively small deployment of civilians, usually from foreign government aid agencies, and military personnel that would be based in the provinces to assist with reconstruction activities. From conception, their role provoked outcries from the assistance community about the narrowing of humanitarian space and worries that the PRTs blurred the line between the military, still engaged in war-fighting, and NGOs. These concerns were exacerbated by the fact that until late 2003, with the exception of Paktya province, the PRTs were based in the relatively safe provincial capitals of Kunduz, Mazar-i-Sharif, and Bamiyan where NGOs were already working, not in the violence-plagued Pashtun belt where NGO activity was under threat. PRTs were building wells, clinics, and schools—traditionally the work of NGOs—rather than focusing on large infrastructure projects like administrative buildings, roads, and bridges that would help advance the authority of the central government. Due to security restrictions on PRT missions, projects tended to be concentrated around the urban centers where PRTs were based, rather than in remote areas where they were most needed. The Afghan government leveled additional criticism that PRT projects were often not in line with government-identified priorities. As reconstruction providers, the early PRTs were modest and offered little improvement in security, but they were an entry point.

Through engagement with the UN, government, and NGO community, the PRT concept evolved and expanded. Despite early resistance from the coalition and ISAF to using the PRTs for presence patrols, force multiplication, and limited security sector reform, PRTs gradually became a platform for projecting Afghan government institutions, although differences in individual commanders, lead country approach, and area of operation meant variations in PRTs' respective approaches. The UK-led PRT in Mazar-i-Sharif demonstrated early on that proactive engagement can have a positive impact in unstable areas. Other PRTs are limited by restrictions from home governments concerned about how casualties will play in domestic politics.

The expansion of ISAF, though long called for, has failed to damper insurgent activity. Several factors bear consideration. First, deployment of international troops in Afghanistan was not equitable with other peace operations. Using late 2006 troop levels, there are 32,600 ISAF troops and 10,000 US-led troops, which works out to 1 per 15 square kilometers or 1 per 681 Afghans, based on 2004 population figures. Although these numbers marked an improvement from June 2004, when Afghanistan had a peak of 20,000 coalition troops and 6,000 ISAF troops, Afghanistan ranks far behind other recent peace operations.[28] When one considers that the Coalition Forces in Afghanistan were not a security force and that until 2005 ISAF was disproportionately concentrated in Kabul, these figures are even starker. These numbers demonstrate that, despite the overwhelming international commitment to unseating the Taliban after September 11, 2001, similar commitment to securing the statebuilding process in Afghanistan does not exist.

Second, the coalition and ISAF were two different international forces with separate command structures and different mandates: one to fight a war and the other to support statebuilding. At times, their goals have been fundamentally at odds. The coalition's "strategic partnership" with factional leaders during the military action against the Taliban not only undermined its ability to capture the Al-Qaida leadership but strengthened the position of militias vis-à-vis the central government. ISAF expansion was initially opposed by the United States, which did not want it to interfere in combat operations. Elsewhere, ISAF was ill-equipped and unwilling to intervene to quell factional violence. Neither force demonstrated an interest in proactively challenging drug traffickers. Indeed, the number of independent actors pursuing their own goals created a diffusion of accountability for the success of the peace operation in Afghanistan.

Third, prisoner abuse at Bagram air base, culturally inappropriate door-to-door searches in the conservative Pashtun belt, and civilian casualties eroded public trust in the Coalition Forces while handing propaganda opportunities to antigovernment insurgents. As the ISAF has expanded and taken on a greater counterinsurgency role, it, too, has found itself the object of resentment over mounting civilian casualties and criticism over excessive use of force. Such actions inside Afghanistan (and elsewhere in the Muslim world) not only have a profound effect on public opinion within the country but influence wider Muslim views of the West as well.

DDR and Domestic Security Institutions

Security sector reform—helping Afghan security institutions move toward civilian control and greater ethnic plurality—was a primary goal of the government. First among these priorities was defactionalization of the Ministry of Defense. The MOD was unwilling to disband the power structures that enabled its leadership to rival the reformist bloc, nor did rival militias want to relinquish their arms to the Panjshiri Tajik-led ministry. Marginalizing the MOD leadership had to be undertaken in a way that would not cause it to seek redress outside the peace process. The process was plagued by stalling on the part of the MOD, but professionalization and ethnic diversification of staff is underway, DDR was completed, and the ANA is being set up. This reform culminated in the replacement of Marshall Fahim with Abdul Rahim Wardak as minister of defense. Further defactionalization is still needed within MOD, but attention must be broadened to encompass the Ministry of Interior (MOI) and NSD, which have largely been untouched.

Security sector reform (SSR) in Afghanistan encompasses five pillars. Until 2006, each was managed by a lead donor country: Japan for DDR, the United States for training the ANA, Germany for training the police, Italy for legal reform, and the UK for counternarcotics. The "lead nation" arrangement encouraged sectoral ownership, ensured commitment, and did so without excluding additional donors. However, the division of responsibility did not guarantee that donor strategies would be collaborative. The model inhibited coordination and policy adjustment once plans were set. Certain elements, like corrections and intelligence reform, were left out entirely, depriving them of comparable financial support and overall policy guidance.

From the outset, SSR in Afghanistan has prioritized the state's immediate security challenges. As one commentator notes, this "slide towards expediency" came at the expense of a long-term holistic vision.[29] This is true both across the security sector writ large and within its individual pillars. The lack of an overarching plan for justice is evidence of the first; the inattention to capacities for planning, budgeting, administration, logistics, and training functions within the ANA/MOD of the second.

In the long term, effective Afghan security institutions are needed to maintain security and the rule of law. To do so, these institutions will need to become operationally and financially self-sufficient. For fiscal year (FY) 2004–2005, the ANA alone accounted for 17 percent of gross domestic product (GDP), funded primarily through the external budget (i.e., via donor support).[30] The Law and Order Trust Fund for Afghanistan, administered by the United Nations Development Programme and set up to cover the cost of police salaries and other related expenses, has been consistently underfunded. There is a fundamental tension between Afghanistan's security needs and what it can afford. Sustainability cannot come at the expense of security; in the near term the government and international community must be more concerned with the survival of the state than with its solvency. However, the government is aware that it will not be able to maintain these forces at their present size without support from the international community and that it cannot count on this support indefinitely. Funding appropriate and financially viable forces—and determining how they will reinforce rather than replicate one another—remains a critical priority.[31]

Disarmament, demobilization, and reintegration. In Afghanistan, the process of DDR has principally been a means of demobilizing the *victors*—the militias that filled the power vacuum after the fall of the Taliban. The process aims to undercut the military support base of factional leaders, thereby removing the primary obstruction to the emergence of centrally loyal security institutions. Afghans consistently and overwhelmingly identify DDR as the number one priority for their personal and communal security.[32] And yet despite this awareness of the importance of DDR, it did not commence until nearly two years after the Bonn Agreement was signed. During those years, factional commanders had considerable time to entrench themselves, to deepen patronage networks, and to gain a major foothold in both the licit and illicit economy. Thus the Bonn Agreement, in deferring the details of disarmament, potentially jeopardized the whole of the statebuilding enterprise.

Until mid-2005, the DDR process focused exclusively on dismantling militias within the Afghan Military Forces structure—what were, in fact, quasi-independent armed groups representing and projecting the power of different political factions. Without an international or centrally loyal military force with which to enforce mandatory demobilization and disarmament and with an ambivalent MOD, the process was ostensibly voluntary. Not surprisingly, the DDR process experienced serious setbacks following its inception in October 2003. The slow pace of professionalizing and broadening the ethnic composition of the MOD drew out the process, though pressure from the government and international community kept it from derailing. The pilot project, which focused on rank-and-file soldiers, underestimated the resistance of the MOD to cooperation—which became visible in the demobilization of large numbers of "reservists" rather than full-time soldiers—and the hold of commanders over their troops, many of whom faced intimidation and extortion. The pilot project exposed serious shortcomings in the design and execution of DDR, but, critically, galvanized the United States and the coalition to exert pressure on MOD and factional leaders to comply.

Still, the factions were militarily weakened by DDR. Commanders stayed within the peace process; many factional leaders translated factional support into strong support in the political arena. By July 7, 2005, the final day of disarmament and demobilization for AMF units, nearly 63,000 soldiers from 250 units had undergone the process.[33] Relatively few former AMF soldiers met the stringent criteria for positions within the new ANA and ANP and were instead offered vocational and educational training. A special "Commanders

Incentive Program" was set up to offer more robust reintegration options for commanders and MOD generals. As of August 2005, some 460 commanders had been awarded a "financial redundancy package" or other bonuses for cooperating with the process. Many commanders sought positions in the civil service or new security forces, but insufficient education, human rights violations, and sheer numbers will keep all but a few from realizing this goal. With some commanders already deeply involved in illegal economic activities in their areas, some may stake their future on criminality and maintaining influence through "unofficial" militias.[34]

According to UN estimates, some 1,800 illegal militias—those outside the MOD structure—maintain a presence throughout the country, especially in remote areas far from the reach of the central government. They are frequently loyal to and supported by some of the very same commanders previously in charge of AMF units. Thus, the decommissioning of the AMF is not the end point of DDR. Kabul has begun to turn attention to illegal forces through the Disarmament of Illegal Armed Groups (DIAG) program. It is a considerable undertaking, especially because where the army and police are not in place, militias may have already filled the void left by the AMF. The weakness of the ANP and, to a lesser extent, the ANA also afforded nonstate militias with the justification that they have a legitimate security role. The situation was complicated by the widening threat posed by antigovernment insurgents moving into previously stable areas, like the northeast.

Heavy weapons cantonment. In parallel with decommissioning of AMF units, a cantonment process surveyed, collected, and disabled over 9,000 tanks, armored personnel carriers, artillery, anti-aircraft guns, and, from the Panjshir Valley, at least one Scud missile from factional forces. The program has been effective in reducing factional violence. By effectively limiting commanders to small arms, it has reduced the intensity of clashes and their likelihood of success, contributing to an overall reduction in factional violence. Importantly, it also leveled the playing field between factional militias and the ANA, enabling the new army to better project itself into areas it had not previously controlled. The decision to make registration of candidates and political parties contingent upon nonaffiliation with armed groups greatly aided compliance. In November 2004, General Dostum turned over fifty tanks in order to get his Jumbesh Party registered. A similar measure for the parliamentary and provincial council elections collected over 4,300 small arms from candidates.[35]

Afghan National Army. The AMF, created immediately after the fall of the Taliban, was less an army than a collection of factional militias on the payroll of the MOD. Replacing the disreputable AMF with a new, unified, multiethnic Afghan National Army that would serve the state was viewed as essential if the armed forces were to gain the trust of the people and the military were to become a tool of the central government.

The development of the ANA is providing the central government with a loyal and professional armed force, one that is largely perceived as impartial and well regarded by the population at large—characteristics that are not shared by other security forces in the country, including the majority of police and border guards. Limitations were placed on the integration of demobilized mujahidin into the ANA. Recruits were vetted for previous human rights violations. With training from embedded US soldiers, the ANA is proving itself against hardened Taliban fighters, as an intervention and peacekeeping force during factional tensions, and as a capable security presence during national elections. It has redressed the lack of ethnic balance via measures like provincial volunteer recruiting centers. Likewise, the number of new recruits undergoing training at any one time has been increased. Nonetheless, the force—especially its beleaguered units in the south—suffers from low morale due to low pay and high casualty rates.[36]

Afghan National Police. In comparison to the ANA, professionalization of the police—and the MOI as a whole—has been much less successful. Until 2006, the MOI had yet to undertake meaningful change, leaving its senior and middle ranks dominated by former United Front commanders. The majority of police are untrained former jihadi fighters brought into the ranks by their military commanders, themselves "transformed" into police after the fall of the Taliban. Rather than protecting communities and fighting crime, it is the police who are too often responsible for it, committing human rights violations with impunity and engaging in criminal activity. There are professional and committed, if undertrained, police, but they are largely understaffed, underequipped, and poorly (and irregularly) paid.

After years of training and other support offered by international sources under German coordination, renewed efforts at reform, including salary structures and personnel rationalization, were initiated in 2006. Newly trained officers would eventually form the backbone of the new ANP. In the interim, the urgency of reestablishing the rule of law in the provinces—and, more immediately, providing security for the Bonn process—necessitated a parallel, regionally focused, crash basic training for existing rank-and-file police. Some 50,000 police had received training by late 2005. The training has improved the quality of policing, and the salary increase that accompanies completion of the course has improved police morale. Unfortunately, the impact of this training is mitigated by shortages of police equipment (vehicles and fuel, communications, office supplies, etc.), by a shortage of professional police administrators, and by the maintenance of corrupt and factionalized police commanders in their posts. Unlike the ANA, there has been no vetting of police trained under the latter program.

Legal Institutions:
Building the Foundation of the Rule of Law

Rule of law is rooted in strengthening the institutions of justice and the legal framework of the state: a credible and independent judiciary in which disputes are peacefully decided in accordance with the laws of the country, rather than bribery or affiliation; a humane correctional system that upholds minimal international standards; and a law enforcement system that protects rather than persecutes. A functioning justice system depends on all three tracks operating simultaneously. To date, progress toward each of these goals has been disappointing.

The Bonn Agreement mandated the creation of two institutions to help drive this process: the Judicial Reform Commission (JRC) and the AIHRC. It was envisioned that the JRC would manage revision of the legal code, survey existing infrastructure and needs, and develop training programs. Yet a fundamental aspect of the JRC's work—the nature of the legal system itself—was not resolved until the Constitutional Loya Jirga, a full year after the commission was established. The JRC also clashed with the Office of the Attorney General, the Ministry of Justice (MOJ), and the Supreme Court, the three permanent judicial institutions. Islamic conservatives within the MOJ and court proved highly resistant to modernist-oriented legal reform. Fazil Hadi Shinwari, who served as chief justice of the Supreme Court through mid-2006 and whose ideal of justice closely resembled that of the Taliban, appointed hundreds of religious officials as judges across the country.[37] Consequently, the JRC never gathered sufficient momentum to lead reform. Emphasis has since shifted to the permanent institutions of justice, leaving the JRC to fade quietly into the background. The permanent justice institutions, however, have proved themselves no more prone to agreeing to a strategy without the JRC than with it.

The process has also suffered from Italy's role as lead nation. The Italian Justice Project relied on foreign experts unfamiliar with Afghan context, yet was initially set on "modernizing" the Afghan judiciary without due regard to the critical state of legal institutions in the provinces and the important role played by traditional institutions. Coordination with police or corrections has been minimal.

Modest progress has been made in some areas. Making a list of all laws throughout the country has been completed, key court facilities are being renovated, and several hundred judges and prosecutors have been trained. A new criminal procedure code was completed in February 2005, which may address the shortage of district judges and hopefully help shift criminal cases into the formal justice system.[38] The law reflects the reliance in the countryside on informal justice mechanisms like *shuras,* or local councils. These traditional forums provide an alternative to nonexistent, distant, ineffective, factionalized, or corrupt formal institutions for the settlement of both criminal and civil cases. The development of the formal judicial system should recognize the contribution of informal institutions, balancing their important role with the need to increase state jurisdiction over the criminal sphere. Accomplishing that goal necessitates the rehabilitation of infrastructure and continued training of qualified legal professionals, as well as the opening of political space in the provinces to impartial institutions. At the provincial and district level, judges often have training only in sharia, and their independence is compromised by local commanders. Meanwhile, women's access to justice is severely restricted by cultural norms in which women are regarded as property, their movement is severely restricted, and their testimony is not equivalent to that of men.

Absent the rule the law, the AIHRC is the principal human rights body in the country. Its outspoken criticism of violations has enhanced its credibility. In contrast to the JRC, the AIHRC has emerged as a strong national advocate for human rights with authority exceeding that accorded to more localized human rights NGOs operating in the country. The AIHRC closely protects its independence, but has worked well together with the UNAMA human rights component.

Within UNAMA's structure, the human rights unit reports to the head of the political unit. This situation, coupled with the ongoing participation of factional leaders in the political process, generated criticism that the UN prioritized "peace before justice." Brahimi was blamed early on for his perceived willingness to place short-term political stability ahead of a strong public stance on human rights.[39] The Bonn Agreement did not establish any mechanisms for accountability—an unpopular decision, as public reactions to the ELJ and CLJ demonstrated. In 2002, the UN reported, "Given ethnic reprisals, insurgency and factional clashes, there was a strong demand to . . . bring Afghan leaders into the peace process and reduce human rights violations."[40] It is not clear, however, that these goals are compatible. The government did not have sufficient means to challenge commanders' de facto military control on the ground. The alternative chosen has gradually marginalized the warlords. But had the international community made a stronger show of intolerance for serious human rights violations or, where security permitted, if commanders had been disarmed by the coalition after the Taliban were swept from power, the situation likely would have turned out quite differently.

In 2004, the AIHRC began a national consultation on transitional justice in order to determine whether past crimes should be addressed and, if so, how. There are strong public demands for some measure of accountability for past crimes. According to the AIHRC, "the vast majority of people . . . have a deeply eroded trust in public authorities due to the absence of justice and protection of their rights, and they desire deeply that their suffering be recognized."[41] Their cause was dealt a major blow in March 2007 when the parliament passed an amnesty law preventing the state from independently prosecuting alleged war criminals without a complaint from the victims.[42] Many Afghans are outraged that former mujahidin-turned-lawmakers are using their powers to shield themselves. Whichever view prevails, how to deal with past violations of human rights remains a stumbling block on the road to rule of law.

The Illegal Drug Economy:
Balancing Law Enforcement and Livelihoods

Afghanistan's illegal drug economy has been a complicating and important factor in the statebuilding process. In 2006, net cultivation increased to 165,000 hectares, yielding a potential 6,100 metric tons of opium. This is 59 percent more than 2005, and the largest area under cultivation ever recorded in Afghanistan. Cultivation now engages nearly 13 percent of households. The dependency of such a large portion of Afghanistan's poor on the drug trade for credit and access to land, as well as the vast profits—some $2.3 billion in 2006—undermines the emergence of a stable, strong, and democratic state.[43] By reinforcing the indebtedness of the poor, out-competing legal economic activity, encouraging the monetization of opium, and partly financing Afghanistan's international trade deficit, the drug economy finances armed groups, hinders reintegration of ex-combatants, fuels corruption, taints electoral politics, and complicates the ability of the state to receive revenues and control economic policy. The drug trade has led to increased insecurity in the northeast, previously one of the calmest areas of the country; in the south it finances an ever-widening gap between the state and citizens.

One of the interim government's first acts was to outlaw all aspects of the drug production chain. Numerous institutions and legal codes have since been established to combat drugs, including a Counternarcotics Directorate (given ministerial status in December 2004), a specialized eradication and interdiction police force, an anti–money laundering law in 2004, and the formation of a criminal justice task force to fast-track counternarcotics cases.

Yet as Jonathan Goodhand has observed, "the drug control and eradication agenda tends to homogenize and criminalize the processes at work by drawing upon a simplistic narrative of predation and profit."[44] Solutions to the drug economy are complicated by its role in financing livelihoods, particularly of the poor, and economic development of peripheral regions where cultivation is prevalent. The integration of the drug economy with the nondrug economy has meant that counternarcotics strategies, which have disproportionately focused on eradication, have failed to check—and in some cases have unintentionally encouraged—cultivation.[45]

The growth of cultivation generated differences within the international community about the response. For the 2004–2005 growing season, the United

States contributed $778 million, in addition to the United Kingdom's $180 million campaign as the lead donor for counternarcotics. But the main recipient of this significant windfall was eradication; only $120 million of the US allotment went to establishing alternative livelihoods.[46] Eradication negatively impacts farmers reliant on sharecropping arrangements, while complicated maneuverings by politicians insulate poppy cultivation upon which their own client-patronage systems depend. Moreover, by reducing the opium supply, eradication benefits traffickers, who profit from higher prices that in turn fuel the spread of cultivation. Greater attention is needed to creating incentives for all economic actors involved in the drug economy to turn away from narcotics. The task becomes more difficult when state institutions cannot provide security and services and when corruption prevails within local administration, police, and border units. But single-minded attempts to tackle the illegal economy without considering its interconnectedness to wider markets, social institutions, and networks are destined to fail.[47]

State-Led Reconstruction, Public Finance, and Administrative Reform

Just as security is necessary for short-term stability, economic recovery is essential in the long term. The Afghan government inherited a country in which intellectual capital and physical infrastructure had been devastated. Its transportation networks, power grids, irrigation systems, and cities were destroyed. Many of its civil servants, teachers, lawyers, doctors, and other trained professionals had fled or had been killed. Policymaking, revenue generation, and service delivery are priorities for the Afghan government.

Faced with the daunting challenges of reconstruction, the central government, led by the Ministries of Finance and of Rural Rehabilitation and Development, exerted strong ownership over its development priorities. One of the first acts of the Interim Administration was to formulate a strategic framework for reconstruction that focused on rebuilding capacity within government, civil society, and the private sector. The resulting National Development Framework, completed in April 2002, identified twelve priority programs in three areas: humanitarian and social capital, physical reconstruction of infrastructure and natural resources, and trade and investment. The National Development Budget, in setting clear goals, became the government's main policy instrument. The government requested that donor contributions be channeled through itself or the World Bank–managed Afghanistan Reconstruction Trust Fund, instead of the standard UN Consolidated Appeal Process. In reality, however, most external assistance was still not channeled through the national budget; during FY 2002–2004, more than 70 percent, or more than $3 billion, went through the external development budget rather than the government's core budget.[48]

Concerned with guaranteeing long-term donor commitment beyond the Bonn time frame and ensuring its own eventual financial sustainability, the government, in collaboration with donors and technical experts, completed a ten-year strategic investment plan and estimate of reconstruction costs—including security, drug control, and demining requirements, all of which have been financed through the external budget. The study, *Securing Afghanistan's Future,* was presented at the Berlin donor conference in April 2004. In exchange for multiyear commitments, the government agreed to specific benchmarks in security sector reform, institution building, and sectoral programming.[49] Donors committed some $8.2 billion for 2004–2005 including $4.4 billion—more than the government had sought—for the 2004–2005 fiscal year. These commitments, representing 69 percent of all funds requested by the Ministry of Finance for the period, were a strong endorsement of the government's financial management and policy direction, as well as an acknowledgment of the challenges still ahead. In 2005 the government released the Interim Afghanistan National Development Strategy, which included five-year strategic economic, political, and security policy targets—the Afghanistan Compact—agreed upon with the international community. The compact is intended to follow the lead of the Bonn process by providing benchmarks for both the government and its international donors.

Afghanistan is highly dependent on external assistance. In its pursuit of sustainability, the central government has emphasized competitive private sector growth and revenue collection reform. Accordingly, major financial reforms were undertaken early on to stabilize the economy, increase donor confidence, and attract investment. A high value was placed on financial transparency and accountability. The Afghan Assistance Coordination Authority was created to track the flow of resources from donors to the government. International accounting firms were brought in to ensure transparency, increase efficiency, and reduce corruption. A new central bank, mandated by Bonn, was established to oversee monetary policy. A new currency was successfully introduced, which helped to unify the country under a single economic sphere. Nearly six years after Bonn, however, investment is lagging, deterred by lack of infrastructure, insecurity, mounting corruption, and delays in developing and enforcing a regulatory framework.

The lack of investment is but one indicator of the enormous challenges the government faces in generating self-sustaining levels of revenue. Government seeks to keep private sector taxes low to encourage investment. Poverty and weak institutions hinder income and property tax collection. During 2002–2003, expenditure was some $349 million, whereas revenue was only $132 million; for 2004–2005, the gap was even larger.[50] In the absence of ready private sector sources of tax revenue, or any means to collect it, the government depends on customs (on imports largely financed by drug money) for its primary source of state revenue. Inroads have been made in redirecting the country's vast customs revenues from the pockets of regional commanders to the coffers of the central government, though for 2005–2006, revenue collection is expected to be only 5.2 percent of GDP.[51] As one study noted, "Without its own sources of revenue, the government will be forever dependent on foreign aid, with all that this implies for control over policy and accountability to its people."[52]

Although these measures have helped to protect the government from being sidelined by the UN and international donors, they have also helped create unreasonably high expectations among the Afghan people about what the government—and by extension the peace process—is able to deliver. A central principle of the light footprint approach was its reliance on Afghan capacities. The emphasis on a government-led recovery effort, regardless of the reality, generated tensions between the imperative to deliver essential humanitarian and reconstruction assistance as quickly as possible and pressure not to outpace the government. Government-led reconstruction requires rehabilitation of the institutions of state and supporting legal frameworks responsible for national and local governance and administration, for strategic planning and program implementation, and for financial and economic policy. The success of such an approach ultimately depends on widely varying capacities within the ministries and their line departments in the provinces.

The legitimacy of the national government depends in large part on its ability to provide basic services. The National Solidarity Program (NSP), the National Emergency Employment Program/National Rural Access Program (NRAP), and the former Afghanistan Stabilization Program (ASP) were the main vehicles for meeting subnational needs. NSP, which aims to give communities a direct voice in development, has delivered block grants for locally planned development projects available to nearly 18,000 villages. By mid-2007, block grants totaling some US$300 million had been distributed, resulting in the completion of more than 12,000 subprojects.[53] NRAP, meanwhile, delivered rural employment through the rehabilitation of over 5,500 miles of roads in thirty-four provinces. The ASP, intended to drive administrative reform at the provincial and district levels, faced greater setbacks. As one study points out, "The difficulties encountered by the program have rendered it largely unable to play an overall coordinating role at a provincial level, and in many provinces it has been largely sidelined."[54]

Extremely low and irregularly paid salaries remain a significant obstacle to retaining and recruiting qualified civil servants. The Priority Reform and Restructuring Decree of July 2003 is the main instrument for overhauling public administration. The decree mandated government institutions to increase the pay scale of key staff for a fixed term, provided that the entities are able to meet certain criteria, including a difficult application process, which many are not able to do.[55] As the state increases its ability to raise and distribute revenue, scarce funds have been allocated to funding the decree. So far, funds have mostly been distributed at the ministerial level; its expansion to the subnational level has experienced delays and, where it has gone ahead, has been less effective.[56]

The system of administration laid out in the 1964 constitution was still largely intact when the Interim Administration took over, despite years of war, neglect, and successive regime changes.[57] It provides, at a minimum, a base for rebuilding and strengthening the government. Training and placing a new generation of civil servants is a long-term process, and there are many questions, both political and bureaucratic, about what form these changes should take. The role of district councils is one such critical question. Meanwhile, the diversity of development actors and programs has led to a number of ad hoc political and administrative structures being created at the subnational level without clear indications of how they will relate to formal governance structures.[58] NSP's community development councils, for example, provide local communities with a choice regarding decisionmaking, which is especially important where traditional village-level institutions are viewed as corrupt or illegitimate. Circumventing ineffective or undemocratic district and provincial government offices is critical, but such parallel structures also risk undermining the development of formal subnational-national administrative links. Whether the focus on NSP-style local governance is the right approach will depend not only on whether such institutions are representative and independent, but also whether they ultimately reinforce administration and governance by the center.

Conclusion

International statebuilding in Afghanistan has largely been motivated by the desire to combat international terrorism. Since the coalition military intervention to unseat the Taliban, the UN and donor community have had a principal role in implementing political and economic rehabilitation—a task ostensibly led by the Afghan government, though shaped by the priorities of the coalition and its ongoing counterinsurgency. As an assistance mission, UNAMA often had to lead Bonn processes without an explicit mandate and without the benefit of a nationally deployed security force.

Across a wide swath of the country, elements of the statebuilding process have been conducted in the midst of an insurgency targeting this very progress. Powerful factional leaders have also worked from within and without to impede the emergence of a strong central state. In spite of this, there have been major achievements. Political space has gradually widened, leading to an increasingly broad-based government and to the emergence of political parties. The ethnic domination of the state's security apparatus is ending without creating spoilers. National elections were held with minimal violence, providing momentum for continued defactionalization of the administration and legal system. The ANA has gained the confidence of the people, and DDR is proceeding apace. Progress in many areas has faced setbacks, but they only underscore the complicated nature of institutional and legal development in a complex political environment.

Indeed, Afghanistan demonstrates that nationally led statebuilding can generate needed legitimacy in postconflict states, providing momentum early in the process. But it also demonstrates that legitimacy will erode if essential services, above all justice and security, are not delivered. As Katia Papagianni points out in Chapter 3 of this volume, legitimacy is based on the willingness of the public "to support new state institutions and to pursue their interests through these institutions." This willingness implies a trade-off between public perceptions of costs and benefits. Afghans overwhelmingly pinned their hopes on the "post-Taliban" period as a new beginning. The measure of this future is the ability of the state to live up to their expectations.

Lack of security creates a significant obstacle. Absent a state monopoly on force, public engagement is a matter of choice. In the south, the Taliban has been able to increase the cost of engaging with state institutions. Although the state may be able to provide some services, the Taliban also kill those who engage with the state. When engagement with the state risks *decreasing* security, people become willing to "wait it out" to see if engagement with the state is worth the risk, both in terms of getting services and security.

This raises the question of for whom the state is being built. The Bonn process was intended to inject legitimacy into the government by steadily widening the political spectrum. In so doing, it exposed the fundamental tension between democratic participation and the need to give antidemocratic, often anti-Western leaders a stake in the political process. The majority provided the government with a mandate for continued reform. At the same time, factional leaders removed from office in response to public sentiment expressed at the presidential ballot gained reentry to politics through the parliamentary ballot. "Legitimacy" is therefore relative, both in terms of individuals and institutions.

What, then, does "nationally led" statebuilding mean? Certainly, policymaking has become more Afghan-led than donor-led. The government has gradually asserted its own voice above the din of donors. But most assistance was still delivered outside government control. To what extent can one lead when one is vitally dependent on those ostensibly being led? Paradoxically, international support for statebuilding can compromise the very leadership and legitimacy it is attempting to foster.

There are a multitude of demands on the attention and purse strings of the international community. But Afghanistan is far from a self-sustaining state. The United States and its NATO allies must not lose sight of the initial reason for their involvement in Afghanistan. Military action alone will not bring stability. It must make way for justice, reconciliation, and other difficult reforms that will enhance the legitimacy of the Afghan government in the eyes of all its citizens, regardless of their ethnicity, location, or past ideology. The outcome of the statebuilding process will affect not only the long-term security and well-being of Afghans, but that of its neighbors and the broader international community.

Notes

The author would like to thank Alex Thier and Charles T. Call for their comments on earlier versions of this chapter, and David Haeri for his guidance during the author's time with UNAMA.

1. United Nations, *Report of the Panel on United Nations Peace Operations* (Brahimi Report), UN Doc. A/55/305-S/2000/809, August 21, 2000.

2. See UN Security Council Resolution 1333, December 19, 2000, UN Doc. S/RES/1333.

3. Up until just before September 11, 2001, the UN had unsuccessfully attempted to persuade the Taliban to enter into negotiations with the United Front.

4. *Agreement on Provisional Arrangements in Afghanistan Pending the Reestablishment of Permanent Government Institutions* (Bonn Agreement), December 22, 2001. Importantly, Bonn recognized the full sovereignty of the Interim Administration.

5. On February 11, 2004, Jean Arnault, the Deputy SRSG for Political Affairs, replaced Brahimi as SRSG.

6. Benchmarks included convening the Emergency Loya Jirga, drafting a new constitution, organizing national elections, monitoring the human rights situation, and assisting with the disarmament of the country's militias.

7. UNAMA's mandate appears in UN General Assembly and Security Council, *Report of the Secretary-General on the Situation in Afghanistan and Its Implications for International Peace and Security,* UN Doc. A/56/875-S/2002/27, March 18, 2002, para. 97.

8. The ELJ marked the entry of women into the political life of the country for the first time. Of the 1,000 delegates, 200 of those selected were women and more than 20 others were elected. It opened the way to the inclusion of women in government at the cabinet level, the right to vote in and stand for national elections, and the enshrining of equality between men and women in the constitution. These gains have raised long-term questions about how to make women's participation "real," rather than merely token, given strong social norms to the contrary.

9. Astri Suhrke, Kristian Berg Harpviken, and Arne Strand, "Conflictual Peacebuilding: Afghanistan Two Years After Bonn," Prepared for the Norwegian Ministry of Foreign Affairs (Bergen, Norway: Chr. Michelson Institute, 2004), pp. 29–30.

10. The lack of checks and balances on the presidency has been an issue among primarily non-Pashtun factional leaders, perceived as the losers in the transition after the ELJ.

11. Barnett Rubin, "Presentation to the Constitutional Commission of Afghanistan," Kabul, Afghanistan, June 5, 2003, http://www.cic.nyu.edu/archive/pdf/Presentation to.pdf, accessed June 27, 2007. The Center for International Cooperation, in a series of papers, outlined various options on the structure of state governance for the drafters.

12. See, for example, Christina Bennett, Shawna Wakefield, and Andrew Wilder, "Afghan Elections: The Great Gamble," Briefing Paper (Kabul: Afghanistan Research and Evaluation Unit, November 2003).

13. Human Rights Watch, "Afghanistan: Blood-Stained Hands—Past Atrocities in Kabul and Afghanistan's Legacy of Impunity," in *World Report 2006,* pp. 220–226 (New York, 2006).

14. "Preamble," *Agreement on Provisional Arrangements in Afghanistan Pending the Re-establishment of Permanent Government Institutions* (Bonn Agreement).

15. Anne Evans, Nick Manning, Yasin Osmani, Anne Tully, and Andrew Wilder, *A Guide to Government in Afghanistan* (Washington, DC, and Kabul: World Bank and AREU, 2004), p. 1.

16. Or, at the very least, the state should seek to impose its norms on nonstate security forces that it cannot actually remove. In other words, it may need to accept that, certainly in the short term, it will not gain an absolute monopoly, but can try to ensure that militias are providing positive security to community members.

17. Anne Evans et al., *A Guide to Government in Afghanistan,* p. 24.

18. The predominantly ethnic Tajik faction of slain United Front leader Ahmad Shah Massoud.

19. UN General Assembly and Security Council, *Report of the Secretary-General on the Situation in Afghanistan and Its Implications for International Peace and Security,* UN Doc. A/57/850-S/2003/754, July 23, 2003, para. 3. One of the more successful aims of the measure was to end extralegal taxation, including lucrative customs levies.

20. It also signaled to certain factional leaders elsewhere that power-sharing arrangements with the government, some dating back to the start of the Bonn process, could be reversed by force. Around this time, factional forces prevented the changing of the governor in Faryab, Samangan, and Sar-i-Pul provinces. Changes were eventually made, but not without negotiations between the government and local power holders. See UN General Assembly and Security Council, *Report of the Secretary-General on the Situation in Afghanistan and Its Implications for International Peace and Security,* UN Doc. A/58/868 S/2004/634, August 12, 2004, paras. 22, 24, 26.

21. As Goodhand points out, "Afghanistan is part of a regional conflict complex. . . . The outer borders of this complex are unclear, but . . . the core Central Asian regional complex is defined as Afghanistan and the neighboring countries of Pakistan, Iran and all the Central Asian states. . . . Beyond this core regional complex, China, India, Kashmir, the Caucasus and the Middle East, particularly Saudi Arabia, are also significant." See Jonathan Goodhand, "From War Economy to Peace Economy? Reconstruction and State-building in Afghanistan," *Journal of International Affairs* 58, no. 1 (Fall 2004): 155–174.

22. More US soldiers have died in each successive year from 2001 to 2005; Bryan Bender, "US Endures Deadliest Year in Afghanistan," *Boston Globe,* July 3, 2005, p. 6-A. The International Stabilization Assistance Force (ISAF) has also suffered a growing casualty rate. By June 2007, ninety troops had been killed in southern Afghanistan alone. BBC News, "Taleban 'Shifting Focus to Kabul,'" http://news .bbc.co.uk/2/hi/south_asia/6224900.stm, accessed June 21, 2007.

23. Radio Azadi, "Two Former Taliban Win Seats in Afghanistan's Parliament," October 25, 2005, http://www.azadiradio.org/en/specials/elections/features/ 2005/10/5763D47B-235A-4699-B050-ACBA12A32967.ASP, accessed on June 25, 2007.

24. See, for example, Sarah Lister and Adam Pain, "Trading in Power: The Politics of 'Free' Markets in Afghanistan," Briefing Paper (Kabul: Afghanistan Research and Evaluation Unit, 2004).

25. Afghanistan Independent Human Rights Commission, *A Call for Justice: A National Consultation on Past Human Rights Violations in Afghanistan* (Kabul, 2005), p. 41.

26. ISAF deployment was limited to Kabul by Security Council Resolution 1386, but the Bonn Agreement envisioned its expansion, allowing that, "Such a force could,

as appropriate, be progressively expanded to other urban centres and other areas."
See *Agreement on Provisional Arrangements in Afghanistan Pending the Re-establishment of Permanent Government Institutions* (Bonn Agreement), Annex I, para. 3.
    27. Center on International Cooperation, *Annual Review of Global Peace Operations 2007* (Boulder, CO: Lynne Rienner, 2007), pp. 52–53.
    28. Compared to Afghanistan, the peace operation in Sierra Leone had 18,000 troops (1 per 4 sq. km or 1 per 300 people); Bosnia, 60,000 (1 per 0.85 sq. km or 1 per 66 people), Kosovo, 40,000 (1 per 0.3 sq. km or 1 per 50 people); and East Timor, 9,000 (1 per 1.6 sq. km or 1 per 111 people). Michael Bhatia, Kevin Lanigan, and Philip Wilkinson, "Minimal Investments, Minimal Results: The Failure of Security Policy in Afghanistan," Briefing Paper (Kabul: Afghanistan Research and Evaluation Unit, 2004), p. 10.
    29. Mark Sedra, "Security Sector Reform in Afghanistan: The Slide Towards Expediency," *International Peacekeeping* 13, no. 1 (March 2006): 94.
    30. Islamic Republic of Afghanistan, *Afghanistan National Development Strategy: An Interim Strategy for Security, Governance, Economic Growth, and Poverty Reduction,* January 2006, vol. 1, p. 54.
    31. Afghanistan's security needs are not just a question of numbers; more efficient and effective forces should enable it to do more with less, and at lower cost.
    32. See, for example, Human Rights Research and Advocacy Consortium, *Speaking Out: Afghan Opinions on Rights and Responsibilities* (Kabul, November 2003), p. 2.
    33. UNAMA Press Briefing, "DDR 'Double D's' (Disarmament and Demobilization) Come to an End," Kabul, Afghanistan, July 7, 2005, http://www.unama-afg.org/news/_pb/_english/2005/_july/05jul07.htm, accessed June 25, 2007. The MOD originally claimed 700,000 soldiers and officers. DDR initially targeted 100,000, but this number, too, proved inflated, with units regularly one-tenth of the size officially claimed.
    34. Jake Sherman, "Disarming Afghanistan's Warlords," *Praxis: The Fletcher Journal of Human Security* 20 (2005): 5–16.
    35. UNAMA Press Briefing, "Reintegration of Ex-Combatants," Kabul, Afghanistan, August 15, 2005, http://www.unama-afg.org/news/_pb/_english/2005/_august/05aug15.htm, accessed June 25, 2007.
    36. Tom Coghlan, "Toughing It in the Afghan Army," BBC World Service, June 15, 2005, http://news.bbc.co.uk/2/hi/south_asia/4080578.stm, accessed June 15, 2005.
    37. Shinwari's position reflected the power that Ittihad-i-Islami commander Abd al-Rabb al-Rasul Sayyaf, an adherent of the conservative Wahabbi sect of Islam, held over Karzai, owing to the proximity of his forces to Kabul.
    38. UN General Assembly and Security Council, *Report of the Secretary-General,* UN Doc. A/58/742–S/2004/230, March 19, 2004, para. 27.
    39. Suhrke, Harpviken, and Strand, "Conflictual Peacebuilding," p. 50.
    40. See *Report of the Secretary-General,* UN Doc. A/56/875-S/2002/27, March 18, 2002, para. 53.
    41. AIHRC, *A Call for Justice,* p. 5.
    42. Ron Synovitz, "Afghanistan: Amnesty Law Draws Criticism, Praise," Radio Free Europe/Radio Liberty, March 14, 2007, http://www.rferl.org/featuresarticle/2007/03/69572c45-d232-4fc4-b4be-a5de9f9fb97c.html, accessed March 14, 2007.
    43. All figures in US dollars; from United Nations Office on Drugs and Crime (UNODC), *World Drug Report 2007* (Vienna: UNODC, 2007), p. 195, http://www.unodc.org/pdf/research/wdr07/WDR_2007.pdf, accessed June 27, 2007.
    44. Jonathan Goodhand, "Frontiers and Wars: The Opium Economy in Afghanistan," *Journal of Agrarian Change* 5, no. 2 (April 2005): 213.

45. Goodhand, "Frontiers and Wars," p. 212.

46. Barnett R. Rubin and Omar Zakhilwal, "A War on Drugs, or a War on Farmers?" *Wall Street Journal (Eastern Edition),* January 11, 2005, p. A20.

47. Goodhand, "Frontiers and Wars," p. 213.

48. Islamic Republic of Afghanistan, *Afghanistan National Development Strategy,* p. 39. Extrabudgetary items were financed through the establishment of trust funds, timely disbursement of which has been often been problematic.

49. Islamic Republic of Afghanistan, Asian Development Bank, World Bank, UNAMA, and UNDP, *Securing Afghanistan's Future;* see also "The Berlin Declaration, Annex 1—The Way Ahead: The Workplan of the Afghan Government," April 1, 2004.

50. Islamic Republic of Afghanistan, *Afghanistan National Development Strategy,* vol. 1, p. 43.

51. Ibid., p. 43.

52. Chris Johnson and Jolyon Leslie, *Afghanistan: The Mirage of Peace* (London: Zed Books, 2005), p. 191.

53. Government of Afghanistan, Ministry of Rural Reconstruction and Development, "National Solidarity Program Implementation Progress as of 31 May 2007," p. 8, http://www.nspafghanistan.org/content/e101/e234/e237/e239/box_file360/07-National StatusReportMay07_eng.pdf, accessed July 9, 2007.

54. Sarah Lister, "Caught in Confusion: Local Governance Structures in Afghanistan," Briefing Paper (Kabul: Afghanistan Research and Evaluation Unit, 2005), p. 8.

55. Other initiatives have also been introduced to provide incentives for Afghans to join the civil service by enabling payment of salaries comparable to NGOs, as well as recruit qualified nationals as long-term advisers. UN General Assembly and Security Council, *Report of the Secretary-General on the Situation in Afghanistan and Its Implications for International Peace and Security,* UN Doc. A/58/868-S/2004/634, August 12, 2004, paras. 56–57.

56. Lister, "Caught in Confusion," p. 8.

57. Evans et al., *A Guide to Government in Afghanistan,* p. xvii.

58. Lister, *Caught in Confusion,* p. 7.

14

Liberia: The Risks of Rebuilding a Shadow State

Mike McGovern

L iberia, a small West African country of some 3 million inhabitants, was
founded as a colony of manumitted American slaves and free-born blacks
in 1822. For almost 150 years, the country operated like a European colony,
except that in Liberia's case, the internal apartheid of the colonial regime
was based upon a nonracial distinction: that between those "Americo-
Liberians" who traced their ancestry back to the United States and the
"country people" who populated the hinterland. Over the years, an intimate,
though still hierarchical, relationship developed between these groups
through institutions like that of the fosterage of "indigenous" Liberian children by Americo-Liberian families. Still, until 1980, every Liberian president had been an Americo-Liberian man.

It is probably fair to blame many of Liberia's governance problems on
this unjust and exploitative system, as is often done in the cases of former
European colonies. That said, the "indigenous" administration of Samuel Doe
and Charles Taylor proved no better for most Liberians, and the fourteen-year
civil war pummeled civil society, sending most of its middle class and best-
educated citizens into exile in the United States. For a variety of reasons,
Liberia was held hostage by warlords and criminals from 1989 through 2005.
The transitional government that assumed power in October 2003 was implicated in granting long-term rights to Liberia's iron, diamonds, and rubber
plantations under obscure circumstances, and audits of such parastatals as
Monrovia's port and the petroleum refining company showed that their managers were unable to account for huge sums. At the time of the October–
December 2005 elections, Liberia hosted 15,000 international peacekeepers;
had a disarmament, demobilization, reintegration, and rehabilitation (DDRR)
program; and had received hundreds of millions of dollars of recovery assistance.[1] Although basic security had returned in most of the country, neither
the capital, Monrovia, nor anywhere else in the country had electricity, piped
water, a sewage system, or land-line phones.

335

The 2005 elections that brought Ellen Johnson-Sirleaf to power were meant to usher in a new era of accountable postconflict governance, but international donors and Liberian citizens seemed to have little faith that the Liberian political elite was capable of jumping the country off the tracks of governance-as-pillage.[2] Diplomats from Africa, Europe, and North America proposed a series of intrusive measures aimed at fencing in state revenues and imposing more transparent management in the areas of budgeting, expenditures, and procurement, as well as judicial reform that would facilitate prosecutions in corruption cases. These measures have been hotly debated both in Monrovia and the hinterland, and ordinary Liberians and Liberian civil society came out strongly for the intrusive approach, though many Liberian elites denounced it as a neocolonial breach of Liberian sovereignty.[3]

In this chapter, I focus on the contentious two-and-one-half-year period between Charles Taylor's August 2003 departure from power to exile in Calabar, Nigeria, and the January 2006 inauguration of Ellen Johnson-Sirleaf as Liberia's new president. The interim period was presided over by the National Transitional Government of Liberia (NTGL) on one hand, and the United Nations Peacekeeping Mission in Liberia (UNMIL) on the other. Because of the accusations of financial impropriety by members of the transitional administration and the structural problems inherent in the international community's approach to postconflict statebuilding, the situation reached a crisis point in mid-2005.

In what follows, I detail both the historical and institutional sources of this crisis and analyze the innovative solutions proposed for the Liberian case. Because the central problem identified in mid-2005 was that of economic governance, I focus mostly on that issue, touching briefly on other crucial areas, including security sector reform, elections, and judicial reform. Each of these pieces is essential to supporting the success of the others, but it is in the area of intrusive economic governance oversight that the Liberian case is most different from other similar international attempts to rebuild postconflict weak or failed states. I argue that addressing economic governance in a serious manner was an unpopular decision, both among Liberian elites and international actors whose tendency in the Liberian case was to follow the one-size-fits-all approach of what I call the "technocratic fix." Even though such an approach has the obvious advantage of being built out of the "lessons learned" in other, similar interventions, it risks failure precisely because its emphasis on checking all required boxes may allow for the particular problems that caused a war to continue as before. In mid-2005, both Liberians and their international partners were faced with the difficult choice of making unprecedented intrusions into the functioning of a sovereign state or risking rebuilding the shadow state that had collapsed during the country's fourteen-year war.

Historical Background

The period that began with Samuel Doe's 1980 assassination of President William Tolbert and the coup that followed brought to the surface a variety of contradictions within Liberian society that had remained just below the surface to that point. Doe's catastrophic mismanagement of the economy and suppression of dissent proved to be just as stultifying to the development of democratic institutions as the preceding Americo-Liberian hegemony. As the Cold War drew to a close, US largesse to Doe's government, which had reached the hundreds of millions of dollars, dried up, and the United States appeared eager to see Doe replaced in the presidential seat. On Christmas Eve 1989, Charles Taylor, only recently imprisoned in the United States on the basis of charges that he had embezzled $900,000 from the Liberian government, invaded Liberia's northeast from Côte d'Ivoire and began a bloody civil war that would kill as many as 250,000 Liberians and send over 1 million into exile. On September 9, 1990, President Samuel Doe was murdered by Prince Johnson's Independent National Patriotic Front of Liberia (INPFL) faction, which had broken off from Taylor's National Patriotic Front of Liberia (NPFL). Over the next six years, the fighting waxed and waned. During this period, Taylor controlled most of the Liberian hinterland, while a Nigerian-led contingent held Monrovia. By early 1997, peace broke out, and by July of that year, Taylor was overwhelmingly elected by Liberians, many of whom chanted, "You killed my Ma, you killed my Pa; I don't wanna hear about it. I'll still vote for you!"

Taylor's mandate, as those words imply, was to fix what he had broken. He did not; he used the Liberian state in the same way he had used the Liberian hinterland for seven years—as a site of pillage and self-enrichment. The state provided virtually no services, did not pay its employees, and tacitly encouraged them to continue with the logic best captured by the name given to the April 1996 rebel offensive on Monrovia—Operation Pay Yourself. Thus police and army provided predation and almost no protection, schools barely functioned, and medical services were provided almost exclusively by international nongovernmental organizations.[4] By the rainy season of 1999, Taylor's main opponents, then in the process of transforming themselves from the United Liberation Movement for Democracy in Liberia—Kromah (ULIMO-K), led by Alhaji Kromah, to Liberians United for Reconciliation and Democracy (LURD), led by Sekou Conneh, began attacking northern Lofa County from Guinea, and a series of clashes between 1999 and 2001 blossomed into a full-fledged war, with LURD marching toward and then being pushed back from Monrovia.[5]

As LURD and the Movement for Democracy in Liberia (MODEL) pushed ever-closer to Monrovia in 2003, the international war crimes tribunal in Freetown released an indictment for Taylor as he attended June peace talks in Accra, Ghana. By August, the rebels had entered Monrovia, and Taylor left for Nigeria. On August 18, 2003, the parties to the conflict signed the Comprehensive Peace Agreement (CPA), arranging for a National Transitional Government of Liberia, composed of representatives of each warring faction, and headed by Gyude Bryant, a businessman unconnected to any armed group who would thereafter be ineligible for elected office.[6] According to the provisions of the CPA, the United Nations established a peacekeeping mission in Liberia on October 14. The mission was charged with deploying 15,000 peacekeepers, undertaking a DDRR program, repatriating refugees and returning internally displaced persons (IDPs) to their homes, and holding elections in October 2005. It was also charged with peacebuilding and statebuilding activities, such as retraining the police and the army, establishing rule of law, and working with the NTGL and its legislative arm to get the government up and running again, providing services to the Liberian population.

These schematic paragraphs give a rough idea of the timeline of the Liberian wars and peaces. They do not, however, give a sense of the exceptionally brutal and arbitrary nature of the ensuing violence. During the Liberian wars it was primarily civilians who were murdered, raped, mutilated, and dispossessed. They do not give a sense of the intimate connections between Liberia and Sierra Leone in war and peace. Taylor was the sponsor of the Revolutionary United Front (RUF), the principal rebel group in Sierra Leone. Conversely, in the ongoing Liberian peacebuilding process, many of the personnel and approaches have come from the United Nations Mission in Sierra Leone (UNAMSIL).

For this reason, from time to time I make reference to the parallel situation in Sierra Leone, several years further ahead of Liberia on the peacekeeping-to-statebuilding continuum. It appears likely that Liberia will face many of the problems faced by Sierra Leone today, where a five-year UN mission and $3 billion to $4 billion invested do not seem to have guaranteed a durable peace or to have guaranteed the provision of the most basic services to the population. I argue in this chapter that the reasons for this failure lie in the fact that international actors have treated the problems of peace- and statebuilding in West Africa as technical ones and have not addressed the underlying political problems that caused each country's war.

Defining the Problem

How should the international community undertake the statebuilding process in places like Liberia, where the postwar transitional "government" was composed of former warlords and their proxies who showed few signs of assuming responsibility for reconstructing their war-destroyed countries? "There is a fundamental legal and moral problem with agreements like Liberia's Accra

Accords," said Kofi Woods, a Liberian civil society leader, "based as they are on traditional assumptions that two parties are coming to the table with clearly defined ideological positions and visions for the future of the country. Our case is different, in that our war has been led by the criminal element of society."[7] In such a context, it is a mistake to heed calls for sovereignty that may be thinly veiled justifications for the further looting of the national treasury.

The problem in Liberia lies also in determining the root causes of a situation in which, in war as in peace, those in positions of power blithely sacrificed the lives of their compatriots for their own self-enrichment. Liberia, which after the war was so devastated that it had no data on such subjects as child mortality and literacy rates, was still "clawing its way up to the last place on the UN Human Development Index," in the words of former US ambassador John Blaney. In such a context, it became clear to ordinary Liberians (including many ex-combatants) that the grand theft that took place during the NTGL's rule actually amounted to the continuing murder of the country's most vulnerable: children, the elderly, and pregnant women, who consequently went without medical care for easily treated sickness, had no potable water, and had no recourse to a justice system worthy of the name.

The international community's role in such extreme cases as Liberia's has been first to restore security and second to prepare the conditions for credible presidential and legislative elections that will presumably move the country toward accountable governance. In a show of rare unanimity, the international community, ranging from the subregional Economic Community of West African States (ECOWAS) to donors to Liberian civil society, decided in 2005 to go one step further and attempt to address some of the root problems of governance and criminality that plagued the country before, during, and after its war. The cornerstone of this attempt was a programmatic attempt to assert intrusive oversight over certain economic functions of the state, particularly of revenue collection. The program, called the Governance and Economic Management Assistance Program (GEMAP), was signed into law by Chairman Gyude Bryant on September 10, 2005. The money thus consolidated was to be deposited in a transparent and public manner into a single bank account in Liberia's Central Bank in a way that fully accounted for all its sources. At the time of Johnson-Sirleaf's January 2006 inauguration, elections were widely considered a success, security was largely ensured by peacekeepers, security sector reform was under way, and governance reforms were also on track. External support for these and other undertakings, such as judicial reform and rebuilding shattered infrastructure, will be essential for many years to come. By buttressing Liberian capacities in these key areas, international partners can free Liberian government, civil society, and voters to work toward the longer-term goals of addressing other causes of their war and the bad governance that was both its cause and effect.

The situation in Liberia is still in its early stages. Whether, and to what extent, Liberians address issues like citizenship, tensions between customary and national law, the excessive power of the executive, and the exaggerated centralization of government remains to be seen. In the short term, multinational organizations like the UN, the African Union (AU), and ECOWAS, as well as donors like the United States, European Commission (EC), World Bank, and International Monetary Fund (IMF), are speaking with one voice, calling for intrusive oversight of economic activity in order to dissociate politics from criminal economic activity. Liberian democracy, human rights, environmental, and religious representatives, although somewhat resentful not to have been included in the discussion that went into forming the international consensus, have supported these intrusive measures almost unanimously.

One argument for abrogating classical sovereignty is the failure of the approach in Sierra Leone to diminish the hemorrhaging of money that passes through the state. The Sierra Leonean postconflict experience shows existing peace- and statebuilding strategies to be structurally flawed, inasmuch as they either treat symptoms, rather than causes, or risk sabotaging their own attempts to address root causes (for instance, through security sector reform) by turning a blind eye to criminal activity in other arms of government. Many have expressed fear that fighting might resume in the country, given that conditions are the same as or worse than they were at the onset of war in 1991, despite a five-year UN mission presence and billions of dollars spent by major donors.[8] Political and security analysts inside and outside the UN system agree that the major security threat in Sierra Leone remains civil unrest caused by general dissatisfaction at the lack of progress, and the widely held belief that this stagnation has been caused primarily by theft and corruption within the government.

The approach applied in Sierra Leone, described here as "the technocratic fix," begins with the deployment of peacekeepers; proceeds to DDR, the repatriation of refugees, the beginning of judicial and security sector reform; and culminates in elections. Although such a technocratic fix may be necessary to address the problems of a failed state like Liberia, it is not sufficient. To have a chance of leading to long-term stability, intervention must take on both the technocratic and the much messier political issues that in Liberia's case led to the civil war in the first place: lack of rule of law, unjust distribution of wealth, predatory security forces, and corruption.

Interventions based upon the technocratic fix model are weakened by four built-in problems, which risk the waste of billions of dollars and mortgage the future of whole populations. First, the interventions are too short. Western governments are now only willing to plan and pay for interventions with a two- to five-year time frame. Second, present approaches to the challenge of disarmament and reintegration perpetuate a series of myths about the possible futures that await ex-combatants in countries like Liberia. Third, the negotiated peace agreements from which they issue are usually structured so that individuals with criminal pasts are treated as legitimate political actors, while voices from civil society, religious groups, or others who could catalyze change are marginalized in order to facilitate the working compromise in place. Fourth, although the technocratic approach takes away the option of capturing the state by force of arms, it leaves the national economy vulnerable to criminal capture. Because revenue flows are obscured from the beginning, it becomes infinitely easier to obscure theft in procurement and expenditures. Stopgap measures taken in Liberia tried to insert accounting mechanisms at the final stages of this process, which is akin to bailing out a sinking ship with a teaspoon.[9]

It is not the political sphere of countries like Liberia that need to be put into trusteeship, but the process of revenue collection.[10] With viable funds entering the national coffers in a manner that can be verified and challenged by any Liberian, it should be up to Liberians to find a solution to how to manage and spend the money. This process, however, will only have a chance of succeeding within a much longer time frame for international support than is usually envisioned. Liberia took decades to decay and will take decades to restore sustainable security, political, and economic structures. Through GEMAP, the international community in Liberia has begun to address the thorny issue of depriving warlords of incentives to try to capture the state but continues to meet fierce resistance in some quarters, especially among representatives of other African countries who may see economic oversight programs in Liberia as a threatening precedent for eroding African sovereignty. In this regard, it is worrying that before the GEMAP agreement was even finalized, there was reportedly discussion of its application to other postconflict states such as Haiti and the Democratic Republic of Congo. African leaders' fears that the program might become a disastrously one-size-fits-all approach (like structural adjustment plans before it) may be well-founded.[11]

The stakes in Liberia are high. The international community has sunk billions of dollars into the country, and UN officials already express fears regarding the durability of the present peace, built as it is on flimsy foundations. If the Liberian peacekeeping mission fails to achieve durable solutions, there is unlikely to be another attempt at intervention. Liberia could well join Somalia on the list of unmentionable names in Washington, London, Paris, and New York. Skirmishes surrounding the GEMAP, discussed below, pitted those willing to defend the principle of sovereignty at all costs against the donors, who signaled their willingness to cut Liberia off completely rather than continue pouring money into the present system. It was a dangerous test of wills, and the Liberian population stood to lose most.

One year into the peacebuilding process, Jacques Paul Klein, the Special Representative of the Secretary-General (SRSG) to Liberia, said in his

September 15, 2004, progress report to the UN Security Council, "there is still a deficit of political commitment on the part of some factions and members of the transitional government."[12] He also noted, "Corruption appears to be very much alive and there is still lack of transparency by the transitional government in the management of public funds." The same could also be said prior to GEMAP's imposition.[13] More importantly, these comments accurately described the situation in Liberia *before* the civil war began in 1989.

The assumptions implicit in the technocratic fix are that the international community, usually led by the UN, can enter war-torn countries where states provide few services and, by introducing a package of interlinked reforms culminating in transparent elections, can leave two to three years later with some confidence that the newly elected government will be in a position to provide services to its population. In Liberia, these assumptions are unfounded for at least two reasons. First, the Liberian war existed, and the Liberian peace- and statebuilding processes exist, within a regional dynamic whose main characteristic is a nomadic war that has migrated across at least four countries (Liberia, Sierra Leone, Guinea, and Côte d'Ivoire) and has involved a hard core of sponsors, organizers, and fighters who have little to gain from peace. These spoilers will continue to seek the most lucrative zones for fighting and looting unless they are actively denied access.

The second reason is that contemporary Liberia emerged out of a shadow state.[14] In shadow states, the bureaucratic apparatus of the government is hollowed out from within, leaving only the façade of free-standing institutions that make up the state, while power and wealth are in fact redirected into personalized, patrimonial channels. Shadow states are predisposed by their institutional weakness to collapse into failed states, especially with a push from warlords like Charles Taylor or Foday Sankoh. Although less frequently noted, it is also true that failed states can retransform themselves back into shadow states, as appears to have been the case in postwar Sierra Leone. The transitional government in Liberia put its country on the same track. If a shadow state is susceptible to collapse into state failure, then a "reconstituted" shadow state recently emerged from warlordism and state failure is doubly fragile.

Broken DDR Promises and the Dialectic of Contempt

Young men will remain dangerous as long as they do not have a project.[15]

In essence, the central problem with the technocratic fix is that it is perceived as sufficient in itself. As a result, practitioners fail to make the jump from short-term to medium-term approaches, from "buying peace" to community reintegration, or from treating symptoms to treating causes. This shortsighted approach is often accompanied by a series of broken promises, both to ex-combatants and their former civilian victims. What has emerged in Liberia is a kind of "dialectic of contempt" in which ex-combatants, realizing that they have real potential as spoilers, hold the peace process hostage, demanding short-term payouts and openly stating that they expect little in the long term. International actors, even while caving in to such demands in situations where threats are credible, categorize further claims for reintegration as "just another way of squeezing a little more money out of us."[16] Those involved in statebuilding in postconflict situations like Liberia's need to expect such behavior from ex-combatants, and it is up to them to have a credible medium-term plan to offer as a rejoinder.

In 1997, Liberia experienced a flawed DDR program, followed by refugee resettlement and elections.[17] The result was Charles Taylor's election, the continued pillage and abuse of the Liberian population, and ultimately a resumption of the country's civil conflict. Seven years later, the international community was implementing a similar strategy for setting Liberia's failed state back on the road to self-sufficient and accountable governance. Ex-combatants were unambiguous about the probable outcome. As one former pro-Taylor fighter put it, "The UN will be back in 2007."[18] With Ellen Johnson-Sirleaf's victory over George Weah in the presidential elections, it is all the more important not to repeat the mistakes of 1997, given that many young Weah supporters became violent for a brief period after his defeat.

Although the Liberian program was officially dubbed "Disarmament, Demobilization, Reintegration, and Rehabilitation," there have been few, if any, meaningful attempts either to demobilize or to rehabilitate Liberian ex-combatants. Original plans to keep disarmed fighters barracked for several weeks of psychosocial and medical follow-up that would help them navigate postconflict life were reduced to three days that included filling out a questionnaire, having a medical checkup, and a lot of sitting around. At the end of this period, those who had turned in ammunition or weapons received the first half of their $300 disarmament payment. I thus focus on disarmament and reintegration as the two moments in the process of redirecting ex-combatants toward other activities. Because the disarmament process was widely considered by both civilians and ex-combatants to be an arms-for-cash exchange, it was inherently short term in nature. Although reintegration was intended to follow closely on the heels of disarmament, it did not, largely because of UNMIL's poor management of the disarmament stage. Thus disarmament represents the necessary but far from sufficient short-term side of the DDR process, whereas reintegration represents the program's medium-term goals. One of the central problems with DDR in

Liberia is the significant gap between disarmament and reintegration, which has left many ex-combatants milling around towns like Monrovia, Ganta, Zwedru, and Voinjama aimless, unemployed, and angry. Successful reintegration would require a larger budget, programming that targets the communities into which ex-combatants settle, and a reconsideration of the goals of the program.[19] If the end goal is providing former combatants and the communities in which they live viable alternatives to making a living with a gun, then it is clear the Liberian plan has not been sufficient to the task. Worse, much reintegration programming actually perpetuates a kind of myth about future lives and livelihoods that contradicts reality altogether. Some ex-combatants may be fooled for a short time, but the resultant resentment and frustration that come from failed reintegration promises only create a greater likelihood that violence will break out later.

In order for DDR to be part of a consequential approach to peacebuilding and statebuilding, it is important to distinguish the different stages of a DDR process so as not to confuse one with another. The first, short term stage evident in Liberia's Comprehensive Peace Agreement amounts simply to "buying peace." The international community accomplished that at Accra, where the CPA was negotiated, by giving the leaders of the three armed factions places in the transitional government for two years. The offer of asylum in Nigeria made to Charles Taylor was also part of the peace-buying process. In such a situation, serious tensions exist between the expectations of the leaders of the combatant groups and the desire of the international community for respect of minimal standards of human rights, transparency, and rule of law.

The second, medium-term stage in the process can play an important role in resolving this contradiction. This is the period when international and local partners create the conditions for reintegration. Reintegration of ex-combatants must be the foundation of any peacebuilding process because it is the first step in bringing combatants and civilians together in communities and in rebuilding those communities. It is also a vitally important opportunity for outside actors to show rank-and-file fighters that they have more to offer ex-combatants (in the medium to long term, if not the short term) than their former commanders. Reintegration, if used cannily, is an invaluable tool in separating fighters from their bosses by demonstrating how few actually benefit from the kinds of bush warfare that destroyed Liberia. The DDR process in Liberia, because it utilized criteria for demobilization that were too lax, set itself up for large-scale manipulation that resulted in some 105,000 people (nearly three times the number that UNMIL said it had expected) being paid a $300 disarmament indemnity. The focus on achieving impressive numbers of nominally disarmed persons not only used up much of the money that had been earmarked for reintegration, but also distracted from the important work of driving a wedge between leaders and the rank and file. As a result, many Liberian ex-combatants today openly state that they consider the search for new wars in the region more interesting than the UN's broken promises.[20]

The third, long-term stage in the process from disarmament to peacebuilding is setting the scene for job creation. It requires a holistic, long-term program in a place like Liberia, including attention to the rule of law, security sector reform, reconstruction of infrastructure, food security, and attraction of foreign investment. However, if the second step (reintegration) has been botched, it is unlikely that security will be solid enough to allow for such large-scale work to take place. Liberia is still in the position of trying to jump-start serious reintegration, and thus is a long way off from addressing root problems like youth unemployment.

In other postconflict situations where countries faced the challenges of both DDR and creating postconflict employment for ex-combatants, the approach has often been to simply integrate former rebels or faction members into the national army. This has given countries like Chad, Sudan, and the Congo bloated militaries with problems of rank inflation and the possibility of internal schisms. Liberia chose the opposite route, demobilizing not only the members of the LURD and MODEL rebel armies, but subsequently the Armed Forces of Liberia (AFL) and the Taylor-era military.[21]

The United States, which has taken responsibility for training the new Liberian army, chose to demobilize all these forces, cashiering the AFL, many of whom were nearing retirement age anyway, as well as Taylor's rebels-turned-paramilitaries. Using private military company DynCorp, the United States committed $200 million to the training of a new 2,000-person army, recruited from scratch. Having learned a lesson in Iraq, where the policy of total debaathification of the army and elsewhere backfired, the United States decided that recruitment for the new Liberian Army would be open to all, including former fighters from the AFL, Taylor's militias, LURD, or MODEL, but it will include a rigorous vetting process that gathers information on each recruit's potential history as a perpetrator of human rights abuses or other crimes. New recruits' names will be published in Liberian newspapers and on handbills, giving all Liberians who can access those media the opportunity to come forward with any claims that they have been abused (i.e., raped, robbed, tortured) by the recruit.

The training of a new military in circumstances like Liberia's, where the military has historically been a Praetorian guard at best and a group of roving war criminals at worst, must strongly emphasize socialization of the new soldiers to their responsibilities as citizens and as protectors, not predators. Whether a private military company is well suited to this type of responsibility is a pertinent question.[22] Regardless of who is undertaking the work, it cannot be emphasized too much that the necessary training is not simply technical and that it will require long-term mentoring and monitoring.

The Centrality of Agriculture
and Incentives for Rural Resettlement

People living in what has long been called Liberia's "hinterland" often like to remind their interlocutors that "Monrovia is not Liberia." That is true: much of Liberia's wealth originates in Nimba County's iron mines, the timber and artisanal gold mines of the southeast, and the rice harvested and rubber tapped all over the country. The central government had almost no presence in the towns and villages of the interior during the 2003–2005 period. Provision of justice was left to local chiefs. Senators and even county superintendents often spent virtually all their time in the capital, and local police simply presented villagers with the challenge of feeding a few extra mouths out of their limited resources.

Two crucial parts of the process of Liberia's postconflict reintegration have to be rebuilding communities and reestablishing food security. In the rural hinterland where the majority of Liberians live, and where the majority of internally displaced persons and refugees were returning, the basis for both community renewal and food security was local agricultural production. Yet putting Liberian agriculture on a solid footing is not a straightforward affair. The picture that emerges is a complex one steeped in the micropolitics of village life.[23] Some of the elements involved might seem like ethnographic curiosities, but taking them into account could make the difference between long-term economic growth and a brief hiatus between wars. The local sociopolitical factors have to do mostly with intergenerational tensions that center on access to land, the availability of marriageable women, and the legal and political system overseen by chiefs.

In most of Liberia outside Monrovia, access to land is traditionally organized around strict lineage hierarchies. The descendants of the man considered to have been the original settler of a village usually own all the land within that village's territory, and rather than selling or giving land to others, they apportion rights to use parts of it. Over time, use rights harden into de facto ownership, and the second, third, fourth, and fifth lineages to have settled in a village often have considerable security in laying claim to large swathes of land for cultivation. However, use rights for relative newcomers, young men, and all women are insecure. Even though all land is theoretically revocable by the local landowning lineage, legitimate long-term rights to use a plot of land in the traditional system derive from the amount of work put into improving that land. Felling trees, clearing brush, and in the case of swamp rice, preparing a plot for cultivation (a time- and labor-intensive activity) all give a farmer priority for using the same plot of land again.

This precolonial system was "modernized" differently in various West African countries. In Guinea and Côte d'Ivoire, national governments applied the law of *mise en valeur,* which argued that any person who put land to good use became its de facto owner (regardless of his or her position in the community—landowner or newcomer, man or woman, elder or youth). Conversely, in Sierra Leone and Liberia, nineteenth-century land tenure laws like those described above were strengthened by the state, giving elder men strong control over land and perpetuating considerable insecurity for women and young people. Moreover, these laws invested "traditional" land-owners with an inordinate level of power. In reality, this region of West Africa had been subject to major migrations, wars, and population movements, and the hierarchy in any village at a given moment was usually in the process of being renegotiated, with the group that held political and/or military preeminence turning itself (often through strategic marriages) into fictive "landowners."[24] Alternately, they might lay claim to the title of the powerful "nephews" of landowning groups. The imposition of chieftaincies by the Liberian government in the early to mid-twentieth century froze these constantly shifting processes, creating powerful "chiefly" landowner groups and relatively powerless "newcomers."

This dynamic has had three major effects on Liberian society. First, in some cases, it has fueled ethnic tensions, particularly between Loma, Mano, and Gio "landowners" and Mandingo "newcomers" in northern Liberia.[25] The landowner groups, especially in Lofa and Nimba Counties in northern Liberia, have increasingly challenged the legitimacy of the Mandingo presence in "their" territories. This is largely the result of a process of elision through which people of Mandingo ethnicity have become assimilated into the ULIMO-K and LURD combatant groups, to Guinean nationality, and to Muslim religious identity. Mandingoes are thus rejected by self-designated landowner groups on the basis of claims that Mandingoes are not "really" Liberian and/or that they are responsible by extension for the destruction wreaked by LURD.

Second, this system also hardened hierarchical relations between groups, transforming fluid landowner-newcomer relations into a sort of class distinction. Finally, it rendered life precarious for young men and all women, as neither group had guaranteed access to land. These disadvantages were often compounded by the fact that elder men were able to monopolize young women, marrying many wives, often through alliances among elder men who could "give" their daughters, granddaughters, and nieces to other older men in marriage in order to seek political advantages of their own. Young men caught in a liaison with one of the junior wives of an older man could be fined so heavily for the offense in traditional courts (presided over by the village's elder men) that they became de facto indentured servants, cultivating rice, cocoa, coffee, and cassava for the old man to pay off their debt.[26]

In Liberia, these abuses have long been present, though they are not as exaggerated as in Sierra Leone. In the wake of Charles Taylor's departure, several Liberian women lawyers took the opportunity to push forward laws that outlawed many of the practices that supported this system, doing away with a husband's ability to reclaim bridewealth payments from his ex-wife's family in the case of divorce, giving women inheritance rights, and explicitly banning elder men's use of young wives to lure in lovers who would then become indentured servants.

Non-Liberians involved in Liberia's statebuilding project need to understand such local dynamics, which constrain ordinary Liberians from pursuing productive activities that lead, in aggregate, toward macroeconomic growth. The fact that young men can invest tremendous labor into preparing a field for cultivation and then have it revoked by a chief is a serious disincentive to their pursuing agriculture. The fact that they might not be able to marry before the age of thirty-five or even forty in the village setting because elder men have monopolized young women through polygynous marriages is also a serious disincentive. Although development specialists and Liberian elites take it as an article of faith that village life could not be interesting to young people who have lived in cities, they offer few details as to what hinders these young people.

In the age of electric generators and satellite television, young people could just as easily watch international football matches and Brazilian soap operas in their villages as in town, if that were the sticking point, and if just two or three trunk roads (to Voinjama, to Zwedru, and to the Sierra Leone border) were properly repaired, young people in the vast majority of Liberian villages could go to the capital inexpensively within a few hours to spend a few days and enjoy the city. The dire situation of the roads today means that the trip from Voinjama or Zwedru to Monrovia is a massive undertaking. Despite elites' assumptions to the contrary, not one of several hundred Liberian ex-combatants and refugees interviewed by the author has expressed an unwillingness to practice farming. One group of former combatants working in an agricultural project in Ganta stated in 2005 that they found their present jobs very tiring but were glad, because they went home and went to bed early rather than spending the night in bars and getting involved in fights that often turned lethal. If young men and women see other citizens prospering through agriculture and they have reason to believe that they too will have a fair opportunity at that prosperity, they will return to rural areas. In the absence of any such incentives, it may be true that they prefer dire poverty in the cities to dire poverty in the hinterland.

Roads are also an important part of pushing the agricultural sector forward from subsistence production toward higher productivity. Despite the fact that it has tremendously fertile soil, abundant rainfall, and a population of (mostly) rice farmers, Liberia is a net importer of rice.[27] If village producers are to begin selling surpluses to the city, and even outside Liberia, decent roads, rice-hulling machines, and an increased cultivation of swamp rice, which is more productive than and also requires less land than upland rice, should all be part of peace- and statebuilding plans. Planners involved in the statebuilding process in Liberia were not addressing the effects of the importation of cheap Asian rice, uncertain land tenure, and the lack of viable infrastructure during the transitional period. All these factors discouraged local rice farmers from growing and selling surpluses, which could start a process leading to a resumption of cash crop production (cocoa, coffee, cola) and later to agricultural diversification.

Another challenge for reintegration might be described as a crisis of expectation. If postconflict statebuilding projects are to have a chance of succeeding, their (ostensible) beneficiaries must be involved in the decision-making process. But what should the representatives of the international community do when the requests of ex-combatant beneficiaries or civilians resettling in their villages, perfectly reasonable in themselves, are out of line with the macroeconomic and political realities of the country where they live? The discussions required to align expectations and reality take time and energy because they are uncomfortable and ultimately tragic. However, there is no way out of the hole Liberia has dug for itself, if not through steady, durable economic growth.

What is tempting but irresponsible for representatives of the UN mission and Liberian politicians is to foster the illusion that there are easy solutions to these questions, and that young Liberians can have what they want quickly or simply. They cannot. Most are handicapped by lack of education, lack of infrastructure, lack of transparency in governance, and the fact that there will be no significant foreign investment in their country until security is thoroughly solidified and economic growth has begun locally. This will necessarily be a decades-long process. To suggest otherwise is at best a way of buying time and at worst a cynical calculation that when things fall apart, those who fostered the illusion will be far away.

Because the UN had not yet made the shift from the "buying peace" to the "consequential reintegration" stage of peacebuilding in 2003–2005, ex-combatants and representatives of the UN became locked in a cycle of bad faith. Sadly, Liberia will not experience major growth in the industrial sector any time soon. Nor in the service sector, nor in tourism, nor in high tech. Where the country could experience dramatic growth over the next five years is in the agricultural sector. If agricultural production grows while an increasing number of citizens go to school and gain access to decent health care, and the security forces provide protection instead of predation, other sectors will certainly follow.

A Viable Path to Building a Durable Liberian State

So far, this chapter has criticized the technocratic fix as an approach to stabilizing countries after conflict. The risk is that in Liberia, a perfectly competent implementation of these steps could lead to the recreation of a shadow state and thus favor the return of war. This remains a worry in Sierra Leone, and experience there has shown that once entrenched, such parallel political-economic networks are extraordinarily difficult—if not impossible—to change by the use of such means as the introduction of technical advisers in ministries. As noted above in the discussion of security sector reform, what the internationals intervening in countries like Liberia and Sierra Leone are involved in is a process of resocialization, or even social engineering. Few of them would admit this, even though many ordinary Liberians openly call for an imposed reform of their country's political culture. Marina Ottaway, who has correctly described this as the "Leninist option"[28] to engineering democracy in Africa, has expressed skepticism about the international community's tendency to bite off more than it can chew: "There can be little disagreement about the desirability of democracy as a solution to the problems of war-torn countries. The model of democratic reconstruction favored by the international community at present, however, is too complex and too costly to be implemented. There is a need for realistic alternatives."[29]

Although others have argued for more robust interventions that might resemble trusteeship, I echo Ottaway's call for self-restraint: interventions in states such as Liberia should not be organized around an ideal goal and an expensive and technically complex set of interlinked reforms.[30] Such programs have shown mediocre results, even in the rare cases where the imposing institutions and governments have been willing to put their money where their mouths were, as in Bosnia. In most instances, and Liberia falls squarely into this category, donors lose interest soon after peacebuilding processes begin, and so end up asking for reforms that weak postconflict governments are in no position to deliver and which donors do not even pay for in the end.

Under such circumstances, reformers must focus on establishing a set of minimal conditions that could simultaneously satisfy basic international standards (for instance, in the area of human rights) and enable Liberians to decide on the next steps to be taken. These conditions would include DDR, refugee repatriation, and elections from the technocratic approach, plus thorough security sector reform and intrusive attempts to diminish criminal economic activity within the government. These basic steps and continuous monitoring of respect for human rights and such civil rights as freedom of speech and the press could create conditions under which local actors can themselves take over the process and move it forward with a degree of accompaniment, rather than control, by foreigners. In the second half of 2005, Liberia surprisingly took this route. The process is still in its earliest stages, so no evaluation can yet be made. However, for a variety of reasons, Liberia and its international partners began augmenting the technocratic approach with interventions that addressed some of the underlying causes of the country's war and state collapse.

The Time Frame

The previous section's focus on agricultural and rural development as the basis for sustainable peace and statebuilding underlines the fact that such interventions must take place within a significantly longer time frame than currently envisioned. Economic recovery will take decades, as will the ongoing process of building self-standing bureaucratic institutions for the first time.[31] The horizon for most peacekeeping interventions is between two and five years, although extra months or even years may be tacked on when it becomes apparent that everything risks falling apart with the departure of peacekeepers. These ad hoc extensions of peacekeeping mandates are proof that peacekeeping operations are often successful at first imposing, then maintaining, peace but seldom at building durable peace, let alone state structures.

Places like Liberia require a long-term security engagement, probably a fifteen- to twenty-five-year commitment with a small financial and operational "footprint." Such an approach could well spread the same amount of money as is currently planned, simply by disbursing less per year for a longer time. Even if the total in the end is more than currently envisioned, it would be far less expensive than yet another emergency intervention in three or five years if Liberia slides back into war. Such a decision has already been made in an ad hoc manner in Sierra Leone, where the UNAMSIL presence stretched from 2000 until the end of 2005, and the British International Military Advisory and Training Team (IMATT) training program for the army was slated to continue until at least 2010. The peacekeeping and security sector reforms have been backed by a British "over the horizon" guarantee to intervene within seventy-two hours in the case of a serious downturn in the Sierra Leonean security situation.

Sierra Leone may well be the model for a long-term security sector commitment in Liberia. For example, initial training of the new Liberian army will have to be followed up by a continuing program of mentoring, perhaps by a small number of US military officers. Such security commitments should be coordinated with economic and political interventions where root problems remain unchanged. A long-term security sector commitment will do little if, for instance, corruption and mismanagement in government means that soldiers go unpaid for long periods. Otherwise, they will simply stage more efficient and technically competent coups than the coups they would have staged without security sector reform.

GEMAP, Accountability, and Sovereignty

At the Liberia donors' conference in Copenhagen in May 2005, many of Liberia's development partners suddenly began using remarkably undiplomatic language to discuss the problems they had identified in the Liberian government. In pointed language, they noted that "economic governance [in Liberia] requires a more robust response with immediate and strong remedial efforts surpassing the 'critical strengthening measures' proposed by the NTGL." Stating both that "the future of Liberia is at stake" and that "the absence of accountability to the Liberian people can not be allowed to continue," the group, which included the UN, the EU, ECOWAS, the United States, the IMF, and the World Bank, promised an economic governance action plan for the country.

The plan had crystallized around donor anger at the results of two sets of investigations. The first, undertaken by ECOWAS, studied the operations of the transitional government itself. The second, sponsored by the European Commission, audited Liberia's Central Bank as well as five parastatal companies: Monrovia's free port, Robertsfield International Airport, the Forestry Development Authority, the Bureau of Maritime Affairs, and the Liberian Petroleum Refining Company. All of them reached the same conclusion: the level of theft going on under the transitional regime was crippling the government's ability to provide services to its people and was facilitating the restructuring of the post-Taylor state into the type of shadow state described above.

The economic governance document demanded co-signatory rights for international experts monitoring revenue collection, expenditures, management of parastatals, granting of contracts, procurement, and judicial reform. Because of the risks of abuse, it was essential that this system be held accountable to an international governing body so that the governance mechanism would operate in the greatest possible transparency. The oversight committee was to include representatives of the UN, EU, United States, IMF, World Bank, Liberian Ministry of Finance, Central Bank of Liberia, Liberian Contract and Monopolies Commission, Liberian government's Governance Reform Commission, Liberian civil society, and ECOWAS.

This proposal raised a tremendous furor in Liberia, with many political figures coming out angrily against it, calling it a form of international trusteeship.[32] Other politicians came out for it.[33] Most ordinary Liberians I have interviewed have supported the plan, casting doubt on the motivations of political actors who talk about the sovereignty of the same country they have, in many cases, been pillaging until quite recently by force of arms. Members of civil society, including human rights, democratization, and religious groups, came out strongly for the plan. Most Liberians grasped the underlying reasons why the international community should oversee the revenue-collecting functions of their state. Ports, airports, customs, and other sectors (such as the Liberian shipping registry) had long served as "cash cows" for those who controlled the state. Because the Liberian state offered little institutional resistance to the capture of these sectors, warlords like Charles Taylor fought to control the state and thus its revenues. Because revenues had been diverted before they reached national coffers, lack of transparency in revenue collection facilitated lack of transparency in expenditure, since it was impossible to know the sums that ought to have been in the system.

In July 2005, the transitional government came back with its own proposal for a softened intervention, renamed the Governance and Economic Management Assistance Program (GEMAP). Further negotiations led to a document acceptable to all, signed in September 2005, just a month before the presidential and legislative elections.

The GEMAP approach promised to complement the technocratic fix in important ways. First, by removing both insurgency *and* economic pillage as incentives and by doing so over a relatively long period, it should radically reduce the attraction of the political sphere for the "vampires" and allow a new class of more service-oriented politicians to enter the scene. It is worth noting that the new system requires a sufficiently long mandate for parasitic actors to drift away from the current political system. As with other parts of the approach, a mandate of fifteen years would probably be most effective. Warlords and corrupt politicians could easily wait out a five-year hiatus, and such a period would not be long enough for a newer class of service-oriented politicians to develop a toehold in national politics.

GEMAP, if properly implemented, could achieve the collection of far greater sums than are currently being collected by the Liberian government. The transparent deposit of an increased sum into the national coffers could allow for sustainable budgets, with which government—and voters—set policy for themselves, rather than undertaking programs because donors require them or are willing to fund them. This in turn could have the effect of forcing Liberians to take greater, not less, responsibility for running the day-to-day affairs of their state, in a way that is accountable to the Liberian population.

Both capacity building and real restraint in the area of directing state expenditures need to be part of the implementation of GEMAP. The international community might, for a certain period, do a better job of running Liberia than some of the warlord figures who made up the transitional government. The question one should pose is, What will happen when that period of receivership comes to an end? Such a question points to the need for capacity building, access to information, and an acceptance that even Liberians acting in good faith will make some bad decisions and may find the temptation of state monies too strong to resist. This is a reality in all the countries from which the would-be overseers originate and is part of politics anywhere. What is important is to give the majority of Liberians information and the ability to act on it so that they can make informed decisions about such failures. If Liberian citizens decide that it is worth pursuing these individuals, whether through the legal system or by voting them out of office, then the program will have achieved its ends. However, there is no program so intrusive (or in Ottaway's terms, "Leninist") that it can force Liberians to make such decisions. As we shall see below, by opening even a small space for Liberians to make claims on their leaders, significant pressure to hold political figures accountable has grown over the course of the two-year transition.

The Political Sphere

Between 2003 and 2005, UNMIL officials often stated that many of their problems stemmed from the fact that their mandate was too weak and that in the context of failed states only a protectorate could solve the deep-seated problems of governance that existed in Liberia.[34] I argue the opposite: that for Liberia to reach sustainable solutions to its political problems, changes can and must be generated from within and not imposed from without. Some Western diplomats admit that they remain engaged with Liberia so as to maintain influence over developments there. Some might reply that "engagement" has too often amounted to turning a blind eye to corruption and human rights abuses by successive governments while "influence" comes at the price of forming coalitions with those in power and marginalizing those truly interested in reform. Liberian peasants are more direct: they complain that although they see rich politicians and rich expatriates driving in expensive new four-wheel-drive vehicles, they have seen few benefits except the imposition of a peace that may dissolve soon after the peacekeepers leave.

By the end of the transitional period, acceptable levels of security had been ensured for most people most of the time; transparent elections and the GEMAP governance package buttressed this security. Liberians could thus take on some of the thorny issues confronting them, including debates over citizenship, ethno-religious fractures, the highly centralized government and lack of local government structures, and constitutional changes that might be necessary if Liberia were to diminish the extremely broad powers held by the president.

One of the essential problems with the 2003–2005 transitional period was that it was based upon compromises with fundamentally problematic interlocutors. Negotiations like the Comprehensive Peace Agreement signed in Accra placed war criminals on the same level as legitimately elected governments and international mediators.[35] What some have called the "Linas-Marcoussis effect"[36] provides incentives to African rebels to attack mostly civilian targets in order to gain a place at the negotiating table and claim a portion of the nation's political and economic spoils. The often well-founded perception that political control provides opportunities to empty the national coffers makes this route attractive to rebels. If they inflict enough suffering on civilian populations, they have a reasonable degree of assurance that the international community will step in on behalf of those civilians and force the government in place to share power with them. International negotiators are caught in a moral and political conundrum in that they are forced to treat murderers, rapists, and their proxies as their political peers in order to save civilians whose lives are held hostage.

This paradox may simply be proof (if proof were needed) that politics is a morally ambiguous undertaking. Over the medium to long term, the work of the international community must be oriented toward moving criminal elements out of the political sphere and opening spaces for the majority of the population, who are not thugs, to take control of that sphere. It might be argued that this should be the *fundamental* objective of peacebuilding and statebuilding processes in postconflict failed state settings.

This is a somewhat more direct way of describing the problem that former SRSG Klein has described as working with a "coalition of the unwilling, that is a government that is quite often not interested in what we are."[37] The danger is in taking this unfortunate necessity for granted. Although the international community had to do business with this "coalition," it should have worked harder to cultivate a broad constituency in Liberia, including those elements of the political class, civil society, and Liberian diaspora who wanted to change the way Liberian politics works. As security was solidified, UNMIL and other leading actors from the international community began to distance themselves from the spoilers who continued to use their leverage to extract wealth from the Liberian countryside.[38]

Liberians must take the lead in this process of political renewal. Even in the 2003–2005 NTGL, there were people who were not involved out of self-interest alone. There were individuals like Rufus Neufville, the youth representative in the National Transitional Legislative Assembly (NTLA), who parked his new $35,000 Jeep and called on the other members of the NTLA to park theirs as well until the twenty-five buses they had promised to Monrovia's citizens were delivered. As a result of his call and the fact that it went unheeded, Monrovians attacked several of Neufville's Jeep-driving colleagues, and he was held responsible. The legislature voted to suspend him for three months for "inciting" the public against it.[39] Figures like Neufville had few allies in the Liberian political class, and they received little public support from UNMIL and others who ostensibly supported transparent governance.

Civil society in Liberia has to be one of the sources for new ideas, as well as for calling the political class to account. Such organizations as the Foundation for International Dignity, the Center for Democratic Empowerment, Green Advocates, the Sustainable Development Institute, and the National Human Rights Commission, among others, took many risks during the Taylor years, with their members spending time in prison and undergoing torture in the name of defending basic rights. Those same organizations, as well as leaders of various religious groups, took an active role in pointing out abuses and illegal activities during the Taylor and transitional periods. As the discussions around the GEMAP plan progressed, they found that there was a space for the kinds of advocacy they have been involved in, and the transitional government was forced into following up on many of their allegations.

Between May 2005 and the NTLA's January 2006 dissolution, the assembly's speaker, deputy speaker, and replacement speaker were all suspended, and government officials in a number of agencies, from the Social Security corporation to the National Petroleum Refining Company and the Liberian International Ship and Corporate Registry were investigated and in some cases charged with criminal offenses. Since the elected government assumed office, the speaker of the house, Edwin Snowe, was impeached by his peers for improprieties, and several questionable contracts entered into by the transitional government were annulled and renegotiated under terms more favorable to the government. The elected government has also indicted several members of the transitional government, including Gyude Bryant, its president, for misappropriating state funds.

Many figures in Liberian civil society move in and out of the Liberian diaspora, estimated at 450,000 by UNMIL and based predominantly in the United States. Many of these Liberians are university educated, employed in all sectors of the US economy, and could bring essential skills to Liberia. There are many figures in the diaspora who could become central players in building a new type of politics in Liberia. This process began in the context of the presidential and legislative elections, with many returning to run for office. It continued as President Johnson-Sirleaf named her cabinet in 2006. Overall, the political objective of international actors should be to open a space for Liberians to argue, debate, and reach their own solutions to the difficult issues surrounding governance, accountability, and representation in their societies, while the objective of Liberian civil society and press should be to push this process forward.

Conclusion

Until now, most approaches to failed states have been based upon the negotiation or imposition of peace, followed by the introduction of transitional peacebuilding and statebuilding mechanisms built out of a set of compromises between the erstwhile troublemakers and the international community. Through day-to-day contact, the pressure to "push money through the door," and exhaustion, these working compromises too often serve either to give combatant factions the chance to regroup and rearm or to facilitate the (re)creation of shadow states. In this chapter I suggest that the international community look hard at the built-in motivations of the corrupt, the violent, and the dishonest who make up an important proportion of their interlocutors in such cases. What motivates them? Why do they engage in such destructive forms of war that overwhelmingly target civilians? Who are their international associates and facilitators?

The game during Liberia's transitional period was based on a single, ugly wager: civilian populations were held hostage by warlords and their proxies, and the international community paid to bring the violence down to a level it could stomach. The same can be said of many other postconflict transitions, from Côte d'Ivoire's to the Democratic Republic of Congo's. In return for ceasing (or pausing) in their destruction, erstwhile warlords are given a place at the table and are guaranteed the ability to "eat," to use a common African metaphor.[40] This situation is frankly unacceptable, and we need new thinking. One way to approach the problem is simply to ask about the incentives and the means at the disposal of the spoilers. The incentives have been and continue to be economic pillage. The means have been violence during wartime and the creation of parallel systems of hierarchy and patronage during peacetime. Peacekeeping operations act, more or less effectively, to diminish the belligerents' possibilities of taking what they want by force, but they have done little to put the spoils of the state beyond reach. The objective of international postconflict interventions must be to distance the warlords and spoilers from the ability to assert themselves by force of arms and also to deny them the possibility of draining the lifeblood of the states trying to emerge out of postconflict situations. That is why attention to governance issues, especially the revenue flows attached not just to natural resources but also to parastatal companies and customs revenue, is as vital a concern as the deployment of blue-helmeted peacekeepers in the peace- and statebuilding process.

When investing billions of dollars in peacekeeping, the international community has the right to set its expectations higher than it has done in the past. In Liberia, two years after the peace agreement, most roads were still impassable for much of the year, and the country had no electrical, piped water, sewage, or land-line telephone systems. Provision of education and health services was still minimal, though improving. After fourteen years of on-and-off warfare, Liberians certainly had the right to ask for more. A guarantee of basic security was the international community's first step in meeting Liberia's statebuilding needs. Organization of credible elections was the second. Revenue collection oversight could become the third step in the process, accompanied by support for an open local dialogue about governance. Such a dialogue would need international guarantees that basic civil rights, such as freedom of speech and of the press, be respected, with local civil society, intellectuals, and returnees from the diaspora taking the lead in negotiating new relations between rulers and ruled. The security and economic governance aspects of this approach need to be assured for a period heretofore unimaginable—of ten years and more.

Such a radical intervention runs up against questions of sovereignty and legitimacy and was much easier to apply in Liberia prior to the October 2005 elections. The approach probably would not work in troubled but higher-functioning states like Côte d'Ivoire or Nigeria, or even in a vast, mostly ungoverned failed state like the Democratic Republic of Congo. In places like Haiti and Somalia, resource flows may be too diffuse for such a program to work. However, in small, resource-rich failed states, this combination of approaches could deprive spoilers of their usual incentives while opening the way for more transparent governance. The lessons to be learned from this case study, as well as many of the discussions currently surrounding the GEMAP and its application, raise a fundamental question about statebuilding in general: Do deeply intrusive forms of intervention risk long-term failure even as they may achieve medium-term success? Here we have limited and idiosyncratic data but could probably borrow some insights from the development literature, which reminds us that unless they are rooted in consultation and a sense of local ownership, even the best development projects have a tendency to collapse soon after their expatriate managers head back home.

Notes

1. Liberia's program has added "rehabilitation" to the usual disarmament, demobilization, and reintegration. When referring specifically to the Liberian program in this chapter, I will use the "DDRR" acronym, while I will opt for the more common "DDR" to talk about disarmament and reintegration more generally.

2. In an essay in *Foreign Affairs,* Liberia expert Stephen Ellis quotes Liberians as referring to the alleged criminal behavior of members of the transitional government as "business more than usual." See Stephen Ellis, "How to Rebuild Africa," *Foreign Affairs* 84, no. 5 (September/October 2005): 135–148.

3. This has been especially true of the legal fraternity, which bitterly opposed outside incursions by other Africans or any other foreigners, both during the transitional period and since President Johnson-Sirleaf's inauguration.

4. See International Crisis Group, "Liberia and Sierra Leone: Rebuilding Failed States," Africa Report no. 87, December 8, 2004, for a case study of the unintended consequences of this parallel system of service provision.

5. The ethnically Mandingo–dominated ULIMO-K had split with the Krahn-dominated ULIMO-J, which took its "J" from the initial of its leader, Roosevelt Johnson. ULIMO-K largely reformed itself as LURD, whereas many of the former ULIMO-J elements combined with Liberians living in refugee camps in Côte d'Ivoire to form MODEL. Just as the Guinean government supported LURD in its 2003 push toward Monrovia, the Côte d'Ivoire government supported MODEL.

6. In addition to the chairman of the NTGL, the vice chairman, the cabinet ministers, the speaker, and deputy speaker of the National Transitional Legislative Assembly (NTLA) would all be ineligible for the 2005 elections.

7. Woods was appointed minister of labor in the Johnson-Sirleaf government.

8. From July 2001 to June 2005, $2.81 billion was spent or budgeted for Sierra Leone by the UN, the British Department for International Development (DfID), the United States Agency for International Development (USAID), and the European Union (EU). These figures do not include monies spent by other UN agencies. The figure for Liberia is $2.27 billion from October 2003 to June 2005.

9. As political scientist and former Liberian minister of finance Byron Tarr has pointed out, there have been some two dozen such interventions by foreign powers—usually the United States, since 1871. Various versions of receivership included one sponsored by the League of Nations in 1930, another by the International Monetary Fund in the 1960s, and a third, called the Operational Experts program, sponsored by

the Reagan administration in the 1980s. All have been failures, largely because they have been unilateral, have not focused on training and mentoring, and have often intervened at the end of a complex economic chain. See Tarr, "Liberian Economic Governance Action Plan: Some Historical Antecedents," unpublished manuscript, 2005; Nicholas Jahr, "Corruption and Reconstruction in Liberia," *Dissent* (Summer 2006).

10. Though nearly everyone recognized that Liberia in 2003 was indeed a failed state, most failed to take the next step and acknowledge that such a situation called for qualitatively new approaches. Those who did, like UNMIL's first Special Representative of the Secretary-General (SRSG), Jacques Paul Klein, argued for a full trusteeship mandate, citing East Timor as a model. Bureaucrats such as Klein, with little or no experience in Africa, did not calculate the fact that people along the West African coast have been managing heavy-handed, patriarchal attempts to control their politics for the past 500 years and that what was needed was a way to simultaneously take the economic spoils of the state away from the warlords and to throw Liberians back upon themselves to start debating what *they* intended to do to politically resuscitate their country.

11. It is important to note that the combination of factors that might make the program effective in Liberia—the clear links between war making in Liberia and the economic incentives provided, especially by the possibility of "milking" the state; the clear revenue streams originating in parastatal institutions like the shipping registry, port, and petroleum refinery; and the relatively small size of the country and the large international peacekeeping contingent that together could facilitate effective enforcement—are rare among postconflict countries.

12. Briefing to the Security Council on the Fourth Progress Report of the Secretary-General on UNMIL, New York, September 15, 2004.

13. On March 13, 2007, the head of the 2003–2005 transitional government, Gyude Bryant, was arrested and charged with converting $1.4 million of government money for his personal use.

14. William Reno, *Warlord Politics and African States* (Boulder, CO: Lynne Rienner, 1999).

15. Interview with humanitarian source, Monrovia, August 9, 2004.

16. Interview with administrator of nongovernmental organization, Ganta, Liberia, May 22, 2005.

17. In 1997, the disarmament exercise offered ex-combatants chits for reintegration training and other benefits that were never delivered. In 2005, ex-combatants, many of whom had fought in both the first and second civil wars, drew the parallel that if they were not reintegrated, they might take up arms again, as they did after the 1997 elections.

18. Interview with former pro-Taylor fighter, Ganta, Liberia, May 20, 2005.

19. Liberia, like other places with UN peacekeeping interventions, has thus suffered from the fact that reintegration does not have an assessed budget line within the mission's plans, and so those reintegration activities are beholden to the goodwill of donors who have largely forgotten the crisis by the time they are asked to pay for these crucial programs.

20. Human Rights Watch, "Youth, Poverty and Blood: The Lethal Legacy of West Africa's Regional Warriors," New York, 2005.

21. The latter two groups were not necessarily the same thing, as the AFL tended to stand for the Samuel Doe–era ethnic Krahn-dominated army, whereas Taylor's former rebel soldiers mostly operated under the guise of various paramilitary groups—such as the "Anti-Terrorist Unit" and the "Special Security Service"—after his election.

22. DynCorp, along with Pacific Architects and Engineers, obtained a five-year monopoly on all military contracting in Africa for the US Department of State on the basis of a single bid. DynCorp's employees have been accused of various abuses, particularly the trafficking of women and girls as young as twelve in the Balkans. See Jamie Wilson and Kevin Maguire, "American Firm in Bosnia Sex Trade Row Poised to Win MOD Contract," *Guardian,* November 29, 2002.

23. See Paul Richards, Khadija Bah, and James Vincent, *Social Capital and Survival: Prospects for Community-Driven Development in Post-Conflict Sierra Leone,* Social Development Paper no. 12 (Washington, DC: World Bank, 2004).

24. See William P. Murphy and Caroline H. Bledsoe, "Kinship and Territory in the History of a Kpelle Chiefdom (Liberia)," in Igor Kopytoff, ed., *The African Frontier: The Reproduction of Traditional African Societies* (Bloomington: Indiana University Press, 1987), pp. 123–147.

25. This tension mirrors those in Côte d'Ivoire and in the forest region of Guinea. Mandingoes (known as Manya or Koniyanke in Guinea and Dyula in Côte d'Ivoire) have often been in their present home villages for many generations, though they may have come after the area's first settlers. In Liberia, tensions related to land access have been exacerbated by interethnic massacres and other violence, including the destruction of traditional sacred groves by Mandingo combatants and Mandingo mosques by non-Muslims.

26. Krijn Peters and Paul Richards, "'Why We Fight': Voices of Youth Combatants in Sierra Leone," *Africa: Journal of the International Africa Institute* 68, no. 2 (1998): 183–210. See also George Schwab, *Tribes of the Liberian Hinterland,* edited with additional material by George W. Harley, papers of the Peabody Museum of American Archeology and Ethnology (Cambridge, MA: Harvard University, Peabody Museum, 1947).

27. This could be attributed to the recent end of the war and continuing insecurity in the hinterland. However, the same situation holds in Sierra Leone several years after the end of fighting.

28. Marina Ottaway, "African Democratization and the Leninist Option," *Journal of Modern African Studies* 35, no. 1 (1997): 1–15.

29. Marina Ottaway, "The Post-War 'Democratic Reconstruction Model': Why It Can't Work," paper presented at "Building Democracy After War?" conference, Brown University, April 3–4, 2002.

30. Stephen D. Krasner, "Sharing Sovereignty: New Institutions for Collapsed and Failing States," *International Security* 29, no. 2 (Fall 2004): 85–120; James D. Fearon and David D. Laitin, "Neotrusteeship and the Problem of Weak States," *International Security* 28, no. 4 (Spring 2004): 5–43.

31. In a recent article, Keith Krause and Oliver Jutersonke argue that postconflict state formation is a slow, organic process that cannot in fact be accelerated by even the most well-intentioned social engineering. See Krause and Jutersonke "Peace, Security, and Development in Post-Conflict Environments," *Security Dialogue* 36, no. 4 (2005): 447–462.

32. See "'EGAP Is Colonisation,' Says Prof. Somah," *Analyst,* July 20, 2005.

33. Among the best known were presidential candidate George Weah and LURD-appointed transitional minister of justice Kabineh Janneh. Ellen Johnson-Sirleaf initially made it clear that she would resist or discontinue the GEMAP program upon taking office. After assuming the presidency, she softened her position, choosing rather to undertake many GEMAP-type reforms on her own and at an even quicker pace than required by the document. Her long-term commitment to the program remains an open question.

34. Interviews with UNMIL officials, Monrovia, September 2004.

35. It is difficult to predict what will happen to these actors in the post-transition period. The Liberian Truth and Reconciliation Commission has the power to recommend prosecution of certain actors, and the Liberian justice system may choose to prosecute some perpetrators.

36. Linas-Marcoussis was the site of the January 2003 peace negotiations for the Ivorian civil war, which made the rebels part of a power-sharing government.

37. Integrated Regional Information Networks, "Where Are the Weapons? Is Disarmament Really Working?" July 28, 2004.

38. See International Crisis Group, "Liberia: Resurrecting the Justice System," Africa Report no. 107, April 6, 2006.

39. See "Legislative 'Axe' Falls on Youth Rep," *News,* October 8, 2004.

40. See Jean-Francois Bayart, *The State in Africa: The Politics of the Belly* (New York: Longman, 1993).

PART 3

Conclusion

15

Building States to Build Peace?

Charles T. Call

This volume opened with several questions about the role of the state in building peace. Is statebuilding essential to postwar peacebuilding? Are there functional priorities in fostering legitimate states in war-torn societies, and how should they be advanced? How does the process of building states relate to the process of building peace? What are the tensions between peacebuilding and statebuilding?

One of the most striking impressions left by the case studies and thematic chapters in this book is that efforts to consolidate peace and to strengthen war-torn states are fraught with problems that leave war-torn countries vulnerable to weak institutions and to renewed or intensified conflict. Despite the potential to play a positive role, international actions more often tend toward the inadequate, misguided, or perverse, according to most of the contributors to this book.

Having detailed the challenges and problems of peacebuilding, the contributors do not propose that international actors walk away from the potentially harmful enterprise of postwar statebuilding. Instead they urge smarter, better resourced, more strategic, and more context-sensitive efforts by outsiders. Although cases like Somalia, Palestine, and Bosnia and Herzegovina were selected precisely because they challenge conventional notions about externally recognized states, these cases and the other chapters illustrate the importance of some minimal national state. Without a minimally effective and legitimate state at least regulating alternative sources of authority and service delivery, peace is likely to prove unsustainable. Despite the advantages of informal institutions, private actors, substate authorities, and suprastate institutions, such bodies are unlikely to sustain both the internal and external legitimacy required for stability in the absence of a state minimally capable of mediating the relationship of these bodies with the populace. In other words, although nonstate forms of authority are increasingly relevant, the need for a state to mediate and regulate those authorities throughout the national territory is as important as ever.

And although states are central to peace, *building* such states does not lead, directly and unproblematically, to peace. On the contrary, the very process of statebuilding exhibits serious tensions with the goal of consolidating peace. One of the most important contributions of this project is to provide analysis and examples of these persistent tensions.

The contributors offer suggestions on how to build states in ways that build peace. The volume identifies a number of core activities in postconflict statebuilding, including the provision of security, public finance, justice, and a sense of representing people's identities and interests. At the same time, the thematic chapters and cases suggest that there is no one-size-fits-all formula for building state institutions. Most chapters point to pitfalls to avoid rather than straightforward models or pathways to effective and legitimate state institutions. In this conclusion I identify these pitfalls, even as I suggest helpful approaches, linkages, priorities, and sequences.

Most of the contributions underscore the centrality of national actors and their interactions with the populace in building sustainable peace in postwar or conflict-ridden territories.[1] Although international actors certainly have an important role to play, their engagement is rarely the key to ensuring the effectiveness of states or to consolidating peace in war-torn societies. By virtue of their self-interest or their lack of interest, international actors can prove more harmful than helpful. In the volume's thematic essays and case studies, international actors are generally seen as holding the potential both to facilitate peace and to undermine peace and the institutionalization of authority.

The very use of the term *building* in peacebuilding and statebuilding conveys agency and optimism. It also implies an institutional blank slate in war-torn societies where, in fact, some meaningful institutions always survive and exercise local power. Yet the story of postconflict statebuilding is one of long-term processes, internal contradictions, and severe limitations on resources and commitment. A number of core conclusions stand out from the volume and serve to organize this chapter:

1. Peacebuilding is not simply a matter of rebuilding state institutions. Efforts to consolidate peace in postwar societies, no matter how well-intentioned, can be harmful in a number of ways.
2. Nevertheless, legitimate states remain crucial for the sustainability of peace.
3. The process of building legitimate and effective states, however, can be destabilizing. Six main tensions characterize the relationship between statebuilding and peacebuilding.
4. Statebuilding is a deeply political process, one that creates winners and losers. This has implications for two aspects of statebuilding: de-

signing states to perform certain core functions and ensuring the capacity of state institutions.

5. Central to managing these tensions is the need to balance the twin imperatives of legitimacy and capacity, extending to both national and international institutions and processes.

These conclusions frame some of the main challenges for managing the complex process of building peace and its relation to building states.

"Doing No Harm" in Peacebuilding

The volume's contributors are united in one attitude: their dissatisfaction with the way statebuilders, especially international actors, act in war-torn societies. The case studies provide vivid illustrations of the frustrations of lost or squandered opportunities, while the thematic chapters identify bad habits and specify ways in which peacebuilders should modify their approaches and programs. Some chapters—such as those on economic policy, public finance, and practical approaches to institution building—reflect frustrations with international financial institutions or UN agencies or nongovernmental organizations (NGOs) for not following an alternative path or model in wartime or postwar societies. The remainder of the contributions push in the opposite direction, rejecting universal models or approaches and arguing instead for greater attention to how difficult choices and trade-offs must be managed in ways particular to contexts and cognizant of existing local institutions and potential spoilers. Yet all these chapters emphasize the past and current negative effects of peacebuilding or statebuilding done poorly. Just as the development community has rallied around the "Do No Harm" mantra, so these contributors point out the harm, or at least lost opportunities, of external and internal approaches to fostering and sustaining peace.[2]

The volume illustrates several different ways in which international actors harm war-torn peoples and their aspirations for peace: the harm caused by (1) what external actors fail to do, (2) what they do, and (3) how they do it. Harm may result from inadequate international efforts, from blind or shortsighted international approaches, or from perversely self-interested international proclivities.

The Harm of Neglect

Donors and other states are driven by interests, and sometimes these interests dictate an unwillingness to provide the money or mandate necessary to foster peace processes or state-strengthening activities after war. The case of Afghanistan demonstrates the harm done by insufficient commitment, as manifest in scarce resources devoted to an effort, in limited mandates, or in an otherwise circumscribed external response. Many attribute that country's persistent internal warfare and the rise of the Taliban during the 1990s to disinterest among Western powers who, once the Soviets had withdrawn, showed little urge to resolve the deficiencies of society and the state. Following the fall of the Taliban regime in 2001, the United States and the International Security Assistance Force (ISAF) failed to deploy troops outside Kabul. This circumscribed commitment of troops in Afghanistan left the warlords relatively unchecked militarily, severely undercutting the ability of Hamid Karzai's nascent transitional government and of international actors to consolidate a national state. Similarly, both Michael McGovern's chapter on Liberia and Rex Brynen's chapter on Palestine (see Chapters 14 and 10, respectively) indicate that greater international backbone could have curbed the behavior of corrupt elites.

The Harm of Excessive International Presence and Prerogatives

In contrast to the harm caused by international failure to act or to provide sufficient resources, a number of chapters in the volume exemplify the opposite danger: excessive international presence and prerogatives. The most obvious instance is East Timor, where the United Nations assumed the reins of the state, administering national ministries and local municipalities while overseeing the transition to self-rule by national actors. In Chapter 12, Edith Bowles and Tanja Chopra agree with much of the prevailing analysis on East Timor: that the UN mission became too occupied with its own capacities at the expense of fostering local capacities and that the mission was slow and clumsy in involving highly legitimate Timorese in decisionmaking structures. Kosovo, although not covered in this book, serves as a similar example. Although international organizations may in exceptional circumstances have to assume sovereign state functions, such transitional administrations should be oriented early and explicitly toward strengthening legitimate and capable institutions.

Several chapters provide examples of how international prerogatives short of executive authority undermine the sustainability of state institutions. The Governance and Economic Management Assistance Program (GEMAP) program in Liberia, whereby a coalition of international actors oversee national revenues and expenditures, may well curb corruption among elites and help ensure that the state's wealth reaches the population. However, in Chapter 14 McGovern criticizes the program's insufficient attention to building Liberian public finance capacity and ensuring that this usurpation of a state function, while necessary, is only temporary. Marcus Cox acknowledges the severity of the problems that led international donors to expand the authority of the Office of the High Representative in Bosnia and Herzegovina (see Chapter 11). Yet he argues that the office wielded its heavy-handed powers for too long, with perverse effects on that country's state institutions and on the legitimacy of its elected officials and democratic processes. In a similar vein, Michael Carnahan and Clare Lockhart lament how donors, humanitarians, and UN agencies preserve their own institutional interests in delivering assistance at the expense of strengthening states' public finance capacities and their role in legitimizing states vis-à-vis citizens (see Chapter 4).

In each case, the contributors argue that international actors' assumption of sovereign state functions, often adopted in response to real short-term challenges, undermine the long-term strengthening of state ministries and capacities, ultimately delaying or undercutting the foundation for self-sustaining peace. In this sense, the harm done by excessive international interests relates to the privileging of short-term solutions over long-term needs identified by Sarah Cliffe and Nick Manning in Chapter 8.[3]

The Harm of Blind Interests

Beyond these critiques of international actors for doing too little or doing too much, others criticize *how* international peacebuilders go about their work. The Somalia case shows the harm done when international actors actively pursue the forging of a state without due regard for the violence such an endeavor might produce. Rex Brynen's case study of Palestine in Chapter 10 shows the harm wrought on legitimacy and coherence of a state apparatus by international actors excessively privileging the pursuit of peace. Bosnia and Herzegovina and East Timor (and Kosovo and Iraq) illustrate the dangers of launching military operations without sufficient planning and programming for forging a legitimate national state that can command the buy-in of major ethnic or social groups.

One cluster of harmful effects of international statebuilding operations stems from their effects on local economies. The large "footprint" of international missions, with tens of thousands of foreign soldiers and police, millions of dollars in short-term aid, and hundreds of international and local civilians employed, can provide both jobs and new markets for local products. However, these missions also tend to create markets for the sex industry; aggravate human trafficking; and distort housing, food, and labor markets.[4] In terms of contributing to state institutions, the high salaries and generous benefits offered by UN missions, bilateral donors, and international NGOs tend to attract the most qualified national personnel, depriving the state of these valuable resources. The UN Development Programme and others have sought to mitigate this problem by placing internationally paid consultants inside state ministries, but some complain that is a partial and often ephemeral solution. Doing no harm in postconflict peacebuilding requires measures to mitigate the effects of large-scale international operations, partly through efforts at supporting national and local capacities and partly through checks on the worst effects of the external presence.

Related to this harm is the presence of large-scale international private contractors who operate outside state direction and directly compete with nationals for jobs. Although the private sector can be useful and efficient, the risk of displacing national actors and capacities, as well as the difficulties of oversight, pose serious challenges.

Several contributors criticize international peacebuilding agencies and donors for showing too little awareness of the state in their priorities and programming. In Chapter 4, Carnahan and Lockhart make a sustained critique of international actors, especially humanitarian groups and UN agencies, for channeling resources directly to beneficiaries often without even informing relevant government ministries, undermining the legitimacy of those state institutions in the eyes of the public. In Chapter 8, Cliffe and Manning identify four perverse tendencies of international actors in approaching postwar societies, all of which undermine the consolidation of a national state. Erik Jensen's discussion of the rule of law shows the harm issuing from the deficient priorities and policy frameworks used by international actors (see Chapter 6). And Katia Papagianni criticizes international organizations' lack of sophisticated attention to issues of legitimacy in Chapter 3. This includes questions such as who already holds legitimacy, how international action affects legitimacy, and how legitimacy can be built, by whom, and who selects any local stakeholders in legitimation processes. These assorted concerns reflect a need for international actors to take into consideration the potentially adverse effects of their interventions in all dimensions.

How Important Is Statebuilding for Peacebuilding?

Given the deep reservations about statebuilding expressed by many of this book's contributors, one may ask whether a legitimate, effective state is really necessary to ensure peace. As I discussed in Chapter 1, some of the case studies presented here were initially selected to challenge this conventional wisdom. The Oslo agreement for Palestine suggested that a peace process could succeed without a sovereign state, and Somalia's experience suggested that alternatives to the state might function adequately and peacefully without a functioning central state.

Nevertheless, the answer appears to be that, yes, a minimally legitimate and effective state is necessary for sustained peace. Despite the problems with states themselves and the deficiencies of statebuilding efforts, the contributions to this volume underscore the importance of the state. Postwar societies and international actors have tended to underemphasize the state and its relevance to peace. Even the recent policy attention to statebuilding has not redressed this condition. The situation in Afghanistan, as explored in Jake Sherman's case study in Chapter 13 and the thematic chapters by Rubin (Chapter 2) and by Carnahan and Lockhart (Chapter 4), exemplifies the tight link between the successful creation of a national state and the preservation of peace among the main ethnic and political groups that reached agreement in Bonn in 2001. East Timor and Liberia also show the degree to which peace is jeopardized by a state that falls short of expectations in delivering basic services and providing representation to the main social and political groups of eclectic societies. Even in Palestine, the failure of the Oslo peace process was (arguably) linked to the question of juridical statehood—a question that also loomed in Kosovo as of mid-2007.

But it is a qualified yes. The importance of the state for peacebuilding is contingent and problematic. The essential character of the state may be challenged in two ways: by empirical and by juridical alternatives to the state. On the empirical front, as William Reno argues here in Chapter 7 and elsewhere, institutions both below and above the state have long provided statelike political authority and basic services. Especially in African countries, informal or tribal authorities continue to provide authority and services alongside "shadow" states. Transnational or regional organizations and networks, as well as private actors, increasingly provide state functions, supplanting "empirical" sovereignty in law enforcement, defense, and in the case of Liberia, public finance. These alternative institutions call into question the newfound emphasis on the state.

And yet, although these alternatives to state institutions are increasingly important, they do not mean that the state can be ignored. In a world of sovereign states, internal peace requires that informal institutions be recognized and mediated within a territory, a function that falls to the national state. Similarly, when states fail to authorize and regulate private or transnational providers of state functions, then a lack of certainty prevails, inviting violent challenges and undermining long-term peace. We can reasonably conclude that the context and circumstances of particular cases dictate how much of a state is necessary, but that peace requires a state sufficiently competent and legitimate to authorize, recognize, and regulate the functioning of institutions both below and above the state. Even where authorities below, above, and alongside the state perform statelike functions, they are all highly susceptible to violence unless a national state is authorizing and regulating them. Hence, we come back to the state, but perhaps emphasizing its monitoring and oversight functions.

On the juridical front, Somalia at first seems to suggest that an externally recognized state is not necessary for effective governance or peace. Faced with total neglect by the international community for over fifteen years, substate authorities in Somaliland and Puntland enjoyed significant internal legitimacy, while their territories produced economic growth and suffered less violence than many neighboring states. By providing minimal levels of legal stability, economic management, and security, they demonstrated empirical sovereignty without juridical sovereignty.

Nevertheless, Somalia's experiments in stateless governance proved untenable. Facing a complete international refusal to recognize substate entities,

Somali elites and international actors episodically sought to reconstitute the state. But the access to power and wealth that comes with control over the state—the ability to dole out state jobs, to capture international aid and loans, to tax and deploy troops, all with the mantle of legitimacy of a recognized state—proved too attractive. As Kenneth Menkhaus describes in Chapter 9 (and indeed foresaw at the time this project was launched in 2004), the external impulse to recreate a state in Somalia fostered a zero-sum game among clans, leading to significantly higher levels of violence by 2006. Ethiopia's external intervention represented a response to, rather than a cause of, this renewed civil war that followed most directly from moves to create a new national state and exercise its authority in Mogadishu.

In arguing for creating a minimal national state, not one overburdened with full-scale state functions as advocated by the West, Menkhaus acknowledges the economic imperative of some minimally functioning national state even in Somalia. In doing so, he also advocates a process of statebuilding, albeit one that takes care not to spark organized violence. Similarly, recognition of the weak capacities of Liberian institutions requires a modest approach to statebuilding in that society. Consequently, even some of the toughest cases— Liberia and Somalia—illustrate the importance of building contextualized states to build peace.

Of course, the need to create a minimal state does not mean that getting there will either be a peaceful process or result in greater peace. In this sense, the distinction between *states* and *statebuilding* parallels the difference between *democracy,* which is accepted to be good for interstate peace, and *democratization,* which is known to spark violence.[5]

The Role of International Actors in Postwar Statebuilding

The contributors' doubts and critiques raise another question: Is there any role for international actors here? At first glance, it may seem not. Critiques of deficient international resources, strategies, knowledge, and cognizance of local contexts permeate these contributions. Certainly one should be skeptical of international actors, their motives, and their impact. Recognition of the primacy of national level actors and of the difficulty of infusing new or imported institutional adaptations with legitimacy runs through the volume.

Yet virtually none of the contributions seems to favor a retreat by international actors from the enterprise of statebuilding. On the contrary, the frustration with neglect of states among international actors leads several contributors to plead for placing particular state institutions front and center in postwar programming. Some of the authors take it as a given that external actors like the World Bank and the United Nations should shift more attention and resources to building state institutions. In this vein, Collier identifies how international policies can and should do more to prevent war recurrence. Carnahan and Lockhart make a sustained appeal for the primacy of national state institutions over virtually all other interests. They appeal to international actors (especially UN agencies) to sacrifice their institutional interests and break longstanding habits that undermine the state in order to strengthen the state, especially through greater attention to the state's public finance capacities. This disposition reflects years of frustration at international organizations' repeated mistakes, some of which are described by Cliffe and Manning, whose broad and practical analysis crystallizes policy lessons.

Interestingly, even the most critical accounts of statebuilding efforts seem to wish for more thoughtful international efforts to foster legitimate and capable states. Thus, McGovern's critique of Liberia's GEMAP program, of which he was an early champion, centers on how the program is conceived. He particularly bemoans the inclusion of expenditures in the program and the seemingly open-ended commitment to international displacement of state capacity. Similarly, Rubin's critique of how international actors approach security urges international actors to build into their approaches the link between legitimacy and capacity, explicitly including the legitimacy and resources wielded by international programs in that calculus. Erik Jensen's critique appears frustrated with recurrently flawed international judicial reform programs, yet he implicitly holds out hope that international justice reformers can reduce their expectations and become more context-sensitive.

Along these lines, several authors appeal to the need for greater attention to the legitimacy of both national processes and international operations. Papagianni's reasoned argument for the importance of participatory processes illustrates several ways in which the interests of individuals and groups can play a role in postwar peacebuilding. Although relatively stable outcomes can derive from exclusionary processes, the advantages of consultation seem clear. Jensen's chapter echoes these concerns, but again, argues along liberal lines for a more active knowledge and inclusion of local actors in efforts to enhance the rule of law. Of course, these appeals do not overcome the two main dilemmas of participatory efforts: (1) the inevitability of exclusion at some point in choosing who gets to participate in participatory exercises; and (2) the likelihood that legitimation exercises and outcomes will produce inefficient processes and less technically able personnel and institutions. Papagianni's examples from numerous transitions illustrate these dilemmas, but also offer some lessons in how these dilemmas can be handled.

Even the most skeptical authors in the volume nevertheless cling to the conviction that international actors *do* have a role in postwar peacebuilding, and that state institutions are somehow important in this process. Despite the harm caused and potentially lurking in postwar operations, international actors should not shrink from these efforts. Instead, they need to act with more thought, more caution, more deference to national actors, and more humility. How can they do so?

Managing Tensions Between Peacebuilding and Statebuilding

The contributions to this volume ratify many ideas about peacebuilding that have gained prominence in the past few years. These include the general neglect of the state by peacebuilders, the negative effects of donor practices on the state (and thus on sustainable peace), and the presence of some common imperatives in crafting legitimate states and strengthening state capacity.[6]

Yet the most provocative findings of the volume question much of the new conventional wisdom about fragile states and the dangers they pose to peace and stability. These findings point to tensions between the process of consolidating peace in a war-torn society and building a self-sustaining state. Such tensions do not exist in every case; consequently, attention to the particular context of a conflictual or postconflict society is of the utmost importance. Aspiring peace engineers can be effective only by discerning from the context whether particular measures will provoke spoilers, bolster warlords, weaken state institutions, undermine a fragile peace process, or add capacity at the cost of legitimacy among certain ethnic or religious groups. The contributions suggest that one of the most important ways that international and national actors can engage in peacebuilding more thoughtfully is by recognizing and managing the tensions between peacebuilding and statebuilding.

Six tensions stand out based on the case studies and the thematic contributions to the volume.

1. *Although states may be essential to peace, the process of building states can spark or facilitate armed conflict, especially if the emergent state is endowed with too many powers too quickly.*

Somalia exemplifies this tension. As Menkhaus argues, by endowing the central state with too many powers too quickly (i.e., with most of the functions of a typical state), statebuilding eventually engendered the armed resistance of those who stood to lose in the process. By building a "state-lite"—one whose functions would be minimal so that armed clans might retain some of their authority—statebuilding might have proceeded without sparking the widespread renewed violence that Somalia experienced in 2006.

Afghanistan provides a different example of how this tension has been managed. The construction of a national state has proceeded with diligent attention to the potential security hazard of usurping warlords' prerogatives too much or too quickly. Although warfare among the signatories to the Bonn agreement has been averted, some criticize the inability of the state to deliver services or command national allegiances. The state's relatively weak capacities may have helped preserve internal peace but have eroded the legitimacy of the new state, jeopardizing the long-term prospects of both state and peace. The case highlights the important (though elusive) role of legitimacy in balancing the imperatives of peace and of strengthening state capacity and reach throughout the territory.

One overlooked factor in this process is a widely held set of expectations about what states are supposed to do. A Western norm of state functions includes all the functions we emphasize in this volume—security, public finance, the administration of justice—as well as basic services such as public health, public education, and public transportation. Yet in weak or war-torn societies, these commonly held ideas should be questioned, as Chapter 7 by William Reno suggests. Certainly, functions such as education, minimal access to health care, the administration of justice, the resolution of conflicts, and basic security for the populace are functions that *someone* should provide. International donors and NGOs should not regard themselves as long-term providers of these services. Instead, states, or entities recognized by and regulated by states—such as substate authorities or suprastate arrangements—should be seen as the sustainable source of these functions in the long run. In most cases, the state can and should provide the range of services normally associated with statehood. At the same time, would-be statebuilders tend to be blind to the possibilities of creative arrangements involving substates, suprastates, or ad hoc arrangements involving the state and international organizations as well as regional or private sector bodies.[7]

2. *International peacebuilding undermines statebuilding when it bypasses state institutions, even though doing so may at times make sense.*

In Chapter 1, I described how international actors, just by their everyday operations, tend to undermine the state. The following international behaviors, although quite reasonable, also have a negative effect on the state: an insistence on delivering aid directly to recipients, refusal to channel aid through state agencies in order to demonstrate accountability to constituents back home, avoidance of domestic decisionmaking in order to expedite apolitical service delivery, and reliance on international NGOs for service delivery. All these behaviors may be justified when the state is corrupt, exclusionary, or predatory. Nevertheless, working to reform and enhance the state under such circumstances remains essential to sustainable peace.

The contributors here point to other ways in which external actors undermine sound state design and state capacity. In Chapter 8, Cliffe and Manning analyze four recurrent problems of international activities—lessons that are underlined by the case studies. First, outsiders (and sometimes insiders) ignore or dismiss preexisting institutions of authority, needlessly reinventing the wheel or creating new institutions that could have enjoyed greater legitimacy and effectiveness by selectively drawing on prior people, relationships and capacities. Second, statebuilding requires prioritization, which requires discipline. Third, statebuilders must anticipate the negative side effects of transitional or short-term measures. They must plan to redeploy resources and adjust institutions accordingly, depending partly on whether confidence builds among former enemies. Fourth, and related, international organizations whose policies routinely sap the strength and legitimacy of postconflict states must adjust or suppress these perverse practices.

The point on the collateral damage of international presences is often overlooked but comes through clearly in our case studies. A strong international presence, especially one with adequate military troop levels, may be successful at maintaining a cease-fire but not contribute to statebuilding—that is, it may keep the peace while undermining peacebuilding. The case of Bosnia and Herzegovina (and less uniformly East Timor) shows the negative long-term consequences of an international mission that dominates the political landscape. Such a mission can leave central state institutions weak, artificial, and bereft of legitimacy and capacity; it can foster dependency by distorting democratic process; it can create disincentives for compromise; and it can suppress the emergence of effective and accountable institutions.

The contributions to the volume indicate ways in which the UN, bilateral donors, and international NGOs can try to mitigate the worst effects of a corrupt state without bypassing it altogether. One mechanism is the voting booth. Although democracy is a blunt instrument in curbing corruption in transitional periods after wars, elections can eventually push corrupt powerholders out of office. Liberia's experience is a good example. Both before and after the election of Ellen Johnson-Sirleaf, legislative leaders were suspended for corrupt practices, and the electorate supported a candidate perceived to be distant from warring and corrupt parties. Other cases, such as Palestine and Bosnia and Herzegovina in the mid-1990s, show the limits of elections in curbing corrupt state practices. Here creative mechanisms to simultaneously strengthen state capacities while enacting greater oversight and accountability mechanisms—emanating from civil society, the legislature, and the courts—are the only means to curb short-term predation and strengthen long-term state institutions. Although Liberia's GEMAP program relies on international actors, it does not supplant the state entirely. Such a combination of international, regional, and state capacities can help external actors work through states while trying to overcome their deep flaws in governance.

3. *One principle of Weberian statebuilding—meritocracy—often must be balanced with central principles of peacemaking—compromise and power sharing—in order for peace to survive the short run and make sustainable statebuilding possible.*

This point reflects the broader finding that the steps necessary to consolidate peace may undermine the creation of a state that proves effective in the long run. Like Weber, many statebuilding advocates emphasize merit-based selection criteria to build apolitical and efficient state bureaucracies.[8]

Such criteria favor institutions that can outlive individual leaders and survive shifts in which party or faction controls the state. However, it is unrealistic to expect the population to immediately rely upon and trust state institutions in societies where people have historically been exploited by state bureaucracies and had to depend on their personal connections or informal networks to protect them and provide needed services. In the aftermath of warfare, distrust of the state will be high if an enemy faction seems to control it.

Under such circumstances, confidence-building measures are necessary, including measures more common to peacemaking: power sharing and compromise.[9] Thus, power-sharing arrangements that guarantee representation of various social groups in the cabinet, military, police, justice system, and other state bureaucracies may help get the state through a transitional period full of fears and uncertainty, even if such measures permit corrupt cabinet secretaries, illiterate cops, less qualified judges, and incompetent civil servants. Similarly, the need to employ ex-combatants may lead to a more bloated government payroll than the state's economic base can sustain over the long term. The exigencies of peace, therefore, may produce a different sort of state than one generally prized by international technical programs. Bosnia and Herzegovina's complicated, multilayered power-sharing arrangements are just one example of this approach. Palestine is a prime example of a related phenomenon in which international actors seeking to consolidate peace take advantage of practices such as patronage and clientelism. Ideally, meritocracy can be combined with measures to ensure adequate representation for ethnic or other important groups in society, with incentives for meritocratic criteria to assume greater precedence over time.

4. *A single-minded focus on strengthening state security forces, if done without attention to inclusiveness, accountability, and political processes, can foster human rights abuses, political exclusion, state delegitimation, and even war.*

In the security sector, the logic of postconflict peacebuilding is to support a cease-fire and to reduce the armament, troop levels, and areas of operation of all military factions, including the state army. In contrast, the logic of statebuilding is to strengthen state military and police capacities to ensure the suppression of any threats to instability or disorder. It is easy to see how efforts to build the capacity of the army or police may jeopardize the security of former insurgent forces engaged in laying down their arms and dismantling their units—or, for that matter, the security of civilian populations who have recently suffered under abusive security forces. This delicate and highly political process of security sector reform is the clearest instance in which statebuilding programs must be modified and contextualized in order not to threaten the perceived security of former insurgents or their associated social/ethnic groups. Even where elections have supposedly granted legitimate power to one party, every step in strengthening the state must take into account the potential impact on former enemies who may feel disenfranchised. Some form of incorporating former enemy factions into the state usually occurs in postwar statebuilding. Even in such circumstances, the perceived neglect of one segment of society may reignite war. The disillusionment of former Falintil fighters from the west of the country, whose rampages in 2006 jeopardized peace in East Timor, exemplifies the political delicacy of security sector reforms.

Similarly, enhancing coercive capacities without due attention to oversight mechanisms can strengthen opportunities for unaccountable forces to engage in abuse. The absence of accountability mechanisms virtually always leads to abuses of authority, and in military and police organizations such conduct can be lethal and have serious repercussions on the legitimacy of the state itself. The imperative in postconflict settings tends to privilege operational capacities. However, both national and international actors must work doubly hard to ensure that internal affairs police units, intelligence oversight mechanisms, and military criminal investigative capacities (among other management capacities) receive prompt and sustained resources and support.[10]

5. *Appeasing spoilers in the interest of peace, while neglecting the development of a sustainable state, can strengthen the hand of repressive or authoritarian state rulers and jeopardize the sustainability of both the state and peace.*

Here, the experience of Palestine during the 1990s is illustrative. Rex Brynen makes clear in Chapter 10 that, had the peace process flourished, the Palestinian Authority's institutions were adequate to sustain a state on a par with most developing world regimes, perhaps stronger than its neighbors in the region. Yet the cronyism and patronage exhibited by Yasser Arafat disillusioned many supporters of the Authority, for which international donors bore some of the blame. Fearing that they would be perceived as failing to support one side in a delicate peace process, and perhaps seeing few alternatives, donors did not sufficiently condition their generous assistance to Arafat's government-under-occupation on improvements in transparency and accountability. They pressed for security sector reforms, financial management reforms, and greater internal democracy, but chose not to use their leverage to demand that Arafat abandon some of the practices that left the nascent state unaccountable and less effective. This external preference for peace over improved state performance was certainly not the most significant factor in the demise of the Oslo process and Palestinian political authority, but it set a poor precedent for state conduct and performance.[11]

6. *Transitional mechanisms that help resolve short-term problems for either peace or state capacity can later create difficulties for both.*

We can think of this challenge as the "Transition Paradox." National elites and international actors often enthusiastically erect transitional mechanisms that are helpful—indeed necessary—to get a peace process through a challenging period or to help jump-start a disrupted state. Such mechanisms include transitional administrations, which allay the insecurities of warring parties and demonstrate to their followers that laying down arms will not cost them their lives. They may fall under international control (e.g., Kosovo, East Timor, Iraq), but are generally under the control of national actors.[12]

Yet transitional administrations tend to freeze politics in ways that undermine the sustainability of long-term peace. For example, commanders of the Kosovo Liberation Army cited their exclusion from the Dayton peace accords for Bosnia and Herzegovina as a factor in their decision to take up arms against the Serbian authorities. Conversely, the inclusion of abusive or controversial military commanders in a political pact may erode its legitimacy over time. Some of the compromises made during Afghanistan's Bonn negotiations privileged warlords in ways that later weakened the hand of the Karzai government. Civil society may also see itself as excluded by transitional arrangements that privilege the concerns of former combatants. Bilateral donors and international organizations have recently devised ways to ameliorate these tensions. Examples include the incorporation of civil society in peace negotiations and the linking of demobilization, disarmament, and reintegration (DDR) programs with projects to meet the needs of communities of displaced civilians.

Similarly, statebuilding programs can provide "transitional" capacity by hiring international actors as civil servants or providing support for returned exiles who have technical skills but may not intend to stay for the long run. Yet by "buying" capacity rather than "building" it, to use Cliffe and Manning's terms from Chapter 8, international actors may negatively affect long-term statebuilding. Again, the judiciary's trajectory in East Timor reflects some of the difficulties of these choices. As Cliffe and Manning suggest, success requires unclouded judgment about when and where to buy capacity versus build it, as well as serious efforts to supplant bought capacity in areas where long-term needs will require national rather than imported capacity.

Statebuilding Without Harm?
State Design and State Capacity

The recent focus on building national states as a means to consolidate peace is clearly fraught with the possibility of doing harm. Do the chapters permit us to draw further conclusions about *how* to do statebuilding in war-torn societies? This section synthesizes some of the guidance that runs throughout the book, especially from the thematic chapters, as to how to advance state institutions even while avoiding pitfalls. Here we start with the distinction drawn in Chapter 1 between state design and state capacity.

State Design and the Prospects for Peace

One of the contributors' most frequent criticisms is the tendency of analysts and practitioners to approach statebuilding as a technical exercise devoid of political significance and risks. In Chapter 14, Michael McGovern strongly discourages international actors from seeing statebuilding as a narrowly technocratic exercise. Consonant with this tendency is an overemphasis on state *capacity* rather than paying heed to opportunities to support national actors in modifying state *design*. Once focused on statebuilding, donors tend to embark on training and advising meant to enhance the human and material capacity of state ministries and agencies. Too often, national and international actors take for granted the prevailing design of state institutions. In fact, negotiations on reorganizing the architecture of the state, and their outcomes, play a fundamental role in subsequent legitimation and peace consolidation.

To be fair, elites of a society rarely have an opportunity to revamp the design of the structure of state institutions. From Botswana to France, from Argentina to Zambia, even constitutional assemblies rarely transform a federal structure of authority into a centralized one, from a consociational to a majoritarian democracy, from a national state to one with autonomous regions. Yet the end of wars—especially where challengers emerge victorious or are sufficiently strong to force a negotiated settlement—provide unique windows of opportunity for rethinking the design of the state. Elites have neglected potential opportunities for redesigning the state in countries such as Haiti, Somalia, and Liberia. In high-profile places like Iraq, Afghanistan, Kosovo, and South Africa, state design received a good deal of attention and deliberation by national elites and external actors. Yet even here, the importance of state design (relative to state strength) is evident—though sometimes with tragic consequences. In Iraq after the 2003 invasion, for instance, the negotiated constitutional representation granted to Shiites, Sunnis, and Kurds shaped the onset of civil war.

The volume's contributors suggest four findings regarding state design. First, the range of options considered for state design is highly constrained by historical precedent. State design options are limited by the historical, institutional fabric woven over decades or centuries by colonial legacies, land tenure patterns, industrial development, and social relations among ethnic and religious groups. In this context, elites in transitional periods tend not to look very far from previous models, reverting to familiar forms of governance.[13] This is true largely because previous forms of governance hold some level of acceptance even among those who are not advantaged by them, whereas any deviation will find opposition from those who think they might possibly be left disadvantaged vis-à-vis familiar prior structures. Prior structures serve as an obvious point of convergence in bargaining, be it explicit or tacit. Even when old forms of governance are discredited or demolished after a war or regime collapse, old state designs serve as points of reference and sources of legitimacy. Postwar Afghanistan, Kosovo, and East Timor all adopted constitutions or legal regimes that predated those associated with the defeated regime. Even though the parameters of state design in postconflict societies are often wider than in societies not experiencing conflict, both international norms of democratic rule and national recourse to familiar forms will likely restrict creativity to the margins.

Second, national elites, not international actors, are in the driver's seat in state design. In most cases of transitions from war, external actors are secondary players. Even where external actors have defeated a state by military force and enjoy apparent predominance, national elites retain a determinant role. The cases of Afghanistan, Palestine, Kosovo, Somalia, and even Iraq illustrate the centrality of national elites' preferences in forging state design, either in constitution-drafting processes or otherwise.

Third, elites' self-interest vis-à-vis other sociopolitical actors drive their decisions about state design more than principled commitments. It is unsurprising that ethnic majorities tend to favor majoritarian electoral formulas rather than power-sharing arrangements, given that "one person, one vote" preserves their power. Even where elites have creatively stepped out of past models in redesigning state structures, their interest in preserving power remains a driving force. Consider the decision by Jean-Bertrand Aristide to eliminate Haiti's armed forces. Along the same lines, in Chapter 12 Edith Bowles and Tanja Chopra discuss decisions made by the Fretilin-dominated Constituent Assembly in East Timor that anticipated Fretilin's dominance of the political landscape. In each case, newly empowered democratic leaders sought not just to advance civilian democracy but to remove future threats to their rule.

Fourth, process is as important as outcome. The redesign of state institutions will acquire legitimacy to the extent that those with veto power have bought into new structures. To the extent that important religious or ethnic groups feel that their voice has been taken into account in constitutional assemblies or other decisions about federalism, regional autonomy, or power-sharing arrangements, then the new state architecture has a chance to succeed. In Chapter 3, Papagianni underscores the importance of participation for sustainability. International actors can usefully expose national elites to models drawn from other places (or indeed from political science), but the process remains intensely political, not just among elites but among important constituencies.

State Capacity and Legitimacy

Several contributors—Carnahan and Lockhart, Cliffe and Manning, McGovern, Bowles and Chopra, Sherman—emphasize state capacity as a crucial factor in the consolidation of peace. As discussed in Chapter 1 and reflected in the organization of the volume, state capacities to provide *security, public finance and economic policy management, and justice and the rule of law* are generally urgent statebuilding priorities unless unusual circumstances dictate otherwise. The case studies show how important each of these sectors can be. Afghanistan, Palestine, and Bosnia and Herzegovina (and more saliently Iraq) demonstrate not only the urgency of security, but also the importance of its interaction with political processes and development progress. Public finance and economic policy capacities have played an especially important role in the peace processes of Liberia and Afghanistan. And East Timor, Liberia, and Bosnia and Herzegovina each demonstrates in different ways the importance of the ability of the state to administer justice, both for wartime atrocities and for present-day crimes.

Cliffe and Manning identify a number of important questions about institutional capacity in Chapter 8, particularly what sort of capacities are needed, and who is best positioned to provide them. They point out that international actors should only in certain circumstances step in and supplant state capacities, and should offer criteria and various rationales for doing so rather than simply providing oversight during an agreed-upon period. And they insist that strategies for capacity building should always accompany any international provision of state services. By privileging the *function* of state institutions over their form, Cliffe and Manning diminish the chances that culturally or socially ill-fitting models will be promoted by external actors. Because both legitimacy and effectiveness are ends of statebuilding, they argue that tradeoffs between building capacity and enhancing legitimacy are not straightforward and require contextual judgments. This guidance is useful for any consideration of either state capacities or state design.

One of the central findings of this volume is the highly complex and context-dependent nature of statebuilding in the shadow of warfare. In particular, the chapters show the significance of the interaction of *capacity and legitimacy*. The core functions that a state performs—generating revenue, administering justice, and providing security—are intertwined with one another and with political legitimation. Too often security provision is seen as a neutral act enabling political deals to be cut or economies to grow. But political negotiations both depend upon and alter the military capacity of the parties. Security provision is necessary for political processes, but it is a factor shaping those deals and is in turn affected by those deals in a spiral of political reforms and security reforms—or reversals. Similarly, although economic growth may require a secure enabling environment, the forces that provide that security will require material resources in the way of salaries and equipment in order to do their jobs. The size of military and police forces must be based on a realistic assessment of the state's capacity to generate the revenue necessary to sustain them. Most postconflict countries—certainly most of the cases explored in this volume—have a very limited revenue base and even more limited capacity to extract revenues, compounding the challenge of ensuring that security institutions are financially viable. Many of the cases have highlighted the importance of border customs revenue and its link to security.

International actors and internationalized peace operations are not exempt from this interdependent evolution of political legitimacy, economic resources, and security provision. On the contrary, an international security presence is part of the political, economic, and security panorama, not separate from it in some illusion of neutrality. In Chapter 2, Barnett R. Rubin points to the importance of the legitimacy of international peacekeepers and the resources they bring to a country.

Consider the following combinations of legitimacy and resources for security in international peace operations. In the view of most analysts, international actors failed to provide sufficient troops or resources for security in post-Taliban Afghanistan, even though the degree of legitimacy of the UN mission was initially high. The low level of resources was a fundamental constraint not only on the political strategy adopted (as discussed above), but also on the potential for the security reform strategy of creating a national army to supplant roving warlord armies and the national government's ability to raise taxes. Consequently, the limits on international security provision were a fundamental reason why hopes were not met that the national state would co-opt and defeat regional warlords and their armies and sources of revenue. Iraq offers a case of an intervention with low legitimacy, coupled with an initially low commitment of troops to police the country, especially once the Baathist army was disbanded. Alternatively, where high levels of resources and legitimacy accompanied intervention, for instance, in Liberia and East Timor, then the security element proved generally successful during the international peace operation.

Finally, Rubin also suggests that, because international statebuilding exercises occur where states almost "by definition" lack both security and legitimacy, the processes of restoring legitimacy and enhancing security are intertwined. The initial steps to create or strengthen a national state necessarily undercut the power of regional military commanders, requiring a security strategy for armed resistance. Preparations to prosecute military leaders for past atrocities generally carry their own serious requirements for security capacities, both to detain suspects like Bosnia and Herzegovina's Radovan Karadzic and to quell potential armed resistance from the suspects' loyalists. To the extent that postconflict states are unable to maintain security for the general population amid possible common criminal, ethnic, or political violence, then the legitimacy of the state itself may be jeopardized. In short, efforts to consolidate peace require deft management of the interaction among security, state capacities, and legitimation.

What of democracy? Democratic forms of authority are virtually indispensable in the present global normative environment. Yet as recent research shows, democratic governance is not synonymous with internal peace. Formal democracies suffer from civil war, and authoritarian regimes are less likely to experience interstate warfare than regimes moving toward democracy.[14] However, global expectations about electoral events make it easy for internal dissidents to rally against a government perceived as acting undemocratically, especially if its defiance of norms of legitimation is accompanied by a failure to provide socially expected services or security. External incentives make it difficult for national elites to mobilize support unless they claim to empower the people, either through Western-supported democratic processes or through populist platforms that make claims of participation in the absence of democratic substance (e.g., Hugo Chavez's Venezuela). Moreover, international actors themselves may exercise power in profoundly undemocratic ways, acting instead as what Simon Chesterman has termed "benevolent autocrats."[15] Use of the term *democracy* now encompasses such divergent regimes and practices (including those many consider undemocratic) that it is more useful to analyze particular mechanisms of participation and legitimation as they relate to specific institutions of postconflict states than to speak of macro strategies of democratization.

The authors of the chapters in the book highlight the important interaction of democracy with goods such as security and capacity. Because democracy is a primary currency of international legitimacy, the forms of democracy and their substance cannot be ignored in transitional societies. Although legitimacy transcends claims of democracy, such claims form a part of state legitimation. Papagianni stresses in Chapter 3 that processes of democratic transformation trump their content, especially in postconflict states. How democracy proceeds is often more important than the substance of that democracy.

Managing the Complexities of Building States to Building Peace

In this volume we have sought to examine critically the newfound wisdom about the centrality of state institutions to the sustainability of peace. Simply put, we concur with the main premise: statebuilding is crucial for peacebuilding. Past scholarship on peace has tended to neglect the state. This neglect extends to the once dominant scholarly focus on reaching negotiated agreements, which are now recognized as a midpoint, rather than the endpoint, of peace processes. It also includes naive assumptions that economic growth and neoliberal policies can readily consolidate peace; that effective DDR programs readily translate into peace; that civil society, once unleashed from the constraints of wartime, can bring about sustainable peace; and that international humanitarians, UN peacekeepers, or any other international actor with enough resources and determination, can make peace stick. All these lines of thinking have understated the complexity and difficulty of peacebuilding—and failed to emphasize the centrality of effective state institutions for self-sustaining peace.

At the same time, the thematic and case chapters make clear the deficiencies of present efforts to build states in the context of building peace. The volume's contributors provide disparate examples of harmful practices in peacebuilding efforts. From the neglect of state institutions to the deliberate bypassing of such institutions, from favoring international capacities over national capacities to disinterest in investing in peace once a cease-fire is reached, international practices could improve simply by doing less harm. Recognizing and planning around some of the under-recognized tensions between statebuilding and peacebuilding is one step that could improve strategic planning and programs for consolidating peace and fostering legitimate and effective state institutions. These tensions expose the hazards of equating peacebuilding with statebuilding. Nevertheless, the authors share a conviction that international and national actors could manage these tensions more nimbly.

Some basic difficulties underlie statebuilding in war-torn societies. First, although the state is a necessary component of ensuring self-sustaining peace, it also poses a perpetual obstacle. States tend to adopt policies that favor certain groups over others, to provide services to some populations more than others, to impinge on the rights of certain social groups, and to undermine nonstate mechanisms for conflict resolution and service delivery. Moreover, long-lived states have historically emerged from the violent consolidation of power by certain social groups over others, with clear winners and losers.[16] Whereas international actors exhibit self-interested (often self-defeating) behavior, national efforts to build state strength often result in exclusion, displacement, and death. Donor agencies and the UN Peacebuilding Commission, among others, will cause considerable damage if they fail to grasp the multivalent and complex roles of states themselves.

Second, even as this volume draws attention to key state sectors or functions, an overarching analysis or approach to the state is also necessary. Technical understandings and approaches must be informed by comprehending the state as an arena of competition and sometimes cooperation among self-interested national elites, private actors, nongovernmental organizations, and international donors and organizations. The interrelated politics of economic gain, security provision, and principled appeals frame the challenges of institution building and capacity building in war-torn countries. Strategic peacebuilding by international actors requires recognition that the state is not a neutral ground for technical programs, but a central locus of social conflict.

This volume offers no straightforward answers to the challenges of statebuilding in war-torn societies. Most of the authors not only fail to provide a how-to manual for statebuilding, but dismiss the idea that such a manual should exist. The US effort in Iraq since March 2003 underscores the need for humility in such enterprises, although its tragic flaws were in many ways overdetermined. That experience highlights the hard lesson that traditional military instruments cannot by themselves secure peace, even in a highly militarized setting. Building peace is a complex process requiring extensive planning, coordination, and harmonization of multiple civilian capacities with the appropriate military and policing instruments and with attention to the legitimacy of international actors.

Building legitimate states and building peace are not synonymous, nor are they without tensions, as detailed above. These tensions, although not easily surmountable, can be ameliorated through four principles: cognizance, context, sequencing, and patience. First, national and international actors must be cognizant of these tensions, anticipating them and developing strategies to overcome them. Naive presumptions that "all good things go together" are harmful, and planners can take foresighted measures to mitigate tensions between peace and state institution building.[17]

Second, context is crucial. No single sequence or combination of peacebuilding activities and institution building will work for all cases. The particulars of a society and place must guide the sequencing and adjustment of policies and programs. For instance, adjusting merit-based selection criteria to allow former enemies entry into the police or civil service may be sensible in some cases but not in others. Temporarily using international jurists may be necessary under some circumstances but not in others. Decisionmakers must repeatedly ask, "How relevant are the past experiences of statebuilding or peace implementation for the society in question?"

Third, sequencing of efforts to strengthen state institutions and support peace processes is vital to accomplishing both. Sequencing does not refer here to the overall pursuit of state institutionalization before peace consolidation (or vice versa). Instead, it refers to the need to sequence particular activities—such as issuing indictments for war criminals who can spoil the peace, forming a transitional government, ramping up public finance capacity, demobilizing combatants, rewriting the constitution or foundational laws, holding local or national elections that may begin to mark the end of transitional authorities, reining in patronage-based leadership styles (or leaders)—so that they will not overturn the applecart of peace and send factions back to war. Conversely, overly hasty, ambitious, or politically tone-deaf efforts to build states may alienate certain social groups, jeopardizing peace and toppling the state. Myriad postconflict activities must be sequenced in such a way that the trust and buy-in necessary for peace have room to grow, as do legitimacy and effectiveness.

Finally, related to the need for cognizance, context, and sequencing is patience. Self-sustaining peace in an effective and legitimate state takes time, resources, hard work, and good fortune. The risk of failure is high, and its dangers are potent.

In the coming decades, efforts to secure peace and to foster legitimate states are likely to become even more pertinent not only for international stability, but for human security, human development, and human rights. Practitioners of development, diplomacy, and defense now recognize, at least dimly, the links between building peace and building states. The political volatility of such efforts and their outcomes is apparent, as we have seen over the past twenty years in West Africa, Central America, southern Africa, southwestern Asia, and the Middle East. We are now in the early stages of serious analysis of these processes. The experiences and analysis offered here should contribute to clearer and more effective approaches to durable peace.

Notes

1. Although seemingly forgotten in much scholarship, the limits of international influence have been widely noted. See Elizabeth Cousens, Chetan Kumar, and Karin Wermester, eds., *Peacebuilding as Politics: Cultivating Peace in Fragile Societies* (Boulder, CO: Lynne Rienner, 2000); Stephen J. Stedman, "Conclusion," in Stedman, Elizabeth Cousens, and Donald Rothchild, *Ending Civil Wars* (Boulder, CO: Lynne Rienner, 2002).

2. See Mary B. Anderson, *Do No Harm: How Aid Can Support Peace—or War* (Boulder, CO: Lynne Rienner, 1999); Susan Woodward, "On the Problem of the Postwar State and the Need for a Doctrine of 'Do No Harm,'" paper presented at the Workshop on Building Peace in Fragile States, University of California at San Diego, December 2006.

3. Even the insistence on persisting in military exports and arms sales, whose effects are analyzed by Paul Collier, privilege Western interests in profit over peace.

4. Michael Carnahan, William Durch, and Scott Gilmore, "Economic Impact of Peacekeeping: Final Report," Study conducted for the United Nations Department of Peacekeeping Operations, March 2006, http://www.stimson.org/fopo/pdf/EIP_FINAL_Report_March2006doc.pdf.

5. Edward D. Mansfield and Jack Snyder, "Democratic Transitions and War: From Napoleon to the Millennium's End," in Chester Crocker, Fen Osler Hampson, and Pamela Aall, eds., *Turbulent Peace,* pp. 113–126; and Jack L. Snyder, *From Voting to Violence* (New York: W. W. Norton, 2000).

6. See, for example, Roland Paris, *At War's End: Building Peace After Civil Conflict* (Cambridge: Cambridge University Press, 2004); Simon Chesterman, Michael Ignatieff, and Ramesh Thakur, eds., *Making States Work: State Failure and the Crisis of Governance* (Tokyo: United Nations University Press, 2005); Ashraf Ghani, Clare Lockhart, and Michael Carnahan, "An Agenda for State-Building in the 21st Century," *Fletcher Forum for World Affairs* 30, no. 1 (Winter 2006): 101–123.

7. For another perspective on alternative approaches to sovereignty, see Stephen D. Krasner, "Sharing Sovereignty: New Institutions for Collapsed and Failing States," *International Security* 29, no. 2 (Fall 2004): 85–120.

8. For instance, see Francis Fukuyama, *State-Building: Governance and World Order in the 21st Century* (Ithaca, NY: Cornell University Press, 2004).

9. Philip G. Roeder and Donald Rothchild, eds., *Sustainable Peace: Power and Democracy After Civil Wars* (Ithaca, NY: Cornell University Press, 2005).

10. See Gordon Peake, Eric Scheye, and Alice Hills, "Introduction," in "Managing Insecurity: Field Experiences of Security Sector Reform," special issue, *Civil Wars* 8, no. 2 (2006); and Charles T. Call, *Constructing Justice and Security After War* (Washington, DC: US Institute of Peace Press, 2007).

11. The absence of juridical statehood for Palestine conditioned these processes in significant ways.

12. For an in-depth study of UN transitional administrations, see Simon Chesterman, *You, the People: The United Nations, Transitional Administration, and State-Building* (Oxford: Oxford University Press, 2004).

13. See José Antonio Cheibub and Fernando Limongi, "Democratic Institutions and Regime Survival: Parliamentary and Presidential Democracies Reconsidered," *Annual Review of Political Science* 5 (June 2002): 151–179; and Juan J. Linz and Alfred C. Stepan, *Problems of Democratic Transition and Consolidation: Southern Europe, South America, and Post-Communist Europe* (Baltimore: Johns Hopkins University Press, 1996).

14. Mansfield and Snyder, "Democratic Transitions and War," pp. 113–126.

15. Simon Chesterman, "Building Democracy Through Benevolent Autocracy: Consultation and Accountability in UN Transitional Administrations," in Edward Newman and Roland Rich, eds., *The UN Role in Promoting Democracy: Between Ideals and Reality* (Tokyo: United Nations University Press, 2004).

16. See Charles Tilly, "War Making and State Making as Organized Crime," in Peter B. Evans, Dietrich Rueschemeyer, and Theda Skocpol, eds., *Bringing the State Back In* (Cambridge: Cambridge University Press, 1985).

17. Robert Packenham first criticized this liberal tendency in US aid programs in his *Liberal America and the Third World* (Princeton, NJ: Princeton University Press, 1973).

Acronyms

AFL	Armed Forces of Liberia
AIHRC	Afghan Independent Human Rights Commission
AMF	Afghan Military Forces
ANA	Afghan National Army
ANP	Afghan National Police
ASP	Afghanistan Stabilization Program
AU	African Union
CAVR	Commission for Reception, Truth, and Reconciliation Timor-Leste
CDF	Civil Defense Forces (Sierra Leone)
CEP	Community Empowerment and Local Governance Project (World Bank)
CEPR	Center for Economic Policy Research
CIA	Central Intelligence Agency
CIC	Council of Islamic Courts (Somalia)
CLJ	Constitutional Loya Jirga (Afghanistan)
CIVPOL	United Nations Civilian Police
CNRM	Conselho Nacional de Resistencia Maubere (East Timor)
CNRT	Conselho Nacional de Resistencia Timorense (East Timor)
CNRT	National Congress for Timorese Reconstruction (East Timor)
CPA	Comprehensive Peace Agreement (Liberia)
CPIA	Country Policy and Institutional Assessment (World Bank)
CPR	Conflict Prevention and Reconstruction Unit (World Bank)
CSAE	Center for the Study of African Economies

DDR	demobilization, disarmament, and reintegration
DDRR	disarmament, demobilization, reintegration, and rehabilitation (Liberia)
DFID	Department for International Development (UK)
DHS	Department of Health Services
DIAG	Disarmament of Illegal Armed Groups (Afghanistan)
DRC	Democratic Republic of Congo
ECOSOC	Economic and Social Council (United Nations)
ECOWAS	Economic Community of West African States
EGAP	economic governance action plan
ELJ	Emergency Loya Jirga (Afghanistan)
EU	European Union
EUPM	EU Police Mission (Bosnia and Herzegovina)
FDTL	Forças de Defesa de Timor Leste
F-FDTL	Falintil–Forças de Defesa de Timor Leste
FY	fiscal year
GDP	gross domestic product
GEMAP	Governance and Economic Management Assistance Program (Liberia)
HDZ	Croatian Democratic Union
HPC	High Preparatory Commission (Iraq)
ICTY	International Criminal Tribunal for the Former Yugoslavia
IDPs	internally displaced persons
IFI	international financial institution
IFOR	Implementation Force (Bosnia and Herzegovina)
IHA	Interim Health Authority
IMATT	International Military Advisory and Training Team (Britain)
IMF	International Monetary Fund
INGOs	international nongovernmental organizations
INPFL	Independent National Patriotic Front of Liberia
INTERFET	International Force for East Timor
IPTF	International Police Task Force
ISA	independent service authority
ISAF	International Security Assistance Force (Afghanistan)
JEMB	Joint Electoral Management Body (Afghanistan)
JRC	Judicial Reform Commission (Afghanistan)
KLA	Kosovo Liberation Army
KRT	Khmer Rouge Tribunal
LDK	Democratic League of Kosovo
LICUS	Low-Income Countries Under Stress
LURD	Liberians United for Reconciliation and Democracy

MCA	Millennium Challenge Account
MCC	Millennium Challenge Corporation
MOD	Ministry of Defense (Afghanistan)
MODEL	Movement for Democracy in Liberia
MOI	Ministry of Interior (Afghanistan)
MOJ	Ministry of Justice (Afghanistan)
NATO	North Atlantic Treaty Organization
NC	National Council (East Timor)
NGOs	nongovernmental organizations
NPFL	National Patriotic Front of Liberia
NRAP	National Emergency Employment Program/National Rural Access Program (Afghanistan)
NSD	National Security Directorate (Afghanistan)
NSP	National Solidarity Program (Afghanistan)
NTGL	National Transitional Government of Liberia
NTLA	National Transitional Legislative Assembly
OECD	Organization for Economic Cooperation and Development
OHR	Office of the High Representative
OSCE	Organization for Security and Cooperation in Europe
PA	Palestinian Authority
PD	Partido Democratico (East Timor)
PDCs	peace and development committees
PLO	Palestine Liberation Organization
PRT	provincial reconstruction team (Afghanistan)
PSF	Preventive Security Force (Gaza)
RRA	Rahanweyn Resistance Army (Somalia)
RUF	Revolutionary United Front (Sierra Leone)
S/CRS	Office of the Coordinator for Reconstruction and Stabilization (US Department of State)
SCU	Serious Crimes Unit (East Timor)
SDS	Serbian Democratic Party
SFOR	Stabilization Force (Bosnia and Herzegovina)
SPLA	Sudan People's Liberation Army
SRSG	Special Representative of the Secretary-General
SSR	security sector reform
TAP	Tripartite Action Plan on Revenues, Expenditures, and Donor Funding
TFET	Trust Fund for East Timor
TFG	Transitional Federal Government (Somalia)
TNG	Transitional National Government (Somalia)
UDT	Timorese Democratic Union
ULIMO-J	United Liberation Movement for Democracy in Liberia—Johnson

ULIMO-K	United Liberation Movement for Democracy in Liberia—Kromah
UN	United Nations
UNAMA	United Nations Assistance Mission in Afghanistan
UNAMET	United Nations Mission to East Timor
UNAMSIL	United Nations Mission in Sierra Leone
UNDP	United Nations Development Program
UNMIL	United Nations Peacekeeping Mission in Liberia
UNMISET	United Nations Mission of Support in East Timor
UNMIT	United Nations Integrated Mission in Timor-Leste
UNOSOM	United Nations Operation in Somalia
UNOTIL	United Nations Office in Timor-Leste
UNPROFOR	United Nations Protection Force
UNRWA	United Nations Relief and Works Agency
UNSCO	Office of the United Nations Special Coordinator in the Occupied Territories
UNTAET	United Nations Transitional Administration in East Timor
USAID	United States Agency for International Development
WBG	West Bank and Gaza

Bibliography

Abbas, Mahmoud (Abu Mazen). *Through Secret Channels.* Reading, UK: Garnet, 1995.

Afghanistan Independent Human Rights Commission. *A Call for Justice: A National Consultation on Past Human Rights Violations in Afghanistan.* Kabul, 2005.

African Rights. *Land Tenure, the Creation of Famine, and the Prospects for Peace in Somalia.* New York, 1993.

Agreement on Provisional Arrangements in Afghanistan Pending the Re-establishment of Permanent Government Institutions [The Bonn Agreement]. December 22, 2001.

Ahmad, Ehtisham, Piyush Desai, Thierry Kalfon, and Eivind Tandberg. "Priorities for Reform in Post-Conflict Finance Ministries." In *Reforming Fiscal and Economic Management in Afghanistan,* edited by Michael Carnahan, Nick Manning, Richard Bontjer, and Stephane Guimbert, 67–80. Washington, DC: World Bank, 2004.

Anderson, Benedict. *Imagined Communities: Reflections on the Origin and Spread of Nationalism.* London: Verso, 2006.

Anderson, James H., David S. Bernstein, and Cheryl W. Gray. *Judicial Systems in Transition Economies: Assessing the Past, Looking to the Future.* Washington, DC: World Bank, 2005.

Arato, Andrew. "Interim Imposition." *Ethics and International Affairs* 18, no. 3 (Winter 2004–2005): 25–50.

Arbitration Commission of the Peace Conference on Yugoslavia (Badinter Commission). "Opinion No. 4." *International Legal Materials* (Paris) 31 (January 11, 1992).

Armstrong, Andrea, and Barnett Rubin. "The Great Lakes and South Central Asia." In *Making States Work: State Failure and the Crisis of Governance,* edited by Simon Chesterman, Michael Ignatieff, and Ramesh Thakur, 79–101. Tokyo: United Nations University Press, 2005.

Ayoob, Mohammed. "The Security Problematic of the Third World." *World Politics* 43, no. 2 (1991): 257–283.

Babo-Soares, Dionísio. "Nahe Biti: Grassroots Reconciliation in East Timor." In *Roads to Reconciliation,* edited by Elin Skaar, Siri Gloppen, and Astri Suhrke. Lanham, MD: Lexington Books, 2005.

Badie, Bertrand. *The Imported State: The Westernization of the Political Order.* Translated by Claudia Royal. Stanford: Stanford University Press, 2000.

Barakat, Sultan, and Gareth Wardell, eds. *After the Conflict: Reconstruction and Development in the Aftermath of War.* London: I. B. Tauris, 2005.

Barnett, Michael. "Bringing in the New World Order: Liberalism, Legitimacy, and the United Nations." *World Politics* 49, no. 4 (July 1997): 526–551.

———. "Building a Republican Peace: Stabilizing States After War." *International Security* 30, no. 4 (2006): 87–112.

———. "The New United Nations Politics of Peace: From Juridical Sovereignty to Empirical Sovereignty." *Global Governance* 1, no. 1 (Winter 1995): 79–97.

Bastian, Sunil, and Robin Luckham, eds. *Can Democracy Be Designed? The Politics of Institutional Choice in Conflict-Torn Societies.* London: Zed Books, 2003.

Bayart, Jean-Francois. *The State in Africa: The Politics of the Belly.* New York: Longman, 1993.

Bayley, David H. *Changing the Guard: Developing Democratic Police Abroad.* Oxford: Oxford University Press, 2005.

Beauvais, Joel C. "Benevolent Despotism: A Critique of U.N. State-Building in East Timor." *New York University Journal of International Law and Politics* 33, no. 4 (Summer 2001): 1101–1178.

Bennett, Christina, Shawna Wakefield, and Andrew Wilder. "Afghan Elections: The Great Gamble." Afghanistan Research and Evaluation Unit (AREU) Briefing Paper. Kabul, November 2003.

Benomar, Jamal. "Constitution-Making After Conflict: Lessons for Iraq." *Journal of Democracy* 15, no. 2 (April 2004): 81–95.

Berdal, Mats, and David Malone. *Greed and Grievance: Economic Agendas in Civil Wars.* Boulder, CO: Lynne Rienner, 2000.

Berkowitz, Daniel, Katharina Pistor, and Jean-Francois Richard. "Economic Development, Legality, and the Transplant Effect." *European Economic Review* 47, no. 1 (February 2003): 165–195.

Bermeo, Nancy. "What the Democratization Literature Says—or Doesn't Say—About Postwar Democratization." *Global Governance* 9, no. 2 (April–June 2003): 159–177.

Bertram, Eva. "Reinventing Government: The Promise and Perils of Peacebuilding." *Journal of Conflict Resolution* 39, no. 3 (September 1995): 387–418.

Bhatia, Michael, Kevin Lanigan, and Philip Wilkinson. "Minimal Investments, Minimal Results: The Failure of Security Policy in Afghanistan." Afghanistan Research and Evaluation Unit (AREU) Briefing Paper. Kabul, 2004.

Bigombe, Betty, Paul Collier, and Nicholas Sambanis. "Policies for Building Post-Conflict Peace." *Journal of African Economies* 9, no. 3 (October 2000): 323–348.

Bienen, Henry, and Jeffrey Herbst. "The Relationship Between Political and Economic Reform in Africa." *Comparative Politics* 29, no. 1 (October 1996): 23–42.

Bildt, Carl. *Peace Journey: The Struggle for Peace in Bosnia.* London: Weidenfeld and Nicholson, 1998.

Bird, Andrew, and Stephen Lister. *Planning and Aid Management for Palestine.* Oxford: Mokoro, 1997.

Blankenburg, Erhard. "Judicial Systems in Western Europe: Comparative Indicators of Legal Professionals, Courts, Litigation, and Budgets in the 1990s." In *Beyond Common Knowledge: Empirical Approaches to the Rule of Law,* edited by Erik G. Jensen and Thomas C. Heller. Stanford: Stanford University Press, 2003.

Boyce, James K. "The International Financial Institutions: Post-conflict Reconstruction and Peacebuilding Capacities." Paper prepared for the Center on International

Cooperation seminar, "Strengthening the UN's Capacity on Civilian Crisis Management," Copenhagen, June 8–9, 2004.

Boyce, James K., and Madalene O'Donnell, eds. *Peace and the Public Purse: Economic Policies for Postwar Statebuilding*. Boulder, CO: Lynne Rienner, 2007.

Bradbury, Mark, Adan Yusuf Abokor, and Haroon Ahmed Yusuf. "Somaliland: Choosing Politics over Violence." *Review of African Political Economy* 30, no. 97 (2003): 455–478.

Brandt, Michele. "Constitution-Making in Cambodia, East Timor, and Afghanistan." Bureau for Crisis Prevention and Recovery, United Nations Development Programme, New York, May 2005.

Bratton, Michael. "State Building and Democratization in Sub-Saharan Africa: Forwards, Backwards, or Together?" Afrobarometer Working Paper no. 43, September 2004, http://www.afrobarometer.org/papers/AfropaperNo43.pdf.

Bratton, Michael, and Nicolas van de Walle. *Democratic Experiments in Africa: Regime Transitions in Comparative Perspective*. Cambridge: Cambridge University Press, 1997.

Brett, Roddy, and Antonio Delgado. "Guatemala's Constitution-Building Processes." Paper submitted to International IDEA's Democracy-Building and Conflict Management Programme, 2005, http://www.idea.int/conflict/cbp/upload/CBP-Guatemala.pdf (accessed July 28, 2007).

Brown, Nathan J. *Palestinian Politics After the Oslo Accords: Resuming Arab Palestine*. Berkeley: University of California Press, 2003.

Brubaker, Rogers. *Citizenship and Nationhood in France and Germany*. Cambridge, MA: Harvard University Press, 1992.

———. *Nationalism Reframed: Nationhood and the National Question in the New Europe*. Cambridge: Cambridge University Press, 1996.

Bryden, Matt. "New Hope for Somalia: The Building Block Approach?" *Review of African Political Economy* 26, no. 79 (March 1999): 134–140.

Brynen, Rex. *A Very Political Economy: Peacebuilding and Foreign Aid in the West Bank and Gaza*. Washington, DC: US Institute of Peace Press, 2000.

Burg, Steven L., and Paul S. Shoup. *The War in Bosnia-Herzegovina: Ethnic Conflict and International Intervention*. Armonk, NY: M. E. Sharpe, 1999.

Burton, Michael, and John Higley. "Political Crises and Elite Settlements." In *Elites, Crises, and the Origins of Regimes,* edited by Mattei Dogan and John Higley. Lanham, MD: Rowman and Littlefield, 1998.

Call, Charles T., ed. *Constructing Justice and Security After War*. Washington, DC: United States Institute of Peace Press, 2007.

———. "Democratisation, War and State-Building: Constructing the Rule of Law in El Salvador." *Journal of Latin American Studies* 35, no. 4 (November 2003): 827–862.

———. "Institutionalizing Peace: A Review of Post-Conflict Peacebuilding Concepts and Issues for DPA." Review conducted for the United Nations Department of Political Affairs, January 31, 2005.

———. "War Transitions and the New Civilian Security in Latin America." *Comparative Politics* 35, no. 1 (October 2002).

Call, Charles T., and Susan E. Cook. "On Democratization and Peacebuilding." *Global Governance* 9, no. 2 (April–June 2003): 233–246.

Call, Charles T., and Elizabeth Cousens. "Ending Wars and Building Peace." Coping with Crisis Working Paper Series. New York: International Peace Academy, March 2007.

Campbell, John L. *Institutional Change and Globalization*. Princeton, NJ: Princeton University Press, 2004.

Caplan, Richard. "A New Trusteeship? The International Administration of War-Torn Territories." Adelphi Paper no. 341. New York: Oxford University Press, 2002.

Carbonnier, Gilles, and Sarah Fleming, eds. *War, Money, and Survival.* Geneva: International Committee of the Red Cross, 2000.

Carnahan, Michael, William Durch, and Scott Gilmore. "The Economic Impact of Peacekeeping: Final Report." Prepared for the Economic Impact of Peacekeeping Project. PBPS/DPKO with Peace Dividend Trust, March 2006.

Casper, Gerhard. "The United States at the End of the 'American Century': The Rule of Law or Enlightened Absolutism?" *Washington University Journal of Law and Policy* 4 (2000): 149–172.

Casper, Karen L., and Sutana Kamal. *Evaluation Report: Community Legal Services Conducted by Family Planning NGOs.* Dhaka: Asia Foundation, 1995.

Center for Strategic and International Studies and Association of the United States Army. *Play to Win: Final Report of the Bipartisan Commission on Post-Conflict Reconstruction.* Washington, DC, January 2003.

Center on International Cooperation. *Annual Review of Global Peace Operations, 2006.* Boulder, CO: Lynne Rienner, 2006. [Published annually.]

Chandler, David. "Introduction: Peace Without Politics?" *International Peacekeeping* 12, no. 3 (Autumn 2005): 307–321.

Chauvet, Lisa, and Paul Collier. "Alternatives to Godot: Inducing Turnarounds in Failing States." October 2005. http://users.ox.ac.uk/~econpco/research/pdfs/Alternatives-to-Godot.pdf.

———. "Policy Turnarounds in Failing States." April 2005. http://users.ox.ac.uk/~econpco/research/pdfs/policy-turnarounds.pdf.

Commission for Reception, Truth, and Reconciliation. *Chega! The Report of the Commission on Reception, Truth, and Reconciliation in Timor-Leste.* Dili, East Timor, 2006.

Chesterman, Simon. *You, the People: The United Nations, Transitional Administration, and State-Building.* Oxford: Oxford University Press, 2004.

Chesterman, Simon, Michael Ignatieff, and Ramesh Thakur, eds. *Making States Work: State Failure and the Crisis of Governance.* Tokyo: United Nations University Press, 2005.

Chopra, Jarat. "Building State Failure in East Timor." *Development and Change* 33, no. 5 (November 2002): 979–1000.

Chopra, Jarat, and Tanja Hohe. "Participatory Intervention." *Global Governance* 10, no. 3 (July–September 2004): 289–305.

Clapham, Christopher. *Africa and the International System: The Politics of State Survival.* Cambridge: Cambridge University Press, 1996.

Clarke, Walter, and Jeffrey Herbst, eds. *Learning from Somalia: The Lessons of Armed Humanitarian Intervention.* Boulder, CO: Westview, 1997.

Cohen, David. "Indifference and Accountability: The United Nations and the Politics of International Justice in East Timor." East-West Center Special Report no. 9. Honolulu, HI, 2006.

Collier, Paul. "Demobilization and Insecurity: A Study in the Economics of the Transition from War to Peace." *Journal of International Development* 6, no. 3 (May–June 1994): 343–351.

Collier, Paul, and Anke Hoeffler. "Aid, Policy, and Growth in Post-Conflict Societies." *European Economic Review* 48, no. 5 (October 2004): 1125–1145.

———. "Conflicts." In *Global Crises, Global Solutions,* edited by Bjørn Lomborg, 129–156. Cambridge: Cambridge University Press, 2004.

———. "Democracy and Natural Resources." Oxford: Centre for the Study of African Economies, Department of Economics, Oxford University, 2005.

————. "Military Expenditure in Post-Conflict Societies." *Economics of Governance* 7, no. 1 (January 2006): 89–107.

————. "Greed and Grievance in Civil War." *Oxford Economic Papers* 56, no. 4 (October 2004): 563–595.

————. "Greed and Grievance in Civil War." Policy Research Working Paper Series no. 2355. Washington, DC: World Bank, 2000.

Collier, Paul, Anke Hoeffler, and Måns Söderbom. "Post-Conflict Societies." Working Paper 2006-12. Oxford: Centre for the Study of African Economies, Department of Economics, Oxford University, August 2006.

Collier, Paul, et al. *Breaking the Conflict Trap: Civil War and Development Policy.* Washington, DC: World Bank and Oxford University Press, 2003.

Conflict, Security, and Development Group. *A Review of Peace Operations: A Case for Change.* London: Kings College, 2003.

Cousens, Elizabeth M., Chetan Kumar, and Karin Wermester, eds. *Peacebuilding as Politics: Cultivating Peace in Fragile Societies.* Boulder, CO: Lynne Rienner, 2000.

Cox, Marcus. "Building Democracy from the Outside: The Dayton Agreement in Bosnia and Herzegovina." In *Can Democracy Be Designed? The Politics of Institutional Choice in Conflict-Torn Societies,* edited by Sunil Bastian and Robin Luckham, 253–276. London: Zed Books, 2003.

————. "State Building and Post-Conflict Reconstruction: The Lessons from Bosnia." Geneva: Centre for Applied Studies in International Negotiations, 2000.

Cox, Marcus, and Madeline Garlick. "Musical Chairs: Property Repossession and Return Strategies in Bosnia and Herzegovina." In *Returning Home: Housing and Property Restitution Rights of Refugees and Displaced Persons,* edited by Scott Leckie. Ardsley, NY: Transnational, 2003.

Crocker, Chester A. "Peacemaking and Mediation: Dynamics of a Changing Field." Coping with Crisis Working Paper Series. New York: International Peace Academy, March 2007.

Daalder, Hans. "The Consociational Democracy Theme." *World Politics* 26 (1974): 604–621.

de Ruggiero, Guido. *The History of European Liberalism.* Translated by R. G. Collingwood. London: Oxford University Press, 1927.

de Soto, Alvaro, and Graciana del Castillo. "Obstacles to Peacebuilding." *Foreign Policy* 94 (Spring 1994): 69–83.

Decalo, Samuel. "Benin: First of the New Democracies." In *Political Reform in Francophone Africa,* edited by John F. Clark and David E. Gardinier, 43–61. Boulder, CO: Westview, 1997.

Diamond, Larry. "Lessons from Iraq." *Journal of Democracy* 16, no. 1 (January 2005): 9–23.

————. *Promoting Democracy in the 1990s: Actors and Instruments, Issues and Imperatives.* New York: Carnegie Commission on Preventing Deadly Conflict, 1995.

————. "Promoting Democracy in Post-Conflict and Failed States: Lessons and Challenges." Paper prepared for the National Policy Forum on Terrorism, Security, and America's Purpose. Washington, DC, September 6–7, 2005.

————. *Squandered Victory: The American Occupation and Bungled Effort to Bring Democracy to Iraq.* New York: Henry Holt, 2006.

Diamond, Larry, Juan Linz, and Seymour Martin Lipset. *Politics in Developing Countries: Comparing Experiences with Democracy.* Boulder, CO: Lynne Rienner, 1995.

Dicey, A. V. *Introduction to the Study of the Law of the Constitution.* 10th ed. London: Palgrave Macmillan, 1985.

Dobbins, James, et al. *America's Role in Nation-Building: From Germany to Iraq.* Santa Monica: RAND, 2003.

Donini, Antonio. *Learning the Lessons? A Retrospective Analysis of Humanitarian Principles and Practice in Afghanistan.* New York: Office for the Coordination of Humanitarian Affairs, June 2003.

Donnelly, Jack. "Human Rights, Democracy, and Development." *Human Rights Quarterly* 21, no. 3 (August 1999): 608–632.

Dorjahn, Vernon R., and Christopher Fyfe. "Landlord and Stranger: Change in Tenancy Relations in Sierra Leone." *Journal of African History* 3, no. 3 (1962): 391–397.

Doyle, Michael W., and Nicholas Sambanis. "International Peacebuilding: A Theoretical and Quantitative Analysis." *American Political Science Review* 94, no. 4 (December 2000): 779–801.

Du Toit, Pierre. *State Building and Democracy in Southern Africa: Botswana, Zimbabwe, and South Africa.* Washington, DC: US Institute of Peace Press, 1995.

Elazar, Daniel J. *Federalism and the Way to Peace.* Kingston: Institute of Intergovernmental Relations, 1994.

Ellickson, Robert C. *Order Without Law: How Neighbors Settle Disputes.* Cambridge, MA: Harvard University Press, 1991.

Ellis, Stephen. "How to Rebuild Africa." *Foreign Affairs* 84, no. 5 (September–October 2005): 135–148.

Elster, Jon. "Constitution-Making in Eastern Europe: Rebuilding the Boat in the Open Sea." *Public Administration* 71, nos. 1–2 (1993).

Enderlin, Charles. *Shattered Dreams: The Failure of the Peace Process in the Middle East, 1995–2002.* Translated by Susan Fairfield. New York: Other Press, 2003.

Esposito, Michele K. "The Al-Aqsa Intifada: Military Operations, Suicide Attacks, Assassinations, and Losses in the First Four Years." *Journal of Palestine Studies* 34, no. 2 (Winter 2005): 85–122.

European Stability Initiative. "Governance and Democracy in Bosnia and Herzegovina: Post-Industrial Society and the Authoritarian Temptation." Berlin, 2004, www.esiweb.org.

———. *Reshaping International Priorities in Bosnia and Herzegovina, Part 1: Bosnian Power Structures.* Berlin, 1999.

Evans, Anne, Nick Manning, Yasin Osmani, Anne Tully, and Andrew Wilder. *A Guide to Government in Afghanistan.* Washington, DC, and Kabul: World Bank and AREU, 2004.

Evans, Peter, Dietrich Rueschemeyer, and Theda Skocpol, eds. *Bringing the State Back In.* Cambridge: Cambridge University Press, 1985.

Ewick, Patricia, and Susan S. Silbey. *The Common Place of Law: Stories from Everyday Life.* Chicago: University of Chicago Press, 1998.

Fearon, James D., and David D. Laitin. "Neotrusteeship and the Problem of Weak States." *International Security* 28, no. 4 (Spring 2004): 5–43.

———. "Violence and the Social Construction of Ethnic Identity." *International Organization* 54, no. 4 (Autumn 2000): 845–877.

Ferme, Marianne. "Studying Politisi: The Dialogue of Publicity and Secrecy in Sierra Leone." In *Civil Society and the Political Imagination in Africa: Critical Perspectives,* edited by John L. Comaroff and Jean Comaroff. Chicago: University of Chicago Press, 1999.

Finnemore, Martha. *National Interests in International Society.* Ithaca, NY: Cornell University Press, 1996.

Finnemore, Martha, and Kathryn Sikkink. "International Norm Dynamics and Political Change." *International Organization* 52, no. 4 (Autumn 1998): 887–917.

Forman, Shepard, and Stewart Patrick. *Good Intentions: Pledges of Aid for Post-Conflict Recovery.* Boulder, CO: Lynne Rienner, 2000.

Fortna, Page. "Where Have All the Victories Gone? Hypotheses (and Some Preliminary Tests) on War Outcomes in Historical Perspective." Paper presented at Conference on Order, Conflict, and Violence, Yale University, New Haven, CT, April 30–May 1, 2004.

Franck, Thomas M. "The Emerging Right to Democratic Governance." *American Journal of International Law* 86, no. 1 (January 1992): 46–91.

Fukuyama, Francis. "The Imperative of State-Building." *Journal of Democracy* 15, no. 2 (April 2004): 17–31.

———. *State-building: Governance and World Order in the 21st Century.* Ithaca, NY: Cornell University Press, 2004.

Fuller, Lon. *The Morality of Law.* 2nd ed. New Haven, CT: Yale University Press, 1969.

Galama, Anneke, and Paul van Tongeren, eds. *Towards Better Peacebuilding Practice: On Lessons Learned, Evaluation Practices, and Aid and Conflict.* Utrecht: European Centre for Conflict Prevention, 2002.

Gallagher, Tom. *Modern Romania: The End of Communism, the Failure of Democratic Reform, and the Theft of a Nation.* New York: New York University Press, 2005.

Galtung, Johan. "Three Approaches to Peace: Peacekeeping, Peacemaking, and Peacebuilding." In *Peace, War, and Defense: Essays in Peace Research.* Vol. 2. Copenhagen: Christian Eljers, 1975.

Geertz, Clifford. *Negara: The Theatre State in Nineteenth-Century Bali.* Princeton, NJ: Princeton University Press, 1981.

Gellner, Ernest. *Nations and Nationalism.* Ithaca, NY: Cornell University Press, 1983.

Genn, Hazel. *Paths to Justice: What People Do and Think About Going to Law.* Oxford: Hart, 1999.

Ghani, Ashraf, Clare Lockhart, and Michael Carnahan. "An Agenda for State-Building in the 21st Century." *Fletcher Forum for World Affairs* 30, no. 1 (Winter 2006): 101–123.

———. "Closing the Sovereignty Gap: An Approach to State-Building." Working Paper no. 253. London: Overseas Development Institute, September 2005.

Giddens, Anthony. *The Nation-State and Violence.* Vol. 2, *A Contemporary Critique of Historical Materialism.* Berkeley: University of California Press, 1987.

Gleditsch, Kristian Skrede. *All Politics Is Local: The Diffusion of Conflict, Integration, and Democratization.* Ann Arbor: University of Michigan Press, 2002.

Gleditsch, Nils Petter, et al. "Armed Conflict 1964–2001: A New Dataset." *Journal of Peace Research* 39, no. 5 (2002): 615–637.

Goldstone, Anthony. "UNTAET with Hindsight: The Peculiarities of Politics in an Incomplete State." *Global Governance* 10, no. 1 (2004): 83–98.

Goodhand, Jonathan. "From War Economy to Peace Economy? Reconstruction and State-building in Afghanistan." *Journal of International Affairs* 58, no.1 (Fall 2004): 155–174.

———. "Frontiers and Wars: The Opium Economy in Afghanistan." *Journal of Agrarian Change* 5, no. 2 (April 2005): 191–216.

Goodson, Larry. "Building Democracy After Conflict: Bullets, Ballots, and Poppies in Afghanistan." *Journal of Democracy* 16, no. 1 (January 2005): 24–38.

Gorjao, Paolo. "The Legacy and Lessons of the United Nations Transitional Administration in East Timor." *Contemporary Southeast Asia* 24, no. 2 (August 2002): 313–336.

Greif, Avner. *Institutions and the Path to the Modern Economy: Lessons from Medieval Trade.* Cambridge: Cambridge University Press, 2006.

Guidolin, Massimo, and Eliana La Ferrara. "Diamonds Are Forever, Wars Are Not: Is Conflict Bad for Private Firms?" Discussion Paper no. 4668. London: Centre for Economic Policy Research, 2004.

Gurr, Ted Roberts. *Minorities at Risk: A Global View of Ethno-political Conflict.* Washington, DC: US Institute of Peace Press, 1993.

Hannum, Hurst. *Autonomy, Sovereignty, and Self-Determination: The Accommodation of Conflicting Rights.* Philadelphia: University of Pennsylvania Press, 1996.

Harris, Peter, and Ben Reilly, eds. *Democracy and Deep-Rooted Conflict: Options for Negotiators.* Stockholm: IDEA, 1998.

Hayek, Friedrich. *Law, Legislation and Liberty.* 3 vols. Chicago: Chicago University Press, 1973–1979.

Hechter, Michael. *Containing Nationalism.* Oxford: Oxford University Press, 2000.

Hegre, Håvard. "The Duration and Termination of Civil War." *Journal of Peace Research* 41, no. 3 (2004): 243–252.

Heilbrunn, John R. "Social Origins of National Conferences in Benin and Togo." *The Journal of Modern African Studies* 31, no. 2 (June 1993): 277–299.

———. "Togo: The National Conference and Stalled Reform." In *Political Reform in Francophone Africa,* edited by John Clark and David E. Gardinier, 225–245. Boulder, CO: Westview, 1997.

Hellman, Joel, Geraint Jones, and Daniel Kaufmann. "Seize the State, Seize the Day: State Capture, Corruption, and Influence in Transition." Policy Research Working Paper no. 2444. Washington, DC: World Bank, 2000.

Helman, Gerald B., and Steven R. Ratner. "Saving Failed States." *Foreign Policy* 89 (Winter 1993): 3–20.

Herbst, Jeffrey. "Let Them Fail: State Failure in Theory and Practice: Implications for Policy." In *When States Fail: Causes and Consequences,* edited by Robert Rotberg, 302–318. Princeton, NJ: Princeton University Press, 2004.

———. "Prospects for Elite-Driven Democracy in South Africa." *Political Science Quarterly* 112, no. 4 (Winter 1997–1998): 595–615.

———. "Responding to State Failure in Africa." *International Security* 21, no. 3 (Winter 1996–1997): 120–144.

———. *States and Power in Africa: Comparative Lessons in Authority and Control.* Princeton, NJ: Princeton University Press, 2000.

Hohe, Tanja. "The Clash of Paradigms: International Administration and Local Political Legitimacy in East Timor." *Contemporary Southeast Asia* 24, no. 3 (December 2002): 569–589.

———. "Justice Without Judiciary in East Timor." *Conflict, Security, and Development* 3, no. 3 (December 2003): 335–357.

———. "Totem Polls: Indigenous Concepts and 'Free and Fair' Elections in East Timor." *International Peacekeeping* 9, no. 4 (Winter 2002): 69–88.

Horowitz, Donald L. *Ethnic Groups in Conflict.* Berkeley: University of California Press, 1985.

Human Rights Research and Advocacy Consortium. *Speaking Out: Afghan Opinions on Rights and Responsibilities.* Kabul, November 2003.

Human Rights Watch. "Afghanistan: Blood-Stained Hands—Past Atrocities in Kabul and Afghanistan's Legacy of Impunity." In *World Report 2006,* 220–226. New York, 2006.

———. *Tortured Beginnings: Police Violence and the Beginnings of Impunity in East Timor.* New York, 2006.

———. "Youth, Poverty and Blood: The Lethal Legacy of West Africa's Regional Warriors." New York, 2005.

Human Security Centre. *Human Security Report 2005: War and Peace in the 21st Century.* New York: Oxford University Press, 2005.

Huntington, Samuel P. *The Third Wave: Democratization in the Late Twentieth Century.* Norman: University of Oklahoma Press, 1991.

Hurd, Ian. "Legitimacy and Authority in International Politics." *International Organization* 53, no. 2 (April 1999): 379–408.

International Commission on Intervention and State Sovereignty. *The Responsibility to Protect.* Ottawa: International Development Research Centre, 2001.

International Commission on the Balkans. "The Balkans in Europe's Future." Sofia: Centre for Liberal Strategies, April 2005, http://www.balkan-commission.org.

International Crisis Group. "The Afghan Transitional Administration: Prospects and Perils." Asia Briefing no. 19, July 30, 2002.

———. "Afghanistan: The Constitutional Loya Jirga." Asia Briefing no. 29, December 12, 2003.

———. "Afghanistan's Flawed Constitutional Process." Asia Report no. 56, June 12, 2003.

———. "Counter-Terrorism in Somalia: Losing Hearts and Minds?" Africa Report no. 95, July 11, 2005.

———. "Disengagement and After: Where Next for Sharon and the Likud?" Middle East Report no. 36, March 1, 2005.

———. "Liberia and Sierra Leone: Rebuilding Failed States." Africa Report no. 87, December 8, 2004.

———. "Liberia: Resurrecting the Justice System." Africa Report no. 107, April 6, 2006.

———. "The Loya Jirga: One Small Step Forward?" Asia Briefing no. 17, May 16, 2002.

———. "Negotiating a Blueprint for Peace in Somalia." Africa Report no. 59, March 6, 2003.

———. "Somalia: Countering Terrorism in a Failed State." Africa Report no. 45, May 23, 2002.

———. "Somaliland: Democratisation and Its Discontents." Africa Report no. 66, July 28, 2003.

International Monetary Fund. *Rebuilding Fiscal Institutions in Post-Conflict Countries.* Washington, DC, 2004.

———. *West Bank and Gaza: Economic Performance and Reform Under Conflict Conditions.* Washington, DC, 2003.

International Peace Academy and the Center on International Cooperation. "Next Steps for the Peacebuilding Commission: Seminar Report." June 9, 2006.

Islamic Republic of Afghanistan. *Afghanistan National Development Strategy: An Interim Strategy for Security, Governance, Economic Growth, and Poverty Reduction.* Vol. 1, January 2006.

Islamic Republic of Afghanistan, Asian Development Bank, World Bank, UNAMA, and UNDP. *Securing Afghanistan's Future: Accomplishments and the Strategic Path Forward.* A Government/International Agency Report, March 17, 2004.

Jackson, Robert H. "Quasi-States, Dual Regimes, and Neoclassical Theory: International Jurisprudence and the Third World." *International Organization* 41, no. 4 (Autumn 1987): 519–549.

———. *Quasi-states: Sovereignty, International Relations, and the Third World.* Cambridge: Cambridge University Press, 1990.

Jackson, Robert H., and Carl G. Rosberg. "Why Africa's Weak States Persist: The Empirical and the Juridical in Statehood." *World Politics* 35, no. 1 (October 1982): 1–24.

Jensen, Erik G. "The Rule of Law and Judicial Reform: The Political Economy of Diverse Institutional Patterns and Reformers' Responses." In *Beyond Common Knowledge: Empirical Approaches to the Rule of Law,* edited by Erik G. Jensen and Thomas C. Heller, 336–381. Palo Alto, CA: Stanford University Press, 2003.

Jensen, Erik G., and Thomas C. Heller, eds. *Beyond Common Knowledge: Empirical Approaches to the Rule of Law.* Palo Alto, CA: Stanford University Press, 2003.

Johnson, Chris, and Jolyon Leslie. *Afghanistan: The Mirage of Peace.* London: Zed Books, 2005.

Jolliffe, Jill. *East Timor: Nationalism and Colonialism.* St. Lucia, Queensland: University of Queensland Press, 1978.

Jones, Seth G. "Averting Failure in Afghanistan." *Survival* 48, no. 1 (Spring 2006): 111–128.

Jonas, Susanne. "Democratization Through Peace: The Difficult Case of Guatemala." In "Globalization and Democratization in Guatemala," edited by John A. Booth. Special issue, *Journal of Interamerican Studies and World Affairs* 42, no. 4 (Winter 2000): 9–38.

Joseph, Richard, ed. *State, Conflict, and Democracy in Africa.* Boulder, CO: Lynne Rienner, 1999.

Joseph, Richard, and Jeffrey Herbst. "Correspondence: Responding to State Failure in Africa." *International Security* 22, no. 2 (Autumn 1997): 175–184.

Judicial System Monitoring Programme. "Findings and Recommendations: Workshop on Formal and Local Justice Systems in East Timor." Dili, East Timor, 2002.

Juergensmeyer, Mark. *The New Cold War? Religious Nationalism Confronts the Secular State.* Berkeley: University of California Press, 1993.

Kang, David. *Crony Capitalism: Corruption and Development in South Korea and the Philippines.* Cambridge: Cambridge University Press, 2002.

Karl, Terry Lynn. *The Paradox of Plenty: Oil Booms and Petro-States.* Berkeley: University of California Press, 1997.

Kaufmann, Daniel. "Governance, Security, and Development: An Initial Exploration." Paper presented at joint Rand/World Bank seminar on Security and Development, Rand Corporation, Santa Monica, CA, August 2004.

Keating, Tom, and W. Andy Knight, eds. *Building Sustainable Peace.* Saskatoon: University of Alberta Press and United Nations University Press, 2004.

Kennedy, David. "Laws and Developments." In *Law and Development: Facing Complexity in the Twenty-First Century,* edited by John Hatchard and Amanda Perry-Kessaris, 17–26. London: Cavendish, 2003.

Keohane, Robert O. "International Institutions: Two Approaches." *International Studies Quarterly* 32, no. 4 (December 1988): 379–396.

Kingston, Paul, and Ian S. Spears, eds. *States Within States: Incipient Political Entities in the Post–Cold War Era.* New York: Palgrave Macmillan, 2004.

Knaus, Gerald, and Marcus Cox. "Building Democracy After Conflict: The 'Helsinki Moment' in Southeastern Europe." *Journal of Democracy* 16, no. 1 (January 2005): 39–53.

Knaus, Gerald, and Felix Martin. "Lessons from Bosnia and Herzegovina: Travails of the European Raj." *Journal of Democracy* 14, no. 3 (July 2003): 60–74.

Kornai, János. "The Soft Budget Constraint." *Kyklos* 39, no. 1 (1986): 3–30.

Kramer, Larry D. *The People Themselves: Popular Constitutionalism and Judicial Review.* Oxford: Oxford University Press, 2004.

Krasner, Stephen D. "Approaches to the State: Alternative Conceptions and Historical Dynamics." *Comparative Politics* 16, no. 2 (January 1984): 223–246. Review of

Clifford Geertz's *Negara: The Theatre State in Nineteenth-Century Bali* (Princeton: Princeton University Press, 1981).

————. "Building Democracy After Conflict: The Case for Shared Sovereignty." *Journal of Democracy* 16, no. 1 (January 2005): 69–83.

————. "Sharing Sovereignty: New Institutions for Collapsed and Failing States." *International Security* 29, no. 2 (Fall 2004): 85–120.

Kreimer, Alcira, John Eriksson, Robert Muscat, Margaret Arnold, and Colin S. Scott. *The World Bank's Experience with Post-Conflict Reconstruction.* Washington, DC: World Bank Operations Evaluation Department, 1998.

Kumar, Krishna, ed. *Rebuilding Societies After Civil War: Critical Roles for International Assistance.* Boulder, CO: Lynne Rienner, 1997.

Kurspahic, Kemal. "Is There a Future?" In *Why Bosnia? Writings on the Balkan War,* edited by Rabia Ali and Lawrence Lifschultz. Stony Creek, CT: Pamphleteer's Press, 1993.

La'o Hamutuk. "The World Bank in East Timor." *La'o Hamutuk Bulletin* 1, no. 4 (December 2000), www.etan.org/lh/bulletin04.html.

Lawson, Letitia, and Donald Rothchild. "Sovereignty Reconsidered." *Current History* 104, no. 682 (May 2005): 228–235.

Le Sage, Andre. "Stateless Justice in Somalia: Formal and Informal Rule of Law Initiatives." Geneva: Centre for Humanitarian Dialogue, July 2005.

Lederach, John Paul. *Building Peace: Sustainable Reconciliation in Divided Societies.* Washington, DC: US Institute of Peace Press, 1998.

Licklider, Roy. "The Consequences of Negotiated Settlements in Civil Wars, 1945–1993." *American Political Science Review* 89, no. 3 (September 1995): 681–690.

Lijphart, Arend. "Constitutional Choices for New Democracies." *Journal of Democracy* 2, no. 1 (Winter 1991): 72–84.

————. *Democracy in Plural Societies.* New Haven, CT: Yale University Press, 1977.

Lipset, Seymour Martin. *Political Man: The Social Bases of Politics.* New York: Doubleday, 1960.

Lister, Sarah. "Caught in Confusion: Local Governance Structures in Afghanistan." Briefing paper. Kabul: Afghanistan Research and Evaluation Unit, 2005.

Lister, Sarah, and Adam Pain. "Trading in Power: The Politics of 'Free' Markets in Afghanistan." Briefing paper. Kabul: Afghanistan Research and Evaluation Unit, 2004.

Lister, Stephen, and Anne Le More. *Aid Management and Coordination During the Intifada.* Report to the Local Aid Coordination Committee Co-Chairs. Oxford: Mokoro, 2003.

Lund, Michael, and Carlos Santiso. "National Conferences." In *Democracy and Deep-Rooted Conflict: Options for Negotiators,* edited by Peter Harris and Ben Reilly, 252–262. Handbook Series 3. Stockholm: International IDEA, 1998.

Lydall, Harold. *Yugoslavia in Crisis.* Oxford: Clarendon Press, 1989.

Lyons, Terrence. "Post-conflict Elections and the Process of Demilitarizing Politics: The Role of Electoral Administration." *Democratization* 11, no. 3 (June 2004): 36–62.

Lyons, Terrence, and Ahmed Samatar. *Somalia: State Collapse, Multilateral Intervention, and Strategies of Political Reconstruction.* Washington, DC: Brookings Institution, 1995.

MacMillan, John. "How Not to Rebuild an Economy: The Lesson from East Timor." Graduate School of Business, Stanford University, June 20, 2006.

Mansfield, Edward D., and Jack Snyder. "Democratic Transitions and War: From Napoleon to the Millennium's End." In *Turbulent Peace: The Challenges of*

Managing International Conflict, edited by Chester A. Crocker, Fen Osler Hampson, and Pamela Aall, 113–126. Washington, DC: US Institute of Peace Press, 2001.

———. "Democratization and the Danger of War." *International Security* 20, no. 1 (Summer 1995): 5–38.

Marshall, Monty, and Ted Robert Gurr. *Peace and Conflict 2003: A Global Survey of Armed Conflicts, Self-Determination Movements and Democracy.* College Park, MD: Center for International Development and Conflict Management, 2003.

Martin, Ian, and Alexander Mayer-Rieckh. "The United Nations and East Timor: From Self-Determination to State-Building." *International Peacekeeping* 12, no. 1 (Spring 2005): 125–145.

Matveeva, Anna. "Democratization, Legitimacy, and Political Change in Central Asia." *International Affairs* 75, no. 1 (January 1999): 23–44.

McWilliam, Andrew. "Houses of Resistance in East Timor: Structuring Sociality in the New Nation." *Anthropological Forum* 15, no. 1 (March 2005): 27–44.

Mearns, David. *Variations on a Theme: Coalitions of Authority in East Timor.* Report prepared for Australian Legal Resources International, December 2001.

Menkhaus, Kenneth. "The Crisis in Somalia: Tragedy in Five Acts." *African Affairs* 106, no. 424 (July 2007): 357–390.

———. "From Feast to Famine: Land and the State in Somalia's Lower Juba Valley." In *The Struggle for Land in Southern Somalia: The War Behind the War,* edited by Catherine Besteman and Lee V. Cassanelli, 133–153. Boulder, CO: Westview, 1996.

———. "Somalia: State Collapse and the Threat of Terrorism." Adelphi Paper no. 364. Oxford: Oxford University Press, 2004.

———. "Vicious Circles and the Security-Development Nexus in Somalia." *Conflict, Security, and Development* 4, no. 2 (August 2004): 149–165.

Menkhaus, Kenneth, and John Prendergast. "Governance and Economic Survival in Post-Intervention Somalia." CSIS Africa Notes no. 172. Washington, DC: Center for Strategic and International Studies, 1995.

Migdal, Joel S., Atul Kohli, and Vivienne Shue, eds. *State Power and Social Forces: Domination and Transformation in the Third World.* Cambridge: Cambridge University Press, 1994.

Miller, Norman. "The Other Somalia." *Horn of Africa* 5, no. 3 (1982): 3–19.

Montville, J., ed. *Conflict and Peacemaking in Multiethnic Societies.* New York: Lexington Books, 1991.

Murphy, William P., and Caroline H. Bledsoe. "Kinship and Territory in the History of a Kpelle Chiefdom (Liberia)." In *The African Frontier: The Reproduction of Traditional African Societies,* edited by Igor Kopytoff, 123–147. Bloomington: Indiana University Press, 1987.

Myrdal, Gunnar. *Asian Drama: An Inquiry into the Poverty of Nations.* New York: Pantheon Books, 1968.

Nettl, J. P. "The State as a Conceptual Variable." *World Politics* 20, no 4 (July 1968): 559–592.

Ní Aoláin, Fionnuala. "The Fractured Soul of the Dayton Peace Agreement: A Legal Analysis." *Michigan Journal of International Law* 19, no. 4 (Summer 1998): 957–1004.

Ninh, Kim, and Roger Henke. "Commune Councils in Cambodia: A National Survey on Their Functions and Performance, with a Special Focus on Conflict Resolution." Asia Foundation, May 2005.

Nwajiaku, Kathryn. "The National Conferences in Benin and Togo Revisited." *Journal of Modern African Studies* 32, no. 3 (September 1994): 429–447.

Nzouankeu, Jacques Mariel. "The Role of the National Conference in the Transition to Democracy in Africa: The Cases of Benin and Mali." *Issue: A Journal of Opinion* 21, nos. 1–2 (1993): 44–50.

Offenheiser, Raymond C., and Susan Holcombe. "Challenges and Opportunities in Implementing a Rights-Based Approach to Development: An Oxfam America Perspective." *Nonprofit and Voluntary Sector Quarterly* 32 (2003): 268–306.

Office of the United Nations Special Coordinator in the Occupied Territories (UNSCO). *Rule of Law Development in the West Bank and Gaza Strip: Survey and State of the Development Effort.* Jerusalem: UNSCO Gaza, May 1999.

Olson, Mancur. "Dictatorship, Democracy, and Development." *American Political Science Review* 87, no. 3 (September 1993): 567–576.

Organization for Economic Cooperation and Development, Development Assistance Committee. *Fragile States: Policy Commitment and Principles for Good International Engagement in Fragile States and Situations.* 2007.

Ottaway, Marina. "African Democratization and the Leninist Option." *The Journal of Modern African Studies* 35, no. 1 (1997): 1–15.

———. "Iraq: Without Consensus, Democracy Is Not the Answer." Washington, DC: Carnegie Endowment for International Peace Policy Brief no. 36, March 2005.

———. "Nation Building." *Foreign Policy* 132 (September–October 2002): 16–24.

———. "The Post-War 'Democratic Reconstruction Model': Why It Can't Work." Paper presented at "Building Democracy After War?" conference, Brown University, April 3–4, 2002.

———. "Rebuilding State Institutions in Collapsed States." *Development and Change* 33, no. 5 (November 2002): 1001–1023.

Ottaway, Marina, and Anatol Lieven. "Rebuilding Afghanistan: Fantasy Versus Reality." Policy Brief no. 12. Washington, DC: Carnegie Endowment for International Peace, 2002.

Packenham, Robert. *Liberal America and the Third World.* Princeton, NJ: Princeton University Press, 1973.

Pajiç, Zoran. "A Critical Appraisal of the Human Rights Provisions of the Dayton Constitution of Bosnia and Herzegovina." In *Human Rights in Bosnia and Herzegovina After Dayton: From Theory to Practice,* edited by Wolfgang Benedek. The Hague: Martinus Nijhoff Publishers, 1998.

Papagianni, Katia. "National Conferences in Transitional Periods: The Case of Iraq." *International Peacekeeping* 13, no. 3 (September 2006): 316–333.

———. "State-Building and Transitional Politics in Iraq: The Perils of a Top-Down Transition." *International Studies Perspectives* 8 (August 2007): 253–271.

Pape, Robert. *Dying to Win: The Strategic Logic of Suicide Terrorism.* New York: Random House, 2005.

Paris, Roland. *At War's End: Building Peace After Civil Conflict.* Cambridge: Cambridge University Press, 2004.

Pastor, Santos. *Ah de la justicia: Politica judicial y economia.* Madrid: Civitas and Ministerio de Justicia, 1993.

Patrick, Stewart. "Weak States and Global Threats: Fact or Fiction?" *Washington Quarterly* (Spring 2006): 27–53.

Patrick, Stewart, and Kaysie Brown. *Greater Than the Sum of Its Parts? Assessing "Whole of Government" Approaches to Fragile States.* New York: International Peace Academy, 2007.

Patrick, Stewart, Shepard Forman, and Dirk Salomons. "Recovering from Conflict: Strategy for an International Response." *Paying for Essentials: A Policy Paper Series.* New York: Center on International Cooperation, 2000.

Paul, James C. N. "The Reconstitution of Ethiopia, 1991–1994: A Procedural History." Draft paper prepared for the Constitution-Making Working Group, US Institute of Peace, Washington, DC, 2003.

Peace Implementation Council. *Bosnia and Herzegovina 1998: Self-Sustaining Structures.* Bonn, December 10, 1997.

Perito, Robert M. *Where Is the Lone Ranger When We Need Him? America's Search for a Postconflict Stability Force.* Washington, DC: US Institute of Peace Press, 2004.

Peters, Krijn, and Paul Richards. "'Why We Fight': Voices of Youth Combatants in Sierra Leone." *Africa: Journal of the International Africa Institute* 68, no. 2 (1998): 183–210.

Posner, Daniel N. "Civil Society and the Reconstruction of Failed States." In *When States Fail: Causes and Consequences,* edited by Robert I. Rotberg, 237–255. Princeton, NJ: Princeton University Press, 2004.

Pressman, Jeremy. "Visions in Collision: What Really Happened at Camp David and Taba?" *International Security* 28, no. 2 (Fall 2003): 5–43.

Pugh, Michael. "Post-Conflict Rehabilitation: Social and Civil Dimensions." Geneva: Centre for Applied Studies in International Negotiations, 1998.

Puntland Development Research Centre. "Pastoral Justice: A Participatory Action Research Project on Harmonization of Somali Legal Traditions: Customary Law, Sharia, and Secular Law." Garowe, Somalia, 2002.

Ramsbotham, Oliver, and Tom Woodhouse. *Humanitarian Intervention in Contemporary Conflict: A Reconceptualization.* Cambridge, UK: Polity Press, 1996.

Rawls, John. "Two Concepts of Rules." *Philosophical Review* 64, no. 1 (January 1955): 3–32.

Rawson, David. *The Somali State and Foreign Aid.* Foreign Service Institute, US Department of State, Washington, DC, 1993.

Ray, James Lee. "The Democratic Path to Peace." *Journal of Democracy* 8, no. 2 (April 1997): 49–64.

Raz, Joseph. "The Rule of Law and Its Virtue." In *The Authority of Law: Essays on Law and Morality.* Oxford: Clarendon Press, 1979, 210–229.

Refugee Policy Group. "Hope Restored? Humanitarian Aid in Somalia, 1991–1994." Washington, DC, 1994.

Reilly, Ben, and Andrew Reynolds, eds. *Electoral Systems and Conflict in Divided Societies.* Washington, DC: National Academy Press, 1999.

Reinhold, Wolfgang, ed. *Power Elites and State Building.* Oxford: Oxford University Press, 1999.

Renard-Clamagirand, Brigitte. *Marobo: Une Société Ema de Timor.* Paris: SELAF, 1982.

Reno, William. *Warlord Politics and African States.* Boulder, CO: Lynne Rienner, 1999.

Richards, Paul, Khadija Bah, and James Vincent. "Social Capital and Survival: Prospects for Community-Driven Development in Post-Conflict Sierra Leone." World Bank Social Development Paper no. 12. Washington, DC: World Bank, 2004.

Roberts, Richard. *Litigants and Households: African Disputes and Colonial Courts in the French Soudan, 1895–1912.* Portsmouth, NH: Heinemann, 2005.

Ross, Dennis. *The Missing Peace: The Inside Story of the Fight for Middle East Peace.* New York: Farrar, Straus, and Giroux, 2004.

Roth, Michael, and Jon Unruh. "Land Title, Tenure Security, Credit and Investment in the Lower Shabelle Region, Somalia." Madison, WI: Land Tenure Center, 1990.
Rubin, Barnett R. *Blood on the Doorstep: The Politics of Preventive Action.* New York: Century Foundation Press, 2002.
———. "Crafting a Constitution for Afghanistan." *Journal of Democracy* 15, no. 3 (July 2004): 5–19.
Rubin, Barry M. *The Transformation of Palestinian Politics: From Revolution to State-Building.* Cambridge, MA: Harvard University Press, 1999.
Salamé, Ghassan. *Appels d'empire: Ingérences et résistances à l'âge de la mondialisation.* Paris: Fayard, 1996.
Sadat, Leila Nadya. "Universal Jurisdiction, National Amnesties, and Truth Commissions: Reconciling the Irreconcilable." In *Universal Jurisdiction: National Courts and the Prosecution of Serious Crimes Under International Law,* edited by Stephen Macedo, 193–213. Philadelphia: University of Pennsylvania Press, 2004.
Saldanha, Estanislau S., et al. *Survey on Public Perception of the East Timor National Police's Work.* Centre for Applied Research and Policy Studies, Dili Institute of Technology, September 2004.
Samatar, Ahmed. *Socialist Somalia: Rhetoric and Reality.* London: Zed Books, 1988.
Sayigh, Yezid, and Khalil Shikaki. *Strengthening Palestinian Public Institutions.* Independent Task Force Report. New York: Council on Foreign Relations, 1999.
Schwab, George. *Tribes of the Liberian Hinterland.* Edited with additional material by George W. Harley. Papers of the Peabody Museum of American Archeology and Ethnology, Harvard University. Cambridge, MA: Peabody Museum, 1947.
Scott, James C. *Seeing Like a State: How Certain Schemes to Improve the Human Condition Have Failed.* New Haven, CT: Yale University Press, 1998.
Scott, W. Richard. *Institutions and Organizations.* Thousand Oaks, CA: Sage Publications, 2001.
Secretariat of the Ad Hoc Liaison Committee. "Aid Effectiveness in the West Bank and Gaza." Report produced jointly by Japan and the World Bank, http://lnweb18.worldbank.org/mna/mena.nsf/0/2CDBC52F2D7B18C58525691A0022B56F.
Serafino, Nina. "Peacekeeping: Issues of US Military Involvement." CRS Issue Brief IB94040. Washington, DC: Congressional Research Service, August 6, 2003.
Sewell, David. "Governance and the Business Environment in the West Bank/Gaza." Working Paper Series no. 23. Washington, DC: World Bank, 2001.
Shain, Yossi, and Juan J. Linz. *Between States: Interim Governments and Democratic Transitions.* New York: Cambridge University Press, 1995.
Shinn, David. "Somaliland: The Little Country that Could." Center for Strategic and International Studies Africa Notes no. 9. Washington, DC, 2002.
Silber, Laura, and Alan Little. *The Death of Yugoslavia.* 2nd ed. London: Penguin Books, 1996.
Sisk, Timothy D. *Power Sharing and International Mediation in Ethnic Conflicts.* Washington, DC: US Institute of Peace Press, 1996.
Snyder, Jack. "Empire: A Blunt Tool for Democratization." *Daedalus* 134, no. 2 (Spring 2005): 58–71.
———. *From Voting to Violence: Democratization and Nationalist Conflict.* New York: W. W. Norton, 2000.
Snyder, Jack, and Karen Ballentine. "Nationalism and the Marketplace of Ideas." *International Security* 21, no. 2 (Autumn 1996): 5–40.
Spears, Ian S. "Understanding Inclusive Peace Agreements in Africa: The Problems of Sharing Power." *Third World Quarterly* 21, no. 1 (February 2000): 105–118.

Stanley, William, and David Holiday. "Broad Participation, Diffuse Responsibility: Peace Implementation in Guatemala." In *Ending Civil Wars: The Implementation of Peace Agreements,* edited by Stephen John Stedman, Donald Rothchild, and Elizabeth M. Cousens, 421–462. Boulder, CO: Lynne Rienner, 2002.

Stedman, Stephen John. "Spoiler Problems in Peace Processes." *International Security* 22, no. 2 (Autumn 1997): 5–53.

Stedman, Stephen John, Donald Rothchild, and Elizabeth M. Cousens, eds. *Ending Civil Wars: The Implementation of Peace Agreements.* Boulder, CO: Lynne Rienner, 2002.

Suhrke, Astri. "Peacekeepers as Nation-Builders: Dilemmas of the UN in East Timor." *International Peacekeeping* 8, no. 4 (Winter 2001): 1–20.

Suhrke, Astri, Kristian Berg Harpviken, and Arne Strand. "Conflictual Peacebuilding: Afghanistan Two Years After Bonn." Prepared for the Norwegian Ministry of Foreign Affairs. Bergen, Norway: Chr. Michelson Institute, 2004.

Suhrke, Astri, Jolyon Leslie, and Arne Strand. "Afghanistan: A Snapshot Study." In Conflict, Security, and Development Group. *A Review of Peace Operations: A Case for Change.* London: Kings College, 2003.

Suhrke, Astri, and Ingrid Samset. "What's in a Figure: Estimating Recurrence of Civil War." *International Peacekeeping* 14, no. 2 (April 2007): 195–203.

Svensson, Jakob. "Eight Questions About Corruption." *Journal of Economic Perspectives* 19, no. 3 (Fall 2005): 19–42.

Swaine, Aisling. *Traditional Justice and Gender-Based Violence.* New York: International Rescue Committee Research Report, August 2003.

Swisher, Clayton E. *The Truth About Camp David: The Untold Story About the Collapse of the Middle East Peace Process.* New York: Nation Books, 2004.

Tabeau, Ewa, and Jakub Bijak. "War-Related Deaths in the 1992–1995 Armed Conflicts in Bosnia and Herzegovina: A Critique of Previous Estimates and Recent Results." *European Journal of Population* 21, nos. 2–3 (June 2005): 187–215.

Tamanaha, Brian Z. *On the Rule of Law: History, Politics, Theory.* Cambridge: Cambridge University Press, 2004.

Tilly, Charles. *Coercion, Capital, and European States, A.D. 990–1990.* Cambridge, MA: Basil Blackwell, 1990; *Coercion, Capital, and European States, A.D. 990–1992.* Rev. paperback ed. Oxford: Blackwell Publishers, 1992.

———. *Contention and Democracy in Europe, 1650–2000.* Cambridge: Cambridge University Press, 2004.

———. "Reflection on the History of State Making." In *The Formation of National States in Western Europe,* edited by Charles Tilly. Princeton, NJ: Princeton University Press, 1975.

———. "War Making and State Making as Organized Crime." In *Bringing the State Back In,* edited by Peter Evans, Dietrich Rueschemeyer, and Theda Skocpol, 169–187. Cambridge: Cambridge University Press, 1985.

Timor-Leste Land Law Program. "Report on Research Findings and Policy Recommendations for a Legal Framework for Land Dispute Mediation." Prepared with funding provided by USAID, February 2004.

Timor-Leste Police Service. *Joint Assessment Mission Final Report.* 2002.

Tisné, Martin, and Daniel Smilov. "From the Ground Up: Assessing the Record of Anticorruption Assistance in Southeastern Europe." CPS Policy Studies Series. Budapest, Central European University, Center for Policy Studies, 2004.

Traube, Elisabeth G. *Cosmology and Social Life: Ritual Exchange Among the Mambai of East Timor.* Chicago: University of Chicago Press, 1986.

United Nations. *An Agenda for Peace: Preventive Diplomacy, Peacemaking, and Peace-keeping.* Report of the Secretary-General. UN Doc. A/47/277-S/24111, June 17, 1992.

———. *Report of the Independent Inquiry into the Actions of the United Nations During the 1994 Genocide in Rwanda.* UN Doc. S/1999/1257, 1999.

———. *Report of the Panel on United Nations Peace Operations* (Brahimi Report). UN Doc. A/55/305-S/2000/809, August 21, 2000.

———. *Report of the Secretary-General on the Situation in Somalia.* UN Doc. S/2004/469, June 9, 2004.

———. *Report of the Secretary-General Pursuant to General Assembly Resolution 53/35: The Fall of Srebrenica.* UN Doc. A/54/549, November 15, 1999.

———. *Report of the Special Envoy of the Secretary-General on Kosovo's Future Status.* UN Doc. S/2007/168, March 26, 2007.

———. *Report of the United Nations Independent Special Commission of Inquiry for Timor-Leste.* Geneva, October 2, 2006.

———. *Statement by the Secretary-General on the Report of the Independent Inquiry into the Actions of the United Nations During the 1994 Genocide in Rwanda.* UN Doc. SG/SM/7263, 1999.

———. *Supplement to* An Agenda For Peace: *Position Paper of the Secretary-General on the Occasion of the Fiftieth Anniversary of the United Nations. Report of the Secretary-General on the Work of the Organization.* UN Doc. A/50/60-S/1995/1, January 3, 1995.

———. *Vienna Declaration and Programme of Action.* World Conference on Human Rights, 48th Session, 22nd plenary meeting. UN Doc. A/CONF.157/24, June 25, 1993.

United Nations Development Programme. *Early Warning System.* Sarajevo, Bosnia, July–September 2000.

———. *Somalia Human Development Report 2001.* Nairobi, 2001.

———. *Timor-Leste Human Development Report 2006: The Path Out of Poverty— Integrated Rural Development.* Dili, East Timor, 2006.

United Nations Millennium Project. *Investing in Development: A Practical Plan to Achieve the Millennium Development Goals.* New York: United Nations Development Programme, 2005.

United Nations Office on Drugs and Crime. *Afghanistan Opium Survey 2004.* Vienna, 2004.

United States Department of State. *Foreign Military Training and Department of Defense Engagement Activities of Interest.* Washington, DC: Bureau of Political-Military Affairs, May 2005.

Verdery, Katherine. *National Ideology Under Socialism: Identity and Cultural Politics in Ceausescu's Romania.* Berkeley: University of California Press, 1991.

Vilarrubia, Josep M. "Neighborhood Effects in Economic Growth." Working Paper no. 627. Madrid: Banco de Espana, 2006.

Vlassenroot, Koen, and Tim Raeymaekers. "The Politics of Rebellion and Intervention in Ituri: The Emergence of a New Political Complex?" *African Affairs* 103, no. 412 (July 2004): 385–412.

Voekel, Swen. "'Upon the Suddaine View': State, Civil Society, and Surveillance in Early Modern England." *Early Modern Literary Studies* 4, no. 2 (September 1999): 1–27.

Waldner, David. *State-Building and Late Development.* Ithaca, NY: Cornell University Press, 1999.

Walter, Barbara F. *Committing to Peace: The Successful Settlement of Civil Wars.* Princeton, NJ: Princeton University Press, 2002.

———. "Does Conflict Beget Conflict? Explaining Recurrent Civil War." *Journal of Peace Research* 41, no. 3 (2004): 371–388.

Walter, Barbara F., and Jack Snyder, eds. *Civil Wars, Insecurity, and Intervention.* New York: Columbia University Press, 1999.

Wantchekon, Leonard. "The Paradox of 'Warlord' Democracy: A Theoretical Investigation." *American Political Science Review* 98, no. 1 (2004): 17–33.

Weber, Max. *Economy and Society: An Outline of Interpretive Sociology.* Edited by Guenther Roth and Claus Wittich. 2 vols. Berkeley: University of California Press, 1978.

Weinstein, Jeremy, and Macartan Humphreys. "Disentangling the Successful Determinants of Demobilization and Reintegration." Working Paper no. 69. Washington, DC: Center for Global Development, 2005.

Wendt, Alexander. *Social Theory of International Politics.* Cambridge: Cambridge University Press, 1999.

West, Ronald A. "East Timor." In Charles T. Call, ed., *Constructing Justice and Security After War.* Washington, DC: US Institute of Peace Press, 2007.

White, Stephen. "Economic Performance and Communist Legitimacy." *World Politics* 38, no. 3 (April 1986): 462–482.

White House. *The National Security Strategy of the United States of America.* Washington, DC, September 2002.

Widner, Jennifer. *Building the Rule of Law: Francis Nyalai and the Road to Judicial Independence in Africa.* New York: W. W. Norton, 2001.

———. "Constitution Writing and Conflict Resolution." UNU-WIDER Research Paper no. 2005/51. Helsinki: UNU-WIDER, 2005.

Williams, Phillip J., and Lee Walker. "The Nicaraguan Constitutional Experience: Process, Conflict, Contradictions, and Change." Draft paper prepared for the Constitution-Making Working Group, US Institute for Peace, Washington, DC, 2003.

Williamson, John. "What Should the World Bank Think of the Washington Consensus?" *World Bank Research Observer* 15, no. 2 (August 2000): 251–264.

Woodward, Susan. "On the Problem of the Post-war State and the Need for a Doctrine of 'Do No Harm.'" Paper presented at the Workshop on Building Peace in Fragile States, University of California at San Diego, December 2006.

Woodward, Susan L. *Balkan Tragedy: Chaos and Dissolution After the Cold War.* Washington, DC: Brookings Institution, 1995.

World Bank. *Bosnia and Herzegovina: From Aid Dependency to Fiscal Self-Reliance.* Report No. 24297-BIH 2002. Washington, DC: World Bank, 2002.

———. *Country Assistance Strategy for the Democratic Republic of Timor-Leste, for the Period FY06–FY08.* Washington, DC: World Bank, 2005.

———. *Disengagement, the Palestinian Economy and the Settlements.* Washington, DC: World Bank, 2004.

———. *Four Years—Intifada, Closures, and Palestinian Economic Crisis: An Assessment.* Washington, DC: World Bank, 2004.

———. *The Role of the World Bank in Conflict and Development: An Evolving Agenda.* Conflict Prevention and Recovery Unit, Social Development Department. Washington, DC: World Bank, 2003.

———. *Sectoral Strategy: Health, Nutrition and Population.* Washington, DC: World Bank, 2004.

———. *Stagnation or Revival? Israeli Disengagement and Palestinian Economic Prospects—Overview.* Washington, DC: World Bank, 2004.

————. *Twenty-Seven Months—Intifada, Closures, and Palestinian Economic Crisis: An Assessment.* Jerusalem: World Bank, 2003.

————. *West Bank and Gaza: Country Financial Accountability Assessment.* Report no. 28990-GZ. Washington, DC: World Bank, 2004.

————. *West Bank and Gaza: Strengthening Public Sector Management.* Washington, DC: World Bank, 1999.

World Bank Operations Evaluations Department. *The World Bank's Experience with Post-Conflict Reconstruction.* Vol. 1, *Synthesis Report.* Washington, DC: World Bank, 1998.

Zakaria, Fareed. *The Future of Freedom: Illiberal Democracy at Home and Abroad.* New York: W. W. Norton, 2003.

Zartman, I. William, ed. *Collapsed States: The Disintegration and Restoration of Legitimate Authority.* Boulder, CO: Lynne Rienner, 1995.

————. "Putting Things Back Together." In *Collapsed States: The Disintegration and Restoration of Legitimate Authority,* edited by I. William Zartman, 267–273. Boulder, CO: Lynne Rienner, 1995.

Zifcak, Spencer. *Restorative Justice in East Timor: An Evaluation of the Community Reconciliation Process of the CAVR.* Dili: Asia Foundation, 2004.

The Contributors

Edith Bowles worked for USAID and the World Bank program in East Timor from 2000 to 2007. She is coauthor of *Strengthening the Institutions of Governance in Timor-Leste,* a 2006 World Bank study.

Rex Brynen is professor of political science at McGill University and coordinator of the Montréal-based Interuniversity Consortium for Arab and Middle Eastern Studies. He is author of *A Very Political Economy: Peacebuilding and Foreign Aid in the West Bank and Gaza* and *Sanctuary and Survival: The PLO in Lebanon* and has also edited and coedited numerous volumes. In addition to his academic work, Brynen has served as a consultant to the Canadian government, the World Bank, the United Nations, and other agencies.

Charles (Chuck) T. Call is assistant professor of international peace and conflict resolution in the School of International Service of American University. He is senior peacebuilding adviser to the International Peace Insitute. In 2004 he worked on postconflict peacebuilding issues in the UN Department of Political Affairs. His publications include the recent volume *Constructing Justice and Security After War* and articles in *Comparative Politics, Journal of Latin American Studies,* and *Global Governance.* He has conducted field research in Central America, Haiti, Afghanistan, West Africa, Bosnia, and Kosovo and has served as consultant to Human Rights Watch, the UN Development Programme, the US Justice Department, the US Agency for International Development, the Ford Foundation, and the European Commission.

Michael Carnahan currently works at the Australian Competition and Consumer Commission. He was previously a visiting fellow at the Asia-Pacific School of Economics and Government at Australian National University. He

413

recently led a major study commissioned by the United Nations examining the economic impact of peacekeeping missions, and in 2002–2004 he worked as senior adviser to Afghanistan's finance minister, assisting in the planning of the reconstruction and development program. Previously, he led a team from the Australian Department of Finance and Administration assisting the UN Transitional Authority in East Timor and then the East Timor Transitional Administration.

Tanja Chopra is currently coordinating the World Bank's Justice for the Poor program in Kenya. She has conducted extensive field research in eastern Indonesia, worked for the UN electoral mission in East Timor and the UN Transitional Administration in East Timor, and has advised the World Bank's West Bank and Gaza office on development interventions.

Sarah Cliffe joined the World Bank in 1996. Since the mid-1980s, she has worked on economic reconstruction, governance, and poverty reduction initiatives in postconflict countries. Previously, she worked for the UN Development Program in Rwanda, the government of South Africa, and the Congress of South African Trade Unions.

Paul Collier is professor of economics and director of the Centre for the Study of African Economies at Oxford University. He is author of *The Bottom Billion: Why the Poorest Countries Are Failing and What Can Be Done About It,* which won the 2008 Lionel Gelber Prize.

Marcus Cox is senior editor of the European Stability Initiative, an independent research institute focusing on the political economy of southeastern Europe. He advised the High Representative in Bosnia and has worked extensively on property rights and ethnic reintegration in the former Yugoslavia. His research interests include postconflict reconstruction and statebuilding, and political governance.

Erik G. Jensen co-directs the Rule of Law Programs at Stanford Law School and the Center on Democracy, Development, and the Rule of Law at the Freeman-Spogli Institute, Stanford University. His most recent book, coedited with Thomas C. Heller, is *Beyond Common Knowledge: Empirical Approaches to the Rule of Law.*

Clare Lockhart is a co-founder of the Institute for State Effectiveness. In Afghanistan, she served as an adviser to the UN Bonn Agreement, the Government of Afghanistan, and ISAF-NATO. She has worked at the World Bank and is a specialist in law, history, and economics. She has authored and coauthored several articles, and a book, *Fixing Failed States,* with Ashraf Ghani.

Mike McGovern is assistant professor of anthropology at Yale University. He is completing a book on the dramaturgy, sociology, and political economy of the Ivorian civil war entitled *Making War in Côte d'Ivoire.* He previously served as the West Africa Project Director of the International Crisis Group.

Nick Manning is World Bank public sector manager for Latin America and the Caribbean. Formerly head of the Public Sector Management and Performance Division in the OECD, he has also been senior technical adviser to UNDP in Lebanon and public management adviser to the Commonwealth Secretariat in London. He has published extensively on public sector issues in developing and OECD countries, including governance and public management in Afghanistan.

Kenneth Menkhaus is professor of political science at Davidson College. In 1993–1994, he served as special political adviser in the UN Operation in Somalia and in 2002 received a US Institute of Peace grant to study protracted conflict in the Horn of Africa. He is author of *Somalia: State Collapse and the Threat of Terrorism.*

Katia Papagianni leads the mediation support program at the Centre for Humanitarian Dialogue. She has also worked for UNDP, the UN Office of the High Commissioner for Human Rights, the OSCE, and the National Democratic Institute, focusing on postconflict transitional processes and institutions, constitution-making processes, and governance and human rights. Her research has been published in a number of journals, including *International Peacekeeping* and *International Studies Perspectives.*

William Reno is associate professor of political science at Northwestern University. He is the author of *Corruption and State Politics in Sierra Leone* and *Warlord Politics and African States.* His forthcoming *Evolution of Warfare in Independent Africa* explains the causes of changing patterns of warfare across the continent.

Barnett R. Rubin is Director of Studies and Senior Fellow at the Center on International Cooperation of New York University, where he directs the program on the Reconstruction of Afghanistan. He is the author of numerous books and articles on Afghanistan, conflict prevention, and state formation, including *Blood on the Doorstep: The Politics of Preventing Violent*

Conflict and *The Fragmentation of Afghanistan: State Formation and Collapse in the International System.*

Jake Sherman is a research associate at the Center on International Cooperation. From 2003 to 2005, he was a political officer with the United Nations Assistance Mission in Afghanistan. He coedited *Beyond Greed and Grievance: The Political Economy of Armed Conflict.*

Vanessa Wyeth joined the International Peace Institute in 2004 and currently serves as an adviser to IPI's work on statebuilding and peacebuilding, with a particular focus on the UN Peacebuilding Commission. Prior to joining IPI, she worked for the UN in Kosovo and served as a researcher on the *gacaca* tribunals in Rwanda.

Index

About the Book

There is increasing consensus among scholars and policy analysts that successful peacebuilding can occur only in the context of capable state institutions. But how can legitimate and sustainable states best be established in the aftermath of civil wars? And what role should international actors play in supporting these vital processes?

Addressing these questions, this volume explores the core challenges involved in institutionalizing postconflict states. The combination of thematic chapters and in-depth case studies covers the full range of the most vexing and diverse problems confronting domestic and international actors seeking to build states while building peace.

Charles T. Call is assistant professor of international peace and conflict resolution in the School of International Service of American University. Editor of *Constructing Justice and Security After War,* he has conducted field research on postconflict issues in Afghanistan, Bosnia, Central America, Haiti, Kosovo, and West Africa. **Vanessa Wyeth** joined the International Peace Institute in 2004 and currently serves as an adviser to IPI's work on statebuilding and peacebuilding. She has lived and worked in Kosovo, Rwanda, and Niger.